# Living and Working
## in
# *Spain*
## *2006*

## A Survival Handbook

### by
### David Hampshire

**SURVIVAL BOOKS • LONDON • ENGLAND**

First published 1995
Second Edition 1998
Third Edition 2000
Fourth Edition 2003
Fifth Edition 2004
Sixth Edition 2006

Copyright © Survival Books 1995, 1998, 2000, 2003, 2004, 2006
Cover illustration, map and other illustrations © Jim Watson

Survival Books Limited
26 York Street Street, London W1U 6PZ, United Kingdom
☎ +44 (0)20-7788 7644, 🖷 +44 (0)870-762 3212
✉ info@survivalbooks.net
🖥 www.survivalbooks.net
**To order books, please refer to page 531.**

British Library Cataloguing in Publication Data.
A CIP record for this book is available
from the British Library.
ISBN 1 901130 74 6

Printed and bound in Finland by WS Bookwell Ltd

# ACKNOWLEDGEMENTS

My sincere thanks to all those who contributed to the successful publication of this book, in particular the many people who provided information and took the time and trouble to read and comment on the many draft versions. I would especially like to thank my chief researcher Joanna Styles, who was responsible for updating this edition, for her invaluable help. I would also like to thank Catherine Wakelin (proofreading), Kerry and Joe Laredo (page design and layout), Charles Peard Clarke, Ron and Pat Scarborough, Pam Miller, Charles King, John Knight, Veronica Orchard, Adèle Kelham, Mark Hempshell and everyone else who contributed in any way and whom I have omitted to mention. Also a special thank-you to Jim Watson for the superb illustrations, map and cover.

## TITLES BY SURVIVAL BOOKS

**Alien's Guides**
Britain; France

**The Best Places to Buy a Home**
France; Spain

**Buying a Home**
Abroad; Australia & New Zealand; Cyprus; Florida; France; Greece; Ireland; Italy; Portugal; South Africa; Spain; Buying, Selling & Letting Property (UK)

**Foreigners Abroad: Triumphs & Disasters**
France; Spain

**Lifeline Regional Guides**
Brittany; Costa Blanca; Costa del Sol; Dordogne/Lot; Normandy; Poitou-Charentes; Provence-Côte d'Azur

**Living and Working**
Abroad; America; Australia; Britain; Canada; European Union; The Far East; France; Germany; The Gulf States & Saudi Arabia; Holland, Belgium & Luxembourg; Ireland; Italy; London; New Zealand; Spain; Switzerland

**Earning Money From Your Home**
France; Spain

**Making a Living**
France; Spain

**Other Titles**
Renovating & Maintaining Your French Home; Retiring Abroad; Shooting Caterpillars in Spain; Surprised by France

*Order forms are on page 531.*

# WHAT READERS & REVIEWERS

When you buy a model plane for your child, a video recorder, or some new computer gizmo, you get with it a leaflet or booklet pleading 'Read Me First', or bearing large friendly letters or bold type saying 'IMPORTANT – follow the instructions carefully'. This book should be similarly supplied to all those entering France with anything more durable than a 5-day return ticket. It is worth reading even if you are just visiting briefly, or if you have lived here for years and feel totally knowledgeable and secure. But if you need to find out how France works then it is indispensable. Native French people probably have a less thorough understanding of how their country functions. – Where it is most essential, the book is most up to the minute.

**LIVING FRANCE**

Rarely has a 'survival guide' contained such useful advice. This book dispels doubts for first-time travellers, yet is also useful for seasoned globetrotters – In a word, if you're planning to move to the USA or go there for a long-term stay, then buy this book both for general reading and as a ready-reference.

**AMERICAN CITIZENS ABROAD**

It is everything you always wanted to ask but didn't for fear of the contemptuous put down – The best English-language guide – Its pages are stuffed with practical information on everyday subjects and are designed to complement the traditional guidebook.

**SWISS NEWS**

A complete revelation to me – I found it both enlightening and interesting, not to mention amusing.

**CAROLE CLARK**

Let's say it at once. David Hampshire's *Living and Working in France* is the best handbook ever produced for visitors and foreign residents in this country; indeed, my discussion with locals showed that it has much to teach even those born and bred in l'Hexagone. – It is Hampshire's meticulous detail which lifts his work way beyond the range of other books with similar titles. Often you think of a supplementary question and search for the answer in vain. With Hampshire this is rarely the case. – He writes with great clarity (and gives French equivalents of all key terms), a touch of humour and a ready eye for the odd (and often illuminating) fact. – This book is absolutely indispensable.

**THE RIVIERA REPORTER**

A mine of information – I may have avoided some embarrassments and frights if I had read it prior to my first Swiss encounters – Deserves an honoured place on any newcomer's bookshelf.

**ENGLISH TEACHERS ASSOCIATION, SWITZERLAND**

# HAVE SAID ABOUT SURVIVAL BOOKS

What a great work, wealth of useful information, well-balanced wording and accuracy in details. My compliments!

THOMAS MÜLLER

This handbook has all the practical information one needs to set up home in the UK – The sheer volume of information is almost daunting – Highly recommended for anyone moving to the UK.

AMERICAN CITIZENS ABROAD

A very good book which has answered so many questions and even some I hadn't thought of – I would certainly recommend it.

BRIAN FAIRMAN

We would like to congratulate you on this work: it is really super! We hand it out to our expatriates and they read it with great interest and pleasure.

ICI (SWITZERLAND) AG

Covers just about all the things you want to know on the subject – In answer to the desert island question about the one how-to book on France, this book would be it – Almost 500 pages of solid accurate reading – This book is about enjoyment as much as survival.

THE RECORDER

It's so funny – I love it and definitely need a copy of my own – Thanks very much for having written such a humorous and helpful book.

HEIDI GUILIANI

A must for all foreigners coming to Switzerland.

ANTOINETTE O'DONOGHUE

A comprehensive guide to all things French, written in a highly readable and amusing style, for anyone planning to live, work or retire in France.

THE TIMES

A concise, thorough account of the DOs and DON'Ts for a foreigner in Switzerland – Crammed with useful information and lightened with humorous quips which make the facts more readable.

AMERICAN CITIZENS ABROAD

Covers every conceivable question that may be asked concerning everyday life – I know of no other book that could take the place of this one.

FRANCE IN PRINT

Hats off to *Living and Working in Switzerland*!

RONNIE ALMEIDA

# THE AUTHOR

David Hampshire was born in the United Kingdom, where after serving in the Royal Air Force he was employed for many years in the computer industry. He has lived and worked in many countries, including Australia, France, Germany, Malaysia, the Netherlands, Singapore, Switzerland and Spain, where he now resides most of the year. It was while working in Switzerland that he wrote his first book, *Living and Working in Switzerland*, in 1987. David is the author of around 15 books, including *Buying a Home in France*, *Buying a Home in Italy*, *Buying a Home in Spain*, *Buying, Selling & Letting Property*, *Living and Working in France*, *Living and Working in Spain* and *Retiring Abroad*.

# CONTENTS

# 12. HEALTH 265

# 13. INSURANCE 285

## 14. FINANCE                                 307

## 15. LEISURE                                 359

# INDEX

# ORDER FORMS

# IMPORTANT NOTE

Spain is a large country with myriad faces and many ethnic groups, religions and customs. Although obsensibly the same throughout the country, many rules and regulations are open to local interpretation, and are occasionally even formulated on the spot. Laws and regulations have also been changing at a considerable rate in recent years.

**I cannot recommend too strongly that you check with an official and reliable source (not always the same) before making any major decisions or undertaking an irreversible course of action.** However, don't believe everything you're told or read, even, dare I say it, herein!

To help you obtain further information and verify data with official sources, useful addresses and references to other sources of information have been included in all chapters and **Appendices A** to **C**. Important points have been emphasised throughout the book in **bold** print, some of which would be expensive or even dangerous to disregard. **Ignore them at your peril or cost!** Unless specifically stated, the references to any company, organisation, product or publication in this book *doesn't* constitute an endorsement or recommendation.

# AUTHOR'S NOTES

- Frequent references are made in this book to the European Union (EU) which comprises Austria, Belgium, Cyprus, the Czech Republic, Denmark, Estonia, Finland, France, Germany, Greece, Hungary, Ireland, Italy, Latvia, Lithuania, Luxembourg, Malta, the Netherlands, Poland, Portugal, Slovakia, Slovenia, Spain, Sweden and the UK. The EU countries plus Iceland, Liechtenstein and Norway comprise the European Economic Area (EEA).

- Whenever references are made to the Spanish language, this means Castilian, spoken as a first or second language throughout Spain. Other official languages in Spain include Basque, Catalan and Galician (see **Language** on page 26).

- Spanish place names (shown in brackets below) are often changed when written in English, as in this book. In many cases this means just dropping an accent, e.g. Cadiz (Cádiz), Cordoba (Córdoba), Malaga (Málaga) and San Sebastian (San Sebastián); other changes are more pronounced, e.g. Andalusia (Andalucía), Alicante (Alacant), Majorca (Mallorca), Seville (Sevilla) and Zaragossa (Zaragoza).

- Times in timetables and throughout this book are shown using am for before noon and pm for after noon, e.g. 10am and 10pm. See also **Time Difference** on page 474.

- **Prices quoted should be taken only as estimates**, although they were mostly correct when going to print and fortunately don't usually change overnight. Most prices in Spain are quoted inclusive of value added tax (*IVA incluido*), which is the method used in this book unless otherwise indicated (e.g. *más IVA*).

- His/he/him/man/men, etc. also mean her/she/her/woman/women, etc. (no offence ladies). This is done simply to make life easier for both the reader and (in particular) the author, and **isn't** intended to be sexist.

- The Spanish translation of key words and phrases is shown in brackets in *italics*.

- Warnings and important points are shown in **bold** type.

- The following symbols are used in this book: ☎ (telephone), 🖹 (fax), 💻 (internet) and ✉ (email).

- Lists of embassies and consulates, further reading and useful websites are contained in **Appendices A**, **B** and **C** respectively.

- For those unfamiliar with the metric system of weights and measures, conversion tables are included in **Appendix D**.

- A map of Spain and a list of the regions and provinces is contained in **Appendix E**.

# INTRODUCTION

Whether you're already living or working in Spain or just thinking about it, this is **THE BOOK** you've been looking for. *Living and Working in Spain* is designed to meet the needs of everyone wishing to know the essentials of Spanish life, including immigrants, temporary foreign workers, businessmen, students, retirees, long-stay tourists and holiday homeowners.

Since its first edition in 1995, *Living and Working in Spain* has been the most comprehensive and up-to-date book available to people wishing to live and work in Spain and it's the only one revised annually. Since Spain joined the European Union in 1986, the country has changed beyond recognition and every year further changes take place as Spain catches up with its more modern fellow members. These are the changes newcomers need to know about and this is the book to tell you about them! Herein you'll find the latest information on tax figures, residence permits, the new points system for driving licences and regional health services, as well as a wealth of other essential information to help you make a success of your stay in Spain. *Living and Working in Spain* is worth its weight in saffron!

You may have visited Spain as a tourist, but living and working there is another matter altogether. Adjusting to a different environment and culture and making a home in any foreign country can be a traumatic and stressful experience, and Spain is no exception. You need to adapt to new customs and traditions and discover the Spanish way of doing things, for example finding a home, paying bills and obtaining insurance. As anyone who has lived in Spain knows only too well, accurate, up-to-date information for foreigners is difficult to find, particularly in the English language. My aim in writing this book was to help fill this void and provide the comprehensive practical information necessary for a relatively trouble-free life. With a copy of *Living and Working in Spain* to hand you will have a wealth of information at your fingertips.

Information is derived from a variety of sources, both official and unofficial, not least the hard won personal experiences of the author, his friends, colleagues and acquaintances. *Living and Working in Spain* is a comprehensive handbook covering a wide range of everyday subjects and it's the most up-to-date source of general information available to foreigners in Spain. It isn't, however, simply a monologue of dry facts and figures but a practical and entertaining look at life in Spain.

Adapting to life in a new country is a continuous process and, although this book will help reduce your beginner's phase and minimise the frustrations, it doesn't contain all the answers. What it will do is help you to make informed decisions and calculated judgements, instead of uneducated guesses and costly mistakes. Most important of all, it will help you to save time, trouble and money and will repay your investment many times over.

Although you may find some of the information a bit daunting, don't be discouraged. Most problems occur once only and fade into insignificance after a short time (as you face the next dozen!). The majority of foreigners in Spain would agree that, all things considered, they relish living there. A period spent in Spain is a wonderful way to enrich your life, broaden your horizons and hopefully please your bank manager. I trust that this book will help you avoid the pitfalls of life in Spain and smooth your way to a happy and rewarding future in your new home.

*¡Mucha suerte!*

David Hampshire
December 2005

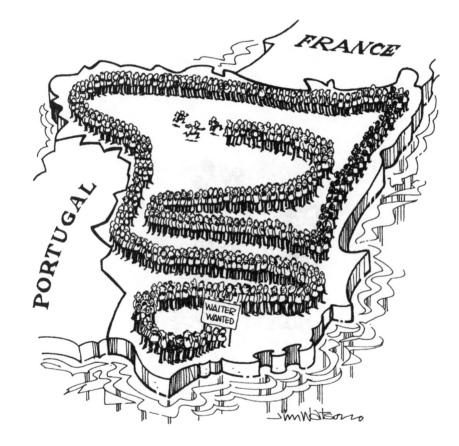

# 1.

# FINDING A JOB

Finding a job in Spain isn't easy, particularly outside the major cities where unemployment is high in many regions. Furthermore, if you don't qualify to live and work in Spain by birthright or as a national of a European Union (EU) country, obtaining a residence permit (see page 78) can be even more difficult than finding work. Americans and other foreigners without the automatic right to work in Spain must have their employment approved by the Spanish Ministry of Labour (Ministerio de Trabajo) and obtain a visa before entering Spain. Most EU nationals have the same employment rights as Spanish citizens, but nationals from eight of the new member states (Czech Republic, Estonia, Hungary, Latvia, Lithuania, Poland, Slovakia and Slovenia) require a work permit (see page 81) until at least mid-2006.

Spain attracts a relatively low number of migrants compared with the UK, France and Germany, although the number of foreign residents has been increasing greatly every year since 2001 and more than 8 per cent of the Spanish population is now foreign. There's also a large floating population of unregistered foreign 'residents'. Just over 40 per cent of foreign residents in Spain come from the EU, the vast majority from the UK and Germany; in some provinces (particularly Malaga and Alicante) over 60 per cent of foreign residents are from the EU. Many Spaniards also work abroad, notably in France, Germany and Switzerland, and Spain imports (low-paid) workers from Morocco (the largest group of foreign residents), Colombia, Ecuador and Eastern Europe (mainly Romania and the Ukraine). Spain is a key entry point for North African immigrants into Europe, which causes considerable problems with illegal immigrants.

# ECONOMY

Spain has experienced an economic 'miracle' in the last few decades, during which it has been transformed from a basically agricultural country into a modern industrial nation. However, the booming '80s were followed by a slump (the severity of which shocked Spain's business and political leaders to the core), although there was a strong recovery in the late '90s. The recession coincided with Spain becoming a full member of the EU and highlighted the country's lack of competitiveness, low productivity and high production costs. Over-manning is common in Spain, particularly in the civil service and state-owned industries, which are renowned for their inefficiency. However, in 2004, Spain had the strongest growth rate among the original 15 members of the EU (2.7 per cent) and forecasts for 2005 and 2006 promise at least 3 per cent growth annually – higher than France, Germany, Italy and the UK.

## Workforce

Spanish workers have an affluent lifestyle compared with just a decade ago, and employees (particularly executives and senior managers) enjoy high salaries and good working conditions. Spain has a reasonably self-sufficient labour market and doesn't require a large number of skilled or unskilled foreign workers. Women have professional and salary equality with men, although they still fill most low-paid jobs. However, workers' security has been seriously eroded in recent years with an increasing number of workers employed on short-term rather than indefinite employment contracts. Many Spaniards (particularly low-paid civil servants) hold down two jobs and work overtime and extra shifts in order to pay their bills.

# Employment Prospects

You shouldn't plan on obtaining employment in Spain unless you have a firm job offer, special qualifications or experience for which there's a strong demand. If you want a good job, you must usually be well qualified and speak fluent Spanish. If you intend to arrive in Spain without a job, you should have a detailed plan for finding employment and try to make some contacts before your arrival. Being attracted to Spain by its weather and lifestyle is understandable, but doesn't rate highly as an employment qualification! It's almost impossible to find work in rural areas (apart from low-paid farm work) and it isn't easy in cities and large towns, particularly if your Spanish isn't fluent.

Many people turn to self-employment or starting a business to make a living, although this path is strewn with pitfalls for the unwary. **Many foreigners don't do sufficient homework before moving to Spain.** While hoping for the best, you should prepare for the worst and ensure that you have a contingency plan and sufficient funds to last until you're established. Before arriving in Spain, you should dispassionately examine your motives and credentials. What kind of work can you realistically expect to do? What are your qualifications and experience? Are they recognised in Spain? How good is your Spanish (or other languages)? Unless your Spanish is fluent, you won't be competing on equal terms with the Spanish (you won't anyway, but that's a different matter!). Spanish employers aren't usually interested in employing anyone without, at the very least, an adequate working knowledge of Spanish. Are there any jobs in your profession or trade in the area where you wish to live? Could you be self-employed or start your own business? The answers to these and many other questions can be disheartening, but it's better to ask them **before** moving to Spain than afterwards. Comprehensive information about employment prospects in Spain can be found in this book's sister publication *Making a Living in Spain* by Anne Hall (Survival Books).

## Women

The number of working women in Spain has increased considerably in the last 20 years and some 40 per cent of Spanish women under 40 now work full or part-time. The number of women in the professions has steadily increased over the years in line with the increase in the number of women graduates (which now exceeds that of men). Women represent around 40 per cent of the working population, but two-thirds of Spain's unemployed.

Nowadays, professional women are common in Spain, particularly doctors and lawyers, and there's less sexism in the professions than in other Latin countries. Career women are commonplace and accepted in many fields that were previously closed to them, although they still have difficulty reaching senior management positions. However, the 'glass ceiling' for professional women in Spain is no lower than in most other western countries (although *macho* Spanish men often feel threatened by female bosses) and the government has done much to boost professional women's position by appointing a woman vice-president (Teresa Fernández de la Vega) and women to half the cabinet posts. On the other hand, Spanish employers are often reluctant to hire women for positions with more responsibility, particularly if they think they're planning a family, although employers don't have to pay maternity leave.

Women are protected by law against discrimination on the grounds of their sex. A woman doing the same or broadly similar work to a man and employed by the same employer is legally entitled to the same salary and other terms of employment. Women's average salary is around 20 per cent lower than men's, although this is partly due to the fact that most women work in lower paid industries and hold lower paid positions than men, rather than to discrimination. Most women are employed in distribution and transport, nursing and health care, education, secretarial professions, and service industries such as retailing.

Although there's no official discrimination, in practice it's often otherwise. The fact that 'the best man for the job may be a woman' isn't often acknowledged by Spanish employers (or employers anywhere) and women must generally be twice as qualified as men to compete on equal terms. The situation has improved considerably in recent years, however, and women are exploited less in Spain than in some other western European countries. Spain celebrates a 'day of the working woman' (8th March) and there are associations of business women in many provinces. A new law promoting sexual equality and regulating positive discrimination is on the drawing board: under the proposed legislation, companies whose workforce includes less than 50 per cent women can only employ women for new posts and equal salaries must be paid to men and women performing the same job (it's estimated that women earn up to a third less than men in similar posts).

Sexual harassment is relatively common in Spain and women are now encouraged to report any advances that go beyond complimentary remarks, which are an accepted part of Spanish life and not to be taken too seriously. If you do receive and refuse a sexual advance from your boss, you should report it to your union representative or another superior. Under the proposed sexual equality law, cases of sexual harassment will be given priority in courts and resolved urgently.

# Unemployment

Spain's strong economic recovery in the last few years has had a dramatic impact on its unemployment rate, which has fallen from over 20 per cent in the '80s to under 10 per cent in 2005. Spain's unemployment figures are distorted by the large number of people working illegally and even the official figures are the among the highest in the EU (where the average is just under 9 per cent), although the figure of 8.4 per cent for September 2005 was the lowest in Spain since 1979 and the government expects unemployment to continue to fall over the next six months. Unemployment is particularly high among those aged 20 to 29 (who represent over 40 per cent of the unemployed), women (60 per cent of the unemployed are women) and foreigners whose unemployment figures are nearly 14 per cent. The unemployed are often unskilled or even illiterate, although a significant percentage of university graduates are also unemployed. Unemployment in some areas is much higher than the national average (as high as 30 per cent). Andalucía, Extremadura and Galicia are the regions with the highest unemployment, while Cataluña, La Rioja and Valencia have the lowest figures (around 6.5 per cent). Apart from its debilitating effect on the Spanish economy, unemployment is expensive on account of Spain's relatively high social security benefits. Reducing unemployment continues to be one of the government's main priorities.

The service and construction industries, the 'engines' of growth in Spain, were hit hard by unemployment in the early '90s, although both these sectors have picked up remarkably since 1998 thanks to a boom in tourism and building (over the last decade over one fifth of Spain's 22.5 million homes have been built!) and now employ over 75 per cent of the workforce between them.

## Industrial Relations

Spain has traditionally had more strikes (*huelgas*) and lost more production days due to strikes in the last few decades than any country in the EU, but industrial relations have improved dramatically in recent years, during which the number of working hours lost to strikes has been reduced by over 20 per cent. Despite the squeeze on pay rises to meet the European Monetary Union (EMU) criteria and qualify for the single currency, there has been little industrial unrest in the last few years, with the notable exception of a nationwide general strike in June 2002, in protest against the previous government's proposed unemployment benefit measures, which were shelved after the strike. In 2004, there were around 700 strikes and nearly 4,500 production days were lost.

## SPAIN & THE EUROPEAN UNION

Spain became a full member of the European Union (EU) on 1st January 1986, joining Belgium, Denmark, France, Germany, Greece, Ireland, Italy, Luxembourg, the Netherlands, Portugal (who joined at the same time as Spain) and the United Kingdom. The EU was enlarged to 15 members in 1995 with the admission of Austria, Finland and Sweden, and to 25 members in May 2004 when Cyprus, Czech Republic, Estonia, Hungary, Latvia, Lithuania, Malta, Poland, Slovakia and Slovenia joined. The European Economic Area (EEA) was formed on the 1st January 1994 and comprises the EU member countries plus Iceland, Liechtenstein and Norway.

The Single European Act, which came into effect on 1st January 1993, created a single market with a more favourable environment for stimulating enterprise, competition and trade, and made it easier for EU nationals to work in other EU countries. Today, nationals of all EU states except the Czech Republic, Estonia, Hungary, Latvia, Lithuania, Poland, Slovakia and Slovenia have the right to work in Spain or any other member state without a work permit, provided they have a valid passport or national identity card and comply with the member state's laws and regulations on employment. EU nationals are entitled to the same treatment as Spanish citizens in matters of pay, working conditions, access to housing, vocational training, social security and trade union rights, and families and immediate dependants are entitled to join them and enjoy the same rights.

There are, however, still some barriers to the freedom of movement of EU workers. For example, some jobs require applicants to have specific skills or vocational qualifications in certain countries, and qualifications obtained in some member states aren't recognised in others. Nevertheless, mutual acceptance of EU educational and professional qualifications by member states has made it easier to study, train and work abroad, and all equivalent professional and trade qualifications are recognised throughout the union (although local examinations may be necessary). There are, however, restrictions on employment in the civil service, when the right to work may be limited, in certain cases, on the grounds of public policy, health or security.

# QUALIFICATIONS

The most important qualification for working in Spain is the ability to speak Spanish fluently (see **Language** on page 52 and **Learning Spanish** on page 191). Once you've overcome this hurdle, you should establish whether your trade or professional qualifications and experience are recognised in Spain. Theoretically, all qualifications recognised by professional and trade bodies in any EU country are recognised in Spain. However, recognition varies from country to country and in certain cases foreign qualifications aren't recognised by Spanish employers, professional or trade associations. All academic qualifications should also be recognised, although they may be given less prominence than equivalent Spanish qualifications, depending on the country and the educational establishment that awarded them. A ruling by the European Court in 1992 declared that where EU examinations are of a similar standard, with limited areas of difference, individuals should be required to take exams only in those areas. EU citizens may become public employees, e.g. teachers and postal workers, and fill other civil service positions in Spain, with the exception of the military and police.

Professionals whose training was compulsory (regulated by statute, statutory instrument or a professional college) and consisted of at least three years' degree level training plus job-based training can have their qualifications recognised automatically in member states. These are, however, subject to any professional codes and limitations in force, e.g. in Spain, a medical practitioner must have his qualifications accepted by the medical college of the province where he intends to practise and by any controlling specialist bodies. He must also show that he's in good standing with the professional authorities in his country of origin. However, professional colleges (*colegios*) in Spain can no longer obstruct the practice of professions by EU citizens holding recognised qualifications earned in another EU country.

All EU member states issue occupation information sheets containing a common job description with a table of qualifications. These are intended to help someone with the relevant qualifications look for employment in another EU country and cover a large number of trades, including agriculture, chemicals, clerical and administration, commerce, construction, electrical/electronics, food, hotel and catering, metalworking, motor vehicle repair and maintenance, textiles, tourism, transport and public works.

In order to have your qualifications recognised in Spain, you must go to the provincial office of the Ministry for Education and Science (Delegación Provincial del Ministerio de Educación y Ciencias) in your provincial capital and apply for a *Homologación*, for which you must pay a fee: currently €83.23 for a degree or €41.62 for a lower qualification. You're expected to supply translations of your certificates and a 'transcript', which is a summary of all the examinations, projects and/or course work included in the course(s) you've followed. A transcript is usually obtainable from the university, school or college that awarded the certificate. **The recognition process can take up to 18 months for a degree (six to eight months for lower qualifications), so you should apply for recognition well in advance of your Spanish job hunt.** Further details are available from the Ministry for Education website (☎ 902-218 500, 🖳 www.mec.es in Spain, www.sgci.mec.es/uk in the UK and www.sgci.mec.es/usa/consejeria in the US). Those with British medical or architectural qualifications can use a faster recognition system: go to the National Academic Recognition Information Centre/NARIC website (🖳 www. naric.co.uk) for details or contact NARIC in Spain (☎ 913-106 633, ✉ ricardo. barahona@mec.es).

Information regarding the official validation of qualifications and the addresses of Spanish professional bodies is obtainable from the education department of Spanish embassies. A direct comparison between foreign qualifications and those recognised in Spain can be obtained from any Spanish employment office (*oficina de empleo*/INEM – see below) where there's a representative of the National Reference Point for Academic Qualifications (Punto Nacional de Referencia sobre Cualificaciones Español/PNR). In the UK, information can be obtained from the National Reference Point for Vocational Qualifications, UK NARIC, Oriel House, Oriel Road, Cheltenham, Gloucestershire GL50 1XP (☎ 0870-990 4088, 🖳 www.uk nrp.org.uk).

# GOVERNMENT EMPLOYMENT SERVICE

The National Employment Institute (Instituto Nacional de Empleo/INEM) is the government-run employment and recruitment agency, with some 700 offices (*oficinas de empleo*) throughout Spain, offering local and national job listings. Under the process of decentralisation, all regions now run their own employment agencies under the 'umbrella' of the INEM (see below). Some regions provide a more comprehensive service than others, but all are striving to give a more personalised and helpful service. Jobs in the local province are sometimes advertised on a bulletin board, as well as perhaps a few national positions requiring specialised experience, training or qualifications. INEM offices may also provide a comprehensive career resource library, including Spanish company listings, trade publications and a wide range of reference books. If you have a residence permit (*residencia*), without which you may receive no help, a personal counsellor may be assigned to your case. In addition to offering a job placement service, the INEM also provides assistance to those wishing to start a business or be self-employed. The INEM website (⌨ www.inem.es) provides good basic information, as well as links to regional employment offices and the useful guide *Working in Spain*, downloadable in PDF in English, French, German and Spanish (⌨ www.inem.es/ciudadano/p_empleo).

The following provides a listing of regional employment agency websites, most of which provide information only in Spanish:

- Andalucía – ⌨ www.juntadeandalucia.es/servicioandaluzdeempleo.
- Aragón – ⌨ http://portal.aragob.es.
- Asturias – ⌨ www.princast.es/trabajastur.
- Balearics – ⌨ http://infosoib.caib.es.
- Canary Islands – ⌨ www.gobiernodecanarias.org/empleo.
- Cantabria – ⌨ www.empleacantabria.com.
- Castilla La Mancha – ⌨ www.sepecam.jccm.es.
- Castilla León – ⌨ www.empleocastillayleon.com.
- Catalonia – ⌨ www.gencat.net/treball.
- Extremadura – ⌨ www.empleaextremadura.com.
- Galicia – ⌨ www.xunta.es/emprego.
- La Rioja – ⌨ www.larioja.org.
- Madrid – ⌨ www.madrid.org/servicio_regional_empleo.
- Murcia – ⌨ www.sefcarm.es.
- Navarra – ⌨ www.navarra.es.
- Valencia – ⌨ www.servef.es.

INEM services are available to all EU nationals and foreign residents in Spain. Unemployed foreigners must register as job seekers (*demandantes de empleo*), after which they receive a document permitting them to legally remain in Spain for six months while seeking employment. However, INEM offices are usually unhelpful to foreign job seekers unless you speak fluent Spanish (or even Catalan in certain parts of Spain!), have already been employed in Spain or are unemployed and receiving unemployment benefit. The INEM isn't service-oriented and the quality of service and co-operation varies with the region, the office and the person handling your case, although the regional services are trying to change this. Most Spanish employers advertise in daily newspapers for personnel. The Servicio de Empleo y Acción Formativa/Promoción Profesional Obrera (SEAF/PPO) of the Ministry of Labour reviews such advertising and sends qualified applicants to apply for the positions described.

There's also a European Employment Service (EURES) network, which includes all EU countries. Member states exchange information on job vacancies on a regular basis and you can also have your personal details circulated to the employment service in selected countries, e.g. to the INEM in Spain. Details are available in local employment service offices in each member country, where advice on how to apply for jobs is also provided from ☎ 00-800 4080 4080 (throughout the EU) and 💻 http://europa.eu.int/eures. Note, however, that it isn't a reliable or quick way to find a job in Spain, and with high Spanish unemployment, an application through EURES is protracted and seldom successful. If you're intending to apply through EURES, you should obtain a *Número de Identificación de Extranjero* (*NIE*) in advance (see **Foreigner's Identification Number** on page 309).

# RECRUITMENT AGENCIES

Private employment agencies in Spain may operate as temporary employment bureaux (*empresas de trabajo temporal*) or private employment agencies, although most act as temporary employment bureaux only. Most agencies are based in the major cities and deal with enquiries from within Spain only, although you can consult vacancies on the internet. As well as general temporary agencies handling vacancies in a range of industries and professions, there are agencies specialising in particular fields, such as accounting, banking, computer personnel, construction, engineering and technical staff, hotel and catering staff, industrial recruitment, insurance, nannies and nursing, sales, and secretarial and office staff. Multinational temporary recruitment agencies such as Adecco, Flexiplan and Manpower are common in cities and large towns, and generally hire office staff and unskilled and semi-skilled labour. Many secretarial jobs are for bilingual or trilingual secretaries with word processing experience (an agency usually tests your written language and word processing skills).

To be employed by a temporary agency, you must be legally eligible to work in Spain and have a social security card (see page 288). You must register with most agencies, which entails completing a registration form and providing a curriculum vitae and references (you can register with any number of agencies). **Always ensure you know exactly how much, when and how you will be paid.** Your salary should include a payment in lieu of holidays and a deduction for unemployment insurance. Due to the long annual holidays in Spain and generous maternity leave, companies often require temporary staff, and a temporary job can frequently be used as a stepping stone to a permanent position. Agencies are listed in the yellow pages under *Trabajo Temporal: Empresas* or *Selección de Personal* and most have websites where you can search for jobs (e.g. 💻 www.adecco.com, 💻 www.flexiplan.es, 💻 www.interempleo.com, 💻 www. manpower.es and 💻 www.temps.es).

Several private employment agencies are now active in Spain and specialise in finding employment (mainly on the Costa del Sol and in Gibraltar) for foreigners fluent in at least English and Spanish. Three of the best include Exposure Career Network (☎ UK 0870-446 6400, 💻 www.exposure-eu.com) with a comprehensive listing of vacancies throughout the country and Gibraltar; JobtoasterSpain (☎ 952-763 008, 💻 www.jobtoasterspain.com) offering vacancies in several locations such as the Costa del Sol, Barcelona, Granada and Cadiz; and Recruit Spain (☎ 952-667 986, 💻 www.recruitspain.com) with job opportunities in the Costa Blanca, Costa del Sol and Gibraltar. All three websites also offer comprehensive information about working in Spain.

Executive recruitment and search companies (headhunters) are common in cities and large towns, and have traditionally been used by large Spanish companies to help recruit staff, particularly executives, managers and professionals. Agents place advertisements in daily and weekly newspapers and trade magazines, but don't usually mention the client's name (not least to prevent applicants from approaching the company directly, thus depriving the agency of its fat fee). Unless you're a particularly outstanding candidate with half a dozen degrees, six languages and valuable experience, sending an unsolicited curriculum vitae (CV) to a headhunter is usually a waste of time. There are also recruitment agencies in other European countries which recruit executives, managers and professionals for employers in Spain.

# SEASONAL JOBS

Most seasonal jobs last for the summer tourist season (May to September), although a few are available in the small Spanish winter sports industry (December to April) and some are simply casual or temporary jobs for a few weeks or months only. Spanish fluency is required for all but the most menial and worst paid jobs and is at least as important as experience and qualifications (although fluent Spanish alone won't guarantee you a well paid job).

Seasonal jobs include most trades in hotels and restaurants; couriers and representatives; various jobs in holiday camps and campsites; work in ski resorts; sports instructing (e.g. tennis, golf and watersports); jobs in bars, clubs and discos (particularly on the *costas* and in the Balearic and Canary Islands); fruit and grape picking and other agricultural jobs and diverse jobs in the construction industry. **If you aren't an EU national, it's essential to check whether you're eligible to work in Spain before your arrival and whether you need a visa (see page 76).** Check with a Spanish embassy or consulate in your home country well in advance of your visit. Foreign students in Spain can obtain a temporary work permit (see page 81) for part-time work during the summer holiday period and school terms.

Although a summer job in Spain may be a working holiday to you, with lots of sunbathing and little work, to your employer it means exactly the opposite. Long hours and low pay are par for the course and you're often required to work ten hours a day with only one day a week free. Due to the large number of unemployed, unskilled workers in Spain, it can be difficult to find work in the construction and farming (e.g. fruit or grape picking) industries and, when found, work is hard and low paid. Unemployment is high in resort areas, although foreigners can often find work in bars, clubs and other tourist-oriented businesses where fluent English (or other foreign language fluency) is an advantage. Bear in mind that seasonal workers are often employed illegally and have few rights and little legal job protection in Spain, and can generally be fired without compensation at any time. See also **Recruitment Agencies** on page 29 and **Temporary & Casual Work** on page 34.

# Hotels & Restaurants

Hotels and restaurants are by far the largest employers of seasonal workers and jobs are available year round, from hotel managers to kitchen hands. Experience, qualifications and fluent Spanish are required for all the better and higher paid positions, although a variety of jobs are available for the untrained and inexperienced. Note that, if accommodation with cooking facilities or full board isn't provided with a job, it can be expensive and difficult to find. Ensure that your salary is sufficient to pay for accommodation, food and other living expenses, and hopefully save some money (see **Cost of Living** on page 355).

# Couriers & Representatives

One of the best seasonal jobs for foreigners is as a courier or representative with a foreign package holiday company. There are also various jobs at holiday camps and campsites. Competition for jobs is fierce, however, and Spanish fluency is usually necessary, even for employment with foreign tour operators. Most companies have age requirements, the minimum usually being 21, although many companies prefer employees to be older. Most companies recruit from outside Spain, so you should apply before travelling to Spain. To find out which companies operate in Spain, check the brochures in your local travel agent's or consult a trade travel directory in your local library. Make applications well before the season starts; for example, for summer work you should apply in November or December, as many positions are filled by January or February.

# Further Reading

There are many books for those seeking seasonal jobs abroad, including *Summer Jobs Abroad* (published annually) and *Work Your Way Around the World* (both published by Vacation Work). An invaluable book for anyone looking for a job in a ski resort is *Working in Ski Resorts in Europe and North America*, by Victoria Pybus (Vacation Work).

# TEACHING & TRANSLATING

English teachers are in huge demand in Spain, where learning English (and other languages) has become extremely popular in the last decade. There are over 20,000 English-language teachers in Spain and, due to the constant demand and high turnover, anyone with a Teaching English as a Foreign Language (TEFL) or English as a Second Language (ESL) certificate can sometimes find a job on the spot, although you shouldn't rely on it. In fact, due to the high demand for teachers in some cities, some schools don't insist on formal teaching qualifications and a graduate native English speaker can often get a job without other qualifications.

# Private Language Schools

There are numerous private language schools in Spain (which has the largest number of language schools of any country in Europe) offering English classes for adults and children. The quality of schools and rates of pay vary considerably, and contracts should be carefully examined before committing yourself. Salaries are low – usually between €800 and €1,200 a month or around €8 an hour, although board and lodging may be subsidised by the school (and you can supplement your earnings by giving private lessons). Hours are long and anti-social (depending on whether you're a night owl) and schools occasionally exploit teachers. Teachers are usually employed on short-term contracts, which may run parallel with school terms (September to June). Several recognised international language schools have branches in Spain, including Berlitz, International House and Linguarama, although they often require applicants to attend their own teacher-training courses.

Many teaching jobs, particularly those in smaller schools, are advertised locally only and those advertised abroad tend to be for the larger schools, international agencies and government institutions. Information about language schools is provided by Spanish consulates or you can write to the Association of Language Teaching Institutions in the region you wish to teach in (e.g. in Andalusia, Asociación de Centros de Enseñanza de Idiomas de Andalucía, C/Asunción, 52, 41011 Sevilla (☎ 954-274 517, 💻 www.aceia.es). The organisation TESOL-Spain also offers information about English language teaching in Spain, including schools, contracts and teaching resources (💻 www.tesol-spain.org). Language schools are listed in yellow pages under *Idiomas* or *Escuelas de Idiomas*.

# The British Council

The British Council (💻 www.britishcouncil.org) recruits English language teachers and supervisory staff for two-year placements in its language centres in Barcelona, Bilbao, Madrid, Palma de Mallorca, Segovia and Valencia. It's necessary to have an RSA diploma or PGCE in TEFL and two years' experience for most positions. For managerial posts, postgraduate qualifications and a minimum of five years' experience are required. For further information contact the British Council by phone (☎ UK 0161-957 7755) or online (💻 www.britishcouncil.org) – the website includes vacancies and allows online applications. The British Council ETRC, Paseo Martínez Campos, 31, 28010 Madrid (☎ 913-373 500, 💻 www.britishcouncil.org/spain) can also provide a list of major English-language schools in Spain.

# Private Tuition

There's a high demand for private English teachers in Spain and many teachers employed in language schools supplement their income by giving private lessons. You can advertise in local schools, universities and retail outlets and, once you're established, additional students can usually be found through word of mouth. You could also try placing an advertisement in a Spanish newspaper or magazine. The demand for private lessons is particularly strong during the summer months (e.g. for children who failed their end-of-term English examination). The rate for private lessons varies considerably with the city or area and the competition – between €10 and €25 an hour.

## Language Assistants

The language assistants' scheme enables students from the UK and over 30 other countries to spend a year working in a school or college in Spain assisting language teachers. Assistants spend 12 to 15 hours a week in the classroom under the supervision of the English (or other language) teacher, helping students improve their command of English and gain an insight into the Anglophone way of life. Graduates and undergraduates aged 20 to 30 of any discipline with the relevant foreign language qualification, e.g. at least A Level standard in the UK, are eligible to apply. Students aged 18 to 20 with an A Level or equivalent qualification in Spanish can apply for a position as a junior language assistant at secondary schools in Spain from January to June. Information and a guide to making applications can be found on the British Council website (💻 www.britishcouncil.org). Comprehensive information for language assistants is available on 💻 www. languageassistant.co.uk.

## Translators & Interpreters

Those who are fluent in Spanish and English (and other languages) can also find work as translators and interpreters. The best job prospects for translators are in the major cities, where most translation work involves business correspondence (although it can be low paid and you need a computer). It's also worthwhile contacting major exporters who must translate their technical and other documentation into English and other languages. Translation agencies are listed in yellow pages under *Traductores*.

## Teaching Other Subjects

Other teaching jobs are few and far between in Spain and Spanish qualifications are often required to teach in state schools, even though schools can no longer insist on Spanish teaching qualifications under EU regulations. Jobs are also available in international and foreign schools teaching American, British and other foreign children. Jobs in Spain are advertised in the *Times Educational Supplement* (Fridays) and through the European Council of International Schools (ECIS), 21B Lavant Street, Petersfield, Hampshire GU32 3EW (☎ 01730-268244, 💻 www.ecis.org).

## Publications

For more information about teaching English, obtain a copy of *Teaching English Abroad* by Susan Griffith (Vacation Work) or *English as a Foreign Language Teacher* and *English as a Second Language Teacher* published by AGCAS, Graduate Prospects,

Prospects House, Booth Street East, Manchester M13 9EP (☎ 0161-277 5200, 💻 www.prospects.ac.uk). Two of the best resources for English teachers are the monthly *EL Gazette* and the *EL Gazette Guide to English Language Teaching Around The World* (Unit 3, Constantine Court, 6 Fairclough Street, London E1 1PW, ☎ 020-7481 6700, 💻 www.elgazette.com).

# TEMPORARY & CASUAL WORK

Temporary and casual work in Spain is usually for a fixed period, ranging from a few hours to a few months, or it may be intermittent. Casual workers may be employed on a daily, first-come, first-served basis. Work often entails heavy labouring and is therefore intended mostly for males, although if you're tough enough there's usually no discrimination against the 'fairer' sex. However, anyone looking for casual unskilled work in Spain must usually compete with unskilled immigrants, who are usually prepared to work for less money than anyone else, although nobody **should** be paid less than the minimum wage (see page 39). Many employers illegally pay temporary staff in cash without making deductions for social security (see **Illegal Working** on page 51). Temporary and casual work includes the following:

- Office work, which is well paid if you're qualified and the easiest work to find in major cities due to the large number of temporary secretarial and office staff agencies. You must be fluent in Spanish.

- Work in the construction industry, which can be found by applying at building sites and through industrial recruitment agencies (such as Adecco). The building industry is experiencing a boom at the moment and jobs are abundant, although they may be poorly paid.

- Jobs in shops during the height of the tourist season and during Christmas and annual sales in major cities.

- Promotional work for bars, restaurants and other businesses in the summer season, which usually consists of distributing leaflets to tourists.

- Gardening jobs in private gardens, public parks, and for landscape gardeners and garden centres, particularly in spring and summer.

- Selling ice cream, cold drinks, food or suntan lotion in summer, e.g. on beaches.

- Touting for timeshare property companies; work can be found in many resorts during the summer season (and throughout the year in some areas), although it usually involves dubious practices and high-pressure sales methods (and is usually paid on a commission only). Note that touting for timeshare customers in public has been banned in some resorts, although it's often carried out under another guise, e.g. market research or offering free prize draws.

- Various jobs in ports, including yacht-minding, crewing, servicing, cleaning and boat delivery. Work as a deck-hand on a yacht pays well and usually also includes tips, although you must have sea legs, as the Mediterranean isn't always calm! You should have private medical insurance.

- Market research, which entails asking people personal questions in the street or house to house (an ideal job for nosy parkers with fluent Spanish).

- House sitting, which involves caring for a house and garden (possibly including a pet) while the owners are away. Not usually paid, but provides free accommodation.

- Modelling at art colleges. Both sexes are usually required and not just the body beautiful.

- Nursing and auxiliary nursing in hospitals, clinics and nursing homes (temporary staff are often employed through nursing agencies to replace permanent staff at short notice). The best-paid nursing jobs are in private clinics and hospitals, or working directly for private patients in their own homes.

- Newspaper, magazine and leaflet distribution.

- Courier work (own transport required – motorcycle, car or van).

- Driving jobs, including coach and truck driving, and ferrying cars for manufacturers and car rental companies.

- Office cleaning, babysitting, labouring and other 'menial' jobs, which are available from a number of agencies specialising in temporary work.

Temporary jobs are advertised on notice boards in supermarkets, expatriate clubs, churches and organisations, and in expatriate newsletters and newspapers. See also **Recruitment Agencies** on page 29 and **Seasonal Jobs** on page 30.

# VOLUNTARY WORK

Voluntary work (as described here) is primarily to enable students and young people to visit Spain for a few weeks or months to learn about the country and its people at first hand. The minimum age for volunteers is between 16 and 18 and you must usually be under 30, although some organisations have no upper age limit. No special qualifications are required and the minimum length of service is usually a few weeks. Disabled volunteers are welcomed by many organisations. Voluntary work is (naturally) unpaid and you must usually pay a registration fee, which includes personal liability and health insurance, and your own travel costs to and from Spain and to the workcamp. Although meals and accommodation are normally provided, you may be expected to contribute towards the cost of board and lodging. The usual visa regulations apply to voluntary workers (see page 76, but you should be informed when applying whether you need a visa), although work or residence permits aren't necessary.

Much voluntary work in Spain takes place in international workcamps which provide the opportunity for young people to live and work together on a range of projects, including agriculture, archaeology, building, conservation, gardening, handicrafts, restoration of buildings and monuments, social welfare and community projects. Camps are usually run for two to four weeks between April and October, although some operate all year round. Work is unskilled or semi-skilled and is for around five to eight hours a day, five or six days a week. The work is usually physically demanding and accommodation, which is shared, basic. Most workcamps consist of volunteers from several countries and English is often the common language.

Archaeological and conservation projects are co-ordinated in Spain by the Instituto de la Juventud (INJUVE), C/José Ortega y Gasset, 71, 28006 Madrid (☎ 913-637 521, 💻 www.mtas.es/injuve). INJUVE provides information on all volunteer camps throughout Spain. Some Spanish voluntary organisations are listed in *Green Volunteers* and the *International Directory of Voluntary Work* (Vacation Work).

# JOB HUNTING

When looking for a job (or a new job) in Spain, it's advisable not to put all your eggs in one basket, as the more job applications you make, the better your chances of finding the right job. Contact as many prospective employers as possible, by writing, telephoning or calling on them in person. Whatever job you're looking for, it's important to market yourself appropriately, which depends on the type of job or position you're seeking. For example, the recruitment of executives and senior managers is often handled by recruitment consultants, who advertise in the Spanish national press and trade magazines. At the other end of the scale, unskilled manual jobs requiring no previous experience may be advertised at INEM employment offices, in local newspapers and on notice boards, and the first suitable applicant may be offered the job on the spot. When job hunting, you should use all the resources available (detailed below). Before accepting a job offer from an employer, you should also ask yourself the following questions:

- What are his prospects?
- Does he have a good reputation?
- Does he have a high staff turnover?

## Newspapers

Obtain copies of Spanish national and regional newspapers, all of which contain 'situations vacant' (*trabajo vacante* or *ofertas de empleo*) sections on certain days, e.g. Sundays. There's a specialist paper, *Mercado de Trabajo* published weekly. Most professions and trade associations publish journals containing job offers (see *Benn's Media Directory Europe*). Jobs are also advertised in various English-language publications, including the *International Herald Tribune, Wall Street Journal Europe* and *Overseas Jobs Express*. The expatriate Spanish press (see page 434) also contains 'Situations Vacant' and 'Situations Wanted' advertisements. You can place an advertisement in 'Situations Wanted' (*demanda*) columns in most publications. It's best to place an advertisement in the middle of the week and to avoid the summer and other holiday periods.

When writing for jobs, address your letter to the personnel director or manager and include your curriculum vitae (in Spanish) and copies of all references and qualifications. If possible, offer to attend an interview and state when you're available. Letters should be tailored to individual employers and be professionally translated if your Spanish isn't perfect. Note, however, that Spanish companies are notoriously bad at answering letters and you should follow up letters with a telephone call.

## Employment Offices

Visit your local employment office in Spain (see page 27). Jobs on offer are mainly non-professional skilled, semi-skilled and unskilled jobs, particularly in industry, retailing and catering.

## Recruitment Agencies

Apply to international recruitment agencies acting for Spanish companies. These companies mainly recruit executives and key personnel, and many have offices in major Spanish cities as well as worldwide. Contact recruitment agencies in Spain (see page 29) for temporary positions. Note that many Spanish agencies find positions only for Spanish and EU nationals and non-EU foreigners with a residence permit.

## Internet

There are hundreds of websites for jobseekers, including corporate and recruitment company sites and newspaper job advertisements (you can use a search engine to find them). Job hunting via the internet is becoming increasingly popular. Most job vacancy websites also offer advice and the opportunity to post your CV online. The most popular sites include the following:

- 🖳 www.computrabajo.es or www.tecnoempleo.com – IT and telecommunications jobs.
- 🖳 www.empleomedico.com – medicine.
- 🖳 www.empleotiempoparcial.com – part-time employment.
- 🖳 www.eurojobs.com – jobs throughout Europe.
- 🖳 www.financialwebjob.com – finance.
- 🖳 www.infoagro.com – agriculture and farming.
- 🖳 www.jobpilot.es – an international site in English which includes job vacancies in Spain.
- 🖳 www.laboris.net – general.
- 🖳 www.monster.es – general.
- 🖳 www.sinexperiencia.com – jobs with no experience required.
- 🖳 www.trabajos.com – general.

## Unsolicited Job Applications

Apply to American, British and other multinational companies with offices or subsidiaries in Spain, and make written applications direct to Spanish companies. Useful addresses can usually be obtained from regional and local chambers of commerce (*Cámara Oficial de Comercio e Industria*) and other organisations in Spain. Spanish companies are listed by product, service and province in *Kompass Spain* (🖥 www.kompass.es) and the EU Business Directory, *Euro Pages* (🖥 www.euro pages.com). Making unsolicited job applications to targeted companies is naturally a hit and miss affair. It can, however, be more successful than responding to advertisements, as you aren't usually competing with other applicants. Some companies recruit a large percentage of employees through unsolicited applications. When writing from abroad, enclosing an international reply coupon may help elicit a reply.

## Networking

Networking (making business and professional contacts) is particularly useful in Spain, where it's common to use personal contacts for everything from looking for a job to finding accommodation. It's difficult for most foreigners to make contacts among the Spanish and therefore many turn to the expatriate community. If you're already in Spain, contact or join expatriate social clubs, churches, societies and professional organisations. Finally, don't forget to ask friends and acquaintances working in Spain if they know of an employer looking for someone with your experience and qualifications.

## SALARY

It's often difficult to determine the salary (*sueldo*) you should command in Spain, as salaries aren't generally quoted in job advertisements, except in the public sector, where employees are paid according to fixed grades and salaries are public knowledge. Salaries vary considerably for the same job in different parts of Spain. Those working in major cities, particularly Madrid and Barcelona, are generally the highest paid, primarily due to the high cost of living, especially accommodation.

If you're able to negotiate your own salary, you should ensure that you receive the salary and benefits commensurate with your qualifications and experience (or as much as you can get!). If you have friends or acquaintances working in Spain or who have worked there, ask them what an average or good salary would be for your trade or profession. When comparing salaries, you must take into account compulsory deductions such as tax and social security, and also consider the cost of living (see page 355).

Throughout the '80s, Spanish employees enjoyed huge wage increases – far in excess of inflation – and the average salary doubled. However, salaries remained largely static during the recession and pay increases are now often linked to increased productivity. In recent years, the government has linked civil service pay rises to inflation and reduced government spending, which, along with the booming economy, has led to increased prosperity and a more positive outlook than anyone would have dreamt possible a few years ago. Wage increases in the private sector have averaged around 3.7 per cent over the last few years.

Salaries for managers and professionals compare favourably with those in other western countries and are among the highest in Europe. Directors usually earn between €70,000 and €180,000 a year depending on the size of the company and middle managers between €40,000 and €70,000. Salaried professionals earn around €40,000 to €60,000. Blue-collar workers earn an average of €19,300 a year compared with the European average of €27,000 (only Greek and Portuguese workers earn less), e.g. some 55 per cent less than German workers, 30 per cent less than the French and around 10 per cent less than British workers. Typical salaries start at around €3,300 a month for an IT professional (one of the highest paid professions), around €1,200 a month in nursing and from €980 to €2,000 a month in an administrative post. Most employees in Spain receive a month's extra salary (*paga extraordinaria*) twice a year, at Christmas and before the August summer holiday.

For many employees, particularly executives and senior managers, their remuneration is much more than what they receive in their monthly pay packets. Many companies offer benefits for executives and managers, including a company car (rarer in Spain than in some other European countries); private health insurance and health screening; paid holidays; private school fees; inexpensive or interest-free home and other loans; rent-free accommodation; free public transport tickets; free or subsidised company restaurant; sports or country club membership; non-contributory company pension; stock options; bonuses and profit-sharing schemes; complementary tickets for sports events and shows and 'business' conferences in exotic places.

## Minimum Wage

Spain has a statutory minimum wage (*salario mínimo interprofesional*), which was €513 a month (€3.20 an hour) in 2005 for an unskilled worker aged from 16 to 59, one of the lowest rates in the EU, although the government has pledged to raise the amount to €600 by the end of its four-year term in 2008. Minimum salaries are set for all workers under collective labour agreements, however, and most workers receive more than the minimum; fewer than 600,000 employees are directly affected by minimum wage rates (although an increase in the minimum wage usually serves as a benchmark for wage demands). Unskilled workers (particularly women) are usually employed at or near the minimum wage, while semi-skilled and skilled workers receive a premium of up to 100 per cent.

## SELF-EMPLOYMENT

If you're an EU-national or a permanent resident, you can be self-employed (*trabajador autónomo*) or work as a sole trader (*empresa individual*) in Spain. Under

Spanish law every self-employed person must have an official status and it's illegal simply to hang out a sign and start business.

If you want to be self-employed in a profession or trade, you must meet certain legal requirements and register with the appropriate organisation, e.g. a professional must become a member of the relevant professional college (*colegio*). Members of some professions and trades must possess professional qualifications (see page 26) and certificates recognised in Spain, and are usually required to sit a written examination in Spanish. You're subject to any professional codes and limitations in force, e.g. a medical practitioner must have his qualifications accepted by the medical college of the province where he intends to practise and any controlling specialist bodies before he can practise. You must also show that you're in good standing with the professional authorities in your own country. In certain professions, such as the legal profession, it's unusual to be permitted to practise in Spain without Spanish qualifications.

As a self-employed person you don't have the protection of a limited company should your business fail, although there are certain tax advantages. It may be advantageous to operate as a limited company, for example (see page 43). However, you should obtain professional advice before deciding whether to operate as a sole trader or form a company in Spain, as it has far-reaching social security, tax and other consequences. All self-employed people must register for income tax, social security and value added tax (VAT/IVA), and anyone with an income in Spain requires a fiscal identification number (*Número de Identificación Fiscal/NIF*), obtainable from your local national police station (*comisaría de policía nacional*). For foreigners this number is called a *Número de Identificación de Extranjeros/NIE*. For further information on the *NIE* see page 309.

Whatever people may tell you, working for yourself isn't easy, but requires a lot of hard work (self-employed people generally work much longer hours than employees), a considerable investment and sufficient operating funds (under-funding is the major cause of business failures), good organisation (e.g. budgeting and planning), excellent customer relations, and a measure of luck (although generally the harder you work, the more 'luck' you will have). Don't be seduced by the apparent relaxed way of life in Spain – if you want to be a success in business, you cannot play at it.

## Social Security

There's a special social security scheme for self-employed workers (*régimen especial de autónomos*). If you're self-employed and employ others, you must register your business in the general social security scheme and must affiliate all your employees and comply with the requirements of the *Inspección Provincial de Trabajo*. Social security contributions for the self-employed are higher than for salaried employees and you receive fewer benefits (which encourages illegal working). In 2005, contributions were a minimum of €229.58 a month irrespective of income. You receive a book of payment slips from your social security office or payments can be made directly by your bank by direct debit. Note that as a self-employed person, you aren't entitled to unemployment benefit should your business fail. Furthermore, if you have two unconnected part-time jobs, you officially require two sets of papers and must pay social security twice!

## Business Tax

Business tax on economic activities, *Impuesto sobre Actividades Económicas* (*IAE*), is only levied on businesses with profits of over €600,000 a year. Anyone conducting a business, however, must still register as a self-employed worker or professional with the tax office, who give you the tax code designated for your profession. This code must be quoted in your annual tax return. Note also that you may need an opening licence (see **Licences & Permits** on page 45).

## Value Added Tax

Most self-employed people must register for value added tax (VAT), irrespective of income, and levy VAT (*Impuesto sobre el Valor Añadido/IVA*) at 16 per cent on all services or goods. VAT must be declared and paid quarterly. See also **Value Added Tax** on page 329.

# STARTING A BUSINESS

Most foreigners find Spain a frustrating country in which to do business. The bureaucracy associated with starting a business there is staggering and ranks among the most pernicious in the western world: the process takes an average of over seven months and there are more than 70 documents and procedures to be completed. Not surprisingly, only some 15 per cent of those who start manage to finish! Nevertheless, Spain is traditionally a country of small companies and sole traders, and there are some 1.5 million family-run businesses (of all sizes) employing over 80 per cent of the working population.

In an attempt to facilitate the process and encourage self-employment, the government has recently introduced new measures. Every province is Spain now has a 'one-stop' office (*ventanilla única*) for businesses, where all information and documents are available and where you can present everything related to your application. Information (in Spanish only), including the addresses of provincial offices, is available from ☎ 902-100 096 or 🖳 www.ventanillaempresarial.org. Nevertheless, foreigners can still find the red tape impenetrable, especially if they don't speak Spanish; you're inundated with official documents and must be able to understand them. (It's only when you come up against the full force of Spanish bureaucracy that you understand what it **really** means to be a foreigner in Spain!)

One way to get round the red tape is to employ a *gestor* (a licensed professional, expert in administrative and tax affairs – see page 461) to do the paperwork for you. His fee depends on the amount of work involved, but is usually well worth paying – not for nothing do many Spaniards use the services of a *gestor* for paperwork! If you decide to 'go it alone', among the best sources of help and information are your local chamber of commerce (*Cámara de Comercio*) and town hall (*ayuntamiento*).

**Starting a business can be one of the quickest routes to bankruptcy known to mankind. In fact, the majority of foreigners who open businesses in Spain would be better off investing in lottery tickets! Many would-be foreign entrepreneurs leave Spain with literally only their shirts on their backs, having learnt the facts of Spanish business life the hard way.**

Most people are far too optimistic about the prospects for a new business and over-estimate income levels (it can sometimes take years to make a profit). Be realistic or even pessimistic when estimating your income, and overestimate the costs and underestimate the revenue (then reduce it by another 50 per cent!). While hoping for the best, you should plan for the worst; new projects are rarely completed within budget.

However, although there are numerous failures for every success story, many foreigners **do** run successful businesses in Spain. Those who make a go of it do so as a result of extensive market research, wise investments, excellent customer relations and most important of all, a lot of hard work.

# Capital

Make sure that you have sufficient working capital and can survive until a business takes off. If possible, you should have enough capital to last a year without taking any money out of a business. Spanish banks are usually wary of lending to new businesses, especially businesses run by foreigners. Lenders usually require a detailed business plan plus security, and a loan may be restricted to the amount of capital you put into a business. If you wish to borrow money to buy property or for a business venture in Spain, you should carefully consider where and in what currency to raise finance.

# Location

Choosing the location for a business is usually more important than the location for a home. As is often said, the three most important points when starting a retail business are location, location and location. Depending on the type of business, you may need access to motorways and rail links or to be located in a popular tourist area or near major attractions. Local plans relating to communications, industry and major building developments, e.g. housing complexes and new shopping centres, may also be important. Plans for new motorways and rail links are usually available from the local town hall.

# Employees

Hiring employees is a big step and should be taken into account **before** starting a business. You must enter into a contract under Spanish labour law and employees enjoy extensive rights. If you're planning to hire staff, you should use the services of a 'labour lawyer' (*asesor laboral*), who's a specialist in employment and self-employment law. It's expensive to hire full-time employees. In addition to their salary you must pay around 30 per cent in social security payments, give them two extra months' salary (see page 60), and allow them 30 days' paid holiday and 14 paid public holidays each year. See also **Social Security** on page 288 and **Chapter 2**.

# Types of Business

The majority of businesses established by foreigners in Spain are linked to the leisure and catering industries, followed by property investment and development, and providing for the miscellaneous needs of foreign residents. The most common businesses operated by foreigners include hotels and other accommodation (particularly in rural areas, where grants are available to encourage 'rural tourism'); caravan and camping sites; farming; catering (e.g. bars, cafés and restaurants); shops and franchises; hairdressers; property development, sales and letting; garden centres; sports centres and tuition (e.g. tennis, golf, squash, bowling, snooker or pool hall, gymnasiums, water and aerial sports, and horse riding); social clubs; business and secretarial services; English-language schools; translations and interpreting; garages and car, motorcycle and bicycle sales and rentals; boat sales and rentals; nursing homes; second-hand furniture stores; new and second-hand book shops and lending libraries; kennels and catteries; discotheques and night clubs and satellite television services.

An overview of popular businesses run by foreigners together with their first-hand experience can be found in *Making a Living in Spain* by Anne Hall (Survival Books).

## Limited Companies

Limited companies cannot be purchased 'off the shelf' in Spain and it usually takes a number of months to set up a company. Incorporating a company in Spain takes longer and is more expensive and complicated than in most other European countries. There are a number of different types of business entity and choosing the right one can be difficult. **Always obtain professional legal advice regarding the advantages and disadvantages of different business structures.**

A Spanish business may assume various legal entities. Most small businessmen operate as sole traders (*empresas individuales*) and must register with the appropriate trade association, paying a small joining fee and a monthly subscription. A small company is usually one of two sorts of 'private limited companies' (*Sociedad de Responsabilidad Limitada/SL* or *Sociedad Limitada Nueva Empresa/SLNE* – see below) and a larger limited company is usually a 'public company' (*Sociedad Anónima/SA* – see below). Other business entities include a general partnership (*Sociedad Regular Colectiva/SRC*), a limited partnership (*Sociedad Comanditaria*), and a joint venture between a Spanish and foreign company (*Asociación de Empresas en Participación*).

**Sociedad de Responsabilidad Limitada:** An *SL* is the simplest and most common form of limited company. It doesn't have any public shares and the capital is divided among the shareholders, of whom there can be a maximum of 50. The minimum set-up capital required is €3,005. Its constitution process is simpler than that of an *SA* (see below) and only two founders are required, although its statutes are more restrictive.

**Sociedad Limitada Nueva Empresa:** In April 2003, a modified version of the *SL* was introduced, called a *Sociedad Limitada Nueva Empresa* (*SLNE*). The idea behind it was to encourage the incorporation of small and medium-sized businesses, and the fact that its fiscal requirements are simpler than those of an *SL* should make it an increasingly popular option. An *SLNE* also differs from an *SL* in terms of the number of shareholders and permissible company names. The maximum number of shareholders allowed with this type of company is five, a move intended to keep *SLNE*s small. The company name must comprise one of the founder's names, a registration number and the letters *SLNE*. The minimum capital required is virtually the same as for an *SL* (€3,012), but the maximum is €120,202.

**Sociedad Anónima:** An *SA* is similar to a British public limited company (plc) or an American corporation (Inc.). To form an *SA* requires a minimum share capital of €60,101 and at least one shareholder, who can be a company or individual of any nationality. An *SA* must have at least 50 employees and a committee on which workers are represented (*comité de empresa*). Only one director is necessary, who may be a foreigner **and** a non-resident.

# Buying an Existing Business

It's much easier to buy an existing business in Spain (or anywhere else) than to start a new one. The paperwork for taking over an existing business is complicated enough, without doing it from scratch. Taking over an established business is also less of a risk than starting something new. However, buying an existing business that's a going concern isn't easy. Most people in Spain simply don't sell thriving businesses without a good reason, at least not at a reasonable price. The Spanish aren't in the habit of buying and selling businesses, which are usually passed from generation to generation.

If you plan to buy a business, obtain an independent valuation (or two). Try to find out why the previous owner is selling, as there may be a hidden motive; for example, a thriving small grocery shop will probably become worthless if a supermarket opens around the corner. It's essential to check local planning permission for rival businesses, roads, factories, public works, housing developments and anything else that may affect your business.

Always ensure that turnover claims can be substantiated and aren't inflated (a common practice). It goes without saying that you should never take actual or projected turnover or profit figures at face value, particularly when they're provided by someone with an interest in selling a business, e.g. an agent or the owner. Note also that the declared turnover for tax purposes is usually lower than actual turnover. The only way to verify the turnover is to spend some time working with the owner or tenant assessing the income at first hand.

It's important to note when buying a business property in Spain, that all debts against the property are automatically transferred to the property's new owners (as with domestic property). Get your lawyer to check whether there are any charges against a business. Many bars and restaurants are sold leasehold and often leases are too expensive to allow the leaseholder to make a profit. Note that there's no statutory security of tenure under the law of industrial leases and, if you rent business premises, it's essential to take legal advice regarding the lease.

When buying a business, two prices are usually quoted; one for the lease/business and a monthly rental. The lease is usually a life lease (*traspaso*), although leases can be from 2 to 20 years. The lease should limit future rent increases to the rate of inflation; otherwise, if your business is a huge success, your landlord can hold you to ransom by demanding an extortionate rent! Business leases must be paid in cash and loans aren't usually available. It's important to obtain **all** necessary licences before signing a lease or purchase contract, or the contract should be conditional on licences being issued. Never sign anything you don't understand 100 per cent and without obtaining independent professional advice from local business experts such as accountants and banks. However, don't expect their advice to be totally unbiased or totally accurate.

There are specialist business agents throughout Spain and many estate agents also sell businesses. Local chambers of commerce can also offer advice and provide contacts. Businesses are advertised for sale through the Spanish and English-language press in Spain (see **Appendix B**).

## Licences & Permits

If your business requires premises, such as a shop, workshop or offices, you must obtain an 'opening' licence (*licencia de apertura*) from the local municipal council before starting business. The cost of an opening licence varies considerably according to the size of the premises (e.g. premises under $100m^2$ pay €350) and the type of business activity, e.g. from €400 for a small shop, a bar or restaurant. To obtain an opening licence you require a lease or title deed for the premises.

If a business may create a risk or inconvenience to the local community, e.g. a bar or discotheque, the council will insist that you fulfil certain requirements before it grants an opening licence. You won't be granted a licence if the business is likely to cause a nuisance or if there are already deemed to be sufficient businesses of that kind in the area. A licence application isn't necessary if the business premises are to be used for the same purpose as previously, e.g. a bar or restaurant, although you must register the ownership of the business in your name.

You may have to wait up to six months for your opening licence to be issued. Many businesses operate without a licence and some continue to operate without one for years, although they're increasingly being closed by the local authorities.

To sell or serve alcohol and food, you require a health licence, and establishments that serve food must also undergo sanitary and technical inspections, and employees must obtain a food handler's certificate (*carnet de manipulador de alimentos*) – possibly even when no food is served!. See also **Work Permits** on page 81.

## Tax

Spanish companies are assigned a fiscal identification number, which is used for all tax purposes. Small businesses (e.g. shops and restaurants) are initially taxed on a modular system (*módulos*), where tax is estimated according to the size of the premises, the number of tables (in a restaurant), the number of employees and other factors. You pay business tax on the estimated amount each quarter and receive a refund or pay the amount outstanding at the end of the tax year. After the first year, you can choose whether to continue with the modular system or pay tax on your actual earnings by the direct estimation (*estimación directa*) method, which requires maintaining detailed records.

All limited companies must file corporate tax returns, which are submitted to the provincial tax headquarters (Delegación de Hacienda) in the area where the business is registered (*domicilio fiscal*). Various returns must be made, including corporation tax, personal income tax, income tax of sole proprietors and value added tax. Corporation tax at a high 35 per cent is levied on profits, although the government plans to reduce this to 30 per cent to increase Spain's competivity. Surcharges and interest are levied for late payment of tax and huge fines are imposed for tax infringements. On the other hand, if you overpay your tax, you can claim a refund when you make your annual tax declaration.

# Grants

There's a wide range of investment incentives available to anyone planning to establish a business in Spain, from central and regional governments and from the European Union. Incentives include investment subsidies, tax relief, low-interest or interest-free loans, social security rebates and reduced registration tax during the start-up period. There are government incentives for investment in 'economic promotion zones' (*zonas de promoción económica/ZPE*), which include all autonomous regions except for Aragón, the Balearics, the Basque Country, Cantabria, Catalonia, Madrid, Navarra and Rioja, as well as numerous regional incentives. No special incentives are offered to foreign investors. However, the Spanish government provides seminars for prospective foreign investors, including advice from banks and lectures from established business people and representatives of companies with subsidiaries in Spain.

# Avoiding the Crooks

To add to your problems with the Spanish authorities, assorted crooks and swindlers are unfortunately fairly common in Spain, particularly in resort areas. You should have a healthy suspicion of the motives of anyone you do business with (unless it's your mum), particularly your fellow countrymen. It's a sad fact of life that foreigners who prey on their fellow countrymen are commonplace. In most cases, you're better off dealing with a long-established Spanish company with roots in the local community (and therefore a good reputation to protect), rather than your compatriots. It's generally best to avoid partnerships, as they rarely work and can be a disaster. In general, you should trust nobody and shouldn't sign anything or pay any money before having a contract checked by a lawyer. If you don't and things go wrong, you may be unprotected by Spanish law.

# Legal Advice

Before establishing a business or undertaking any business transactions in Spain, it's important to obtain legal advice to ensure that you're operating within the law. There are severe penalties for anyone who ignores the regulations. Expert legal advice is also necessary to make the most of any favourable tax and business breaks, as well as to make sense of the myriad rules and regulations. It's important to ensure that contracts are clearly defined and water-tight before making an investment; if you become involved in a legal dispute, it's likely to take years to resolve. You should obtain advice from a lawyer (*abogado*) and an accountant (*asesor fiscal*), and engage an official agent (*gestor*) to shepherd you through the minefield of red tape (see page 461). Many Spanish lawyers, accountants and agents speak English and other languages (lists can be obtained from embassies and consulates in Spain).

# Research

The key to starting or buying a successful business in Spain is exhaustive research, research and yet more research. **If you aren't prepared to thoroughly research the market and obtain expert business and legal advice, you shouldn't even think about starting a business in Spain (or anywhere else for that matter).** Always thoroughly investigate an existing or proposed business before investing any money. **As any expert (and many failed entrepreneurs) will tell you, Spain isn't a country for amateurs, particularly amateurs who don't speak Spanish.** It isn't always necessary to speak Spanish if your customers are exclusively expatriates, although it's important that at least one partner or employee speaks fluent Spanish. Otherwise, you must pay a secretary or business agent to do simple tasks that you could easily do yourself. On the other hand, it's an absolute must to check out the level of competition in a given area. Even when competition is light, there may be insufficient custom to sustain another business.

A saturation of trades and services is common in Spain, particularly in resort areas where there's a glut of bars, cafés, restaurants and retail outlets catering to tourists. In resort areas, some foreigners (e.g. bar and restaurant owners) will do almost anything to lure their competitors' customers, even reducing prices to below cost. In winter, you may be lucky to take a €30 a day in a bar and it often isn't worthwhile even opening your doors. **Your chances of making a good living from a bar, restaurant or retail outlet in a resort area are practically zero, as there's simply too much competition and too few customers to go around.**

In some areas, you may have to put up with petty laws, which may be selectively enforced on foreign businesses by local police and officials (particularly in resort areas). The Spanish survive because they invariably own their business premises, 'employ' family members, have low overheads and live inexpensively. Many small businesses exist on a shoestring, with owners living from hand to mouth, and certainly aren't what could be considered thriving enterprises. Self-employed people usually work extremely long hours, particularly those running bars or restaurants (days off are almost impossible in the high season), often for little financial reward. As in most countries, many people choose to be self-employed for the lifestyle and freedom it affords (no clocks or bosses), rather than the money. It's important to keep your plans small and manageable and work well within your budget, rather than undertake a grandiose scheme.

Many foreigners start businesses in Spain on a whim and a prayer with little business acumen or money and no Spanish. They're simply asking for trouble! **It's pitiful (but all too common) to see newcomers working all the hours under the sun struggling to make a living from a business that's doomed to failure.** Bear in mind that when a couple operate a business together it can put an intolerable strain on their relationship and many marriages fail under the pressures. Many people come to Spain with a grand design **without** doing their homework (research, marketing, etc.), lose all their money, hang on desperately for a few months or years trying to scrape a living in the expatriate community, and are eventually forced to return home much wiser and poorer, having learnt the facts of Spanish business life the hard way.

Generally speaking you shouldn't consider running a business in Spain in a field in which you don't have previous experience. It's often advisable to work for someone else in the same line of business (even without pay) to gain experience, rather than jump in at the deep end. If you're convinced that you have what it takes, don't burn your bridges and sell up abroad, but rent a home in Spain and spend some time doing research before taking the plunge. You should also lease your business premises (at least initially), rather than buying them outright. However, before doing so it's important to ensure that you fully understand your rights regarding possible future rent increases and the renewal and termination of a lease.

## Further Information

Most international accountants have offices throughout Spain and are able to assist (in English and other languages) on subjects such as forming a company, company law, taxation and social security. Many publish free booklets regarding doing business in Spain. The 'Invest in Spain' agency established by the government can provide a series of booklets in English, including the comprehensive *A Guide to Business in Spain*; they're obtainable from the commercial departments of Spanish embassies (London ☎ 020-7467 2330, ✉ londres@mcx.es, Dublin ☎ 01-661 6313, ✉ dublin@mcx.es and New York ☎ 021-2661 4959, ✉ nuevayork@mcx.es) and can be downloaded from the 'Invest in Spain' website (🖥 www.investinspain.org).

Many countries maintain chambers of commerce in Spain, which are an invaluable source of information and assistance. Each province has its own chamber of commerce, each with an international department. For information contact the Association of Spanish Chambers of Commerce, Consejo Superior de Cámaras de Comercio, C/Ribera del Loira, 12, 28042 Madrid (☎ 902-100 096, 🖥 www.camaras.org).

## TRAINEES & WORK EXPERIENCE

Spain is a participant in an international trainee (*aprendiz*) programme designed to give young people the opportunity for further education and occupational training, and to enlarge their professional experience and knowledge of languages. The programme has exchange agreements with different countries depending on the scheme, although Austria, Belgium, Canada, Denmark, Finland, Germany, Ireland, Luxembourg, the Netherlands, New Zealand, Norway, Sweden, Switzerland, the UK and the US are generally included.

If you're aged between 18 and 30 (US 21 to 30) and have completed your vocational training (minimum of two years), you may be eligible for a position as a trainee in Spain. The trainee agreement covers most occupations and employment must be in the occupation in which you were trained. Positions are usually granted for one year and in exceptional circumstances can be extended for a further six months. Information about the trainee programme can be obtained from INEM offices (see page 27) in Spain and government employment offices abroad.

Technical and commercial students who wish to gain experience by working in industry and commerce in Spain during their holidays can apply to the International Association for the Exchange of Students for Technical Experience (IAESTE) in over 60 countries. Applicants must possess a working knowledge of Spanish and be full-time students of agriculture, architecture, applied arts, engineering or science and aged between 19 and 30. Most foreign trainees in Spain are sponsored by employers or colleges under exchange arrangements. For information about trainee and work experience schemes in Spain, contact your country's national employment services agency or the national trade association for the industry in which you wish to train, who may be able to put you in contact with a suitable Spanish employer.

General details about training and apprenticeship programmes in all EU countries are available via the EU Ploteus portal (🖳 http://europa.eu.int/ploteus).

## Leonardo da Vinci Programme

The Leonardo da Vinci Programme is an EU-sponsored programme providing support for young people to benefit from vocational training and work experience in another EEA or Eastern European country. Placements are for between three weeks and twelve months and are targeted at young people in vocational training, young workers and jobseekers, and those taking part in an advanced training programme after starting work. Applications must be submitted through relevant training organisations or colleges or INEM offices.

# AU PAIRS

Single males and females aged between 18 and 30 (ages vary with the agency or employer) are eligible for a job as an au pair. The au pair system provides young people with an excellent opportunity to travel, improve their Spanish and generally broaden their education by living and working in Spain. Au pairs in Spain are accepted from most countries.

If you're an EU national, you need only a valid passport and it's unnecessary to arrange an au pair position before arriving in Spain. In fact it's often better **not** to do so. Some agents allow you to meet families in Spain, before making a decision. This is advisable, as you can interrogate the family, inspect their home and your accommodation, and meet the children who will make your life heaven or hell! If you arrive in Spain without a position, you can usually find one within a few weeks.

Applicants from non-EU countries **must** obtain a visa (see page 76) before arriving in Spain and require an offer of a position from a Spanish family. This must be presented to your local Spanish embassy or consulate (with your passport) in order to obtain a visa.

Au pairs are usually contracted to work for a minimum of six months and a maximum of a year. Most families require an au pair for at least the whole school year, from September to June. The best time to look for an au pair position is therefore before the beginning of the school year in September. You should apply as early as possible and not later than a month before your preferred start date – at least two months if you need a visa. There are also summer au pair programmes of two to three months, for which enrolment must usually be made before 31st March. Au pairs employed for the summer only aren't required to attend Spanish lessons. In addition to regular au pair positions, some agencies offer positions where a room is provided in exchange for around ten hours' work a week (e.g. for full-time students). Agencies charge a registration fee of around €60.

Au pairs are generally placed with Spanish-speaking families with children, although in areas popular with expatriates, families may be of other nationalities. Duties consist of light housework, including simple cooking for children; clothes washing (with a machine) and ironing (children's clothes only); washing up and drying dishes (if the family doesn't have a dishwasher); making beds; dusting; vacuum cleaning and other such jobs around the home. To enjoy life as an au pair you should be used to helping around the house and enjoy working with children. An au pair isn't a general servant or cook (although you may possibly be treated as one) and you aren't expected to look after physically or mentally disabled children.

As an au pair you receive free meals and accommodation and have your own room. Usually you're housed with the family, although this may not always be possible. Working hours are officially limited to 30 a week, five hours a day (morning or afternoon), six days a week, plus a maximum of three evenings' babysitting. You should have at least one full day (usually Sunday) and three evenings free each week, and should be free to attend religious services. In some families, au pairs are expected to holiday with the family, although you may be free to take Christmas or Easter holidays at home. Choose a wealthy family and you may be taken on exotic holidays.

For your labours you're paid the princely sum of between €70 and (in cities) €100 per week 'pocket money'. You're required to pay your own fare to Spain (and back). A family employing an au pair must make a declaration to the Spanish social security administration and make monthly contributions. If you're ill or have an accident during your stay in Spain, you can obtain treatment under the Spanish health system (see page 288).

An au pair position can be arranged privately with a family or through an agency, in Spain or abroad. Au pair positions can also be found through magazines (such as *Lady* in the UK) and newspapers, but you're usually better off using an agency. The best agencies vet families, make periodic checks on your welfare, help you to overcome problems (personal or with your family), and may organise cultural activities (particularly in major cities). Agencies send you an application form (questionnaire) and usually ask you to provide character (moral) references, a medical certificate, school references and a number of passport-size photographs.

Au pairs must usually have had secondary (high) school education (or equivalent) and have a good basic knowledge of Spanish. Au pairs **must** attend Spanish language classes organised for foreign students. An application form can sometimes be completed in your own language, although it's better to complete it in Spanish, even if it means obtaining help (forms are often printed only in Spanish).

Your experience as an au pair will depend entirely on your family. If you're fortunate enough to work for a warm and friendly host family, you will have a wonderful experience and lots of free time, and may even be treated to wonderful holidays in Spain or abroad. Many au pairs grow to love their children and families and form lifelong friendships. On the other hand, abuses of the au pair system are common in all countries and you could be treated as a servant or slave rather than a member of the family, and be expected to work long hours and spend most evenings babysitting. Many families employ an au pair simply because he costs much less than the lowest-paid nanny. If you have any questions or complaints about your duties, you should refer them to the agency that found you your position (if applicable). **There are many families to choose from and you should never remain with a family you're unhappy with.** You're usually required to give notice if you wish to go home before the end of your agreement, although this won't apply if the family has abused the contract.

Au pair agencies in the UK are listed in the *Au Pair and Nanny's Guide to Working Abroad* by Susan Griffith and Sharon Legg (Vacation Work). Several websites (e.g. 🖥 www.aupairs.co.uk and 🖥 www.findaupair.com) also provide lists of agencies and useful general information. You should contact a number of agencies and compare registration fees and pocket money, both of which may vary considerably (although the terms of employment should be the same).

It's possible for responsible Spanish-speaking young women, even without experience or training, to obtain employment as a nanny in Spain (and in many other countries). Duties are basically the same as an au pair, except that a position as a nanny is a real job with a real salary!

# ILLEGAL WORKING

Illegal working (*trabajo ilegal*) thrives in Spain, where it has been estimated that the turnover of the 'black economy' (*economía sumergida*) equals between 20 and 25 per cent of the official gross national product, and that real unemployment is much less than the official figure. After Italy, Spain has the largest black economy in the developed world (it's reckoned to be most widespread in Andalusia, Galicia and Valencia). Official estimates put the number of illegal workers at at least one million, although the real figure is probably at least double this.

In recent years, there has been a clamp-down on illegal labour and there are large fines for employers and workers, and even imprisonment for the most serious offenders. Companies employing illegal foreign labour can be fined for each illegal employee, and illegal workers can be deported and barred from entering Spain for up to three years. A foreigner has the right to a hearing before a court when an expulsion order is made. Occasionally amnesties are declared, during which illegal immigrants are given the opportunity to become legal without reprisals or penalties. One such amnesty in 2005 allowed some 690,000 immigrants to legalise their situation in Spain.

It's strictly illegal for non-EU nationals to work in Spain without a work permit. If you work illegally and don't pay tax or social security contributions, you have no entitlement to state insurance against work injuries, health care, unemployment benefits or a state pension. If you use illegal labour or avoid paying *IVA*, you have no official redress if goods or services are substandard.

# LANGUAGE

Although English is the *lingua franca* of international commerce and may help you to secure a job in Spain, the most important qualification for anyone seeking employment is the ability to speak good Spanish (or the local regional language). Spanish is the official language of 19 countries and is spoken worldwide by some 285 million people. It's the world's second most important commercial language after English and the third most widely spoken after Chinese and English.

What most foreigners refer to as Spanish is actually Castilian (*castellano*), which developed into classical Spanish. Castilian is **the** Spanish language, particularly among the educated classes, and is understood by most Spaniards. All references to Spanish in this section (and elsewhere in this book) are to Castilian, spoken by 65 per cent of Spaniards as their first or only language. The main exceptions are the inhabitants of the autonomous regions of the Basque Country, Catalonia and Galicia, where Basque, Catalan and Galician (respectively) are also official languages (see below). However, most Spaniards speak or understand Castilian (although they may be reluctant to do so). See also **Learning Spanish** on page 191.

## Regional Languages

Regional languages were banned under Franco, schools were forbidden to teach them and books weren't allowed to be published (many existing books were destroyed). Since the death of Franco in 1975 – and with the large degree of autonomy subsequently ceded to the regions – regional languages have made a strong comeback and are now taught in schools alongside Castilian. Basque, Catalan and Galician have also been revived by regional television and radio broadcasts and local film industries. Basque, Catalan and Galician are ancient languages with established literary traditions and you should **never** make the mistake of calling them dialects.

There are, however, also several dialects of Spanish, Catalan and Galician. For example, in the Balearics there are *Mallorquín* (Majorca), *Menorquín* (Menorca) and *Ibicenco* (Ibiza). All three are related to Catalan and similar in vocabulary, many words having their origin in Arabic, French, Italian or Portuguese. Many Spanish gypsies, who arrived with the Moors from North Africa, speak *caló*, a language that includes Spanish and elements borrowed from Sanskrit and other European languages.

In the Basque Country, Catalonia and Galicia, many street and buildings names, road signs, notices and official documents are in Spanish and the relevant regional language. The dominance of regional languages in the autonomous regions is causing increasing problems for foreigners and Spaniards from other regions of Spain. It's an important consideration if you're planning to live in Catalonia, Galicia or the Basque Country (particularly if you have school age children), where Spanish is a 'minor' language. In these regions, all communications from the authorities may be in the local language only and officials may refuse to speak any other language. This practice is especially widespread in Catalonia, where many people are obsessive about speaking Catalan and public notices and even restaurant menus are printed only in Catalan. Do you wish to learn Catalan or Basque, particularly if you already speak Spanish? Do you want your children to grow up speaking a 'foreign' language?

## Catalan

Catalan (*catalán*) is spoken by some 6.5 million people in Catalonia, the Balearics, Valencia, the principality of Andorra and parts of the French Pyrenees. Catalan is by far the predominant language in Catalonia, where Spanish speakers feel linguistically oppressed in much the same way that Catalan speakers were under Franco. This is particularly noticeable in schools, where all lessons apart from Spanish are conducted in Catalan. However, in Barcelona almost everyone speaks Spanish, while less than half are fluent in Catalan. Most Catalans readily speak Spanish, particularly to non-Catalans, although some refuse or pretend not to understand Spanish.

## Galician

Galician (*gallego*) is the language of the north-west province of Galicia. Some 2.5 million Galicians (80 per cent) speak Galician, and half of them (mostly in rural areas) don't speak Spanish. To make matters even more complicated, three dialects of Galician are spoken.

## Basque

Basque (*euskera* or, in Spanish, *vascuence*) is spoken by around 500,000 inhabitants of the Basque Country, mostly in rural areas. Although some words are borrowed from Spanish and French, the basic vocabulary and structure of Basque is unique. It's an ancient tongue of unknown origin and bears no relation to any other modern European language; it's thought by some scholars to be the only remaining representative of a pre-Indo-European language (a possible link has recently been found between Basque and the ancient Etruscan tongues). It's cluttered with consonants, particularly Ks, Xs and Zs, and unfathomable by anyone but native speakers.

# English

Unlike many other European countries, the majority of Spanish businesses don't use English as a working language (although the ability to speak and write good English is required for most jobs in business!) and the vast majority of Spaniards don't speak any foreign languages, particularly older Spaniards and people in rural areas. The amount of English spoken varies hugely with the area or city and the individual (professionals are more likely to speak English than shop assistants). In resort areas, such as the *costas* and the Balearic and Canary Islands, English is widely spoken and understood, as is German. It's also understood by many people in Barcelona and Madrid.

# 2.

# EMPLOYMENT CONDITIONS

Employment conditions in Spain are largely dependent on the 1980 Workers' Statute (*Estatuto de los Trabajadores*). Other governing factors include collective agreements (*convenios colectivos*), an employee's individual employment contract (*contrato de trabajo*) and an employer's in-house regulations. Salaried foreigners are employed under the same conditions as Spanish citizens, although there are different rules for different categories of employee, e.g. directors, managers and factory workers. As in many countries, part-time, seasonal and temporary workers aren't protected by employment laws and have few rights. Consequently, an increasing number of employers are engaging staff on a temporary basis, on short-term contracts, and it's estimated that nearly a third of workers (the highest in the European Union/EU) are in temporary or short-term employment.

There has traditionally been a link between a labour contract and a job for life in Spain. However, the situation has changed dramatically in recent years, during which Spain's economic problems have been exacerbated by the unions' uncompromising defence of high wages and rigid employment terms, which has become outdated in today's increasingly competitive world. Spain has the most rigid and costly labour market in Europe and critics claim that the requirements of the Workers' Statute are a major disincentive to investors and employers, and restrict employment due to the high cost of hiring and firing employees. In spite of a historic agreement reached between the employers and unions in 1997, whereby unions reduced their entitlement to redundancy payments in return for permanent jobs, many employers hire most new employees on short-term contracts, rather than permanent ones. The government is keen to introduce measures to reduce temporary employment, including increasing social security contributions on temporary contracts and reducing contributions for those employees with permanent contracts.

Those fortunate enough to be permanent employees enjoy excellent employment conditions and social security benefits, and extensive rights under Spanish law. The Workers' Statute details the minimum conditions of employment, including labour contracts, terms of hiring and dismissal, working conditions, employee representation and trade union rights. Spain has a statutory minimum wage (see page 39) and pay and employment conditions in many industries are governed by collective agreements, negotiated nationally or regionally for each industry, which stipulate the rights and obligations of employees and employers in a particular industry or occupation.

Employees are protected by the Workers' Statute prohibiting discrimination on the grounds of sex, marital status, age, race, language (i.e. between Spain's various official languages – see page 52), social status, religious belief, political opinion or trade union membership. Discrimination is also illegal with respect to mental or physical disability, provided a disabled person is able to perform the work required. Children under 16 cannot be employed, and certain restrictions apply to under 18s, e.g. a prohibition on working overtime, night work, and certain dangerous and unhealthy jobs.

# EMPLOYMENT CONTRACTS

Employees usually have an employment contract (*contrato de trabajo*), stating such particulars as job title, position, salary, working hours, benefits, duties and responsibilities, and the duration of employment. Note that the legally binding minimum terms of employment and minimum wages are usually decided by agreement between employers and trade unions and also apply to employees with individual contracts.

All contracts must be written in Spanish. (Note that the relationship between employer and employee is legally binding, even if there's no written contract, although you're strongly recommended to obtain one.) All contracts are subject to Spanish labour law, although references may be made to other applicable regulations, such as collective agreements. Anything in contracts contrary to statutory provisions may be deemed null and void. There are usually no hidden surprises or traps for the unwary in a Spanish employment contract. Nevertheless, as with any contract, you should know exactly what it contains before signing it. If your Spanish isn't fluent, you should try to obtain an English translation (your Spanish must be excellent to understand the legal jargon in some contracts) or at least have it translated verbally so that you don't get any nasty surprises later.

Employment conditions usually contain a paragraph stating the date from which they take effect and to whom they apply. There are two main types of employment contract in Spain: an indefinite term contract and a temporary or short-term contract (see below). Note that a short-term contract covering another employee's period of sickness or maternity leave, for example, or when there's a temporary increase in business, is classed as a temporary contract and should specify this; otherwise, a temporary contract is the same as a short-term contract.

In addition to a contract, you should receive a copy of your employer's standard conditions, containing general rules and regulations regarding behaviour and benefits that are applicable to all employees (unless stated otherwise in your employment contract).

## Short-term Contracts

Short-term contracts are usually for a minimum of a year and up to three years, after which an employer must let someone go or hire him permanently. At the end of the three-year period, an employer can fire an employee and it costs him nothing; if he does so one day later, it can cost him hundreds of euros!

The salary of an employee hired on a short-term contract mustn't be less than that paid to a similarly qualified person employed in a permanent job, and a short-term contract can be terminated before the end of its period in specific circumstances only, for example, when the employer or employee has committed a serious offence, in the case of an event beyond the control of both parties, or with the agreement of both parties. There are special contracts for seasonal workers, who have few legal rights.

# SALARY & BENEFITS

Salaries in most industries in Spain are decided by collective bargaining between employers and unions. Salary increases are usually in line with inflation, including those of public employees. Government attempts to freeze public employees' salaries have been overruled by the Spanish Supreme Court. Salary increases usually take effect from 1st January. See also **Salary** on page 38.

Your salary (*sueldo*) is stated in your employment contract, where details of salary reviews, planned increases and cost of living rises may also be given. In job contracts, salaries may be stated in gross or net terms. Salaries are paid weekly, fortnightly or monthly, depending on the employer. If a bonus is paid, such as 13th and 14th months' salaries (see below), this should be stated in your employment contract. General points, such as the payment of your salary into a bank account and the date of salary payments, may be included in your standard employment terms and conditions. Each time you're paid, you should receive a pay slip (*nómina de sueldo*) itemising your salary and deductions.

# Extra Month's Salary & Bonuses

Most employers pay their employees a number of extra months' salary (*pagas extraordinarias*), usually two – one in July before the annual summer holiday and the other in December. Some companies pay as many as four months' extra salary, although this is exceptional. Extra months' salary aren't mandatory unless part of a collective agreement, when they should be stated in your employment contract; in practice, however, their payment is universal and taken for granted by most employees. In your first and last years of employment, your extra months' salary and other bonuses should be paid pro rata if you don't work a full calendar year. Where applicable, extra months' salary are guaranteed bonuses and aren't pegged to a company's performance (such as with profit-sharing). Senior and middle managers may receive extra bonuses, perhaps linked to profits, equal to around 10 to 20 per cent of their annual salary.

# Expenses

Expenses (*gastos*) paid by your employer are usually listed in your employment conditions. These may include travel costs from your home to your place of work, which may consist of a rail season ticket or the equivalent amount in cash (paid monthly with your salary). Travelling expenses to and from your place of work are tax deductible. Companies without an employee restaurant or canteen may pay a lunch allowance or provide luncheon vouchers. Expenses paid for travel on company business or for training or education may be detailed in your terms and conditions or be listed in a separate document.

## Relocation Expenses

Relocation expenses to Spain depend on your agreement with your employer and are usually included in your employment contract or terms and conditions. If you're hired from outside Spain, your air ticket and other travel costs to Spain are usually paid for by your employer or his representative. In addition, you can usually claim any extra travel costs, for example the cost of transport to and from airports. If you travel by car to Spain, you can usually claim a mileage rate or the equivalent air fare cost.

An employer may pay a fixed relocation allowance based on your salary, position and size of family, or he may pay the total cost of removal. The allowance should be sufficient to move the contents of an average house (*castillos* aren't usually catered for!) and you must normally pay any excess costs yourself. If you don't want to bring your furniture to Spain or have only a few belongings to ship, it may be possible to purchase furniture locally up to the limit of your allowance (check with your employer). When it's liable for the total cost, a company may ask you to obtain two or three removal estimates.

Generally, you're required to organise and pay for the removal in advance. Your employer usually reimburses the equivalent amount in euros after you've paid the bill, although it may be possible to get him to pay the bill directly or provide a cash advance.

If you change jobs within Spain, your new employer may pay your relocation expenses when it's necessary for you to move house. Don't forget to ask, as he may not offer to pay (it may depend on how keen he is to employ you).

# Checklist

- Is the salary adequate, bearing in mind the cost of living in Spain (see page 355)?

- Is your salary index-linked and protected against devaluation? This is particularly important if you're paid in a foreign currency that fluctuates wildly or could be devalued. Are you paid an overseas allowance for working in Spain?

- Is the total salary (including expenses) paid in euros, or will the salary be paid in another country in a different currency, with expenses for living in Spain?

- When and how often is the salary reviewed?

- Is the annual salary paid in 14 instalments and are annual or end-of-contract bonuses paid (see page 60)?

- Is overtime paid or time off given in lieu of extra hours worked?

- Is free transportation or a travel allowance paid from your home to your place of work?

- Is free or subsidised parking provided at your place of work?

- Is a free or subsidised company restaurant provided? If not, is an allowance paid or luncheon vouchers provided? Many companies provide staff restaurants, which not only saves you money, but also time.

- Is a company nursery provided or an allowance paid for nursery care?

- Is professional training or education provided or paid for, if necessary abroad?

- Are free work clothes or overalls provided? Is the cleaning or laundering of work clothes paid for?

- Are fringe benefits provided such as subsidised banking services, low interest loans, inexpensive petrol, employees' shop or product discounts, sports and social facilities, and subsidised tickets for social/sports events?

- Are removal expenses or a relocation allowance paid?

- Does the allowance include travelling expenses for all family members?
- Is there a limit and is it adequate?
- Are the costs of selling your home, employing an agent to let it for you, or storing household effects reimbursed?
- Are you required to repay your relocation expenses (or a percentage) if you resign before a certain period has elapsed?
- Are you required to pay for your relocation in advance? This can run into several thousand euros for normal house contents.
- If employment is for a limited period only, will your relocation costs be paid when you leave Spain?
- If you aren't shipping household goods and furniture to Spain, is there an allowance for buying furnishings locally?
- Do relocation expenses include the legal and agent's fees incurred when moving home?
- Are the services of a relocation consultant (see page 97) provided?
- Is there a business entertainment allowance?
- Is a car provided? With a chauffeur?
- Is there a clothing allowance? For example, if you arrive in Madrid from the tropics during the winter, you will probably need to buy new winter clothes.
- Is private schooling for your children financed or subsidised? Does it include the cost of a boarding school in Spain or abroad?
- Is domestic help provided or a contribution made towards the cost of hiring a servant or cook?
- Are you entitled to any miscellaneous benefits, such as membership of a social or sports club or free credit cards?
- Is extra compensation paid if you're made redundant or fired? Redundancy or severance payments (see page 69) are compulsory for all employees in Spain (subject to length of service), but executives often receive a generous 'golden handshake' if they're made redundant, e.g. after a takeover.
- Will a hotel or lodging allowance be paid until you find permanent accommodation?
- Is subsidised or free, temporary or permanent accommodation provided? If so, is it furnished or unfurnished? Some Spanish companies provide subsidised housing.
- Must you pay for utilities such as electricity, gas and water?
- If accommodation isn't provided, is assistance given to find suitable accommodation? If so, what sort of assistance?
- What will accommodation cost?
- Are your expenses paid while looking for accommodation?

# WORKING HOURS

The standard working week in Spain is 35 to 40 hours and the average with overtime around 43. The normal working day is from 9.30am to 1.30pm and from 4.30 or 5pm until 7.30 or 8pm, although from June to September the working day may be continuous from 8am to 3pm (called *horario intensivo*). Foreign companies (and an increasing number of Spanish companies) often operate from 8.30 or 9am to 5.30 or 6pm, with a one-hour break for lunch. There are usually no scheduled coffee or tea breaks, although drinks can usually be taken at any time and it's common for workers to pop out for food or a cup of coffee once or twice a day during working hours.

The long afternoon siesta isn't as common as it used to be, particularly in the cities, and many hard-pressed workers and mothers no longer have time for an afternoon nap. In winter, banks and some businesses work on Saturday mornings. An attempt has been made to reduce working hours in recent years, in an effort to create more jobs, although this has usually foundered on employees' refusal to accept any reduction in their wages.

## Overtime

Overtime is never compulsory and cannot exceed 80 hours per year. It must be paid at not less than 175 per cent of the normal hourly rate. Employees cannot be obliged to work on Sundays unless collective agreements state otherwise, although when an employee agrees to work on a Sunday, normal overtime rates apply. Overtime may be compensated for by time off rather than extra pay, provided there's a written agreement to this effect. Employees are entitled to a minimum of one and a half days (including Sundays) free each week plus public holidays (see page 64). Twelve hours must elapse between the end of one working day or shift and the start of the next.

Salaried employees, particularly executives and managers, aren't generally paid overtime, although this depends on their employment contracts. Managers and executives generally work long hours, even allowing for their often long lunch breaks. Weekends are sacrosanct, and few people in Spain work on Saturdays and Sundays.

It may come as a nasty surprise to some foreigners to discover that many Spanish employers (including most large companies) require all employees to clock in and out of work. Employees caught cheating the clock are liable to instant dismissal.

## Checklist

- What are your weekly working hours?
- Are you required to clock in and out of work?
- Can you choose to take time off in lieu of overtime or be paid for it?

# HOLIDAYS & LEAVE

When public and annual holidays are taken into account, the average Spanish worker works fewer hours each year than those in other EU countries.

# Annual Holidays

Under Spanish labour law, a full-time employee is entitled to one month's (20 working days') paid annual holiday (*vacaciones*). Employers cannot count official Spanish public holidays (see below) as annual holidays. Some collective agreements grant extra holidays for long service.

Most employees take three or four weeks' summer holiday between July and August and perhaps a week in winter (often around the Christmas and New Year holiday period) and at Easter. August is traditionally the month for summer holidays, many businesses closing for the whole month or operating on a skeleton staff. When a company closes during the summer, all employees are obliged to take their holiday at the same time. Some businesses also close for two weeks over Christmas and the New Year.

Before starting a new job, check that any planned holidays will be honoured by your new employer. This is particularly important if they fall within your trial period (usually the first three months), when holidays may not be permitted.

# Public Holidays

The central government allows for 14 national holidays (*días de fiestas*) per year – more than any other country in Europe – but only nine (indicated by an asterisk below) are celebrated in all parts of Spain. Of the remaining five, regional authorities may choose up to four and add regional or local holidays (not listed below) to make up the total of 14.

| Date | Holiday |
|---|---|
| *1st January | New Year's Day (*Día del Año Nuevo*) |
| *6th January | Epiphany or Holy Kings' Day (*Día de los Reyes Magos*) |
| 19th March | St Joseph's Day (*Día de San José*) |
| March/April | Maundy Thursday (*Jueves Santo*) |
| *March/April | Good Friday (*Viernes Santo*) |
| March/April | Easter Monday (*Lunes de Pascua*) |
| *1st May | Labour Day (*Día del Trabajador*) |
| May/June | Corpus Christi (*Corpus Christi*) – second Thursday after Whitsun |
| 25th July | St James' Day (*Día de Santiago*) |
| *15th August | Assumption of the Virgin (*Asunción*) |
| *12th October | Virgin of Pilar or National Day (*Día de Virgen del Pilar*) |
| *6th December | Constitution Day (*Día de la Constitución*) |
| *8th December | Immaculate Conception (*Inmaculada Concepción*) |
| *25th December | Christmas Day (*Día de Navidad*) |

When a holiday falls on a Saturday or Sunday, another day isn't usually granted as a holiday. However, when a public holiday falls on a Tuesday or Thursday, the Monday or Friday is usually declared a holiday as well, although this depends on the employer. This practice is called making a bridge (*hacer un puente*). If a holiday falls on a Wednesday, employees may take the two preceding or succeeding days off, a practice known as making a viaduct (*viaductos*). When two public holidays fall midweek, many people take the whole week off (known as a *superpuente*)!

All public offices, banks and post offices are closed on public holidays and only essential work is performed. Foreign embassies and consulates in Spain usually observe all Spanish public holidays, **as well as** their own country's national holidays.

Most regions, towns and even neighbourhoods (*barrios*) have their own carnival and feast days (*ferias*). Although these aren't always official public holidays, most local businesses are closed, sometimes for a whole week. Due to the 'floating' nature of some holidays, such as Easter, an official annual public holiday calendar (*calendario laboral*) is published. Public holidays are marked on most calendars, many of which also show saints' days (calendars are distributed free by local businesses such as banks in December/January).

## Compassionate & Special Leave

All Spanish companies must (by law) provide additional days off for certain occasions, including moving house (one day); your own or a family marriage (one day); the birth of a child (two days for the father, the mother being subject to maternity leave regulations – see below); the death of a family member or close relative (two days). Grounds for compassionate leave are usually defined in collective agreements. Employees who have worked for a company for a number of years may be entitled to take a sabbatical, e.g. for one year (naturally **without** pay!).

## Pregnancy & Confinement

Female employees are entitled to benefits with regard to pregnancy (*embarazo*) and confinement (*baja por maternidad*). The family is of fundamental importance in Spain and employers are flexible regarding time off work necessitated by pregnancy. Social security benefits are generous and are designed to encourage large families (see page 291). Maternity leave is guaranteed for all women irrespective of their length of employment. The permitted leave period is 16 weeks; e.g. two weeks before birth and 14 weeks following birth. A doctor may authorise additional time off, before or after the birth, in which case a company must continue to pay your salary. A husband is allowed two days' leave on the birth of his child and a wife can transfer two weeks of her maternity leave to her husband.

## Sick Leave

If you fall ill and cannot go to work, you must inform your employer by phone as soon as possible on the first day. If you're still ill after three days, your doctor must complete and sign a social security sick leave form (*impreso de incapacidad temporal*), which you (or someone on your behalf) must present to your employer. This process must be completed every seven days until you're able to return to work. Sick leave lasting from 4 to 20 days is paid at the rate of 60 per cent of your basic salary; longer sick leave is paid at 75 per cent.

## Checklist

- What is the annual leave entitlement? Does it increase with length of service?

- What are the paid public holidays? Is Monday or Friday a free day when a public holiday falls on a Tuesday or Thursday respectively?

- Is free air travel to your home country or elsewhere provided for you and your family and, if so, how often?

# INSURANCE

All Spanish employees, foreign employees working for Spanish companies and the self-employed must contribute to the Spanish social security (*seguridad social*) system. Social security for employees covers health care (plus sickness and maternity), injuries at work, unemployment insurance, retirement benefits, and invalidity and death benefits. Contributions are calculated as a percentage of your gross income and are deducted at source by your employer. Social security contributions are high and total an average of 28.8 per cent of gross pay, although 75 per cent of this is paid by employers (see **Social Security** on page 288).

## Health Insurance

Most Spanish employers don't provide free private health insurance for employees, although they may have a group policy offering employees large savings over individual policies. Some employers, particularly foreign companies, provide free comprehensive private health insurance only for executives and senior managers and their families. For further information about health insurance see page 295.

## Salary Insurance

Salary insurance (*pago de seguro*) pays employees' salaries during periods of sickness or after an accident and is provided by social security. After a certain number of consecutive sick days (the number varies with the employer and in some cases with your length of service), your salary is no longer paid by your employer, but by social security. Employees in Spain don't receive a quota of sick days as in some countries (e.g. the US) and there's no limit to the amount of time you may take off work due to sickness or accidents.

You're normally required to notify your employer immediately of sickness or an accident that prevents you from working. If you're away from work for longer than two days, you're usually required to produce a doctor's certificate (*certificado de médico*). The actual period is stated in your employment conditions. For information see **Benefits** on page 291.

## Unemployment Insurance

Unemployment insurance (*pago de desempleo*) is compulsory for all employees of Spanish companies and is covered by social security contributions (see page 288).

## Checklist

- For how long will your salary be paid if you're sick or have an accident?
- Is extra insurance cover provided besides obligatory insurance?
- Is free life insurance provided?
- Is free health insurance provided for you **and** your family?

# RETIREMENT & PENSIONS

There's no compulsory retirement age in Spain, although the traditional retirement age is 65 for men and women. This is gradually being lowered to 60 and some companies have 'pensioned off' workers in recent years between the ages of 50 and 55 to reduce costs. Company pension schemes are often designed to induce employees to retire at a specific age, although an employee can be forced to retire (i.e. dismissed) only if his age restricts his ability to perform his job. If you wish to continue working after you've reached 65, you may need to negotiate a new employment contract.

## Company Pension Fund

In addition to contributing to social security (which provides a state pension), some employers have a company pension scheme (*plan de pensiones*), which is increasingly common in Spain. Where applicable, annual contributions to a company pension plan are tax-deductible and amounts range from €8,000 to €24,250 depending on the age of the policy holder. For further information see **Supplementary Pensions** on page 295.

## Checklist

- Is a company pension scheme provided? If so, is it contributory or non-contributory? If it's contributory, what percentage of your salary must you pay?
- Are you required or able to pay a lump sum into your pension fund in order to receive a full or higher pension?
- Is the pension transportable to another employer?

# EDUCATION & TRAINING

Most employers provide education and training schemes for their employees, many of which are subsidised by central government through a reduction in employer social security contributions. The government promotes industrial training through technical colleges and arrangements with business enterprises. Training may include management seminars, technical courses, language lessons or any other form of continuing education. However, the vast majority of the average company's training budget is spent on managers and executives rather than 'workers'.

If you need to learn or improve your language proficiency in order to perform your job, the cost of language study may be paid or subsidised by your employer. It's in your own interest to investigate courses of study, seminars and lectures, that you believe are of direct benefit to you and your employer. Most employers give reasonable consideration to a request to attend a course during working hours, providing you don't make it a full-time occupation!

## Checklist

- Will your employer provide or pay for professional training or education, if necessary abroad?
- Are free or subsidised Spanish lessons provided for you (and your spouse)?

# UNION MEMBERSHIP

There isn't a strong trade union (*sindicato*) movement in Spain and only some 2 million of Spain's 15 million workers belong to a union. Nevertheless, the two main union confederations, the socialist Unión General de Trabajadores (UGT) and the Communist Comisiones Obreras (CCOO), play a major role in industrial negotiations. Collective labour agreements negotiated between companies, employers' associations and worker representatives are legally binding on all parties. Employees aren't obliged to join unions, but all businesses with 50 or more employees are required to have some sort of employee representation.

Unions have the right to elect employee delegates to company committees or workers' councils, which should receive quarterly information on the company's performance and can express opinions on company strategy. Workers' councils in Spain aren't a joint management-employee structure, and neither unions nor employees have a say in management decisions.

With the exception of certain public sector employees, e.g. the police, employees are guaranteed the right to strike under Spanish law and cannot be dismissed for striking. Spain has had more strikes (*huelgas*) and lost more production days due to strikes in the last few decades than any country in the EU, although industrial relations have improved considerably in recent years and the number of productive days lost in 2004 when there were around 700 strikes was nearly 4,500. The government can enforce an imposed settlement (*laudo*) if a strike impairs public services or disrupts important sectors of the economy and industry.

# Checklist

- Is there a relevant union which you may join and, if so, what are the conditions and benefits?
- Is there a workers' council and how effective is it?

# OTHER CONDITIONS

## Changing Jobs & Confidentiality

Companies in a high-tech or highly confidential business may have restrictions on employees moving to a competitor in Spain or within Europe. You should be aware of these restrictions, as they're enforceable under Spanish law, although it's a complicated subject and disputes may need to be resolved by a court of law. Spanish law regarding industrial secrets and general employer confidentiality are strict. If you breach this confidentiality, you will be dismissed and may be unable to find further employment in Spain.

## Dismissal & Redundancy

It has traditionally been very difficult for employers to legally dismiss workers in Spain without paying a large redundancy sum (except in cases of gross misconduct), but the law has recently changed. In addition to obvious reasons such as mutual agreement and death, an employment contract can be terminated on 'technological and economic' grounds, for 'objective' causes or for disciplinary reasons.

Employees can be made redundant (*despedido*) on technological and economic grounds if there's to be a major restructuring of a company's workforce, provided the labour authorities agree to the company's redundancy plan. A formal procedure must be followed, allowing employees an opportunity to be heard. The company's plan must include an indemnity for each employee, equivalent to 20 days' salary for each year of service up to a maximum of 12 months' salary. In exceptional circumstances this may be paid by the government from a 'salary guarantee fund' (*fondo de garantía salarial*).

Objective causes for dismissal include employee ineptitude disclosed after a trial period, the inability to adapt to technological changes after a reasonable period (minimum two months) and retraining, and absences constituting over 20 per cent of working days in two consecutive months. An employee can also be dismissed in certain cases where his position is deemed to be redundant (in companies with fewer than 50 employees). To dismiss an employee for an objective cause, an employer must give the employee an indemnity (immediately on notice of dismissal) of 20 days' salary for each year of service up to a maximum of 12 months' salary.

Legal grounds for dismissal for disciplinary reasons include insubordination or disobedience, repeated absenteeism or lateness, physical or verbal abuse of your employer, fellow employees or family members, fraud, disloyalty or abuse of confidence, persistent laziness, working on your own account or for a third party without the consent of your employer, and habitual drug or alcohol abuse which negatively affects your performance. You must be given written notice of dismissal for these causes, stating the effective date of dismissal.

An employee dismissed for objective or disciplinary reasons may challenge the decision in the labour courts (*magistratura de trabajo*). However, you must first submit to conciliation between you and the employer, during which an agreement can be sought. If you're deemed to have been dismissed improperly, the employer may re-engage you or pay you compensation. If you're re-engaged, you're entitled to back pay from the date of dismissal to the date of judgement. If you aren't re-engaged, the compensation consists of back pay plus 33 days' salary for each year of service, up to a maximum of 42 months' salary.

Top executives can be dismissed without cause, in which case they're entitled to compensation of seven days' salary for each year of service, with a maximum of six months' salary (unless other terms are agreed in their contract). If the dismissal of an executive is successfully challenged in the court and judged to be unjustified, the executive is entitled to compensation of 20 days' salary for each year of service (up to a maximum of 12 months' salary), unless otherwise agreed by contract. Although the minimum compensation for executives is less than that for 'ordinary' employees, it's common practice for contracts to allow for higher compensation than the minimum.

If you run a small business and are planning to employ a part-time or temporary employee, you should get him to sign a written statement agreeing to terms of termination, or you could be sued for unfair dismissal.

# Medical Examination

Apart from the employees of a few large Spanish companies, prospective employees in Spain aren't usually required to undergo a pre-employment medical examination, although some must pass a psychological examination. However, a medical examination may be required for employees in specific occupations, e.g. where good health is of paramount importance for safety reasons, in which case an examination may be necessary periodically (e.g. every one or two years) or when requested by the employer. Where applicable, an offer of employment is subject to a prospective employee being given a clean bill of health. Medical examinations may also be required as a condition of membership of a company health, pension or life insurance scheme. Some companies insist that key employees undergo regular health screening, particularly executives and senior managers.

# Part-time Job Restrictions

Restrictions on part-time employment (*media jornada* or *trabajo a tiempo parcial*) may be detailed in your employment conditions. Most Spanish companies don't allow full-time employees to work part-time (i.e. 'moonlight') for another employer, particularly one in the same line of business. You may, however, be permitted to take a part-time job in a completely different line; for example, you could write a book!

# Trial & Notice Periods

For most jobs in Spain there's a trial period (*período de prueba*) of between 15 days and six months, depending on the type of work and the employer. It's usually 15 working days for unqualified workers, six months for university graduates and three months for other employees. The length of a trial period is usually stated in collective agreements, which impose restrictions on the maximum period. During the trial period, either party may terminate the employment contract without notice or any financial penalty, unless otherwise stated in a collective agreement.

Notice periods vary according to your position and length of service. Generally, the higher the position, the longer the notice period. Although many employees prefer to leave immediately after giving notice, they have the right to work their notice period. However, both parties can agree that an employee receives payment in lieu of notice. Compensation must also be made for any outstanding paid annual holidays up to the end of the notice period. See also **Dismissal & Redundancy** on page 69.

# Checklist

- If a dispute arises over your salary or working conditions, under the law of which country will your employment contract be interpreted?
- Is extra compensation paid if you're made redundant or fired (executives often receive a generous 'golden handshake' if they're made redundant, e.g. after a takeover)?

# 3.

# PERMITS & VISAS

Before making any plans to live or work in Spain, you must ensure that you have a valid passport (with a visa if necessary) and the appropriate documentation to obtain a residence or work permit.

The European Union (EU) allows the free movement of goods, services, capital and people between member states, and any EU citizen has the right to live, study, work or start a business in Spain. European Economic Area (EEA) and Swiss nationals who are employees, self-employed or full-time students in Spain don't require a residence permit. In order to qualify for this exemption, employees must have a legal contract of employment and pay monthly social security contributions and taxes. The self-employed must be registered with the local authorities, as well as with the tax office and pay monthly social security contributions.

Non-working and retired EEA nationals must still apply for a residence permit, and **all** foreigners require an identification number (see page 309). Citizens of non-EU countries must also obtain a visa from a Spanish consulate in their home country before coming to Spain to work, study or live (see page 76).

When in Spain you should always carry your foreign identity card, passport or Spanish residence permit (or a copy certified by a national police station) and produce it on demand to the authorities (if you don't have it, you can be fined). Permit infringements are taken seriously by the Spanish authorities and there are penalties for breaches of regulations, including large fines, deportation and even imprisonment for flagrant abuses. Spain has been criticised in recent years for its strong-arm, repressive tactics with regard to the deportation of illegal African immigrants, of whom there are many. On the other hand, thousands of illegal immigrants are granted residence permits under periodic amnesties and under a foreigners' law (*Ley de Extranjería*) passed in 2000. The latest amnesty in spring 2005 allowed around 690,000 immigrants who were working (illegally) and had been in the country since August 2004 to legalise their situation and obtain residence permits. The government has pledged that this is the last amnesty.

Immigration is a complex subject and the information in this chapter is intended only as a general guide. **You shouldn't base any decisions or actions on the information contained herein without confirming it with an official and (hopefully) reliable source, such as a Spanish consulate**.

Most official offices are open from 8.15 or 9.15am until 1.30 or 2pm and are closed for the rest of the day. The more important the office, the longer the queue outside **before** it opens, so it usually pays to arrive at 6 or 7am, unless you want to queue for hours inside and risk being sent home without seeing anyone!

In many cases, it simply takes too long or is impossible to get anything done through 'official' channels and many people give up or turn to unofficial channels; if you have a friend who knows someone in the administration or can afford to pay someone to 'speed things up a bit', it's often worth a try. Some police stations have backlogs of hundreds of applications for residence permits, where the stock reply is 'come back next month'. If you're refused a permit, you shouldn't accept it as the end of the matter, but should obtain legal advice.

Many people employ a lawyer or *gestor* (see page 461) to act on their behalf. A *gestor* is a professional who's trained to deal with the reams of paperwork involved in dealing with government officials. Although it isn't always necessary to employ a lawyer or *gestor* and may result in unnecessary expense, they can usually save you much time and trouble. Some town halls, particularly in municipalities with a lot of foreign residents, have established a foreigners' department (*departamento de extranjeros*) with staff who speak English and other foreign languages. If such a department exists in your municipality, it's worthwhile obtaining free counsel before going to the expense of employing a *gestor*.

A *gestor*'s fees are usually reasonable (lower than a lawyer's) and depend on the complexity of your case. However, the total sum required to make an application, e.g. for a work permit, can amount to €1,000 when all the costs are taken into account. Before employing a *gestor* to make an application for a permit on your behalf, obtain quotations from a number of *gestores'* offices (*gestorías*) and ensure that all expenses, translations, registrations and certificates are included. For anything other than a straightforward case, it's advisable to obtain professional help, particularly if you're starting a business, purchasing or renting property for commercial use, or employing staff.

Information (in Spanish only) regarding permits is available on the Ministry of the Interior website (💻 www.mir.es) in the *Extranjeros* section. You can download application forms for residence permits from the website. A free telephone information service is also available during office hours (☎ 900-150 000), although the operator will probably speak only Spanish.

# VISITORS

Visitors from EEA countries, North and South America, Andorra, Australia, Brunei, Bulgaria, Costa Rica, Croatia, Gibraltar, Grenada, Hong Kong, Israel, Japan, South Korea, Malaysia, Monaco, New Zealand, Romania, San Marino, Seychelles, Singapore and Switzerland don't need a visa for stays in Spain of up to 90 days. All other nationalities require a visa to visit Spain (see below).

Most visitors require a full passport, although EEA nationals and nationals of Andorra, Monaco and Switzerland can enter Spain with a national identity card. The period a visitor can remain in Spain depends on his nationality (e.g. 182 days for EU citizens).

If you're a non-EU national, it isn't possible to enter Spain as a visitor and change your status to that of an employee, student or resident. You must normally return to your country of residence and apply for a visa, although it's possible to obtain an exemption.

After 90 days, anyone permitted to remain in Spain as a visitor for only 90 days must apply for a 90-day extension (*prórroga de estancia*, also referred to as a *permanencia*, which means 'stay' in Spanish, not 'permanence') or cross the border to a neighbouring country which permits them to return to Spain for another 90 days. An extension (only one is granted per calendar year) should be applied for at a national police station (*Comisaría de Policía Nacional*) with a foreigners' department (*departamento/oficina de extranjeros*) at least two weeks before the 90-day period has expired. A person travelling around Spain and staying in different places doesn't need to leave the country or obtain an extension after three months.

Leaving Spain and re-entering after a brief period is easier than obtaining an extension and is quite legal, although your stay in Spain mustn't exceed a total of six months (182 days) in a calendar year. However, if you wish to prove you've left, you must have your passport stamped.

After 182 days, you must leave Spain or apply for a residence permit (see below), although if you're unemployed or have insufficient financial means, your application will be refused. After staying three months in Spain, a person with a permanent address must obtain an extension, leave the country or apply to become a resident.

# VISAS

All citizens of non-EU countries, including non-EU spouses and dependants of EU nationals, must obtain a visa (*visado*) from a Spanish consulate in their home country before coming to Spain to work, study or live. There are various categories of visa, including those for pensioners, investors, business people, employees of multi-national companies (transferees), other employees, teachers, students, extended-holidaymakers, and those performing cultural or sporting activities.

A non-EU visitor wishing to remain in Spain for longer than 90 days must obtain a special entry visa (*visado especial de entrada*) at a Spanish consulate before arrival in Spain. Spanish immigration officials may require you to produce a return or onward ticket and proof of accommodation, health insurance and financial resources (e.g. €100 a day for each day you plan to stay in Spain), although this is unlikely. Non-EU nationals planning to take up residence in Spain must obtain a residence visa (*visado de residencia*) before entering the country. The visa is stamped in your passport, which must be valid for a minimum of six months, and is valid for entry into Spain within 60 days of the date of issue. Some nationalities require an in-transit visa when passing through Spanish airports or ports for in-transit stays of less than five days.

Applications for visas must be made to the Spanish consulate that has jurisdiction over your place of residence and must be made in person by you or your authorised representative. Applicants (other than EU nationals) living in a country other than their country of nationality must have been resident there for at least a year. The following documentation is required by all applicants:

- A full passport valid for at least six months plus a copy of the pages showing your particulars.

- A number of completed application forms (the number varies and you should check how many are required).

- A number of passport-sized photographs, one of which must be firmly fixed to each application form.

- A small stamped, addressed envelope.

In addition, the following documentation may be required, depending on your reason(s) for visiting Spain:

- Proof of private health insurance if you aren't eligible for health treatment under Spanish social security (see page 288).

- A medical certificate (*certificado médico*) proving that you don't have yellow fever, cholera or the plague. This certificate should also state that you're in good health, free from drug addiction and don't suffer from mental illness. Medical certificates for employees must state that they're fit to work.

- A certificate of good conduct or a certificate confirming that you have no criminal record (*certificado de antecedentes penales*) issued by the police or another official authority in the country or countries where you've lived during the five years before the application. (A statement from your local police that you have no criminal record is usually sufficient to meet the requirements.)

Certain categories of visitor require additional documentation, as follows:

- Employees require a pre-contract for a job, stamped and signed by both parties, or a letter on the headed paper of the prospective employer in Spain. Note that your prospective employer must have filed the job offer with the Ministry of Labour in Spain.

- The self-employed require a copy of their Work Authorisation Application, filed with the Ministry of Labour in Spain, and must submit an application for a residence visa to the Spanish consulate within 30 days of the date the Work Authorisation Application was filed.

- Those planning to retire or start a business in Spain must present proof of financial resources. There's no fixed income required to obtain a visa to retire to Spain, but an income of around €930 per month or €11,200 a year is usually the minimum for a retired couple (although the recipient of an EU state pension will qualify even when it's less than this). A minimum investment of €120,000 (around US$120,000) is usually necessary for a non-EU national wishing to start a business in Spain.

- Retirees must also present a copy of the title deeds if they own a property in Spain.

- Students require proof of admission from an approved Spanish educational establishment, proof of sufficient funds to support yourself (at least €500 a month) and to pay for your studies plus proof of medical insurance.

- Au pairs require an agreement with a family in Spain (see page 49).

- A non-EU national married to a Spanish citizen or a foreigner resident in Spain needs a marriage certificate.

Various other documents may be required, depending on the purpose of the visa, many of which must be translated into Spanish. All translations must be made by an official translator approved by your local Spanish consulate (a list provided on request). Copies are also required of most documents, some of which may require an official stamp (*apostille*) on the back. The certificate of no criminal record and the medical certificate are valid for a limited period only, e.g. three months, so don't apply for them too far in advance.

Applications usually take six to eight weeks to be approved, although they can take much longer (up to four months for the investor or self-employment visa if you apply in the US). Successful applicants must collect their visas in person when advised by the consulate that they're ready. You require your passport and the fee of around €100 in local currency.

Visas are valid for 60 days from the date of issue. Those wishing to reside in Spain, other than those exempted from this requirement (see above), must apply for a residence permit (see below) within 15 days of their arrival.

**If you require a visa to enter Spain and attempt to enter without one, you will be refused entry.** If you're in any doubt as to whether you require a visa to enter Spain, enquire at a Spanish consulate abroad before making plans to travel.

# RESIDENCE PERMITS

A residence permit (*tarjeta de residencia*, commonly referred to simply as a *residencia*) is required by anyone wishing to work or start a business in Spain or planning to live there for more than 182 days in a calendar year, with the exception of EEA and Swiss nationals who are employees, self-employed or full-time students in Spain. EU nationals from eight of the ten new member states (Czech Republic, Estonia, Hungary, Latvia, Lithuania, Poland, Slovakia and Slovenia), holders of a residence visa (*visado de residencia*) and retired or non-working EU nationals planning to stay longer than 90 days must apply for a residence permit within one month of their arrival in Spain.

EU nationals who are retired or not working and planning to stay for a limited period (e.g. for under three months) are issued with a temporary residence permit for the period requested. If you require a permit and the period of your stay is indefinite, a five-year residence permit (*tarjeta comunitaria europea* or *tarjeta de residente comunitario*) is issued.

A non-EU residence permit is initially valid for two years or the length of a contract and on renewal is valid for five years.

If a husband or wife has a residence permit, his or her spouse is also considered to be a resident of Spain. Permits for dependants are issued for the same period as the principal applicant (children under 18 may be included on a parent's permit).

Although many EU nationals and their dependants no longer legally require a residence permit, many people have found that, in practice, it's useful to have one for identification purposes (it's considerably smaller than a passport), particularly British citizens who don't have a national identity card. Some transactions (e.g. opening a resident's bank account or applying for a mortgage) still require proof of residence, usually in the form of a residence permit. This can be obtained from your nearest police station, where you must present proof of identity and status in Spain (e.g. salary slip, social security documentation or student card). A residence permit is issued fairly quickly – within a few days in some cases.

**Irrespective of whether you have a residence permit, if you remain in Spain for more than 182 days in a calendar year you will be regarded as a resident for tax purposes and will be liable to pay income tax on your total worldwide income.**

In recent years, local authorities have tried to encourage foreigners spending over 182 days a year in Spain to register as residents (a process called *empadronamiento*) with their local council office, where they must present identification and proof of accommodation in the municipality. (The central and regional governments allocate funds for public services to each municipality according to the number of residents, so it isn't surprising that they're anxious that all bona fide residents register.) In any case, if you remain in Spain for longer than six months a year without obtaining a permit or registering as a resident, you can be fined up to €300 and be excluded from Spain for three years, although the law isn't strictly enforced, particularly for EU nationals.

A permanent residence permit is available to all foreigners who have held a normal residence permit for a period of six years. On the other hand, a resident of Spain isn't required to remain in Spain for any period of time and can spend as much time out of Spain as he wishes.

A resident in Spain must pay Spanish taxes on his worldwide income, may not own a car with foreign registration plates and must apply for a Spanish driving licence unless he holds a valid EU driving licence, which must be registered and stamped by the Spanish authorities (see **Chapter 11**).

# Applications

**It can take up to six months to obtain a residence permit, although backlogs have recently been considerably reduced, so it's wise to apply as soon as you arrive in Spain.**

Residence permits are issued by the provincial central police station (*Comisaría de Policía Provincial*) in the province where the applicant is resident, and applications must be made in person to the nearest national police station (*Comisaría de Policía Nacional*) with a foreigners' department (*departamento/oficina de extranjeros*).

It's advisable to obtain a list of the documents required (and the fee) in advance; if you don't have the correct paperwork, you will be sent away. Usually original documents must be accompanied by one or two copies. The documentation required depends on your situation, but usually includes the following:

- A passport valid for at least six months and a photocopy of the pages showing your particulars*.

- A marriage or divorce certificate or other papers relating to your marital status plus a Spanish translation.

- A number (usually three or four) of completed application forms (which can be downloaded from the Ministry of the Interior's website, 💻 www.mir.es).

- A number of passport-sized photographs (one for each application form)*.

- Proof of residence, e.g. your property purchase contract (*escritura*), a long-term rental contract or receipts for rent.

- The fee. The amount depends on your nationality and whether your country has a bilateral agreement with Spain (it's around €6.50 for EU citizens).

- A medical certificate (*certificado médico*), obtainable from any Spanish doctor.

- A certificate of registration (consular inscription) confirming that you're a resident in Spain, available from your country's consulate in Spain.

- A certificate of good conduct (*certificado de antecedentes penales*) declaring that you don't have a criminal record in your home country (you can request a statement from your local police authorities).

* If you're accompanied by any dependants, they also require a passport and photographs.

Additional documents are required by certain categories of person, as follows:

- Retirees require proof that they belong to a private health insurance scheme that's valid in Spain (the company must have an office in Spain) or that they have the right to medical treatment under the Spanish public health system (see page 288).

- Employees (other than EEA and Swiss nationals) require a job contract or an offer of employment in the form of a pre-contract stamped and signed by both parties. A contract issued to non-EU nationals must be one approved by the Ministry of Labour.

- The self-employed (other than EEA and Swiss nationals) require evidence that they meet the requirements to operate a business or perform a particular profession in Spain (see page 39) and a written presentation of a business proposal, including estimated investment required, details of business premises, number of jobs to be created, estimated income and your salary. Non-EU citizens require proof of their investment in order to be self-employed in Spain, as well as proof of sufficient funds, which must be a minimum of 30 per cent of the amount invested.

- Pensioners and people of independent means require evidence of sufficient funds or the receipt of regular monthly pension or other income. The minimum monthly income required is usually considered to be equal to the Spanish minimum monthly wage (€513 per month in 2005), although the recipient of an EU state pension qualifies. Non-EU nationals need sufficient funds or income for accommodation, living expenses and healthcare for the family. Non-EU pensioners must show proof of an annual income in the form of a pension, in addition to owning a home in Spain. Non-working non-EU nationals must show an annual income of at least US$75,000 and proof of accommodation; they're issued with a *visado de residencia sin finalidad lucrativa*.

- Dependants require evidence of their relationship and proof that they will be wholly maintained by the applicant if they're over 21 years of age.

- Students (other than EEA and Swiss nationals who are full-time students) require proof of enrolment with a recognised educational establishment, proof of sufficient funds to meet the cost of their studies and living expenses (at least €400 per month) and proof of health insurance.

- Au pairs require an au pair contract and a certificate of registration for Spanish-language classes (see page 191).

Some documents must be translated into Spanish by an official translator or endorsed by a public notary (*notario*). It isn't advisable to have documents translated or notarised in advance, as it's expensive and the requirements may vary with the area or office and your nationality. Always check in advance what is required.

When your application for a residence permit is approved, you're issued with a receipt (*resguardo*) as proof of your application. It's valid for two months and renewable until your permit is issued. The receipt also permits you to travel abroad and return to Spain without a visa, if applicable. When your permit is ready for collection, you're summoned to the local police station, where a print of your right index finger is taken.

Residence permits for foreigners (*tarjeta de extranjero*) are plastic and the size of a credit card. Cards are no longer colour coded and are the same irrespective of the type of permit. On one side is a photograph and your personal details, and on the other your fingerprint and the type of permit. Your permit also bears a foreigner's identification number (*número de identificación de extranjero/NIE*), which must be quoted when opening a Spanish bank account or paying Spanish taxes (see page 309). You should carry your residence permit with you at all times, as it constitutes an identity card.

If you lose your card or any of your details change (such as your address), you must report to a police station or foreigners' office within a month. When you leave Spain for good or cease to be a resident, you can have your residence status cancelled by simply handing your residence permit in to a police station with a foreigners' department (*departamento de extranjeros*).

## Renewals

The application for the renewal of a residence permit must be made at least two months before its expiry date. The procedure is the same as for the initial application (see above), although the documents required include (in addition to those listed above) proof of having paid your Spanish income tax, VAT and social security (as applicable). Non-EU citizens also require a certificate of good conduct from the Spanish Ministry of Justice.

The onus is currently on you to renew your permit before it expires, but it's expected that in the near future the Spanish authorities will contact permit holders directly reminding them of the permit's expiry and giving them an appointment for its renewal.

# WORK PERMITS

The requirements regarding work permits (incorporated into residence permits and known as *autorización de trabajo y residencia*) in Spain are set out below. Fees for work permits are up to €100, although they're usually paid by employers.

## Employees

The following regulations apply to employees; for information about work permits for the self-employed, see below.

## EU Nationals

Nationals of Austria, Belgium, Denmark, Finland, France, Germany, Greece, Ireland, Italy, Luxembourg, the Netherlands, Portugal, Sweden and the UK don't require a work permit to work in Spain. Until May 2006, all other EU nationals require a residence and work permit (*autorización de residencia y trabajo*), which is usually issued for five years.

If you're an EU national you can enter Spain as a tourist and register with the Spanish national employment office (Instituto Nacional de Empleo/INEM – see page 27) as a job-seeker. If you visit Spain to look for a job, you have 90 days in which to find employment, although if you enter as a visitor you can obtain an extension after 90 days or leave Spain and re-enter for a further 90 days (see page 76). EU nationals receiving unemployment benefit can be paid their benefit in Spain for 90 days. However, if you wish to continue to receive unemployment benefit after this period, you must return to your home country. When you're offered a job, you should obtain an employment contract (*contrato de trabajo*); with this, you no longer need to obtain a residence permit unless you're from Cyprus, Czech Republic, Estonia, Hungary, Latvia, Lithuania, Malta, Poland, Slovakia or Slovenia.

## Non-EU Nationals

Non-EU nationals must obtain a visa (see page 76) for the purpose of employment before arriving in Spain, the granting of which is subject to the approval of the work permit. When applying for a visa, a copy of the application form, passport and medical certificate certified by the consulate are returned to the applicant as proof of his application. These must be sent by the applicant to the prospective employer in Spain with other relevant documentation, who then applies for a work permit to the provincial office of the Ministry of Labour (Delagación Provincial del Ministerio de Trabajo).

The employment of non-EU nationals must be approved by the Ministry of Labour and Social Security (Ministerio de Trabajo y Seguridad Social), which can propose the employment of an EU national in place of a non-EU national. A position must have been advertised to EU citizens through the INEM before it can be given to a non-EU citizen and a work permit is issued only when it's demonstrated that there isn't an unemployed EU citizen available to do the job. Applications must also be approved by the provincial office of the Ministry of Labour, where the prospective employer is registered.

Spain has an annual quota of work permits for non-EU nationals, which in 2005 was 6,600 contracts, mainly in construction and agriculture. Quotas are allocated to individual provinces (Barcelona and Madrid have around 1,000 each) and are for specific jobs. Before work permits are granted or renewed, certain factors are taken into account, including the level of unemployment in the relevant profession or activity, the number of vacancies in the profession or trade, and whether a reciprocal agreement exists between Spain and the applicant's country of origin. Certain non-EU nationals are given preference, including those married to Spaniards; people closely related to a Spaniard or to someone who previously held Spanish nationality; nationals of Latin American countries, Andorra, the

Philippines, Equatorial Guinea, Portugal and Jews of Spanish origin; the family of a work permit holder and those born and living legally in Spain or who have been resident there for the past five years.

Certain categories of employee don't require work permits, including technical personnel invited by the state; foreign teachers invited by Spanish universities; the management of cultural teaching centres of another state or private centres recognised in Spain; civil and military personnel working with the Spanish government; accredited foreign press staff and members of international scientific missions carrying out investigations in Spain. Temporary and restricted work permits valid for six months (and not renewable) are issued to artists, journalists, performers, professors or other 'skilled' people performing temporary jobs in Spain. A temporary work permit is also required by non-EU students studying in Spain and is available from INEM offices (see page 27). Note, however, that although temporary employment may be permitted for students, it's usually extremely difficult to find work due to Spain's high unemployment.

A non-EU foreigner who doesn't fall into any of the above categories and who carries out an activity for monetary gain (*fines lucrativos*) in Spain requires a work permit and a residence permit, unless he falls into a certain category of worker (see below). The work permit is initially valid for a year, after which a two, three or five-year permit may be issued, no longer restricting the holder by area, activity, employer or industry. The spouse and children under 21 years of age of a non-EU work permit holder are also granted certain rights to work in Spain. A work permit isn't required to buy a property, make an investment, start a Spanish company or register a foreign company in Spain, although the person responsible for a company's activities in Spain must have a work permit.

The type and duration of work permits vary according to a number of factors, including the job to be performed, the region and whether the job is permanent or temporary. The following classes of work permit are issued to non-EU nationals:

- **Permit A** – For seasonal or temporary work in a particular area; valid for a maximum of one year and renewable.

- **Permit B** – For employees in a specified profession or trade, working for a specified employer in a particular location; valid for one year and renewable for a further two years.

- **Permit C** – An unrestricted permit allowing an employee who previously held a Permit B to work   anywhere in Spain in any occupation, but not as a self-employed person; valid for a maximum of three   years and renewable.

- **Permit E** – Allows any type of activity, including self-employment, anywhere in Spain; valid for three years and renewable.

- **Permit F** – Issued to workers who cross the frontier each day to work in Spain; valid for three years and renewable.

# Self-employed

A non-EU citizen wishing to be self-employed in Spain must obtain a visa before arriving in Spain (see page 76) and must then apply (see **Applications** on page 79) for a work permit D, limiting him to working in a particular activity and location. A permit is valid for a year and renewable twice for two years after which it becomes a Permit E (see above) with no location restrictions.

An EU national doesn't require a work or residence permit to start a business in Spain. However, a non-EU citizen wishing to do so must make an investment of around €120,000 in foreign currency in order to be granted a permit. You must also show that your professional activities will produce a profit and benefit to Spain. A licence issued for a business owned by a non-EU national may be conditional on the employment of a minimum number of EU citizens (the authorities can no longer insist that you employ Spanish nationals). Businesses that create jobs are welcomed with open arms, particularly in areas with high unemployment, where financial incentives are also available. Note that a Spanish consulate may insist that the investment is made, employees are hired and the business ready to operate before they grant a visa. You should apply for a work permit D well in advance of your planned move to Spain, as applications take around 11 months! For further information see **Self-employment** on page 39 and **Starting a Business** on page 41.

# 4.

## ARRIVAL

Spain is a signatory to the Schengen agreement (named after a Luxembourg village on the Moselle River where the agreement was signed), which came into effect on 1st January 1995 and introduced an open-border policy between member countries, which are Austria, Belgium, Denmark, Finland, France, Germany, Greece, Iceland, Italy, Luxembourg, the Netherlands, Norway, Portugal, Spain and Sweden. Under the agreement, immigration checks and passport controls take place when you first arrive in a member country, after which you can travel freely between member countries.

If you cross into Spain by road, you may drive through the border post without stopping, unless asked to do so. However, any goods and pets that you're carrying mustn't be subject to any prohibitions or restrictions (see page 465). Customs officials can still stop anyone for a spot check, e.g. to check for drugs or illegal immigrants. Not all border posts are open 24 hours a day; some smaller posts open only from early morning until some time in the evening and times may vary with the season. **If you plan to enter Spain via a minor border post, check the opening times in advance.**

If you arrive at a seaport by private boat there are no particular customs formalities, although you must produce the boat's registration papers on request. A vessel registered outside the European Union (EU) may remain in Spain for a maximum of six months in any calendar year, after which it must be exported or imported (when duty and tax must be paid). However, you can get the local customs authorities to seal (*precintar*) your foreign-registered boat while you're absent from Spain and unseal it when you wish to use it, thus allowing you to keep it in Spain all year round (although you can use it only for six months of the year). Foreign-registered vehicles and boats mustn't be lent or rented to anyone else while in Spain.

In addition to information regarding immigration and customs, this chapter also contains a list of tasks that must be completed before (or soon after) arrival in Spain, and includes suggestions for finding local help and information. Note that in Spain you should always carry your foreign identity card, passport or Spanish residence permit (or a copy certified by a Spanish police station).

# IMMIGRATION

If you arrive in Spain from another EU country, there are usually no immigration checks or passport controls (see above). If you're a non-EU national and arrive in Spain by air or sea from outside the EU, however, you must go through immigration (*imigración*) for non-EU citizens.

This involves completing an immigration registration card, which is usually provided on the aircraft or ship, and having your visa checked on arrival in Spain. If you have a single-entry visa (see page 76), it will be cancelled by the immigration official. **If you require a visa to enter Spain and attempt to enter without one, you will be refused entry.** You may wish to get a stamp in your passport as confirmation of your date of entry into Spain.

If you're coming to Spain to work, study or live, you may be asked to show documentary evidence, e.g. a return ticket and proof of accommodation, health insurance and financial resources. Spanish regulations require visitors to have a minimum of €100 per day on entry to Spain or a total of €700, although this doesn't apply to visitors on pre-paid package holidays (this rule was brought in mainly to deter illegal immigrants from Morocco).

The onus is on visitors to show that they're genuine and that they don't intend to breach Spanish immigration laws. Immigration officials aren't required to prove that you will breach the law and can refuse you entry on the grounds of suspicion only. Young people may be liable to interrogation, particularly if they're of unusual appearance or non-white, and will find it advantageous to carry international credit and charge cards, a return or onward travel ticket, and a student identity card or a letter from an employer or educational establishment stating that they're on holiday. Visitors from 'exotic' regions, e.g. Africa, South America, the Middle and Far East, may find themselves under close scrutiny from customs officials seeking illegal drugs.

# CUSTOMS

The shipment of personal (household) effects to Spain from another EU country isn't subject to customs (*aduanas*) formalities, although an inventory must be provided. Anyone arriving in Spain from outside the EU (including EU citizens), however, is subject to customs checks and limitations on what may be imported duty-free. There are no restrictions on the import or export of Spanish or foreign banknotes or securities, although if you enter or leave Spain with €6,000 or more in cash or 'negotiable instruments' (see page 310) you must make a declaration to Spanish customs.

Information about duty-free allowances can be found on page 441, importing pets on page 465 and importing vehicles on page 230. Further information can be obtained from the Dirección General de Aduanas, Ministerio de Economía y Hacienda (☎ 917-289 608, 💻 www.aeat.es – go to *Aduanas e I. Especiales*).

## Visitors

Visitors' belongings aren't subject to duty or value added tax (VAT/*IVA*) when they're visiting Spain for up to six months (182 days). This applies to the import of private cars, camping vehicles (including trailers or caravans), motorcycles, aircraft, boats and personal effects. Goods may be imported without formality, provided their nature and quantity doesn't imply any commercial aim. All means of transport and personal effects imported duty-free mustn't be sold or given away in Spain, and must be exported before the expiration of the visitor's stay in Spain.

## Residents

EU nationals planning to take up permanent or temporary residence in Spain are permitted to import their furniture and personal effects free of duty or taxes, provided they were purchased tax-paid within the EU or have been owned for at least six-months. Non-EU nationals must have owned and used all goods for at least six months to qualify for duty-free import; otherwise, goods are liable for 12 per cent VAT.

Non-EU nationals require an application form for a 'change of principal residence' (*cambio de residencia*) or for a secondary residence (*vivienda secundaria*), as applicable – available from Spanish consulates – plus a detailed inventory (in Spanish) of the items to be imported, listing their estimated value in euros. All items to be imported should be included on the list, even if some are to be imported at a later date. (You should include the make and serial number of all electrical appliances.) These documents must be signed and presented to a Spanish consulate with the owner's passport. If the owner isn't present when the goods are cleared by customs in Spain, a photocopy of the principal pages of his passport, legalised by a Spanish embassy abroad, are required.

Goods must be imported within three months of your entry into Spain and may be imported in one or a number of consignments, although it's best to have only one. If there's more than one consignment, subsequent consignments should be cleared through the same customs office. Items subject to special customs requirements such as electrical appliances, carpets and works of art should be packed near the container door to facilitate customs inspection. Goods imported duty-free mustn't be sold in Spain within two years of their importation and, if you leave Spain within two years, everything imported duty-free must be exported or the duty paid.

If you use a shipping company to transport your belongings to Spain, they will usually provide all the necessary forms and take care of the paperwork. Always keep a copy of all forms and communications with customs officials, both with Spanish customs officials and officials in the country from where you're shipping your belongings. **If the paperwork isn't in order, your belongings may end up incarcerated in a Spanish customs storage depot for a number of months.** If you personally import your belongings, you may need to employ a customs agent (*agente de aduanas*) at the point of entry to clear them. You should have an official record of the export of valuables from any country, in case you wish to re-import them later.

## Permanent Residence

Applicants importing personal effects for a permanent home must present to the consulate their residence permit (*residencia*) or, if the permit hasn't yet been granted, evidence that an application has been made. In this case, non-EU citizens must deposit with a Spanish bank an amount equal to 65 per cent of the value of their belongings; the bank then provides customs with a guarantee 'exempting' the owner from customs duties; the deposit is returned when a residence permit has been obtained. Non-EU citizens have one year in which to obtain a residence permit (see page 78) and request the return of their deposit. **If you take longer than a year without, you may lose your deposit!**

## Secondary Residence

Applicants importing personal effects for a secondary residence must present the title deed (*escritura*) of a property they own in Spain or a rental contract (lease) for a minimum period of two years. Non-EU citizens must deposit with a Spanish bank an amount equal to 65 per cent of the value of their belongings; the bank then provides customs with a guarantee that the goods will remain in the same dwelling, that the property won't be sub-let by the foreign owner or lessee, and that the property will be reserved for his (or his family's) exclusive use. After two years, you must obtain a certificate from your local town hall verifying that the goods are still in your possession. When customs receive the certificate, they issue you with a document authorising the bank to release your funds. It can take you some time after this to actually reclaim your deposit!

## Prohibited & Restricted Goods

Certain items are subject to special regulations in Spain and in some cases their import and export is prohibited or restricted. This applies in particular to animal products; plants (see below); wild fauna and flora and products derived from them; live animals; medicines and medical products (except for prescribed medicines); firearms and ammunition (see below); certain goods and technologies with a dual civil/military purpose; and works of art and collectors' items. **If you're unsure whether any goods you're importing fall into the above categories, you should check with Spanish customs.**

To import some types of plants into Spain, you must obtain a plant health certificate. There's usually a limit on the number that can be imported, but when they're included in your personal effects they aren't usually subject to any special controls.

If you're planning to import sporting guns into Spain, you must obtain a certificate from a Spanish consulate abroad, which is issued on production of a valid firearms licence. The certificate must be presented to customs on entry into Spain and can be used to exchange a foreign firearms licence for a Spanish licence when taking up residence.

# EMBASSY REGISTRATION

Nationals of some countries are required to register with their local embassy or consulate after taking up residence in Spain. For example, non-EU residents may require a certificate from their country's consulate in Spain (a consular inscription) declaring that they're registered with them in order to obtain a residence permit. In any case, most embassies like to keep a record of their country's citizens who are resident in Spain and registration can be in your interest if there's a national emergency or natural disaster, for example. Many countries (particularly European countries with a lot of residents in Spain) maintain consulates throughout Spain, which are an important source of local information for residents and can often provide valuable contacts (see **Appendix A** for a list of addresses).

# FINDING HELP

One of the major problems facing new arrivals is how and where to get help with matters such as finding accommodation, schooling, insurance and so on. In addition to the comprehensive information provided by this book, you will need detailed local information. How successful you are at finding local help depends on your employer, the town or area where you live (e.g. residents of resort areas are far better served than those in rural areas), your nationality, your Spanish proficiency (there's an abundance of information available in Spanish, but little in English and other foreign languages) and your sex (women are generally better catered for through women's groups).

An additional problem is that much of the available information isn't intended for foreigners and their particular needs. You may find that your friends and colleagues can help, as they can often offer advice based on their own experiences and mistakes. But take care! Although they mean well, you're likely to receive as much useless and conflicting information as helpful (it may not be wrong, but it may not apply to your particular situation).

Your local town hall (*ayuntamiento*) may be a good source of information, but you usually need to speak Spanish to benefit and may be sent on a wild goose chase from department to department. However, town halls in areas where there are many foreign residents often have a foreigners' department (*departamento de extranjeros*) where staff speak Spanish and English, and possibly other languages, such as Danish, French, German, Norwegian and Swedish (an advantage of living somewhere where there are many other foreigners). Some foreigners' departments also publish useful booklets in English and other languages. A foreigners' department can help you save on fees that you would otherwise have to pay to a legal professional such as a *gestor* or a lawyer.

Some companies employ staff to help new arrivals or contract this job out to a relocation consultant (see page 97). However, most Spanish employers are totally unaware of (or uninterested in) the problems and difficulties faced by foreign employees and their families.

In major cities and resort towns, a wealth of valuable information is provided by English-speaking clubs and expatriate organisations. Most consulates provide their nationals with local information, including details of lawyers, translators, doctors, dentists, schools, and social and expatriate organisations. Contacts can also be found through many expatriate magazines and newspapers (see page 434).

# CHECKLISTS

## Before Arrival

The following checklist contains a summary of the tasks that should (if possible) be completed before your arrival in Spain:

- Obtain a visa, if necessary, for you and all your family members. Obviously this **must** be done before arrival in Spain.

- Visit Spain in advance of your move to compare schools and organise schooling for your children.

- Find temporary or permanent accommodation.

- Buy a car, register it and arrange insurance.

- Obtain an international driving permit, if necessary.

- Arrange the shipment of your personal effects to Spain.

- Arrange health insurance for yourself and your family. This is essential if you won't be covered by Spanish social security.

- Open a bank account in Spain, transfer funds and give the details to your employer (you can open an account with many Spanish banks abroad). It's also wise to obtain some euros before your arrival in Spain, as this saves you having to change money on arrival.

- Obtain an international credit or charge card, which will be invaluable during your first few months in Spain.

- Don't forget to bring all your family's official documents with you to Spain, including birth certificates, driving licences, marriage certificate, divorce papers or death certificate (if a widow or widower), educational diplomas, professional certificates and job references, school records and student identity cards, employment references, medical and dental records, bank account and credit card details, insurance policies and receipts for any valuables that you have.

- You will also need the documents necessary to obtain a residence permit (see page 78) plus certified copies, official translations and numerous passport-sized photographs (students should take at least a dozen).

# After Arrival

The following checklist contains a summary of tasks to be completed after arrival in Spain (if not done before):

- On arrival at a Spanish airport or port, have your visa cancelled and your passport stamped, as applicable.

- If you don't own a car, you may wish to rent one for a week or two until you buy one. It's practically impossible to get around in rural areas without a car.

- Apply for a residence permit at your local town hall within 15 days of your arrival (see page 78).

- Register with your local embassy or consulate (see page 91).

- Register with your local social security office (see page 288).

- Find a local doctor and dentist (see **Chapter 12**).

- Arrange whatever insurance is necessary (see **Chapter 13**).

# 5.

# ACCOMMODATION

In most areas of Spain, finding accommodation to rent or buy isn't difficult, providing that your requirements aren't too unusual. There are, however, a few exceptions. For example, in major cities such as Madrid and Barcelona rented accommodation is in high demand and short supply, and rents can be astronomical. Accommodation accounts for around 25 per cent of the average Spanish family's budget, but can be up to 50 per cent in the major cities. Property prices (see page 98) and rents in Spain vary considerably depending on the region and city. For example, an apartment with a rent of €500 a month in Almería will cost at least €1,200 a month in Madrid and Barcelona, and at least €600 a month in most northern cities. In cities and large towns, apartments are much more common than detached houses, which are rare and prohibitively expensive.

Most Spaniards live with their parents until well into their 20s, and some 50 per cent of those aged between 25 and 30 still live in their parents' house, often because high property and rental prices mean they cannot afford to live away from home. However, nearly 90 per cent of Spaniards own their own homes, compared with some 75 per cent in the UK and Italy, 55 per cent in France and 45 per cent in Germany. Around 10 per cent of Spanish families also own a second home in Spain and the proportion is increasing annually. There are more than 2 million foreign property owners in Spain, which is Europe's favourite country for second homes, particularly among buyers from the Benelux countries, the UK, Germany, Ireland and Scandinavia. British and German property owners account for some 70 per cent of the total. Most foreigners are concentrated on the Mediterranean coast (the *costas*) and in the Balearic and Canary Islands. Officially, some 20 per cent of foreign property owners in Spain are residents, the majority of whom are retired, although the real figure is much higher, as many foreigners fail to register as residents.

Property prices generally rise at a steady rate annually, but over the last four years have soared throughout the country, increasing by 17 per cent in 2003 and 15.5 per cent in 2004. These figures were somewhat higher in many regions, e.g. Murcia (26.7 per cent), Andalucía (21 per cent) and Catalonia (19 per cent), and in many areas prices have increased by more than 50 per cent over the last six years. The most expensive cities to buy a property are Madrid (average €3,440 per m²), Barcelona (€3,105 per m²) and Bilbao (€2,590 per m²). In complete contrast are the cities of Lugo (average €736 per m²), Ourense (€1,094 per m²) and Zamora (€1,140 per m²).

The property boom has brought with it a massive increase in construction with some 675,000 new homes started in 2004 alone (a quarter on the Mediterranean coast) and many areas have an endless skyline of cranes. In resort areas, rising prices are fuelled by the seemingly endless demand for holiday homes, particularly from foreigners (especially British) and nearly one third of homes in Spain are holiday or second homes.

Many experts, including the Bank of Spain and *The Economist*, consider the current property situation to be inflated with properties overvalued by as much as 20 per cent and have warned of the dire consequences a drop in prices would have on Spain's economy and an individual paying a mortgage (see page 324). Property experts generally agree, however, that this won't happen in the near future and figures published by one of the leading valuers' associations (TINSA) showed a national price rise of 17 per cent in the year June 2004 to June 2005. Despite the price increases, property remains good value in most areas and is expected to remain so for the next few years.

You've probably heard a number of horror stories concerning property transactions in Spain, many of which are unfortunately true, although some stories are hugely exaggerated by the press. Nevertheless, buying property in Spain isn't the lottery it once was and most problems in recent years have been due to bankruptcies rather than outright fraud and a surprisingly high percentage have been caused by foolish buyers who are seemingly prepared to confide in complete strangers, hand over huge amounts of money or commit themselves to buying property they don't want or cannot afford! **It's vital to obtain expert, independent legal advice (see page 460) and beware of fraudsters when buying and selling property in Spain. Make your maxim for all property transactions: 'if you wouldn't do it in your home country, don't do it in Spain'.**

# TEMPORARY ACCOMMODATION

On arrival in Spain, you may find it necessary to stay in temporary accommodation for a few weeks or months, e.g. before moving into permanent accommodation or whilst you're waiting for your furniture to arrive. Some employers provide rooms or self-contained apartments for employees and their families, although this is rare and is often only for a limited period. Many hotels and hostels (see pages 365 and 369) cater for long-term guests and offer reduced weekly and monthly rates. In most areas, particularly in Madrid and other large cities, self-contained, service apartments are widely available with private bathrooms and kitchens. These are cheaper and more convenient than hotels, particularly for families, and are usually let on a weekly basis. In cities and resorts, self-catering holiday accommodation (see page 368) is widely available, although it's prohibitively expensive during the main holiday season (June to mid-September). See page 97 for more information about temporary accommodation (e.g. hotels).

# RELOCATION CONSULTANTS

If you're fortunate enough to have your move to Spain paid for by your employer, it's likely that he will engage a relocation consultant to handle the details. There are an increasing number of relocation consultants in Spain and many deal with corporate clients and/or individuals. Fees are usually around €250 per day or you can choose a package of services for a set fee, e.g. €2,500. The main service provided by relocation consultants is finding accommodation to rent or buy and arranging viewing. Other housing services include conducting negotiations, drawing up contracts, arranging mortgages, organising surveys and insurance, and handling the house move. Relocation consultants also provide reports on local schools, health services, public transport, sports and social facilities, and other amenities and services. Some companies provide daily advice and assistance, e.g. assisting clients in their dealings with local officials and businesses.

Finding rental accommodation for single people or couples without children can usually be accomplished in a few weeks, while housing families may take longer, depending on the location and requirements. You should usually allow at least two months between your initial visit and moving into a purchased property in Spain.

# BUYING PROPERTY

Buying property in Spain is usually a good long-term investment and is preferable to renting (see page 100). However, if you're staying only for a short term, say less than three years, then you may be better off renting. For those staying longer than this, buying is usually the better option, particularly as buying a house or apartment is generally no more expensive than renting in the long term and could yield a handsome profit. Property in Spain is relatively inexpensive compared with many other European countries, although the fees associated with a purchase add around 10 per cent to the cost.

The Spanish don't generally buy property as an investment and you shouldn't expect to make a quick profit when buying property. In spite of the high rises in prices over the last few years, you need to own a house for up to three years simply to recover the fees associated with buying (around 10 per cent of the price). Capital gains tax (see page 346) can also take a large chunk out of a profit made on the sale of a second home, particularly for non-residents.

As when buying property anywhere, it's never advisable to be in too much of a hurry. Have a good look around your preferred area(s) and make sure that you have a clear picture of the prices and the types of properties available. There's a huge variety of properties in Spain ranging from derelict farmhouses requiring complete restoration to new luxury apartments and villas with all modern conveniences. Some people set themselves impossible deadlines in which to buy a property or business (e.g. a few days or a week) and often end up bitterly regretting their impulsive decision. Although it's a common practice, mixing a holiday with a property purchase isn't advisable, as most people are inclined to make poor business decisions when their mind is on play rather than work.

It's a wise or lucky person who gets his choice absolutely right first time, which is why most experts recommend that you rent before buying unless you're absolutely sure what you want, how much you wish to pay and where you want to live. To reduce the chances of making an expensive error when buying in an unfamiliar region, it's often prudent to rent for 6 to 12 months, taking in the worst part of the year (weather-wise). This allows you to become familiar with the region and the weather, and gives you plenty of time to look around for a permanent home at your leisure. There's no shortage of properties for sale in Spain and whatever kind of property you're looking for, you will have an abundance from which to choose. Wait until you find your 'dream' home and then think about it for another week or two before signing a contract.

## Publications & Exhibitions

For anyone planning to buy a home in Spain, our sister publications, *Buying a Home in Spain* (also written by David Hampshire) and *The Best Places to Buy a Home in Spain* by Joanna Styles (both Survival Books), are essential reading (see **Order Forms** on page 531). A comprehensive list of other reference books is contained in **Appendix B**. Outbound Publishing (1 Commercial Road, Eastbourne, East Sussex BN21 3XQ, UK, ☎ 01323-726040, 💻 www.outboundpublishing.com) publish *World* *of Property*, a quarterly publication containing many properties for sale in Spain (and other countries), and stage property exhibitions in the north and south of England. Property is also advertised for sale in many newspapers and magazines in Spain and abroad (see pages 434). See also **Appendix A**.

## Independent Advice & Information

A useful source of information for foreign property buyers in Spain is the Foundation Institute of Foreign Property Owners (Fundación Instituto de Propietarios Extranjeros/FIPE, Apartado de Correos 418, 03590 Altea (Alicante), ☎ 965-842 312, 💻 www.fipe.org). The FIPE publishes an English-language magazine called *Boletín* for members which contains valuable information, including an early warning system for owners who are the subject of official municipal notices regarding tax and other debts. The FIPE is 'the voice of foreign homeowners in Spain' and provides free advice to members about buying and renting accommodation, a free document check and legal scrutiny of contracts (for a fee). They can also help you choose an agent or lawyer and avoid the crooks, and they publish a wealth of information, much of which is free to members.

Another excellent source of property information is Spanish Property Insight (💻 www.spanishpropertyinsight) whose advice and information is up to date and, most importantly, objective. The site also has a forum and a free monthly 'e-newsletter' offering the latest developments in Spanish property.

# RENTED ACCOMMODATION

If you're planning to stay in Spain for only a few years (say less than three), renting is usually the best solution. (In this section, rentals for longer than a year are referred to as long-term rentals.) Long-term rental is also the answer for those who don't want the trouble, expense and restrictions associated with buying a property. It saves you tying up your capital and can be surprisingly inexpensive in many regions (some people let out their family homes abroad and rent one in Spain, and sometimes make a profit). Renting also affords you maximum flexibility should you wish to move to another region in Spain, return home or even move to another country. In today's uncertain financial climate, there can be considerable risks associated with buying property, particularly if you're unsure of your long-term plans.

**Even if you're looking for a permanent home in Spain, it's wise to rent for a period until you know exactly what you want, how much you wish to pay and where you want to live.** This is particularly important for those who don't know Spain well. Renting allows you to become familiar with an area, its weather, amenities and the local people; to meet other foreigners who have made their homes in Spain and share their experiences and not least, to discover the cost of living at first hand. Rentals for up to a year are referred to here as short-term rentals; note, however, that this section isn't concerned with holiday rentals (for information about holiday rentals see **Self-catering** on page 368).

If you're looking for a property in a resort area, short-term rentals are good value, particularly during the winter, although in most resort areas there's a shortage of short-term rental accommodation because property owners prefer the higher returns from holiday (mainly summer) rentals. You may be able to rent a property from October to May quite easily, but have to vacate it for the summer. The majority of properties in major cities are rented – mostly small, one or two-roomed apartments; large apartments and houses are difficult to find and prohibitively expensive.

Many long-term rental properties in Spain are let unfurnished. Note that 'unfurnished' doesn't simply mean 'without furniture' in Spain. An unfurnished property, particularly in major cities, is usually an 'empty shell' with no light fixtures, curtain rods or even a television aerial. There's also no cooker, refrigerator or dishwasher and there may even be no kitchen units, carpets or kitchen sink! Always ask before viewing, as you may save yourself a wasted trip. If the previous tenant has fitted items such as carpets and kitchen cupboards, he may ask you to reimburse him for the cost. You should be prepared to negotiate the price and make sure that you receive value for money.

Furnished (*amueblado*) properties can be difficult to find in cities, although they're common in resort areas, particularly for short-term rentals. In any case, if you're looking for a short-term rental, you're better off renting a furnished apartment or house.

In an attempt to alleviate the saturated rental market and to provide low-cost housing for the under 35s, many of whom cannot afford their own accommodation, several government incentives are available such as payments of up to €240 per month towards rental expenses over a two-year period for under 35s whose annual income is less than €15,792 and grants of up to €6,000 for property owners who let their property. These grants are to be used towards the cost of indemnity insurance, repair of wear and tear, and any restoration needed on the property. In order to qualify, properties cannot be larger than 120m$^2$ and must be let for a minimum of five years.

See also **Temporary Accommodation** on page 97 and **Self-catering** on page 368.

# Finding a Rental Property

Your success or failure in finding a suitable rental property depends on many factors, not least the type of rental you're looking for, how much you want to pay and the area where you wish to live. Finding a property to rent in Madrid or Barcelona is similar to the situation in London or Paris, where the most desirable properties are often found through personal contacts. There are a number of ways of finding a property to rent, including the following:

● Ask your friends, relatives and acquaintances to help spread the word, particularly if you're looking in the area where you already live. A lot of rental properties, particularly in major cities, are found by word of mouth. You can also look out for 'to rent' (*se alquila*) signs in windows. If you're looking for an apartment in a block in Madrid or Barcelona, ask the concierge (*portero*) if there are any vacancies in a building or if anything will be vacant soon.

● Check the advertisements in local Spanish newspapers and magazines under *alquiler*. If you cannot speak Spanish, you may prefer to respond to advertisements in expatriate newspapers and magazines (see page 434), where advertisers are likely to speak English or other foreign languages. In major cities, there are property newspapers and magazines. There's little jargon or abbreviations in Spanish rental advertisements and most can be deciphered without too much trouble.

● Visit accommodation and letting agents. Most cities and large towns have estate agents (*agentes de propiedad inmobiliaria*) who also act as letting agents for owners. It's often better to deal with an agent than directly with owners, particularly concerning contracts and legal matters. Some agents advertise abroad in property publications and many companies handling holiday rentals also offer longer term rentals, particularly during the winter. **Agents usually charge commission equal to a half or one month's rent for long-term rentals.** If you wish to avoid agency fees ask before viewing, as advertisers who appear to be private individuals are often agencies.

● Check the advertisements in shop windows and on notice boards in shopping centres, supermarkets, universities and colleges, and company offices.

● Obtain copies of newsletters published by churches, clubs and expatriate organisations, and also check their notice boards.

To find accommodation through advertisements in local newspapers you must usually be quick off the mark. Buy the newspaper as soon as it's published and start phoning straight away. You must be available to inspect properties immediately or at any time. Even if you start phoning at the crack of dawn, you're still likely to find a queue when you arrive to view a choice property in Madrid or Barcelona. The best days for advertisements are usually Fridays and Saturdays. Advertisers may be private owners or letting agencies (particularly in major cities). You can insert a 'rental wanted' advertisement in many newspapers and on notice boards, but don't count on success using this method.

Young people aged between 18 and 35 in the regions of Aragon, Baleares, Canaries, Cantabria, Castilla-La Mancha, Castilla y León, Catalonia, Madrid and Navarra have access to the regional 'Young Person's Accommodation Centre' (*Bolsa de Vivienda Joven*) where general information about accommodation, legal advice and a selection of rental accommodation are available. Further information about the centre is provided by the Youth Services (*Servicios de Juventud*) at regional government offices.

# Rental Costs

Rental costs vary considerably depending on the size, quality and age of a property, and the facilities provided. However, the most significant factor affecting rents is the region, the city and the particular neighbourhood. In major cities, particularly Madrid and Barcelona, rental accommodation is in high demand and short supply, and rents are high. A two bedroom, unfurnished apartment (e.g. 75m$^2$) which rents for around €1,200 a month in Madrid or Barcelona, costs around 50 per cent less in most smaller cities, and rural and resort areas. However, rents have risen considerably on the Costa del Sol and in other resort areas, where there's a relatively small long-term rental market. Rents are lowest in small towns and rural areas, although good rental accommodation is often difficult to find.

Many Spanish families live in communal property developments called *urbanizaciones* (which surround Spanish cities), where rents may be lower than in city centres. Rents are also dictated by supply and demand and are higher in cities than in rural and resort areas (except for short lets during the high season). In an apartment block, generally, the higher the apartment, the more expensive it is. However, if a block doesn't have a lift, apartments on lower floors may be the most expensive. A **rough** guide to rents in Spain as a whole is shown below:

| Property | Monthly Rent (€) | |
|---|---|---|
| | Provincial Towns | Major Cities/Resort Areas |
| Studio | From 250 | From 275 |
| 1/2-bedroom apartment | From 400 | 500 – 1,300+ |
| 3-bedroom apartment | From 500 | 600 – 2,200+ |
| 2/3-bedroom townhouse | From 600 | 700 – 2,300+ |
| 3+ bedroom villa with pool | From 800 | 2,500+ |

A **rough** guide to rents in Barcelona and Madrid is shown below:

| Property | Monthly Rent (€) | |
|---|---|---|
| | Barcelona | Madrid |
| Studio | 275 – 550 | 490 – 1,050+ |
| 1/2-bedroom apartment | 550 – 800 | 1,100 – 1,300+ |
| 2/3-bedroom apartment | 610 – 1,200 | 1,900 – 2,200+ |
| 4+ bedroom apartment | 750 – 2,500+ | 3,000+ |

The rents listed above are for good quality new or recently renovated properties and, with the exception of villas, don't usually include a garage. **They don't include apartments located in the central area of cities or properties in exclusive residential areas.** It's possible in some areas to find cheaper, older apartments, but they're rare, generally small and don't usually contain the standard 'fixtures and fittings' of a modern apartment. Rents in resorts are similar for furnished and unfurnished properties, although some owners and agents charge 10 to 20 per cent more for a furnished property. In cities, most properties are let unfurnished. Expect to pay up to 50 per cent more than the rents indicated above, for a furnished property in a city.

## Extra Costs

Long-term contracts usually require tenants to pay gas, electricity and telephone bills, and may also include community (*comunidad*) fees, property taxes (*IBI* – see page 324) and water rates, although these are usually paid by the owner. However, if these charges aren't mentioned in your contract, they're the landlord's responsibility. If a property has a telephone installed you must usually pay a large deposit, e.g. €200. Always have a contract checked by a lawyer if you don't understand it. Tenants should take out third party insurance (see page 303) for a property they're renting and if the property is let unfurnished you should take out contents insurance for your belongings.

## Seasonal Letting

Rents for short-term lets (of less than one year), are usually higher than for longer lets. However, many agents let furnished holiday homes in resort areas (except for the Canaries) at a considerable reduction during the 'low season', which may extend from October to May. Some holiday letting agents divide the rental year into three seasons, e.g. low (October to March), medium (April to June) and high (July to September). The rent for a one or two-bedroom furnished apartment or townhouse during the low season ranges from between €500 and €800 a month for a minimum one or two-month let. Rent is usually paid one month in advance with one month's rent as a deposit (which is forfeited if you leave before the end of the contract). Lets of less than one month are more expensive, e.g. €300 per week for a two-bedroom apartment in the low season, which is around half the rental in the high season. Note that many hotels and hostels also offer special low rates for long stays during the low season (see page 361).

# Rental Contracts

A rental contract (*contrato de arrendamiento*) is necessary when renting any property in Spain, whether long or short term. A short-term or temporary (*arriendo de temporada* or *contrato de arrendamiento de finca urbana amueblada, por temporada*) contract is usually for holiday letting (although it also applies to lets of up to a year) and provides tenants with fewer rights than a long-term (*arriendo de viviendas*) contract (for lets of more than a year). You can rent a property without a contract, although it's advisable to have a written contract. Rental contracts are usually standard state-sponsored tenant/landlord agreements available from tobacconists (*estancos*) for €12. If you don't understand a contract you should have it checked by a lawyer before signing it. When a landlord accepts a rent payment there's an implicit contract, although this is only for the period for which you've paid. **You should receive a written receipt for all rental payments.**

The current law of urban lettings (*ley de arrendamientos urbanos*) balances the rights of landlords and tenants (in the long-term rental market). A rental contract for a principal home has a minimum duration of five years and is renewable annually by mutual consent. A contract is tacitly increased for one year if the tenant doesn't give the landlord 30 days' notice before the end of a year and rent increases are limited to the rise in the consumer price (inflation) index (*indice de precios al consumo/IPC*). If a landlord wishes to recover a property for his own use he can refuse to extend the contract beyond five years. The right to pass on a tenancy is limited to a spouse or child.

A tenant must pay a deposit of one month's rent (two month's rent if the property is furnished) against damages, which may be held by the landlord, an independent agency or the housing department of the regional government. Tenants may be required to pay property tax (see page 344) and community fees if it's specified in the contract.

**If you're a landlord, you must be careful not to fall into the trap whereby you sign a temporary contract, say for one year, which is later interpreted by a court as a long-term contract valid for five years. This is common practice when the tenant is a resident of Spain and is the reason why many foreigners refuse to rent to Spaniards.**

A tenant can be evicted under certain circumstances, although the owner may require a court order (*demanda de desahucio*) to force him to leave the property. Reasons for eviction include failure to pay the rent, damage to property, use of property for immoral purposes, sub-letting a property without permission from the owner, and causing a serious nuisance to neighbours. A tenant can terminate the contract (and is entitled to compensation) if the landlord has caused changes or disturbances in the property, doesn't carry out any necessary repairs to keep the property in adequate condition, or doesn't offer the services that are stated in the contract.

If you have a complaint regarding a long-term rental, you should report it to the local municipal consumers' information office (Oficina Municipal de Información al Consumidor/OMIC). If they're unable to help you, they will direct you to the office where you can make a formal complaint.

# Inventory

When renting a property you may be required to complete and sign an inventory (*inventario*) of the fixtures, fittings and furnishings, and make a report of its general condition. This usually includes the condition of fixtures and fittings, the state of furniture and carpets, etc. (if furnished), the cleanliness and state of the decoration, and anything missing or in need of repair. **Don't sign the inventory until after you've moved in.** If you find a serious fault after signing the inventory, send a registered letter to your landlord asking for it to be attached to the inventory.

An inventory document should be provided by your landlord or letting agent and normally includes every single item in a furnished property. Note, however, that many rental companies in resort areas in Spain are negligent when it comes to providing an inventory. This is to your advantage, as the landlord or agent can hardly charge you for breakages or missing items when no inventory was provided. If an inventory isn't provided, you can ask for one to be prepared and annexed to the lease. Where applicable, an inventory should be drawn up when moving in and when vacating rented accommodation. If the two inventories don't correspond, the tenant must make good any damages or deficiencies or the landlord can do so and deduct the cost from the tenant's deposit. Although Spanish landlords are no worse than landlords in most other countries, some use any excuse to prevent repaying a deposit. When leaving rented accommodation you may be required to pay for cleaning, unless you leave it in a spotless condition. Check that you aren't overcharged; the going rate in most areas is from €8 to €12 an hour, although some landlords may try to charge you €15 or more an hour.

# HOME SECURITY

When moving into a new home it's often wise to replace the locks (or lock barrels) as soon as possible, as you have no idea how many keys are in circulation for the existing locks. This is true even for new homes, as builders often give keys to subcontractors. In any case, it's advisable to change the external lock barrels regularly, e.g. annually, particularly if you let a home. If they aren't already fitted, it's advisable to fit high security (double cylinder or dead bolt) locks. Most modern apartments are fitted with an armoured door (*puerta blindada*) with individually numbered, high security locks with three sets of levers. Note, however, that in order to withstand a crowbar, an armoured door must be made of steel, which costs around €1,000. In areas with a high risk of theft (e.g. most resort areas and major cities), your insurance company may insist on extra security measures such as two locks on external doors, internal locking shutters, and security bars or metal grilles (*rejas*) on windows and patio doors on ground and lower floors. A policy may specify that all forms of protection on doors must be employed when a property is unoccupied and that all other forms (e.g. shutters) must also be used after 10pm and when a property is left empty for two or more days.

You may wish to have a security alarm fitted, which is usually the best way to deter thieves and may also reduce your household insurance (see page 300). It should include all external doors and windows, internal infra-red security beams, and may also include a coded entry keypad (which can be frequently changed and is useful for clients if you let) and 24-hour monitoring (with some systems it's possible to monitor properties remotely via a computer from another country). With a monitored system, when a sensor (e.g. smoke or forced entry) detects an emergency or a panic button is pushed, a signal is sent automatically to a 24-hour monitoring station. The person on duty telephones to check whether it's a genuine alarm (a password must be given) and if he cannot contact you someone is sent to investigate. Some developments and urbanisations have security gates and are patrolled 24-hours a day by security guards, although they often have little influence on crime rates and may instil a false sense of security.

You can deter thieves by ensuring that your house is well lit at night and not conspicuously unoccupied. External security 'motion detector' lights (that switch on automatically when someone approaches); random timed switches for internal lights, radios and TVs; dummy security cameras; and tapes that play barking dogs, etc. triggered by a light or heat detector may all help deter burglars. In rural areas it's common for owners to fit two or three locks on external doors, alarm systems, grilles on doors and windows, window locks, security shutters and a safe for valuables. The advantage of grilles is that they allow you to leave windows open without inviting criminals in. **However, security grilles must be heavy duty, as the bars on cheap grilles can be prised apart with a car jack.** Many people also wrap a chain around their patio security grille and secure it with a padlock when a property is unoccupied (although it may not withstand bolt-cutters). You can fit UPVC (toughened clear plastic) security windows and doors, which can survive an attack with a sledge-hammer without damage, and external steel security blinds (which can be electrically operated), although these are expensive. A dog can be useful to deter intruders, although it should be kept inside where it cannot be given poisoned food. Irrespective of whether you actually have a dog, a warning sign showing an image of a fierce dog may act as a deterrent. You should have the front door of an apartment fitted with a spy-hole and chain so that you can check the identity of visitors before opening the door. **Remember, prevention is better than cure, as stolen property is rarely recovered.**

Holiday homes are particularly vulnerable to thieves, especially in rural areas, and are often ransacked. No matter how secure your door and window locks, a thief can usually gain entry if he's sufficiently determined, often by smashing a window or even breaking in through the roof or by knocking a hole in a wall in a rural area! In isolated areas, thieves can strip a house bare at their leisure and an un-monitored alarm won't be a deterrent if there's no-one around to hear it. If you have a holiday home in Spain, it's inadvisable to leave anything of real value (monetary or sentimental) there and to have full insurance for your belongings (see page 300). One 'foolproof' way to protect a home when you're away is to employ a house-sitter to look after it. This can be done for short periods or for six months (e.g. during the winter) or longer if you have a holiday home in Spain. It isn't usually necessary to pay someone to house-sit for a period of six months or more, when you can usually find someone to do it in return for free accommodation. However, you must take care who you engage and obtain references.

An important aspect of home security is ensuring you have early warning of a fire, which is easily accomplished by installing smoke detectors. Battery-operated smoke detectors can be purchased for around €9 and should be tested periodically to ensure that the batteries aren't exhausted. You can also fit an electric-powered gas detector that activates an alarm when a gas leak is detected. When closing up a property for an extended period, e.g. over the winter, you should ensure that everything is switched off and that it's secure. If you vacate your home for an extended period, you may also be obliged to notify a caretaker, landlord or insurance company, and to leave a key with a caretaker or landlord in case of emergencies. If a robbery takes place, you should report it immediately to your local police station (see page 469) where you must make a statement (*denuncia*). You will receive a copy, which is required by your insurance company if you make a claim.

There are many specialist home security companies in Spain who will inspect your home and offer free advice on security, although you should obtain at least two quotations before having any work done. See also **Crime** and **Home Security** on pages 452 and 105.

# MOVING HOUSE

After finding a home in Spain it usually takes only a few weeks to have your belongings shipped from within continental Europe. From anywhere else it varies considerably, e.g. around four weeks from the east coast of the US, six weeks from the US west coast and the Far East, and around eight weeks from Australasia. Customs clearance is no longer necessary when shipping your household effects between European Union (EU) countries. However, when shipping your effects from a non-EU country to Spain, you should enquire about customs formalities in advance. If you fail to follow the correct procedure you can encounter problems and delays, and may be erroneously charged duty or fined. The relevant forms to be completed by non-EU citizens depend on whether your Spanish home is your main residence or a second home. Removal companies usually take care of the paperwork and ensure that the correct documents are provided and properly completed (see **Customs** on page 89).

It's advisable to use a major shipping company with a good reputation. For international moves it's best to use a company that's a member of the International Federation of Furniture Removers (FIDI, 🖳 www.fidi.com) or the Overseas Moving Network International (OMNI, 🖳 www.omnimoving.com), with experience in Spain. Members of FIDI and OMNI usually subscribe to an advance payment scheme providing a guarantee, whereby, if a member company fails to fulfil its commitments to a client, the removal is completed at the agreed cost by another company or your money is refunded. Some removal companies have subsidiaries or affiliates in Spain, which may be more convenient if you encounter problems or need to make an insurance claim. If you engage a shipping company in Spain, it's wise to avoid small unregistered companies ('man with a van'), as some have been known to disappear with their client's worldly possessions. A Spanish shipping company should have a Spanish business address, a registered licence number, a value added tax (VAT/*IVA*) number and must be licensed to do removals in Spain. For information about Spanish removal companies contact the Federación Española de Empresas de Mudanzas (FEDEM), C/ López de Hoyos 322, 28043 Madrid (☎ 917-444 703, 🖳 www.fedem.es).

You should obtain at least three written quotations before choosing a company, as rates vary considerably. Removal companies should send a representative to provide a detailed quotation. Most companies will pack your belongings and provide packing cases and special containers, although this is naturally more expensive than packing them yourself. Ask a company how they pack fragile and valuable items, and whether the cost of packing cases, materials and insurance (see below) are included in a quotation. If you're doing your own packing, most shipping companies will provide packing crates and boxes. Shipments are charged by volume, e.g. the square metre in Europe and the square foot (ft2) in the US. You should expect to pay from €4,000 to €7,000 to move the contents of a three to four-bedroom house within western Europe, e.g. from London to the south of Spain. If you're flexible about the delivery date, shipping companies will usually quote a lower fee based on a 'part load', where the cost is shared with other deliveries. This can result in savings of 50 per cent or more compared with a 'special' delivery. Whether you have an individual or shared delivery, obtain the maximum transit period in writing, otherwise you may have to wait months for delivery!

Be sure to fully insure your belongings during removal with a well established insurance company. **Don't insure with a shipping company that carries its own insurance, as they will usually fight every euro of a claim.** Insurance premiums are usually 1 to 2 per cent of the declared value of your goods, depending on the type of cover chosen. It's prudent to make a photographic or video record of valuables for insurance purposes. Most insurance policies cover for 'all-risks' on a replacement value basis. Note, however, that china, glass and other breakables can usually be included in an 'all-risks' policy only when they're packed by the removal company. Insurance usually covers total loss or loss of a particular crate only, rather than individual items (unless they were packed by the shipping company). If there are any breakages or damaged items, they must be noted and listed before you sign the delivery bill (although it's obviously impossible to check everything on delivery). If you need to make a claim be sure to read the small print, as some companies require clients to make a claim within a few days, although seven is usual. Send a claim by registered post. Some insurance companies apply an 'excess' of around 1 per cent of the total shipment value when assessing claims. This means that if your shipment is valued at €25,000 and you make a claim for less than €250, you won't receive anything.

If you're unable to ship your belongings directly to Spain, most shipping companies will put them into storage and some offer a limited free storage period before shipment, e.g. 14 days. **If you need to put your household effects into storage, it's important to have them fully insured, as warehouses have been known to burn down!** Make a complete list of everything to be moved and give a copy to the removal company. Don't include anything illegal (e.g. guns, bombs, drugs or pornography) with your belongings, as customs checks can be rigorous and penalties severe. Provide the shipping company with **detailed** instructions how to find your Spanish address from the nearest motorway (or main road) and a telephone number where you can be contacted.

After considering the shipping costs, you may decide to ship only selected items of furniture and personal effects, and buy new furniture in Spain. If you're importing household goods from another European country, it's possible to rent a self-drive van or truck, although if you rent a vehicle outside Spain you must usually return it to the country where it was hired. If you plan to transport your belongings to Spain personally, check the customs requirements in the countries you must pass through. Most people find it isn't advisable to do their own move unless it's a simple job, e.g. a few items of furniture and personal effects only. It's no fun heaving beds and wardrobes up stairs and squeezing them into impossible spaces! If you're taking pets with you, you may need to get your vet to tranquillise them, as many pets are frightened (even more than people) by the chaos and stress of moving house. See also **Pets** on page 465.

Bear in mind when moving home that everything that can go wrong often does, so allow plenty of time and try not to arrange your move to your new home on the same day as the previous owner is moving out. That's just asking for fate to intervene! **Last but not least, if your Spanish home has poor or impossible access for a large truck you must inform the shipping company (the ground must also be firm enough to support a heavy vehicle).** Note that if large items of furniture need to be taken in through an upstairs window or balcony, you may need to pay extra. See also **Customs** on page 89 and the **Checklists** on page 488.

## Inventory

When moving into a property that you've purchased, you should make an inventory of the fixtures and fittings, and check that the previous owner hasn't absconded with anything which was included in the contract or paid for separately, e.g. carpets, light fittings, curtains, fitted cupboards, kitchen appliances or doors.

# ELECTRICITY

Spain's main electricity companies include Grupo Endesa (the largest, with 44.5 per cent of the market share), Gas Natural, Hidrocantábrico, Iberdrola and Unión Fenosa. In January 2003, the energy market was completely liberalised and clients can now choose which company provides their electricity, but in many areas there's still only one company providing electricity and unless you live in a large city, as yet you have no choice. Grupo Endesa (☎ 902-509 509, 🖳 www.endesaonline.com) provides electricity under the following names: Fecsa in Catalonia; Gesa in the Balearics; Sevillana Endesa in Andalusia and Unelco in the Canaries. Gas Natural (☎ 900-710 720, 🖳 www.gasnatural.com) provides electricity to most of Spain except the islands. Hidrocantábrico (☎ 902-860 860, 🖳 www.h-c.es) provides electricity in Asturias and Madrid. Iberdrola (☎ 901-202 020, 🖳 www.iberdrola.es) provides electricity in Asturias, the Basque country, Cantabria, Catalonia, Comunidad Valenciana (including the Costa Brava), Galicia and Madrid. Unión Fenosa provides electricity in central Spain, including Madrid (☎ 901-404 040, 🖳 www.unionfenosa.es).

In autumn 2005, Gas Natural made a takeover bid for Grupo Endesa, whose management initially rejected the offer, although this had yet to be studied by the group's shareholders. If the bid is successful, the resulting electricity company would be one of the largest in Europe. When the euroopean union (EU) electricity market is completely liberalised in 2007, it's expected that several large EU-based companies will show an interest in their Spanish counterparts.

# Power Supply

The electricity supply in most of Spain is 220 volts AC with a frequency of 50 hertz (cycles). However, some areas still they have a 110-volt supply and it's even possible to find dual voltage 110 and 220-volt systems in the same house or the same room! All new buildings have a 220-volt supply and the authorities have mounted a campaign to encourage homeowners with 110-volt systems to switch to 220 volts. Note that most appliances, e.g. televisions (TV) made for 240 volts, will function with a power supply of 220 volts.

Power cuts are frequent in many areas of Spain – in 2004, Andalusia, the Balearics and Extremadura were the regions with most power cuts while Asturias, the Basque Lands, Cantabria and Madrid suffered the least. When it rains heavily the electricity supply can become very unstable, with frequent power cuts lasting from a few micro seconds (just long enough to crash a computer) to a few hours (or days). If you use a computer it's advisable to fit an uninterrupted power supply (UPS) with a battery backup (costing around €150), which allows you time to save your work and shut down your computer after a power failure. If you live in an area where cuts are frequent and rely on electricity for your livelihood, e.g. for operating a computer, fax machine and other equipment, you may need to install a back up generator. **Even more important than a battery backup is a power surge protector for appliances such as TVs, computers and fax machines, without which you risk having equipment damaged or destroyed.**

If you buy a rural property (*finca rústica*), there are usually public guarantees of services such as electricity (plus water, sewage, telephone, etc.) and you aren't generally obliged to pay for the installation of electricity lines or transformers, only the connection to your property. However, you may be obliged to pay for the installation of electricity lines or transformers plus the connection to your property if the mains services don't run near your home. In many remote areas, there's no mains electricity and you **must** install a generator if you want electricity, although some people make do with gas and oil lamps. Note that in some urbanisations, water is provided by electric pump and, therefore, if your electricity supply is cut off, so is your water supply.

If the power keeps tripping off when you attempt to use a number of high-power appliances simultaneously, e.g. an electric kettle and a heater, it means that the power rating (*potencia*) of your property is too low. This is a common problem in Spain. If this is the case, you may need to contact your electricity company and ask them to upgrade the power supply in your property (it can also be downgraded if the power supply is more than you require). The power supply increases by increments of 1.1KW, e.g. 2.2KW, 3.3KW, 4.4KW, 5.5KW. Note, however, that it can take some time to get your power supply changed. The power supply rating is usually shown on your meter. Your standing charge (see page 122) depends on the power rating of your supply, which is why owners tend to keep it as low as possible and most holiday homes have a power rating of just 3.3KW.

**Make sure your power supply is high enough for your needs.** If you install air-conditioning, you will probably need to increase your power supply. Electrical fires caused by overloading the power supply in homes are common.

### Converters & Transformers

Assuming that you have a 220-volt power supply, if you have electrical equipment rated at 110 volts AC (for example, from the US) you will require a converter or a step-down transformer to convert it to 220 volts. If you have a 110-volt supply, you can buy converters or step-up transformers to convert appliances rated at 220 volts to 110 volts. However, some electrical appliances are fitted with a 110/220-volt switch. Check for the switch, which may be inside the casing, and make sure it's switched to 220 volts **before** connecting it to the power supply. Converters can be used for heating appliances, but transformers are required for motorised appliances. Total the wattage of the devices you intend to connect to a transformer and make sure that its power rating **exceeds** this sum.

Generally, small, high-wattage, electrical appliances, such as kettles, toasters, heaters, and irons need large transformers. Motors in large appliances such as cookers, refrigerators, washing machines, dryers and dishwashers, will need replacing or fitting with a large transformer. In most cases it's simpler to buy new appliances in Spain, which are of good quality and reasonably priced, and sell them when you leave if you cannot take them with you. Note also that the dimensions of cookers, microwave ovens, refrigerators, washing machines, dryers and dishwashers purchased abroad, may differ from those in Spain, and therefore may not fit into a Spanish kitchen. See **Household Goods** on page 433 for more information.

An additional problem with some electrical equipment is the frequency rating, which, in some countries, e.g. the US, is designed to run at 60Hertz (Hz) and not Europe's 50Hz. Electrical equipment **without** a motor is generally unaffected by the drop in frequency to 50Hz (except TVs). Equipment with a motor may run okay with a 20 per cent drop in speed, however, automatic washing machines, cookers, electric clocks, record players and tape recorders must be converted from the US 60Hz cycle to Spain's 50Hz cycle. To find out, look at the label on the back of the equipment. If it says 50/60Hz it should be okay; if it says 60Hz you can try it, **but first ensure that the voltage is correct, as outlined above.** Transformers and motors of electrical devices designed to run at 60Hz will run hotter at 50Hz, so make sure that apparatus has sufficient space around it to allow for cooling.

# Wiring Standards

Most modern properties (e.g. less than 20 years old) in Spain have good electrical installations. However, if you buy an old home you may be required to obtain a certificate (*boletín*) from a qualified electrician stating that your electricity installation meets the required safety standards, even when the previous owner already had an electricity contract. You should ensure that the electricity installations are in a good condition well in advance of moving house, as it can take some time to get a new meter installed or to be reconnected.

# Plugs, Fuses & Bulbs

Depending on the country you've come from, you may need new plugs (*enchufes*) or a lot of adapters. Plug adapters for most foreign electrical apparatus can be purchased in Spain, although it's wise to bring some adapters with you, plus extension leads and multi-plug extensions that can be fitted with Spanish plugs. There's often a shortage of electric points in Spanish homes, with perhaps just one per room (including the kitchen), so multi-plug adapters may be essential. Most Spanish plugs have two round pins, possibly with an earth built into the plug, although most sockets aren't fitted with earth contacts. Sockets in modern properties may also accept three-pin plugs (with a third earth pin), although few appliances are fitted with three-pin plugs.

Small, low-wattage electrical appliances such as table lamps, small TVs and computers, don't require an earth. However, plugs with an earth must always be used for high-wattage appliances such as fires, kettles, washing machines and refrigerators. These plugs must be used with earthed sockets, although they also fit non-earthed, two-pin sockets. Electrical appliances that are earthed have a three-core wire and must never be used with a two-pin plug without an earth socket. **Always make sure that a plug is correctly and securely wired, as bad wiring can be fatal.**

In modern properties, fuses (*fusibles*) are of the earth trip type. When there's a short circuit or the system has been overloaded, a circuit breaker is tripped and the power supply is cut. If your electricity fails, you should suspect a fuse of tripping off, particularly if you've just switched on an electrical appliance. Before reconnecting the power, switch **off** any high-power appliances such as a stove, washing machine or dishwasher. Make sure you know where the trip switches are located and keep a torch handy so you can find them in the dark (see **Power Supply** 107).

Electric light bulbs are of the Edison type with a screw fitting. If you have lamps requiring bayonet bulbs you should bring some with you, as they cannot be readily purchased in Spain. You can, however, buy adapters to convert from bayonet to screw fitting (or vice versa). Bulbs for non-standard electrical appliances (i.e. appliances that aren't made for the Spanish market) such as refrigerators and sewing machines may not be available in Spain, so it's advisable to bring some spares with you.

# Registration

Immediately after buying or renting a property (unless utilities are included in the rent), you must sign a contract with the local electricity company. This usually entails a visit to the company's office to register, although most companies now offer the possibility of registering online or by telephone. You need to take some identification with you (passport or residence permit) and the contract and bills paid by the previous owner (and a good book, as queues can be long). In order to register for electricity via the internet or telephone, you will need to give some identification (your name and your passport or identity card number), as well as the reference number for the electricity supply (usually found on the top left-hand corner of a bill under *Contrato de Suministro Nº*). If you've purchased a home in Spain, the estate agent may arrange for the utilities to be transferred to your name or go to the offices with you (no charge should be made for this service). Make sure all previous bills (*facturas*) have been paid and that the contract is put into your name from the day you take over, otherwise you're liable for debts left by the previous owner. If you're a non-resident owner, you should also give your foreign address in case there are any problems requiring your attention, such as a bank failing to pay the bills. You may need to pay a deposit. Some electricity companies have service lines where foreign customers can obtain information in English and German, in addition to Spanish.

# Connection Costs

The cost of electricity connection (*acometida*) and the installation of a meter is usually between €100 and €300, although it varies considerably depending on the region, power supply and the type of meter installed. When you buy a community property, the cost of connection to utility services is included in the price of the property and it's illegal for developers to charge buyers extra for this.

# Tariffs

Electricity is generally cheap in Spain (the second cheapest in the EU) and the cost has remained stable since 1995, although in 2004 prices rose for the second time in eight years by 1 per cent and further rises are expected in the future as electricity companies are forced to pay the cost of keeping to the limits of emission of gases under the Kyoto agreement. The actual charges depend on your local electricity company (the rates shown in the example below are those charged by Sevillana Endesa in Andalusia). The tariff depends on your power rating (*potencia*), which for domestic users with a power rating of up to 15KW is 2.0 (above 15KW it's 3.0). This tariff is used to calculate your bimonthly standing charge. For example, if your power rating is 3.3KW this is multiplied by the tariff of 2.0 and then multiplied by the standing charge rate per KW (e.g. €1.46), i.e. 3.3 x 2.0 x €1.46, making a total of €9.64. The standing charge is payable irrespective of whether you use any electricity during the billing period.

The actual consumption is charged per KW, e.g. €0.08 in Andalusia. To save on electricity costs, you can switch to night tariff (*tarifa nocturna, 2.0N*) and run high-consumption appliances overnight, e.g. storage heaters, water heater, dishwasher and washing machine, which can be operated by a timer. If you use a lot of water, it's better to have a large water heater (e.g. 150 litres) and heat water overnight. If you use electricity for your heating, you can install night-storage heaters that run on the cheaper night tariff. The night tariff rate consists of paying 2.7 per cent more than the normal tariff during the day and evening (from 7am to 11pm), but provides a reduction of 53.3 per cent for electricity used overnight (between 11pm and 7am). In the summer, night hours start at midnight and run until 8am. VAT at 16 per cent must be added to charges.

## Cuota Fija

Some electricity companies allow their customers to pay a set amount (*cuota fija*) monthly, irrespective of consumption. At the end of the year the actual consumption is calculated and the customer pays the outstanding amount to the electricity company or has money returned to them. This is a good idea if you need to stick to a monthly budget.

# Bills

Electricity is billed every two months, usually after meters have been read. However, electricity companies are permitted to make an estimate of your consumption each second period without reading the meter. You should learn to read your electricity bill and check your consumption, to ensure that your electricity company isn't overcharging you. The most important figures on bills (which are now more consumer friendly) are:

| Item | Description |
| --- | --- |
| *Resumen de la factura* | Summary of the bill |
| *Fecha de emisión* | Date of issue of bill |
| *Periodo de facturación* | Period billed |
| *Total factura* | Total amount |
| *Consumo* | Consumption |
| *Lectura real* | Meter reading |
| *Consumo del periodo* | Total consumption |
| *Factura* | Bill |
| *Término de potencia* | Type of supply |
| *Coste del consumo* | Cost of consumption |
| *Impuesto sobre electricidad* | Electricity tax (4.864%) |
| *Alquiler equipos* | Meter rental charge |
| *Base imponible* | Amount before VAT |
| *IVA 16%* | 16% VAT |

It's advisable to pay your utility bills by direct debit (*domiciliación*) from a Spanish bank account. If you own a holiday home in Spain, you can have your bills sent to an address abroad. Bills should then be paid automatically on presentation to your bank, although some banks cannot be relied on 100 per cent. The electricity company and your bank should notify you when they've sent or paid a bill, but several banks no longer do this. If this is the case with your bank, it's a good idea to check your bank statements regularly via the internet. Alternatively, you can pay bills at a post office, local banks (listed on the bill) or at the electricity company's office (in cash).

Electricity companies aren't permitted to cut your electricity supply without authorisation from the proper authorities, e.g. the Ministry of Industry and Energy, and without notifying the owner of a property. If you're late paying a bill, you should be sent a registered letter demanding payment and stating that the power will be cut on a certain date if you don't pay. If you disagree with a bill, you should notify the Servicio Territorial de Ministerio de Industria y Energía in writing; if your complaint is founded, your electricity company will be refused permission to cut your supply. If your supply is cut off, you must usually pay to have it reconnected (*enganche*).

## Meters

In an old apartment block there may be a common meter, with the bill shared among the owners according to the size of their apartments. It's obviously better to have your own meter, particularly if you own a holiday home that's occupied for only a few months of the year. Meters for an apartment block or community properties (urbanisations) may be installed in the basement in a special room or in a meter 'cupboard' in a stair well or outside a group of properties, e.g. in an apartment or townhouse development. You should have free access to your meter and should be able read it (some meters don't have a window to allow you to read the consumption).

## GAS

Mains gas is available only in major cities in Spain, although with the recent piping of gas from North Africa (Algeria and Libya) it may soon be more widely available. When moving into a property with mains gas, you must contact the local gas company to have the gas switched on, the meter read and to sign a supply contract. As with electricity, you're billed every two months and bills (*facturas*) include VAT at 16 per cent. Like all utility bills, gas bills can be paid by direct debit from a Spanish bank account. In rural areas, bottled gas is used and costs less than half that of mains gas in most northern European countries. Many people use as many gas appliances as possible, including cooking, hot-water and heating. You can have a combined gas hot-water and heating system (providing background heat) installed, which is relatively inexpensive to install and cheap to run.

In most areas of Spain, gas bottles (*bombonas*) are delivered to homes by Repsol Butano (the company responsible for distributing gas bottles), for which a contract is required. You must pay a deposit of around €25 and an exchange 12.5kg bottle costs around €9.30 (the price fluctuates frequently) delivered to your home or less when purchased from a depot. A contract is drawn up only after a safety inspection has been made of the property where the gas appliance is to be used. In some areas, you must exchange your bottles at a local supplier. Bear in mind that gas bottles are very heavy and have a habit of running out at the most inconvenient times, so keep a spare bottle handy and make sure you know how to change them (get the previous owner or a neighbour to show you). A bottle used just for cooking can last an average family up to three months. If a gas boiler is installed outside, e.g. on a balcony, it must be protected from the wind, otherwise you will continually be re-lighting the pilot light.

You must have your gas appliances serviced and inspected at least every five years. If you have a contract with Repsol Butano, they will do this for you or it will be done by your local authorised distributor. Some distributors will try to sell you a package which includes third party insurance and free parts should they be required, although it isn't necessary to have this insurance and is a waste of money. **Beware of 'bogus' Repsol Butano representatives calling unannounced to inspect gas appliances.** They may represent legitimate companies, but their charges are extortionate and they will give you a large bill for changing tubing and regulators (which usually don't need changing at all), and demand payment in cash on the spot. If you wish, you can let them make an inspection and give you an estimate (*presupuesto*) for any work that needs doing, but don't let them do any work or pay any money before checking with your local Repsol Butano distributor. Incidentally, plastic tubes have an expiry date printed on them and you can buy them from a hardware store (*ferretería*) and change them yourself.

# HEATING & AIR-CONDITIONING

Central heating (*calefacción*) is essential in winter in northern and central Spain. If you're used to central heating and like a warm house in winter, you will almost certainly miss central heating everywhere in Spain except the Canaries. Central heating systems may be powered by oil, gas, electricity, solid fuel (usually wood) or even solar power (see below). Oil-fired central heating isn't common in Spain due to the high cost of heating oil and the problems associated with storage and deliveries. Many modern houses now include under-floor heating operated by electricity. In rural areas, many houses have open, wood-burning fireplaces and stoves, which may be combined with a central heating system. Whatever form of heating you use, it's important to have good insulation, without which up to 60 per cent of the heat generated is lost through the walls and roof. Note, however, that many homes, particularly older and cheaper properties, don't have good insulation and even with new homes builders don't always adhere to current regulations. In cities, apartment blocks may have a communal central heating system providing heating for all apartments, the cost of which is divided among the tenants. If you're a non-resident or absent from Spain for long periods, you should choose an apartment with a separate heating system, otherwise you will be contributing towards your neighbours' heating bills.

## Electric Heating

Electric heating isn't particularly common in Spain, as it's too expensive and requires good insulation and a permanent system of ventilation. It's advisable to avoid totally electric apartments in regions with a cold winter, such as Madrid, as the bills can be astronomical. However, a system of night-storage heaters operating on night tariff can be economical. Some stand-alone electric heaters are expensive to run and are best suited to holiday homes. If you rely on electricity for your heating, you should expect to pay between €50 and €125 a month during the coldest months, i.e. November to February. An air-conditioning system (see below) with a heat pump provides cooling in summer and economical heating in winter. Note that if you have electric central heating or air-conditioning, you will probably need to upgrade your power supply (see page 110).

# Gas Heating

Stand-alone gas heaters using standard gas bottles cost from €60 to €150 and are an economical way of providing heating in areas that experience mild winters (such as the Costa del Sol). Note that gas heaters must be used only in rooms with adequate ventilation, inspected and approved by Repsol Butano, and it can be dangerous to have too large a difference between indoor and outdoor temperatures. Gas poisoning due to faulty ventilation ducts for gas heaters (e.g. in bathrooms) isn't uncommon in Spain. It's possible to install a central heating system operating from standard gas bottles, which costs around €2,000 for a small home. The Spanish oil providers Cepsa (🖳 www.cepsa.es) and Repsol (🖳 www.repsol-ypf.com) offer good deals on gas central heating, including low-cost financing of the installation. Primus of Sweden (☎ 934-850 949, 🖳 www.vertical.es – representatives in Spain) is the leading foreign manufacturer. Mains gas central heating is popular in cities and is the cheapest to run.

# Solar Energy

The use of solar energy to provide hot water and heating (with a hot-air solar radiator) is surprisingly rare in Spain, where the amount of energy provided by the sun each year per square metre (m$^2$) is equivalent to eleven gas bottles. A solar power system can be used to supply all your energy needs, although it's usually combined with an electric or gas heating system, as it cannot usually be relied upon for year round heating and hot water. If you own a home on Spain's Mediterranean coast (or on the islands), solar energy is a viable option and the authorities (both regional and national governments) offer grants and interest-free finance to encourage homeowners to install solar-energy systems.

The main drawback is the high cost of installation, which varies considerably depending on the region and how much energy you require. A 400-litre hot-water system costs around €2,500 and must be installed by an expert. The advantages are no running costs, silent, maintenance-free operation, and no (or very small) electricity bills. A system should last 30 years (it's usually guaranteed for ten years) and can be upgraded to provide additional power in the future. Solar power can also be used to heat a swimming pool. Continuous advances in solar cell and battery technology are expected to dramatically increase the efficiency and reduce the cost of solar power, which is forecast to become the main source of energy worldwide over the next decades. A solar power system can also be used to provide electricity in a remote rural home, where the cost of extending mains electricity is prohibitive.

# Air-conditioning

In some regions of Spain, summer temperatures can reach over 40°C (104°F) and although properties are built to withstand the heat, you may wish to install air-conditioning (*aire acondicionado*). Note, however, that there can be negative effects if you suffer from asthma or respiratory problems. You can choose between a huge variety of air-conditioners, fixed or moveable, indoor or outdoor installation, and high or low power. Air-conditioning units cost from around €600 (plus installation) for a 2,000 BTU (*frigorías*) unit, which is sufficient to cool an average sized room. Some air-conditioners are noisy, so check the noise level before buying one. Although slightly more expensive, it's advisable to buy an inverter air-conditioner, which maintains a low electric current once the desired temperature has been reached and is up to 30 per cent cheaper to run than a standard model. An air-conditioning system with a heat pump provides cooling in summer and economical heating in winter – a system with an outside compressor providing radiant heating and cooling costs around €1,200 per room. Many people fit ceiling fans for extra cooling in the summer (costing from around €65), which are standard fixtures in some new homes.

## Humidifiers

Note that central heating and air conditioning dry the air and may cause your family to develop coughs and other ailments. Those who find the dry air unpleasant can install humidifiers to add moisture to the air. These range from simple water containers hung from radiators to electrical or battery-operated devices. Humidifiers that don't generate steam should be disinfected occasionally with a special liquid available from chemists (to prevent diseases).

# WASTE DISPOSAL

Most municipalities now recycle glass (green bins), paper and cardboard (blue bins), aluminium, cans and plastic (yellow bins), batteries and other materials, although there are sometimes few collection points. Many municipalities also recycle garden waste, which is then sold as compost. Some municipalities publish leaflets detailing where and when to dump your household rubbish. The amount of waste produced per head in Spain is fortunately one of the lowest in the EU, but little effort is made to educate citizens regarding recycling and waste reduction, although there are now TV and radio publicity campaigns, and schools make a conscious effort to 'teach' recycling. Although the dumping of rubbish (*basura*) is strictly forbidden, many people dump their rubbish in the countryside and the Spanish seem to have little respect for their environment. In Spain, most rubbish goes into landfill sites, although more municipalities are now incinerating it (which creates smoke pollution). The problem of landfill sites, some of which pollute ground water used for household consumption, is a serious and growing problem and many municipalities have a shortage of available sites. When buying a property in Spain, make sure that you aren't within 'smelling' distance of the local rubbish dump (or that one isn't planned close by), as they're sometimes located close to residential areas (although this is illegal).

Rubbish collection is efficient in most towns and cities, although in some rural areas residents are required to take their rubbish to a collection point, which may be located some kilometres away from an urbanisation. However, most community properties have communal skips or rubbish bins where residents are required to deposit their rubbish in sealed plastic bags. Bins are usually emptied daily (at night) except on Sundays. In some areas, residents have personal bins. If this is the case, ask your neighbours when you should put out your rubbish for collection, as some municipalities levy fines if rubbish is put out for collection too early, e.g. before 9pm. By the year 2002, residents in municipalities with over 5,000 inhabitants were supposed to have to deposit different types of rubbish in separate containers, although this has been postponed (yet again) until 2006 due to lack of planning!

Most municipalities charge an annual fee for rubbish collection, which varies depending on whether you live in a town or a rural area, e.g. from €30 to €150 a year. Costs are usually reduced for the elderly on low incomes. Check with your town hall and have the bill sent to your bank and paid directly by them, as (like all municipal bills) if you don't pay it on time it's increased by 20 per cent.

# WATER

Water, or rather the lack of it, is a major concern in Spain and the price paid for all those sunny days. Like some other countries that experience regional water shortages, Spain as a whole has sufficient water, but it isn't distributed evenly. There's (usually) surplus rainfall in the north-west and centre and a deficiency along most of the Mediterranean coast and in the Balearic and Canary islands. In the Canaries, there's a permanent water shortage and most drinking water is provided by desalination plants, while in the Balearics, 20,000 wells are employed to pump water to the surface (there are also desalination plants in Majorca and Ibiza). There are three large desalination plants on the mainland located at Carboneras (Almería), Marbella and San Pedro del Pinatar (Murcia) and a further 17 plants are under construction along the Mediterranean and expected to be working by 2008.

On the Costa del Sol, purification plants recycle waste water from urban areas for crop irrigation and watering golf courses. Shortages are exacerbated in resort areas, where the local population swells five to tenfold during the summer tourist season, the hottest and driest period of the year. The government has presented an ambitious water plan for eastern and southern Spain based mainly on better use of water resources (e.g. repair of broken water pipes – nearly 20 per cent of the country's water supply is lost through broken or leaking pipes! – and recycling of waste water) and the construction of numerous desalination plants along the Mediterranean coast. The plan is controversial, although less so than the previous government's plan to pipe water from the river Ebro in northern Spain to the Comunidad Valenciana and

Murcia, a plan that was overturned by the Socialist government immediately after they gained power. Meanwhile, Spain's regions fight over the allocation of water, particularly for crop irrigation (intensive and often wasteful agricultural irrigation accounts for around 80 per cent of all water used). In 2005, Castile-la Mancha and Murcia were particularly divided over the government's decision to pipe extra water from the Tagus water reserves in Castile-la Mancha to Murcia's crops. However, politicians from all regions and political parties are unanimous in that Spain urgently needs long-term effective measures against drought.

There's also relatively little emphasis on water conservation in Spain, particularly considering the frequent droughts, although consumption has reduced considerably in the last decade in many areas. The Costa del Sol uses double the national average per person for its numerous swimming pools, lawns, gardens and golf courses. Even in autumn 2005 in the midst of the driest year for the last six decades with water reserves down to a historic low, gardens and golf courses on the Costa del Sol were as green as ever! Inhabitants of towns and cities consume more water per person, per day than any other Europeans. At the same time, hundreds of rural towns and villages have water on tap for just a few hours a day during the summer months and farmers regularly face ruin due to the lack of water for irrigation.

# Supply

One of the most important tasks before renting or buying a home in Spain is to investigate the reliability of the local water supply (over a number of years) and the cost. Ask your prospective neighbours and other local residents for information. In most towns and cities, supplies are adequate, although there may be cuts in summer. It's not advisable to buy a property where the water supply is controlled by the developer, some of whom charge owners many times the actual cost or charge for a minimum quantity, even when they're non-residents. In rural areas, there are often severe shortages in summer unless you have your own well. Note, however, that a well containing water in winter may be bone dry in summer and you may have no rights to extract water from a water channel (*acequia*) running alongside your land. Dowsing (finding water by holding a piece of forked wood) is as accurate as anything devised by modern science (it has an 80 per cent success rate) and a good dowser can also estimate the water's yield and purity to within a 10 or 20 per cent accuracy. Before buying land without a water supply, engage an experienced dowser with a successful track record to check it. Although rare, some people in remote areas have spent a fortune (e.g. €50,000 or more) ensuring a reliable, year-round water supply, which may need to be piped from many kilometres away.

## Storage Tanks

If you have a detached house or villa, you can reduce your water costs by collecting and storing rainwater and by having a storage tank installed. Tanks can be roof-mounted or installed underground, which are cheaper and can be any size, but require an electric pump. Check whether a property has a water storage tank or whether you can install one. Most modern properties have storage tanks which are usually large enough to last a family of four for around a week or even longer with careful use. It's also possible to use recycled water from baths, showers, kitchens and apparatus such as washing machines and dish washers, to flush toilets or water a garden. In recent years, it has become common to have a storage tank installed that refills itself automatically when the water supply is restored after having been cut off.

# Restrictions

During water shortages, local municipalities may restrict the water consumption or cut off supplies altogether for days at a time. Restrictions can be severe and householders may be limited to as little as three cubic metres ($m^3$) per month, which is sufficient for around 10 baths or 20 showers. You can forget about watering the garden or washing your car unless you have a private water supply. If a water company needs to cut your supply, e.g. to carry out maintenance work on pipes and other installations, they will usually notify you in advance so that you can store water for cooking. In some areas, water shortages can create low water pressure, resulting in insufficient water to take a bath or shower. Note that in many developments, water is provided by electric pump and therefore if your electricity is cut off, so is your water supply. In urbanisations, the tap to turn water on or off is usually located outside properties and therefore if your water goes off suddenly you should check that someone hasn't switched it off by mistake. In the hotter parts of Spain, where water shortages are common, water tankers deliver to homes. Some properties don't have a mains supply at all, but a storage tank (*depósito*) that's filled from a tanker. If you have a storage tank, water will be pumped into it and you will be charged by the litre plus a delivery charge.

# Quality

Water is supposedly safe to drink in all urban areas, although it can be of poor quality, possibly brown or rust coloured, full of chemicals and can taste awful. Many residents prefer to drink bottled water. In rural areas, water may be extracted from mountain springs and taste excellent, although the quality standards applied in cities are usually absent and it may be of poor quality. Water in rural areas may also be contaminated by the fertilisers and nitrates used in farming, and by salt water in some coastal areas. If you're in any doubt about the quality of your water you should have it analysed. **Although boiling water will kill any bacteria, it won't remove any toxic substances contained in it.** You can install filtering, cleansing and softening equipment to improve its quality or a water purification unit (costing around €1,300) to provide drinking water. Note, however, that purification systems operating on the reverse osmosis system waste three times as much water as they produce. Obtain expert advice before installing a system, as not all equipment is effective.

Many areas of Spain have hard water containing high concentrations of calcium and magnesium. Water is very hard (*muy dura*) in the east, hard (*dura*) in the north and most of the south, and soft in the north-west (e.g. Galicia), and central and western regions. You can install a water softener that prevents the build-up of scale in water heaters and water pipes which increases heating costs and damages electric heaters and other appliances. Costs vary considerably and can be thousands of euros for a sophisticated system, which also consumes large quantities of water for regeneration. **It's necessary to have a separate drinking water supply if you have a water softener installed in your home.**

# Registration

After buying or renting a property (unless utilities are included in the rent), you should arrange for the water contract to be registered in your name. Always check in advance that all water bills have been paid by the previous owner, otherwise you will be liable for any debts. You must usually visit the local town hall to register your ownership and have the water contract transferred into your name. Take along some identification (passport or residence permit) and the previous contract and bills paid by the former owner. When registering, non-resident owners should also give their foreign address in case there are any problems requiring their attention, such as a bank failing to pay water bills.

# Connection Costs & Standing Charges

Water is a local matter in Spain and is usually controlled by local municipalities, many of which have their own wells. In some municipalities, water distribution is the responsibility of a private company. The cost of connection to the local water supply for a new home varies considerably from around €75 up to €500 (when a private company controls the distribution), or even €1,500 in an isolated area. In most municipalities, there's a standing quarterly charge or a monthly charge for a minimum consumption (*canon de consumo*), e.g. 14m³ a month or €10 a month plus VAT at 7 per cent, even if you don't use any water during the billing period. Water shortages don't stop municipalities from levying high standing charges for a water supply that's sometimes non-existent.

# Rates

The cost of water has risen dramatically in Spain in recent years and in some towns, water bills have increased by over 300 per cent or more, although the price of water is surprisingly low and one of the cheapest in Europe. The cost of water varies considerably from an average of around €1 per cubic metre (m³) on the mainland to between €1.50 and €2.50 per m³ in the Canaries and some parts of the Balearics, where drinking water is often provided by desalination plants and is very expensive. In some areas, tariffs start with a low basic charge of say €0.50 per cubic metre (e.g. for the first 15m³ a month), but becomes prohibitively expensive above this consumption. Many municipalities levy a standing charge, which is usually for a minimum amount of water per quarter or month, e.g. 45m³ a quarter or 15m³ a month, whether any water is used or not (which hits non-residents hardest).

Some municipalities levy a quarterly surcharge (*canon de servicio*) and regional governments may also levy a charge for water purification. Sometimes a higher water rate is charged for holiday homeowners or owners in community developments, where the water supply isn't controlled by the local municipality, while in others the cost of water is included in community fees. Water bills usually include sewerage and may also include rubbish collection, e.g. when a city provides all services, in which case the cost of rubbish collection may be calculated on how much water you use. There's also a rental charge for the water meter, e.g. around €4 per quarter. **Always check your water bill carefully, as overcharging on bills is widespread.** Sometimes water company meters show a huge disparity (increase!) in consumption compared with a privately installed meter and when confronted with the evidence water companies often refuse to reply! Some municipalities arbitrarily levy higher tariffs on certain urbanisations, although this is illegal.

To reduce your water costs, you can buy a 'water saver' that mixes air with water, thus reducing the amount of water used. The cost of fitting an apartment with water savers is only around €40, which can reportedly be recouped in six months through lower water bills. Water savers can be purchased from El Corte Inglés and Hipercor stores, hypermarkets and DIY stores (see **Chapter 17**).

# Bills

Bills (*facturas*) are generally sent out quarterly. If you don't pay your water bill on time you should receive an 'enforced collection' (*recaudación ejecutiva*) letter demanding payment of your bill (plus a surcharge). If you don't pay your bill your water supply can be cut off. Many people have their water supply cut off each year for non-payment. If your supply is cut, you must pay a reconnection fee, e.g. €40, plus any outstanding bills. Note that VAT is levied at 7 per cent on water bills.

# Hot Water

Water heating in apartments may be provided by a central heating source for the whole building or apartments may have their own water heaters. If you install your own water heater, it should have a capacity of at least 75 litres. Many holiday homes have quite small water boilers, which are often inadequate for more than two people. If you need to install a water heater (or fit a larger one), you should consider the merits of electric and bottled gas heaters. An electric water boiler with a capacity of 75 litres (sufficient for two people) costs from €130 to €250 and usually takes between 60 and 90 minutes to heat water to 40°C in winter.

A gas flow-through water heater is more expensive to purchase and install than an electric water boiler, but you get unlimited hot water immediately whenever you want it and there are no standing charges. Make sure that a gas heater has a capacity of 10 to 16 litres per minute if you want it for a shower. A gas heater costs from €150 to €275 (although there's little difference in quality between the cheaper and more expensive heaters), plus installation costs. Note that a gas water heater with a permanent flame may use up to 50 per cent more gas than one without one. A resident family with a constant consumption is better off with an electric heater operating on the night-tariff (see page 122), while non-residents using a property for short periods will find a self-igniting gas heater more economical. Solar energy can also be used to provide hot water (see page 117).

# Sewerage

Surprisingly for a western industrialised country, around a third of the population isn't connected to a sewage treatment system, with untreated waste water going straight into the ground, rivers or the sea. In some areas, there are no sewage plants and sewage is drained into cesspools (*pozos negros*) or septic tanks (*fosas sépticas*) which are emptied by tankers. Septic tanks can cause problems in summer in some buildings, for example when holiday homes are fully occupied and the septic tank isn't emptied frequently. Note that cesspools are illegal in many areas and properties must be connected to mains drainage. Most sewage treatment deficiencies are found in central Spain and along the northern Atlantic coast, although raw sewage is dumped into the sea throughout the country. A special tax (*canon*) is levied in many areas to pay for the installation of sewage treatment plants. Towns with 15,000 inhabitants or more were expected to have a sewage treatment system by the year 2001 and municipalities of between 2,000 and 15,000 people by the year 2006, although poor planning means little has been done and as a result many large towns (e.g. Fuengirola) are still without proper sewage treatment.

# 6.

# POSTAL SERVICES

There's a post office (*oficina de correos*) in most towns and at major railway stations, airports and ports in Spain, a total of over 6,000 (a list is available). In addition to the usual post office services, a limited range of other services are provided, including telegrams, fax and telex transmissions, and domestic and international giro money orders. Post offices also operate as agents for Deutsche Bank offering a full range of banking services. Telephones aren't available in most Spanish post offices. Unlike almost all other European post offices, the Spanish post office produces few leaflets and brochures and you may even have difficulty obtaining a tariff. However, this has improved in recent years. You shouldn't expect post office staff to speak English or other foreign languages, although main post offices may have an information desk with multilingual staff. The identifying colour used by the Spanish post office (and most European countries) is yellow, which is the colour of Spanish post boxes (*buzones*), post office signs and post vans. Postmen (*carteros*) usually wear yellow and navy uniforms.

The Spanish post (*correo*) delivery service has a reputation for being one of the slowest and most unreliable in Europe, with deliveries taking anything from a few days to a few weeks or months (or post disappearing altogether). Delivery times are well below the European Union (EU) average and while deliveries within and between major cities are adequate, deliveries to (and between) small towns and rural areas in different provinces can be very (very) slow. In some areas, deliveries are delayed or stop altogether when the local postman goes on holiday! It's advisable to send all international post by airmail (*por correo aéreo*). There's a cheaper surface post (*por barco* or *correo ordinario*) service outside Europe, but it takes aeons, e.g. six weeks or more to North America. Delivery times in Europe vary considerably depending on the countries concerned and where letters are posted in Spain (possibly even the post box used). Letters may arrive more quickly when posted at a main post office – but don't count on it!

Although letters posted in Spain often arrive at European destinations in two to four days, it's advisable to allow around seven days. Airmail letters between Spain and North America usually take five to ten days, although you should allow up to two weeks. Sending letters by express (*exprés/urgente*) post isn't the answer, as there's no guarantee they will arrive earlier than ordinary post. **Although international post delivery can be fairly fast, delivery times cannot be relied upon.** The only guaranteed way to send something urgently, within Spain or internationally, is by courier (*mensajería* or *transportes*), e.g. the post office's *EMS postal exprés* service or by private couriers (or to send correspondence by fax or email). Most European post offices are models of efficiency compared with the Spanish post office (which is, it must be said, better than Italy's), which handles around 5.2 million items of postage a year of which it manages to lose over 100,000! Spanish business is badly let down by the failings of the country's postal system and many businesses routinely send important post by courier.

There are usually long, slow-moving, queues at post offices although service has improved in recent years. In main post offices there are usually several windows dealing with all services (*admisión polivalente*), including stamps, registration of letters, giros, telegraphs, telegrams and telex, except the collection of parcels (*entrega*). In smaller post offices there may be one window for stamps (*venta de sellos*), another to register a letter or send an express letter (*certificados – postal exprés*) and yet another to prepare and post a parcel (*prep. paquete*). Some larger post offices have introduced a numbered ticket system. Customers take a numbered ticket for the service they require (e.g. A for most transactions, B for collection of parcels and registered post and C for giros and telegrams) from a machine (usually by the door) and wait for their number to be displayed over the corresponding desk. The system is designed to alleviate queues, but at peak times you can still expect to wait at least 30 minutes to be served. If you just want to buy stamps, it's quicker to buy them from a tobacconist's (*estanco* or *estancos*), although they don't always have postal scales and therefore may be unable to tell you the cost.

Complaints (*reclamaciones*) about the postal service can be made at any post office and don't need to be made at the post office where the problem occurred or originated (if applicable). In the case of loss of post, the person sending the post must make the complaint. If you don't receive satisfaction you can take your complaint to the Jefatura Provincial de Correos or the Inspección General de Correos, Plaza de la Cibeles s/n, 28014 Madrid. There's also a phone service (☎ 902-197 197) from Mondays to Fridays between 8am and 9pm and on Saturdays between 9am to 1pm or alternatively you can make your complaint online (🖳 www.correos.es – look under *Quejas y Reclamaciones*). Two different types of complaint forms (*hojas de reclamaciones*) are available in post offices, depending on the nature of the complaint. If you have a complaint about bad service, the service **may** be improved, but no compensation will be paid. More information about post office services is available via the telephone (☎ 902-197 197) or you can consult the comprehensive post office website (🖳 www.correos.es – in Spanish only).

Postal and telegraphic tariffs are listed in a free booklet, *Tarifas Postales y Telegráficas*, obtainable from post offices or are available online under *Tarifas*.

# GENERAL INFORMATION

When sending letters or parcels to or from Spain, always ensure that they're securely sealed or wrapped, otherwise they may arrive in tatters. When sending anything heavy, use strong cloth envelopes (e.g. Tyvek), which even the Spanish post office has a problem tearing to shreds (also ask your correspondents to use them when sending post to you). The post office sells a selection of good value stationery, including padded envelopes in three sizes (200 x 275mm for €0.58, 250 x 325mm for €0.76 and 333 x 450mm for €1.33); reinforced envelopes in three sizes: small (€0.46), medium (€0.58) and large (€0.79); boxes in four sizes costing from €1.15 to €2.90; special packs for sending bottles (€2.25 for one bottle and €4.35 for three) and normal envelopes in two sizes priced at €0.10 for the small size and €0.20 for the medium. **You aren't supposed to use coloured envelopes.**

If you live in an apartment block in a town or city, your post is placed in your post box (make sure that it has a lock) located in a central area such as the foyer. Often post boxes aren't big enough for magazines and large packets, which are left in a common storage area. If you prefer, you can arrange to have a post office box (see page 136) and collect your post from there. Postmen aren't required to deliver parcels weighing over 500g, which must usually be collected from a post office (however, parcels up to 10kg can be delivered if a surcharge is paid).

Letters are supposedly delivered once a day to your door if your letter box is placed on a public road, but in many areas (even within large towns) you may receive a delivery only a couple of times a week. If you don't have a letter box outside your house, you must install one on the boundary of your property on the street (often a number of boxes are grouped together at the end of a road). In some rural areas, there isn't a home delivery (*reparto*) service at all, and post must be collected from a local post office, a postal 'depot' or even a shop, which functions as a post drop off and collection point. Post for rural urbanisations is usually deposited in numbered post boxes, which may be located kilometres away (this may be something you wish to take into account before buying or renting a home in Spain).

In addition to post offices, stamps are also sold by tobacconists, shown by a sign of a yellow letter 'T' on dark red background, hotels and some shops. Shops selling postcards don't usually sell stamps. Stamps are always sold at face value and no surcharge is added. Main post offices also have vending machines that print postage labels (*estampillas*) for the amount required. Stamps purchased at main post offices are usually printed postage labels of the 'peel-off' type, i.e. they don't need to be moistened. Official fiscal stamps (*papeles del estado*), used to legalise documents and pay government taxes are sold exclusively by tobacconists.

A domestic and international express service (*urgente*) is available for urgent post, which can be deposited in special red post boxes at main post offices in major cities. Express post guarantees 48-hour delivery within Spain, although there's no such guarantee for international post, which can take up to ten days to European destinations (or the same as ordinary post). The express post surcharge (payable in addition to ordinary postage) for a letter weighing up to 20g is €1.95 for destinations within Spain, €2.40 for Europe and €2.75 for other international destinations. The post office offers a 'tracking' facility for express letters whose progress can be followed via the internet (🖳 www.correos.es) or by phone (☎ 902-197 197).

You should affix an airmail (*por avión*) label or use airmail envelopes for international airmail, although this isn't necessary for post between European countries, as most post is automatically sent by air. Aerograms (*aerogramas*) are available from post offices and cost €0.60 to anywhere in the world. Note, however, that aerograms are often difficult to obtain.

Post boxes (*buzones*) are bright yellow with red stripes circling the base and are usually free standing. In cities, post boxes often have two slots, one for local post (*ciudad* or *localidad*) and the other for international post (*provincias y extranjero*) and post to other provinces (*provincias*). However, there may be separate boxes for Madrid (*Madrid Capital*), local post, the rest of Spain (*resto España*) and international (*extranjero*) post. There are also red post boxes at main post offices in cities for express (*urgente*) post. You may also see green post boxes which are reserved for the use of postal staff.

Post boxes can sometimes be scarce and difficult to locate, although there's always one outside a post office or railway station. It's best to post letters at main post offices or railway stations, as collections are more frequent and delivery may be expedited. During the winter in resort areas, some post boxes may be emptied infrequently, irrespective of the collection times (*horas de recogida*) listed on them, which may be hand written and illegible (some post boxes look abandoned and any post deposited in them may still be there in a year's time!). Some urbanisations have a box (which may be marked *Sólo Para Recogida de Correo para su Despacho*), where you can deposit letters for collection.

The international postal identification for Spanish postal or zip codes (*el distrito* or *código postal*) is 'E', which is placed before the postcode (as shown below), although its use isn't mandatory or widespread. Spain uses a five-digit post code, where the first two digits indicate the province code and the last three the town. Small villages often use the postcode of a nearby town, when the village name should be included in the address before the postcode. Freepost (*franqueo en destino*), where the addressee pays the cost of postage, is available to large companies only in Spain and isn't as widely used as in many other countries.

Spanish addresses (*dirección*) often include a number of abbreviations, for example 'C/España, 33, 3° A dcha'. This means España street (C/ is short for *calle* meaning street) number 33, third floor (3°), apartment 3A on the right (*derecha* or *dcha*). An apartment on the left (when facing the front of an apartment block) is indicated as *izda* (*izquierda*) and one in the centre is *cto* (*centro*). Often a house will have no street number, indicated by s/n (*sin número*). On many roads (*carretera* or *ctra*), the address includes a kilometre marker, e.g. N-340, km 148 or N-V, km 64. Others may include '*Ctra* town 1-town 2, km 25', meaning 25km along the road between town 1 and town 2 or '*Ctra de* town, km 7' means 7km along the road from town (name). Confusion may arise over the use of regional languages (Basque, Catalan or Gallego) in street and town names, which replace or are written alongside their Castilian (Spanish) counterparts. A typical Spanish address is shown below:

> Sr. Don Pulpo
> C/Pescado, 16
> E-12345 Fruta del Mar
> Spain/España

The Spanish post office publishes a guide to postal codes (*guía de códigos postales*), listing each street in cities and individual houses in small villages. You can also look up postcodes on the post office website (🖥 www.correos.es).

If a letter is unable to be delivered due to being wrongly addressed or the addressee having moved, it will be stamped 'return' (*devuelto*) or 'return to sender' (*a su procedencia*). A box headed *devuelto* may be stamped on the reverse of a letter stating the reason for non-delivery. You should write your name and address on the back of all letters and parcels marked 'sender' (*remitente/rte*), as the Spanish post office won't usually open post to obtain a return address. If you send post with insufficient postage (*insuficiencia de franqueo*), the addressee must pay double the amount that's underpaid for national post. For international post you must pay double the underpaid amount plus €0.58.

If you want your post to be redirected (*reenvío postal*), you should fill in the official form at your local post office, you must give your name, your old address and your new address. The cost (which includes 20 pre-stamped cards for you to send out your new address) is €21 for one month, €31.50 for two months and €42 for six months within Spain. International costs are €31.50 for one month, €47.25 for two months and €63 for six months.

The Spanish post office runs a digital postal service (*Correo Digital*) whereby you can send a letter electronically. You have to register (free of charge) on the website before you can use this service. Once you've entered the site, you choose the format you wish to give your letter, including logos and pictures, fill in the recipient's name and address, and write your letter. The letter is then sent electronically to the post office where it's printed and sent. This service costs €0.48 for letters within Spain, €0.73 for Europe and €€€98 for the rest of the world. Letters sent via this service are **supposed** to arrive quicker than conventional post.

The Spanish post office provides a service for stamp collectors and publishes leaflets for new editions (in English, French, German and Spanish). For information contact Correos y Telégrafos, Servicio Filatélico, Vía de Dublín, 7, 3°, 28070 Madrid (☎ 902-213 120, ✉ atcliente.filatelia@correos.es). The post office website also offers extensive information and services, including a shop for stamp collectors.

**Always carefully check your post and don't throw anything away unless you're certain it's junk mail (unsolicited post, circulars, newspapers, etc.)** It isn't unknown for foreigners to throw away important bills and correspondence during their first few weeks in Spain. Look between the pages of junk post for 'real' post.

## Business Hours

Business hours (*horas de oficina*) at main post offices in cities and large towns are usually from around 8am until around 9.30pm, Mondays to Fridays and from 9am to 2pm on Saturdays. Main post offices in major towns don't close for lunch and may also provide limited services outside normal business hours. Some post offices in major cities also open for a period on Sundays, although the range of services may be limited. There are also post offices at international airports, generally only open in the morning, and mobile post offices in some areas usually operating from around 10am to 1pm. In small towns and villages, post offices usually open from 8.30 or 9am until between noon and 2.30pm, Mondays to Fridays, and from 9.30am to 1pm on Saturdays. Note also that some services may be available at post offices for a limited number of hours only each day, including sending telegrams and faxes; the preparation, posting and collection of parcels and poste restante (*lista de correos*).

## Telecor

Under an agreement with Spain's flagship department store, El Corté Inglés, the post office runs Telecor shops, a kind of 'one-stop' shop for telephone (fixed and mobile), television and utility services. The shops, available in main post offices and in provincial capitals, offer clients the chance to sign up for these services from a choice of different companies.

# LETTER POST

There's one set of rates for all domestic post (*interurbana*), although there's a special low (and very slow) rate for domestic publicity post (*publicorreo*) of €2.20 for up to 1kg to addresses in the same town and €3.25 for up to 1kg for all other destinations.

International letter rates depend on the destination, as shown in the table below. It costs the same to send letters (*cartas*) and postcards (*tarjetas postales* or *postales*), irrespective of the destination, the maximum weight for domestic and international letters being 2kg. The cost of posting a letter up to 100g in Spain is as follows (for letters or parcels over 100g see **Parcel Post** on page 133):

| Weight | Spain | Cost (€) Zone 1* | Zone 2** |
|--------|-------|---------|----------|
| Up to 20g | 0.28 | 0.52 | 0.78 |
| 21 – 50g | 0.40 | 1.18 | 1.66 |
| 51 – 100g | 0.55 | 1.39 | 2.38 |

\* Zone 1: Europe

\*\* Zone 2: Rest of the world

# PARCEL POST

Parcels (*paquetes*) are usually dealt with at a separate window in main post offices. The post office provides a range of parcel services, both domestic and international. Parcel services are also provided by Spanish railways and airlines, and by international courier companies such as DHL and UPS. International letters and small packets (*pequeños paquetes*) are limited to a maximum weight of 2kg, as are periodicals (*periódicos*). For domestic parcels weighing up to 2kg, the letter rate applies. Domestic and international parcels containing printed matter (*impresos*), e.g. books and magazines, are limited to 5kg (and take 'for ever' to be delivered). Domestic and international parcels are limited to a maximum of 20kg, although there are special rates for heavier items. Parcels to non-EU addresses abroad must have an international customs label (*impreso para la aduana*) affixed to them (these are no longer required for parcels sent within the EU).

The standard surface domestic parcel service (*paquete azul*) costs €4.30 up to 2kg, €€ between 2 and 5kg, €5.90 between 5 and 10kg, €8.20 between 10 and 15kg, and €10 between 15 and 20kg. There's also a fast domestic service (*postal exprés*), the cost of which varies depending on the destination, e.g. parcels sent to an address within the same province cost €5.55 up to 1kg and €6.10 between 1 and 2kg. Nationwide parcels cost €9.50 up to 1kg and €10.65 between 1 and 2kg Heavier parcels (e.g. 10kg) can also be sent via the domestic and nationwide services. An international small packet (*pequeño paquete*) service is available costing €1.40 (up to 100g), €2.80 (100 to 200g), €5.25 (200 to 350g), €8.75 (350g to 1kg) and €15.35 (1 to 2kg). Two kilos is the maximum permitted weight for airmail within Europe. When sending small parcels, newspapers and magazines, books and brochures, or other printed matter, use a post office window marked *entrega paquetes, reembolso*.

Parcels posted in Spain must be securely packaged. A post office will make up your parcel and seal it at a special window in main post offices only (*Prep. Paquete*). This is an inexpensive service costing from €1 (depending on size) and ensures that parcels comply with regulations. Boxes, bags, large envelopes, padded envelopes and other packing materials are sold by the post office, but supplies often run out so you may save time by buying from a stationery shop before you go to the post office.

The fastest and most convenient way to send domestic or international letters or parcels is via the post office's *postal exprés/EMS* service (serving around 160 countries). Within Spain, *EMS* packages up to 20kg are guaranteed to arrive at their destination within 24 hours and post sent to EU countries is usually guaranteed delivery within 48 hours, depending on the country. The maximum time for delivery to any country is three or four days. Although it's expensive, it can be much cheaper than some private courier services. An item weighing from 500g to 1kg costs €31.05 to zone A (Europe, including the UK, France and Germany); €37.25 to zone B (Europe, including Ireland); €50.60 to North America (zone C) and €59.95 to the rest of the world (zone D). Items can be insured for up to €3,000. **EMS is one of the few reliable services provided by the Spanish post office!**

Spanish railways also operate an express package and parcel service within Spain (24-hour) and to most European countries. Charges vary depending on the speed of delivery, the distance, and whether the package is to be collected or delivered. Many private courier and transport companies also provide an express parcel delivery service, nationally and internationally.

# REGISTERED & RECORDED POST

You can send important letters and parcels by registered post (*certificado*), with or without proof of delivery (*aviso recibo*), and send items that need to be paid for (e.g. if you're running a mail-order business) by cash on delivery (*reembolso*) nationally or internationally. The sender (*remitente*) is required to complete a form, which includes their name and address, and the name and address of the recipient (*destinario*). The sender's address must also be written on the back of registered post, for which you receive a receipt. The registration fee (plus postage) for national letters and parcels is €2.21, for post to Europe €2.73 and for post to the rest of the world €2.98. Proof of delivery (*aviso recibo*) costs €0.48 for domestic post (also for Gibraltar and Andorra) and €0.95 for international post. Payment on delivery (*pago contra reembolso*) costs €1.05 for national post and €1.40 for international post, which must also be registered. Note that the payment on delivery service isn't available to some countries, including the UK.

Registered letters require a signature and proof of identity on delivery, normally from the addressee. If the addressee is absent when a delivery is made, a notice is left and the letter must be collected from the local post office (see **Post Collection** on page 135). Registration is common in Spain when sending official documents and important communications. You can insure (*asegurar*) registered domestic and international post. The cost for domestic post is 1 per cent of the declared value up to a maximum of €3,000. If you have a complaint about registered post (plus giros or postage to be paid by the receiver) you can make a claim (*reclamaciones reglamentarias*) and obtain compensation. Compensation (*indemnización*) is paid for the loss or damage of registered post (*pérdida o sustracción de certificado*), e.g. €1.67 per €50 declared for domestic post and €2.04 per €50 declared for international post, up to a maximum of €2,400. Special pre-paid envelopes for registered postage up to 1kg can be purchased.

Spanish courier services offer similar services at competitive prices for letters and parcels, and some companies (such as DHL and Seur) have branches in most cities and large towns.

# POST COLLECTION

If the postman calls with post requiring a signature or payment when nobody is at home, he will leave a collection form (*aviso*). This also applies to post weighing over 500g, which must usually be collected from a post office (although parcels up to 10kg will be delivered on payment of a surcharge). Normal post is kept at the post office for one month, after which it's returned to the sender, therefore if you're going to be away from home for longer than this you should ask the post office to hold your post. There's no charge for this service. Note that proof of delivery and registered post are kept for three or seven days respectively.

To collect post, you present the collection form at your local post office or postal 'depot', the address of which is written on the form. In large post offices there may be a special window (*Lista, Poste Restante*). You need some form of identification, for example, your passport, residence permit (*residencia* – see page 78) or Spanish driving licence. A post office may refuse to give letters to a spouse addressed to his or her partner, or to give letters to a house owner addressed to his tenants or guests. You can give someone authorisation to collect a letter or parcel on your behalf by entering the details on the back of the collection form in the box marked *autorización*, for which the addressee's and collector's identification is required.

You can receive post at any post office in Spain via the international poste restante (*lista de correos*) service. If you choose a large town or city, address post to the main post office (*Correo Central*) to avoid confusion. Sometimes a post office displays a list of people for whom they have poste restante post. Letters should be addressed as follows:

> Blenkinsop-Smith, Marmaduke Cecil
> Lista de Correos
> Correos Central
> Postcode, City Name (Province)
> Spain/España

Post sent to a poste restante address is returned to the sender if it remains unclaimed after 30 days. Identification (e.g. a passport) is necessary for collection and there's no fee. Post can be forwarded from one main post office to another.

If you have an American Express card or use American Express travellers' cheques, you can have post sent to an American Express office in Spain. Standard letters are held free of charge (registered letters and packages aren't accepted). Post, which should be marked 'client mail service', is kept for 30 to 90 days before being returned to the sender. Post can be forwarded to another office or address, for which there's a charge. Other companies that also provide post-holding services for customers include Thomas Cook and Western Union.

You can obtain a post office box (*apartado de correos*) at most post offices for a fee of €46.10 for the first year and €39.40 for subsequent years. If you have a post box, all your post will be stored there and the postman will no longer deliver to your home. Post boxes are allocated on a first come, first served basis and may be unavailable. You can arrange to be informed when registered or express post arrives. There's a window in a post office where you can register to receive all types of correspondence, packages and money orders (*giro postal*), which can also be forwarded to another post office in the same city for no charge. Proof of identity must be provided to collect post.

# MONEY MATTERS

The Spanish post office acts as an agent for Deutsche Bank, which provides the usual range of banking services, including cheque and savings accounts, house purchase, savings and retirement plans. These accounts provide the same services as bank accounts, including international money transfers (by post and telegraph to many countries), payment of bills, and cheque, cash and debit cards. Post offices don't operate cash machines (ATMs).

Cash transfers can be made within Spain and to Algeria, Morocco and Tunisia, with a postal giro (*giro postal*), by completing a form at any post office. You can choose between an ordinary giro (*giro ordinario*), which takes around two to three days to reach its destination, whether in Spain or abroad, and an urgent giro (*giro urgente*), which takes between 4 and 24 hours for Spanish and international destinations. You're required to complete a form and pay the amount to be transferred plus the fee in cash. Fees for national giro payments depend on whether the recipient has a post office giro account and whether the payment is sent by post or made by telephone. There are set fees plus 0.7 per cent of the amount being transferred. International giros also have set fees depending on the sort of giro plus an additional 0.7 per cent of the amount sent.

There are usually various giro windows at main post offices, these include: sending ordinary giros (*giro ordinario admisión*); sending urgent and international giros (*giro urgente e internacional admisión*); paying for ordinary giros (*giro ordinario pago*) and paying for urgent and international giros (*giro urgente y internacional pago*). Note that it isn't possible to make giro transfers to some countries and some countries only accept ordinary giro payments. Domestic postal giros are useful for sending money to someone in Spain when you don't have a Spanish bank account or when sending money to someone without a Spanish bank account. Some companies insist on payment by postal giro, as the cost of processing bank cheques is prohibitive.

The Spanish post office also has an agreement known as 'Money in Minutes' (*Dinero en minutos*) with Western Union by which you can send money fast to anywhere in the world from Spain up to a maximum amount of €3,000. Examples of rates are €33.50 for €600 and €69 for €2,000. There are special rates and deals for certain countries such as Russia.

# 7.

## TELEPHONE

Spain has one of the lowest numbers of telephones per head in the European Union (EU), around 38 telephones per 100 people, with a total of around 16 million lines in service. The Spanish aren't habitual telephone users and don't usually spend hours on the telephone (many business men prefer to meet in person or exchange letters). However, the last few years has seen the cost of mobile phones fall considerably and Spain now has around 32 million users and consumers now spend more on mobile phone calls than on fixed line services.

The Spanish telephone service is operated by one main company, Telefónica, offering a complete service, including the installation of telephone lines, and numerous others which currently only provide call and internet services, although Telefónica retains a huge percentage of the market share. In 2005, the main telecommunication providers for private phone use were Âlo (USA Communications), Auna (owned largely by Endesa and Telecom Italia), BT (British Telecom), Jazztel (Nortel), SpanTel (Spantel Comms Inc), Tele2 (Netcom), Telefónica and Uni2 (owned mainly by France Télécom and Santander Bank). Competition in the market has resulted in a sharp reduction in the costs of calls and international call charges have more than halved.

In recent years, telephone services in Spain have improved significantly in terms of quality of service and value for money, with less than 1 per cent of calls having problems and most faults being fixed within 24 hours. The waiting time for new telephone installations has also fallen dramatically and is now similar to other EU countries. Telefónica have made a huge investment in advanced technology (such as fibre-optics) and standards in Spain now compare favourably with the best European and North American standards.

Costs listed in this chapter are exclusive of value added tax (VAT/*IVA*) at 16 per cent, where applicable, unless otherwise stated. Information regarding emergency numbers is provided below.

# EMERGENCY NUMBERS

The main national emergency numbers (*servicios de urgencia*) in Spain are as follows:

| Number | Service |
| --- | --- |
| 112 | All-purpose emergency number (if you dial this number you're then connected to the emergency service you require. |
| 061 | Ambulance Service (*ambulancia*) |
| 062 | Civil Guard (*guardia civil*) |
| 080 | Fire Service (*bomberos*) |
| 092 | Local/Municipal Police (*policía local/municipal*) |
| 900-202 202 | Maritime rescue and security (*salvamento y seguridad marítimo*). |
| 091 | National Police (*Policía*) |

All emergency numbers are listed at the front of all telephone directories (white and yellow pages). They include the above numbers and the following: civil protection (*protección civil*); crisis lines such as the Samaritans (*Teléfono de la Esperanza*); drug addiction (*fundación de Ayuda contra la Drogadicción*); first aid posts (*casas de socorro*); poison information (*información toxicológica*); the Red Cross (*Cruz Roja*); social security (*seguridad social*) and urgent health services (*servicio de salud – urgencias*).

You should make a note of emergency numbers, including your doctor, and keep them by your phone. When reporting a medical emergency, you should state the type of emergency, e.g. accident (*accidente*), serious illness (*enfermedad grave*), heart attack (*ataque cardiaco* or *infarto*) and whether an ambulance or doctor (*médico*) is required.

Calls to emergency numbers cost €0.09 from private telephones. You must insert at least €0.10 or a telephone card when using a public telephone, although your money is returned when the emergency service answers. Calls to ☎ 112 are free. There are free SOS telephones on motorways and main roads. For service numbers see below. Dial ☎ 1002 to report telephone breakdowns or line problems. See also **Emergencies** on page 268.

# SERVICE NUMBERS

Useful service numbers are listed at the front of all telephone directories after the emergency numbers in the information pages under the heading 'other services of interest' (*otros servicios de interés*). They include regional government information (*información ciudadana*), water (*agua*), electricity (*electricidad*), gas, airports (*aeropuertos*), post offices (*oficinas de correos*), rail (RENFE), bus (*estaciones de autobús*), telegrams (*telegramas*) and road information (*ayuda en carretera*). Local useful telephone numbers (*teléfonos útiles*) are listed in English-language and other expatriate newspapers and magazines, generally by town, and usually include local emergency and hospital numbers. The following Telefónica and general information numbers can be dialled throughout Spain. For information on how to contact directory enquiries see page 152.

| Number | Service |
|--------|---------|
| 096** | Automatic alarm call |
| 095** | News (*Radio Nacional de España/NE*) |
| 1008 | Operator assisted calls – Europe |
| 1005 | Operator assisted calls – rest of the world |
| 097** | Sports information |
| 1002 | Telephone technical assistance |
| 1004 | Telefónica commercial enquiries/operator services for Spain |
| 093* | Time |

\*   Calls to this number cost €0.45.
\*\*  Calls to these numbers cost €0.72.

# INSTALLATION & REGISTRATION

When moving into a new home in Spain with a telephone line, you must have the account transferred to your name. If you're planning to move into a property without an existing telephone line and want to have one installed, this costs around €80. To have a telephone installed or reconnected, you can visit your local Telefónica office. Telefónica has an *Oficina Comercial* or an *Oficina de Atención al Usuario* in each province. You must take along your passport or residence permit (*permiso de residencia* – see page 78), proof of your address such as a recent electricity bill, and a copy of your property deed (*escritura*) or rental contract.

Alternatively, you can phone Telefónica (☎ 1004) or fill in a form online (🖳 www.telefonica.es). If you're renting and don't have a residence permit, you must pay a deposit of around €200. Staff don't usually speak English, but Telefónica also operates an English-language service (☎ 952-449 020, 🖳 www.telefonica inenglish.com), which includes phone and internet connection, a number of products and services plus tariff information. The service doesn't deal with bills and technical problems, which must be referred to the usual Telefónica number (☎ 1004). If you're taking over a property from the previous occupants, you should arrange for the telephone account to be transferred to your name from the day you take possession. **Before buying or renting a property, check that all the previous bills have been paid, otherwise you may find yourself liable for them.**

You aren't required to rent or buy a telephone from Telefónica and renting doesn't work out to be very cost effective, especially long term. The cheapest model that can be bought from Telefónica is the *Domo Uno* (€33.05), although you can buy telephones from other retailers that cost less. You can choose from a wide range of all-singing, all-dancing models.

Note that if you're using a callback service (see page 146), you should buy a phone with a memory facility – unless you like the idea of dialling around 20 numbers every time you make a call! Cordless (*inalámbrico*) phones (starting from around €50) are useful, as they can be used throughout the house or garden, e.g. when you're lying in the sun. Cordless digital phones are also available. All telephones must be approved (*aprobado*) by Telefónica, which means that you cannot officially buy a telephone abroad and use it in Spain. In any case, any telephone purchased abroad may not work in Spain.

## Registering with Other Companies

Registering with telephone companies other than Telefónica is usually straight forward and can be done by phone or online. You must provide your personal details, including passport or residence permit number and a bank account number. Contact details for the main companies are as follows:

- **Âlo** – ☎ 902-107 701, 🖳 www.alo.es.
- **Auna** – ☎ 015, 🖳 www.auna.es.
- **Jazztel** – ☎ 1565, 🖳 www.jazztel.com.
- **Spantel** – ☎ 902-020 709, 🖳 www.span-tel.com.

- **Tele2** – ☎ 901-107 366, 🖳 www.tele2.es.
- **TeleConnect** – ☎ 900-810 545, 🖳 www.teleconnect.es.
- **Uni2** – ☎ 902-011 414, 🖳 www.uni2.es.

If you choose to use the company's pre-set dialling service (you therefore avoid dialling the company's prefix every time you make a call) you must sign a form provided by the company.

In the past, terminating your contract with a telephone company was time-consuming and difficult – some consumers have found it almost impossible to terminate a contract. Telephone and internet services are one of the main sources of consumer complaints (there were over 13,000 in 2004 alone) and most complaints involved the difficulty of terminating a contract. In response to this, new legislation was introduced in April 2005 designed to make terminating a telephone services contract as easy as initiating one. Telephone companies are now obliged to terminate a contract within 15 days of receiving communication from a client and cannot charge for any services after this date.

The Ministry of Industry has set up a special office for telephone services complaints from consumers and has guaranteed that all complaints will be resolved within six months. The office (☎ 901-336 699) is open from 9am to 7pm Mondays to Fridays and 9am to 2pm on Saturdays. Complaints can also be made online (🖳 www.usuarioteleco.es).

## Temporary Disconnection

If you're leaving your Spanish home for a certain length of time, you can arrange for Telefónica to temporarily disconnect your line. **This can only be done for a maximum of three months per year** and you msut specify the exact dates for disconnection and reconnection in writing. You must continue to pay the standing charge during this time and in addition €3 for the disconnection and another €3 for the reconnection.

# USING THE TELEPHONE

Each province in Spain has its own area code (*prefijo* or *códigos territoriales*), all of which are listed below. All telephone numbers consist of nine digits and include the area code, which must be dialled whether you're making a local call or calling Spain from abroad.

The codes listed below are shown on a map in telephone directories (the provinces are also shown on the map in **Appendix E**):

| A Coruña | 981 | Córdoba | 957 | Ourense | 988 |
| Alava | 945 | Cuenca | 969 | Palencia | 986 |
| Albacete | 967 | Girona | 972 | Pontevedra | 986 |
| Alicante | 96 | Granada | 958 | La Rioja | 941 |

| | | | | | |
|---|---|---|---|---|---|
| Almería | 950 | Guadalajara | 949 | Salamanca | 923 |
| Asturias | 98 | Guipúzcoa | 943 | Sta Cruz Tenerife | 922 |
| Avila | 920 | Huelva | 959 | Segovia | 921 |
| Badajoz | 924 | Jaén | 953 | Seville | 95 |
| Baleares | 971 | Las Palmas | 928 | Soria | 975 |
| Barcelona | 93 | León | 987 | Tarragona | 977 |
| Burgos | 947 | Lleida | 973 | Teruel | 978 |
| Cáceres | 927 | Lugo | 982 | Toledo | 925 |
| Cadiz | 956 | Madrid | 91 | Valencia | 96 |
| Cantabria | 942 | Malaga | 95 | Valladolid | 983 |
| Castellón | 964 | Melilla | 95 | Vizcaya | 94 |
| Ceuta | 956 | Murcia | 968 | Zamora | 980 |
| Ciudad Real | 926 | Navarra | 948 | Zaragoza | 976 |

**Note:** The code for Andorra is 376 and for Gibraltar it's 9567.

When making a domestic call within the same province, i.e. to a number with the same provincial code, you must still include the code. For example, to call Malaga (95) 123 4567 from within Malaga, you must dial 951-234 567. When calling from outside Spain you must add the international dialling code (e.g. 00 from the UK) followed by 34 for Spain. So to call the above Malaga number you must dial 00-34 951 234 567. For information on making international calls from Spain see page 146.

Note that if you're using a service other than Telefónica, then you must dial the company's prefix, e.g. 1050 for Auna and 1073 for Tele2, before making a call. So to call Madrid 912-345 678 with Auna, you would dial 1050-912 345 678. Note that most telephone companies offer a pre-set dialling service where the company's prefix is automatically set on your telephone line and precedes all numbers you dial, although if you wish to use another company, including Telefónica, you must still dial that company's prefix.

Numbers beginning with 900 are free, although they aren't widely used in Spain and aren't nearly as common as in the UK or (particularly) the US. Numbers beginning with 901 and 902 are charged at cheaper or local call rates. Don't confuse these with numbers beginning with 8 (e.g. 803, 806 and 807), these are expensive and used by companies providing services such as weather forecasts, financial and health information and 'leisure' services such as horoscopes. The 80 numbers cost from €0.25 a minute (reduced rate) to a massive €3.40 a minute (peak rate), plus VAT. 80 numbers are the most common source of complaints from consumers and the government has introduced legislation designed to reduce the incidence of fraud. You can ask Telefónica to make it impossible to dial 80 numbers from your phone. Sex chat lines with 80 numbers were banned in 1993 after many consumers (including children) ran up huge bills, but these lines are still advertised in newspapers, with an international prefix (usually for a country in the Far East), meaning calls cost a small fortune.

All mobile phone numbers in Spain begin with the digit 6 and are **generally more expensive** to call than fixed-line phones.

The tones used in Spain are similar to other European countries, e.g. the dialling tone (*señal para marcar*) is a low continuous tone (similar to the UK and the US), a ringing tone is a repeated long tone, and the engaged (busy) signal is a series of rapid pips. If you get a recorded message after dialling, it may be telling you that all lines are engaged and to try again later. The message may also be telling you that the number you've dialled doesn't exist (e.g. *el número marcado no existe*). If this happens, check that the number is correct and redial; if you're dialling an international number, make sure you haven't dialled the first zero of the area code. To make a reverse charge/collect call (*cobro revertido*) dial 1009 for numbers within Spain, 1008 for countries in Europe and 1005 for all other countries.

Person-to-person (*persona a persona*) calls can also be made via the operator (*operadora*). A surcharge is made for reverse charge and person-to-person calls, which can also be made to certain countries via the home direct service (see page 146). As with anything that requires interaction with the operator, this can be a very slow process and it may be easier to make a short direct call and ask the party to call you back.

The usual Spanish response when answering the telephone is hello (*diga*) or literally 'speak to me' (*dígame*). The caller may begin what he has to say with 'listen' (*oiga*). 'I'm trying to connect you' is *le pongo/paso con* and 'go ahead' may be simply *adelante*. A call is *una llamada* and to call is *llamar*. Other useful words include 'to answer the telephone' (*coger*), hang up (*colgar*), dial (*marcar*), connect me (*póngame con*) and wrong number (*número equivocado*).

In Spain, telephone numbers are usually dictated on the telephone two digits at a time. If someone asks you to spell (*deletrear*) something on the telephone, such as your name, you should use the telephone alphabet. Obviously, to use it you must be able to pronounce the alphabet in Spanish and the words listed below. For example if your name's Smith you say, '*S* (*essay*) *para Sábado, M* (*emay*) *para Madrid, I* (*ee*) *para Inés, T* (*tay*) *para Tarragona y H* (*achay*) *para Historia*'.

| | | | |
|---|---|---|---|
| A (ah) | Antonio | N (enay) | Navarra |
| B (bay) | Barcelona | Ñ (enyay) | Ñoño |
| C (thay) | Carmen | O (oh) | Oviedo |
| CH (chay) | Chocolate | P (pay) | Paris |
| D (day) | Dolores | Q (ku) | Querido |
| E (ay) | Enrique | R (eray) | Ramón |
| F (efay) | Francia | S (essay) | Sábado |
| G (zhay) | Gerona | T (tay) | Tarragona |
| H (achay) | Historia | U (oo) | Ulises |
| I (ee) | Inés | V (oo-bay) | Valencia |
| J (hota) | José | W (oo-bay-doblay) | Washington |
| K (kah) | Kilo | X (ekiss) | Xiquina |
| L (elay) | Lorenzo | Y (ee greeyay ga) | Yegua |
| LL (elyay) | Llobregat | Z (thayta) | Zaragoza |

# International Calls

It's possible to make international direct dialling (IDD) calls from Spain to most countries, from private and public telephones. To make an international call from Spain, first dial 00 to obtain an international line, then dial the country code, e.g. 44 for the UK, the area code **without** the first zero and the telephone number of the person you're calling. So to call the London number 020-8123 4567 you must dial 00-44 20 8123 4567. To make a call to a country where there isn't IDD you must dial 9198 for European countries plus Algeria, Lebanon, Syria or Tunisia, and 9191 for all other countries.

A full list of IDD country codes is shown in the information pages (*páginas informativas*) of your local white pages (*páginas blancas*), plus codes for main cities and tariffs.

Competition for customers is fierce and in the last few years a price war has been waged by telephone companies. Auna, Tele2 and Telefónica levy a €0.12 connection fee for each call, a service provided free by most others. Most companies have a flat rate at all times for calls to Europe and the US. Examples of call charges range from €0.08 per minute (Tele2 and Teleconnect) to €0.12 per minute (Telefónica) for calls to Western Europe and the US. Note that tariffs are constantly being reduced and you should consult companies to find the cheapest rate for particular countries. Calls to Gibraltar are charged at the domestic rate for inter-provincial calls. There's a high surcharge for operator connected international calls.

Spain subscribes to a home direct service (*servicio directo país*) that enables you to call a number giving you direct and free access to an operator in the country you're calling, e.g. for the UK dial ☎ 0800-890034 (BT) or 0800-5593145 (C&W). The operator connects you to the number required and also accepts credit card calls. Countries with a home direct service include Argentina, Australia, Austria, Belgium, Bolivia, Brazil, Canada, Chile, China, Cyprus, Czech Republic, Denmark, Finland, France, Germany, Greece, Guatemala, Hong Kong, Hungary, Iceland, India, Indonesia, Ireland, Israel, Italy, Japan, South Korea, Malaysia, Malta, Mexico, Morocco, Norway, the Netherlands, New Zealand, Portugal, Russia, South Africa, Sweden, Switzerland, the UK, Uruguay and the US. Note, however, that this service can be expensive, particularly when making reverse charge calls. Information about home direct services is provided in the 'international communications' (*comunicaciones internacionales*) section of telephone directories, on the Telefónica website (🖥 www.telefonica.es) under *España Directo* or by calling ☎ 11825.

To obtain an operator from one of the three major US telephone companies, call ☎ 1-800-247 7246 (AT&T), ☎ 1-800-937 7262 (MCI) or ☎ 1-800-676 4003 (Sprint). You're connected directly with a US operator and you can place calls with a domestic US telephone card or make a collect (reverse charge) call. International calls can also be made from Telefónica telephone booths (*locutorios públicos*) in major towns and cities (see page 154), where you can pay for calls costing over €3 with a credit card. There are also numerous private telephone offices in resort towns.

## Callback Companies

Many expatriates (and Spaniards) make use of a callback service, such as those provided by Satel (🖥 www.satelcard.com) or Telegroup Global Access (🖥 www.

affinitytele.com) in Spain. Subscribers call a local freephone number or simply dial a code before numbers. In some cases, you call a number abroad (e.g. in the UK or the US) and are called back and given a new line on which to make calls.

## Internet Telephone Services

If you have correspondents or friends who are connected to the internet, you can make international calls for the price of a local telephone call. Once on the internet there are no other charges, no matter how much distance is covered or time spent online. Internet users can buy software from companies such as Quarterdeck and Vodaltec that effectively turns their personal computer into a voice-based telephone (both parties must have compatible computer software). You also need a sound card, speakers, a microphone and a modem, and access to a local internet provider (which may be free or cost a fixed monthly fee plus connection costs).

Users of the MSN Messenger service can speak to fellow users when online – you just need a microphone (from €7) – and Skype (🖳 www.skype.com), currently revolutionising the internet telephone service, is another alternative. You can download the software from the website and speak to any other Skype user free. While the quality of communication isn't always as good as using a telephone (it's similar to using a CB radio) and you must arrange call times in advance (Messenger and Skype users can automatically see if fellow users are available when they go online), international calls cost virtually nothing.

# Custom & Optional Services

Telefónica provides a range of custom and optional services (*líneas multiservicios*), although to take advantage of them your telephone must be connected to a digital exchange and you must have a touch-tone telephone. Most custom or optional services are already included in the cost of your telephone line, while others have a €6.01 initial charge (*alta inicial*) and/or a €0.60 or €0.90 monthly fee (*abono mensual*). Custom services include the following:

## Answerphone

An answerphone (*contestador automático*) service is available and it operates when you don't answer the phone within a certain number of rings (usually six) and when you're already on the phone. There's a standard pre-recorded message in Spanish, but other languages can be selected or you can record your own message. Note that this service is activated automatically on a new line. If you wish to deactivate the service, lift the receiver and press **#10#**. To reactivate it, lift the receiver, press **\*10#** and replace it. The service can be activated and deactivated whenever you wish. To listen to messages, simply lift the receiver and wait seven seconds and a recorded message informs you whether there are any messages and plays them. There's no fee for this service. **If you activate the answerphone service you automatically activate the call waiting service.**

## Automatic Dialling

Automatic dialling (*llamada sin marcar*) is where you programme a number into the phone, take the phone off the hook and after a few seconds the number is dialled automatically. There's an initial charge of €6.01 plus a fee of €0.90 per month. A cheaper option may be to buy a phone which can store numbers.

## Call Diversion

You can ask the exchange to divert calls (*desvío de llamadas*) to another number when your number is engaged (*desvío si comunica*) or when your telephone isn't answered within 15 seconds (*desvío por ausencia*). There's a monthly fee of €0.60 for each service. You can also have calls diverted after you move house (*desvío en bajas y cambio de domicilio*): for two months (fee €7.21); six months (€45.08) or indefinitely (€42.07 plus a monthly fee of €21.04).

## Call Transfer

Call transfer (*desvío inmediato*) allows you to divert calls to another telephone number automatically, e.g. from home to the office (or vice versa) or to a mobile telephone. There's a monthly fee of €0.60.

## Call Waiting

Call waiting (*llamada en espera*) lets you know when another caller is trying to contact you (you hear two short pips on the line) when you're already making a call and allows you to speak to the new caller without terminating your current call. This service is free.

## Caller Identification

Caller identification (*identificación de llamadas*) displays the number of the caller on the telephone. You need a telephone with a screen for this service, which is free.

## Change of Number

The change of number (*cambio de número*) service lets the caller know your new number unless he has programmed his number not to appear. There's an initial charge of €6.01 plus a fee of €0.60 per month.

## Three-way Conversation

Three-way conversation (*llamada a tres*) allows you to hold a conversation with two other people, in Spain or abroad. There's a monthly fee of €0.60.

# CHARGES

Line rental and call charges in Spain are among the highest in Europe, although they've reduced considerably in recent years with increased competition. Telephone charges from Telefónica include line rental; telephone and other equipment rentals; custom services such as call transfer and three-way conversation; credit card calls and general call charges. If you have a private line (*línea individual*), the monthly line rental or service charge (*cuota de abono*) is from €13.43 (levied monthly). People who are disabled or over 65 who have an income below the Spanish minimum pension pay a reduced tariff on monthly rental and call charges. Telephone charges from other companies include general call charges and may include a fixed monthly fee. There's intense competition for business among the numerous companies and tariffs change continuously.

To save money, you should shop around and choose a company with the lowest rates depending on the type of calls you wish to make. Be aware that rates for calls may not be consistently low in the same company and that some companies have aggressive marketing campaigns with cheap offers which often expire once the client has signed up. For a list of the main companies see **Registering with Other Companies** on page 142.

There are two primary tariffs in Spain: national and international. National (i.e. domestic) tariffs are divided into local/metropolitan calls (*metropolitana*), calls within your province (*provincial*) and calls outside your province (*nacional/interprovincial*).

## Local Calls

Local calls are offered by a number of providers. Competition for clients is intense and call charges are expected to continue to fall over the next year. Most providers charge an initial connection fee of €0.07 and typical rates are €0.07 (Tele2), €0.01 (Auna) or €0.02 (Telefónica) per minute during normal times and €0.01 (Auna and Telefónica) per minute at reduced rate. Normal hours (*hora normal*) are from 8am to 6pm, Mondays to Fridays, and reduced (*reducida*) hours from 6pm to 8am Mondays to Fridays, plus weekends and national public holidays.

## Provincial & Inter-provincial Calls

Most companies offer these services and prices vary considerably, as do the peak and normal periods. Tele2, Telefónica and Auna charge a connection fee for each call (€0.08 or €0.12), a service which is provided free by most others. Some companies, such as Auna and Telefónica, have two rate bands on weekdays, e.g. 8am to 8pm (normal) and 8pm to 8am (reduced). Weekends and public holidays are also at a reduced rate. Others such as Tele2 have a flat rate. Note that matters are further complicated by special deals offered by practically all companies.

Examples of provincial call charges are from €0.02 per minute (Tele2) and from €0.04 per minute (Telefónica). Examples of inter-provincial call charges are €0.03 a minute flat rate (Tele2) and €0.06 (Auna and Telefónica) at normal tariff. It's worth noting that Telefónica hardly ever offers the cheapest rate available! **Because of the price war raging, it's worthwhile shopping around and using the services of several different companies (even all of them!) depending on the time of day and call destination, to ensure you get the best value for money.**

Note that there's a surcharge for operator connected calls, the tariffs for which are shown in telephone directories.

# BILLS

Bills (*facturas*) are sent at varying intervals depending on the company, although they're usually sent monthly and you're given 20 days to pay. VAT at 16 per cent is levied on all charges. Itemised bills (*factura detallada*) are provided, listing all numbers called with the date and time, duration and the charge. Bills can be paid in cash at most banks, via a bank account or in cash at a Telefónica office; cheques aren't normally accepted. Simply present the bill with your payment and you receive a receipt. You can also have your telephone bill paid by direct debit (*domiciliación bancaria*) from a bank account, which is advisable for holiday-home owners, as it ensures that you aren't disconnected for non-payment. If your bill isn't paid within 20 days, your line may be cut without further warning, although a new system has been introduced where lines with unpaid bills are reduced for ten days to incoming calls only, before cutting the service completely. If your line is cut, there's a reconnection fee, which depends on the amount owing and the elapsed period, after which it should be reconnected within two working days. All companies offer the possibility of checking your bills and telephone usage online.

If you complain about your bill being too high, Telefónica may install a counter on your telephone for a number of days to check for a malfunction. If the test fails to discover any line problems, Telefónica won't reduce your bill. **You must pay your telephone bill, even if the amount is contested, otherwise Telefónica may cut your line.** If you're unable to pay the whole amount of a contested bill, you should pay your usual amount and contest the rest. Telefónica's bills include the following details (reading from top to bottom):

| Item | Description |
| --- | --- |
| *Datos del cliente* | Name and address of subscriber plus your fiscal number, the phone number the bill is for, details of the bank account (if paid by direct debit), including the date the bill will be paid. The last four digits of your bank account are obscured by asterisks for security reasons. |
| *Conceptos de la factura* | Information about the amount for each part of your bill |
| *Cuotas de abono* (date) | Standing charges |
| *Cuotas otros servicios* | Charges for other services (e.g. telephone plans or call transfer) |

| | |
|---|---|
| *Consumos** | Charges |
| *Descuentos** | Discounts |
| *Total (base imponible)* | Total (amount before VAT) |
| *IVA 16%* | 16% VAT |
| *Total a pagar (euros)* | Total payable (in euros) |
| *Importe medio de consumo diario* | Average daily cost of phone use |

\* Calls and discounts are itemised on the page(s) attached to the bill. Calls show the date, time, duration and number called.

# DIRECTORIES

Telephone directories (*guías telefónicas*) are published by province, with each province having its own telephone book and code number (see page 143). Some provinces have more than one volume, e.g. the Madrid white pages and yellow pages (*páginas amarillas*) each have two volumes. The directories for the province where you live or have your business are provided free of charge. If you want other directories they're available from provincial Telefónica offices for around €3 each.

The white pages directory contains a number of information pages, including: emergency and useful local numbers; Telefónica service numbers; national and international codes; instructions on how to use the telephone (in English, French, German and Italian) and possibly tourist information. The second section in the white pages is the alphabetical list of subscribers. White pages information can also be accessed via the internet (🖳 www.paginasblancas.es). The yellow pages directory contains useful local numbers at the front, a list of towns covered by the directory and local information. Yellow pages information is also available by phone (☎ 11888) or via the internet (🖳 www.paginasamarillas.es). The blue pages (*páginas azules*) are also published in Spain and contain an alphabetical index of streets and subscribers by street number. New directories are published annually. Euro pages is a European business directory containing some 150,000 suppliers (🖳 www.euro pages.es for information). In some areas, there are English-language directories, e.g. the English Speaker's Telephone Directory (ESTD) for the Costa del Sol and Gibraltar (☎ 956-776 958, 🖳 www.esp.gi/publishing.htm). Free local telephone directories (e.g. Tu Distrito (🖳 www.tudistrito.com) and QDQ (🖳 www.qdq.com) are also published in some areas.

When you have a telephone installed, your name and number is automatically included in the next edition of your local white pages directory. You can choose to have an unlisted number (*no registrado*), for which there's no charge. Subscribers are listed in the white pages under their town or village (*ciudad*) and not alphabetically for the whole of a province. When looking for a subscriber's number, you must know the town, not just the province where they live. You will receive little or no help from directory enquiries (*servicio de información*) unless you know the town where the subscriber is located.

# Directory Enquiries

Numerous companies offer directory enquiries services and tariffs vary greatly and not all companies have up to date databases or can provide all numbers. The following are the most common numbers and tariffs for national directory enquiries:

- Telefónica (☎ 11818, 💻 www.paginasblancas.es) – A flat rate of €0.55. This service is free from public telephones.
- Telefónica (☎ 11822) – €0.22 initial connection fee, €0.01 a second.*
- Telegate (☎ 11811, 💻 www.telegate.es) – €0.40 a minute plus €0.40 connection fee.*
- Yellow Pages (☎ 11888, 💻 www.paginasamarillas.es) – €0.75 a minute plus €0.50 connection fee.

International directory enquiries:

- Telefónica (☎ 11825) – A flat rate of €2.*
- Telefónica (☎ 11886) – €1.60 for the first minute, €1.10 for subsequent minutes.
- Telegate (☎ 11880) – €1 a minute plus €0.60 connection fee.

\* These services provide a direct connection service to the number requested for an additional fee.

A consumer watchdog association, Federación de Consumidores en Acción (FACUA), recommends using a public telephone (☎ 11818) or the internet for directory enquiries (both are free services) and to avoid the direct connection service, which, although convenient, is usually more expensive than if you phone the number yourself (☎ 11822 is the only exception to this).

# PUBLIC TELEPHONES

Public telephones (*cabinas telefónicas* or *teléfonos públicos*) are located in bus depots, railway stations and airports; bars, cafés and restaurants; motorway rest areas; various business premises and in streets in towns and villages. Public telephones aren't found in post offices with the exception of a few main post offices in major cities. All payphones allow IDD, but international calls can also be made via the operator. Most old-style call boxes have been replaced by new 'vandal-proof' telephones (both are blue and green). Virtually all public telephones accept coins and many also accept telephone cards (**credit cards aren't accepted in public telephone boxes**). Some public telephones accept only telephone cards, although they're usually placed immediately next to a coin public telephone.

Telephone cards (*tarjetas telefónicas*) costing €5, €10 or €15 are available from post offices, newsagents (*papelerías*), tobacconists (*estancos*) and some retailers, and save you having to find change or carry around piles of coins. The procedure for using public telephones depends on whether you're using an old style telephone or a new one. The instructions for using modern public telephones are as follows:

1. Lift the receiver and check that there's a dialling tone, as some public telephones don't work. The message 'insert coins or a telephone card' (*inserte moneda o tarjeta*) is displayed on the screen. If you wish to see instructions in English, French or German press the top 'select language' (*selección de idioma*) button below the display (depicting a flag marked with an 'L') until the language you require is displayed. Thereafter, follow the instructions on the display. You can increase or lower the volume by pressing the *volumen* button, which is the third button below the display. Instructions on how to use the telephone are usually posted in telephone boxes in English, French, German and Spanish. A selection of national and international code numbers are also listed in some public telephones.

2. Insert coins or a telephone card. Telephones accept €2, €1, 50, 20, 10, 5 and 2 cent coins. You must insert at least €0.20 for a local call (within the same province), €0.40 for a national call (to another province) and €1 for an international call or a call to a mobile phone. If you don't insert enough money you're unable to make a call. If you dial the wrong number or don't insert coins fast enough you must start again and the message 'please wait' (*por favor, espere*) may be displayed. Make sure you have plenty of €0.50 or €1 coins for international calls. **Don't insert large denomination coins for short local calls as they will be lost unless you have a number of calls to make** (see below). If you have a problem inserting coins or coins don't register on the display, press the coin return button next to the coin slot.

   If you're using a telephone card (*tarjeta telefónica*), simply insert it in the card slot and dial. The message 'Dial Number Credit XXXX' is displayed. As your call continues the remaining credit on your card is displayed. When you've finished your call, hang up the receiver and remove your card when 'Remove Card Credit XXXX' is displayed.

3. After you've inserted some money or a card the instruction 'dial number – credit XXXX' (*marque número – crédito XXXX*) is displayed (where 'XXXX' is the amount inserted in coins). The credit amount is permanently updated as you insert more coins or coins are used.

4. Insert new coins as necessary (a high pitched tone indicates when more money is needed). If you're using a telephone card and your credit expires, press the 'card change' (*cambio de tarjeta*) button and insert a new card. If you don't have a new card, you can continue your call by pressing the manual payment button (*botón de cobro manual*) and inserting coins.

5. If you wish to make another call, don't hang up the receiver, but press the (follow on call) button marked 'R' located beneath the handset rest. This ensures that any partly used coins aren't lost, but are reserved as credit towards your next call.

6. When you've finished your call(s) hang up the receiver. Any completely unused coins are returned in the coin box (partly used coins are lost). **Don't forget to retrieve your telephone card.**

**When making an emergency call (see page 140) from a public telephone, you must insert at least €0.10 (which is later returned) or use a telephone card.**

Public telephones can also be found in bars, cafés and restaurants, they set their own charges, which are slightly higher than usual public telephones. Many businesses also allow customers to make calls on metered telephones and make a surcharge on calls. To make a call from a hotel room, you may be able to dial direct or you may need to make a call via the hotel receptionist. **However, making calls from hotels is best avoided, as they levy a high surcharge in addition to the cost of calls.** There are free SOS telephones on motorways and main highways for use in the event of accidents, breakdowns and other emergencies.

You can obtain a telephone calling card (*tarjeta personal*) from Telefónica (currently free of charge). Cards can be used from any public telephone, with calls being charged to your Spanish telephone account. To use a Telefónica card you dial ☎ 083 and give your card number and personal identity number (PIN). **Take care when using telephone calling cards and make sure that nobody discovers your PIN, as card fraud is rife.** For information call ☎ 901-501 083.

## Telephone Booths

You can also make calls from telephone booths (*locutorios públicos*) in Telefónica offices. These booths (usually blue) can be found in major towns and resort areas. Office opening hours vary and may be from 8 or 9am until 10pm on working days (*días laborables*) and from 9am until 9pm on Sundays and public holidays (*domingos y festivos*). **However, Sunday hours vary considerably and offices are often open only for a few hours.** Telephone cards and most credit cards are accepted for calls costing over €3. Reverse charge (collect) calls can also be made. You can make an unlimited number of calls and receive an itemised receipt which includes the surcharge and VAT. In smaller towns, these offices are often franchised businesses, where you pay a 35 per cent surcharge on all calls.

There are also booths (*centros telefónicos or cabinas*) which are leased from Telefónica by private companies (they're usually blue and green and are advertised as *centros telefónicos*). *Centros telefónicos* have shorter business hours than Telefónica offices, e.g. 10am to 2pm and 5 to 10pm daily. They charge a high commission on all calls and don't handle reverse charge calls, as they make no profit on them.

Many businesses in resort areas (such as restaurants) have telephone booths and may also offer a fax service. **Note that (according to the Spanish Consumers' Union/UCE) some operators charge excessive rates, which can be over ten times higher than Telefónica rates.** However, in recent years new companies, such as Call Box and Call Home, have entered the market in resort areas, offering calls at **much** lower rates than from other public phones, as well as fax and mailbox services.

Most booths have a full set of telephone directories.

# MOBILE TELEPHONES

Mobile telephones (*telefonía móvil*) were relatively slow to take off in Spain, but in the last few years prices have fallen dramatically and sales have rocketed, making Spain the fastest-expanding country in the European Union for mobile phones with around 32 million users. All the major population areas are covered by analogue and digital networks, although sparsely populated areas aren't served or reception is difficult. Spain has three digital (Amena, Movistar and Vodafone) networks which cover around 90 per cent of the country and 98 per cent of the population. All mobile telephone numbers start with the number 6.

Mobile telephones are relatively cheap and the cheapest models start at around €60, including at least €20 in calls. Many people choose a mobile phone because the cost of connection is less than a standard 'cable' phone and is instantaneous, you can move house and retain the same number, and you can use the phone almost anywhere, in Spain and internationally.

Tariffs have fallen dramatically due to the price war that has been raging between the three service providers in the last few years. The three main mobile telephone providers offer pre-paid ('pay as you talk') and contract arrangements. Competition is fierce and so prices and packages are constantly changing. Tariffs can be found on the mobile telephone company websites (🖳 www.amena.com, 🖳 www.movi star.com and 🖳 www.vodafone.es). For easy comparison (in Spanish only), consult The Phone House website (🖳 www.phonehouse.es). If you have a pre-paid phone, you can top it up (*recargar*) in many shops and supermarkets or ATM cash machines at many banks (simply key in the telephone number and the amount and it's debited directly from your account). As with fixed-line telephone companies, tariffs (for national and international calls) are constantly changing, as are the times of peak and reduced rates. **It's worthwhile shopping around and comparing offers before deciding which service to buy.**

If you arrive from the UK or another European country, you can usually use the mobile telephone from your home country in Spain, which operates on the GSM network. However, calls are routed via your home country and therefore expensive, so it's advisable to buy a Spanish mobile telephone as soon as you can, or have a Spanish SIM card fitted to your existing telephone. This system works well if you're travelling frequently between Spain and your home country, as you can simply change the SIM card whenever you're in a different country.

As in many other countries, text messaging is extremely popular in Spain and all providers offer very competitive rates for sending text messages. Much to linguists' and teachers' dismay, the use of text messaging has brought with it many new spellings for Spanish, such as the widespread use of 'k' instead of 'qu'. Some messages are almost impossible to read unless you're *au fait* with text message spelling!

Recently, numerous mobile phone scams have come to light, including many which leave you a message asking you to phone a number urgently for important news regarding your family or a prize. The number you must ring is invariably a high charge number (e.g. 806) and you're deliberately kept on the line by an answering machine or telephonists for as long as possible, resulting in a very expensive phone call. Needless to say, the important news or prize doesn't exist. The Consumers' Association advises mobile phone users to ignore all such messages. You should also be aware that mobile phones are highly prized by petty thieves and mobile phone theft is big business. **Keep your mobile phone in a secure place and never leave it on show in your car.**

The use of mobile phones while driving is prohibited. No exceptions are allowed and fines start at €300 with a three-point deduction from your licence. You should install a 'hands free' unit in your car if you wish to use your mobile phone while driving.

# FAX & TELEGRAMS

Despite the advent of email and text messaging, telegrams (*telegramas*) and faxes (*burofax*, often used instead of a registered letter) are still used and can be sent from any post office. Main post offices have a separate 'telegram desk or window' (*telegrama y burofax*), often with a telex and fax cabin (*cabina telex/burofax*), although business hours for these services may be restricted.

## Fax

There has been a huge increase in the use of fax (facsimile) machines in the last decade or so, helped by lower prices, the introduction of cheaper international call rates, and the unreliability of the Spanish post office. They can be purchased from Telefónica and purchased or rented from telephone and business equipment retailers (shop around and compare prices). **If you're planning to take a fax machine to Spain, check that it will work there or that it can be modified.** Most fax machines made for other European countries operate in Spain, although getting them repaired locally may be impossible unless the same machine is sold in Spain.

Public fax services (*burofax*) are provided by main post offices in most towns, from where you can send and receive faxes (you can also have them delivered to your home). Faxes sent within Spain cost €1.55 for the first page and €0.65 for each additional page. Faxes sent to Europe cost €6.40 for the first page and €1.60 for each additional page. Faxes can also be sent from major hotels, business offices (that provide 'business services') and newsagents, which may be cheaper than using a post office and is certainly a simpler way (note, however, that some levy high charges). The cost of receiving faxes at private offices is usually around €1 per page.

## Telegrams

Telegrams can also be sent from a private telephone (☎ 902-197 197; dial 1 after the recorded message or 💻 www.correos.es), but don't expect the telephone operator to speak English or other foreign languages.

To avoid mistakes when sending telegrams or spelling words on the telephone, you should use the phonetic table of code names for individual letters (see page 145). The cost of sending a domestic telegram is €6.10 for under 50 words for home delivery (*domicilio*) or to another post office (*no domicilio*). Telegrams to European addresses (*continental*) cost €11.75 plus €0.38 per word, and telegrams to other destinations cost €9.10 for the first seven words and €1.30 for each word thereafter. You can also send radio telegrams.

# INTERNET

The internet (*internet*) in Spain got off to a slow start due to the high cost of local calls and the relative lack of computers, although there has been a spectacular increase in its usage due mainly to lower prices for calls and computers, and Spain now takes the internet seriously. Around a third of households are online, a huge increase compared to 23 per cent in 2002 and a mere 0.7 per cent in 1996. However, Spain still lags behind in EU ratings where many countries, including new members Estonia and Slovenia, have a higher uptake, although where broadband is concerned, Spain (with over 2 million lines) is within the top ten countries worldwide. All state primary and secondary schools are online and it's now unusual to find a medium or large company without a website. Competition for clients is fierce and there has been a prolific growth in servers (*servidores*) over the last few years, although many small servers have been absorbed by larger ones. Some provide free internet and email (*correo electrónico* or *email*) services, but the majority make an annual charge. It's worth comparing prices, particularly as the internet service provided free by some companies can be extremely slow and/or clogged up with their publicity, making access difficult and expensive in telephone charges.

Connecting to the internet costs the same as local calls, although most companies offer discount services, which generally allow you to buy a fixed number of access hours per month at a discount. Telefónica offers several discounts, including *Bono Ciudad Plus* which provides 600 minutes of local and internet calls at any time and costs €8.21 a month. *Bono Ciudad* offers 600 minutes during off-peak hours (6pm to 8am, Mondays to Fridays and at weekends) and costs €4.21 a month; and *Bononet* with seven or twenty hours internet use a month for €6 (seven hours) or €16. Most companies also offer the possibility of combining local and internet call charges under the same discount scheme. Note that any unused time in a month isn't refundable and if you go over your contracted number of hours the excess time is charged at the normal rate.

# Broadband

Broadband (ADSL) internet connection is now available in most of Spain's urban areas, although you should check with Telefónica. Rural areas are less well-served and some more remote areas don't have ADSL facilities at all, although the government plans to rectify this in the near future. Advantages of ADSL include fast internet access, continuous connection and access to your phone line at the same time. On the other hand, monthly charges are high (at least €20) and your computer is more vulnerable to virus attacks. Unless you use the internet for several hours a day, it's probably cheaper to use the conventional internet connection with a discount service.

Some 50 companies provide ADSL access and the top five are Telefónica (☎ 1004, 🖳 www.telefonicaonline.com), Terra (☎ 902-152 015, 🖳 www.terra.es), Tiscali (☎ 902-444 333, 🖳 www.tiscali.es), Wanadoo (☎ 1414, 🖳 www.wanadoo.es) and Ya.com (☎ 902-903 633, 🖳 www.ya.com). Competition for ADSL clients is fierce and there are occasional good deals (e.g. free installation) and initial charges and monthly rates for 24-hour access vary from €19.95 (Ya.com) to €39.95 (Telefónica). Most companies also offer flexible tariff systems similar to 'normal' internet discounts. Speed on ADSL connections varies from a minimum of 512/128 kbps, although many companies (e.g. Telefónica and Tíscali) now offer 1 Mb as the minimum speed.

All companies use the same broadband infrastructure, which is controlled and maintained by Telefónica. ADSL is, as yet, unregulated in Spain and subject to numerous consumer complaints, particularly with regard to speed of connection and customer service. Before committing yourself to an ADSL line, read the terms and conditions carefully, and check the minimum duration of the contract (usually at least six months), although several companies now offer ADSL with no minimum contract length requirements.

## Satellite Internet Services

If you cannot get cabled broadband connection in your property, you may want to consider a satellite connection. Speed of transmission is the same as conventional ADSL, but installation costs are much higher (around €1,300) with monthly charges starting from around €60, and you must install a satellite dish. The other disadvantage of satellite internet connection is that European satellite broadband capacity is shared, so if you have a lot of material to transfer, this can be a problem. Some companies offer a monthly 'priority traffic' allocation, but above this you must share the service with other users and, at peak times, you may experience a reduction in connection speed. However, satellite internet connection is better than none at all.

Satellite internet providers covering Spain include Avonline (🖥 www.avonline broadband.co.uk), Business Comm (🖥 www.bcsatellite.net) and Global Telephone and Telecommunication (🖥 www.globaltt.com).

# 8.

# TELEVISION & RADIO

Spanish television (TV) isn't renowned for its quality, although it has improved in recent years and is probably not much worse than the 'rubbish' dished up in many other European countries. In addition to terrestrial TV, satellite TV reception is excellent in most areas of Spain and is particularly popular among the expatriate community (not that much of its output is any better than Spanish TV). Cable TV isn't common in Spain compared with northern European countries and is subscribed to by just some 6 per cent of the population. Digital TV is now available (offered by various companies) and will eventually allow hundreds of channels to be transmitted by satellite and cable. Spanish radio (including many expatriate stations) is generally excellent and equal to most other European countries.

Public TV (Televisión Española/TVE) has for years been controlled by the government with TV news and current affairs programmes heavily in favour of the ruling party. In an attempt to rectify this and guarantee TVE's independence, new legislation will be passed in early 2006 under which TVE will become an independent body subject to parliamentary (not cabinet) control. The director will be nominated by TVE's governing body (rather than the cabinet) and the company's monumental debt (over €7,000 million at the end of 2005) will be absorbed by the state. It remains to be seen how successful this bid for independence will be.

The Spanish are avid TV viewers (over 90 per cent of Spanish homes have a TV) and according to surveys rate around fourth in Europe (after Portugal, the UK and Italy) in average viewing time per day, per head (around four hours). Some 90 per cent of Spaniards over the age of 14 watch TV every day and most get their news from the TV (only some 20 per cent of Spaniards buy a newspaper). Spain produces some of the worst TV in Europe, much of which is termed 'junk TV' (*telebasura*) by its critics, with sex and violence prominent, even during children's viewing times, although standards and quality are improving and under new legislation television unsuitable for children can only be broadcast after 10pm. The consolation is that there's no TV or radio licence in Spain (so at least the rubbish is 'free')!

# TELEVISION

The standards for TV reception in Spain **aren't the same as in some other countries**. Due to the differences in transmission standards, TV sets and video recorders operating on the British (PAL-I), French (SECAM) or North American (NTSC) systems won't function in Spain, which, along with most other continental European countries, uses the PAL-BG standard. It's possible to buy a multi-standard European TV (and VCR) containing automatic circuitry that switches between different systems. Some multi-standard TVs also offer the North American NTSC standard and have an NTSC-in jack plug connection allowing you to play back American videos. A standard British, French or US TV won't work in Spain, although British TVs can be modified. The same applies to a 'foreign' video or DVD recorder, which won't operate with a Spanish TV unless dual-standard. Some people opt for two TVs, one to receive Spanish TV programmes and another (e.g. SECAM or NTSC) to playback their favourite videos or DVDs.

If you decide to buy a TV in Spain, you will find it advantageous to buy one with teletext (*teletexto*), which, apart from allowing you to display programme schedules, also provides a wealth of useful and interesting information. A portable colour TV can be purchased in Spain from around €90 for a 36cm (14 inch) with remote control. A 55cm (21 inch) TV costs from around €140 and a 62.5cm (25 inch) model from around €300. Many TVs feature Nicam stereo sound, a high quality, digital TV sound system available in most areas of Spain. Digital widescreen TVs are also available and although still relatively expensive, prices continue to fall and start at around €850. Home cinemas (prices start at around €1,200) are widely available and increasingly popular.

It's now difficult to rent a TV in Spain, even in resort areas and most furnished rental property comes equipped with a TV. In any case, it's usually cheaper to buy one in the long run.

# TV Stations

Most areas of Spain receive five channels with a standard external aerial, although those with an in-house 'cable' or digital system may receive dozens more. Spanish TV consists of a surfeit of moronic game shows, chat shows, football, basketball and bullfighting, although there are also excellent news programmes, documentaries, wildlife and history programmes. Football reigns supreme in Spain, where TV companies pay a staggering sum to televise live football matches, which has had a significant effect on the restaurant trade (live matches are screened several nights a week). One thing you can be sure of, whatever is showing on one of the three main channels, a similar programme will be showing on the others (called counter-programming).

The introduction of commercial TV has provided much needed competition for the state-run channels and has helped improve the choice, if not always the quality.

Dramas and sit-coms such as *Hospital Central*, *Los Serrano* and *Aquí No Hay Quien Viva* are hugely popular and regularly top the audience ratings. Other popular programmes include *Cuéntame cómo pasó* ('Tell Me How It Happened', a drama recounting events in recent Spanish history starting from the '60's), *Operación Triunfo* (Spain's 'Pop Idol' into its fourth series), *CSI* and *Mira Quién Baila* (a celebrity dancing competition). *Gran Hermano* ('Big Brother') continues to appear annually and is still very popular, although audience ratings dropped during the sixth series. In 2005, South-American soap operas made a comeback and were many Spaniards' staple TV diet in the summer. Gossip programmes such as *Corazón Corazón*, *Gente* and *Salsa Rosa* are also widely followed, reflecting the Spaniards' seemingly insatiable interest in other people's lives. Popular current affairs programmes include *Informe Semanal* (La Primera) and *Los Reporteros* (Canal Sur). Chat shows with a magazine-type format such as *Sabor a ti* (Antena 3) and *A Tu Lado* (Tele 5) are also popular and have largely replaced children's programmes in the afternoon. Political satire has found a niche among the Spanish, who regularly watch programmes such as *El Guiñol* and *Caiga quien caiga*. TV news (newscasters and presenters are well-known personalities), domestic and international, is comprehensive and upbeat and contains regular items about the arts, e.g. ballet or opera. There's generally no censorship on Spanish TV and 'sexy' and risqué programmes are commonplace, particularly on the autonomous channels. The main Spanish TV stations are:

- **TVE** – TVE (Televisión Española) is the state television and currently subject to major reform in an attempt to reduce its government control. Despite increased competition, TVE remains Spain's largest and most popular TV network with its two channels, La Primera and La2, claiming around 30 per cent of viewers, although La Primera hasn't topped audience ratings since May 2004. La Primera places emphasis on light entertainment such as game and chat shows, music shows, comedy, soap operas, children's shows, news and films, while La2 puts more emphasis on sports, live cultural broadcasts, regional shows, serials, documentaries and films. Not surprisingly, La Primera attracts around triple the audience of La2. Both TVE channels broadcast 24 hours a day.

- **Antena 3** – Antena 3 went on air in January 1990 and is now mainly owned by Telefónica. Its output consists of fairly conservative programming such as game shows and 'home-made soaps' aimed at a family audience. Antena 3 regularly attracts around 20 per cent of the TV audience (not far behind TVE).

- **Tele 5** – Tele 5 claims to be Spain's entertainment channel and broadcasts popular children's programmes, highly popular 'home-made' soaps, blockbuster films and political satire. Tele 5 is the most independent of central government control among the Spanish channels and its news broadcasts are the least politically biased. In May 2004, Tele 5 topped the audience ratings for the first time ever and broadcasts at least five of the top ten weekly programmes.

- **Cuatro** – Spain's first new national private channel for several years started broadcasting in November 2005 on the same frequency as Canal Plus, which moved to a completely digital and scrambled frequency. Cuatro's output intends to appeal to a wide audience and offer quality entertainment television.

- **Canal Plus** – Canal Plus (also often written as Canal+) is Spain's only scrambled national television channel and offers films, sports and documentaries. Many films are fairly recent and are often screened with the original soundtrack and Spanish subtitles. It also shows National Geographic documentaries and live sports events, including Spanish first division and English Premiership football matches. It offers decoders to subscribers for a refundable deposit of around €100 (special offers usually include this free of charge), a connection fee of €30, plus a monthly subscription of €24.97. As from November 2005, Canal Plus subscriptions also include Digital Plus programmes.

- **Localia TV** – Localia TV, launched in 2004, broadcasts in main towns and cities throughout the country with an emphasis on local events and news with films, current affairs and culture.

- **Regional Stations** – There are regional channels broadcasting in the local language in the Basque Country (two), Catalonia (two) and Galicia, and others in Andalusia (two), Castile-la Mancha, the Canaries, Madrid (two) and Valencia. Most are controlled and sponsored by regional governments and serve as supplements to the national network (and most are deep in debt). Aragon, Asturias, the Balearics, Extremadura and Murcia plan to start broadcasting in the near future. Around 1,000 municipalities also have their own local TV stations (usually embarrassingly amateur!), which usually serve as little more than a platform for the ruling political party in the town.

- **Expatriate TV** – There are no stations for foreigners in Spain and the only option is the Gibraltar TV channel GBC (showing BBC programmes), which can be received in southern Spain, for which a decoder is necessary. However, there have been numerous complaints about poor reception and if you want English-language TV you're better off with satellite TV.

Scheduling of programmes in Spain can be extremely 'flexible', with programmes often being shown half an hour earlier or later than scheduled and sometimes not at all. All Spanish TV channels carry advertising and there's a continuous battle for advertising revenue. Although advertising time has increased considerably in recent years, advertising revenue has decreased. Advertising is pervasive (currently 12 minutes an hour, although this will be reduced to nine in 2006) and there's even advertising during live sports events such as football matches (at the bottom of the screen) whenever the ball goes out of play (football coverage is also constantly interrupted by replays, which are often shown while play is in progress).

TV programmes are listed in all Spanish newspapers and in special TV guides such as *TelePrograma*. Some Spanish TV programmes are also listed in English-language newspapers and magazines, along with satellite TV programmes.

# Digital TV

Digital TV, offering better quality of sound and image as well as numerous more channels than analogue TV, has been slow to take off in Spain, mainly because of lack of decoders and digital televisions, but in 2005 the government introduced the new digital TV rulings under which analogue broadcasting will disappear by 2010. Until then there will be a transitional period when the main TV channels (see above) will broadcast in analogue and digital (known as *simulcast*). TVE will broadcast seven digital channels, private stations four and regional stations eight. Local stations will have four channels, increased to eight in Barcelona, Bilbao, Madrid, Seville and Valencia.

To watch digital TV you require a digital TV (costs are currently between €850 and €1,200) and a digital decoder (*terminal digital terrestre/TDT*), often known as a Digibox, costing from €100 to €400. Alternatively, you can subscribe to Digital Plus (🖥 www.csatelite.es), offering a complete package (including a subscription to Canal Plus) with over 150 channels for €49.80 a month, plus a refundable deposit of €90; if you need a decoder, you must pay an additional €8 monthly. There are also 'specialist' channels such as *Canal Caza y Pesca* for hunting and fishing fanatics and *Canal Barça* or *Real Madrid* for those who think football should be on all day, instead of just most of the day. These channels each cost around €5 extra per month.

Telefónica offers its own digital TV product (Imagenio) broadcast via broadband internet access (ADSL), so you can only watch it if you subscribe to ADSL through Telefónica. Imagenio is currently available in large cities only, but Telefónica plans to extend services to most of the country by mid-2006. Imagenio costs €30 subscription fee and €19 a month for around 50 channels, with the possibility of adding further channels for between €5 and €7.20 a month.

# Satellite TV

There are a number of satellites positioned over Europe carrying over 200 stations broadcasting in a variety of languages. Satellite TV has been growing apace in Europe in recent years, although most homes in Spain with satellite TV are owned by foreigners.

## Astra

The Astra satellites offer a huge choice of English and foreign-language channels, at least 100 (or over 500 with digital TV) of which can be received throughout Spain with a 60 or 85cm dish. Among the many English-language channels available on Astra are Channel 5, The Discovery Channels, The Disney Channel, Eurosport, Film Four, Plus, Sky Cinema 1 & 2, Sky Movies 1–9, Sky News, Sky One, Sky Sports (three channels), TCM, UK Gold and UKTV Gold. Other channels are broadcast in Dutch, German, Japanese, Swedish and various Indian languages. The signal for many channels is scrambled (the decoder is usually built into the receiver) and viewers must pay a monthly subscription to receive programmes. The best served by unscrambled (clear) channels are German-speakers. Further information can be found on Astra's website (💻 www.astra.lu).

A bonus of Astra is the availability of radio stations, including all the national BBC stations (see **Cable & Satellite Radio** on page 170).

## Sky Television

In order to receive Sky television you need a Sky digital receiver (digibox) and a dish. There are two ways to obtain the equipment and the necessary Sky 'smart' card. You can subscribe in the UK or Ireland (personally, if you have an address there, or via a friend) and then take the Sky receiver and card to Spain, although for the first year of your contract the digibox must be connected to a telephone line (so that Sky can sell you interactive services); if you export it during this period and connect it to a foreign telephone line, Sky will terminate your contract (Sky's call centre can tell what country a call/connection is being made from). After the first year, the digibox no longer needs to be connected to a telephone line and so can (although strictly should not) be exported. Similarly, a Sky card shouldn't be used outside the UK.

Alternatively, you can buy a digibox and obtain a Sky card 'privately' in Spain (a number of satellite companies supply Sky cards); however, you're subject to the same restrictions as noted above. Moreover, Sky receivers and cards are much more expensive in Spain: a receiver and card cost around €400 plus the monthly subscription, while the card on its own costs around €200 (plus the subscription). To receive Sky TV in France, a dish must be at least 1.2m in diameter (costing from around €200).

You must subscribe to Sky to receive most English-language channels (other than Sky News, which isn't scrambled). If you subscribe to the basic package, costing around GB£15, you will have access to around 100 channels, including BBC1, BBC2,

ITV1, CH4 and CH5. Various other packages are available costing up to around GB£42.50, for which you have access to the Movie and Sports channels, along with many interactive services such as Sky News Active.

Further information about Sky installation (in the UK) and programme packages can be found on Sky's website (🖳 www.sky.com).

## Eutelsat

Eutelsat was the first company to introduce satellite TV to Europe and it now runs a fleet of communications satellites carrying TV stations to over 50 million homes. The English-language stations on Eutelsat include Eurosport, BBC World and CNBC Superchannel. Other stations are broadcast in Arabic, French, German, Hungarian, Italian, Polish, Portuguese, Spanish and Turkish. Further information can be found on Eutelsat's website (🖳 www.eutelsat.org).

## BBC

The BBC's commercial subsidiary, BBC Worldwide Television, broadcasts two 24-hour channels: BBC Prime (general entertainment) and BBC World (24-hour news and information). BBC World is free-to-air, while BBC Prime is encrypted and requires a D2-MAC decoder and a smartcard, available on subscription from BBC Prime, PO Box 5054, London W12 0ZY, UK (☎ 020-8433 2221, 🖳 www.bbc prime.com). For more information and a programming guide contact BBC Worldwide Television, Woodlands, 80 Wood Lane W12 0TT, UK (☎ 020-8433 2221). A programme guide is also available on the internet (🖳 www.bbc. co.uk/schedules) and both BBC World and BBC Prime have websites (🖳 www.bbcworld.com and 🖳 www.bbcprime.com). When accessing them, you need to enter the name of the country (e.g. Spain) so that schedules appear in local time.

## Equipment

A satellite receiver should have a built-in Videocrypt decoder (and others such as Eurocrypt, Syster or SECAM, if required) and be capable of receiving satellite stereo radio. A system with an 85cm dish (to receive Astra stations) costs from around €300 plus the cost of installation, which may be included in the price. Shop around, as prices vary hugely. With a 1.2 or 1.5 metre motorised dish, you can receive hundreds of stations in a multitude of languages from around the world. If you wish to receive satellite TV on two or more TVs, you can buy a satellite system with two or more receptors. To receive stations from two or more satellites simultaneously, you need a motorised dish or a dish with a double feed antenna (dual LNBs). There are many satellite sales and installation companies in Spain, most of which advertise in the expatriate press. Shop around and compare prices. Alternatively, you can import your own satellite dish and receiver and install it yourself. **Before buying a system, ensure that it can receive programmes from all existing and planned satellites.**

## Location

To receive programmes from any satellite, there must be no obstacles between the satellite and your dish, i.e. no trees, buildings or mountains must obstruct the signal. **Before buying or erecting a satellite dish, check whether you need permission from your landlord or the local municipality.** Some towns and buildings (such as apartment blocks) have strict laws concerning the positioning of antennae, although generally, owners can mount a dish almost anywhere without receiving any complaints. Dishes can usually be mounted in a variety of unobtrusive positions and can also be painted or patterned to blend in with the background.

## Communities

When an apartment or townhouse is advertised as having satellite TV, it often means that it has a communal system and not its own satellite dish. When this is the case, stations are received via a communal satellite dish (or a number) and transmitted via cable to all properties in an urbanisation. Only a limited number of programmes are usually available and no scrambled programmes may be included. Only two English-language stations are currently unscrambled on Astra, Sky News and Eurosport, although some urbanisations pay to receive more.

## Programme Guides

Many satellite stations provide teletext information and most broadcast in stereo. Sky satellite programme listings are provided in a number of British publications such as *What Satellite, Satellite Times* and *Satellite TV Europe*, which are available on subscription and from newsagents in Spain. Satellite TV programmes are also listed in expatriate newspapers and magazines in Spain. The annual *The Directory of Global Broadcasting* (available from WRTH – ☎ UK 01865-514 405, 💻 www.wrth.com) contains over 600 pages of information and the frequencies of all radio and TV stations worldwide.

# DVDs & Videos

DVD and video films are popular in Spain and there are rental shops in all towns, although DVDs have almost replaced videos in many of them. DVD films are expensive to buy in Spain (from €12) and most have an English-language option. In major cities and resort areas, there are English-language rental shops, where films can be rented from around €3 per day. Alternatively you can rent three 'standard' films for €8 per day or three 'classic' films for three days for only €6.

If you aren't a permanent resident with proof of your address, you usually need to pay a deposit, e.g. €60 and show your passport. Rental costs can sometimes be reduced by paying a monthly membership fee or a lump sum in advance. If you have a large collection of SECAM or NTSC video tapes, you can buy a multi-standard TV and video recorder (VCR), or buy a separate TV and VCR to play back your favourite videos.

VCRs cost from €150 and DVD players are increasingly lower in price with the cheapest models (allowing replay only) costing from €60 and a DVD with recording facilities from €400.

BBC Television has leapt on the video and DVD bandwagon and produces three-hour videos and DVDs of its best programmes (including entertainment, humour, sport, natural history, news and current affairs), available for purchase. For information contact the BBC Shop, PO Box 308 Sittingbourne, Kent ME9 8LW, UK (☎ 08700-777 001 (UK only), 🖳 www.bbcshop.com).

# RADIO

The Spanish are a nation of avid radio listeners and spend more time listening to the radio than they do watching TV (which is saying something). Spain has an estimated 35 million radios (for 40 million people) and radio has a regular average daily audience of 16 million people (much higher than in most other European countries).

There are numerous high-quality, public and private, local, regional, national and foreign radio stations in Spain. Among the most popular national radio stations are SER (consistently top of audience ratings), Radio Nacional de España (RNE), COPE (owned by the church and the second-largest network of private stations) and Onda Cero. In the autonomous regions, many stations broadcast in the local regional language. Most stations and networks broadcast on FM, rather than medium wave (there are no long-wave stations in Spain).

There's a wealth of excellent FM stations in the major cities and resort areas, although in remote rural areas you may be lucky to receive one or two FM stations clearly. Spain has many excellent music stations playing mainly American and British pop songs, although relaxing classical or 'easy listening' music is rare. RNE 2 is one of the few stations to play classical music around the clock. As in all countries, Spanish radio stations plumb the depths to unearth their banal DJs, who babble on (and on) at a zillion words a minute in a secret language intelligible only to other DJs and teenagers. (When you can understand Spanish DJs, you're ready to go native!)

## English & Other Expatriate Stations

There are English and other foreign-language commercial radio stations in major cities and resort areas (there are around eight stations on the Costa del Sol and around five on the Costa Blanca), where the emphasis is on music and chat with some news. Some expatriate stations broadcast in a variety of languages, including English, Dutch, German and various Scandinavian languages at different times of the day. Unfortunately (or inevitably), expatriate radio tries to be all things to everyone and not surprisingly falls short, particularly with regard to music, where it tries to cater for all tastes. However, it generally does a good job and is popular among expatriates. The main drawback of expatriate radio (and all commercial radio) is the advertising, which is agonisingly amateurish, and which is also obtrusive and repetitive, and makes listening a chore. Some English-language radio programmes are published in the local expatriate press in Spain.

## BBC

The BBC World Service is broadcast on short wave on several frequencies (e.g. short wave 12095, 9760, 9410, 7325, 6195, 5975 and 3955Khz) simultaneously and you can usually receive a good signal on one of them. The signal strength varies depending on where you live in Spain, the time of day and year, the power and positioning of your receiver, and atmospheric conditions. The BBC World Service plus BBC Radio 1, 2, 3, 4 and 5 are also available on the Astra (Sky) satellite. For a free BBC World Service programme guide and frequency information contact the BBC World Service (BBC Worldwide, Woodlands, 80 Wood Lane, London W12 0TT, UK, ☎ 020-8433 2000). The BBC publishes a monthly magazine, *BBC On Air*, containing comprehensive programme listings for BBC World Service radio, BBC Prime TV and BBC World TV. It's available on subscription from the BBC in the UK (☎ 020-7557 2211, ⊠ on.air.magazine@bbc.co.uk) and from some newsagents in Spain.

# Cable & Satellite Radio

If you have cable or satellite TV, you will also be able to receive many radio stations via your cable or satellite link. For example, BBC Radio 1, 2, 3, 4 and 5, BBC World Service, Sky Radio, Virgin 1215 and many foreign-language stations are broadcast via the Astra satellites. Ask a satellite expert for advice regarding equipment and installation. Satellite radio stations are listed in British magazines such as the *Satellite Times*. If you're interested in receiving radio stations from further afield, obtain a copy of *The Directory of Global Broadcasting* (available from WRTH – ☎ UK 01865-514 405, ⊟ www.wrth.com), published annually.

# 9.

# EDUCATION

Although Spain's state schools aren't among the best in Europe, the Spanish educational system has improved dramatically in the last few decades. Until the '80s, there were insufficient places in state schools in many areas and parents who could afford it were forced to pay for private education (many children just didn't attend school). However, since those dark days, the education budget has increased considerably (although at 4.5 per cent of gross domestic product/GDP it's still one of the lowest in the European Union/EU) and Spain's educational system underwent profound (and long overdue) reforms in the '80s and early '90s, during which it was in a constant state of development. Most changes were necessary, although some have been controversial and haven't met with universal support from parents and teaching staff.

The educational system continues in a state of flux and several new reforms are pending. The latest, known as the *Ley Orgánica de Calidad* (*LOE* – proposed by the current Socialist government), are due to come into effect during the 2006-7 academic year and intend to improve the quality of Spanish education. The Organisation for Economic Co-operation and Development (OECD) education report released in September 2005 placed Spanish education in one of the worst positions and highlighted the fact that Spain has the highest percentage of unqualified school leavers in OECD countries. In the light of this report, the government has promised a huge (and long overdue) injection of public funds into the education system. On the other hand, education in Spain is one of the most egalitarian and accessible in the world (the PISA report – see below – placed Spain eighth in terms of equal access to education, well ahead of the UK and the US).

Education is compulsory for all children aged between 6 and 16. The Spanish take education very seriously and have a deep respect and thirst for learning that isn't found in many other countries. In the current highly competitive labour market, parents and students are acutely aware that academic qualifications and training are of vital importance to obtain a good job.

Spain's state-funded school system (*escuelas públicas*) is supported by a comprehensive network of private schools (*escuelas privadas*), including many foreign and international schools. Around one-third of Spain's schoolchildren attend private schools, most of which are co-educational day schools. State education in Spain is almost exclusively co-educational and is entirely free, from nursery school through to university (and includes the children of foreign residents).

Over 90 per cent of children aged three to five attend nursery school and over 55 per cent of students remain in full-time education until they're 18, around 25 per cent going on to vocational training and 30 per cent to university. Education standards at Spain's finest universities are comparable with the best in Europe, although they're generally overcrowded. Foreign parents who can afford it often send their children to foreign universities, particularly American and British universities, where courses are shorter and more flexible than in Spain.

Critics of the Spanish education system complain that its teaching methods are too traditional and unimaginative, with the emphasis on learning by rote. It has also been plagued by poor teacher training, badly motivated and poorly paid teachers, and a high student failure rate, although all have improved in the last decade. However, Spain's results in the Programme for International Student Assessment (PISA) in 2002 highlighted the country's poor academic record. PISA assessed students in some 31 countries in three areas, language comprehension, mathematics and science, and Spanish students came 18th, 23rd and 19th respectively, far behind France, New Zealand and the UK, although ahead of Germany and Italy.

Generally, the younger a foreign child is when he enters the Spanish system, the easier he copes. Conversely the older he is, the more problems he has adjusting, particularly as the school curriculum is more demanding. Teenagers often have considerable problems learning Spanish and adjusting to Spanish school life. Many foreign parents prefer to educate younger children in Spanish nursery and primary schools, where they quickly learn Spanish, and to send children of secondary school age to a private school.

Despite the difficulties, however, for many children, the experience of schooling and living in a foreign country is a stimulating change and a challenge they relish, and it offers invaluable cultural and educational experiences. Children become 'world' citizens and are less likely to be prejudiced against foreigners and foreign ideas. This is particularly true when they attend an international school with pupils from different countries, although many state schools also have students from a number of countries and backgrounds, especially in Barcelona, Madrid and resort towns on the *costas*. **Before making major decisions regarding your children's future education, it's important to consider their ability, character and individual needs.**

Information about Spanish schools, state and private, can be obtained from Spanish embassies and consulates abroad, and from foreign embassies, educational organisations and government departments in Spain. Information about local schools can be obtained from town halls (*ayuntamientos*). The Ministry of Education and Science (Ministerio de Educación y Ciencia) provides a general information service at its central office open Mondays to Fridays from 9am to 2.30pm (Servicio de Información, C/Alcalá, 36, 28071 Madrid, ☎ 902-218 500, 🖳 www.mec.es). The autonomous regions also have their own education offices in regional capitals.

In addition to a detailed look at the Spanish state school system and private schools, this chapter also contains information about higher education and language schools in Spain.

# STATE OR PRIVATE SCHOOL?

If you're able to choose between state and private education, ask yourself the following questions in order to make the best choice for your child(ren):

- How long are you planning to stay in Spain? If you're uncertain, it's best to assume a long stay. Due to language and other integration problems, enrolling children in Spanish state schools is advisable for a minimum of one or two years, particularly for teenage children who aren't fluent in Spanish.

- What is the choice of schools in the area you wish to live? For example, it's usually necessary to send your child to a state school near your home. If you choose a private day school, you must take into account the distance and travelling time from your home to the school.

- Do you know where you're going when you leave Spain? This may be an important consideration with regard to your child's language of tuition and system of education in Spain. How old is your child and what age will he be when you plan to leave Spain? What plans do you have for his subsequent education and in which country?

- What educational level is your child at now and how will he fit into a private school or the Spanish state school system? The younger he is, the easier it will be to place him in a suitable school.

- How does your child view the thought of studying in Spanish? What language is best from a long-term point of view? Is schooling available in Spain in his mother tongue?

- Will your child require your help with his studies, and more importantly, will you be able to help him, particularly with his Spanish?

- Is special or extra tutoring available in Spanish or other subjects, if necessary?

- What are the school hours? What are the school holiday periods? How will these holidays and hours affect your and your family's work and leisure activities?

- Is religion an important aspect in your choice of school? Religion is no longer a mandatory subject in Spanish schools.

- Do you want your child to go to a co-educational or a single-sex school? Spanish state schools are usually co-educational.

- Should you send your child to a boarding school? If so, in which country?

- What are the secondary and further education prospects in Spain or another country? Are Spanish examinations or the examinations set by prospective schools in Spain recognised in your home country or the country where you plan to live after leaving Spain? If applicable, check whether the Spanish baccalaureate (*bachillerato*) examination is recognised as a university entrance qualification in your home country (see page 186).

- Does a prospective school have a good academic record? Most schools provide exam pass rate statistics.

- How large are the classes in a particular school? What is the pupil-teacher ratio? The legal maximum size of classes in state schools is 25 pupils in primary education and 30 in secondary. There's no limit in private schools, although they generally have smaller classes than state schools.

Obtain the opinions and advice of others who have been faced with the same decisions and problems as yourself, and collect as much information from as many different sources as possible before making a decision. Speak to students, teachers and the parents of children attending the schools on your shortlist. Finally, you should discuss the alternatives with your child before making a decision. See also **Choosing a Private School** on page 184.

# STATE SCHOOLS

Although state-funded schools are termed public schools (*colegios públicos*) in Spain, the term 'state' has been used in preference to public in this book to prevent confusion with the term 'public school', which, in the UK, refers to a private, fee-paying school. The state school system in Spain differs considerably from the school systems in, for example, the UK and US, particularly regarding secondary education.

Spain's state schools have undergone profound changes in the last decade and standards, which were low, are now the equal of those in most of the rest of Europe. State education is ultimately the responsibility of the Ministry of Education and Science (Ministerio de Educación y Ciencia), although the 17 autonomous regions now have responsibility for their own education system (including higher education). State education is free, but parents must usually pay for school books (which are expensive, although they're provided free in some regions, e.g. Castilla-La Mancha and many town councils partially or completely subsidise purchases in certain cases), school supplies, and extra-curricular activities such as sports and arts and crafts. Pupils usually go to local village (*pueblo*) nursery and primary schools, although attending secondary school may entail travelling long distances (buses are usually provided).

For most Spanish children, school starts with nursery or pre-school (*preescolar*), from around the age of three or four (places for three-year olds are available in many regions). Compulsory education (*escolaridad obligatoria*), termed the basic general education (*Educación General Básica/EGB*), begins at six years of age in a primary school (*escuela primaria*) and lasts for six years. At the age of 12 (equivalent to sixth grade), pupils move on to secondary education (*educación secundaria obligatoria/ESO*) for the next four years. When they're 16, and if they've completed the four years, students are awarded a *graduado en educación secundaria* certificate and may attend a higher secondary school (or the same school in some cases) to study for their baccalaureate (see page 186) leading to university entrance. Less academically-gifted pupils who haven't successfully completed four years secondary education are awarded a school certificate (*certificado de escolaridad*). At 16, students may attend a vocational school (*formación profesional*) providing specialised training for a specific career (see page 187).

A general criticism of Spanish state schools made by many foreigners is the lack of extra-curricular activities such as sport, music, drama, and arts and crafts. State schools don't have school clubs or sports teams and if children want to do team sports they must usually join a local club. However, sports and other activities are often organised through parents' and sports associations. Fees are low and activities usually take place directly after school.

Attending a state school helps children integrate into the local community and learn the local language (see below and page 191), and is highly recommended if you plan to remain in Spain indefinitely. Although it may not appeal initially, given the choice many foreign children prefer to attend a Spanish school and become part of the local community. **Note that while it's fairly easy to switch from a state school to a private school, the reverse isn't true.** If you must move a child from a private school to a state school (e.g. due to financial reasons), it can be difficult for a child to adjust, particularly a teenager. Having made the decision to send a child to a state school, you should stick to it for at least a year to give it a fair trial, as it can take a child this long (or longer) to fully adapt to a new language, the change of environment and the different curriculum. **If you choose to send your child to a**

**Spanish school you should learn to speak Spanish well enough to communicate with your child's teachers – few Spanish teachers speak English.**

There are also special state schools in Spain for pupils with special education needs, e.g. learning difficulties due to psychological, emotional or behavioural problems and slow learners. However, pupils are taught in special education units or schools only when their needs cannot be catered for in a mainstream school.

In Spain, children must attend a state school (primary or secondary) within a certain distance of their home, so if you have a preference for a particular school, it's important to buy or rent a home within that school's catchment area. Town halls and provincial Ministry of Education offices can provide a list of local schools at all levels. In some rural areas, there's little or no choice of schools, while in Madrid and other cities there are usually a number of possibilities. Naturally, the schools with the best reputations and exam results are the most popular, and therefore the most difficult to gain acceptance to. You should plan well ahead, particularly if you wish your child(ren) to be accepted at a superior school.

# Language

There are many considerations to take into account when choosing an appropriate school in Spain, not least the language of study. The only schools in Spain using English as the teaching language are foreign and international private schools, although in September 2005 several schools introduced pilot schemes where some subjects are taught in English or French. A number of multilingual international schools also teach pupils in the English and Spanish languages. If your children attend any other school, they must study all subjects in Spanish. For most children, studying in Spanish isn't such a handicap as it may at first appear, particularly for those aged below ten. The majority of children adapt quickly to a new language and most become reasonably fluent within three to six months. However, not all children adapt equally well to a change of language and culture, particularly children aged ten or over, many of whom have great difficulties during their first year. Children who are already bilingual, such as Dutch and Scandinavian children, usually have little problem learning Spanish, while American and British children tend to find it more difficult. Spanish children are generally friendly towards foreign children, who often acquire a 'celebrity status' (particularly in rural schools) which helps their integration.

Some state schools provide intensive Spanish lessons ('bridging classes') for foreign children, although this depends on the school and the province or region (e.g. the regional government of Andalusia operates a scheme for non-Spanish primary pupils, some 6,000 children from 122 different countries, although the scheme is at present implemented only in Malaga and Almeria). It may be worthwhile enquiring about the availability of extra Spanish classes before choosing where to live. Foreign children are tested and put into a class suited to their level of Spanish, even if this means being taught with younger children. Children who don't read and write Spanish are often set back a year to compensate for their lack of Spanish and different academic background. Once a child has acquired a sufficient knowledge of spoken and written Spanish, he's assigned to a class appropriate to his age.

If your local school doesn't provide extra Spanish classes, your only choice will be to pay for private lessons or send your children to another (possibly private) school, where extra Spanish tuition is provided. Some parents send children to an English-speaking school for a year, followed by a move to a bilingual or Spanish school, while other parents believe it's better to throw their children in at the deep end, rather than introduce them gradually. It all depends on the character, ability and wishes of the child. Whatever you decide, it will help your children **enormously** if they have intensive Spanish lessons before arriving in Spain.

An added problem in some regions is that state schools teach most lessons in a regional language such as Basque, Catalan and Galician, although parents may be offered a choice of teaching language. For example, in Catalonia and Valencia (including the Costa Blanca) children aged between 3 and 12 are generally taught most subjects in Catalan except for Spanish which is taught for a few hours a week. Learning a regional language can be a huge problem, not only for foreign children, but also for Spanish-speaking children. However, immersion courses in the local language are usually offered to Spanish-speaking children. **If you live in an area where education is dominated by a regional language, you may need to consider educating your child at a private school.** See also **Learning Spanish** on page 191.

# Enrolment

State schools have an annual quota for pupils and places are allocated on a first-come, first-served basis. The enrolment period usually lasts for two months early in the year e.g. February to March or April to May, although it varies from region to region. Individual schools will provide exact dates. The process of enrolment depends on the age of your child, but may require an interview and in rare cases an examination. To enrol a child in a Spanish state school you must provide the following documents:

● Your child's birth certificate or passport (original and photocopy), with an official Spanish translation (if necessary) and the parents' passports (originals and photocopies).

● Proof of immunisation.

● Proof of residence (*empadronamiento*) from your town hall (*ayuntamiento*).

● Proof of verification, if applicable (see below).

● Two passport-sized photographs (for a student identity card and school records).

## Verification

If the child is going to start a Spanish secondary school in the third year of *ESO* (around age 14) you must also present proof that your child's education record has been verified by the Spanish Ministry of Education. The process is known as *homologación* or *convalidación*. You must complete the official form provided by the Ministry, which is available from Spanish consulates and embassies abroad, from regional departments of education or directly from the Ministerio de Educación y

Ciencia, C/Alcalá 36, 28071 Madrid (☎ 902-218 500, ⌨ www.mec.es). **The form is downloadable from the website** in the section on *homologación* (the form is referred to as the *modelo oficial*). You should also submit your child's school record book and/or exam qualifications, plus his birth certificate.

If possible, this process should be completed before arriving in Spain, as a child may not be accepted at a school until the official papers (confirming verification) have been received and stamped by the Spanish Department of Education. The process takes around three months, although if you show a school proof of the Ministry's receipt of the verification documents, your child should have no problems being accepted.

# School Hours

School hours vary from school to school, but are usually from 9am until 4pm with a one-hour break for lunch, although an increasing number of schools don't have a lunch break and finish classes at 2pm. Lessons are usually divided into teaching periods of 45 minutes. Some schools offer school lunches, although many children bring a packed lunch or go home for lunch if they live nearby. Most schools provide a subsidised or free bus service to take children to and from their homes in outlying regions. Some schools are now opening early (e.g. at 8am) and providing activities after school until 5 or 6pm in an attempt to make childcare provision easier for working parents.

# School Holidays

The academic year in Spain runs from mid-September to mid-June, with the main holidays at Christmas, Easter and the long summer break. Spanish schoolchildren have very long school holidays (*vacaciones escolares*) compared with those in many other countries. The school year is made up of three terms, each averaging around 11 weeks. Terms are fixed and are generally the same throughout the country, although they may be modified in autonomous regions to take account of local circumstances and special events (such as local *fiestas*). The following table shows the main school holidays for the 2005/2006 school year (all dates inclusive):

| Holiday | Dates |
|---|---|
| Christmas & New Year (*Navidad*) | 23rd December – 8th January |
| Easter (*Semana Santa*) | 8th – 16th April |
| Summer (*Verano*) | 23rd June – 14th September |

Some autonomous regions (e.g. Andalusia) also include a week's holiday in the middle of the spring term (usually in February), known as 'white week' (*semana blanca*). Pupils transferring from primary to secondary school are sometimes given an additional two weeks' summer holiday, which usually includes an 'end of school' trip (*viaje de estudios*) with fellow pupils. Schools are also closed on public holidays when they fall within term time.

School holiday dates are published by schools and local communities well in advance, thus allowing parents plenty of time to schedule family holidays. Normally, you aren't permitted to withdraw a child from classes during the school term, except for visits to a doctor or dentist, when the teacher should be informed in advance.

# Pre-school

Spain has a long tradition of state-funded pre-school (*educación infantil*), with over 90 per cent of children aged three to five attending for at least a year before starting compulsory schooling. The term pre-school embraces play school, nursery school (*guardería*), kindergarten (*jardín de la infancia*) and infant school (*escuela infantil*). Note, however, that the provision of public and private pre-school facilities varies considerably with the town and the region, particularly regarding state schools.

State pre-school education is divided into two cycles: First Cycle (*primer ciclo/ciclo 1°*) for children aged one to three and Second Cycle (*segundo ciclo/ciclo 2°*) for ages three to six. Attendance is voluntary and free in public centres in many areas.

There are also many private, fee-paying nursery schools, usually taking children aged from two to six, some of which are part of a primary school. Arrangements are generally flexible and parents can choose attendance during mornings or afternoons, all day, or only on selected days. Many schools provide transport to and from homes. Fees are generally low and schools are popular, well organised and good value.

Note that some nursery schools are more nurseries than schools, and simply an inexpensive way for parents to obtain supervised childcare. The best pre-schools are designed to introduce children to the social environment of school and concentrate on the basic skills of co-ordination, encouraging the development of self-awareness and providing an introduction to group activities. Exercises include arts and crafts (e.g. drawing, painting and pottery), music, dancing, educational games, perceptual and motor activities, and listening skills. During the final years of nursery school, the rudiments of reading, writing and arithmetic are taught in preparation for primary school. There are plans to teach English from the age of three or four in state schools throughout Spain. Children are also taken on outings and it's common to see groups of small children 'roped' together (for their own protection), being shepherded by a teacher.

Nursery school is highly recommended, particularly if your children are going to continue with a state education. After one or two years of nursery school they will be integrated into the local community and will have learnt Spanish in preparation for primary school. Research (in many countries) has shown that children who don't attend pre-school are at a distinct disadvantage when they start primary school.

# Primary School

Compulsory education (*escolaridad obligatoria*), also called 'basic general education' (*educacion general básica/EGB*), begins at the age of six in a primary school (*escuela primaria*) and lasts for six years. Primary school is split into three cycles: First Cycle (*primer ciclo/1er ciclo*), years 1 to 2; Second Cycle (*segundo ciclo/2° ciclo*), years 3 to 4; and Third Cycle (*tercer ciclo/3er ciclo*), years 5 to 6.

The primary curriculum includes natural and social sciences (*conocimiento del medio*), Spanish (*lengua*) and an autonomous language (if applicable), literature, mathematics, arts (*dibujo y plástica*), physical education and a foreign language (usually English or French), which is compulsory from the second cycle, although many state schools now offer English from the age of six. Catholic religion is optional and when your child starts school you're asked whether you want your child to attend religious classes. Alternatives may include extra-reading, ethics or theatre studies. Under the new education reforms (*LOE* – see page 174), pupils in year 1 will also study a new subject, *Educación para la Ciudadanía* (Education for Citizens), covering moral and social values such as sexual equality and care of the environment.

In most schools, pupils have three evaluations (*evaluaciones*) each year. If a child fails to achieve the required standard set for a particular cycle, he may be required to repeat the previous year unless he can show considerable improvement in the autumn (many private and state schools offer 'recovery' classes during the summer holidays to help pupils catch up). The opinion of the teachers, tutors, inspectors and the sector's psychological and pedagogical team are taken into account when deciding whether a pupil must repeat a year. Pupils aren't required to repeat more than one year during their primary education.

## Secondary School

Compulsory secondary education (*enseñanza secundaria obligatoria/ESO*) was created in 1990 for pupils aged 12 to 16 and completes their compulsory education. It provides pupils with more specialised training than their previous education and prepares them for the baccalaureate (see below) or vocational training. The four years of compulsory secondary school are divided into two, two-year cycles, the curriculum containing compulsory and optional subjects. Compulsory subjects during the First Cycle (*primer ciclo/1° ciclo*) include natural and social sciences, history and geography, physical education, plastic and visual arts, Spanish, an autonomous community language (if applicable), a foreign language, literature, mathematics, music, and information technology (IT). During the last year of the first cycle, pupils must choose two optional subjects from natural sciences, plastic and visual arts, music and technology. The Catholic religion is an optional subject in all four years, and a second foreign language, classical culture and other subjects can be studied for at least one year during the Second Cycle (*segundo ciclo/2° ciclo*).

Under the *LOE* reforms (see page 174) pupils in the first three years of *ESO* will study a common curriculum of eight subjects (nine in regions with an autonomous language). Six subjects (natural sciences, Spanish, geography and history, mathematics, physical education and a foreign language) are compulsory. Students can choose the remaining two subjects from *Educación para la Ciudadanía* (moral and social education), art, music, IT and a second foreign language. In the fourth year the curriculum will become more specialised and each pupil will choose his subjects based on his future studies. In this year music, art and IT will be optional.

As with primary education, a pupil can be required to repeat a year if he hasn't passed the end of term exams (pupils who fail four or more subjects in the end of term exams must repeat the year) or the autumn repeats, and pupils aren't required to repeat more than two years in secondary education. The *LOE* intends to make provision for small groups to help pupils who struggle academically – all pupils currently study the same topics at the same level.

Upon completion of *ESO*, pupils who have achieved the set standards are awarded a 'graduate of secondary education' (*graduado en educación secundaria*) certificate enabling them to study for the baccalaureate or undergo specialised vocational training (see below). This certificate is a basic requirement for most jobs in Spain. All pupils, whether or not they've achieved the course objectives, receive a document stating the school years completed, the marks obtained in each subject, and recommendations regarding their academic and vocational future. Under the *LOE*, Pupils aged 16 to 21 who have repeated two years of ESO study and failed to pass a further year are eligible for the Professional Qualification Programme (*Programa de Cualificación Profesional*) whose aims are to provide these pupils with a further opportunity to gain their 'graduate of secondary education' certificate or to gain other professional qualifications to allow them to get a job.

# PRIVATE SCHOOLS

There's a wide range of private schools (*escuelas privadas*) in Spain, including parochial schools, bilingual schools, international schools and a variety of foreign schools (e.g. American and British). Around a third of children in Spain are educated at private school. Most private schools are co-educational, Catholic day schools, although a number of schools (including some American and British schools) take weekly or term boarders.

Your choice of foreign schools depends on where you live in Spain. There's a good choice of English-speaking schools (accepting children from 3 to 18) in Barcelona, Madrid, Palma de Mallorca, Tenerife and on the *costas*. For example, there are British schools in Alicante, Barcelona, Cadiz, Fuengirola, Ibiza, Lanzarote, Las Palmas, Madrid, Menorca, Palma de Mallorca, Marbella, Tenerife, Torremolinos and Valencia. In other cities and areas, there may be only one English-speaking school or none at all. There are also French, German, Swedish and other foreign-language schools in Spain. Under Spanish law, all foreign schools must be approved by their country's embassy in Spain. Like state schools, most private schools operate a five-day, Monday to Friday timetable, with no Saturday morning classes.

Private schools teach a variety of syllabi, including the British GCSE and A Level examinations, the American High School Diploma and college entrance examinations (e.g. ACT, SAT, achievement tests and AP exams), the International Baccalaureate (IB) and the Spanish *bachillerato*. However, most Spanish private schools, i.e. schools teaching wholly in Spanish, are state-subsidised and follow the Spanish state-school curriculum. Some international schools are also subsidised and follow a totally bilingual (English/Spanish) curriculum and are authorised to accept Spanish pupils. They must teach the Spanish curriculum, including primary and secondary education, and the *bachillerato*. They provide the opportunity for children to become completely bilingual and to choose between a Spanish and English-language university or career. To receive state subsidies and accept Spanish pupils,

25 per cent of a school's total number of pupils must be Spanish and at least 20 per cent in each class. As a condition of receiving government funding, schools with Spanish pupils are subject to inspection by the Spanish school authorities. Many international private schools have mixed Spanish and foreign student bodies, e.g. one-third American or British students, one-third Spanish and one-third other nationalities, although they may be called American or British.

Private school fees vary considerably according to, among other things, the quality, reputation and location of a school, but are generally low compared with those of private schools in northern Europe and North America. Not surprisingly, schools in Madrid and Barcelona are among the most expensive. Fees at subsidised Spanish schools are around €700 a year, whereas fees at independent foreign schools range from around €4,000 a year to well over €8,000 a year (for boarders) at senior schools. Fees don't usually include registration, books, materials, laundry, insurance, extra-curricular activities, excursions, meals and transport (most private schools provide school buses), for which you should allow around €800 per term. Most private schools subscribe to insurance schemes covering accidents, in school and during school-sponsored activities. Some schools award scholarships or offer grants to parents with low incomes.

Private foreign and international schools usually have a more relaxed, less rigid regime and curriculum than Spanish state schools. They provide a more varied and international approach to sport, culture and art, and a wider choice of academic subjects. Many also provide English-language summer school programmes combining academic lessons with sports, arts and crafts, and other extra-curricular activities. Their aim is the development of a child as an individual and the encouragement of his unique talents, rather than teaching on a production-line system. This is made possible by small classes, which allow teachers to provide pupils with individually-tailored lessons and tuition. The results are self-evident and many private secondary schools have a near 100 per cent university placement rate. On the other hand, one of the major problems of private foreign-language education in Spain is that children can grow up in cultural 'ghettos' and be 'illiterate' as far as the Spanish language and culture are concerned. **Although attending a private school may be advantageous from an academic viewpoint, integration into Spanish society can be severely restricted.**

You should make applications to private schools as far in advance as possible, as many international schools have waiting lists for places. You're usually requested to send school reports, exam results and other records. Before enrolling your child in a private school, make sure that you understand the withdrawal conditions in the school contract.

# Choosing a Private School

To help you choose an appropriate private school for your child(ren), you should ask the following questions:

- How long has the school been established?
- Does it have a good reputation?

- Does the school have a good academic record? For example, what percentage of pupils obtain good examination passes and go on to good universities? All the best schools provide exam pass-rate statistics.

- What does the curriculum include? What examinations are set? Are examinations recognised in Spain and internationally? Do they fit in with your child's long-term education plans? Ask to see a typical pupil's timetable to check the ratio of academic to non-academic subjects. Check the number of free study periods and whether they're supervised.

- What languages does the school teach as obligatory or optional subjects?

- Are intensive English or Spanish lessons provided for children who don't meet the required standard?

- What are the facilities for art and science subjects, e.g. arts and crafts, music, computer studies, biology, science, hobbies, drama, cookery and photography? Ask to see the classrooms, facilities, equipment and pupils' projects.

- What religion(s) are taught?

- How large are the classes and what's the pupil/teacher ratio? Does the stated class size tally with the number of desks in the classrooms?

- What are the classrooms like? Check their size, space, cleanliness, lighting, furniture and furnishings. Are there signs of creative teaching, e.g. wall charts, maps, posters and pupils' work on display?

- What are the qualification requirements for teachers? What nationalities are the majority of teachers? Ask for a list of the teaching staff and their qualifications.

- What is the teacher turnover? A high teacher turnover is a particularly bad sign and usually suggests poorly paid teachers and/or poor working conditions.

- Which countries do most pupils come from?

- What is the pupil turnover?

- What are the school hours?

- What are the school terms and holiday periods? Private school holidays are usually longer than state schools' (e.g. four weeks at Easter and Christmas and ten weeks in summer) and they often don't coincide with state school holiday periods.

- Is transport provided to and from school and for extra-curricular activities?

- What sports instruction and facilities are provided? Where are the sports facilities?

- What sort of excursions and supervised school holidays are organised?

- What is the quality and variety of food provided? What is the dining room like? Does the school have a dietician?

- What standard and type of accommodation is provided (in the case of a boarding school)?

- What medical facilities does the school provide, e.g. infirmary, resident doctor or nurse? Is medical and accident insurance included in the fees?

- What kinds of punishment are applied and for what offences?
- What reports are provided for parents and how often?
- What are the withdrawal conditions, should you need or wish to remove your child? A term's notice is usual.
- What are the fees?
- What extras must you pay? For example, are lunches, art supplies, sports equipment, excursions, clothing, health and accident insurance, text books and stationery included in fees? Some schools charge extra for every little thing.

It's advisable to check whether a school is recognised by the Spanish education authorities and whether it belongs to an accredited organisation. Most British schools in Spain belong to the National Association of British Schools in Spain (NABSS, 🖥 www.nabss.org), whose members are visited and approved by British school inspectors. Advice about British schools in Spain can be obtained from the British Council, Paseo Martínez Campos, 31, 28010 Madrid (☎ 913-373 500, 🖥 www. britishcouncil.org/spain) or from the European Council of International Schools/ECIS (☎ UK 01730-268244, 🖥 www.ecis.org). Information is also obtainable from embassies in Spain.

Before making a final choice, it's important to visit the schools on your shortlist during term time and talk to teachers and pupils (if possible, also speak to former pupils and their parents). Where possible, check the answers to the above questions in person and don't rely on a school's prospectus or director to provide the information. If you're unhappy with the answers, look elsewhere.

Finally, having made your choice, monitor your child's progress and listen to his complaints. Compare notes with other parents. If something doesn't seem right, try to establish whether the complaint is founded or not; if it is, take action to have the problem resolved. Never forget that you (or your employers) are paying a lot of money for your child's education and you should ensure that you receive good value. See also **State or Private School?** on page 175.

# THE BACCALAUREATE

The Spanish baccalaureate (*bachillerato* or *bachiller*) programme consists of two years' academic training to prepare pupils for higher education or high-grade vocational training (see above) or to start a career. All students are required to study Spanish language and literature, philosophy, a foreign language, an autonomous regional language (if applicable) and physical education, and must choose one of four specialities – art (fine art, technical drawing, history of art, and design); natural and health sciences (maths, biology, chemistry, physics, geology and technical drawing); technology (maths, physics, chemistry, mechanics and technical drawing); or humanities and social sciences (Greek, Latin, economics and history). Under the *LOE* reforms (see page 174), baccalaureate pupils will choose one of the four specialities in their first year and must also study philosophy. Pupils who don't choose an option including a science (e.g. pupils who choose the art or humanities and social sciences options) must study a new subject called 'Science for the Modern World' (*Ciencias para el Mundo Contemporáneo*) covering topics such as genetics, the origin of the universe and the latest scientific advances.

At the end of the second year, pupils take an examination known as the *Prueba General de Bachillerato/PGB*. If they pass this exam and have also passed the exams during the two-year course, they're awarded the *título de bachiller* (called simply *bachiller*), which includes the average mark obtained. The *bachiller*, together with an oral exam in a foreign language (usually English), also allows pupils to study at Spanish universities and is recognised as an entrance qualification by universities throughout the world, provided the student's proficiency in the language of study is up to the required standard. Pupils who fail the *PGB* are awarded a certificate of attendance and can proceed to vocational training (see below). Pupils who fail three subjects in their first year of the baccalaureate are required to repeat the year.

# VOCATIONAL TRAINING

Vocational training (*formación profesional/FP*), traditionally taken by pupils who failed to achieve the standards required to study for the baccalaureate (*bachillerato*) and long discredited as only for those who aren't bright enough to pursue an academic career, has recently been given a higher status in an attempt to foster interaction between educational establishments and the labour market, which is of vital importance to Spain's economic future. In particular, new vocational training courses have been introduced, enabling successful pupils to take specialist baccalaureate courses and proceed to higher education.

Vocational training consists of cycles of between 1,300 and 2,000 teaching hours depending on the profession. The first phase of *FP* (*grado medio*) is open to pupils who have been awarded a *graduado en educación secundaria* certificate (see above) and wish to opt for vocational training rather than study for the baccalaureate. The second phase (*grado superior*) is open to pupils who have passed the baccalaureate or the *examen de prueba de acceso a formación profesional*, which includes subjects from the baccalaureate.

*FP* pupils divide their time between school studies and practical on-the-job training in commerce or industry, where they spend about 25 per cent of their learning time. Vocational training is free for most pupils, whether it takes place in a public centre or a private institution, as the latter are financed by the state (but employ their own teachers and have different rules from state centres). In recent years, emphasis has been placed on IT and telecommunications skills and EU languages, particularly English and German.

Pupils who complete a *grado medio* course receive a 'technical specialist' (*técnico especialista*) certificate and those who complete a *grado superior* course receive a 'superior technical' (*técnico superior*) certificate. Holders of the latter certificate may continue their studies at university.

# HIGHER EDUCATION

Spain has 70 universities (*universidades*), 48 of them state-run (and attended by 90 per cent of higher education students) and 22 run by private enterprises or by the

Catholic church. There are a number of other higher education institutes specialising in physical education, tourism, dramatic arts, dance and music, as well as a number of highly rated business schools (mostly American).

In addition to Spanish higher education establishments, there are a number of US universities with faculties in Spain, including the Schiller International University, the St Louis University and Suffolk University (all in Madrid). All classes at American universities are taught in English. The European university has branches in Barcelona and the University of Surrey (in the UK) also a branch in Madrid.

Although few Spanish universities are world-renowned, Spain has a long history of university education, the university system dating back to the middle ages. Spain's oldest university (Salamanca) was founded in 1218 and even before this, the Moors had 'universities' in Spain long before anyone else had even thought of them. The largest and most highly regarded Spanish universities are Complutense in Madrid and Central in Barcelona, with student bodies of around 89,000 and 55,000 respectively. The Basque Country, Granada and Seville universities each have over 50,000 students.

There are some 1.5 million university students in Spain, a figure generally considered to be too high for a country with a population of 42 million. Overcrowding is a huge problem, particularly in first-year classes (you must usually arrive early to get a seat at a lecture). However, many students drop out after the tough exams set at the end of the first year. The number of female students has increased by around 40 per cent in the last decade and they now outnumber male students (more women also complete their courses and obtain degrees than men). Foreign students comprise just 3 per cent of students, a third coming from EU countries.

# Types of University

There are four different types of university establishment in Spain:

- **University Schools** (*escuelas universitarias*) – These offer three-year courses of a vocational or non-academic nature leading to a *diploma* (see **Studies** below).

- **University Colleges** (*colegios universitarios*) – These offer three-year courses of an academic nature leading eventually to a *licenciatura* or *tesina* (see **Studies** below) and two-year courses for those with a *diploma* who want to obtain a *licenciatura* or *tesina*.

- **Faculties** (*facultades*) – These offer five-year academic courses leading to a *licenciatura* or *tesina* and two-year courses for graduates of a university college who wish to obtain their *licenciatura* or *tesina*.

- **Higher Technical Schools of Engineering & Architecture** (*escuela superior de ingeniería y arquitectura*) – These offer five-year vocational and technical courses leading to an *ingeniero superior y arquitecto* degree (see **Studies** below).

The Spanish university system is rigidly structured: students must follow a fixed curriculum and aren't permitted to change universities during their studies (except for family or health reasons).

# Studies

Studies at Spanish universities are divided into three cycles. The first cycle, lasting three years, leads to a *licencia* (in academic subjects) or a *diploma* (in vocational or technical subjects, which are studied by twice as many students as academic subjects). The second cycle, lasting two years, leads to a *licenciatura* or *tesina* (academic), which is equivalent to an American or British MA or MSc, or an *ingeniero superior y arquitecto* degree (vocational). The third cycle is a PhD (doctorate) programme, which results in the academic title of *doctor* or *Doctor en Filosofía y Letras*.

## University Reforms

University courses are currently in a state of change as Spain starts to bring them into line with EU regulations due to be in place by 2010 and designed to make university studies across the EU as homogeneous as possible. Under the proposals (expected to be adopted in the 2008-9 academic year) the number of available courses will be reduced from around 140 to less than 80 and courses will typically last four years instead of five. Architecture, dentistry, veterinary science and pharmacy will continue to last five and a degree in medicine will take six. It will no longer be possible to study one language only and several specialist degrees currently available will be integrated into other subjects.

The names of degree awards will be known as *Grado* (instead of *licenciaturas* or *diplomaturas*), *Posgrado* (replacing *máster*) and *Doctorado*. Degree awards will include a certificate (*Suplemento al Título*) with a detailed description of the student's completed studies in an attempt to make recognition of qualifications within the EU easier. The government plans to publish a definitive list of changes in 2006.

# Applications

Competition for places at Spanish universities is high, as there are too few places for all the students wishing to attend. Applicants must pass the *Prueba General de Bachillerato* (*PGB*) examination (see **The Baccalaureate** on page 186) and acceptance depends on the result obtained in this exam, as well as the average mark gained during the two years of study for the baccalaureate. Those who pass the *PGB* with a high mark are generally awarded a university place in July, while others may have to wait until August to find out whether they've been accepted.

EU nationals are entitled to compete for places at Spanish universities on equal terms with Spanish nationals. In addition, a small number of places at most universities, e.g. 5 per cent, are allocated to non-EU students. In general, qualifications that are accepted as entry requirements in a student's home country are accepted in Spain. Spanish universities accept British A Levels as an entrance qualification, but an American high school diploma isn't usually accepted. American students must usually have spent two years at college or hold a BA, BBA or BSc degree. For information about the recognition of EU diplomas in Spain, contact the Ministerio de Educación y Ciencia, Subdirección General de Cooperación Internacional, Centro de Información sobre Reconocimiento de Títulos y Movilidad de Estudiantes, C/Alcalá, 36, 28071 Madrid (☎ 902-218 500, 🖳 www.mec.es). As with school enrolment, foreign qualifications must be verified via a process known as *homologación* by the Spanish Department of Education and Culture in Spain.

All foreign students require a thorough knowledge of Spanish, although preparatory courses are provided. **Note that in autonomous regions where there's a second official language (e.g. the Basque Country, Catalonia and Galicia), courses may be conducted in the local language.** Many foreign university students (and Spanish students abroad) can study in Spain under European Union exchange programmes for periods ranging from a few weeks to several months.

In general, the academic year runs from October to June and applications should be made as soon as possible (e.g. on receipt of final school exam results). Applications must be submitted to universities and addressed to the student secretariat (*vice-rectorado de alumnos*).

## Costs

In most regions, university fees (*tasas*) are set by the Spanish Ministry of Education and Science. In autonomous regions with responsibility for their own education, fees are set annually by the university council and the local regional government. Private universities under the auspices of the Catholic church set their own fees. Spanish university fees are low for residents and EU nationals, e.g. from €300 to €1,000 a year, depending on the faculty and location. Grants and scholarships are available to Spanish and foreign students and around one in seven students receives a grant. (Note that a disadvantage of moving to Spain is that foreign children resident in Spain may be classified as overseas students by their home countries, making them no longer eligible for grants and possibly liable to pay fees or higher fees.)

In addition to course fees, students should expect to pay €350 to €1,000 a month for meals and accommodation. There's a huge difference in the cost of living between cities and regions, Madrid and Barcelona being the most expensive. Finding a part-time job to help pay your living expenses is difficult and shouldn't be relied upon. Some universities have their own student halls of residence (*colegios mayores*), although places are in high demand and short supply. The availability and cost of private rented accommodation (see page 100) varies with the location.

Spanish students under the age of 28 and registered at a Spanish institute of higher education are covered for health insurance by a students' insurance fund. This fund also covers many foreign students under reciprocal agreements, including those from EU countries. Students over the age of 28 and others who aren't covered must have private health insurance.

Many Spanish students attend the nearest university to their home and treat university as an extension of school, particularly in Madrid and other large cities where accommodation is expensive. Faced with the choice of living with their parents or in a depressing university residence or cheap room, most choose to live at home. Spanish students don't usually work during their studies or during holidays and most go home at weekends. Few university facilities are open at weekends, when foreign students must amuse themselves. Note that, like Spanish state schools, universities offer few extra-curricular, sports and social activities.

# Further Information

Further information about higher education in Spain can be obtained from the cultural sections of Spanish embassies abroad and from the University Council (Consejo de Coordinación Universitaria), Secretaría General, C/ Juan del Rosal, 14, 28040 Madrid (☎ 914-539 800, ▭ www.mec.es/consejou).

A useful book about higher education in Spain is *Studying and Working in Spain* by M. Newton and G. Shields (Manchester University Press), and the Spain Exchange website includes a wealth of useful information about studying in Spain, as well as a detailed description of all universities and higher education establishments in the country (▭ www.spainexchange.com).

# LEARNING SPANISH

If you don't speak Spanish, it's advisable to enrol in a course at a language school, preferably before arriving in Spain. If you're planning to work in Spain, you may wish to obtain a formal qualification for non-native speakers (*diploma de español como lengua extranjera*), administered by the Spanish Ministry of Education, the Instituto Cervantes (see **Further Information** below) and the University of Salamanca, Servicio Central de Idiomas, C/ Libreros, 30, 1°, 37008 Salamanca (☎ 923-294 400, ▭ http://sci.usal.es). Information is also available from Spanish embassies. Courses are held worldwide and diplomas are awarded at three levels (beginner, intermediate and advanced). Diplomas are particularly useful when formal evidence of Spanish proficiency is required, e.g. for employment or study in Spain.

Most people can teach themselves a great deal through the use of books, tapes, videos, CDs and DVDs. However, even the best students require some help. Teaching Spanish is big business in Spain, with classes offered by language schools (see below), Spanish and foreign colleges and universities, private and international schools, foreign and international organisations, local associations and clubs, chambers of commerce and town halls, and private teachers (see below). Classes range from language courses for complete beginners through specialised business or cultural courses to university-level courses leading to higher diplomas. Most Spanish universities offer language courses all year round, including summer courses. These are generally cheaper than those provided by language schools, although classes may be much larger. Free or heavily subsidised courses are organised for resident foreigners in some provinces, e.g. Alicante and Malaga, by the Spanish department of the Escuela Oficial de Idiomas. If you already speak some Spanish, but need conversational practice, you may wish to enrol in an art or craft course at a local institute or club.

# Language Schools

Spain has around 3,000 language schools (*escuelas de idiomas*), the highest number in Europe, and there are schools in all Spanish cities and large towns. Most offer a range of classes depending on your current language ability, how many hours you wish to study a week, how much money you want to spend and how quickly you need to learn. Courses are graded according to ability, e.g. beginner, intermediate or advanced, and usually last from 2 to 16 weeks. Courses are usually open to anyone over the age of 18 and some also accept students aged from 14. All schools offer free tests to help you find your correct level and a free introductory lesson.

Courses generally fall into the following categories: extensive (4 to 15 hours per week); intensive (15 to 30 hours) and total immersion (30 to 40 hours). The most common are intensive courses, providing four hours' tuition a day from Mondays to Fridays (20 hours a week). The cost of an intensive course is usually between €200 and €300 for a two-week course, €225 to €325 for three weeks or €250 to €400 for four weeks. The highest fees are charged in the summer months, particularly during July and August. Commercial courses are generally more expensive, but include more tuition, e.g. €600 for two weeks and a total of 60 hours' tuition. Courses that include accommodation are often excellent value and many schools arrange home stays with a Spanish family (full or half board), or provide apartment or hotel accommodation. Accommodation with a host family typically costs €200 to €250 per week half board.

Some schools offer combined courses where language study is linked with optional subjects, including business Spanish, Spanish art and culture, reading, conversation, and Spanish history, traditions and folklore. Many schools combine language courses with a range of social or sporting activities such as horse riding, tennis, windsurfing, golf, skiing, hang-gliding and scuba-diving.

Don't expect to become fluent in a short time unless you have a particular flair for learning languages or already have a good command of Spanish. Unless you desperately need to learn quickly, it's usually better to arrange your lessons over a long period. However, don't commit yourself to a long course of study, particularly an expensive one, before ensuring that it's the right course for you. Whichever type of course you choose, you should shop around, as tuition fees vary considerably. You may wish to check that a school is a member of a professional association such as the Asociación para la Enseñanza del Español como Lengua Extranjera (ASELE).

# Private Lessons

You may prefer to have private lessons, which are a quicker (although more expensive) way of learning Spanish. The main advantage of private lessons is that you learn at your own speed and aren't held back by slow learners or left floundering in the wake of the class genius. Don't forget to ask your friends, neighbours and colleagues if they can recommend a private teacher. Private Spanish teachers often advertise in English-language publications in Spain (see **Appendix A**). Private lessons cost from €15 per hour with an experienced tutor.

One way to get to know the Spanish and improve your language ability is to find a Spanish partner wishing to learn English (or your mother tongue), called a 'language exchange' (*intercambio*). Partners get together on a regular basis and half the time is spent speaking English (or another foreign language) and half speaking Spanish. You can advertise for a private teacher or partner in local newspapers, on bulletin and notice boards (in shopping centres, supermarkets, universities, clubs, etc.), and through your or your partner's employers.

# Further Information

Information about Spanish language schools can be obtained from the Departamento de Español para Extranjeros, Escuela Oficial de Idiomas, Jesús Maestro s/n, 28003 Madrid (🖳 www.eoidiomas.com). A list of Spanish language schools in Spain (as well as of organisations arranging courses, exchange visits and home stays in Spain for children and adults) can be obtained from the Instituto Cervantes (🖳 www. cervantes.es), which has offices in many countries, including the UK (102 Eaton Square, London SW1 W9AN, UK, ☎ 020-7235 0353, 🖳 http://londres.cervantes.es) and the US (211–215 East 49th Street, NY 10017, New York, ☎ 212- 308 7720, 🖳 http://nyork.cervantes.es). The Instituto also runs Spanish classes in some 30 countries.

Two good sources for Spanish language-learning books and materials in the UK are European Schoolbooks, 5 Warwick Street, London W1B 5LU, UK (☎ 020-7734 5259, 🖳 www.eurobooks.co.uk) and the Spanish Bookshop (☎ UK 01962-773792, 🖳 www.teachertrading.co.uk). For further information about Spanish languages, see **Language** on pages 52 and 178.

# 10.

# PUBLIC TRANSPORT

Public transport (*transporte público*) is generally excellent in Spanish cities, most of which have efficient urban bus and train services, some supplemented by underground railways (*metros*) and, occasionally, trams (*tranvía*). Spanish railways (RENFE) provide an efficient and reasonably fast service, particularly between cities served by *AVE* high-speed trains (see below). Spain has comprehensive inter-city bus and domestic airline services (see pages 206 and 214) and is also served by frequent international coaches, trains and airline services (see pages 208, 196 and 212). On the down side, trains are non-existent in many areas and buses are sometimes infrequent in coastal resorts and rural areas, where it's often essential to have your own transport.

Urban transport in major cities such as Madrid and Barcelona is inexpensive and efficient, and rates among the best in the world. Services include comprehensive bus routes, *metros* and extensive suburban rail networks. Systems are totally integrated and the same ticket (sold at tobacconists) can be used for all services. A range of commuter and visitor tickets are also available. There are travel agencies (such as Viajes Marsans, Halcón Viajes and Viajes Meliá) in all major cities and large towns, and specialist agencies for young travellers such as Viajes TIVE. Students with an International Student Identity Card (ISIC) receive discounts on selected Iberia flights and buses. Pensioners aged 65 or over also receive discounts on most forms of public transport (if you aren't offered a discount, don't forget to ask). A free travel map (*mapa de comunicaciones*) is available from TurEspaña (see page 392).

# TRAINS

The Spanish rail network is operated by the state-owned company RENFE (Red Nacional de los Ferrocarriles Españoles) which operates some 15,000km (over 9,000mi) of track and 2,500 stations (*estaciones*). The RENFE network takes in all major cities, although it doesn't run to many small towns, and is supplemented by a few suburban networks such as the *Ferrocarrils de la Generalitat de Catalunya* (*FFCC*, but commonly referred to as the *Generalitat*) city lines in Barcelona and private narrow-gauge railways. Little freight is transported by train within Spain or to other European Union (EU) countries, compared with the tens of thousands of tonnes shipped by road. Like most state-owned businesses in Spain, the railways were grossly under-funded under Franco and RENFE remains western Europe's most idiosyncratic railway (many lines are still single track), despite huge investments in new rolling stock. Occasional accidents occur on Spain's rail network (2003 was a particularly bad year), but travelling by train is usually very safe and considerably safer than travelling by car.

Spain's railway network is well below average by European standards, particularly regarding punctuality, although it's also one of the continent's cheapest. However, RENFE has undergone a comprehensive modernisation programme in the last decade, during which journey times have been reduced by up to 50 per cent. There are high speed trains (*Tren de Alta Velocidad Española/AVE*) from Madrid to Seville (2 hours 25 minutes), to Zaragoza (2 hours) and Lleida (3 hours). The *AVE* (which also means big bird in Spanish) employs 'disguised' French *TGV* trains running on special lines travelling at speeds of up to 300kph (185mph). Full refunds are offered if an *AVE* train is more than five minutes late arriving at its destination, but before you get ready for a free trip, only 0.23 per cent of *AVE* trains are more than five minutes late!

The *AVE* service is to be extended countrywide by 2007 and when the network is finished, all provincial capitals will be under four hours journey time from Madrid and all provinces under six and a half hours journey time from Barcelona. The stretches that are currently under construction are Madrid-Barcelona (due to be completed in 2006), Madrid-Malaga and Madrid-Valencia (both due in 2007). The *AVE* will eventually comprise part of a Europewide, high-speed rail network (unlike other Spanish trains, *AVE* trains run on European standard-gauge track) connecting to the French and Portuguese networks. There are three classes of *AVE* trains: first (*club*), business (*preferente*) and tourist (*turista*), plus sleeping accommodation for international travel. *AVE* trains are air-conditioned and equipped with reclining seats, televisions (films are shown), a restaurant and cafeteria, a drinks/refreshment trolley service and, in first class, free newspapers and the *AVE* magazine (*Revista Paisajes*).

Other first-class, long-distance (*largo recorrido*) trains include the *Talgo*, which has first and tourist class seats and is similarly equipped to *AVE* trains. *Talgo* trains are generally slower than the *AVE*, although the fastest run at speeds of between 160 and 200kph. The main Talgo routes are from Madrid to Malaga and from Barcelona along the Mediterranean coast.

RENFE operate a mind-boggling variety of trains, most with different services and fare structures. Spanish trains vary greatly in speed. In general, fast trains stop only at main stations, while slow local trains stop at all stations. One of the fastest trains is the *Talgo* (see above) which also includes *Talgo* sleepers (*coches-cama*). A *Trans-Europe Express* (*Talgo TEE*) is a fast train operating on international routes. *Intercity* (*IC*) trains are air-conditioned and fast, while *Electrotrén* (*ELT*) and *Tren Electrico Regional* (*TER*) trains are comfortable and fast, but slower (and make more stops) than a *Talgo*. A *TAF* is a diesel express used on secondary routes and slower than a *Talgo* or *TER*.

There's also a huge variety of slow, local, short-distance trains classified variously as *tranvía*, *semi-directos* or *correos* (post trains), *automotor*, *omnibús* and *ferrobús*. Suburban commuter trains (*cercanías*) are second/tourist class (*turista*) only and stop at all stations. A regional express (*reg. exp.* or *interurbano*) is a second class, air-conditioned diesel train and an *exprés* is a slow night train, usually with sleeping cars. A *rápido* is a daytime version of the *exprés*. Despite the names, the *exprés* and *rápido* aren't particularly fast. Night trains (*estrellas*) are slow trains with various types of couchettes (*literas*) and beds. Car trains run to all parts of Spain (e.g. you can transport your car by train from Barcelona, Bilbao or Madrid to Malaga) and include an *autoexpreso*, which carries cars, motorcycles, light boats and canoes, and (on some routes) there's a *motoexpreso* carrying only motorcycles. If you aren't in a hurry, it's advisable to compare the cost of slow trains with fast trains, as the savings are considerable (slow trains are excellent for tourists, as they allow plenty of time to enjoy the sights).

Long-distance trains usually have first and second class carriages, although there's a bewildering variety of fares within each class and for different train types. Spanish fares are low by European standards, with the base fare around €0.60 per

10km for second class and €1 per 10km for first class. However, supplements can increase fares by up to 80 per cent. Fares are graded according to a train's speed and comfort and there are surcharges (*suplementos*) on fast trains, including *TER*, *Talgo*, *Inter-City* and *ELT* trains. A smaller supplement is payable on *rápido* class trains. A first class ticket costs around 50 per cent more than second/tourist class (*turista*).

Further information is available from the RENFE website (💻 www.renfe.es) or from the telephone helpline (☎ 902-240 202), open from 5am to 11.45pm.

## International Trains

Spain also has many international services, although they're slow and expensive compared with air travel. There are direct trains to many western European cities (e.g. Geneva, Milan, Montpellier, Paris and Zurich) and there's even a train from Madrid to Moscow taking around three days. International trains usually have two classes, first (*gran clase*) and second/tourist (*turista*), plus sleeping cars (*coches camas*) with a choice of individual compartments or couchettes. At border stops it may be necessary to change trains due to Spain's wider gauge than the rest of Europe, except for *Talgo* and *TEE* trains which have adjustable axles. RENFE also operate a Train-hotel (*Trenhotel*) service running from Madrid to Paris (*Francisco de Goya*) and from Barcelona to Milan (*Salvador Dalí*), to Paris (*Joan Miró*) and to Zurich (*Pau Casals*). The *Francisco de Goya* takes just under 25 hours and costs €252 return for an adult travelling first class in low season. The *Salvador Dalí* takes under 24 hours and costs €3206 return for an adult travelling first class. **Beware of thieves on overnight international trains, as there have been robberies in recent years, particularly those travelling between France and Spain.**

Further information is available from the RENFE website (💻 www.renfe.es) or from the telephone helpline for international enquiries (☎ 902-243 402), open from 7am to 11pm.

## Spanish Network & Main Stations

The Spanish railway system is centred on Madrid, from where three main lines radiate out to other parts of the country (two extend to the French border and the other to Andalusia and the Levante). Consequently, there are good links between Madrid and other cities, although to get to a destination without going via Madrid often requires a circuitous journey. Madrid has two main stations:

● Chamartín serves A Coruña, Albacete, Alicante, Barcelona, Bilbao, Cartagena, Irún, León, Lugo, Ourense, Oviedo, Salamanca, Santander, Soria, Vallodolid, Zamora and Zaragossa, as well as destinations in France and the local area.

● Puerta de Atocha station (south of the *Prado* museum and recently extensively restored and renovated) serves Castilla-La Mancha, Andalusia and Extremadura, including Almeria, Badajoz, Cadiz, Ciudad Real, Cordoba, Cuenca, Granada, Malaga, Mérida, Salamanca, Seville, Toledo and Valencia, as well as destinations in Portugal and the local area.

The main stations in Barcelona are França and Sants (the more important), which has a link to Barcelona airport. Trains to all major Spanish cities and to France (via Gerona) leave from Sants, while França has daily international trains to Geneva, Milan, Paris and Zurich. Note that in smaller towns, stations are often located a few kilometres from the town centre and there may be no bus service.

## Tourist Trains

Spain has a number of 'tourist' trains, many of which run on narrow-gauge lines. The *Al-Andalus Express* (🖥 www.alandalusexpreso.com) is a unique travel experience on a luxurious converted '20s train and a wonderful introduction to Spain, with the round trip commencing in Seville or Madrid and taking in Cordoba and Granada. However, with the four day journey costing from €2,100 for one (including food and excursions), it isn't for those on a tight budget. *El Transcantábrico* (🖥 www. transcantabrico.feve.es) is another '20s train operating between León and Ferrol in the north of Spain along the longest stretch of narrow-gauge railway in Europe (1,000km/625mi). It takes in stunning mountain scenery and offers excursions to a number of enchanting villages and towns during its eight day journey. With prices starting at around €4,000 for two people sharing, it isn't for the budget traveller either. Although it isn't a tourist train, one of the most spectacular train journeys in southern Spain is on the RENFE line from Ronda to Jimena de la Frontera (British built in the 1890s).

Other trains include the independent *Ferrocarrils de la Generalitat Valenciana* (*FGV*) narrow-gauge line (1915) operating the *Costa Blanca Exprés* running along the Costa Blanca from Denia to Alicante (93km/58mi) and the *Limón Exprés* operating between Benidorm and Gata de Gorgos. A coal-burning steam train (*Tren de la Fresa*) with wooden seats runs from Madrid to Aranjuez on Saturdays, Sundays and public holidays from May to October. In Majorca, railway enthusiasts can enjoy a trip on the vintage (circa 1900) train running from Palma to Sóller (the only other train in the Balearics runs from Palma to Inca). It travels through tunnels and mountains and provides some of the best views on the island. From Sóller an equally ancient tramcar runs through orange and lemon groves to Puerto de Sóller. RENFE organise many day and weekend excursion trains, including 'tourist trains' to Spain's most historic cities – train tickets usually include entrance to the main tourist attractions and one-night's hotel accommodation. An interesting book is *Spain and Portugal by Rail* by Norman Renouf (Bradt Travel Guides) and the *El Tren* website (🖥 www.eltren.com) is full of interesting information about trains in Spain and includes links to all the train services.

## General Information

- All *AVE* and long-distance trains have a bar-buffet and/or a restaurant car (*wagón restaurante*) with waiter service. Medium distance trains have a refreshment trolley (*carrito de restauración*) offering drinks and snacks at your seat. Note that catering on trains is expensive and isn't good quality by Spanish standards (many passengers prefer to provide their own picnic).

● Main railway stations provide a variety of services, including an information booth; tourist office; post office; accommodation service; luggage lockers and storage; wash, shower and brush-up facilities; car rental; telephones; cafeterias and restaurants; bank with ATMs; currency exchange; photocopiers; instant passport photograph machines and assorted shops and kiosks.

● Smoking is forbidden on all trains, including sleeping cars. Smoking is only permitted on platforms.

● Public telephones are available on *AVE* and other fast trains, and accept domestic and international calls. They must be used with a Telefónica phone card available from train cafeterias.

● Platforms (*andenes*) aren't always clearly numbered, so make sure you're waiting at the correct one. Lines often have different numbers from platforms, which can be confusing. The destination of trains is usually written or displayed on the outside of carriages.

● Car parks are often provided close to railway stations, where long-term parking costs around €12 per day (monthly season tickets are available to commuters).

● You can rent a car from many main railway stations and leave it at another major city station. Cars can be reserved at travel agencies to coincide with your train journey.

● Beware of thieves when travelling on trains and try to store your bags in an overhead rack where you can keep an eye on them.

● Self-service luggage lockers (*consignas*) and left-luggage offices are usually available at major railway stations, but for security reasons (particularly since the train bombings in March 2004) they may be closed. Lockers large enough for large suitcases or backpacks cost around €2 to €4 per day. Main stations also have left luggage offices open from around 8am until 10pm. Luggage forwarding up to 20kg is free for long-distance rail passengers.

# Buying Tickets

Buying train tickets (*billetes*) can be confusing, as there's a baffling range of fares (*precios/importes*) and trains to choose from. Confusion is widespread and ticket office clerks aren't always familiar with the variety of special tickets and reductions available. **You should double check to ensure that you pay the lowest possible fare for a journey.** Fares for long-distance and high-speed trains, such as *AVE*, are published in leaflets available from stations and RENFE offices, and all fare information is available on the RENFE website (🖥 www.renfe.es). Children under four years of age travel free (including sleeping accommodation) and those aged between 4 and 11 (inclusive) travel for half fare on local trains and for a 40 per cent discount on regional (*regionales*) trains.

Tickets can be purchased at station ticket windows (*taquillas de billetes*), from ticket machines (*máquinas de billetes*) accepting cash and credit cards, at RENFE offices, and from RENFE appointed travel agents. Tickets can also be bought online or by telephone through RENFE's secure booking service, *TIKNET*, requiring online registration, a code name and password, both of which must be used in order to buy tickets. TIKNET (☎ 902-157 507) is open from 7am to 11pm. The first time you buy tickets you must collect them in person from any RENFE station where you must show some identification (passport or residence permit) and give the booking reference number. Tickets bought in subsequent purchases can be collected from your departure station (up to one hour before the train leaves), on the train, if it's a long-distance journey, on regional or *Grandes Líneas* trains or at the access point to AVE, *Talgo* and *Lanzadera* trains.

A single ticket is *un billete de ida* and a return (round trip) is *ida y vuelta*. There may be an information (*información*) or international information window at major stations, where staff may speak English and other foreign languages. A ticket must be purchased and validated **before** boarding a train, unless there's no ticket office (or it's closed) at the station where you're boarding. It's possible to buy a ticket on a train from the ticket collector/conductor (*revisor*), although you may need to pay a surcharge, depending on the type of train and the length of your journey.

## Ticket Offices

It usually pays to avoid station ticket windows, where there are usually long queues, and buy your ticket at a RENFE office, from a travel agent, by phone or online. Ticket windows at stations usually open around an hour before train departures (but in some cases, open just a few minutes before a train is due to arrive). To purchase a ticket at some stations you must take a number from a machine and wait for it to be called (so you must understand Spanish numbers). At main stations, there are a number of ticket windows, which may include local trains (*cercanías*) and long-distance (*largos recorridos*), advance tickets (*venta anticipada*) and imminent departure (*venta inmediata*) i.e. up to two hours before departure. There's also usually a window for international tickets (*billetes internacionales*) at some stations in Madrid and Barcelona. A computerised RENFE ticket shows the train number (*No Tren*), carriage (*coche*) and seat number (*No Plaza*).

## Ticket Classes

There are two classes on most long-distance trains: first class (*preferente*) and second/tourist class (*turista*). On some services, such as fast *AVE* trains, there are three fare classes: *turista, preferente* and *club*. Some trains such as *IC* and *TEE* international trains are first class only.

## Fare Tariffs

There are different fares depending on the type of train (*tipo de tren*) and how long the journey takes. The difference between the cheapest and most expensive fare can be as much as 150 per cent. Apart from the extra cost, it's best to avoid travelling on public holidays or over long weekends (*puentes*), when the whole nation takes to the rails (those that aren't on the roads).

## Reservations

Reservations can be made on routes over 200km (124mi) between two months and one hour before departure. On *AVE* trains, open tickets (*billetes abiertos*) are valid for six months and bookings can be made ten minutes before train departures. Many stations have advance booking offices, although it's usually better to book at a RENFE office or a RENFE-appointed travel agent (*agencias de viajes*), displaying the blue and yellow RENFE logo. Seats should be reserved as far in advance as possible, particularly during the main tourist season and before public holidays.

When you make a reservation via the phone or internet you're given a code number. You must then go to any station or RENFE travel agent within two days of making the reservation, quote this number and show identification. Tickets can be paid for with cash and various credit and charge cards, including MasterCard and Visa. **If you pay by credit card you must show identification.** Note that seat and (in particular) sleeper reservations are compulsory on many long-distance trains. Train tickets purchased abroad must be stamped before each journey, at a RENFE office or at a station before departure.

## Changing Tickets & Cancellation

It's possible to change the date and time of travel on pre-booked tickets. Changes can be made up to five minutes before the train's departure and cost 10 per cent of the ticket price, but there's no charge if the change is for travel on the same day. Cancellations are free of charge unless the ticket or reservation is cancelled within two hours of travel in which case a 15 per cent surcharge is charged. You can change the departure date of a ticket with a reserved seat without penalty up to two hours before the scheduled departure. Cancellation and refund of a ticket for *AVE* and *Talgo* trains can be done up to five minutes before departure.

## Season & Special Tickets

Many season tickets (*abonos*) and special discount (*descuento*) tickets are available in Spain. These include discounts for students and youths (16 to 25), senior citizens, disabled passengers, commuters and groups. Most special tickets can be changed or cancelled. Information is obtainable from information and ticket offices at any railway station.

## Senior Citizens & Disabled Passengers

Senior citizens aged over 60 and disabled passengers can obtain a gold pass (*tarjeta dorada*) for €3 a year, offering discounts of 40 per cent on all trains except *AVE* and *Talgo 200* long-distance trains, where the discount is between 25 and 40 per cent.

## Commuters

There are various commuter tickets, including monthly season tickets (*bonos mensuales*) offering discounts of up to 40 per cent. For further information enquire at any RENFE ticket office. Season tickets are also available on long-distance trains such as the *Talgo 200* between Malaga and Madrid, e.g. the *Abono 10* ticket costs €400 for ten journeys in tourist class and is valid for a maximum of three months.

## Students

A student card (*carnet joven*) is available from local municipal youth departments for €3 for students aged between 12 and 26 and provides a 25 per cent discount on RENFE regional trains, but no discount on *AVE* or *Talgo* trains. A passport or residence permit (*residencia*) and a passport-sized photograph are required. Students can also benefit from the *Tarjeta Studio* which is valid for one term and allows unlimited travel on local train networks in Asturias, Barcelona, Cadiz, Malaga, Murcia, Seville and Valencia. Prices depend on the area.

## Children

On *AVE* and *Talgo 200* trains there's a 40 per cent discount for children aged from 4 to 13. On other trains the discount is for children aged from 4 to 11. Children under four travel free on all trains.

## Groups

Groups of 10 to 25 people receive a 15 per cent discount on *AVE* and *Talgo 200* trains (for groups above 25, contact RENFE).

## International Tickets

Holders of a Eurailpass, Eurodomino or Inter-rail pass may travel on *AVE* and *Talgo 200* trains by paying a supplement of €38 (*club*), €22.50 (*preferente*) and €9.50 (*turista*). *Club* and *preferente* discounts are applicable only to holders of first class tickets. Student discounts of up to 40 per cent are available from offices of Wasteels (European travel agents that specialise in train tickets).

# Timetables

If you use trains regularly, you should obtain route maps (*mapas de carreteras*) and timetables (*horarios*) on arrival in Spain. However, bear in mind that most times are **approximate** only, and with the exception of timetables for fast (e.g. *AVE*) and international trains, they shouldn't be relied upon, although local trains are generally punctual. At major stations, arrivals (*llegadas*) and departures (*salidas*) are shown on large electronic boards. It's wise to double-check departure times and not rely on announcements. You also shouldn't trust the list of trains posted at a station, but confirm trains and times at a ticket or information office. When you buy a train ticket with a reserved seat, the train number and departure time are printed on it.

Train timetables (*horarios de trenes*) are published in national, regional and local versions, and also for individual routes and train types (e.g. long-distance). All timetables are available online and RENFE publish a range of special guides and information, plus an 'Atlas of Spanish Railways' (*Atlas de Ferrocarriles Españoles*) containing a selection of maps of Spain. Train timetables are printed for most major domestic and international rail routes, often in the form of a handy pocket card. A commuter train schedule for Madrid costs around €1 at station news kiosks.

Note that many services operate daily (*diario*) or only on working days (*laborables*), which may include Saturdays, and a limited service is operated on Sundays and holidays (*domingos y festivos*).

# UNDERGROUND RAILWAYS

There are underground railway systems (*metros*) in Madrid, Barcelona, Bilbao and Valencia, where public transport tickets and passes permit travel on all modes of public transport, including *metro*, bus and suburban train services. *Metros* offer the quickest way to get around these cities, although they're crowded during rush hours. No smoking is permitted on *metro* trains or in stations, which are clean and fairly safe. Crime is generally rare on Spanish *metros*, although you should watch out for pickpockets especially on the Madrid system. *Metro* systems are also under construction in Malaga and Seville.

## Madrid

Madrid has the largest and oldest *metro* system in Spain with twelve lines and 190 stations covering most of the city, operating from 6am until 2am and is used by over 615 million people a year. The fare is €1.30 per journey and €5.80 for a ten-journey ticket, which may include bus travel (*metrobús*). Monthly or annual season tickets are available for people aged under 21 (*abono joven*), commuters (*abono normal*) and for pensioners over 64 (*abono tercera edad*). Season tickets offer exceptionally good savings for unlimited travel on public transport, including the underground, city buses and local trains (*cercanías*). Pensioners, who pay only €9.55 a month for unlimited travel, get a particularly good deal. A free map (*plano del metro*) showing the lines in different colours is available from ticket offices. Tickets are sold at station ticket booths and from machines. The *metro* is easy to use; simply note the end station of the line you want and follow the signs. When entering or leaving a train, car doors must be opened manually by pressing a button. Apart from Sundays and late at night, trains run around every five to eight minutes (more frequently during rush hour), although no timetable is published.

Madrid has invested heavily in its *metro* system and in 2002 the centre of Madrid (*Nuevos Ministerios* station where check-in facilities are available) was finally connected by underground to Barajas airport, which can be reached in just 15 minutes. Further extension to the south of the city has been finished with the *MetroSur* line, connecting many suburbs such as Alcorcón and Fuenlabrada to the central underground lines. Comprehensive information regarding the *metro* is available by phone (☎ 902-444 403 from 6am to 1.30am) or on the internet (🖳 www. metromadrid.es).

# Barcelona

Barcelona's *metro* is one of the world's most modern and best designed systems, although it has just six lines: L1 (red), L2 (purple), L3 (green), L4 (yellow), L5 (blue) and L11 (light green). Large areas of the city aren't covered by the *metro* and despite having only a few lines, most connections require long walks between platforms (not recommended if you're carrying heavy luggage). Stations are indicated at street level by a large red 'M' within a diamond. Trains are frequent and run every three or four minutes at peak times. There's piped music on platforms to keep you entertained while waiting for trains, most of which are air-conditioned.

A map (*xarxa de metro* in Catalan) is available from tourist offices and at ticket windows in stations (there's also a *metro* map on the back of the free tourist office city map). Lines are marked in colours, and connections between lines (*correspondencia*) and between *metro* and train systems (*enlace*) are clearly indicated. Stops are announced over an intercom and illuminated panels show where the train has come from, the station you're approaching, and as the train departs after stopping, the next station (an excellent idea which should be adopted by all *metro* systems). Flashing red chevrons at the end of each carriage indicate the side of the train from which to exit. Announcements on trains (and in stations) are made in Spanish (Castilian) and not in Catalan.

A single journey costs €1.15. A *tarjeta multiviaje* (*T-10*) pass costs €6.30 and is valid for ten journeys on the *metro* and city buses, and can also be used on the blue tramway (*Tibidabo*), the Montjuic funicular railway and Catalan railways *Generalitat* (*FFCC*) city lines. Numerous other passes are also available such as the *T-mes*, valid for a month's unlimited travel (€40.75 for one zone); the *T-familiar*, valid for up to 70 journeys and transferable; and the *T-joven*, valid for 90 days' unlimited travel for those under 21. One, three and five-day passes are also available.

Tickets and passes can be purchased from automatic ticket machines at most stations, ticket windows, and from ServiCaixa ATMs and special sales' outlets. If you purchase a multi-trip ticket, it must be inserted in the slot of an automatic gate, which clips off a segment of the ticket, illuminates a flashing yellow light and releases the gate. Always keep your pass or ticket until you leave the *metro*, as riding without a ticket incurs a €30 on-the-spot fine. The *metro* is open from 5am and closes at midnight from Mondays to Thursdays, on Sundays and public holidays, and at 2am on Fridays, Saturdays and the day before public holidays.

Barcelona also has the *FFCC* (*Generalitat*), a small underground train service within the city operated by the provincial government of Catalonia. You can use the *T-1* and *T-2* passes on the *FFCC* or buy tickets from machines in stations.

Comprehensive information on all Barcelona's public transport systems is available on the Transports Metropolitans Barcelona website (🖳 www.tmb.net), which includes a useful guide to public transport based on the name of a street. When you type in the name of a street the public transport operating in the area is shown. Transports Metropolitans Barcelona also have a telephone helpline (☎ 933-187 074).

# Bilbao

Bilbao's *metro* system consists of two lines and 32 stations, and transports over 73 million passengers a year. A one-journey ticket costs €1.15 and a day ticket €3. Further discounts and passes are also available. Trains generally run from 6am to 11pm during the week and until 2am at weekends, when a night service runs between certain stations. Information is available from ☎ 944-254 000 and on 🖳 www.metrobilbao.net.

# Valencia

The *metro* system in Valencia consists of four lines. Tickets cost €1.10 for one journey and a ten-journey ticket, *bonometro*, costs €6.30. Further discounts and passes are also available. Trains generally run from 5am to midnight (2am at weekends). Further information is available from ☎ 900-461 046 and 🖳 www.metrovalencia.com, which includes details of other public transport in Valencia.

# BUSES & TRAMS

There are excellent bus (*autobús*) services in all major cities and towns and comprehensive long-distance coach (*autocar*) services between major cities. Buses are the cheapest and most common form of public transport in Spain and most coastal towns and rural villages are accessible only by bus. The quality and age of buses vary considerably from luxurious modern vehicles in most cities to old ramshackle relics in some rural areas. Private bus services are often confusing and uncoordinated, and buses may leave from different locations rather than a central bus station (*estación de autobuses*), e.g. Madrid has eight bus stations and most cities have two or more (possibly located on the outskirts of town). There are left luggage offices (*consignas*) at central bus stations. **Smoking isn't permitted on buses.**

Before boarding a bus at a bus terminal, you must usually buy a ticket from the ticket office or a machine. Otherwise you can buy a single ticket from the driver or conductor as you enter the bus (they usually give change for small banknotes). Passengers usually enter a bus from a front door (marked *entrada*) and dismount from a centre or side exit (*salida*). Most buses are driver-only operated, although some city buses (e.g. blue buses in Madrid) have the entrance at the rear where you pay a conductor who sits by the door. You must usually signal before the stop (*parada*) where you wish to get off by pressing a button (which activates a bell in the driver's cab).

# City Buses

Most bus services in cities run from around 6am until between 11pm and midnight, when a night service normally comes into operation (which is usually more expensive). There's usually a ten-minute service on the most popular routes during peak hours and an hourly night service, although services are considerably reduced on Sundays and public holidays. City buses are often very crowded and buses that aren't air-conditioned can be uncomfortable in the summer. Most city buses have few seats, so as to provide maximum standing room. There are numerous bus routes in major cities and it can be difficult to find your way around. Urban buses are generally very slow and although there are special bus and taxi lanes in some cities (e.g. Madrid), there are still frequent traffic jams. Consequently, many people prefer to use the *metro* (e.g. in Barcelona or Madrid) or taxis (see page 208). In Madrid, a single bus trip costs €1.30 and a ten-trip ticket (*metrobús*) is available for €5.80. Fares are similar in other cities and there are reductions for pensioners and young people up to 21. Tickets are available from bus offices and tobacconists.

Bus and *metro* fares are the same in Madrid and tickets can be used on both systems. In Barcelona, a ten-ride *T-10* pass can be used on all urban public transport, including the *metro* (see page 204). In Madrid and Barcelona (and some other cities), tickets are valid for an entire bus route, but not for transfers to other buses. Day and multi-day passes offering unlimited travel are also available, plus a range of season tickets (*abono*), e.g. for a week, month or a year. In some cities (such as Madrid), those aged between 15 and 21 can buy a youth card (*carnet joven*) providing discounts on public transport and other discounts (e.g. entrance fees to museums). Multi-ride tickets and passes must be stamped in a special machine upon boarding a bus and there are on-the-spot fines for anyone found travelling without a valid ticket. Routes are numbered and terminal points are shown on buses and displayed on signs at stops in most cities. Bus timetables and route maps are available from bus company offices, bus stations and tourist offices. Tourist buses are provided in major cities, most of which follow a circular route, and bus companies offer excursions throughout Spain (packages may include meals, sightseeing and ferry travel).

## Rural Buses

In rural and resort areas, bus services are often operated by the local municipality and services are usually irregular, e.g. four to six buses a day on most routes, although some have an hourly service (there may be no service during the lunch break, e.g. 1.30 to 3pm). The first bus departs at anytime between 6.30 and 9am, and the last bus may depart as early as 4 or 5pm on some routes (most last buses depart before 9pm). However, bus services are usually reliable and run on time. Small towns can often be reached only via their provincial capital and in the centre of Spain it's difficult to get from one major city to another without going via Madrid. Local bus timetables may be published in free newspapers and magazines.

## Long-distance Buses

In addition to local city and rural bus companies, there are many long-distance bus companies, including Alsa (the largest and now part of the National Express group), Auto Res and Continental-Auto. Inter-city buses are usually faster than trains and cost less. Fares on long-distance routes are reasonable and typical return fares are Madrid-Alicante around €44 and Madrid-Barcelona around €60.

Long-distance bus companies are usually privately owned and their fares are quite competitive. The most luxurious buses are comfortable and offer air-conditioning, films and sometimes free soft drinks. All the main companies have telephone and internet information and booking services. Further information can be obtained from Alsa (☎ 902-422 242, 🖳 www.alsa.es), Auto Res (☎ 902-020 052, 🖳 www.auto-res.net) and Continental-Auto (☎ 902-330 400, 🖳 www.continental-auto.es).

## International Coaches

There are regular international coach services between Spain's major cities and many European cities. For example, Eurolines runs coach services from the UK to some 45 destinations in Spain. Journeys are very long, e.g. from London it's 26 hours to Barcelona and 28 hours to Madrid, and fares are often little cheaper than flying (it's worth comparing bus fares with charter flights). Unless you have a fear of flying or a love of coach travel, you may find one or two days spent on a coach a nightmare. Coaches are, however, comfortable, air-conditioned, equipped with toilets and show films.

Most services operate daily during the summer holiday season and two or three times a week out of season. Discounts are provided for students and youths on some routes. Bookings can be made at travel agents in Spain and abroad. Typical return fares with Eurolines are Barcelona-London around €125 and Madrid-London around €140. Apex returns are considerably cheaper.

## Trams

Few Spanish cities have retained their tram systems (*tranvía*), although trams have been reintroduced in Bilbao (through the city centre) and Valencia (where trams are air-conditioned). Barcelona also has a city-centre tramline, called '*Combino*'.

# TAXIS

Taxi ranks (*paradas de taxi*) are located outside railway stations, at airports, and at main intersections in towns and cities. In major cities you can hail a taxi in the street, but in small towns they're available only at taxi ranks. You can also call a radio-taxi in most towns and cities, but you must pay for the taxi's journey to the pick-up point (taxi ranks also have phones). It's advisable to book on the day you want a taxi, preferably close to the time required (if you book too far in advance a taxi may not appear at the desired time). In cities and many towns, you can also rent luxury chauffeur-driven cars (*grandes turismos*), by the hour or for a fixed fee for a particular journey.

Spanish taxi drivers are a pleasant surprise to many foreigners, particularly if you come from a country where taxi drivers are surly, rude and dishonest, as they generally take passengers by the most direct route and don't usually overcharge. What's more, Spanish taxis are relatively inexpensive and many people routinely use them when shopping. Even more astounding is, that contrary to the practice in most other countries, it isn't usual to tip taxi drivers in Spain.

Madrid has more than 16,000 licensed taxis (one of the highest densities in the world) which are black or white with a horizontal red stripe on the side and the city's coat of arms on their doors. Taxis usually have a maximum capacity of four passengers. Tariffs are controlled and the fares for the most popular destinations may be displayed on a board at taxi ranks (particularly when taxis have no meters). All taxis levy a standing charge, a charge per kilometre, a surcharge and/or higher kilometre rates at night and on Sundays, and various surcharges (e.g. for luggage, pets). **Note that many taxis won't carry dogs.** There are special taxis for disabled passengers in many towns which carry wheelchairs (ask when booking). In Madrid the fare is €1.65 (standing charge) plus €0.75 per km within the centre and €0.95 per km outside.

You should only hail a taxi that's travelling in the direction you wish to go, as they won't usually do U-turns. A free (*libre*) sign or a green light at night indicates that a taxi is for hire. If a taxi is displaying a red sign with the name of a local neighbourhood, it means the taxi driver is on his way home and isn't obliged to pick up passengers unless their destination is on his route. If you go outside a city's limits (shown by a *límite taxi* sign), you may be required to pay double the fare shown on the meter (e.g. in Madrid).

In all cities and major urban areas, taxis are fitted with meters (make sure that it's switched on). If a taxi has no meter, you should agree the fare before commencing a journey. If you aren't fluent in Spanish, it's advisable to write down your destination, so that there's no misunderstanding. **Beware of illegal unlicensed and unmetered taxis operating in main cities and preying on foreign visitors.** If you think you've been cheated, ask for an official receipt (*recibo oficial*) showing the taxi licence number, start and finish points of the journey, the date and time, and the driver's signature. Send it to the local licensing authority with your complaint.

# FERRIES & CRUISE SHIPS

Regular car and international ferry services operate all year round between Spain and the UK and Morocco, and domestic ferries run between the mainland and the Balearics, the Canaries and Spain's North African enclaves of Ceuta and Melilla. Spain's most important ports include Algeciras, Almeria, Barcelona, Bilbao, Cadiz, Las Palmas (Gran Canaria), Palma de Mallorca, Santander, Santa Cruz (Tenerife) and Valencia.

Two companies, Brittany Ferries and P&O, operate ferry services between the UK and Spain (see below). Ships provide a variety of facilities and services, including a choice of bars and restaurants (book early for a table during peak hours), swimming pool, Jacuzzi, sauna, cinemas, shops, hairdressing salon, photographic studio, medical service, children's playroom, and evening entertainment (including a nightclub, casino, discotheque and musical shows). There are more shops and diversions on P&O ships, which also tend to have better service and entertainment. Food and drinks are quite expensive, particularly bar drinks and snacks, although Britanny ferries have better food and restaurants than P&O.

Both ferry companies offer various fare tariffs (depending on the time of year) and a choice of single fares, mini-cruises (spending around five hours in Spain or the UK), mini-breaks (five days abroad) and ten-day returns (up to ten days abroad), as well as standard return fares. Children aged under four travel free and those aged from 4 to 14 (Brittany Ferries) or 15 (P&O) travel for half fare. It's advisable to book well ahead when travelling during peak periods and at any time when you require a luxury cabin. If possible, it's best to avoid travelling during peak times, when ships can be uncomfortably crowded.

Travelling between the UK and Spain by ferry will save you around 1,200km (750mi) of driving compared with travelling via France. Ferries can also be a cheaper way to travel, particularly with children and a car, as you don't have to pay for air fares for children or (if you bring your car with you) car rental at your destination. Travelling from the UK to southern Spain by road (via France) entails spending three full days driving and making two overnight stops, plus meals and petrol costs, although it usually works out cheaper than the ferry if you use budget accommodation and don't splash out on gourmet meals.

Note that the seas are often rough between Spain and the UK (the Bay of Biscay is famous for its swell) and travelling isn't advisable during bad weather if you don't travel well (sailings can also be delayed or cancelled due to bad weather in the Bay of Biscay). If you take a mini-cruise during stormy weather, you will have just a few hours' respite from the rolling seas before having to endure the return journey! Check the weather report and be prepared to travel via France or fly. If you do travel by ferry, keep a good supply of seasickness pills handy!

# Brittany Ferries

Brittany Ferries operate an almost year-round, once or twice-weekly service between Plymouth in the UK and the Spanish port of Santander. The days and times of sailings vary according to the time of year. Always check the departure times carefully. The journey time is just over 20 hours between Plymouth and Santander, when one night is spent on board ship. The ferry serving the route is the Port-Aven, with a capacity of 2,140 passengers and 570 cars.

Fares for ferry crossings are published in brochures; you can only consult prices online by using the booking form or quote facility, which is time-consuming if you want to compare several dates and durations. In recent years, fares have fallen considerably in response to increased competition from cheap air fares. The cost for a standard return to Santander for a car (up to 5m/16ft in length) and two passengers is from €293 (October to April) and from €420 (May to September). Foot passengers pay from €59 to €89 for a standard return.

The cost of accommodation isn't included in the fare and, when you book your ticket, you must also book some form of accommodation. An inside double cabin costs from €101 to €132 and exterior cabins start at €173. The best cabins are in the Commodore Class (*Salon Commodore*), which has 14 luxurious wood-panelled suites (€243 to €297) and an exclusive lounge bar overlooking the bow. For those on a budget (and insomniacs), reclining seats are available at a cost of €8.

Bookings can be made via Brittany Ferries' UK office (☎ 0870-366 5333) or Spanish office (☎ 942-360 611) or via the internet (🖳 www.brittany-ferries.co.uk or 🖳 www.brittanyferries.es). Brittany Ferries run a Property Owners' Travel Club for frequent travellers, offering savings of up to one-third off single and standard return fares.

# P&O Ferries

P&O Ferries operates a year-round, twice or three times- weekly service between Portsmouth in the UK to the Spanish port of Bilbao (the ferry port is at Santurtzi, around 13km/8mi to the north-west of the city centre). The route is served by the Pride of Bilbao, the largest cruise ferry operating out of the UK (capacity 2,500 passengers, 600 cars). The journey time is 35 hours from Portsmouth and 29 hours from Bilbao. Fares are similar to Brittany Ferries' (see above). Like Brittany Ferries, P&O offer luxury cabins with a double bed, two easy chairs, writing desk, television (TV), shower, toilet, washbasin, two large windows and room service. Bookings can be made via the UK office (☎ 0870-598 0333) or the Spanish office (☎ 902-020 461) or via the internet (🖳 www.poferries.com). P&O offers several discount schemes, including 'Homeowner Traveller' with discounts of up to 45 per cent and annual season tickets.

# Other International Ferry Services

There are hourly car ferry services from Algeciras to Tangier and Ceuta and an additional hourly service from Algeciras to Tangier in summer (when there are usually long delays when thousands of Moroccan migrant workers return home). There's also a ferry service from Gibraltar to Tangier, a year-round hydrofoil service from Tarifa to Tangier, and ferry services to Melilla from Almeria and Malaga.

# Domestic Ferries

Domestic ferry services operate from mainland ports to the main Balearic and Canary islands, supplemented by inter-island services. Services include Barcelona to Palma, Ibiza and Mahon; Dénia to Ibiza and Palma; Gandía to Ibiza and Formentera and Valencia to Palma, Ibiza and Mahon. Services operate from Cadiz on the mainland to Tenerife, Las Palmas, Lanzarote and Fuerteventura in the Canaries. Tickets should be purchased in advance, particularly in summer, but can also be bought on board, when a surcharge is payable. There are various tariffs depending on the type of seat required (couchettes are available on night trips). The fare from Barcelona to the Balearics (under four hours by high speed ferry or eight hours otherwise) is from €26.20 single (reclining seat), from €43 for a cabin and from €96.70 for a car. Tickets for high speed ferries can sometimes be twice the price. Ferries carry cars, boat-trailers, buses and trucks, and are equipped with restaurants and coffee shops, bar-lounges, TVs, discotheques and shops. **Ferries are very crowded in summer, with erratic schedules and a range of fares** (shop around for the best deal).

There are regular inter-island ferries in the Balearics and Canaries, including a fast two-hour hydrojet service between Palma de Mallorca and Ibiza, and a regular ferry service from Ibiza to Formentera. Frequent inter-island ferry services also operate in the Canaries, including a hydrofoil service between all the islands. Most domestic routes to and from the mainland and the Balearic and Canary islands are operated by Compañía Transmediterránea/TRAS) (for reservations ☎ 902-454 645, 💻 www.trasmediterranea.es). Transmediterránea offers youths and retirees aged 60 or over a 20 per cent discount outside the high season to the Canaries and Africa, and a 38 per cent discount for residents of the Balearics or Canaries (you must present proof of this when you book your ticket). Other companies running services to the Balearics include Balearia (☎ 902-160 180, 💻 www.balearia.net) and Iscomar (☎ 971-437 500, 💻 www.iscomar.com) with ferries from Denia (Costa Blanca) to Ibiza and Palma de Mallorca. In the Canaries, companies running inter-island services include Fred Olsen (☎ 902-100 107, 💻 www.fredolsen.es) and Naviera Almas (☎ 902-456 500, 💻 www.navieraalmas.com).

## Cruise Ships

A number of companies operate cruise ships calling at Spanish ports. In winter, many ships operate out of Malaga, Spain's main cruise port, and ships also call at Las Palmas and Lanzarote in the Canaries and at Gibraltar (which is also a major cruise port). The Cunard (QE2) and Caronia ships offer winter cruises of 10 to 14 days from November to March out of Malaga calling at various ports such as Barcelona, Palma de Mallorca, Cadiz and Vigo. The cost starts at around €2,500 for ten days and a 20 per cent discount is available if you book early. At the other end of the cruise range, those with **very** deep pockets may wish to take a trip on the Queen Mary 2 (QM2), promoted as the world's largest and most luxurious cruise ship, calling at Malaga a few times a year. Most cruise lines offer large discounts for early bookings on winter cruises, e.g. a general 40 per cent reduction or a 50 per cent reduction for the second person. For information contact M.B. Bland & Co Ltd, The Cruise Club, 1st Floor, Cloister Building, PO Box 554, Gibraltar (☎ 956-777 221 from Spain or +0350-77221 from abroad, 💻 www.cruiseclubeurope. com) or your local travel agent.

# AIRLINE SERVICES

Most major international airlines provide scheduled services to Madrid and many also fly to Barcelona and other Spanish cities. The Spanish national privatised airline, Iberia, is Spain's major international carrier. Although it isn't rated as one of the world's best airlines, it has an excellent safety record and its standard of service has improved considerably in recent years. Iberia's fares have become more competitive and the company has been in the black for the last few years. However, in the light of increased competition from the high-speed train network and budget airlines (whose share of the flight market rose nearly 30 per cent in 2004), Iberia needs urgently to implement cost-cutting measures. These include re-negotiating salaries, particularly pilots', and cutting non-profit flights. In common with many airlines,

Iberia has been badly hit by the rise in fuel prices, but in 2005 the company unveiled its new costly uniforms created by top designer Adolfo Domínguez, so Iberia's finances cannot be so bad! Iberia is part of the One World Alliance (🖳 www. oneworldalliance.com), which includes British Airways, American Airlines, Cathay Pacific and Qantas.

# Scheduled Flights

Iberia has good connections to North, Central and South America and throughout Europe, but doesn't offer many flights to the rest of the world apart from a few cities such as Cairo, Tel Aviv, Tokyo, and a number of countries in North and West Africa. Iberia plans to invest heavily in routes to Central and South America over the next few years. Most transatlantic flights from North America travel via Madrid. If you're unable to get a direct intercontinental flight to Spain, it's usually advisable to fly via London, from where there are daily flights to airports throughout Spain. Fares on scheduled flights to and from Spain have fallen in recent years due to increased competition, although they're still high compared to charter fares. However, if you're unable to obtain a cheap charter flight, Iberia's scheduled apex flights are good value for money and allow you to fly more or less when you want. Iberia have low (*baja*) and high (*alta*) season fares on most routes.

# Charter Flights

Cheap charter flights to Spain are common from many countries, particularly the UK, Germany and the US. Around 70 per cent of people visiting Spain from the UK do so on charter aircraft (the UK and Spain are the only countries in the world with such a high percentage of charter flights). The cheapest Spanish destinations from the UK are Malaga, Alicante and Palma de Mallorca, with return fares from around €30 in the low season rising to around €250 in the peak season (mid-June to mid-September). If you're travelling from the UK to the western Costa del Sol or the Costa de la Luz, you can also fly via Gibraltar (fares are similar to flights to Malaga). Charter flights from New York to Madrid cost from $350 scheduled or from $250 charter. It may be cheaper for North Americans and others travelling on intercontinental flights to fly to London and get a charter flight from there, particularly outside the summer high season. Return fares from Spain may be more expensive than from the UK, with typical return fares from around €150 to London and from €80 one-way to Amsterdam, Frankfurt and Paris.

It's worth shopping around for the best price. In the UK, check the advertisements in the London *Time Out* entertainment magazine and British Sunday newspapers such as the *Sunday Times* and the *Observer*. In the US, the best place to look for advertisements for inexpensive flights is the *New York Times*. In the UK, those aged under 26 qualify for discount charter flights offered by student travel agents such as Campus Travel, STA Travel and USIT. **It's also advisable to shop around local travel agents.**

The negative aspect of charter flights is that charter agents and companies can be unreliable. Some agents seem to advertise low fares as bait (they're always 'sold out') and then try to sell you a more expensive flight. It's advisable to reconfirm a flight, especially your return flight, to ensure that you have a seat and the departure time hasn't changed. Although over-booking of charter flights is now illegal in Europe, mistakes can still be made.

As a general rule, the further in advance you buy your ticket, the cheaper it is (and the greater the penalty for cancelling), although late bookings can also be good value. The main disadvantage of charter flights is that they usually have fixed return dates and a maximum of four weeks between the outward and return flights. Most charter flights restrict stays to 7, 14, 21 or 28 days, although you can always throw away the return ticket (it may still be cheaper than a single fare on a scheduled flight). **It's advisable to take out insurance against missing your flight, as there are no refunds for charter flights.** Note that charter tickets aren't transferable and it's illegal to use a ticket issued in someone else's name. Tickets are checked against passports and if the names don't match you're refused boarding (and you can be prosecuted).

## Domestic Flights

There are a number of airlines offering domestic services in Spain, including Iberia (☎ 902-400 500, 🖳 www.iberia.com), Air Europa (☎ 902-410 501, 🖳 www.air-europa.com), Spanair (☎ 902-131 415, 🖳 www.spanair.com) and various small airlines such as Binter Canarias (☎ 928-579 601, 🖳 www.bintercanarias.es) and Air Nostrum (☎ 902-400 500, 🖳 www.airnostrum.es) – both subsidiaries of Iberia. Air Europa and Spanair cover most of the same routes as Iberia and are generally cheaper. Single flights are available to most domestic destinations from €60 (from €90 to the Canaries) and cheaper night (*nocturno*) flights are available to some cities. Youth fares are also available at large discounts. Flights to the Balearics from the mainland are only slightly more expensive than ferries (see page 209), although you must usually book well in advance during the summer season. Residents in the Balearics or Canaries are entitled to discounts of 33 per cent on flights between the islands and the mainland.

Many domestic flights are routed via Madrid or Barcelona, so it can be difficult to get a direct flight between regional cities. There are frequent flights between Spain's international airports and regional airports, with Iberia operating flights from Barcelona and Madrid to around 20 domestic airports. There's a half-hourly or hourly 'air bridge' (*puente aéreo*) shuttle service between Barcelona and Madrid, which carries over two million passengers a year. Tickets for Iberia domestic flights can be purchased from machines at airports (using a credit card). Private aircraft and helicopters can be rented from most Spanish airports to almost anywhere in Spain.

## Fares

When buying a ticket in Spain for an international or domestic flight, it pays to shop around for the best deal. Whatever your destination, it's advisable to consult a travel agent, who can explain the various options and may be able to offer a range of inexpensive flights. In addition to first, business and tourist class tickets, airlines offer a variety of discount fares, including superpex, apex, superapex, weekend returns, youth and senior citizens (Iberia tourist class tickets are available at a 25 per cent discount for those aged over 65), students, families, children and groups. Scheduled airlines usually offer child discounts whilst charter airlines offer none. **Note that scheduled flights booked at short notice can considerably increase the fare, irrespective of the availability of seats.** Special offers for frequent fliers are provided by Iberia ('Iberia Plus') and most international airlines. Bear in mind, that although cheap fares are widely advertised in Spain, they're often unavailable on the dates when you want to fly and you may be offered much more expensive flights.

Iberia are rarely the cheapest, but offer competitive special offers and promotional flights. These include 'open-jaw' flights that allow you to fly into one airport and out of another; minifares (*tarifas-minis*) offering savings of up to 60 per cent on certain domestic flights.

If you're planning to go abroad during school holidays, book **well** in advance, especially if you're going to a popular destination such as London, Paris or New York.

# Airports

Spain's busiest airport with around 34 million passengers a year is Madrid's Barajas airport (*aeropuerto de Barajas*). Barajas is Spain's main airport for intercontinental flights and is also served by direct flights from most European and North and South American cities. Madrid is the hub of Spanish domestic flights and typical flight times are: Barcelona (55 minutes), Bilbao (50 minutes), Seville (50 minutes), Valencia (30 minutes), Palma de Mallorca (one hour) and the Canary Islands (2 hours 30 minutes). Barcelona's airport is Spain's second busiest airport with around 21 million passengers a year. Palma de Mallorca airport handles around 19 million passengers a year (mainly summer charter flights) and Malaga over ten million a year.

International flights are available from many of Spain's 'regional' airports, including Alicante, Almeria, Asturias, Bilbao, Fuenteventura, Gerona (Costa Brava), Granada, Gran Canaria, Ibiza, Jerez de la Frontera (Costa de la Luz), La Coruña, Lanzarote, Las Palmas, Malaga, Melilla, Menorca, Murcia, Palma de Mallorca, Reus (Tarragona), San Sebastián, Santander, Santiago de Compostela, Seville, Tenerife, Valencia, Vigo, Vitoria and Zaragossa. Other domestic airports include Ampurias (Gerona), Asturias, Badajoz, Burgos, Cáceres, Cordoba, Logroño, Mahón (Menorca), Puigcerdá, Pamplona, Salamanca, Seu d'Urgell and Valladolid.

Madrid's Barajas airport is located 15km (9.3mi) outside the city on the A-2 and is one of Europe's five major airports and has recently undergone extensive modernisation, including the building of a second runway. A new terminal has recently been finished and is expected to open in early 2006, increasing the airport's capacity to some 70 million passengers a year. It has separate international and domestic terminals. There are various ways of getting to Madrid city centre: by bus running every 10 to 18 minutes from around 5am to around midnight to the Avenida de América costing around €1.30; *metro* to Nuevos Ministerios station (where check-in facilities are available) open from 6am to 2am, costing €1.15; taxi costing at least €20 and AeroCity's 24-hour airport shuttle services to anywhere in Madrid (€15 to the centre). AeroCity also offers the useful option of advance booking by phone or internet (☎ 917-477 570, 🖳 www.aerocity.com). Flight information is available from ☎ 913-058 436.

Barcelona's airport (*El Prat de Llobregat*), located 14km (9mi) from the city centre, is one of the finest airports in the world and currently under expansion. The fastest and cheapest way to the city is by RENFE train, costing €2.30 and services run from 5.45am to 11.30pm. There's also a special bus service (*aerobús*) running every 11 to 15 minutes from 6am to midnight and costing €3.60. A taxi to the city centre costs from €15. A telephone number for flight information is available (☎ 932-983 838).

Many Spanish airports have been expanded and modernised in recent years, including Barcelona, Malaga and Seville, although you should expect delays at major airports during the summer season (the worst airports for delays in summer include Alicante, Malaga, Palma, Ibiza and Mahon, particularly at weekends). Always carefully check your luggage on collection and report any damage immediately. Most airports have sufficient luggage trolleys, although you usually need a €1 coin to use one (although £1 coins also fit trolleys), and porters (who charge an official rate per piece of luggage) are also usually available to carry bags. All major Spanish airports have duty-free shops, although some are open only during the main tourist season. **Note that it's usually cheaper to buy alcohol in a local off-licence or supermarket.** There's no airport departure tax in Spain. Secure 24-hour parking is provided at most Spanish airports, where parking fees are usually reasonable, e.g. from €8 a day, with discounts for two weeks or longer. There are also parking areas near to airports, but not within the grounds, which cost from around €3 a day. Information about all airports in Spain, including flight arrivals and departures in English and Spanish is available from AENA (🖳 www. aena.es – go to '*elija aeropuerto*' or 'choose airport' on the left and scroll down to the airport you're looking for).

# Holiday & Visitors' Passes

Two holiday passes for air travel are offered by Iberia and are for non-residents only. If you buy a return international ticket with Iberia, you're entitled to purchase an *Iberiabono España*, which includes a minimum of two coupons valid for domestic flights in Spain. Coupons for flights within mainland Spain cost from €62 and from €125 for flights, including the Balearics and Canaries. The pass must be purchased a minimum of five days before your arrival in Spain and some flights have restrictions, e.g. they must be booked in advance or are available only on certain days of the week. Iberia also offers an *Iberiabono Europa* for non-residents arriving in Spain from North or South America, Senegal or South Africa. This pass allows the purchase of at least two coupons (from $125 each, $210 for Cairo and Tel Aviv) valid for flights to around 25 European cities. The pass must be purchased a minimum of five days before your arrival in Spain and you must be in possession of a return ticket. Information regarding the *Iberiabono España* and *Iberiabono Europa* is available on Iberia's American website (🖳 www.iberia.com) under 'Products & Services' or from travel agents in Canada and the US.

There are a variety of train tickets for visitors to Spain and Spanish residents travelling by train in Europe. A wide range of rail passes are also available, some of which are sold only in certain countries, e.g. Canada and the US, or to non-residents of Europe. Passes include a Eurodomino, Spain FlexiPass and Iberic Rail Pass. A range of Eurail passes, allowing travel in 17 countries and valid for 15, 25, 30, 60 or 90 days, are available for those with their permanent residence outside Europe, including the Eurail Pass, the Eurail Flexipass, Eurail Youthpass (under 26), the Eurail Saverpass and the Eurail Flexi Saverpass. The Inter-rail Pass is valid for 12 or 22 days for the first zone of travel and for one month for further zones. It allows unrestricted, second-class travel by train in 27 European countries, including the UK, Ireland and Morocco, and discounts of up to 50 per cent in the country where it's purchased. The Inter-rail pass is better value than Eurail passes and is available to those with their permanent residence in Europe (but must be purchased in your country of permanent residence). Comprehensive information about Inter-rail is available on ⌨ www.interrailnet.com.

Inter-rail and Eurail passes are valid on all RENFE trains, although supplements are payable. For example, you must pay €9.50 extra to travel on a *Talgo* or *AVE* (unless you're resident in Spain) and sometimes on *expreso* and *rápido* trains or on rail bus services. Surcharges seem to be random and may depend on individual conductors. It's advisable to reserve a ticket in advance, in return for which you receive a computer-printed ticket that usually satisfies conductors. Note that international rail passes aren't valid on Spain's private railway lines, such as those operated by Ferrocarriles de Via Estrecha (FEVE). Free Eurail/Inter-rail timetables and a wide range of brochures and maps are available from offices selling passes.

A Eurodomino pass allows unlimited first or second class travel for three, four, five, six, seven or eight consecutive days' travel on trains within Europe, Algeria, Morocco and Tunisia. **Spanish residents cannot use Eurodomino for travel in Spain.** Prices start at €113 for three days in second class. Travellers who aren't resident in Europe can buy the Spain FlexiPass or the Iberic Rail Pass, which allow unlimited travel within Spain or within Spain and Portugal (Iberic Rail Pass) for between three and ten days. The Spain FlexiPass costs from $175 to $385 in second class accommodation (first class is also available) and the Iberic Rail Pass costs from $334 to $660, first class only. Both passes also offer discounts on Trasmediterránea ferry crossings, car hire and Tryp hotels. You can buy the passes at authorised travel agents abroad or at main line RENFE stations. Further information is available on the RENFE website (⌨ www.renfe.es) under *Viajes internacionales*.

An excellent book for European travellers is *Europe by Train* by Katie Wood (Robson Books). It covers accommodation, visas, food, sights, customs and even the idiosyncrasies of local transport. *Europe by Eurail* by Laverne Ferguson (Globe Pequot Press) provides tips on planning a European tour using a Eurail pass and other passes, making day trips from selected base cities. The European Rail Guide website also provides comprehensive information (⌨ www.europeanrailguide. com). Thomas Cook publish a wide range of books, guides and maps for train travellers. These include a *European Timetable*, which is much more than a collection of train times and contains information on shipping services, customs regulations, visa requirements and town plans. Thomas Cook Publications publish a number of other useful maps and timetables for European and world travellers, including a *Rail Map of Europe* and the *European Timetable* (rail and ferry schedules in Europe). All publications are available direct from Thomas Cook Publishing, PO Box 227, Peterborough PE3 8SB, UK (☎ 01733-416177, 💻 www.thomascookpublishing.com).

# 11.

# MOTORING

Motoring in Spain has altered dramatically in the last few decades, during which the number of cars has vastly increased and roads have been improved beyond recognition. The traffic on Spanish roads doubled between 1980 and 1990 and in the five years alone from 1995 to 2000 increased by 27 per cent (heavy goods traffic by some 37 per cent) and there are around 26 million cars on the roads. Not only have new roads and bypasses been built, but existing roads have also been widened, lanes added for heavy traffic, and signs and road markings improved. The road-building programme (and provision of parking spaces) has, however, failed to keep pace with the increasing number of cars and consequently, Spain's roads are rapidly becoming saturated in many regions.

Driving long distances is usually cheaper than using public transport, particularly when the costs are shared between a number of people and you avoid motorways. In any case, unless you're travelling between major cities, you will have little choice but to drive, as public transport is generally poor in rural areas. If you're travelling long distances, you will, however, find it quicker and certainly less stressful to take the train or fly. Those travelling to Spain from the UK may prefer to take the ferry (see page 209) to northern Spain rather than drive through France.

Driving can be enjoyable in rural areas, particularly outside the tourist season, when it's possible to drive for miles without seeing another motorist (or a caravan). If you live in a city, particularly Madrid or Barcelona (where public transport services are excellent), a car is a liability and driving is a nightmare to be avoided if at all possible. A recent nationwide survey found that on an average working day it takes eight minutes to travel one kilometre in a large city. As a result of the *siesta*, Spain has four rush hours (*horas puntas*): 8 to 9.30am, 12.30 to 2.30pm, 3.30 to 5pm and 6.30 to 8.30pm; the quietest period is usually between 3 and 5pm. Traffic jams (*atascos*) are particularly bad in cities such as Madrid and Barcelona, where the rush 'hour' lasts all day. Madrid, where the survey found the average traffic speed was below 10kph (6mph), is to be avoided at any time!

Jams are also common on coastal roads and in resort towns during summer and on roads heading south out of Madrid and Barcelona, particularly at the start and end of holiday periods, when some 12 million Spaniards and foreigners take to the roads.

Anyone who has driven in Spain won't be surprised to learn that it has the worst accident record in the European Union (EU) with 28 deaths per 10,000 cars per kilometre (the EU average is 13). Spain's shocking accident statistics show over 3,500 deaths in 2004 (over half of the victims were not wearing a seat belt), although this figure is down 13 per cent on 2003. The government has made reducing the number of car accident victims one of its top priorities and to this end have introduced a licence points system (see page 227) and greater police vigilance on the roads. However, Spain still has a long way to go before traffic accidents cease to be the largest cause of death among young Spaniards.

Eccentric and impatient drivers, *machismo*, compulsive speeders (including speeds at over 180kph), drunk (around 40 per cent of drivers in fatal accidents are over the alcohol limit) and drugged motorists and pedestrians, blazing hot weather, stray animals, vehicles without lights, badly maintained and marked roads, and sharp bends without crash barriers, all contribute to the hazards of driving in Spain. **The most important thing to bear in mind when driving in Spain is to drive defensively and always expect the unexpected from other road users.**

# CAR INSURANCE

All motor vehicles and trailers must be insured when entering Spain, and you can be fined between €600 and €3,000 for failing to have proper insurance. It isn't mandatory for cars insured in most European countries to have an international insurance 'green' card (see below) and motorists insured in an EU country, Hungary, Liechtenstein, Norway and Switzerland are automatically covered for third-party liability in Spain.

There are an estimated 2 million drivers without insurance in Spain, where there's also more insurance fraud than in any other EU country. Note, however, that driving without obligatory insurance (*seguro obligatorio*) is a serious offence, for which you can be fined up to €3,000 or even imprisoned. You must carry your insurance documents when driving and can be fined €60 for not having them if you're stopped by the police. See also **Insurance Contracts** on page 287.

Car insurance is available from many Spanish insurance companies and a number of foreign insurance companies in Spain, including direct insurance companies (who don't use agents). Always shop around and obtain a number of quotations. **When choosing a company, bear in mind that a number of Spanish car insurance companies have gone bust in recent years, leaving tens of thousands of motorists blissfully unaware that they no longer had any insurance!**

See also **Breakdown Insurance** on page 260.

## Green Cards

All Spanish and most insurance companies in Western Europe provide an automatic 'green' card (*certificado internacional de seguro de autómovil*), which extends your normal insurance cover (e.g. comprehensive) to other European countries. This doesn't include cars insured in the UK, however, where insurance companies usually provide a green card for limited periods only (e.g. 30 or 45 days) and for a maximum number of days per year, e.g. 90. However, you should shop around, as some companies allow drivers a green card for up to six months a year. Green cards are also expensive. Nevertheless, if you're British and have comprehensive insurance, it's wise to have a green card when visiting Spain.

If you drive a British-registered car and spend over six months a year on the continent, you may need to take out a special (i.e. expensive) European insurance policy or obtain insurance with a European company. Another alternative is to insure with a British insurance company in Spain. Note that EU rules require all vehicles to be insured in their country of registration. For example, if you keep a British-registered car in Spain, you can insure it through the Spanish branch of a British-based insurance company, but you **cannot** insure it with a Spanish insurance company. Similarly, if you have a Spanish-registered car, it must be insured with a Spanish insurance company (or a foreign insurance company with an office in Spain).

## Types of Insurance

The following categories of car insurance are available in Spain:

## Third-party

Third-party insurance (*responsabilidad civil obligatoria* or *seguro obligatorio*) is the minimum required by law. It costs from around €300 a year to insure against the minimum third-party claims (€360,000 for personal injury and €100,000 for damage to third-party property). You should make sure that you fully understand the cover provided for the driver and passengers and that it meets your needs. You can choose to pay an extra premium for additional cover up to a specified or unlimited amount (*ilimitada*), which is highly recommended. Unlimited third-party cover usually costs around €35 extra per year. Note that a driver and his family don't count as third parties and must be insured separately (see **Driver & Passenger Insurance** below).

Roadside assistance (*asistencia en viajes*), glass breakage (*rotura de lunas*) and legal expenses (*defensa penal*) in the event of a court case may be included in basic third-party cover or can be added for an additional premium.

## Third-party, Fire & Theft

Third-party, fire and theft insurance (*responsabilidad civil obligatoria, incendio y robo*), known in some countries as 'part comprehensive', includes cover against fire (*incendio*), natural hazards (e.g. rocks falling on your car), theft (*robo*), broken glass (e.g. windscreen), legal expenses (*defensa penal*), and possibly damage or theft of contents (although this is rare). Insurance against the theft of a stereo system is usually available only from the manufacturer (it may be included in the purchase price). You may be able to take out fire cover independently, although it's usually combined with theft cover.

## Comprehensive

Comprehensive (sometimes called 'fully comprehensive') insurance, known in Spain as 'all risks' (*todo riesgo*), covers all the risks listed under third-party, fire and theft (above) plus all other types of damage to your vehicle irrespective of how it's caused. **Note that some insurance companies don't provide comprehensive cover for vehicles more than two or three years old (although it's possible to get comprehensive cover on vehicles up to ten years old).** Comprehensive insurance may be compulsory for lease and credit purchase contracts. Note that Spanish insurance doesn't usually pay for a replacement car when your car is being repaired after an accident.

## Driver & Passenger Insurance

Driver and passenger insurance (*seguro de ocupantes*) is usually optional and can be added to insurance policies. Driver protection allows the driver of a vehicle involved in an accident to claim for bodily injury to himself, including compensation for his incapacity to work or for his beneficiaries should he be killed. There are usually various levels of driver and passenger accident insurance, e.g. from €5,000 to €25,000 for death and permanent disability.

### Special Insurance

Special insurance can be purchased for contents and accessories such as an expensive car stereo system.

# Premiums

Insurance premiums in Spain are among the lowest in the EU, although they vary considerably according to numerous factors, including the following:

- The type of insurance (see above).

- The type of car and its use. Cars are divided into eight categories, based on their performance (some companies don't insure high-performance vehicles), the cost of repairs, where and how much they're used (some premiums are based on the number of kilometres driven each year), whether they're garaged, and whether they're used for business or pleasure.

- Your age and accident record. Drivers with less than two or three years experience usually pay a 'penalty' (*multa*) and drivers under a certain age, e.g. 25, also pay higher premiums. Some insurance companies refuse to insure drivers under 25. Drivers aged over 70 may also pay a penalty, although some companies offer low-cost policies for experienced older drivers, e.g. those over 50 or 55, with a good record. Other companies give discounts of 10 to 20 per cent for experienced drivers of any age.

- The area where you live. Premiums are highest in Madrid and other major cities and lowest in rural areas.

- Whether the car is garaged. Some insurance companies give an additional discount (e.g. 5 per cent) if a vehicle is garaged overnight.

Premiums vary from around €350 a year for third-party insurance for a small family saloon to €1,500 or more a year for comprehensive insurance for a high-performance sports saloon. Short-term policies (for periods of less than a year) are available from some companies, although premiums are high, e.g. 50 per cent of the annual rate for three months and 70 per cent of the annual rate for six months. Value added tax (VAT/*IVA*) at 16 per cent is payable on insurance premiums. You can reduce your premium by choosing to pay an excess (*franquicia*), e.g. the first €150, €180, €300, €450 or €600 of a claim.

If you're convicted of drunk or dangerous driving, your premium will be increased considerably. In fact, if you're convicted of drunk driving, your insurance company will probably refuse to pay on a claim!

Insurance companies must give two months' notice of an increase in premiums.

# No-claims Bonus

A foreign no-claims bonus (*bonificación/sistema bonus-malus*) is usually valid, provided you've had insurance within the last two years, but you must provide written evidence from your present or previous insurance company, not just an insurance renewal notice. You may need an official Spanish translation. **Always insist on having your no-claims bonus recognised, even if you don't receive the same percentage reduction as you received abroad (shop around).**

Most companies offer a 5 per cent discount for each year of no claims up to a maximum discount of 60 per cent, although some offer a maximum of only 50 per cent (or less). Foreign insurance companies may offer a more generous no-claims bonus than Spanish companies.

If you have an accident, you're usually required to pay a penalty (*multa*) or your bonus is reduced, e.g. one accident may lose you two years' no-claims bonus. You can usually pay an extra premium to protect your no-claims bonus. No-claims bonuses usually also apply to a second family car.

# Claims

In the event of an accident, claims are decided on the information provided in accident report forms (*declaración de siniestro de automóvil*) completed by drivers, reports by insurance company experts and police reports (see also **Accidents** on page 255). You must notify your insurance company of a claim within a limited period, e.g. two to five days. Some companies have 24-hour helplines for claims, in Spain and abroad. If you have an accident, the damage must usually be inspected and the repair authorised by your insurance company's assessor, although sometimes an independent assessor's report may be permitted. An inspection may be unnecessary for minor repairs. Note that when a vehicle is a write-off, a Spanish insurance company may pay only a percentage of its 'book' value, which is less than its actual value.

If your car is stolen, you must report it to the local police immediately and submit a copy of the police report with your claim. After reporting your car stolen, 30 days must elapse before an insurance company considers a claim.

There's little communication or co-operation between insurance companies in Spain and trying to recover uninsured losses is a nightmare.

# Cancellation

Spanish insurance companies are forbidden by law to cancel third-party cover after a claim, except in the case of drunk driving or when a driver is subsequently disqualified from driving. A company can, however, refuse to renew your policy at the end of the current period, although they must give you 15 days' notice. Note also that, if you have an accident while breaking the law, e.g. drunk driving or illegal parking, comprehensive insurance may be automatically downgraded to third-party, which means that you must pay for your own repairs and medical expenses.

If you wish to cancel your car insurance at the end of the current term, you must notify your insurance company in writing by registered letter and usually give two months' notice. You may cancel your insurance before the term has expired if the premium is increased, the terms are altered, or your car has been declared a write-off or stolen. If you cancel your policy during the term of the insurance, e.g. you sell your car, and don't take out another policy, your insurance company isn't required to give you a refund.

# DRIVING LICENCES

The minimum ages for driving in Spain are 14 for a motorcycle (moped) up to 50cc, 16 for a motorcycle up to 125cc and 18 for a motorcycle with an engine capacity over 125cc or for a car. There's also a maximum age of 65 for obtaining your first licence, although this doesn't apply to foreigners aged over 65, who can exchange a valid foreign licence for a Spanish licence (*permiso de conducción*).

Many foreign driving licences are recognised in Spain under reciprocal agreements, including all EU licences and some US state licences, in which case you can drive on the licence of your home country and aren't required to obtain a Spanish driving licence. Nevertheless, you must take your existing licence to your local provincial traffic department to be stamped and registered. You must also undergo the same medical exams and eye tests as holders of Spanish licences (see below). **Note, however, that the above rule isn't always known or recognised by the local police, and there have been cases of EU nationals resident in Spain driving Spanish-registered vehicles and being fined for not having a Spanish licence.** For this reason, many people find it's simpler to exchange their foreign licence for a Spanish one!

Holders of licences issued by countries without a reciprocal agreement with Spain must take a Spanish written and/or practical driving test. Previously the written test could be taken in English and other foreign languages, but recent legislation has ruled that the written test must be taken in Spanish. If in doubt, consult a Spanish consulate abroad or your country's embassy or consulate in Spain. All non-resident non-EU licence holders must obtain a Spanish driving licence and are entitled to drive in Spain for a maximum of six months in a calendar year.

To apply for a Spanish licence, you must produce the following documents:

- An international driving permit (IDP), as well as the licence from your home country.

- An official translation of your licence, which can be obtained from a Spanish consulate.

- A certificate of equivalence (*certificado de equivalencia*) issued by the Spanish RAC (RACE – see page 261).

An international driving permit is obtainable in Spain from the Royal Automobile Club of Spain (Real Automóvil Club de España/RACE) on presentation of a valid foreign driving licence, a passport and two photographs. Note, however, that if a non-resident obtains an international driving licence in Spain, it's valid only for driving **outside** Spain.

As from 2004, a Spanish driving licence is a plastic-coated card, the same size as a credit card, with personal information (including a photograph) printed on one side and driving information on the other. The card is similar to those issued in many EU countries such as Germany, Sweden and the UK. The old-style licence is gradually being replaced by the new one when licence holders renew their licence.

You must carry your foreign or Spanish driving licence at all times when driving in Spain (see **Traffic Police** on page 252).

# Validity

The validity period of a Spanish licence depends on your age and the type of licence held, e.g. a motorcycle (A-1/A-2) or car (B-1) licence is valid for ten years if you're under 45 and for five years if you're between 45 and 70. A driver aged over 70 must renew his licence every two years. A commercial, passenger vehicle or heavy goods licence must be renewed every five years up to the age of 45, every three years from 46 to 60 and every two years from 61 to 70.

# Points System

In an attempt to reduce the high accident and mortality rate on Spain's roads, the government has introduced a points system, similar to that used in France, Germany and Italy. The scheme, widely acclaimed by motoring associations and insurance companies, becomes law in late 2005.

Under the system, most drivers receive an initial 'score' of 12 points on their driving licence. Drivers with under 30 months' driving experience or who have committed a serious driving offence within the previous three years receive eight points. When a driver commits an offence, a number of points are deducted from the licence depending on the seriousness of the offence, as in the following examples:

- **Six point deduction** – Drunk driving; speeding at 50 per cent over the limit and over 30kph; dangerous driving.

- **Four point deduction** – Speeding at more than 40kph over the limit; jumping a 'give way', 'stop' sign or a red light.

- **Three point deduction** – Failure to maintain a safe distance between the vehicle in front; driving without lights in poor visibility conditions; using a mobile phone or headphones while driving.

- **Two point deduction** – Stopping on bends or tunnels; not wearing a seatbelt.

Drivers who lose all their designated points automatically lose their licence. To regain their licence, drivers must retake the driving test and take a driving course of around 30 hours. These tests cannot be taken until at least six months after the last driving offence. Those who have lost points, but still have credit on their driving licence regain their points two or three years after their last offence. Professional drivers such as taxi and lorry drivers have a different system.

# Applications

To apply for a Spanish driving licence you require the following:

- A completed application form, TASA 2.3 (*Solicitud de Carnet del Permiso de Conducir*), available from the *información-impresos* counter at the local provincial traffic department.
- Your Spanish residence permit (*residencia*) and a photocopy.
- Your current foreign driving licence and a photocopy.

- The registration number of a Spanish registered vehicle or a sworn statement that you don't own a vehicle with Spanish registration.
- One passport-sized photograph. (Non-EU citizens require three passport-sized photographs, one of which must be signed on the back by the doctor performing the medical examination – see below.)
- The fee of €17 (the same price for the replacement of a lost or damaged licence) payable at the traffic department.

Holders of non-EU driving licences also require an official translation of their licence and a certificate of equivalence (*certificado de equivalencia*) available from the Royal Automobile Club of Spain (see **Motoring Organisations** on page 261), a medical certificate of fitness to drive (see below) and a stamped self-addressed envelope.

You can use a *gestor* (see page 461) to obtain a Spanish driving licence or apply through a Spanish motoring organisation such as the Royal Automobile Club of Spain. A *gestor* will charge you €30 to €60 for the work involved.

It usually takes between one and three months to obtain a Spanish licence. You're given an official receipt for your application and a copy of your foreign licence, which is valid until you receive your Spanish licence. When you receive your Spanish licence, your foreign licence is returned to the issuing authority abroad. If you change your address, you must apply to have the address on your licence changed (there's no fee).

## Renewals

To renew a Spanish driving licence you require the following:

- A completed application form (see above).
- Your current licence.
- Your residence permit and a photocopy.
- A medical certificate (see below).
- Two or more passport-sized photographs.
- The fee of €17 payable at the traffic department (no fee for the over 70s).

If someone other than the licence owner makes the application, he must provide written authorisation from the owner and supply his own residence card and copy.

## Medical Certificate

Holders of non-EU driving licences require a medical certificate to obtain a Spanish driving licence. The medical examination is carried out in designated clinics (*centros de reconocimento médico para conductores*), which are open from 10am to 2pm and from 4 to 8pm Mondays to Fridays. The examination includes eyesight, hearing, pulse and blood pressure tests, and tests for speed of reaction, judgement of the speed of other vehicles and acuteness of visual identification. If you wear glasses or contact lenses, you're tested with them and your licence with be annotated to indicate this (note also that you must carry a spare pair when driving). The examination takes around half an hour and costs around €30. The medical certificate is valid for 90 days, during which time you must make your application for a licence (or a renewal). **Three passport-sized photographs are required.**

# IMPORTING A CAR

Anyone wishing to import a vehicle into Spain must be a permanent resident, own property in Spain or have a rental agreement for a minimum of a year and hold a Spanish driving licence. The regulations and paperwork regarding car importation are now comparatively simple, but many people still find the red tape forbidding and employ a *gestor* (see page 461) to do the paperwork for them. The procedure for the importation of a caravan or motorcycle with an engine capacity over 49cc is the same as for a car, although mopeds with engines below 49cc can be freely imported as part of your personal possessions and require no special paperwork.

After you've completed the importation procedure (outlined below), you mustn't drive your car until your local provincial traffic department has issued temporary (green) registration plates (see page 235). These are valid for a limited period (usually ten days) and allow you to drive to the nearest testing station for an *inspección técnica de vehículos* (*ITV*) test (see page 237), which must be passed before you receive a permanent registration number (see **Registration** on page 235).

**Anyone who illegally drives a vehicle on foreign plates can be fined up to €3,000 and the vehicle can be confiscated.**

The exact paperwork required depends on whether the car you wish to import is new or second-hand and from the EU or outside the EU. Personal documentation for the importer includes proof of residence in Spain (residence card or personal identification from your country of origin plus a certificate from the local police in Spain stating that you live in the locality), proof of owning or renting a property (the rental contract must be for a minimum of one year) and your Spanish driving licence. Documentation for the vehicle includes the technical inspection certificate (see page 237); the completed form for vehicle registration (*Certificado Unico para la Matrícula de Vehículos*) available from your local provincial traffic department; the invoice for the purchase of the car if you've bought it within the last six months; proof of payment of road tax (*impuesto municipal sobre vehículos de tracción mecánica*/IVTM – see page 242); and proof of payment of the appropriate taxes (see **Taxes** below). Cars imported from outside the EU may need to undergo the homologation process as well (see below). A vehicle imported tax and duty-free into Spain mustn't be sold, rented or transferred within one year of its registration.

Details for the exact paperwork and documentation required can be found on the Department of Traffic's website (🖳 www.dgt.es – go to *Vehículos*), where you can also download forms.

## Homologation

Homologation (*homologación*) is the procedure whereby vehicles are made to comply with certain safety and other requirements before they can be registered. A vehicle imported from a country outside the EU must undergo homologation and must be certified by the manufacturer or an officially recognised laboratory and undergo a test before it can be registered in Spain. This costs between €120 and €400, depending on the make of car. It's a long and complicated process and the information demanded by the local authorities often varies with the province or region of Spain.

## Taxes

The following taxes and duty must be paid when importing a vehicle into Spain:

- VAT (*IVA*) at 16 per cent on cars imported from outside the EU or on a tax-free car (on which VAT hasn't previously been paid) imported from an EU country.

- A registration tax (*impuesto sobre circulación de vehículos*) of 12 per cent (11 per cent in the Canaries) on petrol-engined vehicles with a capacity of over 1,600cc and diesel-engined vehicles over 2,000cc, and of 7 per cent (6 per cent in the Canaries) on vehicles with smaller engines. The tax also applies to four-wheel drive vehicles, which were previously taxed at a lower rate. However, residents coming to live permanently in Spain and importing a car on which they've previously paid VAT and which they've owned for at least six months are exempt. An application for exemption must be made within a month of the date of issue of your residence permit, and you must present a certificate of non-residence (*certificado de baja de residencia*) from the country you're leaving.

- Import duty of 10 per cent on vehicles imported from outside the EU unless you're a resident (see above).

Each of the above tax rates is applied to the original price of the vehicle, with a reduction for each year of its age up to ten years, e.g. 20 per cent after the first year, 30 per cent after two years, 50 per cent after four years, and 80 per cent after ten years.

## Driving a Car on Foreign Registration Plates

### Residents

A Spanish resident isn't permitted to operate a car on foreign registration plates. Vehicles registered outside the EU cannot generally be operated in Spain or any other EU country by EU residents, although there are a few exceptions. The importation of right-hand drive (RHD) cars was prohibited in 1991, but this was subsequently reversed (after protests from British residents to the European Commission!). However, only new residents importing an RHD car may register it in Spain; residents aren't permitted to purchase an RHD vehicle abroad and register it in Spain.

### Non-residents

The regulations for non-residents depend on whether you're an EU national:

- **EU Citizens** – Non-residents of Spain resident in another EU country can bring a vehicle registered in another EU country to Spain and can use it (for up to 182 days per year) without paying Spanish taxes. The vehicle must be legal in its country of registration, meaning that it must be inspected (for roadworthiness) as appropriate and taxed there.

- **Non-EU Citizens** – A person resident outside the EU may temporarily import a vehicle registered outside the EU for a total period of six months (which needn't be continuous) within a calendar year. In certain circumstances, the six-month period can be extended. This applies, for example, to those regularly crossing into EU territory to work, full-time students from outside the EU, and people from outside the EU on a special mission for a specified period. The vehicle can be used only by the owner, his spouse, parents and children (who must also be non-residents). Note, however, that it's necessary for non-EU citizens to have a foreign-registered vehicle 'sealed' (*precintado*) by customs during periods of absence from Spain.

# BUYING A CAR

New cars are more expensive in Spain than in some other EU countries (although cheaper than in the UK) and up to double the cost of cars in the US. This also results in higher used car prices. However, although cars may be more expensive to buy, they depreciate more slowly than in most other European countries, so the extra you pay when buying a car is usually gained when you sell it. Spanish-made cars are generally cheaper than imported cars, due to import taxes and duty. If you do high mileage, it may be worth considering buying a diesel car, as diesel fuel costs marginally less than petrol in Spain (it's also cheaper in most other EU countries).

Cars may be bought in Spain by residents or by non-residents owning a property in Spain, renting a property for a minimum of a year or registered as an inhabitant of their municipality (*empadronado*).

## New Cars

A record number of cars (1.52 million) were sold in 2004 and sales in 2005 are expected to be even higher. Many new cars are manufactured in Spain, which is the world's seventh largest car manufacturer and around 80 per cent of new cars are exported to the European market. New cars are more expensive than in many other European countries owing to taxes, which include the registration tax (*impuesto sobre la circulación*) of up to 12 per cent and VAT (*IVA*) at 16 per cent. Most new cars are sold at list price, although you should still shop around for the best deal, as dealers compete in offering discounts, guarantees, financing terms and special deals. To boost new car sales and reduce the number of old cars on Spanish roads (more than a third are over ten years old), anyone who has owned a car over ten years old for more than a year is given a registration tax discount of €600 when buying a new car. The new vehicle must be purchased within six months of scrapping the old vehicle.

Residents can buy cars on a hire purchase agreement (instalment plan), although those who aren't property owners must usually provide a financial guarantee or obtain a guarantor. You also need a certificate from your Spanish bank stating that you pay your bills regularly, a copy of your employment contract and a copy of your previous year's tax return. The deposit (down payment) varies with the dealer and payments can be spread over one to four years. After making the deposit, you're asked to sign a number of 'bills of exchange' (*letras de cambio*), usually one for each monthly instalment due (a reassuringly antiquated system!). These are like cheques or individual direct debit advices and are addressed directly to your bank for payment. Most car dealers also sell car insurance, although you should shop around, as you will probably get a better deal elsewhere.

It's possible to buy a new car VAT-free in another EU country, e.g. from the factory of a European manufacturer or from an exporter in countries such as Belgium, Denmark (usually the cheapest due to high local taxes), Greece and the Netherlands, and personally import it into Spain. In some countries (e.g. the UK) you can buy a VAT-free car up to six months before exporting it. Personally importing any car from the US is usually much cheaper than buying the same car in Spain or elsewhere in Europe. However, before importing a car from outside the EU, you should ensure that it's manufactured to Spanish specifications, or you will encounter problems getting it through the homologation inspection (see page 230). There's no longer any import duty on cars imported from other EU countries, although you must pay Spain's registration tax (*impuesto sobre la circulación*) and 16 per cent VAT (if VAT hasn't already been paid in another EU country).

# Used Cars

Used or second-hand (*de segunda mano/de ocasión*) cars in Spain are more expensive than in many other EU countries, as new cars are more expensive and cars hold their value better. It often pays to buy a used car that's around two years old, as depreciation in the first one or two years is considerable (high mileage cars, particularly ex-rental cars, are good value). Note, however, that older cars in Spain (outside their warranty period) aren't always well maintained.

Used car dealers have the same dreadful (and usually well deserved) reputation in Spain as in other countries, and caution must be taken when buying from them. There are many 'cowboys' in Spain (often foreigners) selling worthless wrecks (the small advertisements in the expatriate press are full of them) and it's generally better to buy from a reputable dealer, even if you pay a bit more, and obtain a warranty.

There are various motoring journals advertising used cars, including *Auto Semanal* and *Coche Actual* (weekly – 🖳 www.cocheactual.es), in addition to most daily newspapers. There are also free magazines in most areas, such as *Mi Coche*, *Motor en Mano* and *Anuncio Motor*. Most national and local (including free) newspapers carry advertisements for used cars, as do expatriate newspapers, which include foreign-registered cars. There are also numerous websites advertising used cars (e.g. 🖳 www.autonetplus.com and 🖳 www.supermotor.com). Second-hand car prices vary with the region of Spain and are generally higher in remote areas and the islands than they are in Madrid and other major cities.

If you intend to buy a used car in Spain, whether privately or from a garage, check the following:

- That it has a current *ITV* test certificate and card (see page 237), if applicable.

- That it hasn't been involved in a major accident and suffered structural damage.

- That the chassis number tallies with the registration document (*permiso de circulación*), which should be in the name of the seller when a car is purchased privately (check his identity card or passport).

- That it has a genuine service history that confirms the kilometres or miles shown on the clock.

- That the service coupons have been completed and stamped and that servicing has been carried out by an authorised dealer.

- That you receive a 'transfer of ownership' (*transferencia*) form from the seller. The form is available from the provincial traffic department.

- Whether a written guarantee is provided; car dealers usually give warranties on used cars up to 12 months old.

When you're buying a used car from a garage, try to negotiate a reduction, particularly when you're paying cash and aren't trading in another vehicle. When you buy a car from a dealer, he will arrange the transfer of ownership, usually for a small fee. Alternatively, you can employ a *gestor* to handle the transfer or do it yourself at the local provincial traffic department.

**Be extremely wary of buying a car with foreign registration plates, as it can be very expensive to register it in Spain if you need to (see page 235).**

When you buy a second-hand car in Spain, the seller must de-register it (see page 234) at the provincial traffic department, after which you receive the registration document (*permiso de circulación*), the *ITV* test certificate and card and photocopies (if applicable), the road tax receipt and a photocopy, and a receipt for the payment of transfer tax. You have 30 days to register the vehicle in your name.

# SELLING A CAR

When selling a car in Spain, you must obtain and complete a transfer of ownership form (*notificación de transferencia de vehículos*, usually simply called a *transferencia*), available from your provincial traffic department. The form must be completed in duplicate; one copy is given to the buyer and the other sent to the traffic department.

When you sell a second-hand car in Spain, you must pay transfer tax (*impuesto sobre transmisiones patrimoniales y actos jurídicos documentados/ITP*), which is 4 per cent of the vehicle's 'fiscal' value. The fiscal value of a car when new is decided by the tax office, which publishes a list of values for all new cars sold in Spain. The fiscal value is reduced each year (e.g. by 12 per cent when a vehicle is between one and two years old) until it's ten or more years old, when the fiscal value is 10 per cent of the new value. It's the responsibility of the seller to pay the tax, and most sellers include the tax in the sales price (so check in advance what it is). The tax must be declared on form 620 (*compra-venta de vehículos usados entre particulares*), obtainable from a tobacconist (*estanco*) or tax office (*hacienda*), and paid within 30 days of selling your car. Payment is made at the provincial tax office (*Consejería de Hacienda*) of the regional government, e.g. the Junta de Andalucía, where you must present your passport or identity card. You can use a *gestor* to handle the paperwork for you.

When selling a car, you should also do the following:

- You must complete, sign and date the reverse of the registration document (*permiso de circulación*) under the section *transferido* and take it directly to the provincial traffic department along with your other car papers, such as the *ITV* test certificate, municipal tax receipt and a form from your local town hall on which you've de-registered your ownership (for municipal tax reasons).

- Inform your insurance company.

- If you're selling your car privately, insist on payment in cash or with a banker's draft (*cheque bancario*), which is standard practice in Spain. If you cannot tell a banker's draft from a personal cheque, insist on cash. **Never accept a personal cheque**.

- Include in the receipt the price paid, the car's kilometre reading and a statement that you're selling the car in its present condition (as seen) without a guarantee (*sin garantía*), signed by the buyer.

Although it's the buyer's responsibility to re-register the vehicle in his name within 30 days of purchase, many fail to do this (to avoid paying a change of registration fee of €41.80), so unless the buyer accompanies you to the tax or government office, it's in your interest to pay this fee (you must present a bill of sale signed by the buyer). If the buyer then fails to re-register the vehicle, you won't receive any fines for parking and motoring offences committed by him, which you would otherwise.

The best place to advertise a car for sale is in local newspapers, expatriate newspapers, on free local notice boards, and in the Friday and Saturday editions of major newspapers. Many people also put a 'for sale' (*se vende*) notice on their car with a telephone number and park it in a prominent place.

Finally, you should be wary of thieves posing as buyers. Never allow a prospective buyer to drive your car alone or even to sit in the driving seat when you aren't in the car (unless you retain the ignition keys). There have been a number of cases of crooks driving off with cars after duping the owner into getting out.

# REGISTRATION

When you import a car into Spain or buy a new or second-hand car, it must be registered (*matriculación*) at the traffic department in the province where you're resident. If you import a car, you must obtain customs clearance and, if it's imported from a country outside the EU, it may need to undergo a homologation inspection before it can be registered (see page 230). When you buy a car from a dealer in Spain, he usually arranges for the issue of the registration certificate (*permiso de circulación*) or the transfer of ownership. If you buy a car privately, you can do the registration yourself or you can employ a *gestor* to do it for you.

When you buy a second-hand car, you must apply for a change of registration (*cambio de titularidad*) within ten days of purchase at the *vehículos* counter of the local traffic department, and pay a fee of €41.80. The following documents are required:

- A completed application form (*notificación de transferencia de vehículos*), obtainable from the local provincial traffic department.

- The current registration document (*permiso de circulación*) with the transfer of ownership listed on the reverse, including the seller's signature.

- The road tax (*impuesto municipal sobre vehículos de tracción mecánica*/IVTM) receipt for the current year and a photocopy (see page 242).

- The current *ITV* test certificate and card (see page 237) and photocopies.

- A receipt for the payment of transfer tax (see **Selling a Car** on page 234).

- Your residence permit (*residencia*) or a photocopy or the title deeds (*escritura*) of your Spanish home if you aren't a Spanish resident and your foreigner's identification number (*NIE* – see page 309). It's usually necessary to be a Spanish resident or own or rent a home in Spain in order to operate a car on Spanish plates, although you can also obtain a certificate (*certificado de empadronamiento*) stating that you're a registered inhabitant of a municipality.

- The receipt for the change of registration fee.

- A stamped, self-addressed envelope (for the return of the new registration document).

If a person other than the new owner makes the application, he must provide written authorisation from the owner and supply his own resident permit and a copy.

If your car is stolen or scrapped, you should complete a *baja de matrícula* form, available from your provincial traffic department. You require the same documents as for registration (listed above), with the exception of the receipt for payment of transfer tax (see **Selling a Car** on page 234). If the vehicle has been stolen, a copy of the police report (*denuncia*) is required. If the vehicle is more than 15 years old, no fee is charged; otherwise, you must pay €6.40. The *baja* ensures that you no longer receive road tax bills or traffic fines, even if someone else puts the vehicle back on the road.

# Registration Plates

Spanish registration plates consist of four digits followed by three letters, e.g. 1234 ABC. You can no longer tell where the car is from or its age from the number plate. However, there are still thousands of cars on the road with the old style (pre-2001) registration plate, which consists of one or two letters denoting the province where the vehicle is registered (e.g. B for Barcelona and M for Madrid), followed by four digits and one or two more letters, indicating the age of the car. The original registration normally remains permanently with a car, although it's possible to re-register a vehicle (see page 235). **If you buy a second-hand car with old style plates, it's best to buy one registered in the province where you live, or you will be permanently identified as a 'stranger' (which could cause you problems in some areas).**

Since 1st July 1995, Spanish registration plates have incorporated the EU flag and an 'E' for *España* on the left-hand side of the plate. Tourist plates (see below) have a T followed by numbers and a date of expiry in red. Green plates signify an imported vehicle or one previously on tourist plates awaiting standard plates.

## Tourist Plates

It's possible for non-residents to register a vehicle under Spain's 'tourist registration' scheme (*matrícula turística*). It must have been bought outright with foreign currency or, if you paid for it in euros, you must provide proof that it was bought outside Spain. The vehicle will be issued with tourist plates, which cost €66.60 and must be renewed annually for a similar fee. They can be renewed indefinitely provided you don't work in Spain.

If you're a non-EU national, you must make a sworn statement (*declaración jurada*) that you don't reside in Spain for more than six months a year and the vehicle may be used only by you and your immediate family and must be 'sealed' (*precintado*) by customs during periods of absence from Spain.

Spanish road tax must be paid on all cars kept in Spain on tourist plates. Most car dealers will handle the registration and renewal of tourist plates, as will a *gestor*, who should charge around €40 to complete the paperwork.

When a non-resident with a vehicle on tourist plates becomes a resident, he has three months from the date of receipt of his residence card to change to standard plates. **Anyone who illegally drives a vehicle on tourist plates can be fined up to €3,000 and the vehicle can be confiscated.**

# TECHNICAL INSPECTION

All cars over four years old must have a regular technical inspection (*inspección técnica de vehículos/ITV*) at an authorised test station. The test must be carried out every two years until the car is ten years old, after which time the test is annual. Motorcycles are first tested after five years, after which the test is due every two years. If a vehicle is involved in a serious accident, it must usually undergo an *ITV* test after repair to establish whether the repair has been carried out correctly.

There are *ITV* test stations in most major towns (listed in yellow pages under *Automóviles Inspección Técnica de Vehículos*). Make an appointment to avoid a long wait or a wasted journey. The test fee varies from province to province and is from €25 to €50, usually only payable in cash.

Most garages will get your car tested for you, although if you ask a garage to take your car in for a test, make sure that you don't pay for unnecessary repairs, either before or after the test. The Real Automóvil Club de España (RACE) will also take members' cars for testing. If you don't speak Spanish, you should get a garage to take your car in for a test or take a Spanish speaker with you so that you understand any instructions given at the test.

If a vehicle fails the test, you receive a blue form listing the faults and you're given 15 days to have it repaired and re-tested. If possible, get the *ITV* examiner to write down the repairs necessary to pass the test, or you could receive a large bill for unnecessary repairs. Tests aren't exhaustive or rigorous, and old wrecks that should have been consigned to the scrap heap decades ago flourish in Spain, particularly in rural areas.

When your car has passed the test, you're given a certificate showing the month and year when the test is next due, which must be displayed in the top right-hand corner of your windscreen. Certificates are a different colour for each year. You also receive an *ITV* card (*tarjeta de inspección técnica de vehículos*), which details the results of each test. You can be fined up to €1,500 for *ITV*-related offences, such as failing to display a valid *ITV* certificate.

Note that the Spanish *ITV* test has no value in other EU countries and, if you operate a car in Spain that's registered in another EU country, it must be tested in accordance with the law of the country where it's registered in order to be legal in Spain. If you import a car into Spain, it must pass the *ITV* test before it can be registered in Spain.

# ROADS

The Spanish road network now covers over 300,000km (around 200,000mi), of which around 8,000km (5,000mi) are motorways (*autovías/autopistas*). Although this is a smaller proportion than in most other northern European countries, there are plans to extend the motorway network to some 13,000km (8,125mi) by the year 2007, including the completion of the long-awaited Cantabrian motorway (*Autovía del Cantábrico*) and toll motorways such as Las Pedrizas-Torremolinos (Malaga), Alicante-Villena and Madrid-Toledo.

Spanish roads have improved considerably in recent years and Spain's best roads are now among the finest in Europe, especially the motorways. Unfortunately, these are also among the world's most expensive roads and consequently main trunk roads (*carreteras*) are jammed by drivers who are reluctant (or cannot afford) to pay the high motorway tolls.

In contrast to the excellent new motorways and trunk roads, many secondary roads in rural areas and small towns are full of potholes and in a dreadful or even dangerous condition. Some main roads are also in poor condition with surprising undulations and dips, and they aren't often up to the standards of roads in northern Europe. Heavy rain in winter can expose major defects in many roads, including relatively new roads (e.g. the A-7 dual carriageway in Guadiaro, Estepona, one side of which collapsed four months after completion!), and some can become treacherous due to inadequate drainage. Heavy rainfall also causes widespread floods, rock falls, landslides and subsidence. A consumer report published in 2005 found that around a third of Spain's roads had a high or very high risk of accident, mainly because of poor road conditions.

In major cities, it's usually wise to park your car (if you can find a parking space) and use public transport. Driving in Madrid is the motoring equivalent of hell and should be avoided at all costs. You should be wary of entering small towns and villages, where streets are narrow and often come to a dead end (so that you must reverse out). It's better to park on the edge of town.

# Types of Road

In 2004, road denominations were changed in order to make them more consistent and easier to understand. Changing all signs (including the kilometre markers on main roads) and maps is expected to take until the end of 2005, until which time you can expect to see roads signposted by their new name, old name or both – not to mention plenty of confused motorists! The old and new prefixes are shown in the table below. (Note also that the numbering of main roads has been changed from Roman to Arabic numerals; e.g. the old N-II is now the A-2.) Comprehensive information on the new road denominations can be found at the Ministry of Public Works website, where an interactive map shows the old and new denominations (💻 www.mfom.es – go to *Carreteras, Nueva denominación* and then click on a region).

| New Prefix | Spanish | Old Prefix | Description |
|---|---|---|---|
| AP | *Autopista* | A | Motorway – usually marked in blue or red/yellow on maps |
| E | *Carretera europea* | E | European motorway-standard highways traversing a number of countries, e.g. the E5 running from the French border at Hendaye to Algeciras |
| A | *Autovía* | N | National trunk road – usually marked in red or yellow on maps |
| N | *Carretera nacional* | N | Primary road – usually marked in red or yellow on maps |
| C | *Carretera comarcal* | C | Secondary road – usually marked in green or yellow on maps |
| Various* | *Carretera autonómica* | Various | Minor road – usually marked in yellow or white on maps |

\* A two-letter prefix indicates the province, e.g. MA for Malaga. Access roads to main cities are prefixed by the city or province code (e.g. B for Barcelona, M for Madrid and SE for Seville) followed by one or two digits, e.g. M-23 and B-21, shown on a blue background. Some minor roads are unnumbered.

The main trunk roads radiate from Madrid to the coast or the Spanish border, i.e. the A-1 (old N-I) to San Sebastian, the A-2 (old N-II) to Barcelona, the A-3 (old N-III) to Valencia, the A-4 (old N-IV) to Cadiz, the A-5 (old N-V) to Badajoz and the A-6 (old N-VI) to A Coruña.

All main roads have kilometre stones located on the right hand side. Distances on the national roads listed above are calculated from the Puerta del Sol in Madrid and shown on red and white kilometre stones at the side of the road.

# Motorways

Spanish motorways are indicated by blue or green signs and often have an international motorway symbol on them. Most are toll roads (*autopistas de peajes*) and are the most expensive in Europe (Spain has the third-largest network of toll motorways in Europe after France and Italy). Tolls vary, as each motorway has its own fee structure, and are generally more expensive in the summer. Typical toll fees are around €16 from Valencia to Alicante and around €11 from Malaga to Guadiaro. Not surprisingly, toll roads are avoided by most motorists and are consequently very quiet. Partly for this reason, motorways are Spain's safest roads – a relative term!

A ticket is issued automatically at a motorway entrance (or shortly afterwards); when you reach another toll-booth or leave the motorway, you hand your ticket to an attendant (the toll due is usually shown on a display). Tolls may also be levied at intermediate points. On some stretches, e.g. around cities, tickets aren't issued and a fixed toll is charged. On these roads, there may be unmanned toll-booths for those with the correct change, shown by the sign *Automático – importe exacto*. Throw the correct amount into the 'basket' and wait for the red light to change to green and the barrier to rise. You can pay tolls with a credit card or in major foreign currencies.

Regular commuters can buy a season card (*tarjeta de la autopista*) offering savings of 10 to 25 per cent. You insert your card in a machine or, on some motorways, simply drive through the toll while a machine reads your number plate, which has been previously registered.

All motorways have service areas with a petrol station, cafeteria or coffee shop, toilets, telephones, and possibly a restaurant and shops. Some have repair workshops, bureau de change facilities, information offices and motels.

Motorway exits (*salidas*) are marked on maps, as are service and rest stops (*apartaderos*). Motorway maps and toll information are available from ASETA, C/Estébanez Calderón, 3, 28020 Madrid (🖳 www.aseta.es). Most motorway operators provide free maps.

# Main Roads

For many Spaniards, driving on motorways is too expensive, so the traffic density is usually low. The same cannot be said of main trunk roads (*carreteras*) running parallel to motorways, which are jammed by drivers (including truckers) who are reluctant or cannot afford to pay the high motorway tolls. (Even an offer of half price for trucks attracts few takers.) If you must get from A to B in the shortest possible time, there's no alternative to the motorway, apart from taking a plane or train. However, if you aren't in too much of a hurry, want to save money and wish to see more of Spain, you should avoid them. The money saved on tolls can pay for a good meal or a hotel room.

Many dual-carriageways (*autovías*), such as the A-4 south of Madrid, have the appearance of motorways and the same maximum speed limit (120kph/75mph). However, they also have left turns and crossings in some places, so take care. The sign *cambio de sentido* (change direction) on a dual-carriageway is an opportunity to reverse your direction by way of an under or overpass, e.g. when you've missed your exit. On national highways there are 'crawler' lanes on gradients for trucks and other slow-moving vehicles. On single-lane highways you shouldn't expect to cover more than around 70 to 80km per hour.

# Secondary Roads

Travelling on secondary roads (particularly mountain roads) invariably takes two or three times longer than travelling on national routes. Mountain passes in Spain are usually open all year, although some are closed intermittently. Most are narrow with hairpin bends, no road markings and unprotected roadsides with sheer drops, and aren't recommended for timid or nervous drivers, particularly in winter.

# Signposts

In general, signposting in Spain is inadequate, especially in most rural areas, although main routes are usually well signposted. Most road signs are international, although Spain still has many Spanish and local idiosyncrasies. In some areas, direction signs disappear (or everywhere is signposted except where you want to go!) and signs out of towns are often non-existent. It's advisable to have a good map, particularly when you aren't travelling on main roads, or to ask someone to give you detailed instructions.

In and around Madrid and other main cities, signs can be extremely confusing, due to the sheer number of roads and destinations signposted. Look out for the road number, as well as the name of your destination. Often only road numbers **or** towns are listed, and not both. When travelling north to south on the E5/A-4 you should follow the signs for Algeciras and Ocaña. Travelling south to north on the same road, follow the signs for the E5 and the A-1 to Burgos.

# Emergencies

Emergency telephones, mounted on orange posts, are sited around every 5km (3mi) on motorways and other main roads. Each telephone is individually numbered and directly connected to the local police station, which will send out a breakdown van or tow truck (*grúa*) with first-aid equipment. There are fixed (and reasonable) charges for emergency repairs and towing. If you've broken down and call from an ordinary telephone, you should ask the operator for the 'rescue service' (*auxilio en carretera*). The *guardia civil* also provides roadside assistance on main roads throughout Spain, as do motoring organisations (see page 261).

If you break down on a motorway, you must park your car on the hard shoulder and place emergency triangles 10m behind and in front of your vehicle, visible at a distance of 100m. You must also put on a reflective waistcoat. **Never remain in your car when it's parked on the hard shoulder, as it's extremely dangerous.** Note that you're only permitted to stop on the hard shoulder in an emergency (e.g. not for a 'call of nature').

# Information

Road information can be obtained by phone (☎ 900-123 505 for general information) or the internet (🖳 www.dgt.es). Note that at holiday times and weekends, phone lines and the website are overloaded and it can be impossible to get through. See also **Road Maps** on page 250.

# ROAD TAX

All Spanish-registered vehicle owners (including motorcycle owners) must pay an annual road tax (*impuesto municipal sobre vehículos de tracción mecánica/IVTM*). Like all Spanish taxes, road tax has increased in the last decade, although it's still lower than in most other EU countries. Minimum and maximum limits are established by law, but within these, tax levels are set by individual municipalities and vary from town to town depending on their size; rates are higher in municipalities with over 100,000 inhabitants, which may double the minimum tax rate. Among the cheapest cities are Madrid (surprisingly), Valencia and Zaragoza, and among the most expensive are Barcelona (around 20 per cent higher than Madrid), Bilbao and Córdoba.

The amount of tax payable also varies with the 'fiscal horsepower' (*potencia fiscal* or *caballos fiscales*) of your car, which is a nominal amount not necessarily related to the engine power of a vehicle, as follows:

| Fiscal Horsepower | Tax Range (€) |
|---|---|
| 0 – 8 | 15 – 30 |
| 9 – 12 | 45 – 70 |
| 13 – 16 | 90 – 150 |
| 17 – 20 | 130 – 200 |
| Over 20 | 160 – 250 |

**It's advisable to check your bill, as some town halls overcharge by up to 100 per cent by using the wrong formula to calculate the horsepower.**

## Payment

Road tax must be paid to your local authority, usually some time between March and May. Contact your local town hall to find out when and how it must be paid and to obtain a payment form. Announcements are made on municipal notice boards and in local newspapers and banks, and the town hall may send you a reminder (but don't count on it!). Tax can be paid in person at the town hall (where there are usually long queues) or tax office (*recaudación* or *oficina municipal de impuestos*), via certain local banks (or by direct debit from your account) or by post.

When a vehicle is purchased, the tax payable is calculated pro rata for the current tax year. If a car is unused for a whole calendar year, you can have its registration temporarily suspended (*baja temporal*) at your provincial traffic department. However, if a vehicle is used for just one month in a year, tax must be paid for the whole year.

There's a late payment surcharge (*recargo*) of 5 per cent in the first month and 20 per cent thereafter, and the unpaid sum is also liable to interest. Some people have been able to avoid paying road tax for many years, although municipalities are now clamping down on non-payers, whose vehicles can be impounded by local police.

Note that a Spanish-registered car is automatically logged by your local municipality when you register your ownership with the provincial traffic department.

A Spanish road tax certificate isn't displayed inside your car's windscreen or on your registration plates. However, you should keep the receipt in your car with your other vehicle documents, as the local police may ask to see it.

# RULES OF THE ROAD

Spanish road rules were extensively revised in 2004 in an attempt to improve safety and the following is a summary of the most important current regulations. Don't, however, expect other motorists to adhere to them (many Spanish drivers make up their own 'rules', which are infinitely variable!).

● The Spanish drive on the right-hand side of the road (when not driving in the middle). It saves confusion if you do likewise! If you aren't used to driving on the right, take it easy until you're accustomed to it. Be particularly alert when leaving lay-bys, T-junctions, one-way streets and petrol stations, as it's easy to lapse into driving on the left. It's helpful to have a reminder (e.g. a luminous sign saying 'Keep right!') on your car's dashboard.

● When driving outside Spain, you must affix the nationality letter (*nacionalidad*) 'E' (*España*) to the rear of a Spanish-registered car unless it has a number plate that incorporates one. Drivers of foreign-registered cars in Spain must have the appropriate nationality plate affixed to the rear of their cars; you can be fined on the spot for not displaying it.

● All cars must carry a reflective waistcoat (to be worn if you stop at the side of the road), two approved red warning triangles (to be placed around 10m in front of and behind the vehicle – or both behind on a dual-carriageway – if you must stop at the side of the road), a full set of spare bulbs and fuses, a spare wheel and the tools for changing a wheel. If you don't have the above when your car undergoes its *ITV* inspection (see page 237), it will fail. It's also advisable (but not mandatory) to carry a fire extinguisher and a first-aid kit.

● In towns, you may be faced with a bewildering array of signs, traffic lights, road markings, etc. If you're ever in doubt about who has priority, give way to emergency (ambulance, fire, police) and public utility (electricity, gas, telephone, water) vehicles attending an emergency, trams, buses and all traffic coming from your RIGHT.

● Most main roads are designated priority roads (*prioridad de paso*). All secondary roads have a stop sign or a give-way sign, the latter often with the words *ceda el paso* (give way) beneath it. An obligation to give way may also be indicated by a triangle painted on the road. When roads have equal status and no priority is indicated, traffic coming from the right has priority. The priority to the right rule usually also applies in car parks, but never when exiting from car parks or dirt tracks. **Failure to observe the priority-to-the-right rule is the cause of many accidents**.

- Traffic flows anti-clockwise round roundabouts (traffic circles) and not clockwise, as in the UK and other countries where driving is on the left, although on a few major roundabouts in cities (e.g. Barcelona) traffic is routed **both** ways round a central island! When approaching a roundabout, you must give way to traffic on the roundabout (coming from your left). There's usually a give-way sign (which may be painted on the road) on all roads approaching the roundabout. Bear in mind that what appears to be a roundabout isn't always one, so check for 'give way' or 'stop' signs.

- The wearing of seat belts is compulsory on all roads at all times (not only outside towns as was previously the law) and includes passengers in rear seats when seat belts are fitted (rear seat belts have been compulsory in new vehicles in Spain since 1st July 1994). Children aged under 12 or less than 150cm (5ft) tall must travel in the back seats of cars unless the front seat is fitted with an approved child seat. Failure to wear a seat belt can result in an on-the-spot fine of €90 and subsequent offences may mean increased fines or even the loss of your licence. If you have an accident and aren't wearing your seat belt, your insurance company can refuse to pay a claim for personal injury.

- Don't drive in bus, taxi or cycle lanes, identified by a continuous yellow line parallel to the kerb, unless necessary to avoid a stationary vehicle or an obstruction (you can be fined for doing so). Be sure to keep clear of tram lines – i.e. outside the restricted area, marked by a line.

- For left-hand turns off a main road with traffic lights, there's often a marked filter lane to the right, where you wait to cross the main road at right angles.

- The use of horns is forbidden at night in towns, when lights should be flashed to warn other motorists or pedestrians of your presence – and not for any other reason (Spanish drivers sometimes warn other motorists of police radar traps and road blocks by flashing their headlights, although this is illegal). In towns, horns should be used during the day only in emergencies. If you use a horn 'unnecessarily', e.g. to wake the driver in front when the traffic lights change to green, you can be fined up to €60, but judging by the noise of car horns on Spanish streets this penalty is rarely applied!

- Headlamps must be used when driving at night, in poor visibility during daylight and in tunnels at any time (you're reminded by a sign). Be extremely careful when driving in tunnels, some of which have very poor lighting. Your headlamps must be dipped (*luces de cruce*) at night when following a vehicle or when a vehicle is approaching from the opposite direction. Failure to dip your lights can result in a fine.

- A vehicle's hazard warning lights must be used to warn other drivers of an obstruction, e.g. an accident or a traffic jam, or if the vehicle is forced to drive at below the minimum speed. Warning triangles and reflective waistcoats must be used as appropriate (see above).

- Most traffic lights are situated on posts at the side of the road, although they may also be suspended above the road. The sequence of Spanish traffic lights (*semáforos*) is usually red, green, amber (yellow), red. Amber means stop at the stop line; you may proceed only if stopping may cause an accident. (Take care before stopping at an amber light when a vehicle is close behind you, as Spanish drivers routinely drive through amber – and even red – lights and may be taken by surprise if you stop!)

- Flashing amber lights at the side of the road usually indicate that you're approaching traffic lights or a built-up area with a restricted speed limit (e.g. 50kph/30mph). At the entrance to many towns, there are flashing amber traffic lights designed to slow traffic; double flashing amber lights mounted vertically are simply a warning to slow down, although some have a light mounted above them that changes to red if you approach them too fast, e.g. at more than 50kph. This would be an excellent (if irritating) way of slowing down traffic, except for the fact that many Spanish drivers are impervious to red lights and simply ignore them. You shouldn't follow their example, however, as you risk a heavy fine (e.g. from €90 to €600).

- An amber or green filter light, usually flashing and with a direction arrow, may be shown in addition to the main signal. This means that you may drive in the direction shown by the arrow, but must give priority to pedestrians or other traffic. In towns, individual lanes sometimes have their own traffic lights showing a green arrow (indicating that you may use that lane) or a red cross (indicating 'no entry'). Flashing amber lights are a warning to proceed with caution and may indicate that you must give way to pedestrians.

- You occasionally see a flashing red light, meaning stop or no entry, e.g. at a railway level crossing. Two red lights mounted vertically one above the other indicate 'no entry'.

- Take care when approaching a railway crossing, indicated by a sign with a large 'X' or an engine in a triangle. You must take particular care at crossings without barriers, as several people are killed every year by trains at crossings without barriers. Approach a railway level crossing slowly and stop as soon as the barrier or half-barrier starts to fall, as soon as the red warning lights are illuminated or flashing or a warning bell rings, or when a train is approaching! Your new car may be built 'like a tank', but there won't be much left of it (or you) if it collides with a speeding train.

- White lines are used for traffic lanes. A solid single line or two solid lines means no overtaking (*adelantar*) in either direction. A solid line to the right of the centre line, i.e. on your side of the road, means that overtaking is prohibited in your direction. You may overtake only when there's a single broken line in the middle of the road or double lines with a broken line on your side of the road. No overtaking is also shown by the international sign of two cars side by side (one red and one black). Overtaking is prohibited within 100m of a blind hill and on all roads where visibility is less than 200m. It's illegal to overtake on an inside lane on a multi-lane road unless traffic is being channelled in a different direction.

- When overtaking, you must indicate before you pull out and again when returning to your lane. Drivers of trucks, buses and other commercial vehicles often flash their right indicator when it's safe to overtake, but they could simply be about to make a right turn! The left indicator means 'don't overtake'. Always check your rear view and wing mirrors carefully before overtaking, as Spanish motorists seem to appear from nowhere and zoom past at a 'zillion' miles an hour, especially on country roads. If you drive a right-hand drive car, take extra care when overtaking (it's advisable to have an overtaking mirror fitted). You're forbidden to overtake a stationary tram when passengers are boarding or alighting. Illegal overtaking can result in a fine of at least €300 and a suspended licence.

- A rule introduced in 2002 requires you to leave at least enough space for another car between you and the car in front.

- Be particularly wary of mopeds (*ciclomotor*) and bicycles. It isn't always easy to see them, particularly when they're hidden by the blind spots of a car or are riding at night without lights. Many young Spanish moped riders seem to have a death wish and tragically many lose their lives each year. They're constantly pulling out into traffic or turning without looking or signalling. **Follow the example set by Spanish motorists, who, when overtaking mopeds and cyclists, always give them a WIDE berth.** If you knock them off their bikes, you may have a difficult time convincing the police that it wasn't your fault; far better to avoid them (and the police). It's also common to encounter tractors, horses, donkeys and sheep in rural areas. Keep an eye out for them and give them a wide berth too.

- In tunnels and underpasses, vehicles must use dipped headlights and follow any instructions on information panels or loudspeakers. If you must stop, turn off the engine, switch on your hazard lights and place your warning triangles in front of and behind the car. Unless there's a fire, you shouldn't leave your car. Overtaking is prohibited in tunnels unless there are two lanes, and you should keep a minimum distance of 100m or four seconds between you and the vehicle in front.

- Three-point turns and reversing into side streets is forbidden in towns. U-turns can be made on main roads where signposted.

- Studded tyres and snow chains may be used in winter in mountainous areas. Snow chains are compulsory on some roads in winter, indicated by a sign.

- Cars mustn't take more people than they have seats for and it's a serious offence to grossly overload a car. You can be fined €300 or more and the police may impound your car. Cars also mustn't be overloaded with luggage, particularly on roof racks, and the luggage weight shouldn't exceed that recommended in manufacturers' handbooks. Loads on the back of a vehicle (e.g. bicycles) may only protrude by up to 10 per cent of the vehicle's length and must display the appropriate sign (white rectangle with diagonal red stripes).

- Drivers towing (*con remolque*) a caravan or trailer must display a sign of a yellow triangle on a blue background on the front of their vehicle. Note that towing a broken-down vehicle is permitted only for a tow truck.

- A dog must be restrained in a car.

- The use of hand-held telephones and the wearing of audio headphones is illegal when driving, and you can be fined up to €300 and lose three points from your licence. 'Hands-free' sets are allowed, although they must be without earphones.

- When filling up with petrol, you must turn off the engine, all lights, electrical equipment (including the radio) and your mobile phone.

- All motorists in Spain must be familiar with the Spanish highway code (*Código de la Circulación*), available from bookshops throughout Spain.

# SPEED LIMITS

The following speed limits (*límites de velocidades*) apply to cars and motorcycles in Spain:

| Type of Road | Speed Limit |
|---|---|
| Motorways (*autopistas*) | 120kph (75mph) |
| Dual-carriageways (*autovías*) | 100kph (62mph) |
| Other main roads (*carreteras*) | 90kph (56mph) |
| Built-up areas (*vías urbanas*) | 50kph (31mph) or as signposted (e.g. 20kph in some residential areas) |

Campervans, cars towing caravans and trailers up to 750kg are restricted to 90kph (56mph) on motorways and dual-carriageways, and 80kph (50mph) on other roads (unless a lower speed limit is in force). Cars towing weights over 750kg are restricted to 80kph on motorways and dual carriageways, and 70kph (43mph) on other roads (unless a lower speed limit is in force). Obligatory speed restrictions are shown on round signs in black figures on a white background with a red rim. Recommended speed limits, e.g. at sharp bends, are shown on square signs in white figures on a blue background.

Most Spanish drivers routinely speed everywhere, particularly on rural roads, and it has been estimated that only some 15 per cent of Spanish drivers observe speed limits. Many drivers are reluctant to slow for 50kph limits in towns, particularly on national highways running through towns, and are often irritated by motorists who do so. However, speed limits are more rigidly enforced in towns, particularly in resort areas, where tourists are among the main contributors to the town halls' coffers. Radar controls are in use throughout Spain, and speed limits are also enforced by motorcycle traffic police operating in pairs. See **Fines & Penalties** on page 252.

# PARKING

Spaniards are parking (*estacionamiento/aparcamiento*) anarchists and are champions at the art of 'creative' parking. They will park on pedestrian crossings, corners, in front of entrances and exits, in fact, almost anywhere it's illegal. Double parking is commonplace, although triple parking or completely blocking the road is frowned upon. Many streets in Spanish villages and towns are very narrow and cars are invariably parked opposite garages making access even tighter. If someone blocks your car in a town, they will usually be shopping or working locally. You should ask around the local shops and businesses or ask a parking attendant for help before calling the police. Failing that, leaning on your horn (although illegal) may help. Some people leave their cars in neutral and the handbrake off when they double park, so that drivers of other parked cars can move it if necessary.

Parking in most Spanish towns and cities is a nightmare – a recent survey found that it takes an average of eight minutes to find a (legal) parking space in main towns, although it takes nearly twice as long in large cities. Parking is restricted in all cities and towns and prohibited altogether in certain areas, although it isn't usually as expensive as in many other European countries. In major towns and cities, it's wise to park on the outskirts and use public transport. In many small towns and villages, it's advisable to park on the edge of town and walk to the centre, as many towns are difficult to navigate with narrow and dead-end streets commonplace.

Parking regulations vary with the area of a city, the time of day, the day of the week, and even whether the date is odd or even. In many towns, parking is permitted on one side of the street for the first half of the month (blue and red parking restriction sign marked '1-15') and on the other side for the second half of the month (marked '16-31'). In one-way streets, parking may be permitted on the side with even house numbers on even-numbered days and on the side with odd numbers on odd-numbered days. Parking should be in the same direction as the traffic flow in one-way streets or on the right-hand side of roads with two-way traffic. Some towns have zones where parking is regulated during working hours (*horas laborables*), when you need a permit covering the period you intend to stay.

When buying a property in Spain, it's important to investigate the parking facilities, as few older Spanish apartment and townhouse developments have underground or lock-up garages, or even adequate off-road parking facilities, particularly in towns. Some cities have on-street resident parking areas, marked with black bands on telephone poles and lampposts. Residents must buy a parking card from the town hall (proof of residence is required) and display it in their windscreen.

# On-street Parking

On-street parking is forbidden in many streets in the centre of main cities. A sign saying '*estacionamiento prohibido*', sometimes accompanied by a sign with a blue background and a red line through it, means that parking is forbidden. Some no parking signs have a large 'E' (for *estacionamiento*) with a diagonal line through it (any sign with a diagonal line means something is prohibited). No parking may also be indicated by yellow, red or white kerb or road markings. A blue and white curb stone indicates that you can stop briefly, but cannot park. No parking signs also indicate the direction (shown by an arrow), i.e. left or right of the sign, where it's illegal to park. If parking is illegal in both directions, a sign will have two arrows. A tow-away zone is usually shown by a sign of a hoist on the back of a truck and the words '*retirada grúa*'.

In many towns, private entrances and garage doors have a 'no parking' (*prohibido estacionar* or *vado permanente*) sign accompanied by a police permit number enforcing the parking restriction. Parking in front of this sign may mean a fine or that your car can be towed away or clamped.

In most Spanish cities, individual parking meters (*parquímetros*) have been replaced by ticket machines (*expendedor de tickets de estacionamiento*) sited every few dozen metres where parking is restricted, e.g. in areas designated as 'blue zones' (*zonas azules*), indicated by blue street markings with blue ticket machines. Parking must usually be paid for from 9 or 9.30am until 2pm and from around 4 until 9pm, Mondays to Fridays, and from 9.30am until 2pm on Saturdays. Parking costs from around €0.70 to €1 per hour, depending on the town (Barcelona has the most expensive on-street parking). The maximum stay is usually two hours. Buy a ticket for the period required and place it behind your windscreen where it can be seen by the parking attendant.

If you exceed your time and are fined, you can often cancel the fine by paying a penalty (*anulación aviso de sanción*) of around €3 (purchased in ticket form from a ticket machine) and either 'posting' it in a special slot in the ticket machine, displaying it in your car window or giving it to the parking attendant. This must, however, be done within a limited period, otherwise you must pay a fine of up to €40.

In some towns, an *ORA* or *OTA ZONA* system is operated (look out for '*ORA ZONA*' or '*OTA*' signs), whereby parking tickets for 30, 60 and 90 minutes, costing €0.30, €0.60 and €1 respectively, are sold by tobacconists (*estancos*) and other shops. You punch holes in the ticket indicating the date and time you parked and display it in your car window.

Some towns operate a monthly card system (e.g. *multi-parking* in Malaga), costing around €15 per month.

In some cities, you may encounter unofficial parking 'attendants' who will demand a fee to 'look after' your car. This may simply be a protection racket and, if you refuse to pay, they may damage your car. However, they usually only want around €1 and although, there's no guarantee that your car will be safe, it may reduce the risk of having it broken into. In some areas (e.g. outside Gibraltar), there are parking touts, who demand a parking fee (e.g. €10) and take your money and run. Official parking attendants (*guardacoches*) are usually uniformed.

# Car Parks

There are off-road car parks in cities and towns, although these are rarely adequate. Parking rates vary considerably and are usually from around €1 per hour or €15 for 24 hours. Spaces available in a multi-storey or underground car park (*aparcamiento subterráneo*) are indicated by a 'free' (*libre*) sign at the entrance, while '*completo*' indicates that it's full. If you park in a multi-storey car park, make a note of the level and space number where you leave your car (it can take a long time to find your car if you have no idea where to start looking!).

On entering most car parks, you take a ticket from an automatic dispenser, usually by pressing a button. You must usually pay **before** collecting your car, at a cash desk (*cajero*) or via a machine. You cannot usually pay at the exit. After paying, you usually have around 15 minutes to find the exit, where you insert your ticket in the slot of the exit machine in the direction shown by the arrow on the ticket. Many multi-storey car parks have video security.

# Fines

Parking fines (*multas*) have skyrocketed in recent years and previously free parking zones are changed almost overnight without warning (or streets become temporary 'no-parking' zones **after** you've parked there!). Many town halls have allegedly targeted motorists as a way of buying their way out of bankruptcy, particularly through extortionate parking fines. In Malaga alone, around €6,000 per day (€1.8 million a year) is collected in parking fines, with unsuspecting tourists often the victims. A fine of €100 (less 20 per cent for prompt payment) is common for a minor parking infringement, which is astronomical considering the relatively low cost of living in Spain, and fines may be drastically increased if you don't pay within the prescribed period (residents are allowed 15 days to pay or formally protest a fine).

A large number of cars are towed away in Spain, particularly as most Spaniards don't pay parking fines (in Madrid, only a fraction of parking fines are paid). If your car has been towed away, there may be an adhesive sticker by the side of the road indicating this. To get it back, you must pay a fee of between €30 and €120 in addition to the parking fine (around €20 per day or part of a day). Non-residents must first pay the fine (in cash) before paying the towing (*grúa*) charge, usually at two different places. You will need to ask a policeman or parking warden where the car pound is.

Wheel clamps (*cepos*) have been introduced in recent years in some cities. When they were first used in Madrid they almost caused a riot and many motorists attacked them with sledgehammers! They aren't, however, used to prevent illegal parking in private parking areas or on private land, as in some other countries.

# ROAD MAPS

A huge variety of road maps (*mapas de carreteras*) is available in Spain, including the following. Unfortunately there are no large-scale maps for rural areas with comprehensive street indexes. A map showing the regions and provinces of Spain is included in **Appendix E**.

● Michelin map 990 covers Spain and Portugal (1cm = 10km) and a set of six maps (440 to 446) covers the mainland in more detail (1cm = 4km). The Canary Islands are shown on a separate map.

● An excellent official map of Spanish roads (*España Mapa Oficial de Carreteras*) is published annually by the Ministry of Public Works (Ministerio de Obras Públicas de Carreteras/MOPU) and is available from most bookshops. It includes street plans, an alphabetic list of towns and villages, emergency telephone numbers and a list of petrol stations.

● The *Motoring Atlas of Spain* (Michelin) and the *Road Atlas of Spain* (Hamlyn) are priceless. The Michelin website (🖥 www.viamichelin.com) provides a useful online map service: you type in your points of departure and destination, and alternative detailed itineraries are provided together with estimated times of arrival and printable maps.

- The Campsa petrol company produces a book (*Guía Campsa*) containing detailed road maps and a guide to hotels and restaurants in major cities.

- Motorway maps are distributed free by motorway operators, and a general map (*Autopistas de España*) can be obtained by post from ASETA, C/Estébanez Calderón, 3, 28020 Madrid (🖳 www.aseta.es).

- A free map of Spain (*Mapa de Comunicaciones*) is obtainable from Spanish National Tourist Offices abroad, and free town and city maps are available from local tourist offices in Spain. Town maps are also available from book shops, news agencies and kiosks.

# SPANISH DRIVERS

Like all Latins, a Spaniard's personality often changes the moment he gets behind the wheel of a car, when even normally tolerant and patient people turn into suicidal maniacs. Many Spaniards are frustrated racing drivers and they rush around at breakneck speed (totally out of character with their celebrated *mañana* attitude) in their haste to reach their destination (or the next life). To many male Spaniards, driving is like a bullfight and an opportunity to demonstrate their *machismo* to their wives and girlfriends. Foreign-registered cars (observing speed limits) are like red rags to a bull to some Spaniards, who **must** overtake them immediately, irrespective of their speed, the speed limit, road markings, adverse weather conditions or oncoming traffic.

Among the many motoring 'idiosyncrasies' you will encounter are a total lack of lane discipline (lane markings are treated as optional), overtaking with reckless abandon on blind bends, failure to use mirrors or indicators (especially when exiting from a motorway or dual-carriageway), driving through red lights and the wrong way up one-way streets, and parking anywhere it's illegal. Many drivers routinely park too close to other cars and bang their doors up against them, damaging the paintwork. In Spain, nearly every car has a dent in it.

**When driving in Spain, you should regard all drivers as totally unpredictable and drive defensively** (although it should be noted, that not all Spanish drivers are mad or incompetent). When driving on narrow country roads, stay on your own side of the road at all times unless you can see a long distance ahead (if you don't, you can bet your life that around the next blind corner will be a large truck with poor brakes and/or steering). Note that some Spanish drivers are confused by roundabouts (as are many other Europeans) and they don't always give way to traffic already on roundabouts when entering them (previously traffic on a roundabout had to give way to traffic entering it). When driving at night, watch out for bicycles, motorcycles, donkeys, and horses and carts without lights. Maniacs on ear-splitting motorcycles and mopeds are a menace to everyone in towns. Motorists should also keep a wary eye out for pedestrians, particularly older people, who often walk across the road without looking.

Although they aren't among Europe's worst tailgaters, some Spanish drivers sit a few metres (centimetres) from your bumper trying to push you along irrespective of traffic density, road and weather conditions, or the speed limit. Always try to leave a large gap between your vehicle and the one in front. This isn't just to give you more time to stop should the vehicles in front decide to come together, but also to give the inevitable tailgater behind you more time to stop.

The most civilised drivers (relatively speaking) are to be found in the north of Spain (e.g. Catalonia), where most drivers follow at least some of the rules and even stop at red lights. In contrast to most car drivers, Spanish truck drivers are competent and courteous, and most use their right indicators to tell you when it's safe to overtake and their left indicators to warn you that there's an oncoming vehicle. Motorists also use their hazard warning lights when forced to slow rapidly, e.g. for an accident or road works.

Driving in cities can be absolutely chaotic and is to be avoided if at all possible. Inexperienced drivers should take extra care, as the accident rate for foreigners is quite high, particularly in Spanish cities. The Germans and the French have the most accidents, being speed-crazy like the Spanish (the sensible British drive more defensively).

Don't be too discouraged by the road hogs and tailgaters on Spanish roads; driving in Spain can be a pleasant experience, particularly when you're using rural roads, which are relatively traffic-free most of the time.

# TRAFFIC POLICE

In towns, the municipal police (*policía municipal*) are responsible for traffic control, while on Spain's highways the 'civil guard' (*guardia civil de tráfico*) undertake the task, patrolling in cars, motorcycles and helicopters. Motorcycle police usually patrol in pairs (*parejas*), at least one of whom is usually a trained mechanic and the other trained in first-aid; they will stop and help anyone in trouble. Always follow the instructions of traffic police and be prepared to stop. Police in towns blow whistles and wave their arms about a lot – if you don't know what's going on, follow the example of other motorists!

## Fines & Penalties

Except on Spaniards and Spanish residents driving a Spanish-registered vehicle with a Spanish driving licence, on-the-spot fines (*multas*) of up to €300 can be imposed for a range of traffic offences, including speeding, overtaking without indicating, travelling too close to the car in front, not being in possession of your car papers (although you're now permitted to carry a photocopy of your papers in your car) and not wearing a seat belt. On-the-spot fines are routinely imposed on non-resident foreigners, whose vehicles can be impounded or immobilised if they're unable to pay a fine, although the police may escort you to a bank or hotel where you can obtain money or change foreign currency to euros. **The police can also impound a foreign-registered car if they believe that it's used permanently in Spain (you must prove that you live abroad, which may be difficult).**

Motoring offences are classified as 'minor' (*leve*), 'serious' (*grave*) and 'very serious' (*muy grave*). Minor offences carry fines of up to €91, serious offences fines of €92 to €301 with a possible three-month licence suspension, and very serious offences fines of up to €602 and an automatic three-month licence suspension. Other fines for offences such as driving without a licence or without a number plate range from €94 to €1,503.

Speeding fines (*multas*) depend on the degree to which you exceed the speed limit and usually range from €150 to €600; you can also lose your licence. There's a 'leeway' of up to 10 per cent above the speed limit to allow for speedometer and radar errors. It's a very serious offence if you're 30 per cent over the limit, e.g. 80kph in a town or 150kph on a dual carriageway. If you're caught by an unmanned radar trap, you will be sent a photograph of your number plate, which is deemed to be irrefutable evidence of speeding.

The police often set up check-points and stop motorists at random to ask for their identity and vehicle documents (and also to look for drugs or terrorists). You should always carry your passport or residence permit (*residencia*), driving licence (Spanish, if held), vehicle registration papers (*permiso de circulación*) and insurance certificate, although copies are accepted. If a vehicle isn't registered in your name, you also need a letter of authorisation from the owner. Police have stepped up their patrols in many areas and may impose fines for the slightest and most obscure infringements, such as not carrying your driving licence, which can carry a €250 fine.

If you're fined, you receive a *boletín de denuncia* specifying the offence and the fine (check that it's the same as the amount demanded). Unless required to pay on the spot, you can pay a fine at any post office using a post office money order (*giro postal*) or at the local traffic department. **Always ensure that you receive a receipt for it.**

If over 60 working days elapse between an offence and your receiving official notification of it, the fine is invalid. **If, however, notification of a fine is sent to you in Spain while you're abroad, your Spanish property can eventually be embargoed for non-payment. Your driving licence may also be suspended without your knowledge and your name listed in the provincial official bulletin (*boletín oficial*).**

Fines must be paid within 30 days, but for minor offences residents (and foreigners who pay on-the-spot) receive a 30 per cent discount if they pay within ten days. The prompt payment discount doesn't apply to serious or very serious offences, although you can attend a special course in lieu of up to 30 per cent of the fine. Some communities offer young traffic offenders the option of doing community service rather than paying a fine, which means that parents no longer have the obligation to pay their children's traffic fines.

If a fine seems unusually high without good reason, you should question it or take legal advice. You can appeal against a fine and there are instructions in English on the back of the *boletín de denuncia* explaining how to do this. A written appeal (in any language) must be made within ten days of an (alleged) offence to the provincial traffic department in the province where the offence took place. The police decide whether to uphold your appeal and there's no appeal against their decision, so unless you have a cast-iron case it's a waste of time and money. You need the assistance of a notary or a lawyer, which can incur costs of €500 or more. To add insult to injury, if you lose your appeal, you no longer qualify for the 30 per cent prompt payment discount!

In some provinces, the authorities seize cars when road taxes and traffic fines are unpaid. This seizure can be expensive for non-residents, who can have their vehicles towed away and stored (at their expense) for a number of months while they're abroad. Their names are also listed in official bulletins (*boletines oficiales*) displayed at town halls.

As from 2005, motorists committing offences lose points from their licence, as well as paying a fine. Once you've lost your allocated 12 points, you lose your licence. See page 227 for further information on the points system.

# MOTORCYCLES

Somewhat surprisingly, given Spain's excellent weather, large touring motorcycles (*motocicletas* or *motos*) aren't particularly common on Spain's roads. However, mopeds (*ciclomotores*), scooters and small motorcycles are a scourge in towns and cities, where their noise may drive you crazy (noise levels are restricted, but not enforced). Approved crash helmets (*casco*) should be worn at all times by all moped and motorcycle riders and passengers (previously helmets weren't necessary in urban areas), although you will see many riders not wearing them. Failure to wear a helmet can result in a fine of €100, although it isn't unusual to see a whole family on a motorcycle, including children and babies, without a helmet between them!

Under new legislation, children must be over seven years of age to ride on a motorcycle with a parent. If a child wishes to ride with an adult other than its parents, written authorisation must be given by the parents. Dipped headlamps must be used at all times by all motorcyclists except moped riders.

When parking a motorcycle in a city, lock it securely (if possible, chain it to an immovable object). Take extra care when parking in a public place overnight, particularly in major cities, where bike theft is rife.

Mopeds and motorcycles of all sizes can be rented throughout Spain. Note that rental insurance doesn't always include theft. You must usually leave your driving licence as security (it isn't advisable to leave your passport; if the bike breaks down or is stolen, you may have trouble getting it back).

# Under 50cc

A 14-year-old (16 if a non-resident) can ride a moped (i.e. a motorbike with an engine capacity of up to 50cc). Riders aged under 16 must pass a simple examination on the rules of the road and obtain written parental consent. Riders of mopeds with an engine capacity of less than 50cc require a provincial licence costing €17 and a moped licence (*permiso de conducir de ciclomotores*), if they don't have a regular driving licence. Third-party insurance is also obligatory, but is expensive (from around €350 per year) and difficult to obtain, as insurance companies have had to pay astronomical amounts in claims for moped accidents in recent years and are now reluctant to insure them. On the other hand, no registration or road tax are required for mopeds.

Mopeds aren't permitted on motorways and riders must use cycle paths where provided. Nevertheless, many riders are killed each year. Car drivers often cannot see or avoid moped riders, particularly when they speed out of side streets without looking or ride at night without lights.

# Over 50cc

A 16-year-old is permitted to ride a light motorcycle with an engine capacity of up to 125cc, requiring an A1 licence. At 18, a motorcycle with an engine capacity above 125cc may be ridden, for which an A motorcycle licence (*licencia de conducción de ciclomotores*) is required. Both types of motorcycle licence are valid for ten years if you're under 45 and for five years if you're between 45 and 70. Riders over 70 must renew their licence every two years.

Speed limits are the same for motorcycles as for cars and motorcycles, above 75cc are permitted to use motorways (tolls are lower than for cars). All motorcycles must be registered with the provincial traffic department. A motorcycle over 500cc must have a manufacturer's certificate, industry certificate, appraiser's certificate and town hall registration. Third-party insurance is obligatory for all bikes, costing around €350 a year. Motorcycles must have their first technical inspection (*inspección técnica de vehículos/ITV*) after five years and thereafter annually (see page 237).

# ACCIDENTS

If you're unfortunate enough to be involved in a road accident (*accidente de tráfico*) in Spain, the procedure is as follows:

1. Stop immediately. If a vehicle is blocking the road, switch on your hazard warning lights or place a warning triangle at the edge of the road 10m behind your car, with a visibility of 100m. If necessary, e.g. when the road is partly or totally blocked, turn on your car's headlights and direct traffic around the hazard. Put on your reflective waistcoat before leaving the car and try to warn oncoming traffic of the danger, e.g. with a torch or by waving a warning triangle up and down.

2. If anyone is injured, immediately call an ambulance. If someone has been injured more than superficially or extensive damage has been caused, the *guardia civil* must also be called to the scene. Don't move an injured person unless it's absolutely necessary to save him from further injury and don't leave him alone except to call an ambulance. Cover him with a blanket or coat to keep him warm.

3. If there are no injuries and damage to vehicles or property isn't serious, it's unnecessary to call the police to the accident scene; contacting the police may result in someone being fined for a driving offence. However, if another driver has obviously been drinking or appears incapable of driving, you should call the police.

4. If you or the other driver(s) involved decides to call the police, don't move your vehicle or allow other vehicles to be moved. In an accident where someone has been injured or killed, any vehicles involved mustn't be moved until the police have been informed. If it's necessary to move vehicles to unblock the road, mark their positions with chalk, take photographs of the accident scene or make a drawing showing the position of all vehicles involved before moving them. There's a space for such a drawing on the Spanish insurance accident report form (see below).

5. Check whether there are any witnesses to the accident and take their names and addresses, particularly noting those who support your version of what happened. Write down the registration numbers of all vehicles involved and their drivers' names, addresses and insurance details. Give any other drivers involved your name, address and insurance details, if requested.

6. If you've caused material damage, you must inform the owner of the damaged property as soon as possible. If you cannot reach him, contact the nearest police station (this also applies to damage caused to stationary vehicles when parking or manoeuvring).

7. If you're detained by the police, ask someone you're travelling with to contact anyone necessary as soon as you realise you're going to be detained. **Don't sign a statement, particularly one written in Spanish, unless you're certain you understand and agree with every word.**

8. In the case of an accident involving two or more vehicles, it's standard practice for drivers to complete an accident report form (*declaración de siniestro de automóvil*) provided by Spanish insurance companies (keep one in your car). This form is an 'amicable statement', where drivers agree (more or less) on what happened and who was at fault. It isn't obligatory to complete an accident report form and, if your Spanish isn't up to it, you should refuse. You may, however, complete it in English or another language if you wish. It's important to check the details included on forms completed by other drivers against official documents, particularly those relating to a driver's identity, driving licence, car registration and insurance details. If police attend the scene of an accident, they will make their own report.

9. Your insurance company must be notified of an accident within 24 to 48 hours and a delay may affect a claim. If you're involved in an accident, you have two months to bring a charge against other parties involved. This involves going to a local police station and making a statement (*atestado*), after which the insurance companies determine the outcome. Bear in mind that, if a court case is required to decide the outcome, it can take years for a case to be heard.

**All motorists are required to stop and help at the scene of a serious accident.**

# DRINKING & DRIVING

In Spain, you're no longer considered fit to drive when your blood/alcohol concentration exceeds 50mg of alcohol per 100ml of blood (or 30mg for drivers with less than two years' experience and professional drivers). Alcohol is a major factor in a high percentage of Spain's road accidents (around a third of drivers in fatal accidents are over the alcohol limit), particularly those that occur late at night. The amount you can drink and remain below the limit depends on how much you normally drink, your sex and your weight. A man weighing around 75kg can usually drink around two glasses of wine with a meal and remain below the limit. Your alcohol level rises considerably if you drink on an empty stomach (which is why the Spanish eat lots of bread!).

Random breath tests (*alcohol-tests*) can be carried out by the police at any time (they're more widespread during the Christmas and New Year holiday period and in July and August), and motorists who are involved in accidents or who infringe motoring regulations are routinely given alcohol and drug tests. Drunken driving can result in a fine of up to €600, loss of points from your licence or its suspension and even imprisonment. Drivers who refuse to take a breath test are liable to a prison sentence of 6 to 12 months. Note that the same regulations apply to cyclists.

**If you have an accident while under the influence of alcohol, your car and health insurance could be nullified. This means that you must pay your own and any third party's car repairs, medical expenses and other damages, which could run to millions of euros.**

# PEDESTRIANS

## Crossings

Pedestrian crossings (*pasos para peatones*) are distinguished by black and white stripes on the road, but aren't usually illuminated, e.g. by flashing or static lights. In towns, pedestrian crossings are usually combined with traffic lights. Motorists are required by law to stop for a pedestrian waiting at a pedestrian crossing **only** if he indicates his intention to cross by giving a clear hand-signal or placing one foot on the crossing. **It's never safe to assume that you have the right of way as a pedestrian crossing in Spain, particularly in cities, where motorists are very reluctant to stop.**

At a pedestrian crossing with pedestrian lights, pedestrians are supposed to wait for a green light (or green man) before crossing the road (sometimes they must press a button), irrespective of whether there's any traffic. The green light may be accompanied by an audible signal, which may be a few short bleeps just before the light changes to red. A blinking green light means don't cross unless you're already on the crossing (note that the light for motorists may change to green when you're half way across the road even when you started to cross on a green light, so always look out for traffic). You can be fined for crossing the road at the wrong place or ignoring pedestrian lights and crossings.

## Footpaths

Usually, pedestrians must share footpaths with bicycles, skateboards, roller skates, assorted animals and the occasional moped and at the same time keep an eye out for broken paving stones and open manholes and drains. Paving stones and tiles can be slippery when wet, and in country areas many roads have loose gravel and stones on which it's easy to lose your footing. Many towns and cities have pedestrian streets (*zona peatonal*) barred to traffic and some have roads barred to pedestrians (shown by a sign).

Pedestrians must use footpaths where provided or may use a bicycle path when there's no footpath. Footpaths are generally rare outside towns, although there may be a narrow 'hard shoulder'. Where there's no footpath or bicycle path, you should usually walk on the left side of the road, facing oncoming traffic. However, on narrow country roads it's advisable to walk on the side of the road which affords the best view of oncoming traffic, as many roads have blind corners and drivers often drive close to the edge of the road at high speed.

# CAR CRIME

All European countries have a problem with car theft and thefts from cars, and Spain's is among the worst (particularly thefts from cars). National figures indicate that there's a theft from a car every three minutes in Spain as a whole and even more frequently in the cities of Barcelona, Madrid and Valencia. **Foreign-registered vehicles, especially camper vans and mobile homes are popular targets.** Some 75 per cent of stolen vehicles are taken from outside the owner's home and 10 per cent from garages, but fortunately 70 per cent of stolen vehicles are recovered.

If you drive anything other than a worthless heap, you should have theft insurance, which includes your car stereo and belongings. If you drive a new or valuable car, it's wise to have it fitted with an alarm, an engine immobiliser (preferably of the rolling code variety with a transponder arming key) or other anti-theft device, and to also use a visible deterrent such as a steering or gear change lock. It's particularly important to protect your car if you own a model that's desirable to professional car thieves, e.g. most new sports and executive models (BMW and Mercedes are favourites), which are often stolen by crooks to order. In the south of Spain, stolen cars often find their way to Africa and may already be on a ferry by the time their owners report them stolen.

Few cars are fitted with deadlocks (Fords are a notable exception) and most can be broken into in seconds by a competent thief. A good security system won't necessarily prevent someone from breaking into your car or even stop it being stolen, but it makes it more difficult and may persuade a thief to look for an easier target.

Thieves often smash windows (in Spain, BMW stands for 'break my window') to steal stereo systems and other articles from cars – even articles of little worth such as sunglasses or cigarettes. When leaving your car unattended, store any valuables, including clothes, in the boot (trunk). Note, however, that if a car is empty, a thief may be tempted to force open the boot with a crowbar. It isn't advisable to leave your original car papers in your car, which will help a thief dispose of it. When parking overnight or when it's dark, you should use a secure car park or garage, or at least park in a well-lit area.

Thieves in Spain operate various scams, which include pretending that you have a flat tyre (they may even puncture your tyre in slow-moving or stopped traffic) or that fuel is leaking from beneath your car. While they're pretending to help fix your car, they steal your belongings (women are popular targets). **View any strangers offering to help you with suspicion.** Some criminals specialise in robbing motorists at motorway toll booths and there has also been an increasing incidence of highway piracy', where gangs deliberately bump or ram cars to force drivers to stop (usually late at night when there's little traffic about). **Be on your guard!**

If your car is stolen or anything is stolen from it, report it immediately to the police in the area where it was stolen. You can report it by telephone, but must go to the station to complete a report (*denuncia*). Don't, however, expect the police to find it or even take any interest in your loss. Report a theft to your insurance company as soon as possible.

# FUEL

Unleaded petrol (*sin plomo*) is available in normal (95 octane) and super (98 octane) grades. Diesel fuel (*gasóleo* or *mezcla*), including 'diesel plus', is available at all petrol stations (*gasolineras*). Leaded petrol (*super*) is no longer available. To prevent errors, petrol pumps and pipes are colour coded: green for unleaded and yellow or black for diesel. Note that there aren't many petrol stations in rural areas off the main highways, so it's advisable to keep your tank topped up when touring. You're permitted to carry a can containing ten litres of petrol.

There are three main fuel companies in Spain: Campsa, Repsol and Cepsa. Prices are no longer fixed by the government and, where there are a number of petrol stations in a town, it's worth shopping around for the lowest price, although the days of cheap petrol are now long-gone. Consumer surveys show the cheapest petrol is generally available in Barcelona, Lleida and Valencia. Prices per litre in late 2005 were around €0.97 for diesel, €1.05 for 'diesel plus', €1 for unleaded and €1.10 for 'unleaded plus'. Information on petrol prices by province is available from 🖳 www6.mityc.es/energia/hidrocarburos/carburantes/index.asp – click on the province and type of fuel you're interested in. (Note that some regions levy a regional tax on vehicle fuel; for example, an extra €0.024 is charged on every litre in Cataluña.)

Most petrol stations are open continuously from around 7am to around 10.30pm, except on *fiesta* days, when opening hours are severely curtailed. In large towns, local petrol stations operate a rota to ensure that at least one station is open 24-hours a day, and many service stations are open 24 hours on motorways and other main highways (although some close overnight).

Self-service (*autoservicio*) stations are now common, although there are still many manned petrol stations, particularly in towns. To have your tank filled at a manned station, say '*Lleno, por favor*'; to ask for '€10/€15/€20 worth' simply say '*deme diez/quince/veinte euros, por favor*'. When paying at self-service petrol stations, simply tell the cashier your pump number. To prevent robberies, some stations don't give change at night and you must fill up to exact cash amounts. In many, you must pay before you can fill up. However, most (but not all) stations accept credit cards such as MasterCard or Visa, and most major chains also provide their own credit cards.

Most petrol stations don't provide any services and it's unnecessary to tip unless an extra service is performed such as checking your oil or tyre pressures, when a tip of around €1 is sufficient. If you need oil (*aceite*) or water (*agua*), ask the attendant. On the other hand, many petrol stations provide services such as car washes, vacuum cleaners and air (although machines are often out of order), and routine servicing and repairs are also carried out at some stations. Petrol stations usually have toilets or there's a bar/café or restaurant nearby, and many have a shop or vending machines for soft drinks, beer, confectionery, snacks and cigarettes.

# SERVICING & REPAIRS

When buying or importing a car, you should take into account the local service facilities, as not all cars can be easily serviced. All the main European manufacturers are well represented in Spain, but garages (*garajes* or *talleres de reparaciones*) servicing North American and some Japanese cars can be difficult to find. If you drive a 'rare' car, it's advisable to carry a basic selection of spare parts, as service stations in Spain may not stock them and you may have to wait several weeks for them to be sent from abroad. In fact, some garages keep very few spares, particularly for Japanese and Korean makes, and can take weeks to obtain spares for cars manufactured in the last decade. If you find yourself in this position, you can buy most spares abroad, e.g. in the UK or Germany (where they're also likely to be around 50 per cent cheaper) and have them shipped to Spain by courier. Spanish mechanics may try to repair parts rather than simply replacing them. This is because labour has traditionally been cheaper than spare parts, although this is changing fast, particularly in the cities. Mechanics can often come up with creative solutions to problems if parts are unavailable.

Repair work is usually of a high standard and prices are competitive (many garages offer fixed prices for routine servicing). However, you shouldn't rely on a Spanish garage to repair a car when they say they will, as it's common for repairs to take days (or even weeks) longer than scheduled due to the Spanish *mañana* attitude (although a delay may also be due to a lack of spare parts). You should receive a three-month or 2,000km guarantee for any major work done and should be given any parts that have been changed. Always ask for a written estimate (*presupuesto*) before having a car repaired (you may be billed for this, although it isn't usual).

It's generally cheaper to have your car serviced at a village garage rather than at a main dealer, although the quality of work can vary considerably from garage to garage. If a car is under warranty, it must usually be regularly serviced by an approved dealer in order not to invalidate the warranty. However, if you need urgent assistance, particularly with an 'exotic' foreign car, you're more likely to receive sympathetic help from a small garage than from a large dealer.

Garages in Spain are open from 8 or 9am until 6 or 7pm and usually close for lunch from 1 or 2pm until 3 or 4pm. In major cities, there are garages providing 24-hour breakdown assistance (at a price).

Service stations rarely provide a free 'loan car' (*coche prestado*) while yours is being serviced or repaired, although you can usually hire a car from a large garage for a reasonable fee. Some garages collect your car from your home or office and deliver it after a service, or drop you off at a nearby rail or bus station and pick you up when your car is ready for collection.

# BREAKDOWN INSURANCE

If you're going to be motoring abroad or you live abroad and are going to be driving in Spain, it's important to have motor breakdown insurance (*seguro de asistencia en carretera*), which may also include holiday and travel insurance, including repatriation for your family and your car in the event of an accident or breakdown.

Motor breakdown insurance covering Spain and other European countries is provided by car insurance companies (see page 223) and Spanish motoring organisations (see page 261). Insurance companies usually offer an optional accident and breakdown service (*asistencia en viaje*), which is adopted by some 75 per cent of Spanish motorists. The breakdown service normally covers the policy holder, his spouse, single dependent children, and parents and grandparents living under the same roof. The 24-hour telephone number of the breakdown service's head office is shown on a card, which should be kept in your vehicle.

If you have an accident or break down, you simply call the emergency number and give your location, and a recovery vehicle is sent to your aid. Although accidents are covered anywhere in Spain, in the event of a breakdown you must be a certain distance from your home, e.g. 15 or 25km (9 or 15mi). The insurance provides for transportation in the event of a breakdown or illness, although transportation to hospital (if necessary) and medical treatment are covered up to a limited amount, e.g. €350. An interest-free loan and an emergency message service is normally provided in the case of a robbery. The retrieval of your vehicle is also guaranteed from within Spain or abroad. If you're unable to find spare parts locally to repair damage, your insurance company will arrange to have them shipped to you (at your expense).

Most foreign breakdown companies provide 24-hour centres where multilingual staff provide help and advice on motoring, medical, legal and travel matters. Some organisations also provide economical annual motoring policies for those who frequently travel abroad, e.g. owners of holiday homes in Spain.

# MOTORING ORGANISATIONS

There are a number of motoring organisations in Spain, although membership isn't as large as in many other European countries. Breakdown insurance is also provided by insurance companies and most motorists take advantage of the low rates offered. Spain has two national motoring organisations: Real Automóvil Club de España (RACE, ☎ 902-414 143, 💻 www.race.es), the larger and better known, and Real Automobil Club de Catalunya (RACC, ☎ 902-453 452, 💻 www.racc.es).

Membership of RACE costs around €30 for registration plus an annual fee of around €105 (fees are lower in the Balearics and Canaries). A breakdown must happen at least 25km (15km in the Balearics and Canaries) from your home and there's a limit of three 'free' breakdown recoveries each year, after which a fee is charged. RACE transport your vehicle to a garage and make alternative travel arrangements if you break down while on holiday. Assistance outside Spain is provided only within 60 days of leaving Spain. Other services include assistance in obtaining a driving licence, registration plates and vehicle importation; insurance and financial services; comparative running costs and reliability information for popular cars; tourism (hotel discounts), leisure and sports services; an information service and legal advice.

The RACC offers similar services and fees (€24.50 for registration and €113 annual fee), and both organisations have agreements with foreign organisations such as the AA, AAA, ACI, ADAC, AvD, DTC, RAC and the TCI.

# CAR HIRE

To hire (rent) a car in Spain, you must usually be at least 22 years old – 25 for certain cars – and most companies also have an upper age limit, e.g. 65. Drivers must produce a valid licence (a copy isn't acceptable) and non-EU licence holders require an international driving permit. All the drivers' names must be entered on the hire agreement.

The major car hire (*alquiler de coches*) companies, such as ATESA, Avis, Budget, Europcar, Helle-Hollis and Hertz, have offices in most cities and at major airports. ATESA are generally cheaper than the international companies, although cheapest of all are small local rental companies. Car hire companies are listed in yellow pages under *Automóviles Alquiler* and local companies are listed by town. You may be approached at airports by representatives of local companies, most of which are reputable (but check their credentials). If you're a visitor, it's advisable to reserve a hire car before arriving in Spain, particularly during peak periods (more visitors hire cars in Spain than any other European country). When booking, you should specify an automatic model if you're unused to a manual (stick-shift) gearbox, as most hire cars in Spain are manual. Fly-drive deals are available through most airlines and travel agents.

Car hire in Spain is the cheapest in Europe, due mainly to the cut-throat competition, particularly during off-peak periods. The rates of major international companies vary little, although you may get a better deal by booking well in advance. One of the advantages of using a national or international company is that you can hire a car in one town and drop it off in another, although you should check the cost of this service. Although cheaper, some small local companies require you to return the car to the office you got it from or to the local airport.

As an example of prices, Hertz charge around €175 for six days for their cheapest (Group A) cars, such as a Kia Picanto (without air-conditioning), including unlimited kilometres, collision damage waiver (CDW) and VAT. Business tariffs are higher. A small company in a resort area might charge €150 per week in winter, e.g. between 15th November until 30th April, for a similar car, rising to around €200 a week in summer. **Note, however, that some inexpensive hire companies cut corners on maintenance and repairs, and cars can sometimes be unsafe.** Always carefully check a car (e.g. for body damage and to ensure that everything works) and the rental contract before setting out. As from 2006, car hire in the Balearics will cost an extra €4.50 or €5 a day depending on the size of the car plus a further one or two cents per kilometre. With this measure, the Balearic government hopes to collect around €12.5 million a year towards paying off the islands' huge healthcare deficit.

Most companies have low rates for weekend hire, e.g. from 4pm on Friday to noon on Monday, and for rentals of 14 days or longer. When comparing rates, check that prices include insurance and taxes (VAT at 16 per cent), that insurance cover (including personal accident) is adequate and that there are no hidden costs. Check the cost of any extras that aren't included in the basic price, such as collision damage waiver/CDW (*cobertura de daños por colisión*), theft cover (*cobertura contra robo*), personal accident insurance/PAI (*asistencia por lesiones personales*), airport tax (*cargo de aeropuerto*), roof rack, baby seat, air-conditioning, and additional drivers. Some companies don't offer unlimited kilometres (*kilometraje ilimitado*), which usually works out more expensive unless you plan to drive only a short distance. If required, check in advance that you're permitted to take a car out of Spain, e.g. to France or Portugal, as you may need extra insurance.

If you're touring, you should ensure that you have sufficient power for mountain driving, e.g. at least a 1.6 litre petrol engine or a 2 litre diesel engine for two people and their luggage. If you're going to be doing a lot of driving in summer, air-conditioning is a must.

Unless you're paying by credit card, you must usually pay a high cash deposit; in some cases, the whole rental must be paid in advance. **When paying by credit card, carefully check your bill and your statement, as extra unauthorised charges aren't unknown.**

# 12.

# HEALTH

The quality of healthcare and healthcare facilities in Spain is generally good and at their best are equal to any country in Europe and the most recent World Health Organisation survey into quality of healthcare ranked Spain as 7th in the world (the UK was ranked 17th). Spanish medical staff are highly trained and major hospitals are equipped with the latest high-tech equipment. Healthcare costs per head in Spain are, however, below average for the European Union (EU) and Spain spends just over 5 per cent of its gross domestic product (GDP) on health, although spending is set to increase by some 30 per cent in the 2006 budget. Hospital nursing care and post-hospital assistance are below what northern Europeans and North Americans take for granted, and spending on preventive medicine is low. Public and private medicine operate alongside each other and complement one another, although public health facilities are limited in some areas. An important contribution is also made by voluntary organisations such as the Red Cross (*Cruz Roja*), which is funded totally by voluntary contributions and membership subscriptions.

Spain has a public health system, providing free or low cost healthcare for those contributing to Spanish social security (see page 288), plus their families and retirees. Huge advances have been made in the last few decades and the public health service is much improved. Waiting lists to see specialists and for non-urgent operations have been drastically reduced in most areas, although waiting lists for surgery are still long in many regions – exact statistics are difficult to obtain because each region has its own way of calculating what a waiting list is! Patients can choose any specialist or surgeon in Spain.

If you don't qualify for healthcare under the public health system, it's essential to have private health insurance (see page 295). **You may not be able to get a residence permit without private health insurance.** This is often advisable in any case if you can afford it, in order to circumvent the shortage of public health services and waiting lists in some areas. Visitors to Spain should have holiday health insurance (see page 303) if they aren't covered by a reciprocal agreement (see **Medical Treatment Abroad** on page 281).

In common with many Western countries, the financing of the public health system in Spain is a growing problem – all regions' health services run huge debts (those in Catalonia, Madrid, Murcia and Valencia are particularly high). One of the main problems is that little financial provision has been made for the large increases in population (Murcia's population has grown by 14.5 per cent in the last five years). Regions also overspend hugely on prescriptions – a third of Catalonia's health budget goes on prescriptions. After months of intense public debate, in September 2005, the central government offered the regions state funds to relieve their health debt and increased taxes on alcoholic drinks and tobacco to help finance healthcare. Regions are also permitted to increase taxes on petrol to pay for healthcare, although to date Catalonia is the only region to have applied this.

The Spanish are among the world's healthiest people and have an average life expectancy of nearly 83 for women and 75 for men, the highest in the EU. The incidence of heart disease in Spain is among the lowest in the world, a fact partly contributed to their diet (which includes lots of garlic, olive oil and red wine). They do, however, have a high incidence of liver problems and other complaints associated with excess alcohol. The infant mortality rate of around four deaths per 1,000 births (2002 figures) is decreasing.

For a country with one of the world's healthiest diets, Spain has a shocking obesity problem: over half of the adult population and over a quarter of children are overweight and of these a third are obese – the highest rate in the EU after Italy and Malta. Sedentary lifestyles and changes in diet from traditional balanced menus with plenty of fruit and vegetables in favour of fast food and high calorie snacks are the main causes. The government has introduced a nationwide campaign to try and reduce Spaniards' weight and encourage better levels of fitness.

Smoking-related ailments and deaths are a serious problem; smoking is the leading cause of death among adults in Spain, directly causing some 56,000 deaths a year (Spain rates second highest after Greece in the number of smokers per capita in Western Europe). New anti-smoking measures designed to reduce the incidence of smoking and effective from 1st January 2006, include a total ban on tobacco advertising, no smoking in work places and most public areas. Smoking is banned in areas that allow access to the under 18s. Legislation for bars and restaurants is different and whether they allow smoking depends on the owner. Premises larger than 100m² may have up to 30 per cent of the space for smoking, but the area must be completely enclosed and with its own ventilation system. Smoking in premises under 100m² is permitted, but a sign on the entrance must clearly state whether smoking is allowed. Spanish smokers have a notorious disregard for no smoking regulations and it remains to be seen how well they will adapt to the new legislation.

Among expatriates, common health problems include sunburn and sunstroke, stomach and bowel problems (due to the change of diet and more often, water, but also poor hygiene), and various problems caused by excess alcohol, including a high incidence of alcoholism. Some health problems are exacerbated by the high level of airborne pollen in spring in many areas, which affects asthma and hay fever sufferers, and noise and traffic pollution (particularly in Spain's major cities). **If you aren't used to Spain's fierce sun, you should limit your exposure and avoid it altogether during the hottest part of the day, wear protective clothing (including a hat) and use a sun block.** It's also important to drink sufficient fluids, replace lost salt and not to over-exert yourself. Too much sun and too little protection dries your skin and causes premature ageing, to say nothing of the risks of skin cancer. Care should also be taken to replace the natural oils lost from too many hours in the sun.

Spain's climate (see page 449) is therapeutic, particularly for sufferers of rheumatism and arthritis, and those who are prone to bronchitis, colds and pneumonia. Spain's slower pace of life (plus the *siesta*) is also beneficial for those who are prone to stress (it's difficult to remain uptight while lying in the sun), although it takes most people some time to adjust. The climate and lifestyle in any country has a marked effect on mental health and people who live in hot climates are generally happier and more relaxed than those who live in cold, wet climates. When you've had a surfeit of Spain's good life a variety of health cures are available at spas and health 'farms'.

Health (and health insurance – see page 295) is an important issue for anyone retiring to Spain – the Costa Blanca and Costa del Sol have one of the highest percentages of retired people in the world, which puts a huge strain on local health services. Many people are ill-prepared for old age and the possibility of health problems. There's a dearth of welfare and home-nursing services for the elderly in Spain, state or private, and many foreigners who are no longer able to care for themselves are forced to return to their home countries. There are few state residential nursing homes and hospices (usually funded by private donations) for the terminally ill, although there are a number of private sheltered home developments, particularly in resort areas. There are occasional scandals over unauthorised private nursing homes where the residents live in dreadful and unhygienic conditions. Before you or a relative enters a private home, you should check its credentials carefully. Spain's provision for disabled travellers is also poor, and wheelchair access to buildings and public transport is well below the average for western Europe, although measures are improving.

There are no special health risks in Spain (apart from over indulgence and falling sick in August when all the doctors are on holiday) and no immunisations are required. You can safely drink the water, although it sometimes tastes terrible and many people prefer bottled water – when not drinking red wine (which isn't only tastier, but beneficial to your health **when consumed in moderation!**). *¡Salud!*

# EMERGENCIES

The action to take in a medical emergency (*urgencias*) depends on the degree of urgency. The emergency medical services in Spain are excellent. **Keep a record of the telephone numbers of your doctor, local hospitals and clinics, ambulance (*ambulancia*) service, first aid, poison control, dentist and other emergency services (fire, police) next to your telephone.** Throughout Spain you can dial a special number for the emergency services (*Servicios de Urgencias*), e.g. ☎ 012 (ambulance, fireman and police). If you're unsure who to call, ask operator information (☎ 11818) or call your local police station, who will tell you who to contact or contact the appropriate service for you. Whoever you call, give the age of the patient and if possible specify the type of emergency, so that the ambulance can bring a doctor if necessary. Some useful words are accident (*accidente*), serious illness (*enfermedad grave*), heart attack (*ataque cardiaco*), ambulance (*ambulancia*) and doctor (*médico*).

In a life-threatening emergency such as a heart attack or a serious accident, you should call for an ambulance (see below) and mention the nature of the emergency. There may be a special three-digit number in a city, or you should call your local social security clinic (*ambulatorio, clínica de salud*) or the Red Cross. (You can become a member of your local Red Cross centre for around €20 a year.) There are also 24-hour private medical centres (*centros médicos*) in resort areas with ambulance services. The numbers are listed at the front of your telephone book and should be kept next to your telephone. See also **Emergency Numbers** on page 140.

If you're physically capable, you can go to a hospital emergency or casualty department (*urgencia*) or a 24-hour public health clinic (*ambulatorio* or *casa de socorro*). The telephone numbers of first aid stations are listed at the front of telephone directories and many are equipped with ambulances. Check in advance which local hospitals are equipped to deal with emergencies and the quickest route from your home. This information may be of vital importance in the event of an emergency, when a delay may mean the difference between life and death. In an emergency, a hospital must treat you, irrespective of your ability to pay. Most chemists post a list of local clinics and hospitals where emergency medical treatment is available. Note that if you're initially treated at a state medical centre (*centro de salud*) or out-patient clinic (*ambulatorio*) you will usually be referred to a public hospital for treatment (which you may not want if you have private health insurance).

If you're ill and unable to visit your doctor's surgery, your doctor will visit you at home (in Spain, doctors make house calls at any time of the day or night). If you need a doctor or some medicine in a non-urgent situation and are unable to contact your doctor, ring the telephone information service (☎ 11818) or your local police station, either of whom will give you the telephone number of a doctor on call or the address of a chemist's (*farmacia*) that's open.

## Ambulances

Private ambulance services provide a 24-hour service in most towns and are listed by town under *Ambulancias* in yellow pages, and most clinics and private hospitals operate their own ambulance services. Ambulance drivers and staff aren't generally highly trained, as paramedics aren't recognised in Spain. Social security patients don't pay for ambulance services and private patients (who have a private health insurance policy) are usually reimbursed. If you must pay, the cost depends on the type of ambulance required (intensive care ambulances are more expensive) and the distance travelled. Standard ambulances cost from around €90, and fully-equipped intensive care ambulances cost from around €120, for a journey of 25 to 30km (15 to 19mi). If your doctor travels with you, the charge is increased by €35 to €100. In an emergency, an ambulance will take a patient to the nearest hospital equipped to deal with the particular emergency.

Taxis must, by law, transport medical emergencies to hospital when requested to do so. A private car can claim priority when transporting a medical emergency by switching on its hazard warning lights and displaying a piece of white material from a window.

## SOCIAL SECURITY HEALTH BENEFITS

If you make Spanish social security (*Seguridad Social*) contributions, you and your family are entitled to free or subsidised medical and dental treatment on the same terms as Spaniards. Over 90 per cent of the population are covered by Spain's public health scheme, which is administered by the regional health authorities (see below), including retired EU residents (with a residence permit) in receipt of a state pension.

### Regional Health Authorities

- Andalusia – ☎ 902-505 060, 🖳 www.juntadeandalucia.es/servicioandaluzde-salud (GP appointments via the internet in the near future).
- Aragon – ☎ 976-765 800, 🖳 http://portal.aragob.es.
- Asturias – ☎ 012, 🖳 www.princast.es.

- Balearics – ☎ 971-175 600, 💻 www.ib-salut.caib.es.

- Canaries – 💻 www.gobiernocanarias.org/sanidad (GP appointments via the internet).

- Cantabria – ☎ 942-202 770, 💻 www.scsalud.es.

- Castile-La Mancha – 💻 http://sescam.jccm.es.

- Castile León – ☎ 983-413 600, 💻 www.jcyl.es.

- Catalonia – ☎ 934-824 220, 💻 www.gencat.es/ics.

- Extremadura – 💻 www.juntaex.es/consejerias/syc/ses (centralised appointment system).

- Galicia – ☎ 981-542 737, 💻 www.sergas.es (GP appointments via the internet).

- La Rioja – 💻 www.seris.es.

- Madrid – 💻 www.madrid.org/sanidad/srs.

- Murcia – 💻 www.murciasalud.es.

- Navarra – 💻 www.navarra.es.

- Valencia – 💻 www.san.gva.es.

If you aren't entitled to public health benefits through payment of Spanish social security or being in receipt of a pension from another EU country, you must usually have private health insurance (see page 295) and must present proof of your insurance when applying for a residence permit. If you're an EU national of retirement age, who **isn't** in receipt of a pension, you may be entitled to public health benefits, if you can show that you cannot afford private health insurance.

Anyone who has paid regular social security contributions in another EU country for two full years before coming to Spain is entitled to public health cover for a limited period from the date of their last social security contribution made in their home country. Legislation in 2000 ruled that illegal immigrants in Spain and their dependants are also entitled to free healthcare. Social security form E-106 must be obtained from the social security authorities in your home country and be presented to the local provincial office of the Instituto Nacional de la Seguridad Social (INSS) in Spain. Similarly, pensioners and those in receipt of invalidity benefits must obtain form E-121 from their home country's social security administration. You're registered as a member of the social security and given an electronic social security card (*tarjeta*), a list of local medical practitioners and hospitals, and general information about services and charges. If you're receiving an invalidity pension or other social security benefits on the grounds of ill-health, you should establish exactly how living in Spain will affect those benefits. In some countries, there are reciprocal rights regarding invalidity rights, but you must confirm that they apply in your case.

Public health benefits include general and specialist medical care, hospitalisation, laboratory services, discounted drugs and medicines, basic dental care, maternity care, appliances and transportation. General and specialist medical treatment is totally free, but you must also pay a percentage of the cost of certain items such as drugs and medicines (see page 273), although these are free to pensioners.

Health services traditionally placed the emphasis on cure rather than prevention and treated sickness rather than promoted good health, although they've now implemented a comprehensive preventive medicine programme, including regular health checks and an immunisation programme for children. The public health service has limited resources for out-patient treatment, nursing and post-operative care, geriatric assistance, terminal illnesses and psychiatric treatment, although these are improving. Perfunctory treatment due to staff shortages, long waiting lists and a general dehumanisation of patients are among the complaints made against Spain's social security health system. Many problems are related to crippling bureaucracy, bad management and general disorganisation. However, attempts at reform have had some success, including a huge reduction in waiting times and there are several public hospitals in Spain run as successful profit-making enterprises. Eventually, the health service intends to make all hospitals and general practices, self-administrating.

When you receive your social security card, you're offered a choice of general doctors (*médicos de cabecera*) in the area where you live. No payment is made when visiting a public health service doctor and once you've registered with a doctor, you aren't required to produce your social security card.

For more information about social security, contact the Instituto Nacional de la Seguridad Social (INSS), Servicios Centrales, Padre Damián, 4, 28036 Madrid (☎ 900-166 565, 💻 www.seg-social.es).

# DOCTORS

There are excellent doctors throughout Spain, although finding a doctor who speaks English can be difficult, particularly in rural areas. However, there are a number of English-speaking Spanish and foreign doctors practising in Spain, particularly in the major cities and resort areas, including American, British, German and Scandinavian doctors. Many embassies and consulates in Spain maintain a list of English-speaking doctors and specialists in their area and your employer, colleagues, friends or neighbours may be able to recommend someone. Tourist offices may also keep a list of English-speaking doctors and the names and telephone numbers of English-speaking doctors and dentists are often listed in local English-language newspapers and magazines. Doctors are permitted to advertise their services and a number advertise in the expatriate press. General practitioners (GPs) or family doctors are listed in yellow pages under *Médicos* and specialists under their speciality such as obstetricians and gynaecologists (*Médicos Obstetricia y Ginecología*) and heart specialists (*Médicos Cardiología*).

The ratio of doctors to inhabitants in Spain (4.4 per 1,000) is higher than all other EU countries except Italy, although it varies considerably from town to town and region to region. In most major cities and resort areas, there are more than enough doctors, although in rural areas and some urbanisations surrounding the major cities there's sometimes a shortage of doctors and those who practise there are often over-worked and can spare patients little time (some public health doctors see as many as 20 to 40 patients an hour!). This may also apply to some doctors working for Spanish insurance companies, although fees have increased in recent years and doctors are now able to spend more time with patients. **Always try to choose a doctor who allocates you sufficient time and who will explain his diagnosis and recommended course of treatment.** Note that if you don't speak Spanish, you may need a translator if you visit a Spanish doctor. If you take regular medication, are undergoing a course of treatment, or suffer from a long-term illness or disability, you should ask your present (i.e. overseas) doctor to provide a short statement regarding your medical history and have it translated into Spanish before arriving in Spain.

If you have private health insurance (see page 295), you can choose to see any doctor at any time and aren't required to register with a doctor or visit a doctor within a certain distance of your home. This also makes it easy to obtain a second opinion, should you wish to do so. If you need the services of a medical auxiliary such as a nurse, physiotherapist or chiropodist, you must usually obtain a referral or prescription from a doctor. Health insurance companies also usually insist on a referral from a family doctor (GP), but if you have a 'free choice' policy you can select your own specialist or other practitioner.

If you attend a doctor at a health centre or clinic (public or private) certain tests, including ECGs, scans, X-rays, and blood and urine analysis, may be conducted on the premises. Alternatively, you may be given a form for X-rays, eye tests or special tests to be carried out at a local hospital or clinic (you may be given your X-ray plates to return to your doctor). Free flu (*gripe*) vaccinations are given each autumn at clinics and medical centres to 'high-risk' groups such as the elderly and young children.

Alternative medical practitioners aren't as common in Spain as they are in some other European countries or North America, although there are a number of expatriates practising in the major cities and resort areas (many advertise in English-language publications). Before choosing an alternative practitioner, you should check whether he's state registered. Note that it's normal practice to pay a doctor (preferably in cash) or other medical practitioner after each visit when you're a private patient, although some charge you only after treatment is completed. A routine visit to a doctor's surgery usually costs from €50, a home daytime call from €70 and a home night time call from €75. A consultation with a specialist costs between €50 and €100. If applicable, obtain a receipt for your insurance company.

Surgery hours vary considerably between public health and private doctors and from day-to-day, e.g. private doctors' surgery hours may be from 9am to 2pm and from 5 until 7pm Mondays to Fridays, while public health doctors in health centres (*centro de salud* or *ambulatorio*) often work from 8am until 6pm without a break. Some public health centres in resort areas provide a volunteer interpreter service for foreigners. It's usually necessary to make an appointment (*cita previa*) by phone or in person (in some regions you can book online – see page 269), although some health centres operate a first-come, first-served system, where patients are given a number and wait until it's called. Appointments with public health doctors can usually be made within 24 or 72 hours, although in some towns it can take a week or more. If your doctor is unavailable, his surgery will give you the name of a standby doctor or you can visit an emergency clinic (*clínica de urgencia*).

Most public health clinics operate a 24-hour service and there are also 24-hour private medical centres (*centros médicos*) in resort areas. If you're unable to attend surgery, doctors will make house calls, although if you live in a rural area you may have trouble getting a doctor to call on you unless you're an urgent case. If you rely on the public health service, try not to get ill in August when many doctors and specialists take a month's holiday! This is a serious point, as a number of medical 'disasters' occur in August when doctors are away. See also **Emergencies** and **Emergency Numbers** on pages 268 and 140.

There are excellent ante-natal facilities in Spain and arrangements for regular check-ups are made through your family doctor who then refers you to an ante-natal (or post-natal) organisation or clinic. Children in Spain are issued with a green vaccination book (*carnet de vacunaciones*), which must be presented when starting school. Once your child is registered at a health centre, you're advised by phone or letter when he's due for vaccinations.

# DRUGS & MEDICINES

Drugs (*medicinas*) and medicines (*medicamentos*) prescribed by a doctor are obtained from a chemist's (*farmacia*) denoted by the sign of a green cross. Most chemists are open from 9.30am to 1.30pm and from 4.30 to 8pm from Mondays to Saturdays. Outside normal opening hours, a notice is posted giving the address of the nearest duty chemist's (*farmacia de guardia*) open after 8pm (a weekly roster may be displayed). There are 24-hour duty chemists in all towns (usually indicated by a red light), although there may also be duty daytime (e.g. from 9.30am until 10pm) and night time chemists (e.g. from 10pm until 9.30am the following day). Legislation permits unlimited opening hours for chemists.

When visiting a duty chemist's outside normal hours, you must usually ring a bell, speak to the pharmacist (*farmacéutico*) behind a bullet-proof glass door and be served through a small hatch (this is particularly common in cities where crime is rife). In some areas, you may even be required to take a policeman with you. **A duty chemist's only fills prescriptions (*recetas*) and there may be a surcharge.** In addition to being displayed in chemists' windows, a list of duty chemists is published in local newspapers, and in some towns an annual schedule and map is published (available from tourist offices). A pharmacist in Spain must own and run his own chemist's (chain chemists are illegal) and their numbers are strictly controlled.

If you have a prescription you must pay 40 per cent of the cost of medicines and drugs or nothing at all if you're a pensioner or disabled. Many private health insurance schemes also reimburse members for drugs and medicines. Note that there's no refund for some prescribed medicines or for medicines purchased without a doctor's prescription. Prescription medicines in Spain are among the cheapest in the EU. However, chemists have a monopoly on non-prescription drugs, which are expensive compared with many other countries. General medication (such as painkillers, cough medicine and eye drops) which can be purchased in supermarkets in other EU countries can cost more in Spain, e.g. 20 paracetamol tablets cost around €1.50.

It's a good idea to buy non-prescription drugs abroad and stock up before arriving in Spain. In order to reduce the public health prescription bill of nearly €9,500 million a year, the public health service has removed almost 1,000 treatments previously available on social security prescriptions. However, public spending on prescriptions increases annually and further measures such as the introduction of more generic medicines and individual doses are planned in order to reduce Spain's huge pharmaceutical bill.

Pharmacists in Spain are highly trained and provide free medical advice for minor ailments, although you must probably speak Spanish. They're often able to sell you the proper remedy without recourse to a doctor and will also recommend a local doctor, specialist, nurse or dentist where necessary. They can supply a wide range of medicines over the counter without a prescription. Some medicines sold freely in other countries require a prescription in Spain. Homeopathic and herbal medicines are stocked by most chemists, some of which specialise in homeopathy.

Brand names for the same drugs and medicines vary from country to country, therefore if you regularly take medication you should ask your doctor for the generic name. If you wish to match medication prescribed abroad, you need a current prescription with the medication's trade name, the manufacturer's name, the chemical name and the dosage. Most foreign drugs have an equivalent in Spain, although particular brands may be difficult or impossible to obtain. It's possible to have medication sent from abroad and no import duty or value added tax (VAT/*IVA*) is payable. If you're visiting Spain for a limited period, you should take sufficient drugs to cover the length of your stay. In an emergency, a local doctor will write a prescription that can be filled at a local chemist's or a hospital may fill a prescription from its own pharmacy.

Spanish chemists aren't cluttered with all the non-medical wares found in American and British chemists, although they also sell non-prescription medicines, baby food and essentials, cosmetics, diet foods and toiletries. Chemists are cheaper than a *perfumería* for cosmetics, but more expensive than a supermarket or hypermarket. Another type of shop is a *droguería*, which sells non-medical items such as toiletries, cosmetics and household cleaning items, but not non-prescription medicines. A *droguería* shouldn't be confused with an American drugstore, which is a general store come fast food outlet. A health food shop (*herboristería*) sells health foods, diet foods and eternal-life-virility-youth pills and elixirs.

# HOSPITALS & CLINICS

All Spanish cities and large towns have at least one hospital (*hospital*) or clinic (*clínica*), many of which are modern establishments with highly trained staff and state of the art, high-tech equipment (most resort areas have a selection of good hospitals and clinics). However, in some areas (particularly poor rural areas) hospitals may not be up to the standard you might expect. There are long waiting lists for beds in some public hospitals (particularly the best ones), although this problem has been alleviated in recent years and is a health service priority. Generally, large towns and resort areas have the best hospital facilities. Hospitals are listed in yellow pages under *Hospitales* and indicated by the international hospital sign of a white 'H' on a blue background. A list of local hospitals and health centres treating social security patients is available from your local social security office.

There are many different categories of hospitals and clinics (often used to refer to all private hospitals) in Spain, including public (*hospitales de la seguridad social*) and private hospitals (*hospitales privados*), plus day hospitals performing specialist tests and minor surgery. Spanish hospitals include general hospitals (*hospitales generales*), district hospitals (*hospitales distritos*), regional hospitals (*hospitales comarcales*), provincial hospitals (*hospitales provinciales*), local hospitals (*hospitales comarcales/locales*), military hospitals (*hospitales militares*), nursing homes (*clínicas de reposo*), private clinics (*clínicas privadas*) and emergency clinics (*clínicas de urgencias*).

Some public hospitals are run by the Red Cross and funded by private donations, although some towns also contribute from public funds, and there are foreign-run private hospitals and clinics in major cities and resort areas. Major hospitals have an outpatients department (*consultas externas/departamento de enfermo externo del hospital*) and an emergency clinic. Red Cross posts throughout the country (staffed by volunteers) deal with minor accidents. Note that not all hospitals have an emergency department (*departamento de urgencias*) and public hospitals with emergency departments are often swamped by patients.

Most private hospitals and clinics specialise in in-patient care in particular fields of medicine such as obstetrics and surgery, rather than being full-service hospitals. A number of private clinics advertise in the expatriate press. Many Spaniards and foreign residents have private health insurance (see page 295) and some 40 per cent of Spanish hospitals treat only private patients, including hospitals owned by Spanish health insurance companies which only treat patients covered by their policies.

In public hospitals in resort areas, up to 40 per cent of patients may be foreigners, many of whom are retired foreign residents who don't speak Spanish. Although the reception staff and telephonists at Spanish hospitals in resort areas and major cities often speak English (and other languages), medical staff may speak only Spanish. In hospitals with many foreign patients, local expatriates may organise a team of volunteer interpreters (speaking a number of languages) for patients who are unable to speak Spanish. Note, however, that if you don't speak Spanish you may be given no information regarding the television (TV), phone, library, interpreting service, meal times and visiting hours, and will be very unlikely to receive any information in English or another foreign language. If your Spanish is poor, you may prefer to be treated at a private hospital or clinic with English-speaking staff. The cost of a bed in a private hospital averages around €150 a day in Spain, less than in northern Europe, although specialists' fees may be higher (resulting in similar overall costs of around €350 a day).

Except for emergency treatment, you're admitted or referred to a hospital or clinic for treatment only after a referral by a doctor or a specialist. If you're a social security patient, you're given a choice of specialists and hospitals offering the treatment you require usually in your own province. If you wish to be treated in hospital by your personal doctor or specialist, you must check that he's able to treat you at your preferred hospital. You can sometimes leave hospital at any time without a doctor's consent by signing a release form, although a doctor's consent is usually required.

Some public hospitals publish a guide (*guía del usario*) containing a hospital plan, public transport and road connections, department phone numbers, details of services such as cafeteria opening hours, visiting hours and other miscellaneous information. Public hospitals may have a library with books in a number of languages (including English) and may provide a mobile library for bedridden patients. The facilities provided in public hospitals are often limited compared with private hospitals and there may be no private rooms. If you wish to have a private room, you must pay a supplement, which may be paid by private health insurance (see page 295). You can usually rent a radio, TV or telephone for a small daily fee (if not already included in the room fee) and must usually provide your own pyjamas, robes, towels and toiletries. Public hospitals often have a pay TV and a pay-phone operated by a special key.

Except in the case of emergencies, you must present your social security card or, if you aren't covered by social security, you must provide evidence of your health insurance or the ability to pay. If your private insurance company doesn't have an arrangement with a Spanish hospital to pay bills direct, you must pay the bill yourself (credit cards are usually accepted) or seek assurance from your insurance company that they will pay the bill. If you have an appointment for treatment or surgery in a public hospital you may have to wait long past your appointment time before you're eventually allocated a bed. Note also that in a hospital with an accident and emergency department, a non-urgent operation may be cancelled a number of times while priority is given to emergency cases.

You may sometimes find nursing staff and your treatment cold and impersonal, particularly compared with hospitals in northern Europe and North America. Hospital accommodation in public hospitals is usually basic (in rooms with two to four beds) and can be very noisy with visitors chattering and the TV blaring. Food is variable and at its worst is terrible.

If you need crutches or other appliances you may need to obtain them yourself, although a public hospital may provide them. Patients are expected to convalesce at home, not in a hospital, and they're often discharged earlier than would be the case in many other countries. In many areas, back-up and nursing care is provided by the local community or expatriate groups. If you need to attend a public hospital out-patient department, bear in mind that it's likely to be totally chaotic. Take a long book (and earplugs) and be prepared to wait a number of hours, even if you have an appointment.

**Despite the criticisms included above**, most foreigners are **very** satisfied with their treatment in Spanish hospitals and expatriate newspapers regularly publish letters from former patients praising their treatment. Many people also report that the difference between the standard of accommodation and treatment varies little between the best public and private hospitals and clinics.

# DENTISTS

There are excellent dentists (*dentistas*) throughout Spain, although finding a dentist who speaks good English can be a problem, particularly in rural areas (although *Aaargh!* is the same in any language). However, there are many English-speaking foreign and Spanish dentists practising in Spain (particularly in major cities and resort areas), including American, British, German and Scandinavian dentists (although their fees may be higher than a Spanish dentist). Many embassies and consulates in Spain maintain a list of English-speaking dentists in their area (or dentists speaking their national language) and your employer, colleagues, friends or neighbours may be able to recommend someone.

Many tourist offices also maintain a list of English-speaking dentists, and dentists may be listed in local English-language newspapers and magazines. Dentists are permitted to advertise their services and a number advertise in the expatriate press and are listed in yellow pages under *Dentistas Odontólogos*. Usually, only names, addresses and telephone numbers are listed, and information such as specialities, surgery hours and whether they treat children (some don't) isn't provided. Many 'family' dentists in Spain are qualified to perform 'special' treatment, e.g. endodontics (*endodoncia*) or periodontics (*periodoncia*), carried out by specialists in many countries.

Dentists' surgery hours vary considerably, but are typically 9.30 or 10am to 2pm and 5 to 8pm. Some dentists have Saturday morning surgeries, e.g. 9.00am to noon. You must make an appointment. Many dentists provide an emergency service and there are special emergency dental services in major cities and resort areas. Note that only extractions and emergency treatment after an accident are available free under the Spanish public health service (treatment may be performed in a public health clinic or a public hospital). If you need emergency treatment under the public health service (see page 268), first visit your doctor. Dentists expect to be paid in cash or by credit card when treatment is completed, although if you're having expensive treatment such as a crown or a bridge made, your dentist may ask for a deposit in advance. Some dentists operate a membership scheme (e.g. €100 a year) which may include two check-ups, consultations, and a scale and polish. Always obtain an itemised bill if you intend to claim on your health insurance.

The cost of treatment varies wildly, but as a rough guide you can expect to pay around €40 for an extraction and €40 to €100 for a filling. Before committing yourself to a large bill, it's advisable to obtain a written quotation for expensive treatment (if you don't receive a written quotation, the final bill may be much higher than estimated). A verbal estimate is often much lower than the final bill, even for a simple filling. If you or your family require expensive cosmetic dental treatment, e.g. crowns, bridges, braces or dentures, you may find it cheaper to have treatment abroad. Alternatively, you can ask your dentist if he can reduce the cost by reducing the work involved. See also **Dental Insurance** on page 299.

# OPTICIANS

As with other medical practitioners in Spain, it isn't necessary to register with an optician or optometrist (*óptico*); simply make an appointment with the optician of your choice. Ask your colleagues, friends or neighbours if they can recommend someone. Opticians are listed in the yellow pages under *Óptica* and ophthalmologists (specialist eye doctors) under *Médicos Oftalmología*. Eye tests and prescriptions for spectacles are available free under the public health system, and low-income families and pensioners also receive free (basic) spectacles. Public health eye tests are generally performed at a public hospital and patients need a referral from their family doctor. However, many opticians also perform free eye tests.

The optical business is highly competitive in Spain. Prices for spectacles (*lentes*) and contact lenses (*lentillas de contacto*) aren't controlled, so it's wise to shop around and compare costs. You may find that special spectacle lenses and contact lenses are more expensive in Spain than in some other European countries. Always obtain an estimate for lenses and ask about charges for such things as eye tests, fittings, adjustments, lens-care kit and follow-up visits. Note that the cost of tinted and special lenses (e.g. high index) increases the cost of spectacles considerably. Ask about the cost of replacement lenses – if they're expensive it may be worthwhile taking out insurance. Many opticians and retailers offer insurance against the accidental damage of spectacles for a nominal fee or even free for a limited period. Disposable and extended-wear soft contact lenses are also widely available, although medical experts believe that extended-wear lenses should be treated with caution, as they greatly increase the risk of potentially blinding eye infections. **Obtain advice from an ophthalmologist before buying them.**

It's advisable to have your eyes tested before arriving in Spain and to bring a spare pair of spectacles and/or contact lenses with you. You should also bring a copy of your prescription in case you need to obtain replacement spectacles or contact lenses urgently. **Note that many people find it essential to wear sunglasses all year round in Spain.** Always buy a good pair that protects your eyes from the sun's harmful ultra-violet rays.

# COUNSELLING & SOCIAL SERVICES

Counselling and help for special health and social problems isn't as widely available in Spain. However, there are a number of public and private organisations providing help for various health and health-related problems, including drug rehabilitation; alcoholism and related problems; gambling; dieting; smoking; teenage pregnancy; attempted suicide and psychiatric problems; rehabilitation; homosexual related problems; youth problems; parent-child problems; child abuse; family violence (e.g. battered wives); runaways; marriage and relationship counselling and rape.

In the first instance, you should contact your family doctor, who can usually offer advice and put you in touch with an appropriate organisation or professional counsellor. In times of need there's usually someone to turn to and all services are strictly confidential. There are expatriate self-help groups in all areas, particularly for alcoholism (e.g. Alcoholics Anonymous), drug dependency and weight control (e.g. Weight Watchers). Voluntary groups are also common among expatriate communities, particularly organisations helping the elderly and infirm.

One of Spain's major health problems is alcoholism, which is directly responsible for the loss of thousands of lives each year. The legal age for drinking alcohol in Spain is 18 and in 2002, the government and autonomous regions introduced a series of measures designed to enforce this, including high fines for establishments who sell to under-age drinkers. Alcoholism is a particular problem among expatriates in Spain, many of whom have little to do, but lie in the sun and drink alcohol all day long. If you already drink more than is good for you, you should take extra care not to over-indulge in Spain. There are English-speaking Alcoholics Anonymous groups in Barcelona, the Balearics (Ibiza and Mallorca), the Canaries, Madrid and on the

Costa Blanca and the Costa del Sol. Many advertise in the expatriate press and details of meetings can be found on the AA Europe website (🖥 www.aa-europe.net/countries – go to 'Spain').

Spain has a relatively small number of social workers and there are few state-funded homes for the mentally and physically disabled, or residential nursing homes for the elderly. In fact, services for the disabled and elderly are generally poor. There are three kinds of social security homes which are operated by the Instituto de Migraciones y Servicios Sociales (IMSERSO) for the elderly in Spain; homes for those able to look after themselves, residences for invalids or the chronically ill, and mixed residences. To qualify for entry you must be aged over 65 (or 60 if an invalid or widowed) **and** be in receipt of a Spanish state pension or be the spouse of a Spanish pensioner. Foreigners who aren't in receipt of a Spanish pension aren't admitted to IMSERSO homes, but may be admitted to homes run by provincial authorities.

# SEXUALLY-TRANSMITTED DISEASES

As in many western countries, AIDS (*SIDA*) has caused anxiety in Spain, which has far more cases of AIDS and HIV, the virus that causes AIDS, than any other EU country. However, the number of new cases is falling by around 20 per cent annually. Since 1990, AIDS has primarily been transmitted by drug users, many of whom are prostitutes (injecting drug-users account for nearly 60 per cent of Spain's victims). There are also as many children infected with AIDS in Spain as in all other EU countries combined.

In an attempt to combat the spread of AIDS, the use of condoms (*preservativos*) has been encouraged and they're widely available from chemists and vending machines in public toilets, although apparently only some 35 per cent of Spaniards use contraceptives in casual encounters. With the growing problem of AIDS, opposition to contraception from the Catholic Church has been muted. A lack of resources and political indifference are considered by medical experts to be the biggest hurdles to curbing the spread of AIDS in Spain, although recent widespread publicity campaigns have helped reduce the incidence. There's a free and confidential AIDS helpline operating throughout Spain (☎ 900-850 000), and there are usually local support groups operating in towns and cities (listed under *Seropositivos* in yellow pages).

# BIRTHS & DEATHS

Births and deaths must be registered at the Civil Registry (*Registro Civil*) at the town hall of the district where they take place. Registration applies to everyone irrespective of their nationality or whether they're residents of Spain or just visitors.

## Births

Registration of a birth must be made within eight days at the local civil registry and may be done by the hospital or clinic where the child was born, or by the midwife when a birth takes place at home. Parents are, however, responsible for ensuring that this is done and may have to do it themselves. There are two forms of birth certificate; a short certificate (*extracto de inscripción de nacimiento* or *certificado simple*), showing only the date of birth, the names of the child and parents, and the inscription number and a full certificate (*certificado literal de nacimiento*). Foreigners should get the full one, which costs only a little more (both are inexpensive) and it may be necessary to register your child at your home country's consulate or embassy in Spain (to obtain a birth certificate and passport for a child).

A birth certificate must state whether a child is legitimate or illegitimate – a **legitimate** child is one born at least 180 days after its parents' marriage or within 300 days of a divorce, annulment of a marriage or the death of the father. Note that the suspected father of a child can be compelled to undergo a biological test (at a cost of €275 to €500) to prove whether or not he's the father. Tests are supposedly almost foolproof (99.9 per cent accurate) and are accepted as such by a court of law. Spain has one of the lowest birth rates in the world at around 1.07 children per woman aged between 15 and 49.

Abortion is legal in Spain, but it remains a contentious issue, and is fervently opposed by the Catholic Church and right-wing circles. It's currently available during the first 12 weeks of pregnancy in certain circumstances, e.g. when a pregnancy threatens the mother's life, the foetus is severely deformed or the pregnancy was the result of rape, but the current government intends to make abortion legal within the first 14 weeks of pregnancy whatever the circumstances may be.

# Deaths

A death must be registered within 24 hours at the town hall of the district where it took place. If the deceased was a foreigner, the town hall needs his passport or residence permit (*residencia*) and the death must also be registered at the deceased's local consulate or embassy in Spain. A death needn't be reported to the police unless it was as a result of an accident or crime (or the death occurred in suspicious circumstances). A death certificate must be prepared and signed by the doctor who attended the death (in a hospital or elsewhere) and be legally certified by a judge. In the case of a foreigner, it must be presented to the deceased person's embassy or consulate in Spain to obtain a certificate valid in the deceased's home country. The certificates are required for insurance claims and to execute a will.

A body can be buried or cremated in Spain or flown to another country for burial. It's expensive (e.g. €900 to €1,800 within Europe) to fly a body to another country for burial, although the cost may be covered by an international insurance policy which includes repatriation. In Spain, a burial must take place through an undertaker (*funeraria*), who arranges everything, including death certificates. A full service funeral costs between €1,200 and €2,500, including five years rent on a cemetery niche (*nicho*). The cost of cremation is cheaper than a full-service funeral at from €300, although there aren't many crematoriums in Spain. A service may be attended before the actual cremation (with the body present) or after it with the urn containing the deceased's ashes. A body cannot be interred sooner than 24 hours after death.

However, burial usually takes place within 48 hours of death and where there's no refrigeration a burial **must** take place within 72 hours. Refrigeration is, however, available in most areas and costs around €35 a day.

Although cemeteries in Spain are mostly Catholic, a person of any creed can be buried there. There are also foreign cemeteries in some cities and towns, e.g. there's a British cemetery in Malaga and an international cemetery in Benalmádena (Costa del Sol). Burials and cremations can be made only in official cemeteries. In most Spanish cemeteries, internment is above ground and bodies are placed in niches set into walls, which are rented for a number of years, e.g. 5 to 50 (the rent is from €30 a year). The cheapest 'graves' are in municipal cemeteries, where typical rentals are around €300 for five years, then €30 per year and up to €1,500 for 50 years. After the rental period has expired, bodies are interned in a common burial ground within the consecrated cemetery grounds. After a number of years (e.g. 25), all graves are exhumed in some areas and the remains buried in a large communal tomb, although this occurs mostly on the islands where land is at a premium. **To avoid this you must buy a plot outright which can cost €3,000 or more.** Note that cemeteries often have limited opening hours and aren't open to the public at all hours, as they are in most countries.

Dying is an expensive business in Spain. Always check the cost of a funeral in advance and make sure that you aren't paying for anything you don't want. The cost of a full service funeral is around €1,200 to €2,500, depending on the area and town, and there may also be extra costs for transportation and cemetery fees. Embalming isn't common in Spain and is expensive, e.g. €1,200. It may be necessary to engage a local funeral company, but undertakers' fees are roughly the same in most areas. Most undertakers expect to be paid in cash. It's possible to take out an insurance policy (*seguro de decesos*) for funeral expenses with a Spanish or foreign insurance company, although it's very expensive.

When a resident of Spain dies, all interested parties must be notified (see **Inheritance & Gift Tax** and **Wills** on pages 349 and 352). You need several copies of the death certificate which are required by banks and other institutions.

# MEDICAL TREATMENT ABROAD

If you're entitled to public health benefits in Spain or another EU country, you can take advantage of reciprocal healthcare agreements in most other European countries. Everyone insured under Spanish social security is covered for medical expenses while travelling abroad, providing certain steps are taken to ensure reimbursement. In some cases, you must obtain an EU health card (*tarjeta sanitaria europea*) from your local social security office before leaving Spain. **This also applies to foreign residents of Spain planning to visit their home EU country.**

Full payment (possibly in cash) must usually be made in advance for treatment received abroad, although you will be reimbursed on your return to Spain. This applies to all EU countries except the UK, where everyone receives free emergency healthcare. You're also reimbursed for essential treatment in countries not mentioned above, although you must obtain detailed receipts. Note that reimbursement is based on the cost of comparable treatment in Spain. In certain countries, e.g. Canada, Japan, Switzerland and the US, medical treatment is very expensive and you're advised to take out travel or holiday insurance (see page 303) when visiting these countries. **This is advisable wherever you're travelling, as it provides considerably wider medical cover than reciprocal healthcare agreements (and includes many other things such as repatriation).** If you do a lot of travelling abroad, it's worthwhile having an international health insurance policy (see page 295).

# Visitors to Spain

If you're an EU resident visiting Spain, you can take advantage of reciprocal healthcare agreements (see **Medical Treatment Abroad** on page 281). Nationals of non-EU countries are also entitled to free healthcare under the Spanish public health service, providing their home country has a reciprocal agreement with Spain. EU residents should apply for a European Health Insurance Card/EHIC (previously the E-111 form) from their local social security office at least three weeks before planning to travel to Spain. The new card will be valid in all 25 EU countries by January 2005. The card is open-ended and valid for life. However, you must continue to make social security contributions in the country where it was issued and if you become a resident in another country (e.g. in Spain) it becomes invalid. It covers emergency hospital treatment, but doesn't include prescribed medicines, special examinations, X-rays, laboratory tests, physiotherapy and dental treatment.

If you use the EU health card in Spain, you must present the card to the medical practitioner who's providing treatment and pay for treatment in cash. You must apply for reimbursement to your home country's social security department (instructions are provided with the card), which can take a number of months. If you travel to Spain or to another EU country **specifically** for medical treatment or maternity care in a public hospital, you need the E-112 form, and prior authorisation from your country's social security department. The form E-112 authorises treatment in a Spanish or other EU public hospital without pre-payment (although it's difficult to obtain).

British visitors or those planning to live in Spain can obtain information about reciprocal health treatment in Spain (and other countries) from the Department for Works and Pensions, Pensions and Overseas Benefits Directorate, Newcastle-upon-Tyne NE98 1BA, UK (☎ 0191-218 7777, 💻 www.dwp.gov.uk).

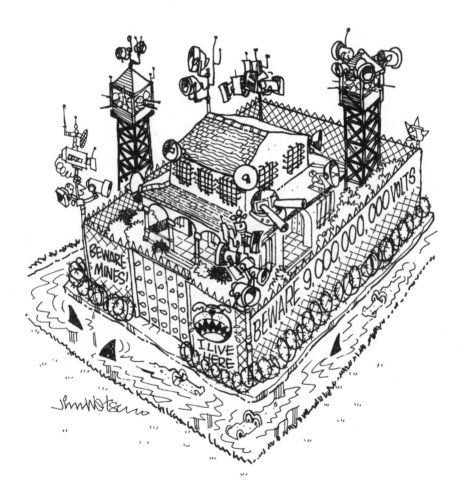

# 13.

# INSURANCE

The Spanish government and Spanish law provide for various obligatory state and employer insurance schemes. These include health, sickness and maternity; work injuries; state pensions; disability and unemployment insurance. However, the average Spaniard is more prone to taking risks than many other nationalities and carries less insurance than, for example, northern Europeans. Most Spanish and European Union (EU) residents and their families receive health treatment under the Spanish social security (*seguridad social*) system. If you don't qualify for healthcare under the Spanish national health system (see page 288), it's essential to take out private health insurance (see page 295), which is obligatory for most non-EU residents. Spanish employees have considerable protection under social security and are entitled to higher benefits than employees in many other EU countries (although in most cases you would be unwise to rely solely on social security to meet your needs).

Ensure your family has full health insurance during the interval between leaving your last country of residence and obtaining health insurance in Spain. One way is to take out a travel insurance policy (see page 303). However, if possible, it's better to extend a private health insurance policy to cover you in Spain, rather than take out a new policy. This is particularly important if you have an existing health problem that won't be covered by a new policy. There are a few occasions in Spain where insurance for individuals is compulsory, including third party car insurance (see page 223), third party property liability insurance (see page 303) for tenants and homeowners, and mortgage life insurance for mortgage holders. If you lease a car or buy one on credit, a lender may insist that you have comprehensive car insurance (see page 223). Voluntary insurance includes private pensions, disability, health, household, dental, travel, car breakdown and life insurance.

It's unnecessary to spend half your income insuring yourself against every eventuality from the common cold to being sued for your last cent, but it's important to insure against any event that could precipitate a major financial disaster, such as a serious accident or your house falling down. As with anything connected with finance, it's important to shop around when buying insurance. Just collecting a few brochures from insurance agents and making a few telephone calls **could save you a lot of money.** Regrettably, you cannot insure yourself against being uninsured or sue your insurance broker for giving you bad advice.

In all matters regarding insurance, you're responsible for ensuring that you and your family are legally insured. Note that if you wish to make a claim on an insurance policy, you may be required to report an incident to the police within 24 hours (in some cases this may be a legal requirement). Obtain legal advice for anything other than a minor claim. Spanish law is likely to differ from that in your home country or your previous country of residence, never **assume** that it's the same. See also **Car Insurance** on page 223 and **Breakdown Insurance** on page 260.

# INSURANCE COMPANIES & AGENTS

There are numerous Spanish and foreign insurance companies to choose from, providing a range of insurance services or who specialise in certain fields only. Many of the British and other foreign insurance companies operating in Spain cater particularly for the needs of expatriates, with major insurance companies having offices or agents throughout Spain (there are also 'direct' telephone insurers). Insurance agents, brokers (*corredor de seguros*) and companies are listed in the yellow pages under *Seguros* and many advertise in the expatriate press. Most insurance companies or brokers provide a free appraisal of your family's insurance needs.

There are many independent brokers in Spain, including many British and other foreign brokers in resort areas, who can offer you a choice of policies and save you money. However, as in many countries, it's often difficult to obtain completely independent unbiased insurance advice, as brokers may be influenced by the commission offered for selling a particular policy. As with all financial matters in Spain, be careful who you choose as your broker and the company you insure with, as a number of companies have gone bust in recent years (particularly in the motor insurance sector) and insurance fraud isn't unknown. **When buying insurance, particularly car insurance (see page 223), shop around.** Obtain recommendations from friends, colleagues and neighbours (but don't believe everything they tell you!). Compare the costs, terms and benefits provided by a number of companies before making a decision. Note that premiums (*premios*) are sometimes negotiable.

Spanish residents are free to insure their car, home or life with any insurance company registered in the EU, **without** the need for the insurer to be registered in Spain. The company must be registered in its home country and insurance cover must correspond to the minimum legal requirements. Note, however, that should a dispute arise over a claim, it will usually be dealt with in the country where the insurance company is registered.

If you take out insurance through a broker in Spain, it's important to check that your insurance premium has been paid to the insurance company concerned and that you receive your policy quickly. It isn't widespread, but there have been occurrences where a policy (e.g. health) has been cancelled when the premium paid to a broker wasn't passed to the insurance company (or was paid late).

If you have a complaint regarding an insurance policy, you should complain in the first instance to the company; large companies usually have a complaints department (*defensores del asegurado*). If you don't receive satisfaction you can send a complaint to the Servicio de Reclamaciones, Dirección General de Seguros y Fondos de Pensiones (DGSFP), Paseo de la Castellana, 44, 28046 Madrid (☎ 913-397 000, 🖳 www.dgsfp.mineco.es – go to *Servicio de Reclamaciones*). Note that the DGSFP concerns itself only with Spanish insurance companies and foreign companies with a registered office in Spain.

# INSURANCE CONTRACTS

Read all insurance contracts before signing them. **If you don't understand Spanish, have your legal advisor check a policy and don't sign it until you clearly understand the terms and the cover provided.** Many foreign insurance companies operating in Spain provide policies and information in English and other foreign languages. Note, however, that an insurance policy issued in Spain is usually written under Spanish law and that the Spanish document is always the legal one. Like insurance companies everywhere, some will use any available legal loophole to avoid paying out in the event of a claim and therefore it pays to deal only with reputable companies (not that this provides a foolproof guarantee). Policies often contain legal loopholes in the small print and if you don't understand them you should obtain independent professional legal advice before signing a contract.

**If you believe that you have a valid claim you should persevere, despite any obstacles placed in your path.** The wheels of justice grind very slowly in Spain and it may take you a number of years to gain satisfaction, but if you have a legitimate claim you will usually eventually receive compensation (plus interest from the date of the claim).

Always check the notice period required to cancel (*cancelar/anular*) a policy. Note that in Spain, most insurance policies are automatically extended for a further period (usually a year) if they aren't cancelled in writing by registered letter two or three months before the expiry date. You may cancel an insurance policy before the term has expired if the premium has increased, the terms are altered, e.g. the risk is diminished, or an insured object is lost or stolen. This must, however, still be done in writing and by registered post. Cancellation is also permitted at short notice under certain circumstances, including when changing jobs, redundancy, retirement, marriage and divorce. You're usually entitled to a refund of any unused premiums paid.

If you wish to make a claim, you must usually inform your insurance company in writing by registered letter within two to five days of the incident (e.g. for accidents) or 24 hours in the case of theft. Thefts should also be reported to the local police station within 24 hours, as the police report (*denuncia*) constitutes evidence of your claim. Usually, an insurance company sends an adjuster to evaluate the extent of damage, e.g. to your home or car.

One of the advantages of taking out a policy with a foreign insurance company is that you have a policy you can understand (apart from all the legal jargon) and can make claims in your own language. This is usually a good option for the owner of a holiday home in Spain. However, bear in mind that insuring with a foreign insurance company may be more expensive than insuring with a Spanish company and in certain cases a policy may still need to be written under Spanish law.

# SOCIAL SECURITY

Spain has a comprehensive social security (*seguridad social*) system covering over 90 per cent of the population. It includes healthcare (plus sickness and maternity); industrial injuries; unemployment insurance; old age (pensions), invalidity and death benefits. Social security benefits in Spain are among the highest in the EU, as are social security contributions. The total contributions per employee are an average of around 30 per cent of gross pay, some 25 per cent of which is paid by employers. With the exception of sickness benefits, social security benefits aren't taxed.

Two-thirds of social security spending is on cash benefits such as pensions (old age, disabled, orphans and widows), sickness and housing benefits, distributed through the Instituto Nacional de Seguridad Social (INSS). The Instituto Nacional de Empleo (INEM) distributes unemployment benefits. Less than a third of revenue is spent on health services, administered through the regional health services (see page

269), and social services, which are the responsibility of the Instituto de Migraciones y Servicios Sociales (IMSERSO). Spain has a separate social security system for members of the civil service and the armed forces, and special schemes for farm workers, seamen, the self-employed, domestic servants and other groups.

The Spanish social security system has been under severe financial strains (partly due to widespread fraud and non-payment of bills by town halls). An ageing population and increasing unemployment have contributed to a huge increase in spending on healthcare, pensions and unemployment benefits, although there have been cutbacks in government spending in recent years. Most analysts agree that present levels of social security benefits (particularly pensions) are unsustainable and payments must be slashed if the system isn't to be bankrupted. However, in recent years, the record number of social security contributions from employees (more than 17.6 million) means the outlook has improved somewhat. A government priority is to increase the pension fund, which in 2005 had a balance of nearly €21,500 million, guaranteeing pensions until at least 2015. Government policy is to continue to add to this fund, rather than reduce Spain's high social security contributions.

For more information contact your local social security office or the Instituto Nacional de la Seguridad Social, Subdirección General de Relaciones Internacionales, Padre Damián, 4, Madrid 28036 (freephone ☎ 900-166 565, 🖳 www.seg-social.es).

# Eligibility & Exemptions

All foreign employees working for Spanish companies and self-employed foreigners in Spain must usually contribute to Spanish social security. Generally, if you're an employee in Spain, you will be insured under Spanish social security legislation and won't have any liability for social security contributions in your home country or country of domicile. However, social security agreements exist between Spain and over 40 countries, including all EU countries, Australia, Canada and the US, whereby expatriates who remain registered as employed in their home country may continue to be members of their home country's social security scheme for a limited period. EU nationals transferred to Spain by an employer in their home country can continue to pay social security abroad for one year (form E-101 is required), which can be extended for another year in unforeseen circumstances (when form E-102 is needed). This also applies to the self-employed. However, after working in Spain for two years, EU nationals **must** contribute to the Spanish social security system.

To qualify for social security benefits, you must have been employed in Spain for a limited period and have made certain minimum contributions. If you're retired and living in Spain and receive a state pension from another EU country, or from a country with a social security agreement with Spain, you and your spouse are automatically entitled to health benefits under Spanish social security (if a wife aged 65 or over is entitled to public health treatment, then a husband aged under 65 may also be entitled to it). You must prove your entitlement to a pension by obtaining form E-121 from your home country's social security administration, which must be produced when registering with Spanish social security (see below). Form E-121 has indefinite validity and doesn't need to be renewed. If, however, you retire to Spain before reaching the Spanish retirement age, you must have private health insurance (see page 295).

If you qualify to pay social security contributions abroad, it may be worthwhile doing so, as contributions in some countries are lower than those in Spain. If you or your spouse work in Spain, but remain insured under the social security legislation of another EU country, you can claim social security benefits from that country. If the spouse and children of an EU national employed in Spain remain in their home country, they will continue to be covered by the social security system of that country.

If you need to claim benefits in Spain and have paid contributions in another EU country, those contributions are usually taken into account when calculating your right to benefits. If you're receiving an invalidity pension or other social security benefits on the grounds of ill-health, you should establish exactly how living in Spain will affect those benefits, as they may cease when you take up residence in Spain. In some countries, there are reciprocal rights regarding invalidity, but you must confirm that they apply in your case before going to live in Spain. Note that the payment and right to foreign (e.g. from other EU countries) social security benefits (apart from pensions) usually ends when you take up permanent residence in Spain. Citizens of an EU country who visit Spain as tourists can also use the Spanish public health system (see page 288).

In the UK, information regarding social security rights within the EU is provided in two booklets: *Your Social Security Insurance, Benefits and Healthcare When Moving within the European Community* (SA29), available from the Department for Works and Pensions, Pensions and Overseas Benefits Directorate, Newcastle-upon-Tyne NE98 1BA, UK (☎ 0191-218 7777, 🖳 www.dwp.gov.uk) and *The Community Provisions on Social Security*, available online only from 🖳 http://bookshop.eu.int.

# Registration

If you're working in Spain, your employer will usually complete the necessary formalities to ensure that you're covered by social security. If he doesn't do it, you must obtain an attestation that you're employed in Spain and register at the nearest social security office to your home. Your local town hall will give you the address of your local office or it's listed under *Seguridad Social* in your local yellow pages. If you're in receipt of a state pension in another EU country and move to Spain, you must take both copies of your form E-121 (see above) to the pension department at your local social security office in Spain. One copy is retained and the other stamped and returned to you. You must produce passports and (certified) birth certificates for all dependants and a marriage certificate (if applicable). You may also need to provide copies with official translations, but check first, as translations may be unnecessary. You also need proof of residence such as a property deed (*escritura*) or a rental contract.

After you've registered you receive a registration card (*tarjeta sanitaria*), similar to a credit card, usually by post around four to eight weeks later. A married couple with one partner working are covered by the same number, as are all dependants (e.g. children under 16), but each dependant receives a separate social security card. When applying for benefits or for social security reimbursements, you must apply to the office listed on your social security card and quote your social security number or produce your card. **Note that there's a compulsory waiting period before a new subscriber can claim certain social security benefits, which varies depending on the particular benefit.**

If you contribute to social security, your dependants will receive the same benefits. Dependants include your spouse (if he or she isn't personally insured); your children supported by you under the age of 16 (or under the age of 20 if they're students or unable to work through illness or invalidity) and ascendants, descendants and relatives by marriage supported by you and living in the same household. Separated, divorced and widowed people continue to receive benefits for at least one year after the 'event', or in the case of separated people, for as long as their spouse is employed providing they aren't eligible for benefits from other sources.

## Contributions

Social security contributions (*cuotas*) for employees are calculated as a percentage of their taxable income, although for certain contributions there's a maximum salary level. Contributions start as soon as you start work in Spain and not when you obtain your residence permit (*residencia* – see page 78). Social security contributions for employees and employers are based on the official salary limit (*nómina*) for a specific occupation. The minimum monthly salary on which you must usually pay social security contributions is the official minimum salary (€513 a month), of which 37.2 per cent is calculated as the monthly payment for social security. A small proportion, i.e. 6.4 per cent, is deducted from the employee's salary and the remainder is paid by the employer.

The self-employed (*cuenta propia*) pay a minimum of around €230 a month (the maximum is around €840), which is subject to a 20 per cent surcharge if you don't pay it on time. **Any self-employed person, even if he works only part-time, must contribute to social security.** However, if you don't work for a **minimum** of a calendar month you aren't required to pay social security during that period, e.g. if you operate a business in Spain and close for the month of January. **Note that if you're self-employed and have a number of separate jobs, you require two sets of papers and must pay social security twice.** Domestic workers (*empleados de hogar*) who are self-employed and work part-time for a number of employers pay reduced social security contributions of €132 a month. However, if they're employed full-time by one employer, they must receive the minimum wage (see page 39) and pay normal employee contributions.

## Benefits

Spanish social security includes benefits for health, sickness, maternity, work injury, housing, unemployment, retirement, invalidity and death. Social security benefits are paid as a percentage of your salary and are subject to minimum and maximum payments. In order to qualify for benefits, you must have made social security contributions for a certain length of time, e.g. 180 days over the last five years to qualify for sick pay. See also **Social Security Health Benefits** on page 269.

## Health Benefits

Public health benefits include general and specialist care, hospitalisation, laboratory services, drugs and medicines, basic dental care, maternity care, appliances and emergency transportation. With the exception of pensioners and the disabled, members must pay a percentage of the cost (around 40 per cent) of certain treatment and items such as drugs and medicines (see page 273). See also **Social Security Health Benefits** on page 269.

## Sickness Benefits

When an employee is ill, he continues to receive a percentage of his salary. A self-employed person can also receive 60 per cent of his base monthly payments for the first 20 days and 75 per cent afterwards, providing he obtains a doctor's certificate stating that he's incapable of carrying out his usual occupation.

## Unemployment Insurance Benefits

Unemployment in Spain is among the highest in Western Europe and although membership of the state social security system is mandatory, only some 50 per cent of unemployed people qualify for benefits (young people who have never been employed don't qualify). There's no such thing as supplementary benefit (e.g. as in the UK) or supplemental security income (e.g. as in the US), although many regions pay a 'social wage' to the unemployed who don't qualify for unemployment benefits. There's a 'safety net' for agricultural workers who can claim the minimum unemployment benefit if they can prove that they've been employed for a minimum number of days a year (most agricultural workers can find seasonal work for a maximum of just three months a year).

Huge deficits in public spending have forced the government to reduce benefits to 75 per cent of the **minimum** salary of €513 a month, irrespective of former earnings. Unemployed people who haven't been employed for at least one year receive only 75 per cent of this sum and don't receive any credit against their state pension. Under a new system, benefits have been cut and the period during which the newly unemployed are eligible for state assistance is from 120 to 720 days, providing they've worked for at least 360 days during the previous six years. Entitlement to unemployment benefit ceases after one or two years, except in the case of families who receive a much reduced benefit for a further two years. An unemployed person planning to carry on a professional activity as a working member of a labour co-operative or an employee-owned company, can receive aggregate unemployment benefit as a one-time payment.

Note that social security payments made in another EU country are taken into account and credited to EU workers in Spain, so that they're eligible for full unemployment benefits during a period of unemployment. If you're entitled to unemployment benefits in another EU country and have been claiming unemployment for at least four weeks, you can continue to receive unemployment benefit (at your home country's rate) in Spain for up to three months while looking for work. You must inform the unemployment office in your home country that you intend to seek work in Spain well in advance of your departure. If you qualify for transfer of benefits to Spain, your home country's unemployment service provides a certificate of authorisation, which is necessary to register in Spain.

You must register for work at your nearest regional unemployment office (see page 29) within seven days of leaving your home country, so that your eligibility for benefits isn't interrupted. **However, there may be a delay of up to three months before you actually start to receive benefits, so you must be able to finance yourself during your job search in Spain.** During this period, you're entitled to healthcare in Spain, for which you require a certificate of entitlement (form E-119). Note that Spanish bureaucrats aren't very co-operative with this scheme and you must persevere to obtain your rights. If, after three months, you don't have a job you must leave Spain, as you're permitted to remain for only three months without a residence permit (see page 78). **A residence permit won't be issued if you don't have a job or an adequate income.**

## Maternity Benefits

Maternity benefits (*baja por maternidad*) are available to women who have paid their social security contributions for the total of 180 days during the last five years. The equivalent of the full salary is paid to the mother by social security for 16 weeks (18 weeks for multiple births) of which a minimum of six weeks must be taken after the birth. Paternity leave is also available and can be taken from six weeks after the birth. Maternity and paternity leave may be taken together or separately and both parents are entitled to the equivalent of their full salaries. Parents who adopt may also take maternity or paternity leave. Check with your local social security office for information.

## Old Age, Invalidity & Death Benefits

The Spanish state retirement (*jubilación*) pension is paid at 65 for men and women. Contributions are paid by employers and employees, and vary according to your income. Spanish state pensions are the highest in Europe, after Sweden. The current minimum pension (after 15 years contributions) for someone aged 65 is €524.01 per month for a couple and €438.71 per month for a single person. The maximum monthly pension is €2,159.12. Spanish pensions are indexed to take account of rises in the cost of living. Pensioners, like salaried employees, receive 14 payments a year instead of 12, with an extra payment in July and December (this also includes retired, self-employed people).

A worker earning over €2,731.50 a month can choose to pay the maximum contributions (around €840 a month for a self-employed person) in order to receive the maximum pension of €2,159.12 a month after 35 years' contributions. No extra contributions can be paid on income above €2,731.50 a month. A worker's final pension is principally based on his payments during the fifteen years before his retirement and in particular, during the last two. To receive a full state pension you must have contributed for 35 years.

The **minimum** number of years you must pay into the system to qualify for a pension is 15 years. Early or partial retirement is permitted under Spanish law and anyone with sufficient credits can choose to retire early. The widowed partner of a state pensioner is entitled to the full pension payable to his or her spouse, while dependant children are entitled to an additional 20 per cent. When there's no surviving parent, dependant children are also entitled to the widow's pension.

If you move to Spain after working in another EU country (or move to another EU country after working in Spain), your state pension contributions can be exported to Spain (or from Spain to another country). Spanish state pensions are payable abroad and most countries pay state pensions directly to their nationals resident in Spain. Under EU regulations, the total contributions paid into different member states insurance systems are taken into account when accessing an individual's rights to a state pension (this also applies to invalidity pensions). The number of years contributions paid in different countries are added together and each country pays the percentage for which it's liable, e.g. if you worked 20 years in the UK, 5 years in Germany and 15 years in Spain, the UK would pay 50 per cent, Germany 12.5 per cent and Spain 37.5 per cent of your state pension. Contributors can ask the authorities in the relevant countries to calculate their entitlements and opt to choose the highest amount. Contact your home country's social security administration for information.

If you retire to Spain before your home country's state retirement age, it's advisable to continue to contribute to the state pension scheme, otherwise your state pension could be reduced. In some countries (e.g. the UK), there are special contributions for those who aren't employed, who can pay contributions annually in one instalment. Most countries pay state pensioners living in Spain the same pension that they would receive in their home country, with annual increases indexed to the cost of living.

If you plan to retire to Spain, you should ensure that your income is (and will remain) sufficient to live on, bearing in mind devaluation if your pension or income isn't paid in euros, rises in the cost of living and unforeseen expenses such as medical bills or anything else that may reduce your income (e.g. stock market crashes). Anyone living in Spain who's in receipt of a state pension in any EU country is entitled to the benefits of Spanish social security. Various organisations, such as the Fondo Nacional de Asistencia Social (FAS), provides old age pensions for those who don't qualify under other schemes.

As in all western European countries, state pensions are under pressure from governments that can no longer afford to pay them, due to the ever dwindling number of workers who are supporting a growing number of retirees. There are around 8 million pensioners in Spain in 2005, and the figure is expected to reach 12 million by the year 2040. Spain has particular problems, as state pensions remain far too generous (for the government – pensions are **never** too high for pensioners!), despite reductions in the last few years, and more people receive their income from the state than from the private sector. The state pension fund was almost bankrupt, although there are now annual large injections of funds in an attempt to ensure that future contributors receive the pensions they've been promised (although it's still expected to run into problems by 2015). The Spanish government is trying to shift some of the burden onto private insurance companies, so far without much success. There are proposals to increase the number of years required to qualify and to drastically reduce benefits.

# SUPPLEMENTARY PENSIONS

Until recent years, supplementary or private pensions (*planes de pensiones*) were unusual in Spain. However, with the long-term future of state pensions in doubt and attempts by the government to encourage company and private pensions, many people are taking out supplementary pensions. Many employees in Spain pay into private insurance schemes which top up their social security benefits, which may be combined with a private health insurance scheme. In many cases, the combined state and supplementary pensions are equal to an employee's final salary.

It's important for anyone who doesn't qualify for a state pension or who will receive only the minimum state pension to contribute to a supplementary or private pension fund. **Note that you must contribute to Spanish social security for 15 years before you're entitled to a state pension.** There are a wide range of private pension funds in Spain (many provided by banks) and it's also possible to continue to contribute to a personal pension plan abroad or to an offshore fund. However, contributions to foreign pension schemes aren't tax deductible in Spain, although many major European private pension companies have offices or agents in Spain.

Most experts advise that the best pension scheme for most people is one that doesn't require fixed monthly payments, but allows you to pay irregular lump sums. In Spain, there's usually a small minimum monthly payment, possibly as low as €50 a month, and lump sum contributions are usually from €600. A pension should be index linked to insure that it keeps pace with inflation. With an index-linked policy, capital is tax free after contributions have been made for 15 years, with an increasing scale of tax penalties for early surrender. If you have an offshore pension, there's no tax relief, but all benefits are paid tax free. Where applicable, annual pension contributions to a company pension plan are tax-deductible for Spanish taxpayers with amounts ranging from €8,000 (for taxpayers under 52) to €24,250, the maximum deduction for taxpayers over 65. Pensions paid to foreign residents in Spain are taxed as regular salary income and a one-time payment is taxed as irregular income. The exception are civil service pensions, which are taxable in your home country and don't usually need to be declared to the Spanish authorities (this doesn't include United Nations pensions, as the UN cannot tax its former employees). Note, however, that civil service pensions are usually taken into account when calculating your Spanish tax rate if you have other income which is taxable in Spain.

# HEALTH INSURANCE

The vast majority of people in Spain are covered for health treatment under social security (see page 288). However, most people who can afford it take out private health insurance, which provides a wider choice of medical practitioners and hospitals, and more importantly, frees them from public health waiting lists. If you aren't covered by Spanish social security, it's important to have private health insurance, unless you have a **very** large bank balance. The policies offered by Spanish and foreign companies differ considerably in the extent of cover, limitations and restrictions, premiums, and the choice of doctors, specialists and hospitals.

Note that the US doesn't have a reciprocal health agreement with Spain and therefore, American students and other Americans who aren't covered by social security **must** have private health insurance in Spain. Proof of insurance must usually be provided when applying for a visa (see page 76) or residence permit (see page 78). Note that some foreign insurance companies don't provide sufficient cover to satisfy Spanish regulations and therefore you should check the minimum cover necessary with a Spanish consulate in your country of residence. See also **Chapter 12**.

## Spanish Companies

There are a large number of Spanish health insurance companies, some of which such as Adeslas, Asisa, Sanitas (owned by the British company BUPA) and Vital Seguros operate nationally, while others are restricted to certain cities or provinces only (although non-national policies have participating hospitals throughout Spain for emergency cases). Spanish insurance companies provide their members with a patient's membership card together with a list of contracted doctors, specialists and hospitals in their area that accept the company's cards. Some insurance companies also operate their own clinics. Usually, it's impossible to freely choose your own doctor, clinic or hospital, although some companies offer a free choice of doctors and hospitals for a higher premium. The main disadvantage of the 'contract' system is that in some areas you may have to travel long distances to see a specialist or to be admitted to hospital. **Note that if you're taken to a hospital in an emergency that isn't on your insurance company's list, you won't be covered under your policy.**

Most companies offer an all-inclusive policy only (a free choice of practitioners and hospitals offering all services), although occasionally a company may offer a choice of plans, e.g. contracted doctors, specialists and other out-patient treatment; and all out-patient consultations and treatment plus hospitalisation and surgery (with contracted practitioners and hospitals) for a limited period each year. An important consideration for many foreigners is being able to choose an English-speaking medical practitioner or a hospital with English-speaking staff (or staff that speak another language). This is impossible with Spanish insurance unless a policy allows a free choice of practitioners and hospitals.

Annual premiums for a family of four (two adults aged 40 years and two children aged under 16) range from around €2,000 or from €450 for a man under 60 (policies for women under 60 are up to twice as expensive). There may be an annual surcharge for those aged over 60, which increases with age, and supplements for certain services such as basic dental treatment or for a pregnant woman. Some insurance companies offer group policies to expatriate clubs and organisations at large savings over individual policies. Major Spanish insurance companies pay 90 per cent of medical expenses and policy holders pay the remaining 10 per cent. When a policy allows a free choice of practitioners and hospitals, clients may be expected to pay the first 20 per cent of bills.

When comparing the cost of Spanish health insurance with a foreign policy, carefully compare the benefits and exactly what's included and excluded. All policies include limitations and restrictions, e.g. injuries as a result of participation in certain high-risk sports aren't usually covered. Many Spanish companies limit costs for a particular specialist or treatment in a calendar year, in addition to having a total overall annual limit for all treatment. Some companies include restrictive clauses, e.g. they may exclude dialysis treatment or may pay for only a limited number of days a year in hospital, e.g. 20 to 60. Steer well clear of policies with severe restrictions (such as a maximum 20-day hospitalisation period) and **always** have the small print checked.

Certain services aren't provided during the first six months cover, e.g. medical check-ups and dental care, and some services may be included only for an extra premium and an excess payment. Most policies don't cover illnesses contracted within a certain period of taking out a policy or pre-existing illnesses for a period, e.g. one or two years (irrespective of whether you were aware of the illness or not). Many policies have clauses allowing annual increases bearing no relation to inflation or increases in the cost of living. **Spanish insurance companies can (and will) cancel a policy at the end of the insurance period if you have a serious illness with endless high expenses and some companies automatically cancel a policy when you reach the age of 65.** You should avoid such a company at all costs, as to take out a new policy at the age of 65 at a reasonable premium is difficult or impossible. Some companies won't accept new clients aged over 60 while others accept new clients up to the age of 75.

It's important to note that Spanish health insurance policies are designed for those living permanently in Spain and most offer only emergency cover abroad. Emergency medical cover abroad is paid up to a limited amount only, e.g. €2,500 or €5,000, which is very little if you must be hospitalised (international travel policies typically include medical expenses equal to €300,000 or more). Spanish policies, not surprisingly, don't include repatriation to another country. The consensus among expatriates is that although Spanish health insurance may sometimes be cheaper, it doesn't offer wide cover and isn't good value for money compared with some foreign health insurance schemes.

# Foreign Companies

There are a number of foreign health insurance companies with agents or offices in Spain, including AXA PPP Healthcare (🖳 www.axappphealthcare.com), BUPA Spain (🖳 www.bupaspain.com), Exeter Friendly Society (🖳 www.exeter friendly.co.uk) and International Health Insurance (Denmark – 🖳 www.ihi.com). These companies offer special policies for expatriates and usually include repatriation to your home country and international cover. If you aren't covered by Spanish social security and need private health insurance to obtain a resident permit (see page 78), you must ensure that your health policy will be accepted by the Spanish authorities (those listed above are all accepted). The main advantages of a foreign health insurance policy are that treatment is unrestricted and you can choose any doctor, specialist, clinic or hospital in Spain, and usually abroad also.

Most foreign policies include repatriation (although it may be optional), which may be an important consideration if you need treatment which is unavailable in Spain, but available in your home (or another) country. Repatriation may also pay for repatriation of your body for burial in your home country. Some companies offer policies for different areas, e.g. Europe, worldwide excluding North America, and worldwide including North America. A policy may offer full cover anywhere within Europe and limited cover in North America and certain other countries (e.g. Japan). Some policies offer the same cover worldwide for a fixed premium, which may be an important consideration for globetrotters. Note that an international policy allows you to choose to have non-urgent medical treatment in another country. Most companies offer different levels of cover, for example, AXA PPP Healthcare offer standard, comprehensive and prestige levels of cover.

Usually there's an excess which may be per visit to a doctor or specialist, or per claim or illness. Obviously, a 'per claim' policy is better, as the excess will include a visit to a family doctor, pharmacy medicines, a consultation with a specialist and hospitalisation, if they're all associated with the same illness. Cover for dental treatment, spectacles and contact lenses may be available as an option, although there may be a hefty excess, which usually means that you're better off paying bills yourself. A basic policy doesn't usually include maternity cover and may offer no benefits or restricted benefits for out-patient treatment (which means that you must pay for visits to a family doctor) and may also exclude out-patient drugs, medicines, dressings, surgical/dental appliances, spectacles, contact lenses or hearing aids. There may also be an annual limit for ambulance costs. Children (e.g. up to age 16) may be covered free on a parent's policy and children up to certain age (e.g. 26) may receive a 50 per cent premium reduction. Note that it's impossible to obtain insurance with some companies if you're above a certain age, e.g. 75. Premiums are usually related to age, although some companies (such as the Exeter Friendly Society) don't relate premiums to age providing you join before a certain age, e.g. 60 or 65.

There's always an annual limit on total annual medical costs (which should be at least €350,000 to €400,000) and some companies also limit costs for specific treatment or costs such as specialist's fees, operations and hospital accommodation. Some policies include permanent disability cover, e.g. €150,000, for those in full-time employment. A medical isn't usually required for most health policies, although pre-existing health problems are excluded for a period, e.g. one or two years. Claims are usually settled in major currencies and large claims are usually settled directly by insurance companies (although your choice of hospitals may be limited). **Always check whether a company pays large medical bills directly.** If you're required to pay bills and claim reimbursement from the insurance company, it may take you several months to receive your money (some companies are slow to pay). It isn't usually necessary to have bills translated into English or another language, although you should check a company's policy. Most companies provide 24-hour emergency telephone assistance.

The cost of international health insurance varies considerably depending on your age and the extent of cover. Premiums can sometimes be paid monthly, quarterly or annually, although some companies insist on payment annually in advance. Annual premiums vary from around €1,000 to over €4,500 for the most comprehensive cover. Some companies have an excess of around €100 per claim (or €150 for dental treatment) and it may be possible to choose an increased voluntary excess of €300 to €1,000 and receive a discount (e.g. 10 or 20 per cent). The maximum annual cover is usually up to around €350,000 to €425,000 per person, per year, and may include permanent total disability cover up €150,000. Payment may be accepted by Visa or Access. Policies usually include repatriation and limited worldwide cover, including North America.

When comparing policies, carefully check the extent of cover and exactly what's included and excluded from a policy (often indicated only in the **very** small print), in addition to premiums and excess charges. In some countries, premium increases are limited by law, although this may apply only to residents in the country where the company is registered and not to overseas policy holders. Although there may be significant differences in premiums, generally you get what you pay for and can tailor your premiums to your requirements. The most important questions to ask are does the policy provide the necessary cover and is it good value for money. If you're in good health and able to pay for your own out-patient treatment, such as visits to your family doctor and prescriptions, then the best value for money policy may be one covering only specialist and hospital treatment.

If you have existing private health insurance in another country, you may be able to extend it to include Spain. If you already have a private health insurance policy, you may find you can save a substantial amount by switching to another company without losing any benefits (you may even gain some). To compare policies, it's best to visit an insurance broker offering policies from a number of companies. If your stay in Spain is short, you may be covered by a reciprocal agreement between your home country and Spain (see **Medical Treatment Abroad** on page 281).

**Make sure you're fully covered in Spain before you receive a large bill.** It's foolhardy for anyone living and working in Spain (or even visiting) not to have comprehensive health insurance. If you or members of your family aren't adequately insured, you could face some very high medical bills. When changing employers or leaving Spain, you should ensure that you have continuous health insurance. If you're planning to change your health insurance company, you should ensure that no important benefits are lost.

# DENTAL INSURANCE

It's unusual to have full dental insurance (*seguro de dentista*), as the cost is prohibitive. Only extractions of bad teeth are possible under the Spanish public health service (see **Dentists** on page 276). Some Spanish insurance companies include coupons for basic dental care such as check-ups, X-rays and cleaning in their standard premium, while others offer more comprehensive dental cover as an optional extra. Some foreign health policies include basic dental care and most offer optional (or additional) dental cover, although there are many restrictions and cosmetic treatment is excluded. Where applicable, the amount payable by a health insurance policy for a particular item of treatment is fixed and depends on your level of dental insurance. A detailed list of refunds is available from insurance companies.

Some dentists in Spain, including a number of foreign dentists, offer a dental insurance scheme. One such scheme costs around €100 a year for one person, €150 for a couple and €25 for each child aged under 17. The fee includes two 6-monthly check-ups, a free scale and polish, and free consultations at any time. Insurance also entitles members to a discount of 50 per cent off the cost of fillings and 25 per cent off the cost of crowns, bridges and dentures, plus discounts on children's orthodontics. The cost of dental insurance may be dependent on the condition of your teeth.

# HOUSEHOLD INSURANCE

Household insurance (*seguro de hogar*) generally includes the building, its contents and third party liability, all of which are contained in a multi-risk household insurance policy. Policies are offered by Spanish and foreign insurance companies and premiums are similar, although foreign companies may provide more comprehensive cover.

## Building Insurance

Although building (*continente*) insurance isn't compulsory, it's advisable for homeowners to take out property insurance that covers damage to a building due to fire, smoke, lightning, water, explosion, storm, freezing, snow, theft, vandalism, malicious damage, acts of terrorism, impact, broken windows and natural catastrophes (such as falling trees). Insurance should include glass, external buildings, aerials and satellite dishes, gardens and garden ornaments. Note that if a claim is the result of a defect in a building or its design, e.g. the roof is too heavy and collapses, the insurance company won't pay up (another reason why it's advisable to have a survey before buying a home). Property insurance is based on the cost of rebuilding your home and should be increased each year in line with inflation. **Make sure that you insure your property for the true cost of rebuilding.** It's particularly important to have insurance for storm damage in Spain, which can be severe in some areas. If floods are one of your concerns, make sure that you're covered for water coming in from ground level, not just for water seeping in through the roof. **Always read the small print of contracts.** Note that if you own a home in an area that has been hit by a succession of natural disasters (such as floods), your household insurance may be cancelled.

## Contents Insurance

Contents (*contenido*) are usually insured for the same risks as a building (see above) and are insured for their replacement value (new for old), with a reduction for wear and tear for clothes and linen. Valuable objects are covered for their actual declared (and authenticated) value. Most policies include automatic indexation of the insured sum in line with inflation. Contents insurance may include accidental damage to sanitary installations, theft, money, replacement of locks following damage or loss of keys, frozen food, alternative accommodation cover, and property belonging to third parties stored in your home. Some items are usually optional, e.g. credit cards, frozen foods, emergency assistance (plumber, glazier, electrician, etc.), redecoration, garaged cars, replacement pipes, loss of rent, and the cost of travel to Spain for holiday homeowners. Many policies include personal third party liability, e.g. up to €300,000, although this may be an option.

Items of high value must usually be itemised and photographs and documentation (e.g. a valuation) provided. Some companies even recommend or insist on a video film of belongings. When claiming for contents, you should produce the original bills if possible (always keep bills for expensive items) and bear in mind that replacing imported items in Spain may be more expensive than buying them abroad. Contents' policies contain security clauses and if you don't adhere to them a claim won't be considered. If you're planning to let a property, you may be required to inform your insurer. Note that a building must be secure with iron bars (*rejas*) on ground-floor windows and patio doors, shutters and secure locks. Most companies give a discount if properties have steel reinforced doors, high security locks and alarms (particularly alarms connected to a monitoring station). An insurance company may send someone to inspect your property and advise on security measures. Policies only pay out for theft when there are signs of forced entry and you aren't covered for thefts by a tenant (but may be covered for thefts by domestic personnel). All-risk policies offering a worldwide extension to a household policy covering jewellery, cameras and other items aren't usually available from Spanish insurance companies, but are offered by foreign companies. See also **Home Security** and **Crime** on pages 105 and 452.

## Community Properties

If you own a property that's part of a community development, the building is insured by the community (although you should ensure that it's comprehensively insured). You must, however, be insured for third party risks (*riesgo a terceros*) in the event that you cause damage to neighbouring properties, e.g. through flood or fire. Household insurance policies usually include third party liability up to a maximum amount, e.g. €300,000.

## Holiday Homes

Premiums are generally higher for holiday homes, due to their high vulnerability, particularly to burglaries. Premiums are usually based on the number of days a year a property is inhabited and the interval between periods of occupancy. Cover for theft, storm, flood and malicious damage may be suspended when a property is left empty for an extended period. **Note that you're required to turn off the water supply at the mains when vacating a building for more than 72 hours.** It's possible to negotiate cover for periods of absence for a hefty surcharge, although valuable items are usually excluded (unless you have a safe). If you're absent from your property for long periods, e.g. longer than 90 days a year, you may be required to pay an excess on a claim arising from an occurrence that takes place during your absence (and theft may be excluded). **It's important to ensure that a policy specifies a holiday home and NOT a principal home.**

In areas with a high risk of theft (e.g. major cities and most resort areas), an insurance company may insist on extra security measures. It's unwise to leave valuable or irreplaceable items in a holiday home or a property that will be vacant for long periods. Note that some insurance companies will do their utmost to find a loophole which makes you negligent and relieves them of liability. You should ensure that the details listed on a policy are correct, otherwise your policy could be void.

# Rented Properties

Your landlord will usually insist that you have third party liability insurance. A lease requires you to insure against 'tenant's risks', including damage you may make to the rental property and to other properties if you live in an apartment, e.g. due to floods, fire or explosion. You can choose your own insurance company and aren't required to use one recommended by your landlord.

# Premiums

Premiums are usually calculated on the size (constructed area in square metres/m²) of a property, its age, the value of the contents and the security protection, e.g. window protection at ground level, the number of entrance doors and their construction. As a rough guide, building insurance costs around €10 a year per €5,000 of value insured, e.g. a property valued at €100,000 will cost €200 a year to insure. Contents insurance costs from around €15 a year per €5,000 of value insured (e.g. a premium of €30 for contents valued at €10,000) and may be higher for a detached villa than an apartment, e.g. up to €20 per €5,000 insured. In general, detached, older and more remote properties cost more to insure than apartments and new properties (particularly when they're located in towns), due to the higher risk of theft. Premiums are also higher in certain high-risk areas.

# Claims

If you wish to make a claim, you must usually inform your insurance company in writing (by registered letter) within two to seven days of an incident or 24 hours in the case of theft. Thefts should also be reported to the local police within 24 hours, as the police report (*denuncia*), of which you receive a copy for your insurance company, constitutes irrefutable evidence of your claim. Check whether you're covered for damage or thefts that occur while you're away from your property and are therefore unable to inform the insurance company immediately. Take care that you don't under-insure your house contents and that you periodically reassess their value and adjust your insurance premium accordingly. You can arrange to have your insurance cover automatically increased annually, by a fixed percentage or amount, by your insurance company. If you make a claim and the assessor discovers that you're under-insured, the amount due will be reduced by the percentage by which you're under-insured. For example, if you're insured for €5,000 and you're found to be under-insured by 50 per cent, your claim for €1,500 will be reduced by 50 per cent to €750.

## Insuring Abroad

It's possible (and legal) to take out building and contents insurance in another country for a property in Spain and some foreign insurance companies offer special policies for holiday homeowners, although you must ensure that a policy is valid under Spanish law. The advantage is that you have a policy you can understand and you're able to handle claims in your own language. This may seem like a good option for a holiday home in Spain, although it can be more expensive than insuring with a Spanish company and can lead to conflicts if, for example, the building is insured with a Spanish registered company and the contents with a foreign based company. Most experts advise that you insure a Spanish home and its contents (*continente y contenido*) with a Spanish registered insurance company through a local agent.

## THIRD PARTY LIABILITY INSURANCE

It's common in Spain to have third party liability insurance (*riesgo a terceros*). This type of insurance covers all members of a family and includes damage done or caused by your children and pets, for example, if your dog or child bites someone. Note that owners of certain types of dog must have third-party liability insurance (see **Pets** on page 465). Where damage is due to severe negligence, benefits may be reduced. Check whether insurance covers you against accidental damage to your home's fixtures and fittings (which may be covered by your household insurance). Third-party liability insurance is usually combined with household insurance (see above). If it isn't included in household insurance, third party liability insurance costs around €15 for each €50,000 of cover.

## HOLIDAY & TRAVEL INSURANCE

Holiday and travel insurance (*seguro de viajes*) is recommended for all who don't wish to risk having their holiday or travel ruined by financial problems or to arrive home broke. As you probably know, anything can and often does go wrong with a holiday, sometimes before you even get started (particularly when you **don't** have insurance). The following information applies equally to residents and non-residents, whether they're travelling to or from Spain or within Spain. **Nobody should visit Spain without travel (and health) insurance!**

Travel insurance is available from many sources, including travel agents, insurance companies and agents, banks, automobile clubs and transport companies (airline, rail and bus). Package holiday companies and tour operators also offer insurance policies, some of which are compulsory, too expensive **and don't provide adequate cover.** You can also buy 24-hour accident and flight insurance at major airports, although it's expensive and doesn't offer the best cover. Before taking out travel insurance, carefully consider the range and level of cover you require and compare policies. Short term holiday and travel insurance policies should include cover for holiday cancellation or interruption; missed flights; departure delay at the start **and** end of a holiday (a common occurrence); delayed, lost or damaged baggage; personal effects and money; medical expenses and accidents (including evacuation home); flight insurance; personal liability and legal expenses and default or bankruptcy insurance, e.g. against a tour operator or airline going broke.

## Health Cover

Medical expenses are an important aspect of travel insurance and you shouldn't rely on insurance provided by reciprocal health arrangements (see page 281), charge and credit card companies, household policies or private medical insurance (unless it's an international policy), none of which usually provide adequate cover. However, you should take advantage of what they offer. The minimum medical insurance recommended by experts is around €300,000 in Spain and the rest of Europe, and €1.5 million for the rest of the world (many policies have limits of between €1.8 and €3 million). If applicable, check whether pregnancy related claims are covered and whether there are any restrictions for those over a certain age, e.g. 65 or 70 (travel insurance is becoming increasingly more expensive for those aged over 65).

Always check any exclusion clauses in contracts by obtaining a copy of the full policy document, as not all relevant information is included in an insurance leaflet. High risk sports and pursuits should be specifically covered and **listed** in a policy (there's usually an additional premium). Winter sports policies are available, which are more expensive than normal holiday insurance ('dangerous' sports are excluded from most standard policies). Third-party liability cover should be €3 million for North America and €1.5 million for the rest of the world. **Note that this doesn't cover you when you're using a car or other mechanically-propelled vehicle.**

## Cost

The cost of travel insurance varies considerably, depending on where you buy it, how long you intend to stay in Spain and your age. Generally, the longer the period covered, the cheaper the daily cost, although the maximum period covered is usually limited, e.g. six months. With some policies, an excess must be paid for each claim. As a rough guide, travel insurance for Spain (and most other European countries) costs from around €35 for one week, €60 for two weeks and €100 for a month for a family of four (two adults and two children under 16). Premiums may be higher for those aged over 65 or 70.

## Annual Policies

For people who travel abroad frequently, whether on business or pleasure, an annual travel policy usually provides the best value, but carefully check exactly what it includes. Many insurance companies offer annual travel policies for a premium of around €100 for an individual, which are excellent value for frequent travellers.

Some insurance companies also offer an 'emergency travel policy' for holiday homeowners who must travel abroad at short notice to inspect a property, e.g. after a severe storm. The cost of an annual policy may depend on the area covered, e.g. Europe, worldwide (excluding North America) and worldwide (including North America), although it doesn't usually cover travel within your country of residence. There's also a limit on the number of trips a year and the duration of each trip, e.g. 90 or 120 days. An annual policy is usually a good choice for owners of a holiday home in Spain who travel there frequently for relatively short periods. **However, check carefully exactly what's covered (or omitted), as an annual policy may not provide adequate cover.**

## Claims

If you must make a claim, you should provide as much documentary evidence as possible to support it. Travel insurance companies gladly take your money, but they aren't always so keen to pay claims and you may have to persevere before they pay up. Always be persistent and make a claim **irrespective** of any small print, as this may be unreasonable and therefore invalid in law. Insurance companies usually require you to obtain a written report and report a loss (or any incident for which you intend to make a claim) to the local police or carriers within 24 hours. Failure to do so may mean that a claim won't be considered.

# 14.

# FINANCE

Spain is one of the poorest countries in the European Union (EU) with an estimated per capita gross domestic product (GDP) in 2004 of US$23,987, compared with US$33,898 in France, US$33,240 in Germany, US$35,658 in the UK and US$40,023 in the US. Spain's GDP has more than doubled since 1986 and currently has the eighth largest economy in the world, as well as the fastest growth rate among the original 15 members of the EU. However, unemployment remains high at around 10 per cent, the cost of living has increased in recent years (although it's still relatively low), and personal debt has risen considerably.

In the last two decades, Spain has become a member of the 'real' world and its cost of living and taxes have increased accordingly. It's no longer a low-tax country as many people still believe – unless, of course, you come from Belgium, Holland or Scandinavia, in which case almost anywhere else is a low tax country! Nevertheless, the cost of living in Spain is still lower than in most other EU countries, inflation was 3.2 per cent in 2004 and for many the quality of life/cost of living ratio is unbeatable.

Family debt is an increasing problem in Spain and in 2004 rose to a total of nearly 600,000 billion euros, more than twice the amount owed just five years ago and up nearly 18 per cent on 2003. Most debt is in the form of mortgages (Spaniards owe 118 per cent more on their homes than ten years ago) and the Bank of Spain is seriously concerned about the effect a rise in mortgage interest rates could have on the average family's economy.

Like all western countries, Spain has extremes of wealth and poverty and there's a vast difference in prosperity between the rich north and the poor south and west of the country (an imbalance which regional policies and vast injections of EU aid have done little to alleviate).

Competition for your money (*dinero*) is considerable, and financial services are offered by clearing and commercial banks, savings banks, foreign banks, the post office, investment brokers and a range of other financial institutions.

If you're planning to invest in property or a business in Spain that's financed with money earned or held in a currency other than euros, it's important to consider present and possible future exchange rates (don't be too optimistic!). If you plan to live permanently in Spain, you should ensure that your income is and will remain sufficient to live on, bearing in mind currency devaluations, rises in the cost of living, unforeseen expenses, such as medical bills, and anything else that may reduce your income (including stock market crashes and recessions!). In the early '90s, many pensioners with a fixed income paid in a foreign currency saw it fall dramatically, as exchange rates worsened and the cost of living rose, although in the last few years some have made gains on the exchange rate.

If you wish to borrow money to buy property or for a business venture in Spain, you should carefully consider where and in what currency it should be raised. Note that it's difficult for foreigners to obtain business loans in Spain, particularly for new ventures, and you shouldn't rely on it. On the other hand, if you earn your income in euros, this may affect your financial commitments abroad, particularly if these currencies are devalued. List all your probable and possible expenses and do your homework thoroughly **before** moving to Spain – afterwards it may be too late!

When you arrive in Spain to take up residence or employment, ensure that you have sufficient cash, travellers' cheques and/or credit cards to last at least until your first pay day, which may be some time after your arrival. During this period you will find that an international credit card is useful; major credit cards, e.g. MasterCard and Visa, are widely accepted in Spain. Note, however, that compared to many other western countries, particularly the UK and US, Spain isn't a credit economy and the Spanish prefer to pay (and be paid) in cash, rather than with a credit card or cheque. Don't assume that a business accepts credit cards, but check in advance.

See also **Chapter 13** for information about social security and pensions.

# FOREIGNER'S IDENTIFICATION NUMBER

All residents and non-resident foreigners with financial affairs in Spain must have a foreigner's identification number (*Número de Identificación de Extranjero/NIE*). This is similar to the fiscal number (*Numero de Identificación Fiscal/NIF*) all Spaniards have (and which is the same as their identity card and passport numbers). An *NIE* works as identification and a kind of tax number. Without an *NIE*, you won't be able to purchase property, open a bank account, arrange credit terms or use temporary employment agencies. When you buy a property, you must apply for an *NIE*, which is required when the property is registered in your name.

Your *NIE* must be used in all dealings with the Spanish tax authorities, when paying property taxes and in various other transactions. Anyone placing money or assets in deposits or other forms or receiving credits or loans in Spain must give his *NIE* to the bank within 30 days of the operation. A bank cannot issue a cheque against a deposit without reporting your *NIE* and must report to the authorities any activity where an *NIE* hasn't been provided. Banks and individuals can be heavily fined for non-compliance with the law regarding identification numbers.

Forms for an *NIE* can be downloaded from the Ministry of Interior website (🖳 www.mir.es – go to *Extranjeros* and then *Modelos de Solicitud*). Applications for an *NIE* can only be made in person and you should go to a national police station (*comisaría*) with a foreigners' department (expect to queue for most of the morning). A representative can apply on your behalf only if you've given him a power of attorney made out abroad and translated into Spanish. (For reasons known only to a select few in the police, powers of attorney made out in Spain are no longer acceptable!) However, once you've applied, anyone can collect the *NIE* on your behalf. If you have an employment contract or a letter from a Spanish employer or business stating why it requires you to have an *NIE*, you can obtain a number in around a week. Otherwise, you may have to wait up to three months.

# SPANISH CURRENCY

Along with 11 other EU countries (Austria, Belgium, Finland, France, Germany, Greece, Ireland, Italy, Luxembourg, the Netherlands and Portugal), Spain's currency is the euro (€). Euro notes and coins became legal tender on 1st January 2002 replacing the peseta. The euro is divided into 100 cents (*céntimo*) and coins are minted in values of 1, 2, 5, 10, 20, 50 cents, €1 and €2. The 1, 2 and 5 cent coins are copper-coloured, the 10, 20 and 50 cent brass-coloured. The €1 coin is silver-coloured in the centre with a brass-coloured rim, and the €2 coin has a brass-coloured centre and silver-coloured rim.

The reverse ('tail' showing the value) of euro coins is the same in all eurozone countries, but the obverse ('head') is different in each country. Spanish coins carry three designs (the king's head on the €1 and €2 coins, Cervantes on the 10, 20 and 50 cent coins, and the cathedral in Santiago de Compostela on the 1, 2 and 5 cent coins), the word '*España*' and the date of minting. All euro coins can, of course, be used in all eurozone countries (although minute differences in weight occasionally cause problems in cash machines, e.g. at motorway tolls!).

As in most other eurozone countries, many people in Spain still claim to have difficulty determining the value of items in euros and the vast majority of Spaniards still 'think' (and talk) in pesetas, particularly for large amounts. As yet, there are no slang terms for euros – there were several for pesetas.

Euro banknotes (*billetes*) are identical throughout the eurozone and depict a map of Europe and stylised designs of buildings (as the member countries couldn't agree which actual buildings should be shown!). Notes are printed in denominations of €5, €10, €20, €50, €100, €200 and €500 (worth over £300 or $600!). The size of notes increases with their value. Euro notes have been produced using all the latest anti-counterfeiting devices. Nevertheless, you should be wary, especially of €200 and €500 notes. The euro symbol may appear before the amount (as in this book), after it (commonly used by the Spanish, e.g. 24,50€) or even between the euros and cents, e.g. 16€50. When writing figures (for example on cheques), a full stop (period) is used to separate units of millions, thousands and hundreds, and a comma to denote fractions.

It's advisable to obtain some euro coins and banknotes before arriving in Spain and to familiarise yourself and your family with them. You should have some euros in cash, e.g. €50 to €100 in small notes, when you arrive, but should avoid carrying a lot of cash. This saves you having to change money on arrival at a Spanish airport (where exchange rates are usually poor and there are often long queues). It's best to avoid €100 notes, if possible, as these sometimes aren't accepted, particularly for small purchases. Note also that many shops and businesses don't generally accept €200 and €500 notes.

# IMPORTING & EXPORTING MONEY

In theory, there are no restrictions on the import or export of funds by residents or non-residents, although you're required to declare amounts over €6,000 (see below). A Spanish resident is permitted to open a bank account in any country and to import (or export) funds in any currency. However, when a resident opens an overseas account, his Spanish bank must routinely inform the Bank of Spain within 30 days of account movements above €3,000. When importing funds for the purchase of a property (or any other major transaction) in Spain, non-residents must have the transfer of funds verified by a certificate from their bank (*certificado de inversiones*).

## Declaration

Sums of €6,000 to €30,000 (per person and journey) must be declared to the customs authorities (on form B-1) when entering or leaving Spain. For sums above €30,000, authorisation is required from the Dirección General de Transacciones Exteriores (DGTE), which can be obtained by completing form B-2 at your bank. Authorisation is routinely granted. These regulations are designed to curb criminal activities, particularly drug-trafficking. Both forms are valid for 15 days only. **Note that, if you don't declare funds, they're subject to confiscation.**

Residents receiving funds from non-residents or making payments to them of over €6,000 (or the equivalent in foreign currency) in cash or cheques must declare them within 30 days. A form must be completed (B-3), which includes the name, address and *NIE* of the resident, the name and address of the non-resident, and the reason for the payment.

If you intend to export funds from Spain, irrespective of the amount, you should declare them, as this certifies that the foreign currency was imported legally and allows a non-EU national to convert euros back into a foreign currency.

# International Bank Transfers

When transferring or sending money to or from Spain, you should be aware of the alternatives and shop around for the best deal.

- **Personal Cheque** – It's possible to send a creditor a cheque drawn on a personal account, although they can take a long time to clear (usually a matter of weeks) and fees are high. Some people prefer to receive a cheque direct (by post) from their overseas banks, which they then pay into their Spanish bank (although you must usually wait for it to clear). **The main problem with sending anything by post to or from Spain is that it leaves you at the mercy of the notoriously unreliable Spanish post office (see Chapter 6).** It's possible to pay cheques drawn on a foreign account into a Spanish bank account; however, they can take weeks to clear, as they must usually be cleared with the paying bank (although some Spanish banks credit funds to accounts immediately).

- **Bank Draft** (*cheque bancario*) – Another way to transfer money is via a bank draft, which should be sent by registered post. Note, however, that if it's lost or stolen it's impossible to stop payment and you must wait six months before a new draft can be issued. Bank drafts aren't treated as cash and must be cleared like personal cheques.

- **Bank Transfer** (*transferencia bancaria*) – A 'normal' transfer should take three to seven days, but in reality it usually takes much longer and an international bank transfer between non-affiliated banks can take weeks! (It's usually quicker and cheaper to transfer funds between branches of the same bank than between non-affiliated banks.) In fact, the larger the amount the longer it often takes (surprise, surprise!), which can be particularly awkward when you're transferring money to buy a property.

- **SWIFT Transfer** – One of the safest and fastest methods of transferring money is via the SWIFT or IBAN system. A SWIFT or IBAN transfer should be completed in a few hours, funds being available within 24 hours, although even these can take five working days. Most banks are members of the SWIFT system or have an

IBAN code. The cost of transfers varies considerably – not only commission and exchange rates, but also transfer charges.

● **Telegraphic Transfers** – One of the quickest (it takes around ten minutes) and safest methods of transferring cash is via a telegraphic transfer, e.g. Moneygram (☎ UK 0800-8971 8971, 🖥 www.moneygram.com) or Western Union (🖥 www. westernunion.com), but it's also one of the most expensive, e.g. commission of 7 to 10 per cent of the amount sent! Western Union services are also available at post offices (☎ 902-197 197, 🖥 www.correos.es) in Spain under the agreement known as 'Money in Minutes' (*Dinero en minutos*). There are special rates and deals for certain countries such as Russia. Money can be sent via overseas American Express offices by Amex card holders (using Amex's Moneygram service) to American Express offices in Spain in just 15 minutes.

The cost of transfers varies considerably, not only in the commission and exchange rates, but also in the transfer charges, e.g. for a SWIFT transfer. Many Spanish banks deduct commission, whether a transfer is made in euros or a foreign currency, although an EU directive limits the costs banks can pass on to customers.

If you intend to send a large amount of money to Spain or abroad for a business transaction such as buying a property, you should ensure you receive the commercial rate of exchange rather than the tourist rate. Some banks levy high charges (as much as 4 per cent) on the transfer of funds to Spain to buy a home, which is the subject of numerous complaints, while others charge nothing if the transfer is made in euros. Always check charges and rates in advance and agree them with your bank (you may be able to negotiate a lower charge or a better exchange rate). If you have your pension paid into a bank in Spain from another EU country, you should have it transferred in euros, for which (under EU regulations) there should be no charge and money must be deposited in your account within five working days.

Spanish (and Portuguese) banks are reportedly the slowest in Europe to process bank transfers. It isn't unusual for transfers to and from Spain to get stuck in the pipeline (usually somewhere in Madrid), which allows the Spanish bank to use your money for a period interest-free. For example, transfers between British and Spanish banks sometimes take from three to six weeks and the money can 'disappear' for months or even completely!

If you routinely transfer large sums of money between currencies, you should investigate Fidelity Money Funds, which operate free of conversion charges and at wholesale rates of exchange. There are many companies specialising in foreign exchange, particularly large sums of money, such as Foreign Currency Direct (☎ UK 0800-328 5884/+44 1494-725353, 🖥 www.currencies.co.uk), Halewood (☎ UK 01753-859159, 🖥 www.hifx.co.uk) and Moneycorp (☎ UK 020-7589 3000, Spain 966-771 068, 🖥 www.moneycorp.com).

# Obtaining Cash

One of the quickest methods of obtaining (usually relatively small amounts of) cash in Spain is to draw on debit, credit or charge cards. Many foreigners living in Spain (particularly retirees) keep the bulk of their money in a foreign account (perhaps in an offshore bank) and draw on it with a cash or debit card in Spain. This is an ideal solution for holidaymakers and holiday homeowners (although homeowners will still need a Spanish bank account to pay their bills). Most banks in major cities have foreign exchange windows (and there are banks with extended opening hours at international airports and main railway stations in major cities), where you can buy and sell foreign currencies, buy and cash travellers' cheques, and obtain a cash advance on credit and charge cards.

Note that most banks charge around 1 per cent commission with a minimum charge of between €3 and €6, so it's expensive to change small amounts. However, some banks charge a flat fee of €3 and no commission, irrespective of the amount, especially if you're a client of the bank.

There are numerous private *bureaux de change* (including most travel agents), many of which are open long hours, and some shops (such as El Corte Inglés department stores) have an in-house *bureau de change*. Note that banks at airports and railway stations often offer the worst exchange rates and charge the highest fees. There are automatic change machines at airports and in tourist areas in major cities accepting up to 15 currencies including US$, £ Sterling and Swiss francs. Most *bureaux de change* charge no commission (but always check) and are also usually easier to deal with than banks. If you're changing a lot of money, you may be able to negotiate a better exchange rate. However, commercial *bureaux de change* don't usually offer the best exchange rates and you're usually better off changing money at a bank. (The posted exchange rates may apply only when changing high amounts, so ask before changing any money.) **Note that 'no commission' usually means a poor exchange rate!**

The euro exchange rate (*cambio*) for most European and major international currencies is listed in banks and daily newspapers, and announced on Spanish and expatriate radio and TV programmes.

There isn't a lot of difference in the cost of changing cash, buying travellers' cheques (see below) and using a credit card to obtain cash in Spain. However, many people simply take cash when visiting Spain, which is asking for trouble, particularly if you have no way of obtaining more cash in Spain, e.g. with a credit card. **When travelling anywhere, don't rely on only one source of funds!**

# Travellers' Cheques

If you're visiting Spain, it's safer to carry travellers' cheques (*cheques de viaje*) than cash, although they aren't as easy to cash as in some other countries. They aren't usually accepted as cash by businesses, except some major hotels, restaurants and shops, which usually offer a poor exchange rate. Most banks charge a commission of 1 per cent when cashing foreign currency travellers' cheques with a minimum fee of between €3 and €6 (so it's wise to avoid changing small amounts), but there's usually no commission when cashing euro travellers' cheques. Banks offer a better exchange rate for travellers' cheques than for banknotes. Note that you must show your passport when changing travellers' cheques.

Always keep a separate record of travellers' cheque numbers and note where and when they were cashed. Most cheque issuers offer a replacement service for lost or stolen cheques, although the time taken to replace them varies significantly. American Express claim a free, three-hour replacement service at any of their offices, provided you know the serial numbers of the lost cheques. Without the serial numbers, replacement can take three days or longer.

# BANKS

Although Spanish banks aren't renowned for their proficiency, the service they offer has changed out of all recognition in the last few decades, during which the number of banks and branches has increased considerably (some have also gone bust!). Spanish banks have become highly automated and their cash dispensers (ATMs) are among the world's most advanced (how many other countries' ATMs 'talk' to you in a number of languages?), although where human involvement is concerned some banks remain Neanderthal.

There are no drive-in banks in Spain, but most banks also offer home banking services via telephone and/or the internet, and there are several internet/telephone-only banks: ING Nationale-Nedenlanden (☎ 901-020 901, 💻 www.ingdirect.es), Openbank/Patagon (☎ 902-365 366, 💻 www.patagon.es) owned by BSCH and Uno-e (☎ 901-111 113, 💻 www.uno-e.es) owned by BBVA and Telefónica. All three internet banks offer (relatively) high interest current accounts with immediate access to your money, as well as the usual banking services.

A strange idiosyncrasy of some Spanish banks is that they sell goods, such as household appliances, bicycles and computers, and other services (e.g. holidays and insurance).

There are two main types of bank in Spain: clearing banks (*bancos*) and savings banks (*cajas de ahorros*). The Spanish clearing banks with the largest branch networks are the two giants, Banco Santander-Central Hispano (BSCH – now the fourth-largest in Europe after its takeover of the British Abbey National) and Banco Bilbao Vizcaya-Argentaria (BBVA), and the smaller Banco Popular, Banesto and Sabadell Atlántico. All banks in Spain are listed in yellow pages under *Bancos*.

Spain also has around 50 savings banks, which were originally charitable organisations granting loans for public interest and agricultural policies. Savings banks are similar to building societies in the UK and savings and loan banks in the US and hold around 45 per cent of deposits and make some 25 per cent of personal loans. The two largest Spanish savings banks are La Caixa (some 3,600 branches) and Caja Madrid (almost 1,900 branches). In general, savings banks offer a more personal, friendly service than clearing banks and are excellent for local business (many have limited regional branch networks). However, although they provide the same basic services as clearing banks, they aren't always best for international business.

There are also some 100 co-operative savings banks (*cooperativas de crédito*), whose members are agricultural co-operatives, although they play only a small part in Spain's banking system and hold just a few per cent of total bank assets.

There are around 50 foreign banks operating in Spain – fewer (and with an overall smaller market share) than in most other European countries. Most major foreign banks are present in Madrid and Barcelona, but branches are rare in other cities. Among foreigners in Spain, the British are best served by their national banks, in the major cities and resort areas. Barclays, Deutsche Bank, Lloyds TSB and Solbank are the most prominent foreign banks in Spain. These banks are full members of the Spanish clearing and payment system and can provide cheque accounts, cash and credit cards, direct debits and standing orders, and loans and mortgages. The Royal Bank of Scotland also operates at some BSCH branches. Note, however, that foreign banks in Spain operate in exactly the same way as Spanish banks, so you shouldn't expect, for example, a branch of Barclays in Spain to resemble a branch in the UK or any other country. Surprisingly, considering the size and spending power of foreign residents and tourists in Spain, most Spanish banks make few concessions to foreign clients, e.g. by providing general information and statements in foreign languages and multilingual staff.

If you have a complaint regarding your bank, don't expect to receive a quick resolution (or any resolution at all). A complaint should be addressed to the ombudsman (*defensor del cliente*, although the title may vary) of your bank. The Bank of Spain (Banco de España, Servicio de Reclamaciones, Alcalá, 50, 28014 Madrid, ☎ 913-385 068, 🖳 www.bde.es – information available under ' *Servicios al Público*) can provide further information on filing a complaint.

# Opening Hours

Normal bank opening hours are from between 8.15 and 9am until between 1.30 and 2pm, Mondays to Fridays, and from between 8.30 and 9.30am until 1pm on Saturdays, except in summer (banks are closed on Saturdays from April to September). Savings banks open all day on Thursdays (until 7pm), but are closed on Saturdays. Some branches in major cities remain open continually from the morning until 4 or 4.30pm from autumn to spring, although they may close earlier on Fridays. Some banks are experimenting with longer hours at certain branches and opening from, for example, 8.15am until 8.30pm (or may open from around 8.15am to 2pm and again from around 4.30 until 7.45pm). Banks in shopping centres may also open all day until late in the evening (some are open the same hours as hypermarkets, e.g. from 10am until 10pm). At major international airports and railway stations in major cities, there are also banks with extended opening hours, although they often have long queues.

Banks are closed on public holidays, including local holidays (when banks in neighbouring towns often close on different days), and they may also close early during local *fiestas*. Note that many *bureaux de change* have long opening hours and some are even open 24 hours in summer in some resort areas.

# Opening an Account

You can open a bank account in Spain whether you're a resident or a non-resident. It's better to open a Spanish bank account in person than by correspondence from abroad. Ask your friends, neighbours or colleagues for their recommendations and just go along to the bank of your choice and introduce yourself. You must be aged at least 18 and provide proof of identity (e.g. a passport), your address in Spain and your passport number or *NIE* (see page 309). If you wish to open an account with a Spanish bank while you're abroad, you must first obtain an application form, available from foreign branches of Spanish banks or direct from a Spanish bank in Spain. You must select a branch from the list provided, which should preferably be close to where you will be living in Spain. If you open an account by correspondence, you must provide a reference from your current bank. Note that all Spanish bank accounts have 20 digits: the first four are the bank code, the next four are the branch code followed by the sort code (two digits) and then your account number (ten digits).

## Non-residents

If you're a non-resident, you're entitled to open a non-resident euro account (*cuenta de euros de no residente*) or a foreign currency account only. An important point to note is that when importing funds for the purchase of a property (or any other major transaction), the transfer of funds must be verified by a certificate from your bank (*certificado de inversiones*). Although it's possible for non-resident homeowners to do most of their banking via a foreign account using debit and credit cards, they need a Spanish bank account to pay Spanish utility and tax bills (which are best paid by direct debit). If you own a holiday home in Spain, you can have your correspondence (e.g. cheque books, statements, payment advices.) sent to an address abroad.

## Residents

To open a resident's account you must usually have a residence permit (*residencia*) or evidence that you have a job in Spain. Note that it isn't advisable to close your bank accounts abroad when you live in Spain, unless you're sure that you won't need them in the future. Even when you're resident in Spain, it's cheaper to keep money in local currency in an account in a country you visit regularly than to pay commission to convert euros. Many foreigners living in Spain maintain at least two cheque (current) accounts: a foreign account for international transactions and a local account with a Spanish bank for day-to-day business.

## Cheque Accounts

The most common account in Spain is a cheque or current account (*cuenta de ahorro con talonario/cuenta corriente*), which are provided by all Spanish banks, although many Spaniards don't trust cheques and prefer to deal in cash. Personal cheques aren't usually accepted for payment by local retailers and cannot be guaranteed, although banks can issue a book of certified cheques and some supermarket chains issue identity cards (which they sometimes misleadingly call 'credit' cards), allowing customers to pay with personal cheques. Cheque account holders are normally issued with cash or debit cards (see page 319), although you must usually ask for one.

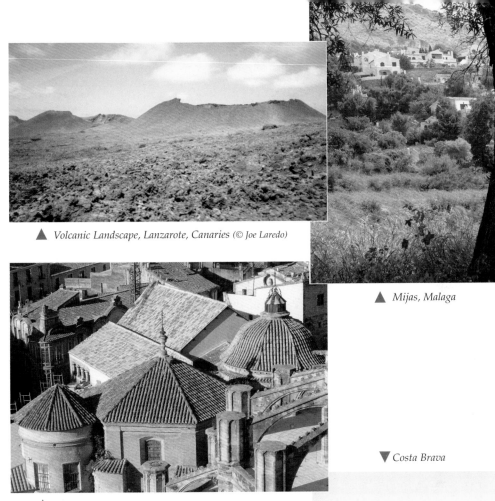

▲ Volcanic Landscape, Lanzarote, Canaries (© Joe Laredo)

▲ Mijas, Malaga

▼ Costa Brava

▲ Tortosa, Tarragona

▲ *Paella* (© Joe Laredo)

► *Casa Batlló, Barcelona*

▲ *Plaza España, Madrid*

◄ *Camels, Lanzarote, Canaries*
(© Joe Laredo)

*Seville Cathedral*

*Villa, Mijas, Malaga*

*All photographs © Survival Books unless otherwise stated*

*Puerto Banús, Malaga*

◀ *Puerto Marina,*
*Benalmádena, Malaga*

▼ *La Rambla, Barcelona*

◀ *Andalusian*
*Riding School,*
*Jerez*

◀ *Mojácar, Almeria*

**Charges:** Spanish banks levy some of the highest charges in Europe for day-to-day transactions such as writing cheques, standing orders, direct debits and credit card transactions. Always obtain a list of charges before opening an account and compare the charges levied by a number of banks. A number of entries (account transactions) per year (e.g. 30) are usually free, after which there's a charge per entry (e.g. €0.25), although a bank manager can waive certain charges. If you arrange to have your salary or pension paid into a Spanish bank account (called *domiciliación de nómina*), you may qualify for a choice of gifts, entry in a grand draw to win a car or other prizes, and low or no-fee services such as a low-interest overdraft or a free credit card. If you wish to change banks, don't maintain a bank account with a small amount of money in it, as you will continue to be charged fees, but write a letter to your bank informing them that you're closing the account.

**Interest:** Spanish cheque accounts pay little interest on account balances, e.g. just 0.1 or 0.2 per cent interest on the average balance. Generally, an interest-paying cheque account (i.e. paying a 'normal' rate of interest) requires a minimum balance of around €1,500 and even then it may pay interest only on the balance above this amount. So there's little point in keeping a lot of money in a cheque account when you can deposit your money in a deposit or savings account (see below) and earn interest on the whole balance.

**Writing Cheques:** Spanish cheques (*cheques* or *talones*) may be different from those you're familiar with. Your account details (*Código cuenta cliente/CCC* with 20 digits – see **Opening an Account** above) are printed at the top right of cheques and statements. This information is required when payments are to be made directly to or from your account, e.g. for direct debits. The payee's (*páguese a*) name should be written in the top left corner (it's usual to write *Sr. D.* in front of a man's name and *Sra. Da.* in front of a woman's). The amount in figures should be written in the top right corner. Many people put a hash (#) sign before and after the amount, e.g. #4.500, 25#, so that it cannot be altered, although this isn't obligatory. The amount should also be written in words (*en letras*) on the line below the payee's name, e.g. *cuatro mil quinientos euros con veinticinco céntimos*. The date must be written in words under the amount (in words) and after the town where the bank is located. Your signature should be written in the bottom right corner below the date. The amount and date in words must usually be written in Spanish, although some banks allow you to write it in English and other languages.

If a cheque is made out to the bearer, the words *al portador* must be added. However, it isn't recommended to pay a cheque to the bearer, which is regarded as currency and could change hands a number of times during its validity period (although people will ask you to do this, so that the payment cannot be traced or so they can cash it immediately). It's usually better to pay someone in cash. Note that, in order to pay a cheque into your bank account, you must sign the back.

When making a cheque out to a named person, you should write, for example, '*Páguese a John Smith por este cheque*'. To ensure that a cheque can be paid only into the account of the payee, you must add *y Cia* between diagonal lines on the front or add *a abonar en cuenta* before the name of the payee. Note that your bank isn't required to reimburse you for a falsified cheque if you've been negligent when writing it.

**Validity:** Spanish cheques are valid indefinitely, although it isn't wise to keep a cheque for longer than six months before cashing it. All cheques, including post-dated cheques, are payable on presentation (if the funds are available). If you write a cheque without sufficient funds in your account, your bank must pay out whatever is in your account as part payment, although this isn't always done. Your bank also sends you a 'notarial protest' (*declaración substitativo de impago/declaración equivalente*), which they must do within 15 days if the cheque is issued and payable in Spain (they have 20 days if it's issued in another European country and 60 days if it's issued outside Europe). You're obliged to pay a penalty of 10 per cent of the unpaid amount of a cheque, e.g. if you write a cheque for €1,000 and have only €750 in your account, you must pay the €250 shortfall plus a €25 penalty. **It's illegal to overdraw a bank account without prior agreement and it can lead to many problems.**

You cannot usually stop payment of a cheque unless the cheque or cheque book has been lost or stolen, when a police report (*denuncia*) must be produced. If your cheque book is lost or stolen, you must notify your bank by telephone immediately and confirm the loss in writing. Once you've informed your bank of a loss, any cheques written after that time cease to be your responsibility.

Beware of accepting cheques from foreigners (even for small amounts), as they often bounce, resulting in a bank fee, e.g. €3, plus the loss of your money!

**Bills of Exchange:** When buying something on credit in Spain, cheques aren't usually used to pay instalments. Instalments are made via bills of exchange (*letra de cambio*), one of which is issued for each payment due. You're required to sign one for each payment to be made (e.g. 24 if you're paying monthly for an item over two years), which are then presented to your bank for payment by your creditor each month. Make sure they're made out in the name of the company that sold the goods and not an individual. If funds aren't available to pay a bill of exchange, you will receive a 'bill of exchange protest' (*letra protestada*) from your bank asking you to pay the amount due plus extra costs. You should never sign *letras* on behalf of a company or someone else, as you're personally held responsible for payment.

**Standing Orders & Direct Debits:** You can have your standing orders (*domiciliación de pagos*) and direct debits (*domiciliación bancaria*) paid by your Spanish bank by simply completing a form at your bank and giving them a copy of a bill. This is the best way to pay all regular bills, such as electricity, gas, water, telephone, local taxes and community charges. However, you should check your statements to ensure that payments have been made, as banks cannot always be relied upon.

**Deposits:** You can pay cheques drawn on a foreign bank into a Spanish account in all major currencies. Your bank may credit your account immediately, which means that you can draw on the money before the cheque has been cleared (which may take weeks). Many banks charge a flat fee per cheque (e.g. €3 or €5), so it pays to write cheques for large amounts, and you receive the exchange rate for cheques and travellers' cheques (which is higher than when changing cash).

**Correspondence:** All correspondence from Spanish banks is in Spanish and it's advisable to learn to interpret your statements and other correspondence you receive. The most common words used in statements are *fecha* (date), *debe* (debit), *haber* (credit), *fecha operación/valor* (date of operation/transaction), *saldo* (balance) and *concepto* (description). Account statements (*estados* or *comunicaciones de movimientos*) are sent to customers monthly or quarterly, although you can request one at any time by asking for an *extracto* or an *avance*. Most banks now provide the option of receiving all correspondence by email or online. **Beware of bogus emails claiming to be from your bank asking for confidential information such as your account numbers and PIN.** These emails are invariably from fraudsters who use this information to access (and empty) your account. Banks **never** ask for confidential details by email.

## Savings Accounts

You can open a savings account (*cuenta/libreta de ahorro*) or deposit account (*cuenta de imposición a plazo*) with any clearing or savings bank in Spain. Savings banks offer savings schemes and loans for buying property and other purchases, although general banking services may be limited compared with those of clearing banks. The post office also provides a range of savings accounts (see page 319) in association with Deutsche Bank.

Most financial institutions offer a variety of savings and deposit accounts, with varying interest rates, minimum deposits, and withdrawal restrictions, depending on the type of account and the bank. For short-term savings and small amounts, it's best to open a savings account where funds are on call and withdrawals can be made at any time. Interest is usually paid twice a year, but is negligible unless the average balance is above a certain sum, e.g. €1,500. Funds in a term deposit account must be deposited for a minimum period or term (e.g. 7, 14, 30 or 90 days, six months or a year), which is the notice you're required to give in order to withdraw funds without a penalty. The longer the period you're willing to have your money tied up, the higher the interest rate paid.

High interest accounts may require a minimum account balance of €1,500, €3,000 or even €6,000. These accounts can usually be in euros or a major foreign currency and some accounts allow for the payment of standing orders and direct debits, although there may be a maintenance charge, e.g. €3 or €5 per year.

Savings account holders receive a pass book in which all deposits and withdrawals are recorded (which can be done via an ATM) and they may also be issued with a cash card, cheque book and a credit card, depending on the type of account.

For residents, the interest earned on bank accounts and deposits is subject to a 15 per cent withholding tax at source in lieu of personal income tax. Tax withheld at source can be deducted from tax payable when the following year's income tax return is filed. Non-residents are now subject to the European Savings Tax Directive (ESTD) under which non-residents with a non-resident account can choose to pay retaining tax at 15 per cent (this will be increased to 20 per cent in July 2008 and to 35 per cent in 2011) or allow an 'exchange of information' whereby the Spanish bank provides details about the account to the tax authorities in their country of residence.

## Cash & Debit Cards

All Spanish banks offer customers combined cash and debit cards (*tarjeta de débito*), which are widely used and accepted throughout Spain. Purchases and cash withdrawals are automatically debited from your cheque or savings account. You don't receive a monthly statement, although you can obtain account balances and mini-statements from cash machines (ATMs), and cannot overdraw your account with a cash or debit card. A card allows you to withdraw up to €600 per day from ATMs operated by your own bank – less from those of other banks.

There are many thousands of ATMs in Spain, where the three main networks are *Red 6000*, *Servired* and *Telebanco 4B* (indicated by a blue and yellow striped logo with the inscription '4B'). Cash can also usually be obtained from a network other than the one your card belongs to, for which there's a fee (from €1.50 to €3). Most ATMs accept a bewildering number of Spanish and foreign cards, usually illustrated on machines, including credit and charge cards (see page 322). Note that, although foreign debit cards such as those belonging to the Visa network, can be used to obtain cash in Spain, they're usually treated as credit cards and a charge is made.

Most ATMs are located outside banks. In cases when they're located inside the bank or in a lobby, you may need to run your card through a card reader to gain access. The procedure for withdrawing money from an ATM is usually as follows:

1. If the machine is in working order, a message such as *Introduzca su tarjeta, por favor* (Insert your card, please) is displayed. If your card is rejected, try again; if it's rejected a second time, try another machine. If a machine is temporarily out of order, a message such as *Cajero temporalmente fuera de servicio* is displayed.

2. Most machines permit you to choose the language in which instructions are displayed. If this is the case, the first screen will show a selection of languages.

3. Next you're asked to enter your personal identification number (PIN) and press the green 'enter' (*anotación*) button. If you make a mistake, press the yellow 'erase' (*borrar*) button and re-enter your PIN. As a security measure, if you enter the wrong PIN three times, your card will be retained by the machine and you must contact your bank for its return.

4. Select the service required, e.g. balance enquiry (*saldo*), statement enquiry (*extracto de saldo*) or cash withdrawal (*sacar dinero*).

5. If you've chosen to withdraw cash, the screen will usually display a choice of amounts, e.g. €20, €50, €100, €150 and €200. Note however, that some machines only offer amounts payable in €20 and €50 notes. If the amount you wish to withdraw isn't displayed, you can press the 'other amounts' (*otras cantidades*) button and enter the amount required. If you make a mistake, press the yellow 'erase' (*borrar*) button and re-enter the correct amount. If you request more than your current credit limit (or account balance), you will be asked to request a smaller amount.

6. Remove your card, receipt (machines may automatically issue a receipt or ask you if you require one – (*¿Desea un recibo?*) and cash when instructed.

The 'cancel' (*cancelar*) button can be used to terminate a transaction at any point and your card will be returned, so you then can start again, if required.

Note that it's inadvisable to rely entirely on a cash or credit card to obtain cash in Spain, as your card may be 'swallowed' by an ATM and it may be some time before it's returned via your bank. If you lose your cash card or it's stolen, you must report it to your bank as soon as possible or phone the appropriate number: Red 6000

☎ 915-965 335; Servired ☎ 902-192 100 or ☎ 915-192 100; Telebanco 4B ☎ 902-144 400 or ☎ 913-192 100.

# Offshore Banking

If you have a sum of money to invest or wish to protect your inheritance from the tax man, it may be worthwhile looking into the accounts and services (such as pensions and trusts) provided by offshore banking centres in tax havens (*paraísos fiscales*) such as the Channel Islands (Guernsey and Jersey) and the Isle of Man (around 50 locations worldwide are officially classified as tax havens). The big attraction of offshore banking is that money can be deposited in a wide range of currencies, customers are usually guaranteed complete anonymity, there are no double-taxation worries, no withholding tax is payable and interest is paid tax-free. Many offshore banks also offer telephone banking (usually seven days a week) and some provide internet banking.

A large number of American, British and other European banks and financial institutions provide offshore banking facilities in one or more locations. Most institutions offer high-interest deposit accounts for long-term savings and investment portfolios in which funds can be deposited in any major currency. Many people living abroad keep a local account for everyday business and maintain an offshore account for international transactions and investment purposes. **However, most financial experts advise expatriates not to invest their savings in an offshore tax haven until they know what their long-term plans are.**

Accounts have minimum deposit levels that usually range from the equivalent of around €750 to €15,000 (£500 to £10,000), with some as high as €150,000 (£100,000). In addition to large minimum balances, accounts may also have stringent terms and conditions, such as restrictions on withdrawals or high early withdrawal penalties. You can deposit funds on call (instant access) or for a fixed period, e.g. from 90 days to a year (usually for larger sums). Interest is usually paid monthly or annually; monthly interest payments are slightly lower than annual payments, although they have the advantage of providing a regular income. There are usually no charges provided a specified minimum balance is maintained. Many accounts offer a cash card or a credit card (e.g. MasterCard or Visa), which can be used to obtain cash from ATMs throughout the world.

**When selecting a financial institution and offshore banking centre, your first priority should be for the safety of your money.** In some offshore banking centres, a percentage of bank deposits up to a maximum sum is guaranteed under a deposit protection scheme in the event of a financial institution going bust (the Isle of Man, Guernsey and Jersey all have such schemes). Unless you're planning to bank with a major international bank, you should check the credit rating of a financial institution before depositing any money, particularly if it doesn't provide deposit insurance. All banks have a credit rating (the highest is 'AAA') and a bank with a high rating will be happy to tell you (but get it in writing). You can also check the rating of an international bank or financial organisation with Moody's Investor Service (💻 www. moodys.com). You should be wary of institutions offering higher than average interest rates; if it looks too good to be true, it probably is!

# INVESTMENTS

When looking for a profitable home for your cash, your decision will probably depend (among other things) on how much money you wish to invest (which may be a lump sum or a monthly amount), how quickly you need access to it in an emergency, whether you want income or capital growth, and whether you're a taxpayer. You must also decide whether you're willing to speculate or want a guaranteed return on your money. Before you invest in anything remotely speculative, you should ask yourself: "Am I prepared to risk losing all or part of my investment?" If the answer is no, you should look for an investment offering a guaranteed return, such as a time deposit. Lastly, you should consider the effect that inflation might have on your nest egg, as inflation is the main enemy of anyone who relies on investment income, particularly if your income is fixed.

Financial advice is offered (often free) by numerous financial institutions and advisers, in Spain and abroad, although the quality of advice is extremely variable and is unlikely to be independent. Any advice you receive should be tailored to your particular situation and requirements, and shouldn't be the advisor's own standard packaged investment portfolio.

**Be VERY careful where and with whom you invest your money in Spain.** There have been many financial scandals in recent years and many investors have somehow managed to 'lose' all their clients' money – no mean feat, even in the most turbulent of times! Not for nothing is it said that the way to create a small portfolio in Spain is to start with a big one! Spain seems to have more than its fair share of 'crooks' and unscrupulous investment advisers (often foreigners), particularly on the Costa del Sol. Whoever you invest with, make sure that they have a good reputation (obtain references), extensive experience, a good track record (documented) and that you receive proper documentation. Bear in mind that many financial advisers in Spain are unregulated, and anyone can set up business without any professional qualifications or experience. Also don't be taken in by endorsements, as some 'celebrities' and businesses will endorse anything to make a fast buck.

Whatever advice you receive, you should do comprehensive personal homework, such as subscribing to specialist financial magazines and newsletters, some of which offer excellent advice. **The best thing to do in the first instance is nothing at all – until you know exactly what your long-term plans are and have investigated all the available investment options.**

# CREDIT & CHARGE CARDS

Credit and charge cards are usually referred to collectively as credit cards (*tarjeta de crédito*) in Spain, although not all cards allow you to repay the balance over a period of time. Visa and MasterCard are the most widely-accepted credit cards and are issued by most Spanish banks. Charge cards such as American Express and Diners Club aren't as widely accepted in Spain as they are in the UK and US (the Spanish wisely prefer cash, which cannot be traced by the tax authorities!).

The annual fee for a credit card varies according to the issuing bank and is usually between €10 and €25 per year for a standard Visa or MasterCard and between €40 and €60 a year for a 'gold' card. Always check annual fees and interest charges, as they can vary greatly. Some credit cards provide free travel insurance (e.g. Europ Assistance) or accident life insurance when travel costs are paid for with the card, or operate a points system whereby you earn points every time you use a card. Before obtaining a credit or charge card, compare the costs **and** benefits. In some countries (e.g. the UK), credit card users are protected against a purchase going 'wrong', such as a company going bust or goods being faulty (which also applies to goods purchased overseas).

It's advisable to retain your foreign credit cards when you live in Spain, at least for a period. One of the advantages of using a credit card issued abroad is that your bill is usually rendered or your account debited around six weeks later, thus giving you a period of interest-free credit, except when cards are used to obtain cash, when interest starts immediately. You may, however, find it more convenient and cheaper to be billed in euros than in a foreign currency, when payments can vary with exchange rate fluctuations.

Most ATMs in Spain accept credit and charge cards. Note, however, that there's a standard charge (e.g. 1.5 per cent) for using a foreign credit card to obtain cash in Spain and, if you use a Spanish credit card, a high interest rate is usually levied from the day of the withdrawal. In order to withdraw cash from an ATM with a credit card, you must obtain a PIN (personal identification number) from the issuing bank. Cardholders can usually withdraw any amount up to their credit balance or personal limit.

Major department and chain stores issue their own free account cards, among them Alcampo, Carrefour, Cortefiel and El Corte Inglés. Some cards allow credit, where the account balance may be repaid over a period, although interest rates are usually high (the El Corte Inglés card allows three months' free credit on certain items).

Note that in rural and resort areas, many small businesses don't accept credit cards. **Never assume that a particular business (such as a restaurant) accepts credit cards or you may discover to your embarrassment that it doesn't.**

Spain has one of the highest incidences of credit card theft in the EU. If you lose a credit card or have it stolen, report it immediately by telephone to the issuing office (see below) or your bank and confirm the loss in writing by registered letter. Your liability is usually limited to around €150 until you report a loss, after which you have no liability. Numbers to call are as follows: American Express ☎ 902-375 637; MasterCard, Visa or Visa Electron ☎ 902-144 400, ☎ 902-192 100, ☎ 913-192 100 or ☎ 915-192 100.

Even if you don't like credit cards and shun any form of credit, they do have their uses, e.g. no-deposit car rentals, no prepayment of hotel bills, the convenience of shopping by phone or via the internet, safety and security and, above all, convenience (although you must be wary of bogus charges and scrutinise statements).

# LOANS & OVERDRAFTS

Theoretically, residents and non-residents can now obtain loans (and mortgages) in any EU country, in any currency (provided they're eligible), but in many cases it's advantageous to arrange these in Spain, particularly for a property there. All Spanish banks provide loans (*préstamos*) and overdrafts (*giros en descubierto*), although they aren't as free with their money as banks in some other European countries, particularly regarding loans to foreigners. Most Spanish banks are happy to make loans to foreign residents in Spain, particularly if they're homeowners, but some are reluctant to do so and may even refuse to lend you money, although, if this is based purely on the fact that you're a foreigner, it's illegal.

To calculate the cost of a loan, you need to know the true rate of interest (*tasa anual equivalente/TAE*), which must be quoted by law. The *TAE* includes all charges (e.g. documentation fees or maintenance charges) and varies with the frequency of payments. It pays to shop around for a loan, as interest rates vary considerably according to the bank, the amount and the period of the loan. Don't neglect smaller banks, as it isn't always necessary to have an account with a bank to obtain a loan. Ask your friends and colleagues for their advice. If you have equity, e.g. Spanish property or an insurance policy, or you can get someone to stand as a guarantor for a loan, you may be eligible for a secured loan at a lower interest rate. Some banks may require you to take out a life insurance policy to cover the term of a loan. The penalty a bank can charge when a client pays off a loan before the due date is limited, and interest on overdrafts is limited to 2.5 times the current interest rate.

# MORTGAGES

Mortgages, or home loans (*hipotecas*), are available from most Spanish banks (for residents and non-residents), foreign banks in Spain, and overseas and offshore banks. In recent years, Spanish and foreign lenders have tightened their lending criteria due to the repayment problems experienced by many borrowers in the early '90s, although over the last few years a record number of mortgages have been taken out, the average amount borrowed being around €120,000. The amount you can borrow depends on various factors, such as your income, your trade or profession, whether you're an employee or self-employed, whether you're married and, if so, whether your partner works. Lenders may also have a maximum lending limit based on a percentage of your income, but this isn't required by law in Spain.

Mortgages are granted on a percentage of a property's valuation, which is usually below the market value. The maximum mortgage in Spain is usually 80 per cent of the valuation for a principal home (*vivienda habitual*) and 50 to 60 per cent for a second home (*segunda residencía*). The normal term is 10 to 15 years, although mortgages can be repaid over up to 35 years. The repayment period may be shorter for second homes. Repayment mortgages are the most common type in Spain, although endowment and pension-linked mortgages are also available. Payments can usually be made monthly or quarterly.

Some banks offer mortgages of up to 80 per cent (usually for new developments) without proof of income, although you must usually provide proof of your monthly income and outgoings such as mortgage payments, rent and other loans or commitments. If you want a Spanish mortgage to buy a property for commercial purposes, you must provide a detailed business plan in Spanish. Some foreign lenders apply stricter rules than Spanish lenders regarding income, employment and the type of property on which they will lend. Foreign lenders, e.g. offshore banks, may also have strict rules regarding the nationality and domicile of borrowers (some won't lend to Spanish residents), and the percentage they will lend. They may also levy astronomical charges if you get into arrears. If you raise a mortgage outside Spain for a Spanish property, you should be aware of any impact this may have on your foreign or Spanish tax liabilities or allowances.

In recent years, Spanish mortgages have been among the most competitive in Europe and in late 2005, variable interest rates were around 4 per cent. Around 90 per cent of home loans have a variable (*interés variable*) instead of a fixed interest (*interés fijo*) rate and they've traditionally been set at 1 to 2 per cent above the base rate (European inter-bank rate or EURIBOR). In September 2005, rates for variable mortgages ranged from 3 to 4.5 per cent and those for fixed mortgages from 5 to 8 per cent. Note, however, that a low interest rate may be more than offset by increased commission charges. Always shop around for the best interest rate and ask the effective rate (*tasa anual equivalente/TAE*), including commissions and fees.

In Spain, it's customary for a property to be held as security for a home loan, i.e. the lender takes a first charge on the property, which is recorded at the property registry office. If a loan is obtained using a Spanish property as security, additional fees and registration costs are payable to the notary (*notario*) for registering the charge against the property.

Note that you must add expenses and fees, totalling around 10 per cent of the purchase price, to the cost of a property. Most lenders levy an 'arrangement' fee (*comisión de apertura*) of 0.5 to 2.5 per cent of the purchase price. Although it's unusual to have a full survey carried out in Spain, most lenders insist on a 'valuation' (usually costing between €150 and €300) before they will grant a loan. Mortgages also usually have a cancellation fee of around 1 per cent. Note that, if you're a Spanish taxpayer, you can claim a deduction for your Spanish mortgage against your tax liability (see **Income Tax** on page 330).

Spanish banks often insist that you take out home insurance cover with them together with the mortgage, although you aren't legally required to do so and should shop around before you take on insurance cover with a bank, as their rates are invariably higher than other insurers. Note that a mortgage can be assumed by the new owner (called *subrogación*) when a property is sold, which is common practice in Spain.

It's relatively easy to change your mortgage lender or re-negotiate mortgage terms with your existing lender: lenders are required to issue a list of conditions and interest rates (*hojas vinculantes*) that are binding on the lender for ten days. This enables applicants to compare rates and allows existing mortgage holders to transfer their mortgage if their present lender cannot meet the terms offered by another·lender.

There are two ways of improving existing mortgage terms: by 'compulsory substitution' (*subrogación forzosa*), whereby the lender offering more favourable terms/interest rates takes over the existing mortgage, and by 'variation' (*novación modificativa*), whereby the existing lender offers a reduced interest rate or changes the repayment period. Some lenders offer to pay all the associated expenses if you switch your mortgage to them. Banks may charge a maximum of 2.5 per cent when a lender wishes to cancel a mortgage with fixed interest and take one with variable interest (a common event when interest rates are falling). If you wish to re-negotiate your mortgage terms, it's a good idea to contact your branch manager to see what sort of deal your bank is prepared to offer you – most banks are keen to keep their mortgage customers.

If you're unable to meet your mortgage payments, lenders are usually willing to re-schedule your mortgage so that it extends over a longer period, thus allowing you to make lower payments. Some banks offer 'flexible' mortgage payments with the possibility of not paying two or three instalments a year. Note that you should make arrangements with your lender immediately you stop paying your mortgage, as lenders are quick to embargo a property and could eventually repossess it and sell it at auction, which can take just a few months.

**Irrespective of how you finance the purchase of a home in Spain, you should obtain professional advice.**

## Second Homes

If you have equity in an existing property, in Spain or abroad, it may be better to re-mortgage (or take out a second mortgage on) that property than to take out a new mortgage for a second home in Spain. It involves less paperwork (and therefore lower legal fees) and a plan can be tailored to meet your requirements. Depending on your equity in your existing property and the cost of your Spanish property, this may enable you to pay cash for a second home. Note, however, that when a mortgage is taken out on a Spanish property it's based on that property and not the individual, which could be important if you get into repayment difficulties.

If you let a second home, you may be able to offset the interest (pro rata) on your mortgage against letting income. For example, if you let a Spanish property for three months of the year, you can offset a quarter of your annual mortgage interest against your letting income.

## Foreign Currency Mortgages

It's also possible to obtain a foreign currency mortgage (i.e. other than in euros) in Spain or abroad. In previous years, high Spanish interest rates meant that a foreign currency mortgage was a good bet for many foreigners. **You should be extremely wary about taking out a foreign currency mortgage, as interest rate gains can be wiped out overnight by currency swings and devaluations.** It's generally recognised that you should take out a mortgage in the currency in which you're paid or in the currency of the country where a property is situated. When choosing between a euro loan and a foreign currency loan, make sure that you take into account all costs, fees, interest rates and possible currency fluctuations. If you have a foreign currency mortgage, you must usually pay commission charges each time you transfer foreign currency into euros or remit money to Spain.

# TAXATION

Spain is no longer the tax haven it was in the '60s and '70s, when taxes were low and tax evasion was a way of life and almost encouraged! Spain's taxes have increased dramatically during the last few decades, although income tax and social security contributions remain among the lowest in the EU and income tax rates have been reduced over the last three years. On the other hand, indirect taxes (e.g. on fuel) have recently been increased. Before you decide to settle in Spain permanently, you should obtain expert advice regarding Spanish taxes. This will (hopefully) ensure that you take maximum advantage of your current tax status and that you don't make any mistakes that you will regret later.

Today it's difficult to avoid paying taxes in Spain and penalties are severe. Nevertheless, tax evasion is still widespread; many non-resident homeowners and foreign residents think that they should be exempt from Spanish taxes and are among the worst offenders.

As you would expect in a country with millions of bureaucrats, the Spanish tax system is inordinately complicated and most Spaniards don't understand it. In fact, even the experts have difficulty agreeing with the tax authorities (Agencia Estatal de Administración Tributaria, previously known as *hacienda*), and tax advisers often giving different advice. It's difficult to obtain accurate information from the tax authorities and, just when you think you have it cracked (ho! ho!) the authorities change the rules or hit you with a new tax.

Taxes are levied by three tiers of government in Spain: central government, autonomous regional governments and local municipalities. Government taxes are administered by the Ministry of Economy and Taxation (Ministerio de Económica y Hacienda), which has its headquarters in Madrid and assessment and tax collection centres in provincial capital towns. It isn't so much the level of taxes in Spain that's burdensome, but the number of different taxes for which individuals are liable. At the last count there were around 15, including the following:

- **Business Tax** (*impuesto sobre actividades económicas/IAE*) – Payable by all businesses with an annual turnover of more than €600,000, including the self-employed. Note, however, that all businesses and the self-employed must register with the tax authorities irrespective of annual turnover.

- **Capital Gains Tax** (*impuesto sobre incremento de patrimonio de la venta de un bien inmeuble*) – Payable by residents and non-residents on the profits made on the sale of certain property and other assets located in Spain (see page 346).

- **Company or Corporation Tax** (*impuesto sobre sociedades/IBI*) – Payable at the rate of 35 per cent on the profits made by partnerships and registered companies such as a *Sociedad Anónima* (*SA*) or *Sociedad Limitada* (*SL*). The government plans to reduce this to 30 per cent to increase Spain's creativity. The Canary Islands, particularly Gran Canaria and Tenerife, are something of a tax haven with a 1 to 5 per cent company tax, depending on a number of factors, including activity and creation of employment.

- **Income Tax** (*impuesto sobre la renta de las personas físicas/IRPF*) – Payable by residents on worldwide income and by non-residents on income arising in Spain (see page 330). Non-residents must also pay an imputed 'letting' or deemed property income tax based on property values (see page 344).

- **Inheritance & Gift Tax** (*impuesto sobre sucesiones y donaciones*) – Payable by residents on the transfer of worldwide assets and by non-residents on Spanish assets (see page 349).

- **Offshore Company Tax** (*impuesto especial*) – Payable by offshore companies that don't declare the individual owner of property in Spain or the source of investment.

- **Property Tax** (*impuesto sobre bienes inmeubles urbanos/IBIU*, formerly called *contribución urbana*) – Payable by all property owners, whether resident or non-resident (see page 344).

- **Social Security** (*seguridad social*) – Not strictly a tax, but payable by employees and the self-employed (see page 288).

- **Value Added Tax/VAT** (*impuesto sobre el valor añadido/IVA*) – Payable on a wide range of goods and services at varying rates (see page 329).

- **Vehicle Registration Tax** (*impuesto sobre circulación de vehículos*) – Payable by all those owning a Spanish-registered vehicle (see **Taxes** on page 231).

- **Waste/Drainage Tax** (*basura y alcantarillado*) – Payable by most property owners, whether resident or non-resident.

- **Wealth Tax** (*impuesto sobre el patrimonio*) – Payable by residents and non-residents on high-value capital assets, including property, in Spain (see page 342).

There are other taxes concerned with building a property in Spain and property purchase, which include transfer tax (*impuesto de transmisiones patrimoniales/ITP*), and a 'value increase' tax (*plus valía*), which is levied by local councils (at various rates) when properties are sold. Property buyers who purchase property in an urbanisation without the proper infrastructure may need to pay an exceptional municipal tax (*impuestos especiales municipales*) to bring the infrastructure up to the required standard. In addition to VAT, supplementary taxes are levied on automobiles, alcohol, petrol and tobacco products.

Most taxes in Spain are based on self-assessment, meaning that individual taxpayers are liable to report and calculate any tax due within the time limits established by law. Tax forms must be purchased by taxpayers and are obtainable from a tobacconist (*estanco*), although some are available only from tax offices (*agencia tributaria*). Penalties and interest are levied for late payment or non-compliance, although there's a five-year statute of limitations (*prescripción*) on the collection of back taxes in Spain, i.e. if no action has been taken during this period to collect unpaid tax, it cannot be collected.

# Fiscal Representation

The term fiscal representative (*representante fiscal*) refers to any person or agent who provides tax and other financial services; this may be a professional, such as an accountant (*contable*) or tax adviser (*asesor fiscal*), or it may be a non-professional who merely deals with your financial affairs on your behalf. (All accountants and tax advisers in Spain act as fiscal representatives for their clients.) It isn't necessary (but is recommended) for non-resident owners of a single dwelling in Spain to have a fiscal representative; however, if you have more than one asset in Spain, e.g. separate title deeds for a property and a garage or garden, or you own a commercial property, you must have a fiscal representative. A foreign company owning a property in

Spain must have a fiscal representative, and a foreigner receiving income from a business in Spain may need it. If you fail to appoint a representative when you're required to have one, you can be fined up to €6,000.

Even if they don't have a professional fiscal representative, non-residents should appoint someone in Spain to look after their financial affairs and declare and pay their taxes. The Spanish tax authorities will communicate with this person, and he can also receive your bank statements and ensure that your bank is paying your regular bills (such as electricity, water and telephone) by standing order and that you have sufficient funds in your account to pay them. Your representative (professional or not) can also apply for an identification number (*Número de Identificación de Entranjero/NIE*) on your behalf (see above).

Your representative can be a Spaniard or a foreign resident in Spain, an individual or a company (such as a bank). The local provincial office of the Ministry of Finance must be notified of the appointment of a representative within two months by letter and the representative must expressly communicate his acceptance of the appointment to the office where your taxes are to be paid. Before employing a representative, you should obtain recommendations from friends, colleagues and acquaintances. However, bear in mind that, if you consult a number of 'experts', you're liable to receive conflicting advice.

**Note also that some representatives fail to pay tax bills on time (or at all), thereby incurring their clients a fine equal to 20 per cent of the amount due.** You should therefore check with the town hall and tax authorities that your bills have actually been paid!

Professional fiscal representation usually costs from €150 per year for a single person and €300 for a couple, depending on the services provided, although many representatives charge only 50 per cent more for a couple than for a single person. There may be additional charges for tax administration and completing tax returns, the cost depending on the complexity of your tax affairs. For the relatively small cost involved, most people (residents and non-residents) are usually better off employing a professional representative to handle their Spanish tax and other financial affairs than doing it themselves, particularly as the regulations change frequently; you can often save more than the representative's fee in avoided tax.

# VALUE ADDED TAX

Value added tax (*impuesto sobre el valor añadido/IVA*) is levied on most goods and services in Spain. Most prices in shops are quoted inclusive of value added tax (VAT), although prices are occasionally quoted exclusive of tax (e.g. the price of office equipment). Bills usually show whether VAT is included (*IVA incluido*) or not (*más IVA*).

Certain goods and services are exempt from VAT, including healthcare (e.g. doctors' and dentists' services), educational services insurance, banking and certain financial services, social security services, sports and cultural activities, postal services, state lotteries, land and second-hand property, the letting of residential property, the transfer of a business (provided the buyer continues the existing business), and certain transactions that are subject to other taxes. Exports are also exempt from VAT.

VAT applies to the mainland and the Balearic Islands, but isn't levied in the Canary Islands, Ceuta and Melilla. Instead, the Canary Islands have an indirect general tax (*impuesto general indirecto Canario/IGIC*), which is levied on goods and services at the rate of 4.5 per cent, and Ceuta and Melilla levy various sales taxes on imports, services and production. Spain has the following rates of VAT (it's the declared aim of the EU to have just one rate of VAT for all members, although this will take some time to accomplish, particularly as only Denmark currently has one rate and all other members have at least two!):

| Rate | Applicability |
|---|---|
| 4% (super reduced rate) | Basic foodstuffs such as bread, flour, milk, cheese, eggs, fruit & vegetables; books, newspapers & magazines; certain pharmaceutical products; disabled vehicles & prostheses; subsidised housing |
| 7% (reduced rate) | Food; drink (other than alcohol & soft drinks); fuel; water; communications; medicines; feminine hygiene products; transport; hotels; restaurants (excluding five-fork rated restaurants); theatres & cinemas; certain sports services; new dwellings |
| 16% (standard rate) | All other goods & services, including utility bills, car hire and five-fork rated restaurants |

All businesses in Spain must be registered for VAT and **it's essential to have legitimate bills showing names and tax numbers (CIF, NIF, NIE) in order to reclaim VAT**. Businesses with a turnover of €6 million or more per year must file a VAT return monthly, paying the tax due within 20 days of the end of the month. Businesses with an annual turnover of less than €6 million must file a quarterly return and pay tax due within 20 days of the end of the quarter. VAT fraud is rife in Spain and payments are often made in cash to avoid it.

VAT is payable on goods purchased outside the EU, but not on goods purchased in an EU country where VAT has already been paid, although you may be asked to produce a VAT receipt. People who are resident outside the EU can obtain exemption from VAT on individual purchases in Spain costing over €100. Retailers can provide information and the necessary forms. You must show your passport and complete a form and the shop posts the refund to your home address. See also **Customs** on page 89 and **Shopping Abroad** on page 440.

# INCOME TAX

Spanish income tax (*impuesto sobre la renta de las personas físicas/IRPF*) is payable on earned and unearned income. Taxable income includes salaries, pensions, capital gains, property and investment income (dividends and interest), and income from professional, artistic, business or agricultural activities. It also includes employee benefits and perks such as overseas and cost of living allowances, contributions to profit sharing plans, bonuses (annual, performance, etc.), storage and relocation allowances, language lessons provided for a spouse, personal company car, payments in kind (such as free accommodation or meals), stock options, home leave or holidays (paid by your employer), and children's private education. If you're a non-resident or own more than one property in Spain, your 'income' also includes 2 per cent of its fiscal value (*valor catastral*) – see **Tax on Deemed Letting Income** on page 340.

Income tax in Spain is below the EU average and isn't supplemented by crippling social security rates as in some other EU countries (e.g. France). Major tax reforms have been introduced in recent years and income tax rates for the 2003 fiscal year fell by around 11 per cent, although critics claim the reforms favour higher taxpayers. The reforms are designed to make taxation simpler for the taxpayer and the authorities and to reduce tax fraud, which is still widespread. Further reforms, including reducing the current five tax bands to four, are planned before 2008. If you're able to choose the country where you're taxed, it can be to your advantage to pay Spanish income tax, as there are more allowances than there are in some other countries; you should obtain advice from an international tax expert.

Moving to Spain (or another country) often provides opportunities for legal 'favourable tax planning'. To make the most of your situation, it's advisable to obtain income tax advice before moving to Spain, as there are usually a number of things you can do in advance to reduce your tax liability, in Spain and abroad. Be sure to consult a tax adviser who's familiar with the Spanish tax system and that of your present country of residence. For example, you may be able to avoid paying tax on a business abroad if you establish residence and domicile in Spain before you sell it. On the other hand, if you sell a foreign home after establishing your principal residence in Spain, it becomes a second home and you may then be liable to capital gains tax abroad (this is a complicated subject and you should obtain expert advice). You should notify the tax authorities in your former country of residence that you're going to live permanently in Spain.

Employees' income tax (*retenciones*) is deducted at source by Spanish employers, i.e. pay-as-you-earn, and individuals aren't responsible for paying their own income tax, although they must still make a tax declaration. Self-employed people must pay their income tax quarterly (*pago fraccionado*). Non-residents who receive an income from a Spanish source and non-resident property owners (see page 340) should instruct their fiscal representative to file an income tax declaration on their behalf (or do it themselves).

Tax evasion is illegal and a criminal offence in Spain, and offenders can be heavily fined or even imprisoned. Although Spanish tax inspectors make a relatively small number of inspections, they target them at those among whom tax fraud is most prevalent, such as the self-employed. **Note that new legislation has been introduced to tackle fraud and 'fiscal nomads' will find it more difficult to avoid Spanish taxation in future.** On the other hand, tax avoidance (i.e. legally paying as little tax as possible, if necessary by finding and exploiting loopholes in the tax laws) is highly recommended! Residents have a number of opportunities to legally reduce their taxes, although non-residents have very few or none at all.

You can obtain free tax advice from the information section (*servicio de información* or *oficina de información al contribuyente*) at your provincial tax office in Spain, where staff will answer queries and advise you on completing your tax declaration (unfortunately, they won't complete it for you!). Some offices, particularly those located in resort areas, have staff who speak English and other foreign languages. The tax office provides a central telephone information service (☎ 901-335 533), open during May and June from 9am to 9pm Mondays to Fridays and from 9am to 2pm on Saturdays, the rest of the year from 9am to 7pm Mondays to Fridays. For information about income tax and obtaining tax labels, the tax office runs an automatic telephone service open 24 hours a day, seven days a week (☎ 901-121 224). There's also a useful website (🖳 www.aeat.es), although your Spanish needs to be fluent to understand most of it; there are few pages in English.

# Liability

Your liability for income tax in Spain depends on whether you're officially resident there. Under Spanish law you become a fiscal resident in Spain if you spend 183 days there during a calendar year **or** your main centre of economic interest, e.g. investments or business, is in Spain. Temporary absences are included in the calculation of the period spent in Spain (or Spanish territories). If your spouse and dependent minor children normally reside in Spain and have residence permits (and you aren't legally separated), you're considered to be a tax resident in Spain (unless you can prove otherwise). Note that the 183-day rule also applies to other EU countries, and the UK limits visits by non-residents to 182 days in any one year or an average of 91 days per tax year over a four-year period.

If you're tax resident in two countries simultaneously, your 'tax home' may be resolved under the rules applied under international treaties. Under such treaties you're considered to be resident in the country where you have a permanent home; if you have a permanent home in both countries, you're deemed to be resident in the country where your personal and economic ties are closer. If your residence cannot be determined under this rule, you're deemed to be resident in the country where you have a habitual abode. If you have a habitual abode in both or in neither country, you're deemed to be resident in the country of which you're a citizen. Finally, if you're a citizen of both or neither country, the authorities of the countries concerned will decide your tax residence between them!

Spanish residents are taxed on their worldwide income, whereas non-residents are taxed in Spain only on income arising in Spain, which is exempt from tax in their home countries (see **Double-taxation** below).

If you plan to live permanently in Spain, you should notify the tax authorities in your previous country of residence. You may be entitled to a tax refund (*devolución*) if you depart during the tax year, which usually requires the completion of a tax return. The authorities may require evidence that you're leaving the country, e.g. proof that you have a job in Spain or have bought or rented a property there. If you move to Spain to take up a job or start a business, you must register with the local tax authorities soon after your arrival.

If your earned annual income from work in Spain is less than €22,000, you're exempt from making a tax declaration, as your salary will have been correctly taxed at source. If you're a pensioner and your earned worldwide annual income (i.e. income from pensions plus a maximum of €1,600 from investments) is less than

€8,000, you aren't required to make a tax declaration or pay Spanish income tax. **However, if you're entitled to deductions for pension plans or housing, you must make a tax declaration irrespective of your earnings.**

The tax year in Spain is the calendar year and runs from 1st January to 31st December.

## Double-taxation

Spain has double-taxation treaties with around 50 countries, including all European Economic Area (EEA) countries (except Cyprus, Estonia and Malta), Argentina, Australia, Bolivia, Brazil, Bulgaria, Canada, Chile, China, Cuba, Ecuador, India, Indonesia, Israel, Japan, Mexico, Morocco, the Philippines, Romania, Russia, South Korea, Switzerland, Thailand, Tunisia, Turkey, the US and Venezuela. Treaties are designed to ensure that income that has already been taxed in one treaty country isn't taxed again in another treaty country. Treaties establish a tax credit or exemption on certain kinds of income, in your country of residence or the country where the income was earned. Where applicable, a double-taxation treaty prevails over domestic law.

The US is the only country that taxes its non-resident citizens on income earned abroad (US citizens can obtain a copy of a brochure, *Tax Guide for Americans Abroad*, from American consulates). Citizens of most other countries are exempt from paying taxes in their home country when they spend a minimum period abroad, e.g. a year.

However, even if there's no double-taxation agreement between Spain and another country, you can still obtain relief from double-taxation through a direct deduction of any foreign tax paid or through a 'foreign compensation' (*compensación extranjera*) formula.

Note that taxpayers entitled to double-taxation relief must still make a tax declaration in Spain and, if their tax liability in another country is lower than that in Spain, they must pay the Spanish tax authorities the difference. If you're in doubt about your tax liability in your home country, contact your nearest embassy or consulate in Spain.

## Expatriate Workers

Innovative tax breaks for foreign workers were introduced in 2004 as an incentive for foreign companies to establish their headquarters or a permanent office in Spain and to encourage executives and employees to work there. Under the scheme, foreign employees living in Spain can choose to be taxed at a flat rate of 25 per cent during the year of their arrival and for the following five years. Under this tax regime, you don't qualify for any allowances or deductions and must meet the following requirements:

- You must be a first-time resident of Spain or have been non-resident during the ten years before you move to Spain.

- You must have a work contract for a job, which must be carried out in Spain.

- Your employer must be a company resident or with a permanent establishment in Spain.

## Leaving Spain

Before leaving Spain permanently, foreigners should pay any tax due for the previous year and the year of departure by applying for a tax clearance. A tax return should be filed before departure and include your income and deductions from 1st January of the departure year up to the date of departure. Your local tax office calculates the tax due and provides a written statement. When departure is made before 31st December, the previous year's taxes are applied. If this results in overpayment, a claim must be made for a refund. Tax clearance permits aren't required by those leaving Spain to live abroad.

# Allowances & Deductions

Before you're liable for income tax, you can deduct certain costs from your gross income (allowances) and others from the sum due after establishing your tax base (deductions). The resultant figure is your taxable income. The following allowances and deductions apply to the fiscal year 2005, i.e. tax declarations made in 2006. Note that there are numerous regional variations on allowances and deductions.

## Allowances

- Any withholding tax paid during the previous year.
- All social security payments (see **Chapter 13**).
- A 'personal minimum' (*mínimo personal*) allowance, i.e. the amount you and your dependants need to live, which is €3,400. If you're over 65, this amount is increased by €800.
- One of the following deductions from your income:
    - €3,500 if your annual salary (i.e. earned from paid employment) is less than €8,200.
    - €3,500 minus 22.91 per cent of the difference between the salary and €8,200, if your annual salary is between €8,200 and €13,000; e.g. if your salary is €12,000, the deduction would be €3,500 - (€3,800 x 0.2291 = €870.58) = €2,629.42.
    - €2,400 if your annual salary is over €13,000 or the income is from other sources, e.g. investments.

    These deductions also apply if you were unemployed and accepted a job in a different locality to where you live.
- One of the following deductions if you're disabled (these allowances may also be claimed by a disabled person's dependants and parents):
    - €2,000 if your disability is between 33 and 65 per cent plus deductions of €2,800 from income and €2,000 for care if you have mobility problems.
    - €5,000 if your disability is above 65 per cent plus deductions of €6,200 from income and €2,000 for care if you have mobility problems.

- The following deductions for dependants:
  - €1,400 for a first child.
  - €1,500 for a second child.
  - €2,200 for a third child.
  - €2,300 for a fourth and each additional child.
  - €1,200 for each child under three (for childcare fees).
  - An additional €1,200 for each child under three (maternity or paternity allowance – to qualify the parent must be contributing to social security); note that the parent can opt for this allowance to be deducted from his gross income or choose to receive a monthly payment of €100.
  - €1,000 if you have someone aged over 75 living with you and their annual income is below €8,000.
- Professional and trade union fees.
- Spanish company pension contributions up to a maximum of €8,000 if you're under 52. If you're between 52 and 65, you may add a further €1,250 for each year over 52; if you're over 65, the maximum amount is €24,250.
- A percentage of an annuity (life or fixed-period), depending on your age.
- If you're a divorced parent, child-support payments made as a result of a court decision (maintenance payments may be taxable subject to provisions made under court orders).

## Deductions

After deducting the allowances listed above, you should apply the percentages shown in the tax tables on page 336, which will give you the amount of tax due. However, before arriving at your final tax bill, you can make certain deductions from the tax due, including the following:

- 75 per cent of any *plus valía* tax paid as a result of a property sale.
- 15 per cent of the cost of the purchase or renovation of your principal residence up to €9,015 (excluding additions such as a garage or swimming pool or normal maintenance and repairs).
- Deductions from mortgage payments (capital plus interest) up to €9,015. If the mortgage loan represents at least half the value of the property and no more than 40 per cent is to be repaid in the first three years, the deduction is 25 per cent on the first €4,508 and 20 per cent on the balance.
- 15 per cent of the amount invested in a 'mortgage savings' account up to €9,015.

Any personal income taxes paid in another country is also deducted from your tax base. However, if you pay higher tax abroad than you would have paid in Spain, you won't receive a rebate from the Spanish tax authorities!

# Calculation

There are no longer different tax rates for couples who choose to be taxed individually or jointly. Income tax rates for individuals (*personas físicas*) start at 15 per cent on income up to €4,080 and rise to 45 per cent on income above €45,900. Tax is divided between the Spanish state (60 per cent) and the autonomous regions (40 per cent), as shown in the two tables below, although some autonomous regions (e.g. the Basque Country, Catalonia and La Rioja) offer deductions from tax due. You must add the two rates to obtain the total tax payable (see below).

**Individual Declaration – General Scale**

| Taxable Income (€) | Tax Rate (%) | Cumulative Tax (€) |
|---|---|---|
| 0 – 4,080 | 9.06 | 369.65 |
| 4,080 – 14,076 | 15.84 | 1,953.02 |
| 14,076 – 26,316 | 18.68 | 4,239.45 |
| 26,316 – 45,900 | 24.71 | 9,078.66 |
| Over 45,900 | 29.16 | |

**Individual Declaration – Autonomous Region Scale**

| Taxable Income (€) | Tax Rate (%) | Cumulative Tax (€) |
|---|---|---|
| 0 – 4,080 | 5.94 | 242.35 |
| 4,080 – 14,076 | 8.16 | 1,058.02 |
| 14,076 – 26,316 | 9.32 | 2,198.79 |
| 26,316 – 45,900 | 12.29 | 4,605.66 |
| Over 45,900 | 15.84 | |

The table below shows the total income tax payable (the above general and autonomous region scales combined).

**Individual Declaration – Total Tax Payable**

| Taxable Income (€) | Tax Rate (%) | Cumulative Tax (€) |
|---|---|---|
| 0 – 4,080 | 15 | 612.00 |
| 4,080 – 14,076 | 24 | 3,011.04 |
| 14,076 – 26,316 | 28 | 6,438.24 |
| 26,316 – 45,900 | 37 | 13,684.32 |
| Over 45,000 | 45 | |

# Declaration

An annual income tax declaration (*declaración sobre la renta de personas físicas*) must be lodged between 1st May and 20th June by residents and non-residents with income in Spain (other than income from property letting). This deadline also applies to declarations for property tax and wealth tax for residents, although if you're entitled to a refund (*devolución*) it's extended until 30th June. Income tax is paid a year in arrears, e.g. the declaration filed in the year 2006 is for the 2005 tax year.

If your earned income is below €8,000 (for an individual declaration), it isn't necessary to complete an income tax declaration. Note that, if you're a Spanish resident, this limit applies to your worldwide family income wherever it arises, but doesn't include income taxed in another country. If you're resident in Spain, the authorities will ask to see your income tax declaration when you renew your residence permit (*residencia*). Rather than try to explain why your income is below the tax threshold (and therefore possibly below the income necessary to obtain a *residencia!*), it's advisable to make a 'negative' tax declaration.

Unless your tax affairs are simple, it's advisable to employ an accountant or tax adviser (*asesor fiscal*) to complete your tax return and ensure that you're correctly assessed. There are 'foreign' tax assessors (*asesores de extranjero*) who specialise in filing returns for foreigners, particularly non-residents. The fees charged for filing tax returns vary and for residents are around €35 for a simple return and €60 for an ordinary return. The fee for filing a tax return for a non-resident is usually around €35. Make sure that you have your tax return stamped as proof of payment by your adviser.

There are four kinds of tax declaration form in Spain, as detailed below.

## Draft Declaration

The draft declaration (*borrador*), which was introduced in 2003, can be used by any taxpayer and is the simplest method of declaring your income. Instead of your having to purchase, complete and return a tax form, a draft declaration is sent to you by the tax authorities, with figures and calculations based on your income the previous year. Taxpayers who request a draft declaration in their previous year's declaration (via the tick box *petición de borrador/datos*) receive the draft by post during March and April; anyone else can request one before 15th June.

Once you receive the draft, you must confirm or contest the figures. If the figures are correct, you can confirm this with the tax office by one of the following methods:

- At a tax office or participating bank.
- By phone (☎ 901-336 633).
- Via the internet (🖳 www.agenciatributaria.es).
- By SMS (☎ 5025) – write the word 'RENTA' followed by a space, then enter your draft reference number, followed by another space and then your NIE.
- At a cash machine following the instructions under the Renta section.

According to tax office statistics, taxpayers whose draft declaration was correct and were entitled to a tax refund received this at the beginning of May – considerably earlier than those using other types of declaration. If the draft isn't correct, you must contact a tax office, explaining the changes to be made.

## Abbreviated Declaration

The *declaración abreviada* (Form 103) consists of two pages. It's used by taxpayers whose income derives entirely from earnings or from pensions and investments that have already been subject to Spanish withholding tax. Note that, if your income consists of a pension that has had deductions made in another country and which you intend to subtract from your Spanish declaration, you cannot use this form, but must use a simple declaration (see below).

## Simple Declaration

The *declaración simplificada* (Form 101) consists of five pages and is for those with the same sources of income (usually below €600,000) as for the abbreviated declaration (see above) plus income from letting, certain business and agricultural income, and capital gains from the sale of a permanent home where the total gain will be invested in a new home in Spain. Form 101 is used for refunds and the declaration and payment of the first stage of income tax, while Form 102 is used for the second payment.

## Ordinary Declaration

The *declaración ordinaria* (Form 100) consists of 13 pages and is for those with incomes from all sources other than those mentioned above, e.g. business or professional activities (this includes the self-employed) and capital gains.

# Procedure

With the exception of a draft declaration, tax returns aren't sent out by the tax office and must be purchased each year from a tobacconist (*estanco*) for around €0.50 each. If you're unable to obtain a tax return from a tobacconist, you can obtain one from a tax adviser or your local tax office (*agencia tributaria*). An instruction booklet is provided with returns, and the tax office publishes a booklet, *Manual Práctico – Renta* (costing €0.75), containing examples of how to complete tax forms and an interpretation of the current Finance Act.

If you can use the abbreviated declaration, you should be able to complete your own tax form, perhaps with a little help from the tax office. However, most people require professional help to complete the *simplificada* and *ordinaria* tax forms. (Until the introduction of the abbreviated declaration, only some 15 per cent of Spain's 14 million taxpayers made their own tax declarations.) If you need assistance with an abbreviated or simple declaration, you can contact the information section (*servicio de información*) of your local tax office, which may have multilingual staff. However, tax offices won't help you complete an *ordinaria* tax form and you must make an appointment (☎ 901-223 344). When you go to the tax office, you should take along the following:

- Your end-of-year bank statements (*estado de cuenta*) showing any interest received and your average balance (*saldo medio*).

- Any papers relating to stocks, shares, bonds, deposit certificates or any other property owned, in Spain or abroad.
- Declarations and receipts for any taxes paid in another country (if you're seeking to offset payment against your Spanish taxes).
- Your passport, residence permit and *NIE*.

If tax is due, you can submit your return to the district tax office where you're resident for tax purposes or at a designated bank in the province. If no payment is due, you must file it at the tax office. If you delay filing your tax return by even a day, you must pay a surcharge on the tax due (see below), although it's possible to request a payment deferral.

You should retain copies of your tax returns for at least five years, which is the maximum period that returns are liable for audit by the Spanish tax authorities.

# Payment

Unless deducted at source, income tax in Spain is paid at the same time as the tax declaration is made. You can pay the whole amount when the form is filed or 60 per cent with your declaration and the balance by the following 5th November. Payment must be made in cash; if you're filing at a bank where you hold an account, they will make an electronic transfer to the tax authorities.

Late payment of any tax bill usually incurs a surcharge of 20 per cent. Large fines can be imposed for breaches of tax law and in certain cases forfeiture of the right to tax benefits or subsidies for a period of up to five years. The fraudulent evasion of €30,000 or more in tax is punishable by fines of up to six times the amount defrauded and/or imprisonment, although it's rare for anyone to be prosecuted for tax evasion in Spain.

# Property Owners

The liability for income tax of property owners depends on whether they're resident or non-resident in Spain. Non-resident property owners and resident owners of more than one property must also pay a so-called tax on deemed letting income (see below).

## Residents

Property income earned by residents is included in their annual income tax declaration and tax is payable at the standard income tax rates (see above). You're eligible for deductions such as repairs and maintenance, security, cleaning costs, mortgage interest (Spanish loans only), management and letting expenses (e.g. advertising), local taxes, and insurance, plus an amortisation deduction of 3 per cent per year of the value of the property. You should seek professional advice to ensure that you're claiming everything you're entitled to.

## Non-residents

Non-resident property owners are liable for income tax at a flat rate of 25 per cent on any income arising in Spain, including income from letting a property. Income must be declared on Form 210 (*Impuestos Sobre la Renta de las Personas Físicas y Sobre Sociedades*) and paid quarterly to the tax authorities. There's a 10 per cent surcharge for late payment. For any part of the year when you don't have rental income, e.g. the winter, you must still make a tax declaration, e.g. for tax on deemed letting income, using Form 214 (*Impuesto Sobre el Patrimonio y Sobre la Renta de No Residentes*), which is obtainable only from a tax office (*agencia tributaria*).

Non-residents owning a single property in Spain can declare their income and wealth taxes together on a single form at any time during the year, e.g. the declaration for 2005 could be made any time up to 31st December 2006. This is done on Form 214. If you own two or more properties in Spain, however, you cannot use Form 214 and must make separate declarations for income and wealth tax (Forms 714 and 210) between 1st May and 20th June (and you must appoint a fiscal representative in Spain).

Form 214 is a simple form and homeowners with a knowledge of Spanish should be able to complete it themselves (instructions in Spanish are printed on the reverse). When a husband and wife own a property jointly, they should complete separate forms, although it's possible for a couple to make their declaration on one form (check with your fiscal representative). When a property is used partly for letting and partly for habitation, an apportionment is made between the amount of time used for each purpose. This tax may be offset against taxes paid in other countries.

Non-residents must pay property income tax at a bank in cash or by debit from a Spanish bank account.

# Tax on Deemed Letting Income

The tax that causes most confusion (and resentment), particularly among non-resident property owners, is the tax on deemed or notional letting income (*rendimientos del capital inmobiliario*, usually referred to simply as *renta*). All non-resident property owners and residents owning more than one property in Spain are deemed to receive an income of 2 per cent of the fiscal value (*valor catastral*) of their property (1.1 per cent if the fiscal value has been revised since 1st January 1994). Non-residents pay tax at a flat rate tax of 25 per cent on this income (for example, if you own a property valued at €100,000, 2 per cent of this is €2,000, on which the 25 per cent 'income' tax is €500); there are no deductions. Residents must add the deemed letting income to other income for income tax purposes. Principal residences are exempt from this tax.

# Pensions

The taxation of pensioners changed in 1992, and since then pensions have been taxed according to the source of the income, as detailed below. Taxation of investment capital and insurance-based pensions can be very complicated and you should obtain expert professional advice from an accountant or tax adviser **before** deciding where and how to receive your pension. See also **Supplementary Pensions** on page 295.

## Employment-based Pensions

Employment-based pensions are taxed in the same way as salary income (see above). You're entitled to the same allowances and deductions, and the same tax rates apply. However, the situation isn't as straightforward if your pension is paid from a savings scheme such as a pension fund established through an employment relationship with tax advantages in your home country.

## Investment Capital Pensions

Investment capital pensions, whereby you pay a sum of money or transfer assets such as property to another party in return for annuity payments (or a monthly income) for a fixed period or until death, may give rise to capital gains and interest income, each of which is taxed differently in Spain.

## Insurance-based Pensions

Insurance-based pensions – insurance schemes that permit you to choose between taking the whole amount accrued under the policy in a lump sum and having it paid in the form of annuities – are taxed as a capital gain (see page 346) or as ordinary income (see above).

## Civil Service Pensions

Foreign civil service pensions are usually tax-free in Spain and don't need to be declared to the Spanish authorities if they're your only source of income, **although this depends on the country paying your pension and whether it has a double-taxation treaty with Spain (see page 333)**. However, you may need to provide the tax office with proof that your pension is taxed at source. Civil service pensions don't include United Nations pensions, as the UN cannot tax its former employees (unlike individual countries). Note, however, that if you have other income that's taxable in Spain, your civil service pension is usually taken into account when calculating your Spanish tax rate and it must usually be declared. If you pay tax in error on a pension that wasn't in fact taxable, you can claim a refund only for the previous five years, which is Spain's statute of limitations (if they aren't collected, taxes also usually lapse after five years).

## Non-resident Pensions

Non-resident pensions received from a Spanish source are subject to special tax rates depending on the amount, as follows:

| Amount (€) | Tax Rate (%) | Cumulative Tax (€) |
|---|---|---|
| Up to 9,616.19 | 8 | 769.30 |
| 9,616.19 – 15,025.30 | 30 | 2,392.03 |
| Over 15,025.30 | 40 | |

# WEALTH TAX

Spain levies a wealth tax (*impuesto sobre el patrimonio, commonly referred to simply as patrimonio*) on residents and non-residents (unlike most other countries, which exempt non-residents). Your wealth is calculated by totalling your assets and deducting your liabilities. When calculating your liability to wealth tax, you must include the value of all your assets, including property, vehicles, boats, aircraft, businesses, cash (e.g. in bank accounts), life insurance, gold bars, jewellery, stocks, shares and bonds. The value of property is whichever is the highest among the purchase price, its fiscal value (*valor catastral*) and its value as assessed by the authorities (e.g. in the case of a house which has not yet been built or a property in an area where there are no property taxes). If you fail to declare your total assets, you can be fined.

Note that it's no longer necessary for most people to declare their average bank balance (*saldo medio*) in Spain for wealth tax. However, if you're a non-resident and your country of residence has a double-taxation treaty with Spain (see page 333), bank balances and interest are taxable only in your country of residence.

Certain assets are exempt from wealth tax, including *objets d'art* and antiques (provided their value doesn't exceed certain limits), the vested rights of participants in pension plans and funds, copyrights (provided they remain part of your net worth), and assets forming part of Spain's historical heritage. Deductions are made for mortgages (for residents and non-residents), business and other debts, and any 'wealth' tax paid in another country. Other exemptions and allowances are detailed below.

## Residents

Residents are entitled to two general allowances against wealth tax: €108,182.18 per person for all assets except a principal residence and €150,253 per person for a principal residence. Therefore, if you're single and own your principal residence in Spain, you qualify for a wealth tax allowance of €258,435.18. If a property is registered in the names of both spouses (or a number of unrelated people), they should make separate declarations and are each entitled to claim the exemption. If you've bought a property with a loan or mortgage, there are deductions from your wealth tax liability.

If your worldwide assets are below the taxable limit and you make an income tax declaration, you're exempt from making a wealth tax declaration.

# Non-residents

There's no allowance for non-residents, who must pay wealth tax on all their assets in Spain, which for most non-resident property owners consists only of the property itself.

# Tax Rates

In 2005, assets were taxed on a sliding scale, as follows:

| Asset Value Above Allowance (€) | Tax Rate (%) | Cumulative Tax (€) |
| --- | --- | --- |
| Up to 167,129 | 0.2 | 334 |
| 167,130 – 334,253 | 0.3 | 836 |
| 334,254 – 668,499 | 0.5 | 2,507 |
| 668,500 – 1,337,000 | 0.9 | 8,523 |
| 1,337,001 – 2,673,999 | 1.3 | 25,904 |
| 2,674,000 – 5,347,998 | 1.7 | 71,362 |
| 5,347,999 – 10,695,996 | 2.1 | 183,670 |
| Over 10,695,996 | 2.5 | |

In the above table, the cumulative tax is the tax payable for each band of asset value, e.g. €2,507 is payable on assets of €668,499. If your assets are valued at €500,000 in excess of any allowance you qualify for (i.e. as a resident – see above), you pay 0.2 per cent on the first €167,129 (€334), 0.3 per cent on the next €167,123 (€502) and 0.5 per cent on the balance of €165,746 (€829), making a total wealth tax bill of €1,665.

# Declaration

Residents in Spain must make a declaration for wealth tax at the same time as they make their income tax declaration, i.e. between 1st May and 20th June. The declaration is made on Form 714 (*Impuesto Sobre el Patrimonio*), which is available from tobacconists and tax offices. The form must be presented with payment to a regional tax office or participating bank. When a husband and wife own a property in Spain jointly, each of them should complete a form, although it's possible for a couple to make their declaration on just one form (check with your financial representative).

Non-residents owning a single property in Spain can make their declarations for tax on deemed letting income (see page 340) and wealth tax on a single form at any time during the year, e.g. the declaration for 2005 can be made any time until 31st December 2006. This is done on Form 214 (*Impuesto Sobre el Patrimonio y Sobre la Renta de No Residente*). Non-residents can have a financial representative in Spain make the declaration and arrange for payment on their behalf.

# PROPERTY TAX

Property tax (*impuesto sobre bienes inmuebles urbana/rústica* or *IBI*) is payable by resident and non-resident property owners in Spain and goes towards local council administration, education, sanitary services (e.g. street and beach cleaning), social assistance, community substructure, and cultural and sports amenities. Before buying a property, check with the local town hall that there aren't any outstanding local taxes for the past five years. As with all property-related taxes and debts, if the previous year's taxes are unpaid, the new owner becomes liable (you can, however, reclaim the tax from the previous owner – if you can find him!). A town hall has five years in which to bill you or take legal action to recover unpaid taxes. It's now obligatory for the vendor to produce his last *IBI* receipt when completing a sale in front of a notary, but it's preferable to uncover any debts before you reach this stage in a purchase!

When you buy a property in Spain, you must register your ownership with the local town hall so that property tax can be applied. Registration must be done within two months of signing the deed and there are fines of up to €1,000 for non-registration.

Many local authorities also levy fees (*tasas*) for services such as rubbish collection, street and beach cleaning, issuing documents, local parking restrictions and fire-fighting services. These vary greatly from one authority to another (e.g. the charge for rubbish collection, which in some cases also includes sewerage, can be as little as €50 or as much as €400 per year).

## Assessment

Property tax is based on the fiscal or rateable value (*valor catastral*) of a property, which has traditionally been around 70 per cent of a property's market value. However, due to the huge increase in property prices in most parts of Spain over the last five years, fiscal values are often far lower than the market price – often less than half. As a result, many municipalities are now reviewing fiscal values in their areas and increases of up to 50 per cent can be expected, with corresponding rises in property taxes. If you receive an official communication (usually in the form of a registered letter) that the fiscal value of your property is about to increase greatly, you should check that it has been correctly calculated.

Property values are calculated according to a variety of measurements and evaluations, including the area (in square metres) of the property (the built, terraced and land areas), building and zoning restrictions in the area, the quality of the building (e.g. whether it's classified as luxury, normal or basic), the date of construction, and the proximity to services and roads. To check that a property is correctly specified, go to the town hall or the *urbanismo* (the office that deals with building regulations), ask to see its dossier (*expediente*) and obtain a *certificación catastral*, which is the property description used to determine the *valor catastral*, sometimes accompanied by plans and photographs. Check that the data recorded is correct, as errors are fairly common.

You can appeal against the valuation of your property or an increase in valuation if you believe it's too high, particularly if it's higher than that of similar properties in the same area, although you have only 15 days in which to lodge an appeal (yet another good reason for non-residents to have a local financial representative). Note that, if an error has been made in your assessment, it can take years to have it corrected, although it's important to persevere.

**It's important that the fiscal value of your property is correct, as a number of taxes are linked to this value, including deemed letting income tax (see page 340) and wealth tax (see page 342), as well as property tax.**

## Tax Rates

Property tax rates depend on the population of the municipality and the level of public services provided and can vary considerably for similar properties in different areas. Rates tend to be higher in resort and coastal areas than in inland areas. Some municipalities have invested huge sums in recent years improving civic amenities, e.g. building indoor sports complexes (with swimming pools, gymnasiums, etc.) and cultural centres, and have increased property taxes to pay for them. General revisions are permitted once every eight years, but rates can be adjusted annually in accordance with coefficients set by the state government in its budget.

The basic property tax rates are 0.3 per cent for agricultural properties (*rústicas*) and 0.5 per cent for urban properties (*urbana*). However, provincial capitals, towns with over 5,000 inhabitants and towns providing 'special services' can increase the rate to up to 1.7 per cent. To calculate your property tax, simply multiply the fiscal value of your property by the tax rate, e.g. if the fiscal value of your property is €100,000 and the tax rate is 1 per cent, your annual bill will be €1,000.

Note that in an attempt to open up the rental market and encourage owners to rent empty properties rather than leave them vacant, some cities (e.g. Seville) charge double the usual rates for empty properties.

Some municipalities, particularly those with a high foreign population, have introduced higher property tax rates for property owners not registered on the council's resident list (*el padrón*). Increases of up to 50 per cent were imposed in Benalmadena and Fuengirola (Costa del Sol) in 2004. Other municipalities are expected to follow suit with the aim of 'encouraging' unregistered property owners living in the area to register (a simple process called *empadronamiento*), so that the municipality is entitled to more government funds (and therefore has less need to increase property taxes).

## Payment

Payment dates of property taxes vary with the municipality, but are usually between 1st September and 31st October. **Note that few town halls send out bills; it's your responsibility to find out how much you must pay and when.** Payment can usually be made in cash or by guaranteed bank cheque at the tax collection office or by postal giro at certain banks, and some municipalities accept payment by recognised credit card, e.g. MasterCard and Visa. Non-resident property owners should pay their *IBI* (and other local taxes) by direct debit from a Spanish bank account.

If the tax isn't paid on time, a surcharge (*recargo*) of 10 to 20 per cent is levied in addition to interest (plus possible collection costs), depending on how late payment is made. If you're unable to pay your property tax, you should talk to your local tax office. They will be pleased that you haven't absconded and will usually agree to a deferred payment schedule.

Some town halls have instituted a system of discounts to encourage residents to pay their bills early and thus spread the municipality's income throughout the year. For example, Mijas (Malaga province) offers discounts of 4 per cent for payments received before 30th April and 2 per cent for payments before 30th June. There's no discount for payments made between 1st July and 20th November and a surcharge of 20 per cent for payment after 20th November.

### Non-payment

In the past, many people have been able to avoid paying property taxes, owing to a *laissez-faire* attitude towards tax collection on the part of municipalities, who considered they were doing well if around 65 per cent of taxes were collected! However, in recent years, local municipal tax authorities have made strenuous efforts to collect unpaid property taxes. **If you owe back taxes and refuse to pay them, your property can be seized and sold at auction, perhaps for as little as 10 per cent of its value. Local authorities also have the power to seize vehicles and place garnishment orders on bank accounts.**

If you don't pay your property taxes, your property will be embargoed by the local tax authorities and your name listed in your province's 'official bulletin' (*Boletín Oficial de la Provincia/BOP*), so that everyone knows! You will usually be given plenty of warning before this happens, but if you're due to be absent from your property for an extended period, you should make sure that your property taxes are being paid; there have been many cases of foreigners arriving in Spain after a long absence to find that their homes have been sold to pay taxes!

# CAPITAL GAINS TAX

Capital gains tax (*impuesto sobre incremento de patrimonio*) is payable on the profit from the sale of certain assets in Spain, including antiques, art and jewellery, stocks and shares, property and businesses. Capital gains revealed as a result of the death of a taxpayer, gifts to government entities and donations of certain assets in lieu of tax payments are exempt from capital gains tax (CGT). Spain's taxation system combines capital gains (*incremento de patrimonio*) and capital losses (*disminución de patrimonio*). Capital losses can be offset against capital gains, but not against ordinary income. Capital losses in excess of gains can be carried forward to offset against future gains for a five-year period.

## Property

Capital gains tax (*impuesto sobre el incremento de patrimonio de la venta de un bien inmeuble*) is payable on the profit from the sale of property and is based on the difference between the purchase price (as stated in the title deed) and the sale price of a property, less buying and selling costs (and costs of improvements).

## Exemptions

Residents over 65 are exempt from CGT on the profit made from the sale of their principal home, irrespective of how long they've owned it. Note, however, that the Spanish Tax Office defines a 'principal home' as the place where you've lived permanently for **at least three years**.

Residents below 65 are exempt from CGT on the profit made from the sale of their principal home, provided that all the profit is invested in the purchase of another principal home in Spain within two years of the sale. Any profit that isn't reinvested is subject to CGT at the residents' tax rate (see below).

## Tax Rates

Non-residents are taxed at a flat rate of 35 per cent. Capital gains made by residents are counted as income, but taxed at a flat rate of 15 per cent.

## Calculation of CGT Liability

The capital gain on a property is calculated in one of two ways, according to the date of purchase, as detailed below. Each calculation involves an adjustment for inflation called a coefficient or inflation index (*coeficiente de actualización*), which is applied when you sell to allow for inflation and the loss of value of the amount originally invested. The coefficients for the years up to 2005 are shown below – new figures are published annually:

| Coefficient or Inflation Index | |
| --- | --- |
| Purchase Date | Index for 2005 Sale |
| 1994 & earlier | 1.169 |
| 1995 | 1.235 |
| 1996 | 1.1928 |
| 1997 | 1.169 |
| 1998 | 1.1463 |
| 1999 | 1.1257 |
| 2000 | 1.104 |
| 2001 | 1.0824 |
| 2002 | 1.0612 |
| 2003 | 1.0404 |
| 2004 | 1.020 |
| 2005 | 1.000 |

- **Property Purchased before 31st December 1996** – Capital gains on assets purchased before 31st December 1996 are calculated on a sliding scale according to how long they've been owned and are also subject to an inflation index (see above). After the first two years of ownership (when CGT is applied to 100 per cent of the value), there's an annual deduction of 11.11 per cent on the profit. This means that gains on property are free of tax after 11 years (i.e. purchases made before 31st December 1986), as shown in the table below:

| Year Purchased | Deduction on Profit (%) |
|---|---|
| 1996 | 0 |
| 1995 | 0 |
| 1994 | 11.11 |
| 1993 | 22.22 |
| 1992 | 33.33 |
| 1991 | 44.44 |
| 1990 | 55.55 |
| 1989 | 66.66 |
| 1988 | 77.77 |
| 1987 | 88.88 |
| 1986 | 99.99 |

**Example:** To calculate the CGT on a home purchased in 1992 for €100,000 with deductible costs totalling €10,000 (the purchase price was therefore effectively €110,000) and sold in 2005 for €200,000 with deductible selling costs of €15,000 (the effective selling price is therefore €185,000):

**STEP 1:** Apply inflation coefficient of 1.169 to purchase price (see table above): €110,000 x 1.169 = €128,590.

**STEP 2:** Deduct adjusted purchase price from effective selling price: €185,000 - €128,590 = €56,410.

**STEP 3:** Apply deduction on profit (see above table): €56,410 x 33.33 per cent = €18,801.

**STEP 4:** Apply CGT rate to net figure:

CGT for non-resident: €18,801 x 35 per cent = €6,580

CGT for resident: €18,801 x 15 per cent = €2,820

● **Property Purchased after 31st December 1996** – Gains arising from property purchased after 31st December 1996 are calculated using the coefficient or inflation index (see table above).

**Example:** To calculate the CGT due on a home purchased in 2001 for €200,000 with deductible costs totalling €10,000 (the effective purchase price was therefore €210,000) and sold in 2005 for €300,000 with deductible selling costs of €20,000 (the effective selling price is therefore €280,000):

**STEP 1:** Apply inflation coefficient of 1.0824 to purchase price (see table above): €210,000 x 1.0824 = €227,304.

**STEP 2:** Deduct adjusted purchase price from effective selling price: €280,000 - €227,304 = €52,696.

**STEP 3:** Apply CGT rate to net figure:
CGT for non-resident: €52,696 x 35 per cent = €18,444
CGT for resident: €52,696 x 15 per cent = €7,904

## Non-resident Sellers

If you're a non-resident and are selling your home in Spain, the buyer (whether he's resident or non-resident) is obliged to subtract 5 per cent from the purchase price and pay it to the Spanish Ministry of Finance within 30 days of the transaction. You must then apply (on Form 212) for a return of the difference between his 5 per cent payment and your CGT liability within three months of the payment. If you don't, the tax office will keep the money. If a representative or agent obtains the refund for you, you should request copies of the above forms and a statement showing the tax paid and the agent's fees.

If you're buying from a resident, ask him to provide a resident's fiscal certificate (*certificado de residencia fiscal*) issued by the tax office (*AEAT*) to prove it. A notary accepts a residence card or even registration with the town hall as proof of residence, but the tax authorities only accept a fiscal certificate as proof of residence in Spain. If the tax authorities aren't satisfied the seller is resident the buyer has to pay the five per cent retention and a fine.

# INHERITANCE & GIFT TAX

As in most countries, dying doesn't free you (or, more correctly, your beneficiaries) from the clutches of the tax man. Spain imposes a tax on assets or money received as an inheritance or gift (*impuesto sobre sucesiones y donaciones*). The estates of residents and non-residents are subject to Spanish inheritance and gift tax if they own property or have other assets in Spain. Inheritance and gift tax is paid by the beneficiaries, e.g. a surviving spouse, and not by the deceased's estate.

The country in which beneficiaries must pay inheritance tax is usually decided by their domicile (see **Liability** on page 332). If they're domiciled in Spain, Spanish inheritance tax is payable on an inheritance, whether the inheritance is located (or received) in Spain or abroad. There are currently numerous proposals for inheritance and gift tax reform, including the abolition of all inheritance tax or a substantial reduction on lower amounts. Several regions have already introduced inheritance tax reductions (see below).

Tax is payable by beneficiaries within six months of a death if the deceased died in Spain, although it's possible to obtain a six-month extension, or within 30 days following the transfer of a lifetime gift. If the deceased died abroad, the inheritance tax declaration and the payment of inheritance tax duties must be made within 16 months.

Tax is assessed on the net amount received and accrues from the date of death or the date of a gift. Some people have managed to avoid inheritance tax by failing to inform the Spanish authorities of a death (after five years and six months the tax can no longer be collected), although this is illegal.

Those who have been Spanish residents for at least three years receive an exemption of 95 per cent of inheritance tax when their principal residence or family business (in Spain) is bequeathed to a spouse, parent or child who has been living with them for at least two years before their death. The principal residence must be valued at less than €122,606 (there's no limit for a business) or the inheritance mustn't exceed €122,606 per heir, above which normal inheritance tax rates apply. For example, if the residence is worth €150,000, you pay tax at only 5 per cent on the first €122,606 and tax at the full rate on the balance of €27,394. The inheritor must retain ownership of the property for a minimum of ten years, although if he dies within the ten-year period no further tax is payable. However, if the property or business is sold during this period, tax may be levied at the discretion of the relevant authorities, e.g. the regional government.

The following regional variations apply: Andalusia has an exemption of 99 per cent on a principal residence; in the Balearics the exemption is 100 per cent up to the amount of €123,000; in Castile-La Mancha and Extremadura the exemption is 100 per cent; and Catalonia has an exemption of €125,060 per heir.

# Liability

Inheritance and gift tax liability depends on your relationship to the donor, the amount inherited and your wealth before receipt of the gift or inheritance.

## Relationship

Direct descendants and close relatives of the deceased receive an allowance before they become liable for inheritance tax, as shown below.

| Group | Includes | Allowance |
|---|---|---|
| 1 | Direct descendants under 21 | €15,956.87 plus €3,990.72 for each year under 21 up to a maximum allowance of €48,000 |
| 2 | Direct descendants over 21, direct ascendants (parents and up), spouse or partner* | €15,956.87 |
| 3 | Relatives to third degree (and ascendants by affinity) including brother, sister, uncle, aunt, niece or nephew | €7,993.46 |
| 4 | Unrelated people and more remote relatives (including common-law partners*) | None |

\* Note that some regions (Andalusia, Aragón, Balearics, Basque Lands, Catalonia, Madrid and Navarra) now recognise common-law partners as spouses for inheritance tax purposes if they're registered as such in the region.

## Amount Inherited

Your inheritance tax liability is calculated as a percentage of the amount inherited (in excess of any allowance), as shown below:

| Value above Allowance (€) | Tax Rate (%) | Cumulative Tax Liability (€) |
|:---:|:---:|:---:|
| Up to 7,993 | 7.65 | 611 |
| 7,994 – 15,980 | 8.50 | 1,290 |
| 15,981 – 23,968 | 9.35 | 2,037 |
| 23,969 – 31,955 | 10.20 | 2,852 |
| 31,956 – 39,943 | 11.05 | 3,735 |
| 39,944 – 47,930 | 11.90 | 4,685 |
| 47,931 – 55,918 | 12.75 | 5,703 |
| 55,919 – 63,905 | 13.60 | 6,790 |
| 63,906 – 71,893 | 14.45 | 7,944 |
| 71,894 – 79,880 | 15.30 | 9,166 |
| 79,881 – 119,757 | 16.15 | 15,606 |
| 119,758 – 159,634 | 18.70 | 23,063 |
| 159,635 – 239,389 | 21.25 | 40,011 |
| 239,390 – 398,777 | 25.50 | 80,655 |
| 398,778 – 797,555 | 29.75 | 199,291 |
| Over 797,555 | 34.00 | |

Note that Catalonia has a different inheritance tax scale.

## Current Wealth

Your current wealth is the value of all your assets **before** the inheritance transfer.

## Calculation

Once you've worked out your relationship group and calculated your inheritance tax liability, use the table below to calculate the inheritance tax payable based on your current wealth by multiplying your inheritance tax liability (shown in the above table) by the percentage shown under the relevant relationship group.

| Current Wealth (€) | Relationship Group | | |
|:---:|:---:|:---:|:---:|
| | 1/2 | 3 | 4 |
| Up to 402,678 | 100% | 158.82% | 200% |
| 402,678 – 2,007,380 | 105% | 166.76% | 210% |

| | | | |
|---|---|---|---|
| 2,007,380 – 4,020,770 | 110% | 174.71% | 220% |
| Over 4,020,770 | 120% | 190.59% | 240% |

For example, if you're in relationship group 3 (giving you a tax allowance of €7,993.46) and you've inherited €79,886.46, you must pay tax on €71,893, so your tax liability is €7,944; if you earn between €402,678 and €2,007,380 (lucky you!), you must pay tax at 166.76 per cent, which amounts to €13,247.41.

## Avoiding Inheritance & Gift Tax

It's important residents and non-residents with property in Spain to decide in advance how they wish to dispose of their Spanish property. Ideally this should be decided even before buying a home in Spain. Property can be registered in a single name, both names of a couple or joint buyers' names, the names of children, giving the parents sole use during their lifetime, or in the name of a Spanish or foreign company or trust. It's advisable for a couple not only to register joint ownership of a property, but to share their other assets and have separate bank accounts, which helps to reduce their dependants' liability for inheritance tax. In most regions, Spanish law doesn't recognise the rights to inheritance of a non-married partner, although there are a number of solutions to this problem, e.g. a life insurance policy.

One way of reducing your liability to inheritance tax is to transfer legal ownership of property to a relative as a gift during your lifetime. However, this is treated as a sale (at the current market price) and incurs fees of around 10 per cent plus CGT (see page 346), which must be compared with your inheritance tax liability (see above). Whether you should will or 'sell' a property to someone depends on the value of the property and your relationship, and it may be cheaper for a beneficiary to be taxed under the inheritance laws. Take, for example, a couple jointly owning a property in Spain who wish to leave it to a child. When one of the parents dies, the child inherits half the property and pays inheritance tax on that amount. Inheritance tax on the other half of the property is paid when the other parent dies. In this way little tax is paid on a property with a low value. If you're elderly, it may pay you to make the title deed directly in the names of your children. **Spanish inheritance law is a complicated subject and professional advice should be sought from an experienced lawyer who understands Spanish inheritance law and the law of any other countries involved.** Your will (see below) is also a vital component in reducing Spanish inheritance and gift tax to the minimum or deferring its payment.

Further information on this subject can be found in *Inheritance*, an information file published by the Foundation Institute of Foreign Property Owners (🖳 www.fipe.org – see **Independent Advice & Information** on page 99) in various languages, including Dutch, English, German, Norwegian and Swedish.

# WILLS

It's an unfortunate fact of life that you're unable to take your hard-earned money with you when you make your final exit. All adults should make a will (*testamento*), irrespective of how large or small their assets (each spouse should make a separate will). If a foreigner dies without a will (intestate) in Spain, his estate may be automatically disposed of under Spanish law and the law regarding compulsory heirs (see below) applied.

A foreigner resident in Spain is usually permitted to dispose of his Spanish assets according to the law of his home country, provided his will is valid under the law of that country. If you've lived in Spain for a long time, it may be necessary for you to create a legal domicile in your home country for the purpose of making a will.

A will made by a foreigner regarding Spanish assets isn't invalidated because it doesn't bequeath property in accordance with Spanish law, as Spanish law isn't usually applied to foreigners and the disposal of property (buildings or land) in Spain is governed by the law of the deceased's home country unless there's a dispute among the beneficiaries, in which case Spanish law is applied. See also **Inheritance & Gift Tax** above regarding ways to delay or circumvent the law of obligatory heirs and reduce inheritance tax.

## Law of Obligatory Heirs

**The following information applies to Spanish nationals only**. Under Spanish law, a surviving spouse retains all assets acquired before marriage, half the assets acquired during the marriage, and all personal gifts or inheritances which have come directly to the spouse. The remaining assets must be disposed of under the law of 'obligatory heirs' (*herederos forzosos*), which is as follows. When a person dies leaving children, his estate is divided into three equal parts. One third must be left to the surviving children in equal parts. Another third must also be left to the children, but the testator decides how it's to be divided. A surviving spouse has a life interest in this second third and the children who inherit it cannot dispose of it freely until the surviving parent dies. The final third can be freely disposed of. If a child has died leaving children of his own, they automatically inherit his share. If the deceased has no children, his surviving parents have a statutory right to one-third of his estate if he has a surviving spouse or half of his estate if he doesn't.

## Types of Will

There are three kinds of Spanish will, each of which is described below. Note that, where applicable, the rules relating to witnesses are strict and, if not followed precisely can render a will null and void.

Although it isn't necessary to have a Spanish will for Spanish property, it's advisable to have a separate will for **any** country in which you own property. When a person dies, assets can be dealt with immediately under local law without having to wait for the granting of probate in another country (and the administration of the estate is also cheaper). Having a Spanish will for your Spanish assets speeds up the will's execution and saves the long and complicated process of having a foreign will executed in Spain. **Note that, if you have two or more wills, you must ensure that they don't contradict or invalidate one another.** You should periodically review your will to ensure that it reflects your current financial and personal circumstances.

## Open Will

An open will (*testamento abierto*) is the normal and most suitable kind of will for most people. It's unnecessary to employ a lawyer to prepare an open will, although it's usually advisable. It must, however, be prepared by a notary who's responsible for ensuring that it's legal and properly drawn up. Its contents must be known to the notary and to three witnesses, who can be of any nationality; each of them must sign the will. The notary will give you a copy (*copia simple* or *copia autorizada*) and send a copy to the general registry of wills (*Registro General de Actos de Ultima Voluntad*) in Madrid. The original remains at the notary's office. If you don't understand Spanish, you need an official translation into a language that you speak fluently.

## Closed Will

A closed will (*testamento cerrado*), whose contents remain secret, must be drawn up by a Spanish lawyer to ensure that it complies with Spanish law. You must take the will to a notary, who seals the envelope and signs it, as must two witnesses, and then files and records it as for an open will.

## Holographic Will

A holographic will (*testamento ológrafo*) is a will made in your own handwriting or orally. If written, it must be signed and dated and must be clearly drafted in order to ensure that your wishes are absolutely clear. No witnesses or other formalities are required. It can be voluntarily registered with the registry of wills. On the death of the testator it must be authenticated before a judge, which delays the will's execution. An oral will must be made in the presence of five witnesses, who must then testify to a notary the wishes of the deceased. The notary then prepares a written will and certifies it. For anyone with a modest Spanish estate, e.g. a small holiday home in Spain, a holographic will is sufficient.

# Cost & Procedure

The cost of preparing a simple open or closed will is around €125 plus the notary's fee (around €50). Spanish wills can be drawn up by Spanish lawyers and notaries abroad, although it's cheaper to do it in Spain.

Executors aren't normal in Spain and, if you appoint one, it may increase the inheritance tax payable. However, if you appoint an executor, you should inform your heirs so that they will know who to notify in the event of your death. It isn't advisable to name a lawyer who doesn't speak Spanish as your executor, as he will have to instruct a Spanish lawyer (*abogado*), whose fees will be impossible to control. If you appoint a lawyer as your executor, he's permitted to charge a maximum of 5 per cent of the estate's value.

Your beneficiaries in Spain must produce an original death certificate or an authorised copy. If you die outside Spain, a foreign death certificate must be legally translated and notarised for it to be valid in Spain. The inheritance tax declaration and the payment of inheritance tax duties must be made within six months of your death if you die in Spain and within 16 months if you die elsewhere (otherwise, a surcharge may result). Inheritance tax must be paid in advance of the release of the assets to be inherited in Spain, and beneficiaries may therefore need to borrow funds to pay the tax before they receive their inheritance. Note that the winding-up of an estate can take a long time in Spain.

Keep a copy of your will(s) in a safe place and another copy with your lawyer or the executor of your estate. Don't leave them in a bank safe deposit box, which in the event of your death is sealed for a period under Spanish law. You should keep information regarding bank accounts and insurance policies with your will(s), but don't forget to tell someone where they are!

Note that in Spain, marriage doesn't automatically revoke a will as in some other countries. **Spanish inheritance law is a complicated subject and it's important to obtain professional legal advice when writing or altering your will(s).**

# COST OF LIVING

No doubt you would like to try to estimate how far your euros will stretch and how many (if any) you will have left after paying your bills. Spain is no longer the El Dorado that it once was and taxes and the cost of living have risen considerably in recent years. Unemployment is high, and many Spaniards have seen a drop in their standard of living in recent years. Inflation is currently at around 3 per cent and the price of many goods and services is now in line with those in most other European countries. Among the more expensive items in Spain are quality clothes (although winter clothes aren't needed in most resort areas) and many consumer goods.

Nevertheless, with the exception of the major cities, where the higher cost of living is generally offset by higher salaries, the cost of living in Spain is lower than in most other western European countries, particularly in rural and coastal areas. Many things remain relatively cheap, including property, rents, food, alcohol, dining out and general entertainment. Food in Spain costs around the same as in the US, but is cheaper than in most northern European countries. A recent Eurostat survey found that food and drink in Spain is 24 per cent cheaper than the EU average. Around €200 will feed two adults for a month, including (inexpensive) wine, but excluding fillet steak, caviar and expensive imported foods.

Overall, the cost of living is lower than in the UK, France and Germany and around the same as in North America. A couple owning their home can 'survive' on a net income of as little as €400 per month (many pensioners live on less) and most can live comfortably on an income of €800 per month (excluding rent or mortgage payments). In fact, many northern Europeans (particularly Scandinavians) who live modestly in Spain without overdoing the luxuries find that their cost of living is up to 50 per cent less than in their home country. Shopping for expensive consumer goods such as hi-fi equipment, electronic goods, computers and photographic equipment in other European countries or North America or via the internet (see page 443) can yield further savings.

It's difficult to calculate an average cost of living in Spain, as it depends on each individual's circumstances and lifestyle. However, a list of the approximate

**minimum** monthly major expenses for an average single person, couple, and family with two children are shown in the table below, although many live on less (most people will agree that the figures are too high or too low). When calculating your cost of living, deduct the appropriate percentage for social security contributions and income tax from your gross salary. The numbers in brackets refer to the notes following the table:

| ITEM | MONTHLY COSTS (€) | | |
|---|---|---|---|
| | Single | Couple | Family of Four |
| Housing (1) | 300 | 400 | 550 |
| Food (2) | 160 | 200 | 350 |
| Utilities (3) | 60 | 60 | 100 |
| Leisure (4) | 100 | 125 | 200 |
| Transport (5) | 50 | 100 | 125 |
| Insurance (6) | 60 | 75 | 125 |
| Clothing | 100 | 150 | 200 |
| **TOTAL** | **830** | **1,110** | **1,650** |

1. Rent or mortgage payments for a modern or modernised apartment or house in an average small town or suburb, excluding high-cost areas. The properties envisaged are a studio or one-bedroom apartment for a single person, a two-bedroom property for a couple, and a three-bedroom property for a couple with two children.

2. Doesn't include luxuries or alcohol.

3. Includes electricity, gas, water, telephone, cable or satellite television, heating and air-conditioning.

4. Includes entertainment, dining out, sports and holiday expenses, plus newspapers and magazines.

5. Includes running costs for an average family car, plus third party insurance, annual taxes, petrol, servicing and repairs, but excludes depreciation and credit costs.

6. Includes 'voluntary' insurance such as inexpensive supplementary health insurance, household (building and contents), third-party liability, travel, car breakdown and life insurance. Expensive private health insurance isn't included.

# 15.

# LEISURE

If you want guaranteed sunshine, miles of sandy beaches, good food and wine, an abundant choice of entertainment and a wide variety of accommodation – and you don't want to pay the earth – then Spain is the place for you. Not for nothing does the Spanish National Tourist Office use the slogan 'Everything Under The Sun'! Although the vast majority of holidaymakers (and residents) come to Spain to recline on a beach, there's much (much) more to the country than the *costas* and a few islands. Spain offers infinite variety with something for everyone, including magnificent beaches; spectacular unspoilt countryside; a wealth of mountains and waterways; vibrant nightlife; bustling sophisticated cities; superb wine and cuisine; a surfeit of art, culture and serious music; numerous festivals and *fiestas* and above all tranquillity. Spain is a nation of *bon viveurs* with an insatiable thirst for fun and pleasure – nobody can throw a better party than the Spanish.

Tourism took off here in the early '60s. The number of visitors grew steadily over the next few decades and currently stands at over 53.5 million a year (the UK with 30 per cent of visitors and Germany account for almost half the market). In 2004, Spain was the second most popular tourist destination (the most popular regions are Catalonia, the Balearics and the Canaries) in the world after France, and tourism accounts for some 12 per cent of gross domestic product (GDP) and employment. However, although mass tourism saved Spain from economic disaster in the '60s, it has irrevocably changed the face of the country. Spain has traditionally catered to the package-holiday market, although it's now attempting to attract a more up-market clientele.

Outside its beach resorts, Spain's main attractions are its lively cities, particularly Madrid and Barcelona, which have an intense rivalry. Barcelona is Spain's most international and European city, elegant and compact, while Madrid is a sprawling metropolis and one of the world's most friendly and free-wheeling cities. Madrid has a wealth of world-class museums and art galleries, and is blessed with magnificent parks and gardens, whereas Barcelona is an architectural masterpiece and one of the world's most handsome cities. Both offer superb cuisine and a bustling, vibrant nightlife, and are just warming up when most other European cities are going to bed. Naturally, there's much more to Spain than Madrid and Barcelona, and the country has a wealth of other beautiful historic cities, including Avila, Burgos, Cáceres, Cadiz, Cordoba, Cuenca, Gerona, Granada, Malaga, Mérida, Palma de Mallorca, Pamplona, San Sebastian, Salamanca, Santander, Santiago de Compostela, Segovia, Seville, Toledo and Valencia, to name just a handful.

Spain's diverse regions accentuate a land of great culture with a colourful history; over the centuries it has been home to Phoenicians, Iberians, Romans, Visigoths and Moors, all of whom have left their mark and added to the country's rich heritage and culture. It's a land steeped in tradition with a wealth of artistic, cultural and historical treasures scattered the length and breadth of the country. There are a surfeit of excellent art galleries and museums throughout Spain, and traditional *fiestas* and music festivals are held in all regions and major towns throughout the year. One of the foremost attractions of Spain is its outstanding countryside, sadly enjoyed by few visitors. Spain's rugged beauty is almost unparalleled in Europe and it harbours a wealth of unique flora, fauna and wildlife, and contains more (and larger) unspoilt areas than any other European country, many preserved as national parks and nature reserves.

Information regarding local events and entertainment is available from tourist offices and is published in local English-language newspapers and magazines. In most cities, there are magazines and newspapers dedicated to entertainment, and free weekly or monthly programmes (e.g. *Guía del Ocio*) are published by tourist organisations in major cities and tourist resorts. Many towns produce a monthly cultural programme and some foreigners' departments also produce newsletters listing local cultural events. Many newspapers publish weekly magazines or supplements containing a detailed programme of local events and entertainment. There are also many excellent guides to Spain, see **Appendix B** for a list.

# ACCOMMODATION

Many types of accommodation are available in Spain, catering to all tastes and pockets, from sumptuous, grand luxury (*gran lujo*) to humble. If you want to rub shoulders with the real Spanish, start at the bottom rather than the top of the accommodation chain. Note, however, that it can be difficult to find good (or any) hotels in small villages and towns or on main roads in many areas, and Spain doesn't have the tradition of charming country hotels that you can find throughout the UK and France, although this is changing. Hotels (and other accommodation in Spain) are regulated by the government and all legally registered establishments must display a blue plaque showing their category and class in white letters, as listed below:

| Category | Description |
| --- | --- |
| *H (*hotel*) | Standard hotels as described on the following pages. |
| *HR (*hotel residencia*) | Residential hotels without a restaurant. |
| *HA (*hotel apartamento*) | Self-contained apartments or chalets with kitchenettes; they offer reasonable weekly or monthly rates, but little service. |
| *RA (*residencia apartamento*) | Similar to ordinary apartments except that they're mainly let for short periods to tourists and may provide breakfast. |
| *M (*motel*) | Roadside lodgings for short stays, located on or close to motorways and other main roads. |
| **Hs (*hostal*) | Basic accommodation and usually family-run; no public rooms, although there may be a television (TV) in the dining room/lounge and meals may be provided. |
| **HsR (*hostal-residencia*) | Similar to a hostel, but usually for long-stay guests and without a restaurant. |
| **P (*pensión*) | A guesthouse with basic accommodation, possibly offering full board only. |

| | |
|---|---|
| CH (*casa de huéspedes*) | A guesthouse which is usually a private home with rooms to let (no star rating) and similar to *hospedajes* (literally 'lodgings'). |
| F (*fonda*) | A small inn offering basic accommodation (no star rating). |
| * One to five stars | |
| ** One to three stars | |

Many of the above categories of accommodation, including hostels, pensions, guesthouses and inns are described under **Budget Accommodation** on page 362. Residential hotels are generally cheaper than standard hotels and offer fewer services and public lounges. Residential hotels and hostels don't provide a restaurant service, but may offer breakfast or a cafeteria service. Hostels often provide better accommodation than inexpensive hotels and better value for money (a three-star hostel is roughly equivalent to a one-star hotel).

# Budget Accommodation

There's a variety of budget accommodation in Spain, including the following:

- *Casas de Huéspedes* – These are a kind of guesthouse that offer basic accommodation. Food isn't usually served. However, long-stay guests (*estables*) are usually preferred.

- *Fondas* – These are generally village inns with basic facilities and rooms, usually located over the bar. Food may be served (some may not offer rooms without full board), although this isn't always the case.

- *Hospedajes* – This type of basic accommodation consists of rooms/lodgings, not very different from the two types of guesthouses. Long-stay guests (*estables*) are usually preferred.

- *Hostals* – These are hostels offering similar accommodation to hotels. They're the most upmarket type of budget accommodation with wash basins in all rooms, but they don't usually offer full board.

- *Pensiones* – These are a kind of guesthouse that offer basic accommodation. Food may be served (some may not offer rooms without full board), although this isn't always the case. Long-stay guests (*estables*) are usually preferred.

Spain doesn't have bed and breakfast accommodation as such, although some private homes (*casas particulares*) offer bed and breakfast off the beaten tourist track, and there are 'bed and breakfast' organisations in cities and large towns. Beds (*camas*) and rooms (*habitaciones*) are advertised in the windows of private houses, and above bars and roadside restaurants such as *ventas*, perhaps with the phrase *camas y comidas* (beds and meals). They often provide the cheapest of all accommodation and are usually spotlessly clean.

In country areas, there are rural cottages and farmhouses (*casas rurales, casas rústicas* and *casas de labranza*), officially referred to as *turismo rural*, providing the opportunity to experience the Spanish country way of life and possibly make contact with Spanish families. Rural tourism is currently experiencing a boom in Spain, with Spaniards and foreign visitors, and you can rent a room in a house (meals are usually provided) or rent the whole house with self-catering facilities. Accommodation is usually in traditional houses, some of which may be centuries old. Several books are published annually on rural tourism, e.g. *Guía ATR* (Guías Azules), *Guía de Alojamiento de Turismo Rural* (Anaya Touring) or *Anuario de Turismo Rural* (Susaeta) and there are numerous websites (e.g. 🖳 www.azrural.com and 🖳 www.top rural.com), which may allow you to book accommodation online. The most popular areas in 2004 were Castile León, Catalonia and Galicia. Book early for the summer months, particularly in coastal areas and in the north of Spain.

Other budget accommodation includes rooms in university dormitories (*colegios mayores* and *residencias*) during the summer holidays and rooms in monasteries. Monasteries offer basic lodgings in real working monasteries where prayer, silence and seclusion are the order of the day (plus a large helping of beauty, serenity, superb architecture and perhaps even Gregorian chant). They accept guests of both sexes or men only and payment is often in the form of a 'donation' (e.g. €15 or €20 per night) rather than a fixed fee. There are set meal times and reservations must usually be made in advance. Many monasteries have hospices or guest quarters (*hospederías*). If you're a fan of Gregorian chant, you may wish to visit the monastery of Santo Domingo de Silos (Burgos), although you must book years in advance since the astounding success of their recording of Gregorian chant.

The cost of budget accommodation varies considerably, although the cheapest is around €20 per person, per day for full board (*pensión completa*) consisting of breakfast, lunch and dinner. Half board (*pensión media*) may also be offered at a slightly reduced rate. Rates at rural cottages and farmhouses usually range from €10 to €20 for a single or double room. Hostels charge from €10 to €20 for singles and €15 to €30 for doubles, plus an extra €4 or so for a room with a bath or shower. The cheapest accommodation is generally found in *casas de huéspedes* and *hospedajes*. If a room doesn't have a private bathroom, which usually contains a shower rather than a bath, you may be charged an additional fee to use a communal bathroom. As with most accommodation in Spain, large discounts are usually offered for long stays during winter.

When booking budget accommodation you should enquire about the exact location and the facilities provided, as standards vary from clean and homely abodes to 'fleapits' unfit for human habitation. **Note that budget accommodation is often basic, usually lacks heating and guests are often subject to curfews.** There's usually a wide variation in the standard of accommodation of establishments within the same category. Budget establishments seldom accept credit cards and 7 per cent value added tax (VAT) is added to all bills. A list of budget accommodation can usually be obtained from local tourist offices and rooms to let can also be found by asking at local bars and restaurants. When staying in budget accommodation, it's advantageous if you speak some Spanish, as your hosts may not speak any foreign languages.

# Camping & Caravanning

Spain has over 800 campsites (*campings* or *campamentos*), two-thirds of which are located on the coast, with a total capacity of over 400,000 places. Campsites are inspected and approved by the Spanish tourist authority and classified under four categories L (luxury), 1st, 2nd and 3rd class (1a, 2a or 3a), according to their amenities. Many camps have a small capacity of 300 to 400 people and some cater exclusively for naturists.

Even the most basic camp grounds must have 24-hour surveillance; a fenced area; unlimited drinking water; first aid and fire prevention; toilets and showers (there may be a fee for hot showers); washing and washing-up facilities and rubbish collection. Most camps also provide a range of other services and facilities which may include a post office, playground, currency exchange, cable TV, telephones, safes, launderette, bottled gas, electricity/water hook-ups for caravans and motor caravans, swimming pools, tennis courts and other sports facilities, shops, supermarket, hairdresser, disco, restaurants and bars.

All campsites post their daily fees (usually from noon until noon the following day) at the entrance, which are calculated per car or caravan, per person and per tent. Fees are around €2.50 to €3 per person, per day plus €2.50 to €3 for a car and around the same for a caravan or camping space (although fees can be as high as €15 a day at a deluxe site). There are reductions of around 20 per cent a day for children, e.g. aged from three to ten years. Motor caravans are charged between €5 and €7.50 a day and electricity hook-ups cost an additional €2 to €4 a day. VAT at 7 per cent must be added to all fees. Some sites charge extra for hot showers, sports (such as tennis courts) and the use of ironing facilities or a freezer. Most campsites offer special rates outside the high season of June to August, although many are open only during the 'summer' season, e.g. April or June to September. It's advisable to book during the high season, particularly for campsites situated in coastal areas in July and August. **Note that many campsites don't accept dogs.**

An international camping carnet isn't necessary in Spain when camping at registered sites, although it's required when camping 'wild'. However, it's advisable to have one, as it's accepted as proof of identification by campsites. Before camping in open country you should check that wild camping is permitted and obtain permission from the owner of private land. Wild camping is often prohibited during the dry season due to the danger of fires or when there's an official campsite in the immediate vicinity (you aren't permitted to camp within one kilometre of an official campsite). Camping is forbidden on beaches, river banks and in mountains, and you can be fined for camping illegally.

The Spanish Federation of Camping Sites (Federación Española de Empresarios de Camping y Centros de Vacaciones, C/San Bernardo, 97–99, 28015 Madrid, ☎ 914-481 234, 🖥 www.fedcamping.com) publishes an annual guide (*Guía de Campings*) listing sites (by region), with illustrations and plans. Another useful guide is the *Guía Ibérica de Campings y Bungalows* (Ocitur), which includes campsites in Portugal. Reservations can be made directly with campsites and through the Spanish Federation of Camping Sites. TurEspaña publish a free camping map (*Mapa de Campings*) showing all official campsites and free regional and provincial maps are available from local tourist offices, as well as an annual official guide *Guía Oficial de*

▲ *Villajoyosa, Alicante*

► *Sherry Barrel, Jerez*

▲ *Pavement Artist, Barcelona*

▲ Prado Museum, Madrid

▲ Roses, Girona

► La Alquería, Malaga

◄ Peñón de Ifach, Calpe, Alicante

▲ *Spring Fair, Jerez*

▲ *Cadaqués, Girona*

◄ *Fiesta, Andalusia*

▼ *Benidorm, Alicante*

▲ *Horseman, Seville*

► Cabo de Gata,
Almeria

▼ Cadaqués, Girona

► Mijas, Malaga

*Campings.* If you're a newcomer to camping and caravanning, it's advantageous to join a camping or caravan club which provide useful information (e.g. the best guides to campsites), approved sites, caravan and travel insurance, travel services, rallies, holidays, reservations and a range of other benefits.

# Hotels

Hotels are officially classified with one to five stars (*estrellas*) by the Ministry of Economy, depending on the facilities they offer, rather than their price (although they're priced accordingly). Note that hotels within the same category can vary considerably in quality and comfort, and that ratings depend on the area, as all regions administer star ratings in different ways. A **rough** guide to room rates is shown below:

| Star Rating | Price Range (€) | Class |
|---|---|---|
| *****GL | 350+++ | Great Luxury |
| ***** | 120-400++ | Luxury |
| **** | 60-210 | Top Class |
| *** | 30-150 | Very Comfortable |
| ** | 20-70 | Comfortable |
| * | 15-50 | Basic |

The prices quoted above are for a double room with bath for one night (prices in Spain are usually quoted per room and **not** per person). VAT (*IVA*) at 7 per cent is added to all hotel bills. In the Canaries, Ceuta and Melilla, a local tax (*IGIC* or *ITE*, similar to VAT) of 4.5 per cent is added to bills. Prices should be quoted inclusive of tax and service charges.

Hotel room rates don't normally include breakfast, which usually costs around €6 (for a continental breakfast), although it's usually cheaper at a local bar or cafe. Hotels are closely regulated by the government. Room prices (including seasonal rates) must be posted in the foyer and in rooms, and it must be stated whether they include tax and service.

Rates vary according to location as well as category, with hotels located in large towns and cities, coastal resorts and spa towns being the most expensive. Hotels are expensive in major cities such as Madrid and Barcelona, where rates are similar to other major European cities. However, inexpensive hotels are plentiful in most towns, where a single room (*habitación individual*) can usually be found for €15 to €20 and a double (*habitación doble*) for €20 to €30 (usually without a private bath or shower). Inexpensive accommodation is mostly found in the old quarter of town centres, often close to the main square or cathedral. Hotel rates vary considerably depending on the region and season, and it's often worth haggling over rates, particularly if you're on your own or during the low season. As in most countries, single rooms are rare and only marginally cheaper than doubles (they usually cost around 20 per cent less).

A double room usually contains two single beds, rather than a double bed (*cama matrimonial*), which should be requested if required. Many hotels have 'family' rooms for three or four guests at greatly reduced rates, or provide extra beds (*camas*) for children in a double room free of charge. An extra bed for an adult normally costs around 35 per cent of the double room rate or 60 per cent of the cost of a single room. Half and full board is common at hotels with restaurants, although it's usually restricted to guests staying three or more days.

Minimum and maximum rates are fixed according to the facilities and the season, although there's no season in major cities. In the Canaries and winter resorts, low season may be in summer (there's usually not much difference in rates). Rates are considerably higher in tourist areas during the high season (*temporada alta*) of July and August (and Easter), when rooms at any price are hard to find. On the other hand, outside the main season, particularly in winter, many hotels offer low half or full board rates, when a double room with bath, including dinner (buffet) and breakfast can cost €35 for two. Many hotels have lower rates at weekends and special rates for groups, and some chains provide discount cards for regular clients reducing rates by 15 to 25 per cent.

It's advisable to make a reservation (*reserva*) during the high season months of July and August, on public holiday weekends, and during international trade fairs, conventions, festivals and *fiestas*. At most other times, it's usually unnecessary to book, particularly in rural areas and small towns. It's advisable to book at least two to three months in advance for summer in major cities (such as Madrid and Barcelona), and around two weeks in advance at other times. A hotel is required to retain a booked room only until around 6pm, after which it can be let to someone else (unless you've paid in advance). If you plan to arrive later than this, you should advise a hotel of your estimated arrival time. Note that staff and owners of small rural hotels don't usually speak English or other foreign languages. Children and animals are usually welcome, although you should check when booking. Numerous websites, including 🖳 www.onlydog.com and 🖳 www.perros.com provide information about hotels accepting dogs and other animals.

You're required by law to show your passport or identity card and complete a registration form when registering at a hotel. If you're staying in a small hotel and wish to leave early in the morning, it's best to pay your bill (*cuenta*) the evening before and tell the proprietor when you plan to leave. Otherwise you may find the hotel locked up like Fort Knox and no-one around to let you out. Check out time is usually noon at the latest and if you stay any later you may be charged for an extra day. If required, hotels will usually store your luggage free of charge until later in the day.

You should be shown a room. No Spaniard would dream of accepting a room without inspecting it first, especially the beds, which are often hard or lumpy and too short for anyone above average height. Beds usually have long, hard, sausage-shaped bolsters (*cabezales*) serving as pillows and running across a double bed, with the bottom sheet running around them and substituting for pillow cases. Many foreigners find bolsters uncomfortable (they can be **very** hard), although they're quite happily used by most Spanish guests. There may be pillows (*almohadas*) in the wardrobe, which, like bolsters, usually have no slips and are placed under the bottom sheet. Duvets aren't common in Spain, even in winter, when sheets (*sábanas*) and blankets (*mantas*) are normally used.

Most hotels are centrally heated in winter, although cheaper hotels are often miserly with the heating and hostels often lack heating altogether. Air-conditioning is generally found only in 3 to 5-star hotels (and is a blessing in summer). If you're staying in a city, it's advisable to ask for a quiet room, i.e. nowhere near a discotheque, bar or restaurant. With the exception of modern and luxury hotels, hotels rooms in Spain aren't always equipped with a radio or TV, irrespective of the price. Satellite TV is provided in top class hotels. All top class hotels provide tea and coffee-making facilities; a radio and colour TV; bath (*baño*) and shower (*ducha*) with a bidet; telephone; room service and a mini-bar or refrigerator. Drinks from a hotel mini-bar are expensive, but they're handy for storing your own food and drinks. Many top class hotels also provide sports facilities such as tennis, squash, swimming pools (mandatory in summer), gymnasium (there may be a fee), billiards/pool, sauna and solarium, plus bars, restaurants, discos, cabaret and a TV/video room with big-screen video. In many mid-range 'tourist' hotels, all meals are served buffet-style. Luxury hotels often have excellent convention facilities.

## Paradores

One national chain of hotels rating a special mention are *Paradores Nacionales de Turismo* (usually referred to simply as *paradores*), a state-owned chain of hotels housed in historic buildings such as castles, palaces, convents and monasteries, plus a few modern buildings with swimming pools and sports facilities. There are some 85 *paradores*, most in the three or four-star category, providing comfortable (even luxurious) rooms and excellent regional cuisine and wines. They're expensive by Spanish standards, with rates between €90 and €250, although prices are lower outside the high season when they offer a 35 per cent discount for those aged over 60 staying half-board, a 20 per cent discount for stays of a minimum of two nights in half-board accommodation and a one-off price of €€2 per person per night for guests aged between 20 and 30. Note, however, that *paradores* can offer excellent value for money and a double room in luxury four-star *paradores* may only cost some €20 more than a basic two-star tourist hotel around the corner!

Reservations can be made through agents in many countries. For a free brochure contact Paradores Nacionales de Turismo, Central de Reservas, C/Requena, 3, 28013 Madrid (☎ 915-166 666, 🖳 www.parador.es). The website includes information and photographs of all the *paradores* and online booking facilities. You can become a 'friend of *paradores*' (*amigo de paradores*) and receive a complementary drink on arrival, free garaging for your car and one point for every €3 you spend (which can be exchanged for free accommodation). A comprehensive book *Paradores de Turismo* by José Mª Iñigo (Everest) is available from bookshops.

As well as *paradores*, there are many 'select' hotels in Spain, more than 130 of which are included in Rusticae's listings, a company that specialises in exclusive hotels. The hotels, around Spain, mainly consist of luxury accommodation at a reasonable price in exquisite settings, often rural, and prices for a double room start at around €120. A brochure is available direct from Rusticae (☎ 902-199 717) or from the website, which includes online booking facilities (🖳 www.rusticae.es).

Most guide books contain a selection of hotels and there are numerous Spanish hotel guides (see **Appendix B**). The most comprehensive hotel (and restaurant) guides are the *Michelin Red Guide España y Portugal* and *Hoteles y Restaurantes de España* (El País Aguilar), which include the humblest and 'poshest' of establishments, and lists weekly closing days and seasonal opening. Both books are published annually. Lists of hotels and other accommodation are published by local municipalities, and provinces and regions also publish hotel guides. TurEspaña publish the *Guía de Hoteles*, containing every classified hotel and hostel in Spain (available from local book shops).

Note that all official establishments offering accommodation must maintain a complaints book and you can also make a complaint to the local tourist office, who may intercede on your behalf to resolve a dispute.

# Self-catering

There's a wealth of self-catering accommodation in Spain which is extremely popular, particularly with Spanish families. It includes apartments, townhouses, villas, farmhouses and country houses (*fincas*). Note that standards vary considerably, from dilapidated, ill-equipped apartments to luxury villas with every modern convenience. You don't always get what you pay for and some properties bear little resemblance to their descriptions. Unless a company or property has been highly recommended, it's best to book through a reputable organisation such as Interhome or a tourist agency. TurEspaña publish a guide to self-catering accommodation entitled *Apartamentos Turísticos*. Tourist apartments (*apartamentos turísticos*) in Spain are graded by one to four keys as shown below:

● **Luxury** (four keys) – A top-quality building in a good location with air-conditioning, heating, 24-hour hot water, parking, reception and information desk, private telephone, bar service, and a restaurant or cafeteria. Lifts are provided if the building is higher than two floors.

● **First Class** (three keys) – A quality building with heating and hot water, reception and information desk, telephone to reception, and lifts if the building is higher than three floors.

● **Second Class** (two keys) – Well-built structure with heating, hot water, a telephone at the reception desk and on each floor, and lifts if the building is higher than three floors.

● **Third Class** (one key) – Hot water, at least a shower in all apartments and a lift if the building is higher than three floors.

Most accommodation is let for a minimum of seven nights (except for public holiday weekends such as Easter). The cost per night usually ranges from €30 for a studio (sleeping two to four people) in low season, to €60 per night in high season (July-August). A two-bedroom apartment or townhouse (sleeping four to six) costs from around €60 per night in low season to €100 per night in high season, although rates depend on the location and the quality of the accommodation. Rates usually include linen, gas and electricity, although heating in winter, e.g. gas or electric heaters, is usually charged extra. It's illegal to install electricity coin meters in rental accommodation in Spain. **Beware of gas heaters with faulty ventilation ducts, as**

**they've been responsible for a number of deaths in self-catering accommodation due to gas poisoning.** Extra beds and cots (e.g. €6 per night or €20 per week) can usually be rented.

In Madrid and other cities, there are luxury serviced apartments costing around €50 to €150 a night (€300 to €900 a week) for a studio or one bedroom apartment sleeping two and €150 to €250 a night (€900 to €1,500 a week) for a two or three-bedroom apartment sleeping four to six. VAT at 7 per cent is added to bills and may be included in quoted rates. **Note that pets are usually prohibited.** During the low season, which may extend from October to May, rates may drop to as little as €300 to €450 a month for a two-bedroom apartment, although there's usually a minimum let of two months. Naturally, you can rent a wide variety of villas and luxury properties throughout Spain, the cost of which can be astronomical.

Properties in resort areas always have a swimming pool (shared for apartments and townhouses), in use from around May to October, and most are also located close to a beach. Some properties have an indoor heated swimming pool and other facilities such as tennis courts. Most holiday apartments are fairly basic, often with tiny kitchens and bathrooms (there may only be a shower), and have a combined lounge/dining room, a patio or balcony. If you need special items such as a cot or high chair, you should mention them when booking.

Properties are generally well-stocked with cooking utensils, crockery and cutlery, although you should check before shopping. Some things that may come in handy are a decent cook's knife, a teapot, egg cups, a pepper mill, a filter coffee machine and a few of your favourite foods such as tea, instant coffee, and relishes and condiments you cannot live without. Most people take a few essential foods and supplies with them and buy fresh food on arrival, although many self-catering properties provide a 'welcome pack' with essentials for when you first arrive.

It's essential to book during the high season and over holiday weekends (e.g. at Easter). There's usually a 25 per cent deposit, with the balance payable on arrival. Normally, you must arrive by 5pm on your first day and vacate the property by noon on your day of departure. Outside the high season of July and August, self-catering accommodation can usually be found on the spot by asking around in bars and restaurants or by obtaining a list from the local tourist office.

# Youth Hostels

There are more than 200 youth hostels (*albergues juveniles*) in Spain, some 100 of which are open all year round and 65 in summer only. They're operated by the Spanish youth hostel association (Red Española de Albergues Juveniles/REAJ) and provide the cheapest accommodation in Spain. International Youth Hostel Federation (IYHF) membership is usually necessary and costs €5 (for those aged from 14 to 30) or €11 (over 30) and is available from REAJ offices, offices of Viajes TIVE and other travel agencies. Cards can also be issued at some hostels.

Most hostels are housed in old buildings without modern plumbing or air-conditioning, and possibly no heating in winter in the south of the country. They're usually situated out of town, packed with schoolchildren, and residents are subject to curfews which exclude guests from making the most of Spain's extensive nightlife.

If you don't have a booking, you should arrive early (e.g. between 8 and 9am) at some hostels, particularly those in Madrid, and you should book for the peak months of July and August. Most hostels allow a maximum stay of around three days. However, unless you're dedicated to staying in youth hostels you may find they aren't worth bothering with as there's a wealth of budget accommodation throughout Spain (see page 362) and hostels can work out more expensive for couples and groups than other types of accommodation. Costs vary depending on the actual hostel, although typical costs per person are as follows:

| Service | Typical Costs (€) | |
| --- | --- | --- |
| | Under 26 | Over 26 |
| Full Board | 18 – 23 | 21 – 28 |
| Half Board | 14 – 18 | 17 – 23 |
| Bed & Breakfast | 8 – 14 | 11 – 18 |
| Dinner | 4 – 5 | 4 – 5 |

For further information contact Red Española de Albergues Juveniles (REAJ), C/Castello, 24 6º dcha, 28001 Madrid (☎ 915-227 007, 🖳 www.reaj.com). The website includes downloadable brochures in Spanish and English with prices and lists of hostels. REAJ also publish an annual magazine *Albergues* with useful information about youth hostels in Spain. In mountain areas, the Spanish Mountain Sports Federation (Federación Española de Deportes de Montaña y Escalada/FEDME), C/Floridablanca, 84, 08015 Barcelona (☎ 934-264 267, 🖳 www. fedme.es) maintains over 200 alpine huts (*refugios*). These are simple, inexpensive, dormitory huts for climbers and hikers, and they're usually equipped only with bunks and a basic kitchen. The Spain Mountains website (🖳 www.spain mountains.com) includes useful information on alpine huts, as well as a wealth of other information in English, French and German about travelling in Spain's mountainous areas.

# BARS & CAFES

One of the delights of living in Spain is the many excellent pavement cafés and bars, and in particular, their delicious coffee and inexpensive prices. Few countries can match Spain for the variety, quality, economy and number of its watering holes. Drinking habits vary considerably from region to region, although it isn't uncommon to see Spaniards taking a brandy with their morning coffee.

## Bars

Spain's cities and resort areas contain a wealth of bars and pubs, including over 8,000 in Madrid alone and reportedly more than the whole of Norway. They include cocktail bars, piano bars, disco bars, live-music bars (e.g. jazz, rock or flamenco), bar-cafeterias, bar-restaurants, cabaret bars, casino bars, beach bars, wine bars (*bodegas*), taverns (*tabernas*), *mesones* (a bar specialising in serving wine and *tapas*), *cervecerías* (a bar specialising in beer, usually with a wide selection of imported beers on tap), gay bars, roof-top bars, pool-side bars, youth bars, topless bars, and a huge variety of foreign bars and pubs. Pubs tend to be flashy bars, often with live music, satellite television, expensive drinks and usually no food.

For homesick Britons there are numerous pseudo British bars in resort areas, usually equipped with satellite television systems showing English football, cricket and other sports events. Television can be even more obtrusive in Spanish bars, where customers are fed a constant diet of soccer, bullfights, game shows and dubbed foreign films. Don't expect to have a quiet conversation in a bar with a TV. **Note that it's cheaper to drink while standing at the bar; sitting at a table may be 50 per cent more expensive and a table on a pavement terrace (*terraza*) can be double the bar price.** You may not be permitted to buy a drink at the bar and take it to a seat outside. Eating is also more expensive at a table than at the bar. Bars are usually open from noon to 4pm and from 8pm until midnight or later, although some are open all day while others only open in the evenings. In resort areas, many bars (and restaurants) are closed outside the high season. There are no official licensing laws in Spain and closing time is usually when the owner decides to shut up shop or when the last customer goes home, which is usually in the early hours of the morning (although some town halls fix bar closing times, e.g. 2am).

# Cafés

Traditional café life can still be found in Spain, where a café is rarely simply somewhere to grab a cup of coffee and a pastry. Its myriad roles include a place in which to read the newspaper (without buying one); a convenient place to make a telephone call or go to the toilet (due to the dearth of public toilets in Spain); somewhere to pass the time; a business or social meeting place; a place to write or study; an academic or debating arena; a refuge from the sun or rain or simply somewhere to watch the world go by. Around 5pm is the hour of *tertulia*, the café get-together that's a national institution. Note that it's customary to buy a drink when you use the toilet in a bar or cafe, although owners don't usually mind non-customers using their facilities. Cafés often have a billiard room and some even entertain customers with a live orchestra or chamber music.

To attract the attention of a waiter (*camarero*) or waitress (*camarera*) in a busy bar or café, it's customary to call out 'attention, please' (*¡oiga, por favor!*) or simply to shout your order at the waiter. In small family bars and cafés, you're usually served by the landlord or landlady (*dueño/dueña*), who won't usually accept tips (*propinas*). Tipping is, however, common in bars, although tips are usually small and often consist of the small change left in saucers. Tips are often kept in a communal tin or box (*bote*) and shared among the staff, although this practice isn't common in restaurants, where waiters prefer to keep their own tips.

# Coffee

Spain is a Mecca for coffee lovers and Spanish coffee is invariably superb and among the best value in Europe. It's served in cafés, ice-cream parlours (*heladerías*), bars and restaurants and is freshly made, piping hot and actually tastes of coffee beans. A 'normal' coffee is an espresso which is served black (*café solo*), while a coffee made with half milk is a *café con leche*, usually drunk by Spaniards for breakfast. Coffee with a dash of milk is a *café cortado*. If you want a large black coffee ask for a *doble* or a *grande*. Should you wish to drink weak milky coffee ask for a *manchada*, which is literally 'stained milk'. Decaffeinated coffee (*descafeinado*) is widely available, which may be from a machine, although many bars just serve a sachet of instant coffee poured into a cup of hot milk. Iced coffee (*café con hielo*) is also available and is usually served black. In some areas, a coffee is routinely accompanied by a glass of cold water. A coffee usually costs around €1, although in tourist haunts and fashionable *terrazas* it can be as much as €3. It's often served spiked with brandy, whisky or anisette, when it's called a *carajillo*, and may be served with a small slice of lemon and a coffee bean floating on top.

## Tea

Tea (*té*) is available in most bars and cafés and is usually drunk black or served with a slice of lemon (*té con limón*). If you want tea with milk it's best to ask for tea with a little cold milk (*té con un poquito de leche fría*), because if you ask for tea with milk you're likely to get tea made with half water and half hot milk! However, it's best not to drink 'English' tea in bars and cafés at all, as it's invariably awful. Herbal teas such as camomile (*manzanilla*) and mint (*mentapoleo*) are also widely available. There are tea rooms (*salones de té*) in the major cities and afternoon tea is often served in luxury hotels, perhaps to a background of live classical music.

## Soft Drinks

A wide variety of non-alcoholic 'soft' drinks (*refrescos*) are available in Spain, including ubiquitous international brands such as Pepsi, Coca Cola and Fanta. Other common drinks include sweetened fruit juice (*zumo* or *jugo*), fresh juice (*zumo natural*), iced fruit juices made from fruit syrups or coffee (*granizados*), orange (*naranja*), lemon (*limón*), tonic (*tónica*) and bitter (*kas*). Mineral water is sold in sparkling (*con gas*) and still (*sin gas*) versions. A popular thirst-quenching drink is a *horchata de chufa*, a concoction made from the tuberous root of the *chufa* (known in English as 'earth almond') and served with crushed-ice (often served in special cafés called *horchaterías*). Others include a black and white (*negro y blanco*), a combination of ice cream (*helado*) and coffee, and creamy milk shakes (*batidos*).

## Beer

Beer is extremely popular in Spain and somewhat surprisingly most Spaniards prefer it to wine. In general, a bar serves one brand of local draught beer and possibly a few different bottled beers. A *cervecería* is a bar that specialises in beer and usually has several brands on tap and a wide range of bottled beers, including imported brands. Spanish beers come in light (*dorada*) and dark (*negra*) varieties, the most famous brands, including *San Miguel*, *Cruzcampo*, *Dorada*, *Aguila*, *Estrella* and *Mahou*.

Bars also serve non-alcoholic beer, inappropriately called *sin* (literally 'without'). A small bottle of beer (300ml) is a *botellín*, while a small glass of draught beer is called a *caña*. A *caña doble* is twice as large as a *caña* (and is often served when you don't ask for a *caña*) and a large beer is a *tubo* (tube) or *jarra* (mug or jar), although this can also mean a large jug or pitcher. In tourist resorts, customers who ask for a beer are often served a *tubo*. Draught beer is generally cheaper than bottled beer and costs around €1 to €1.50 for a small glass (*caña*). **Spanish beer is quite strong and is usually around 5 per cent alcohol by volume.** For something lighter try *clara*, a refreshing shandy made with beer and sweetened seltzer (*gaseosa*).

# Cocktails & Spirits

Cocktails and spirits are much cheaper in Spain than in most other countries and are served in larger measures (the Spanish don't use official measures when pouring drinks, although European Union regulations are supposed to end this practice). An aperitif at midday or in the evening is a ritual in Spain. Most spirits are ordered by brand name, as there are generally cheaper Spanish (*nacional*) equivalents for most international brands. When drinking cocktails, most people notice little difference between Spanish gin, vodka and rum, and more expensive imports. However, Spanish whisky is terrible and to be avoided. Some bars and discotheques reportedly buy inexpensive spirits in bulk to refill well-known brand bottles and charge higher prices. Whisky (scotch, bourbon or rye) is less likely to be substituted, as it's difficult to reproduce the flavour of a particular whisky and it's less likely to be drunk in a cocktail. Drinks are usually served with lots of ice (*hielo*), which those with sensitive stomachs may wish to avoid (depending on the water source).

# Other Drinks

Wine (*vino*) is sold by the glass (*copa*) in bars and cafés and is ordered by simply asking for a glass of red, white or rosé (*una copa de tinto/blanco/rosado*). If you don't specify the colour, you're usually served red wine. It's inexpensive by northern European standards, costing as little as €1 for a glass of house wine (*vino de la casa* or *vino del lugar*) often served from a barrel or a glass jug. If you fancy trying your hand at drinking from a wineskin (*odre/bota de vino*) or *porrón* (a glass carafe with a pouring funnel) don't wear your best clothes. Note that red wine is sometimes served chilled in bars; if you want it at room temperature ask for *no frío* or *normal*.

Table wine (*vino corriente* or *vino de mesa*) is often drunk mixed with sparkling mineral water, soda or lemonade, called *tinto de verano* (literally 'summer red') when made with red wine. *Sangría* is a delicious punch made with peaches, oranges, seltzer, sugar, red wine and a dash of brandy. It's available everywhere and can be surprisingly strong, although it isn't usually well made in bars. A similar drink is *zurra* made with white wine, brandy, vermouth and sugar, garnished with orange and lemon segments and diluted with water and ice. Sherry (*jerez*) is popular, particularly in the south, and cider (*sidra*) is a common drink in the north of Spain. *Pacharán*, made from sloes, is an increasingly popular after-dinner drink.

# Food

Bars and cafés in Spain aren't just somewhere to get a drink, and many serve snacks and complete meals from morning until late at night. In addition to *tapas* (see below), bars (and cafés) serve a variety of snacks, including sandwiches and rolls (*bocadillos*), toasted sandwiches (*tostadas*) and various egg dishes, including fried eggs (*huevos fritos*) and cold Spanish omelette (*tortilla de patata*). In local bars, there's often no menu and you just ask the patron what he has to eat. There's invariably something, usually what the family is eating such as a home-made stew, grilled seafood or fresh salad. You can also find a wide selection of appetising snacks in food shops such as *panaderías* and *croissanterías*.

## Tapas

*Tapas*, meaning 'lids', as they were originally little saucers of snacks served on top of a drink, are the world's greatest snack food. They're a way of life throughout Spain, although more common in the north and the major cities, where it's customary to drop into a bar after work to have a drink accompanied by *tapas*. *Tapas* consist of small dishes usually eaten at the counter in a bar with a glass of draught beer or wine, although they may also be eaten as an *entrée* before a meal. Among the best places to eat *tapas* is a traditional *mesón* or *tasca*, many of which are also restaurants, with a whole counter full of hot and cold appetisers. If you don't speak Spanish, it's best to choose a bar where the dishes are displayed along the bar, rather than one where they're simply listed on a blackboard. A dirty floor is the sign of a good *tapas* bar, as everything that's left is simply dropped on the floor, including leftovers, seafood shells, olive stones, nutshells, cigarette ends and serviettes.

*Tapas* are served in various sizes: a standard *tapa* is an appetiser-like serving, a *pincho* or a *porción* a slightly larger serving, and a *ración* is the same size as a starter. Always state the size of serving you want. *Tapas variadas* is a selection of *tapas* and an excellent introduction for the uninitiated. Most *tapas* can also be ordered as sandwiches in French bread. There are many varieties of *tapas*, including olives, mushrooms, pickled vegetables, kebabs (*pinchos morunos*), ham, seafood (baby eels, tuna, squid, octopus, clams, mussels, lobster, prawns, anchovies), garlic potatoes, pieces of omelette (*tortilla*), meatballs, tripe, huge potato crisps, peanuts, Russian salad, cheese, salami, nuts, pickled carrots, sausage, snails, stewed pimento, cubes of pork in sauce, pig's ear and pickled artichoke hearts (to name but a few). In southern Andalusia, a favourite tapa is *huevos revueltos*, softly scrambled eggs made with a variety of flavourings, including wild asparagus, shrimps, ham, beans and mushrooms. *Tapas* are usually accompanied by draft beer, wine or sherry.

Some bars automatically serve free *tapas* with every drink, midday and evening, although this custom isn't so widespread nowadays. However, it's still possible to find places where you can get a small glass of wine (*chato*) and a tapa for €1. *Tapa* etiquette dictates that you don't usually choose free *tapas*. When not served free, *tapas* cost around €1 to €3 for a serving.

# Paying

In a bar or café, it's usual to 'run a tab' and pay for your drinks when you leave, although you may be asked to pay when you're served in a busy establishment or a tourist spot such as a beach bar. Your account may be chalked on the counter itself or written on a pad kept behind the bar. If your waiter is going off duty, he will also ask you to pay. Service and tax is included in the price and it's unnecessary to tip, although most people leave their small change (e.g. €0.20) and a party may leave €1 after an evening's drinking. When Spaniards have a drink together, usually the one who made the invitation or suggestion pays (although they may argue about it). The foreign habit of trying to work out who has drunk what and splitting the bill is alien to the Spanish, they don't run a mental bill and make sure that everyone pays in turn. If you're invited for a drink by a Spaniard, he will invariably insist on paying, even if he's of modest means.

The legal age for drinking in Spain is 18, although it isn't always enforced (children under 18 are permitted on licensed premises with an adult, but cannot consume alcohol). Although Spaniards are comparatively heavy drinkers by most standards, you rarely see them intoxicated. Drunkenness is associated with a loss of dignity and anyone who cannot hold his drink is scorned. Alcoholism is a serious problem in Spain, particularly among expatriates, many of whom are unable to control their drinking. Newcomers should be particularly wary of drinking too much, which is all too easy with Spain's low prices and generous measures. A surfeit of sun and alcohol can be deadly. See also **Alcohol** on page 426 and **Restaurants** below.

# BULLFIGHTING

A book about Spain wouldn't be complete without a 'few' words about bullfighting (*la lidia*), commonly referred to as the *fiesta nacional*. Foreigners love or loathe bullfights and it provokes controversy even among Spaniards. To many it's a barbaric and sadistic blood sport with no merit whatsoever and should be banned. It's claimed by those opposed to bullfighting that over 80 per cent of Spaniards are against it, although it remains highly popular with over 40 million paying spectators a year and top fights being shown live on television. It is, however, banned in the Canary Islands and in a few areas in mainland Spain, including Barcelona, which joined the anti-bullfighting league in 2004 much to the surprise of many in Spain.

If you're opposed to bullfighting on moral and ethical grounds, it's best not to go, as you certainly won't enjoy it and may well be distressed. If you feel you ought to watch it at least once, it's advisable to watch a bullfight on TV before deciding whether to see one in the flesh. If you decide to go to a fight, you should **never** cheer for the bull, particularly if it has gored the bullfighter (*matador* or *toreros*), otherwise you can expect to be the object of some hostility from the crowd.

Bullfighting isn't considered a sport in Spain, but an art (the art of *tauromachy*), and is reported in the arts and culture section of newspapers. It's certainly not a contest, as there can be only one 'winner', although bullfighters can and do get killed every year (in addition to some 8,000 bulls) and even some spectators (*espontáneos*) who jump into the ring to try their hand. Aficionados hail it as a spectacle encompassing colour, tradition, excitement, pageantry, beauty, danger, bravery, skill, blood and high drama. It's an essential part of Spain's heritage and culture and has probably had more influence on Spanish consciousness than any other phenomenon in the last few centuries.

# History

Andalusia is the birthplace of bullfighting, where Ronda is regarded as the cradle of modern bullfighting, and many of Spain's top bullfighters come from this region. Pedro Romero (immortalised by Goya in his painting *Tauromaquia*), who developed the classical style used today, is considered the father of modern bullfighting and ended his career in the 1820s at the aged of 72, having killed over 5,500 bulls without once being gored. Throughout the last two centuries there have been many famous bullfighters, including Rafael Gómez (*El Gallo*), Manolete (Manuel Rodríquez Sánchez), Joselito, Espartero and Juan Belmonte. Many bullfighters have been hailed by their supporters as the greatest who ever lived, including Manolete, Joselito and Belmonte. Among modern bullfighters, one of the most famous was Manuel Benítez (El Cordobés), who made his name in the '60s and '70s. Over the years, there has been a few American and English bullfighters and even women are beginning to make their mark in the ring. However, women find it hard to gain acceptance in what is the world's most macho (*machista*) 'profession', and some of Spain's top male bullfighters refused to share a bill with Cristina Sánchez, Spain's leading female bullfighter (now retired).

# Season

The official season runs from 19th March until 12th October. The most popular day is Sunday, but bullfights are also held on public holidays and during festivals. The most famous bullfighting fiestas are staged during Valencia's *fallas* (March); in Seville during the April Fair; San Isidro in Madrid (May) with 23 consecutive days of fighting; Granada's Corpus Christi celebrations (June); San Fermín in Pamplona (July); Bilbao's *Semana Grande* (August) and Zaragossa's *Feria de Pilar* (October).

# Bullrings

There are some 500 permanent bullrings in Spain. The most famous, which are usually exactly circular, are Madrid's *Las Ventas* (the biggest in Spain seating 25,000), Seville's *La Maestranza* and Pamplona, followed by Bilbao and Valencia. There are also rings in many smaller towns, including the resort towns of Benidorm, Marbella and Torremolinos. Apart from Madrid, other towns holding over ten bullfights (*corridas*) per year include Malaga, Seville, Valencia and Zaragossa.

A bullfight is held between 4 and 6pm or 5 and 7pm depending on the heat and time of the year, and is one of the few things in Spain that starts on time. Sometimes two fights are held on the same day. Bullfights are announced by posters stating whether it's a full bullfight with senior bullfighters and mature bulls, or a novice bullfight with younger bulls and junior bullfighters (a *novillada, gran novillada* or *corrida de novillos*). Matadors are listed on posters in order of seniority. Note that posters sold outside bullrings as souvenirs rarely advertise the current fight and most feature famous dead or retired bullfighters.

## Tickets

Ticket (*billetes*) prices vary considerably with the bullring, the bullfighters and the occasion. Tickets for small bullfights usually range from €10 to €100. Tickets for top fights may be sold by touts (scalpers) for up to ten times their face value. Ticket prices are generally high in tourist areas, typically between €35 and €100, although locals usually pay nothing like the prices charged to tourists. Seats are usually designated as being in the shade (*sombra*) or the sun (*sol*), with shaded seats being more expensive. Sun and shade (*sol y sombra*) seats are those that become shaded as the fight progresses. The closer you are to the action, the more expensive the seat, with ringside barrier (*barrera*) seats in the shade being the most expensive. Some rings have seats designated as *contrabarrera* which are the next rows to the barrier seats. The seats behind the ringside seats are called *tendidos* and may be divided into high (*alto*) and low (*bajo*) areas. The cheapest seats in the highest rows at the back are *gradas* or simply *filas*, costing around €12 in a large ring. Cushions (*almohadillas*) can be rented for around €1 and are essential, as the 'seats' are usually stone or concrete. **Children aren't admitted to bullfights.**

Tickets show the section name and number (e.g. *tendido* 10), the row (*fila*) and the seat (*asiento*) number. It's best to purchase tickets from the box office (*taquilla*) at the bullring or at an official ticket office. Tickets sold by agents usually have a high surcharge. You should avoid buying tickets from touts.

Live bullfights are shown on Spanish TV almost daily throughout the season and recorded fights are screened twice weekly in the off-season. Top bullfighters are huge stars and feted like pop stars or star footballers and can command fees of anywhere between €20,000 and €200,000. Scores of books about bullfighting are published each year and magazines and newspapers devote many pages to it. Among the many books written about bullfighting are *Death in the Afternoon* by Ernest Hemingway (Grafton), *Or I'll Dress You in Mourning* by Larry Collins (Weidenfeld & N) and *Blood Sport: A Social History of Spanish Bullfighting* by Timothy Mitchell (University of Pennsylvania Press).

## CINEMAS

Spain has over 2,000 cinemas (*cines*) nationwide and around 1,300 cinema clubs. Although it has lost a lot of its former popularity to television and many cinemas have closed in the last few decades, cinema remains reasonably popular in Spain where over 10 per cent of adults see a film each week. In major cities, most cinemas have three or four performances (*sesiones*) a day, at two or three hour intervals, e.g. 4.30pm, 6.30pm, 8.30pm and 10.30pm (some have an extra performance on Saturdays and holidays, shown in listings as *S y F*). Ticket prices are among the lowest in Europe and are generally around €5 (sometimes less in smaller towns). On certain days, e.g. Wednesdays in Madrid (designated the *día del espectador* or 'spectator's day'), tickets are reduced to €3.50 or €4 for all performances. Other discounts are available for students, pensioners and children under 13. Some cinemas also have a 'couple's day' (*día de la pareja*), usually midweek when couples pay half-price. Most cinemas are fairly small, although multi-screen cinemas (e.g. with 15 screens) have sprung up all over the country, particularly in shopping centres. There are outdoor and drive-in cinemas in the summer in many areas and free films are also sponsored in some cities, e.g. in the Parque del Retiro in Madrid.

Most foreign films are dubbed into Spanish (including foreign names), usually indicated by the letters V.E. (*versión española*). However, a number of private theatres in the major cities and resort towns specialise in screening original soundtrack films, indicated by the letters V.O. (*versión original*), with Spanish subtitles (*subtitulada*). Restricted films that aren't recommended for children (minors) less than a certain age (e.g. 13 or 18) are listed as *no recomendada para menores de 13/18 años*, while a film with no age restrictions is classified as *todos los públicos*. Cinema programmes are published in daily newspapers and entertainment guides.

There has been a revival of Spanish films since censorship ended and some 20 per cent of films shown in Spain are now Spanish-made. Spain stages some 40 film festivals each year, notably in Barcelona, Gijón, Madrid, San Sebastian and Vallodolid. However, Spanish film makers (like the French) are under serious threat from US-made films, which dominate most cinemas, particularly those owned by US-companies. In order to protect its indigenous film industry, the Spanish government introduced a highly unpopular quota system in 1994, forcing cinemas to show European films at least one day in three, and in June 2004, the government introduced a new ruling that all television companies must invest a certain amount of their profit in film-making in Spain.

Pedro Almodóvar is Spain's most famous film director and his numerous films depicting complex relationships in often surrealist and *kitsch* settings, are known the world over. In 2000 his film, *All About My Mother* (*Todo sobre mi madre*) won the Oscar for the best foreign film and in 2003 his latest film, *Talk to Her* (*Hable con ella*), won the Golden Globe award for best foreign film and the Oscar for best original script.

# FESTIVALS & FIESTAS

Festivals and *fiestas* are an important part of cultural and social life in Spain, where over 3,000 are celebrated each year. The Spanish are inveterate revellers and almost every village and town has its annual fair (*feria*), lasting from a few days to a few weeks. They're usually held on the local saint's day (*patrón* or *patrona*), appropriately marked in red on Spanish calendars, when an effigy of the saint is paraded around the town in a procession. Village festivals often include a pilgrimage (*romería*) to a local shrine on horseback and in horse-drawn wagons, where a grand celebration is held. Foreigners are usually welcome to join in, although you may need an invitation to take part in some religious festivals.

The first national celebration of the year is *Martes de Carnaval* (Spain's Mardi Gras), held in February and best experienced in Cadiz or Tenerife. Holy Week (*Semana Santa*) is a major tourist attraction in many cities and towns, particularly in

Seville and the rest of Andalusia. The main attractions are huge religious processions with ornate floats depicting scenes from the Passion and masked men decked out in ghostly costumes with pointed hats (imitated by the Ku Klux Klan in the US). Other major festivals include Corpus Christi in May or June; the feast day of Spain's patron saint, Santiago, on 25th July; and the Assumption of the Virgin (*la Asunción*) on 15th August. There are also numerous local *fiestas* for harvests, deliverance from the Moors, safe return from the sea, plus a variety of other obscure occasions (the Spanish use any excuse to have a party!).

Essential ingredients for a *fiesta* include costumes, processions, music, dancing and feasting. Processions often include huge papier-mâché statues called giants or bigheads (*gigantones* or *cabezudos*), which take many months to create and may be ritually burnt during the festival (the most famous is the *fallas fiesta* held in Valencia in March). The largest festivals include bullfights, flamenco, funfairs, circuses, fireworks, plays, concerts, music recitals and competitions. In Extremadura, the Basque Country and Navarre, summer *fiestas* often feature loose bulls stampeding through the streets (*el encierro*). The most famous is the running of the bulls in Pamplona during the *Fiesta de San Fermín* (although there are many others), when the slow of foot and foolhardy (usually foreigners) are often injured or even occasionally killed. A *vaquilla* is the running of bulls, cows or calves through the streets of a town and includes the opportunity to 'fight' the animals. Another tradition, called the *toro del aguardiente*, is to set a table with a bottle of brandy and glasses in the middle of a bullring; those wishing to enjoy a drink must risk being tossed by a small bull (some people will do anything for a free drink!).

There's rarely any violence or serious crime at Spanish festivals and *fiestas*, which are a great occasion for all the family (children often stay up all night), and any drunkenness or hooliganism is likely to be among foreigners. **Pickpockets and bag snatchers are, however, fairly common at major festivals, which tend to attract thieves in droves.** Dates for most festivals are fluid and when they fall on a Tuesday or Thursday the day is usually 'bridged' with the preceding or following weekend to create a four-day holiday. Check exact dates with TurEspaña and local tourist offices in Spain. TurEspaña publish a number of brochures about festivals and *fiestas*, including *Celebrating in Spain* and *Festivals of Special Interest to Tourists*.

# FLAMENCO

Flamenco consists of a flamboyant dance accompanied by guitar music and song (*cante*), the heart of the art of flamenco, which at its best is the true classical performance art of Spain. It has been referred to as the soul of Spain and, like bullfighting, is an essential part of the country's culture and traditions. The history of flamenco, in particular the origin of the name (literally 'Flemish'), is obscure, although it's believed to have originated in the 18th century with the gypsies of Andalusia. Its songs of oppression, lament and bitter romance were taken up by the peasants of Andalusia and spread throughout Spain in the 20th century as they migrated in search of jobs.

Flamenco consists of two main groups of songs, the small song (*cante chico*), which is lively and cheerful, and the big or deep song (*cante jondo*), the genesis of flamenco, lamenting love, sadness, death, hardship and the struggle for life. The classical flamenco repertoire consists of some 60 songs and dances. Castanets, although symbols of Spain to many foreigners, are rarely used by the best dancers. The best flamenco singers tend to live tormented lives and many die of alcohol and drug abuse, including the revered El Camarón de la Isla who died in 1992 (fans are still mourning his loss). Antonio Ruiz Soler, Spain's most famous flamenco dancer, died in 1996 aged 74. In the last few years flamenco has increasingly been blended with music from other cultures such as the salsa, rumba and blues, which is known as the 'new flamenco' (*nuevo flamenco*) or 'flamenco fusion' (one of the most famous and controversial 'fusion' dancers is Joaquín Cortes).

Flamenco has been shamelessly exploited by the Spanish tourist industry and it's commonly performed in commercial tourist shows advertised as 'genuine flamenco *fiestas*', which although enjoyable are a pale imitation of the real thing. Generally, the more commercially orientated the performance, the less authentic it's likely to be. In fact, the idea of a staged performance is alien to the whole concept of flamenco, which is traditionally informal and spontaneous. Real flamenco is said to evoke the indescribable quality of spirit or demon (*duende*) that possesses performers and contains a primitive, ecstatic allure that embraces listeners.

Real flamenco can be experienced in specialist bars and small members-only clubs (*peñas*) in Andalusia and other regions of Spain, where unappreciative foreigners are rarely welcome or invited (although it's possible to find authentic places where guests are admitted). The best chance most foreigners have of experiencing authentic flamenco is at one of the big summer festivals held in Cadiz, Jerez, Granada, Malaga and Seville or during festivals and *fiestas* in small villages off the tourist track. Many books have been written about flamenco, including *Songs of the Outcasts: an Introduction to Flamenco* by Robin Totton (Amadeus Press), *In Search of the Firedance* by James Woodall (Sinclair Stevenson), *Flamenco!* by Gwynne Edwards (Thames & Hudson) and *Duende: a Journey in Search of Flamenco* by Jason Webster (Black Swan).

# GAMBLING

The Spanish are a nation of gamblers and bet a higher proportion of their income than almost any other nation. It's estimated that the Spanish gamble well over €1.9 billion a year equal to around €480 per head or some 15 per cent of the average net household income. They bet on almost anything, including lotteries, football and racing pools, horse racing (illegal betting shops, where punters bet on foreign horse and greyhound racing, are common in resort areas), bingo, slot machines, casinos, and the big *jai-alai* games in the Basque Country and Madrid. Prizes can be huge running into hundreds of thousands of euros.

The most popular form of gambling is the state national lottery (*Lotería Nacional*) run in aid of charities and the Catholic Church. Lottery tickets are sold at lottery offices at face value (€20) or can be purchased from street vendors (10 per cent commission is added) and through ONCE (the Spanish organisation for the blind) kiosks manned by the blind or those with impaired sight. ONCE takes some €60 a year from every Spaniard and has a massive turnover that many companies would be proud of.

Spain's and the world's biggest lottery, 'the fat one' (*El Gordo*), is held at Christmas and consists of 108 series of 66,000 tickets, each costing €200. Not surprisingly, €200 is too much for most people and tickets are divided into ten shares (*décimos*) costing €20 each. Many clubs and charities buy a *décimo* and offer shares (called *partcipaciones*) for a couple of euros, usually adding a small surcharge. The total amount wagered on *El Gordo* is over €1.7 billion, some 70 per cent of which is paid in prizes. The top prize is around €2 million, the second just under €1 million and the third €500,000, each of which is multiplied by the number of series' of tickets (there are usually over 100).

Tickets are usually sold out long before the draw on the 22nd December, which is televised live (it takes three hours) and traditionally made by the children of the San Ildefonso school in Madrid. Winning numbers are published in newspapers on 23rd December and the list is posted in lottery offices for three months following the draw. Winners must claim their winnings, as they aren't sent to them automatically (unclaimed winnings go back to the state). If you win a big prize you can take your ticket to a Spanish bank, which gives you a receipt and collects your winnings on your behalf. Lottery prizes are free of all taxes. Spain's second-largest lottery is called the kid (*El Niño*) after the baby Jesus and takes place on 5th January.

Spain has some 20 casinos, and there's also one in Gibraltar. The most common casino games are American and French roulette, black jack, *punto y banca* and *chemin de fer*, plus the ubiquitous slot machines and private gaming rooms. There's usually an entry fee, e.g. €6, and visitors must show their passports (to identify professional gamblers). Most casinos are open from late afternoon until the early hours of the morning, e.g. 5pm until 4 or 5am. Dress code is smart casual (no jeans, sandals or T-shirts).

# LIBRARIES

Spain has poor public libraries, which bear no comparison to the excellent library systems in, for example, the UK and the US. Most Spaniards don't do a lot of reading and most homes possess few books. However, Spanish public libraries often have an international section mostly containing English-language books, but also with books in Danish, Dutch, French and German (the selection may depend on the predominant resident expatriate community). There may be a small annual membership fee, e.g. €3. Usually, you must know in advance what you want and ask for it at the counter. Opening times are usually severely restricted and libraries may open for a few hours a day only, usually in the morning, on just two or three days a week. The largest library in Spain is the National Library in Madrid containing over two million volumes. The Instituto Cervantes and the Hispanic and Luso Brazilian Council have offices in many countries with extensive Spanish reference (open to non-members) and lending libraries.

Foreign residents will be pleased to know that there are private libraries in many towns run by expatriate organisations and social clubs. There are also second-hand book shops in resort areas, where you can swap books. Like public libraries, private libraries open for only a few hours on two or three days a week, usually including Saturdays. Annual membership normally costs €3 to €10 a year or perhaps more for non-residents (short-term membership is usually available). There may also be a small fee (e.g. €0.50) for each book borrowed. Private libraries welcome new members of all nationalities, residents and non-residents, and are grateful for donations of unwanted books.

# MEALS

The Spanish eat much later than other Europeans, with lunch (*comida* or *almuerzo*) usually being taken between 2 and 4pm and dinner (*cena*) between 9 and 11pm (or as late as midnight at weekends!). People in Barcelona tend to eat dinner around an hour earlier than those in Madrid (which has the latest eating hours in Europe), while in tourist resorts, dinner is usually served from 7 or 8pm. Most establishments serve meals from 1 until 4pm and from 8pm until midnight, and outside these hours the only restaurants that may be open are those catering to foreigners (or those serving 'snacks' rather than full meals). Most restaurants close one day or evening a week, usually Sunday evening and possibly also the whole of Monday or Tuesday. Many restaurants close for holidays in January or August for at least two weeks and some also close for a few days at Easter and over Christmas. In resort areas, many restaurants and bars close for the whole of the winter.

## Breakfast

Breakfast (*desayuno*) isn't usually an important meal in Spain and is often skipped altogether. When eaten it's generally of the continental variety consisting of coffee or hot chocolate and rolls (*bollos*), toast, croissants (*croisantes*), fried fritters (*churros*) or small sponge cakes (*magdalenas*). However, most hotels and many cafes and bars serve a cooked breakfast (*desayuno completo*), particularly in resort areas.

## Lunch

Lunch is the most important meal of the day in Spain and is usually eaten between 2 and 4pm. It consists of an appetiser or starter (*entrada*) of soup or salad, a first course (*primer plato*), possibly followed by an *entrée* or second course (*segundo plato*), often consisting of egg dishes (e.g. omelettes) or vegetables, a main course (*plato fuerte*) of fish or meat with vegetables or salad, followed by fruit or cheese and occasionally a dessert. Often, you must to order vegetables separately and in small family restaurants a salad may be routinely served. Note that modest establishments expect customers to use the same knife and fork for all courses.

## Dinner

Dinner is normally served from 9pm until midnight, although it's usually served earlier in resort towns, and in Spanish cities many restaurants remain open until well after midnight. Usually dinner is a lighter meal than lunch, although judged by international standards, it's certainly no snack. There's often little difference between lunch and dinner menus, except that there isn't always a set menu in the evening and rural establishments may serve dinner only by prior arrangement. A meal eaten late in the evening, perhaps after visiting the cinema or theatre, is called supper (*cena*) and is often eaten in the early hours of the morning in major cities.

It's advisable to book for high class restaurants or any restaurant in a popular resort during the high season. Note, however, that many budget restaurants don't accept reservations and may not even have a telephone. Legislation regarding smoking changes in January 2006 (see page 267) and all restaurants should provide non-smoking sections. Restaurant bills usually include a 15 per cent service charge (plus 7 per cent value added tax or 16 per cent in 5-fork restaurants), usually shown on the bill as *servicio incluido*. Even when service isn't included, the Spanish rarely tip much and may leave only a few small coins. However, many foreigners follow international practice and tip as they would in other countries. **Not all restaurants accept credit cards, particularly budget restaurants, so it's prudent to check in advance.**

There are many excellent guides to Spanish cuisine and restaurants, including *Guía Peñín de los Vinos de España* by José Peñín (Pi & Erre) and a number published (in Spanish) by the Spanish *Club de Vinos Gourmets*, including a monthly magazine entitled *Gourmentour*. *Vinoselección* (Guzmán el Bueno, 133 , 28003 Madrid, ☎ 902-253 525, 💻 www.vinoseleccion.es) is Spain's largest wine club and publishes the gourmet food and wine magazine *El Club*. The club also organises wine tasting trips several times a year. Other guides include *The Wine and Food of Spain* by Jan Read with Maite Manjón and Hugh Johnson (Weidenfeld & Nicolson), *The Spanish Table* by Marimar Torres (Ebury Press), *Cooking in Spain* by Janet Mendel (Santana Books), the pocket *AA Essential Food & Drink Spain* (AA Essential Guides) and the Michelin *Red Guide España and Portugal* (see **Appendix B**).

See also **Alcohol** on page 426 and **Bars & Cafés** on page 370.

# MUSEUMS & GALLERIES

Spain has over 800 museums (*museos*) and important collections, particularly in Madrid and Barcelona, and there has been an explosion in the number of art galleries (*galerías de arte*) in the last decade throughout the country, particularly for contemporary art. Spain has a distinguished history in the field of art and has produced many of the world's greatest artists, including Goya, El Greco, Ribera, Velázquez, Zurbarán, Cano, Murillo, Picasso, Dalí, Miró and Juan Gris. Modern art is a passion with the Spanish and the annual Contemporary Art Fair (ARCO) held in February in Madrid is a highly popular event.

Spain's premier art gallery is the *Museo Nacional del Prado* (called simply the *Prado*, 💻 www.museoprado.es) in Madrid, housing one of the world's richest art collections. It contains over 5,000 paintings, each one a masterpiece, including an unrivalled collection of Spanish masters. The museum has recently been extended to double its floor space to allow many more of its works to be displayed, as well as creating space for temporary exhibitions, theatres and cafés. Complementing the Prado are many other celebrated art collections, including the *Museo Lazaro Galdiano* (💻 www.flg.es), the *Museo Thyssen-Bornemisza* (💻 www.museothyssen.

org), which shows one of the world's best selection of art and has just opened a new wing, and the *Museo Nacional Centro de Arte*, Reina Sofía (💻 www.museoreina sofia.es), Europe's top museum of contemporary art. The museum, housed in a modernised eighteenth century hospital, has also been extended to include three new buildings and boasts a monumental 78,000m² (836,160ft²) of exhibition space. The Prado, Thyssen and Reina Sofía museums are known as Madrid's 'Art Triangle' and the future semi-pedestrianisation of the Paseo de Prado connecting the three and facilitating access will be known as the 'Art Walk'. A Museum Card is available which allows access to all three museums over a three day period; this costs just €7.66.

Although it isn't so richly endowed with museums as Madrid, Barcelona boasts a number of important collections, including the *Museu Picasso* (💻 www.museu picasso.bcn.es), the *Museu d'Art de Catalunya* (💻 www.mnac.es), the *Fundació Joan Miró* (💻 www.bcn.fjmiro.es), the *Museu d'Art Modern* and the Barcelona Museum of Contemporary Art/MACBA (💻 www.macba.es). Modernism is particularly strong in Barcelona which is the capital of modernist architecture. One of its major attractions is the Parc Güell designed by Spain's greatest architect Antoni Gaudí and housing the *Casa-Museu Gaudí*. Also not to be missed are Gaudí's masterpiece *Casa Milà* apartment building and his most famous work, the remarkable unfinished *Temple Expiatori de la Sagrada Familia*. The Barcelona *Articket*, allowing you to visit six major art museums in the city for €17 and valid for three months, is available from art museums in Barcelona, branches of *Caixa Catalunya* bank throughout Spain or from Tel-Entrada (☎ 902-101 212, 💻 www.telentrada.com). The *Museu Dalí* (Dalí Theatre-Museum), itself a surrealist work of art, is located in Figueras (the birthplace of the artist) on the Costa Brava, and is the second most visited museum in Spain after the *Prado*. A futuristic, 21st-century art gallery funded by the Guggenheim Foundation was opened in Bilbao in 1999 and is one of Europe's most beautiful galleries. In late 2003, the long-awaited Picasso Museum (💻 www.museo picassomalaga.org) opened in Malaga (the artist's birthplace) and houses the largest collection of his works in the world.

Most major museums open from 9am to 7pm, Tuesdays to Sundays. Smaller museums may open only between 9 and 10am until 2 or 3pm, although some re-open after the *siesta* from 4 to 7pm. Some museums have extended opening hours in the summer. Opening times vary considerably and are subject to frequent change, so check in advance (they're usually listed in guide books). Many smaller museums disregard 'official' opening hours and open erratically.

Entrance fees to Spain's museums, galleries and other sites are very reasonable, and are usually between €1.50 and €3. The entrance fee of €6 to the *Prado* is a bargain and entrance is free to students with an international student card, pensioners over 65, those under 18 and the unemployed. Many museums provide free entrance to students, some have reduced fees for students and senior citizens, and a few provide free entry on one day a week (including the *Prado*), usually Sundays. A pensioner's card (*tarjeta de pensionista*) allows free entry to state museums and monuments (operated by the *Patrimonio Nacional*) and discounts elsewhere.

The city of Madrid offers tourists the *Madrid Card* system, allowing free entry to museums and monuments, unlimited free travel on public transport and discounts in shops and theatres. The card is valid for one, two or three days and priced €25,

€35 and €45 respectively (discounts are available for online purchases), and can be purchased by telephone (☎ 902-877 996) or online (🖥 www.madridcard.com) and in tourist offices and travel agents in Madrid. In Barcelona, the *Barcelona Card* allows discount entry to museums, shows and attractions, unlimited free travel on public transport and discounts in shops and restaurants. The card is valid for one, two, three, four or five days and priced €17 to €30, and can be purchased at tourist offices and attractions in the city.

Most cathedrals, monasteries and famous churches, many of which house great works of art, charge admission fees to non-worshippers. Student admission is usually half price or less and children under 14 may be admitted free. It's also possible in Spain to visit numerous businesses, particularly those connected with the food and drink industry such as vineyards, distilleries, breweries, mineral water springs, farms and dairies. Spain has numerous zoos, the best of which are Barcelona, Madrid and Fuengirola (Malaga), whose innovative zoo was acclaimed by *National Geographic* as the best in Spain.

# MUSIC

Music of all kinds, from flamenco to rock, jazz to classical, is extremely popular in Spain and an essential ingredient of any festival or *fiesta*. Spain has a wealth of traditional folk music and dance, particularly flamenco (see page 379) and classical guitar, which are popular throughout the country. It's renowned worldwide for its classical guitar, made famous by Andrés Segovia, Carlos Montoyo, Manuel de Falla, Joaquín Rodrigo and Narciso Yepes. An international festival of the guitar is held in Córdoba in July.

Rock and pop music is popular with young Spaniards and there are many excellent home-grown bands, although the most popular music is American and British. Among the most popular forms of Spanish pop music are root-rock (*rock-con-raíces*), a sort of rock version of flamenco singing, and rave music (*bacalao/baKalao*). Madrid has the most lively and varied music scene, although the Catalans are recognised as Spain's most serious music lovers, particularly with regard to opera, jazz and Catalan song. Jazz has a large following in Spain and jazz festivals are staged in many cities in summer, including Barcelona, San Sebastian, Santander and Sitges.

Spain's most popular crooner is Julio Iglesias, who has sold more records in more languages than any other musical artist in history (over 160 million albums) and has earned some 200 gold and platinum records. However, one of Spain's biggest national and international hits in recent years was surprisingly the Benedictine monks of Santo Domingo de Silos (Burgos), whose album of Gregorian chant (*Las Mejores Obras del Canto Gregoriano*) topped music charts around the world selling over 5 million copies.

The Spanish pop music industry, in common with that in most countries, has suffered badly at the hands of pirate copies of compact discs (CD) sold by immigrants on the street for around €3 and popular artists 'sell' more pirate copies than legal ones. Statistics show that since 2000 legal CD sales are down by a third and one out of every four CDs sold is a pirate copy. Despite spectacular police raids and arrests of the copiers and sellers, including one where CD and DVD recorders capable of producing 60 million copies a year were seized, music piracy is a major problem facing the future of the Spanish music industry.

Madrid, Barcelona and Valencia all stage classical music concerts. Major concerts in Madrid are held at the magnificent *Auditorio Nacional de Música* (🖳 www. auditorionacional.mcu.es), home of the Spanish national orchestra (*Orquesta Nacional de España/ONE*), where tickets for most concerts cost between €15 and €70. Annual concert cycles are also performed by the National Orchestra and Choir of Spain, and Spanish Radio and Television at the *Teatro Real* in Madrid. Free open air concerts are held in summer by the city band in the *Templete del Retiro* in Retiro Park. One of the most popular forms of music in Madrid is *Zarzuela*, a form of light opera or comic operetta in the style of Gilbert & Sullivan, performed in the *Teatro de Zarzuela*. In Barcelona, major concerts are held at the eccentric art nouveau *Palau de la Música*. One of the world's most spectacular auditoriums, *El Palau de les Arts*, opened in October 2005 in Valencia.

Spain also stages a wealth of excellent music festivals, including a festival of religious music (*Semanas de Música Religiosa*) in Cuenca at the end of March; the international festival of music and dance (*Festival Internacional de Música y Danza*) in Granada in June/July (Spain's most important musical event); the Santander international festival (*Festival Internacional de Santander*) of music, dance and drama in July/August; the international music festival (*Festival Internacional de Música*) in Barcelona in September/October and the autumn festival in Madrid from mid-September until the beginning of October (includes concerts, opera, drama and ballet). Top international soloists, bands and orchestras give concerts in Spain throughout the year.

# NIGHTLIFE

Spain is famous for its vibrant nightlife, which extends until dawn and beyond in major cities such as Madrid and Barcelona (not for nothing are nocturnal *Madrileños* known as 'the cats' or *los gatos*). In major cities and resort areas, there's a wide choice of nightlife for all ages, including jazz clubs, cabarets, discos, sex shows, flamenco clubs, music clubs and bars, night clubs, music halls, and restaurants with floor shows (*tablaos*). Karaoke is popular in many pubs and clubs in resort areas. For many Spaniards the day doesn't begin until nightfall and most clubs and discotheques don't start to warm up until after midnight (raving is ironically referred to as 'the bad life' – *la mala vida*).

Many young Spaniards literally rock around the clock and in the major cities and resorts some discotheques **open** at daybreak, while others are in business non-stop from Friday night until Monday afternoon. Not surprisingly, Spaniards reportedly sleep less than other Europeans. Ibiza is the spiritual home of the 'Euroraver' and is **the** place to be in summer, when it boasts Europe's most vibrant nightlife and biggest and boldest dance clubs. The authorities in Madrid and Barcelona have been forced to restrict Spain's incessant day and nightlife in some cities, in an attempt to reduce drug use (particularly amphetamines and ecstasy) and the resulting high number of fatal car accidents. Bars in these cities must now close at 2.30am and discos at 4.30am, although most owners ignore the new regulations unless forced to close by the police. Some towns are also cracking down on discos making excessive noise.

Discos are found in the smallest of towns, although they may be no more than a bar with music and a dance floor. The entrance fee is usually around €6, but can be as high as €30 for the most exclusive places (women are often given free entry or are charged less than men). The entrance fee often includes a drink; some have no entrance fee, but **very** expensive drinks, e.g. between €5 and €20. Some discos have early evening sessions for teenagers with an entrance fee of around €3. Live music is common in music bars which have a small dance floor and offer free entrance or charge a small fee, e.g. €2.

It's important to be fashionably dressed to gain access to the most exclusive discos, but in general any casual dress is acceptable, including jeans and T-shirts. There's usually a 'bouncer' on the door checking that guests are suitably attired and haven't had too much to drink.

Discos, night clubs, music bars and clubs, dinner/dancing venues and cabarets are listed in English-language publications and in Spanish newspapers under *salas de fiestas* and *espectáculos*.

# RESTAURANTS

Like most Latins, Spaniards live to eat (and drink) and one of the greatest pleasures of living in Spain is its abundant variety of inexpensive eating places. In fact, anyone who loves good food and wine is guaranteed a happy life in Spain, which boasts one of the healthiest diets in Europe. Dining out is a popular social occasion and a source of great pleasure and it's common for Spaniards to entertain their friends at a restaurant rather than at home. You will often see whole families dining together, perhaps represented by three or four generations, and including children of all ages (children are welcome in all but the most exclusive restaurants in Spain). However, the restaurant trade has been hard hit by live TV football matches, which are usually screened six nights a week in Spain (the most extensive coverage in Europe).

Spain offers a wealth of eating places from luxury international restaurants (with matching prices) to humble *bodegas* and *cantinas* serving homely fare at bargain prices. Traditional eating and drinking places include *mesónes* in urban areas, *ventas* in the countryside, and *merenderos*, *chiringuitos* and *chamboas* (specialising in sea-food) at the beach. *Paradores* (see page 367) and *refugios* specialise in regional cooking. A *marisquería* is an up-market fish restaurant, *cocederos* and *freidurías de pescado* are basic places to enjoy fresh fried fish, while an *asador* specialises in roast meat, poultry or fish. It's also possible to 'dine out at home' in many towns, where restaurants and caterers provide gourmet take-away meals complete with simple cooking instructions, or a chef and waitress will cook and serve dinner in your home for a moderate charge.

Anyone who says Spanish food is boring or always swimming in garlic and olive oil hasn't ventured far off the tourist trail. Spanish cuisine is among the most varied and sophisticated in Europe and is greatly influenced by other Mediterranean countries and Arab cooking. Each region serves its own specialities (*platos típicos*) based on local produce, meats and fish, and every province and most large towns boast their own culinary delights, even if it's just a local sausage or cheese. Spanish cooking largely consists of simple, wholesome fare and is noted for its high-quality fresh ingredients. Spices, particularly hot spices, are used sparingly and the best Spanish cooking is a subtle combination of ingredients and sauces intended to enhance (rather than smother) the flavour.

Generally, the further north you go in Spain, the better the food, with the majority of *haute cuisine* restaurants situated in the Basque Country, Madrid and Barcelona. Basque cuisine is the finest in Spain, where San Sebastian (heavily influenced by France and vice versa) is the gastronomic capital, with around six Michelin-rated restaurants. San Sebastian is also famous for its all-male gastronomic societies (*sociedades populares/cofradías*), where members do the cooking in turn. In addition to the Basque Country, Asturias, Catalonia and Galicia are also noted for the excellence of their cuisine.

Spain isn't noted for its international cuisine, although there's an abundance of good foreign restaurants in Spanish cities and resort areas. There's also a plethora of fast food outlets such as hamburger joints (*hamburgueserías*) and British 'restaurants' that serve 'full English breakfasts all day', although you're unlikely to find any in rural areas. Foreign restaurants cater mostly to foreigners (with menus in Spanish, English or German), as the Spanish generally prefer to stick to Spanish cuisine. Although Spanish food can sometimes be terrible, particularly in some tourist establishments on the *costas*, it usually offers better value-for-money (and often better quality) than foreign cuisine. In general, it's best to follow the locals' example. In resorts, restaurants that open year round may offer better service and value for money than seasonal and beachside restaurants catering primarily to tourists.

Spain's most famous dishes include *gazpacho* (cold tomato, cucumber and onion soup from Andalusia, although the recipe varies depending on the region), *paella* (a seafood saffron rice dish originally from Valencia), and *tortilla española* (Spanish omelette from Castile), found on tourist menus throughout Spain. However, there's much more to Spanish cooking than a few stereotypes and the country boasts many other delicacies, including roast suckling pig (*cochinillo asado*) and lamb (*cordero asado*); superb casseroles and stews such as *cocido madrileño* made from salt pork, beef and stewing hen; 'exotic' dishes such as bull's tail (*rabo de toro estofado*) cooked in a sauce of onions and tomatoes and mouth-watering game such as partridge braised with ham, tomatoes, wine and anchovies (*perdices al torero*). Spain also has a wide variety of desserts (*postres*), although in budget establishments dessert may consist of fresh fruit or the Spanish 'flan' (*créme caramel* or *crema catalana*) only.

The Arab habit of adding fruit and nuts to meat and fish dishes is common in Spain, as are unusual combinations of meat, fish and fowl. Meat is usually excellent throughout Spain, particularly the pork and chicken (often free-range). When ordering steak you should specify how you want it cooked, i.e. **very** rare (*vuelta y vuelta*, literally 'turned'), rare (*poco hecho*), medium (*hecho*) or well done (*muy hecho*). Vegetarians are endangered species in Spain, where there are few vegetarian restaurants (usually run by foreigners) outside the major cities. However there's something vegetarian on most menus and many foreign restaurants serve vegetarian dishes. **Note that many soups and vegetable dishes in Spain contain bacon, ham or sausage and food is often cooked in pork fat.** Your safest bet is salad and eggs, although if you eat fish you will have an abundance of dishes to choose from.

Spain is noted for the quality and variety of its fish (*pescados*) and shellfish (*mariscos*), and fish lovers will think they've died and gone to heaven. Seafood is excellent throughout Spain, even in Madrid and other inland cities, although it's best in the north (particularly Galicia) and the south-west region of Andalusia. However, fish and seafood is rarely cheap and in up-market restaurants can be expensive (fish is usually priced per 100g). In coastal areas, there are numerous seafood restaurants (*marisquerías*) exclusively serving fish and other seafood, and unpretentious open-air, beach restaurants such as *merenderos* or *chiringuitos* serving inexpensive fried fish and chips (although some are sophisticated and expensive). Good fish restaurants often keep a variety of live fish and shellfish in tanks from which you can choose your meal.

The most common seafood dish is *paella*, usually eaten by Spaniards only at lunchtime, and best (and most authentic) in Valencia where it originated. The quality and variety of seafood is unrivalled and includes sea bream, grouper, trout, tuna, salmon, swordfish, turbot, angler fish, sea bass, hake, eels, cod, squid, king crabs, spider crabs, jumbo shrimp, scallops, mussels, lobster, cockles, oysters, prawns, crayfish, octopus, cuttlefish, clams and the most prized of all shellfish, *percebes* (goose barnacles), costing up to €100 a kilo.

# Menus

Menus (*el menú* or *la carta*) are usually written in two or three languages in resorts and some cities, e.g. Spanish plus English and/or German, although in Barcelona they may be written only in Catalan, particularly in high-class establishments. All restaurants must offer a menu of the day or house menu (*menú del día, cubierto* or *menú de la casa*) at lunchtime at 80 per cent of the price each course would cost separately. The house menu is usually written on a blackboard outside restaurants and may not be listed on the menu inside. It usually consists of three courses (e.g. starter, main course with vegetables and a sweet) and may include a glass or small carafe of house wine and bread, although these are usually charged extra. Many restaurants serve a selection of *tapas* before the first course as part of a set menu. Menus usually cost from €7 in small restaurants, *bodegas* and bars, up to €20 or more in high class restaurants. Many restaurants have a €15 set menu and some also have a €30 set menu. Note that prices, quality and the choice of dishes on a set menu vary enormously. In resort areas and major cities, many establishments offer tourist menus (*menú turístico*), with a choice of set meals, including a quarter to half a litre of wine or a beer, service and other charges. Many restaurants, particularly those catering to foreign residents and tourists in resort areas, provide special menus at Christmas and New Year.

# Wine

Wine (*vino*) is inexpensive in Spanish restaurants by northern European standards and costs from just €3 for a bottle (*botella*) or carafe (*garafa*) of house wine (*vino de la casa*) in a modest establishment. However, the price increases rapidly as you go up market, although a good bottle can be purchased in most quality restaurants for €9 (the mark up on wines in Spain is usually around 100 per cent of the supermarket price and can be as low as 50 per cent). Be wary of ordering a bottle of wine in a tourist area unless you've checked the price on the wine list, as rip-offs on wine (and food) are common in some places. Wine is sometimes included in set menus, when two people may receive a bottle between them and one person a half bottle (*media botella*) or a quarter to half a litre. Most house whites and rosés are drinkable and may be produced locally. However, the quality of house red wine varies considerably from good to terrible.

Buying wine by the glass instead of a bottle can be quite expensive at between €1 and €2 a glass, especially considering it's usually cheap 'plonk' which costs €1 to €2 a bottle (or carton) in a supermarket. If you drink more than a few glasses you're better of ordering a bottle. In an inexpensive rural establishment, there may be no choice of wine and you're served whatever comes out of the barrel. If you just order *vino* it's understood to mean red wine, which is often served chilled and drunk with everything from red meat to fish. Spaniards don't drink a lot of alcohol with their meals and many prefer mineral water (*agua mineral*) or lemonade. If you want tap water ask for *agua del grifo* or *agua corriente*.

## Ratings & Prices

Spanish restaurants are officially rated by their number of forks, from one to five, with five denoting the top grade, although they aren't necessarily a sign of quality cooking, but facilities, décor, length of menu and price. Prices per head range from €6 in the cheapest bar-restaurants to around €15 in a two or three-fork restaurant, where two people can dine well for around €20 to €30, including a bottle of good wine. The best value is often found in inexpensive, unpretentious restaurants, particularly the 'dining rooms' (*comedores*) of bars, *pensiones* and *fondas* (see page 362), many of which may serve food only at lunchtime.

There are also budget *cafeterías* (often self-service) in major cities and resort areas graded with one to three cups depending on their facilities. The emphasis is usually on bland 'international' fare, although many serve traditional Spanish dishes and they provide unbeatable value for money, e.g. €5 for all you can eat. *Cafeterías* also offer set meals called *platos combinados* (literally 'combination plates'), which are also available in many bars and inexpensive restaurants, consisting of one-course meals such as egg and chips, steak and/or fish with chips, and squid (*calamares*) and salad. *Platos combinados* usually include bread and possibly a drink and cost from €3 to €6. There are many excellent pizza places in resort areas (e.g. Telepizza), where scrumptious 'real' pizzas are made in proper wood-burning ovens and usually cost around €5 to €12.

## SOCIAL CLUBS

There's a wealth of expatriate clubs and organisations in major cities and resort areas catering for all nationalities. In addition to a multitude of social, sports and special interest clubs, there are also branches of international clubs in most major towns, including Ambassador Clubs, American Women's and Men's Clubs, Anglo-Spanish

Clubs, Business Clubs, International Men's and Women's Clubs, Kiwani Clubs, Lion and Lioness Clubs, and Rotary Clubs. Club listings and announcements are made in English-language and other expatriate publications in resort areas, and many embassies and consulates in Spain maintain lists. Many clubs support local charities.

Most clubs organise a variety of activities and pastimes such as chess, bridge and whist evenings; sports activities and outings; art, music, theatre, cinema and local history outings; informal dances and various other social events. Some clubs have their own facilities such as a clubhouse, library, bar and restaurant. Annual membership fees vary considerably, e.g. from €10 to €100, and some offer daily, weekly and monthly membership for visitors. Many clubs provide important information for new arrivals, organise free or inexpensive Spanish language lessons, and provide foreign newspapers to keep members in touch with home.

Joining a local club is one of the best ways for newcomers to meet people and make friends in Spain. If you want to integrate into your local community or Spanish society in general, one of the best ways is to join a local Spanish club. Most towns also have social centres for retired people (*jubilados*) and pensioners' clubs (*club de pensionistas*) open to residents with a pensioner's card (*tarjeta de pensionista*), available from your local town hall.

# THEATRE, OPERA & BALLET

The vast majority of theatres in Spain are in Madrid and Barcelona, although there has been a huge theatre building programme throughout the country in the last decade and many smaller towns now have municipal-sponsored theatres (*teatros municipales*) housed in cultural centres. The main theatres in Madrid include the *Teatro de Zarzuela*, *Teatro Español*, *Teatro de la Comedia*, *Centro Dramático Nacional*, *Teatro María Guerrero*, *Centro de Nueva Tendencias Escénicas*, and the *Compañía Nacional de Teatro Clásico*, a number of which are sponsored by the state or city. Spain has a long tradition of drama and a number of prolific playwrights such as Lope de Vega (who wrote or co-wrote almost 2,000 plays) and Tirso de Molina (who created Don Juan). Classical and contemporary Spanish and foreign plays are performed throughout Spain and experimental theatre is particularly popular in Catalonia.

Theatre tickets usually range from €5 and €40, but are often reduced on certain days, e.g. Wednesdays or Thursdays. Some offer student discounts. There are often two performances in the same evening at 7 or 7.30pm and 10 or 10.30pm and 'matinee' (afternoon) performances on Saturdays, Sundays and public holidays, starting around 4.30pm. In summer, outdoor plays are performed in many cities, including free sponsored plays. There are also a number of English-language amateur dramatics' groups in the major cities and resort towns, performing in local theatres and 'supper theatre' in restaurants.

Opera is popular in Spain which has produced some of the world's leading performers, including Victoria de los Angeles, Teresa Berganza, Montserrat Caballé, José Carreras, Plácido Domingo and Alfredo Kraus. Regular performances are held in Madrid, Barcelona, Oviedo, Bilbao and other cities, although only Barcelona has a 'proper' opera house, the *Gran Teatro del Liceu* (1847), considered second worldwide only to *La Scala* in Milan. The season in Barcelona lasts from September to July.

Madrid's *Teatro Real* was reopened as the *Teatro de la Opera* in 1992 and stages opera, orchestral music, ballet and *Zarzuela* (a form of light opera or comic operetta in the style of Gilbert & Sullivan). The National Ballet of Spain performs at the *Teatro de la Zarzuela* or the *Teatro Monumental* in Madrid, and the *Teatro de la Zarzuela* in Madrid stages opera from January to July and ballet from December to January. Seville also has a concert hall (*Teatro de la Maestranza*) with 1,800 seats and caters for classical music and opera.

# TOURIST OFFICES

Tourism is promoted at four levels in Spain: by the national Ministry of Industry, Tourism and Commerce (Ministerio de Industria, Turismo y Comercio) through overseas Spanish National Tourist Offices/SNTO (Oficinas Nacionales de España de Turismo) known as TurEspaña (⌨ www.spain.info), by regional and provincial governments, and by local municipalities. TurEspaña maintains offices in Argentina, Austria, Australia, Belgium, Brazil, Canada, Denmark, Finland, France, Germany, Italy, Japan, Mexico, the Netherlands, Norway, Portugal, Singapore, Sweden, Switzerland, the UK and the US. There are tourist offices (*oficinas de turismo*) in all major cities and resort towns in Spain, which are operated by TurEspaña in major cities and by provincial governments and local municipalities in other cities and towns. In cities, there's usually a variety of tourist information outlets, including tourist offices at airports and railway stations, and even street tourist guides during the peak season in some cities.

The quality of information dispensed by local tourist offices varies enormously, as do office opening hours. Offices in resort towns are usually open from 9am to around 1pm and from 4 to around 7.30pm from Mondays to Fridays, and 9am to 1pm on Saturdays. In major cities, offices are open continuously, e.g. from 9am to around 7.30pm, Mondays to Fridays. Offices are usually closed on Sundays. Business hours vary depending on the time of year and are reduced in winter (except in ski resorts).

National, regional and local authorities publish a wealth of free brochures, pamphlets and beautifully detailed maps in many languages, available from TurEspaña offices worldwide and local tourist offices in Spain. TurEspaña publish a free map (*mapa de comunicacions*) of Spain and regional tourist authorities produce a local calendar of events. It's often advisable to collect information before arriving in Spain, as local tourist offices often run out, and local and regional tourist offices don't provide information about places outside their area. Staff at tourist offices in major towns and resorts speak English and can recommend qualified multi-lingual guides. Note that Spanish tourist offices don't usually make hotel bookings, although there are hotel reservation offices at international airports and main railway stations in major cities.

Tourist information is also available by telephone (*teléfono de información turística*) from 8am to 10pm seven days a week (☎ 901-300 600), with information available in English, French, German and Spanish (calls are charged at the reduced rate). You can write to local tourist offices in Spain for information, a list of which is available from TurEspaña offices and their website. When writing requesting information you should include an international reply coupon and shouldn't expect a personal reply in English, although most office staff will understand a letter written in English. Many tourist offices now have email facilities.

# 16.

# SPORTS

Sports facilities in Spain vary considerably depending on the town or area and are usually excellent in major cities and resort areas, although sparse in rural areas. Many towns have municipal, all-weather sports complexes (*polideportivos*) and there's a wealth of private country clubs, sports centres and gymnasiums in cities and resort areas, most of which allow guests to use their facilities. All community developments in resort areas have swimming pools and many also have communal tennis courts and other sports facilities. The cost of participation in most sports in Spain is reasonable and less than in most other European Union (EU) countries, with annual membership of a sports or country club usually between €300 and €600 a year. Most towns have sports centres and organise a wealth of sports activities and courses at all levels during the summer and other school holidays. Fees are low and are usually between €1.50 and €3 a session or €9 to €18 a month (or you can pay annually).

Sports facilities in Spain have been greatly improved in the last decade and now rival most other European countries. Many improvements have been tourist-driven, particularly regarding golf, skiing and watersports. Most Spaniards aren't great sports participants and are more at home watching a football or basketball match on television (TV) in a bar than working up a sweat. In general, Spaniards are more laid-back in their attitude towards sports and pastimes and they don't work as fervently as northern Europeans and North Americans to enjoy themselves.

Spain's athletes are prominent in many world sports, including soccer, basketball, tennis, golf, cycling and athletics. Other popular sports include swimming, handball, fishing, hiking, horse riding, *jai-alai*, *boules*, hunting, motor sports, volleyball and squash. Spain is a Mecca for watersports enthusiasts and sailing, waterskiing and windsurfing have a large following, as do aerial sports. However, football is the national sport and top teams such as Real Madrid and Barcelona enjoy a vast following throughout the world.

General information about sports facilities and events can be obtained from TurEspaña (see page 392), while local information is available from regional, provincial and local tourist offices, all of which publish information regarding sports events and local sports venues. Many towns also publish an annual or monthly sports programme (*programa de actividades deportivas*). Numerous newspapers and magazines devoted to sport are published in Spain, including three daily sports newspapers in Barcelona alone, although they tend to concentrate mostly on football. **Note that a player's licence (which covers all sporting accidents) is necessary to participate in competitive sports in Spain.** Information about particular sports can be obtained from the Spanish Sports Council (*Consejo Superior de Deportes*), Avda Martín Fierro s/n, 28040 Madrid (☎ 915-896 700, 💻 www.csd.mec.es).

# AERIAL SPORTS

Spain is an outstanding country for all aerial sports, including light-aircraft flying, gliding, hang-gliding, paragliding, parachuting, sky-diving, ballooning and microlighting. Spain's many mountain ranges, particularly the Pyrenees, are excellent venues for aerial sports such as hang-gliding and paragliding, due to the strong air currents that allow pilots to stay aloft for hours. Paragliding, which entails jumping off a steep mountain slope with a parachute, is technically easier than hang-gliding. The Pyrenees are reckoned to be the best mountains in Europe for hang-gliding and paragliding, with their warm summers and wide valleys. Participants must complete an approved course of instruction, after which they receive a proficiency certificate and are permitted to go solo. Competitions are held throughout the country, often with cash prizes. If you employ an instructor for any aerial sport, ensure that they're qualified.

A flight in a balloon is a marvellous experience, although there's no guarantee of distance or duration and trips are dependent on wind conditions and the skill of your pilot. A flight usually costs around €150 (often including food and champagne) and is made at dawn or in the evening when the air is more stable. There are balloon meetings and competitions throughout Spain, particularly in summer. It is, however, an expensive sport and participation is generally limited to the wealthy. A list of ballooning clubs is available from TurEspaña and local tourist offices (see page 392).

There are flying clubs at most airfields in Spain, where light aircraft and gliders can be rented. Parachuting and free-fall parachuting (sky-diving) flights can also be made from many private airfields. The south of Spain is an excellent place to learn to fly, as it's rarely interrupted by bad weather. The latest craze to have taken off in Spain is microlight (or ultralight) flying, which is a low-flying go-cart with a hang glider on top and a motorised tricycle below, and one of the cheapest and most enjoyable ways to experience real flying. For information about aerial sports contact the Real Federación Aeronáutica Española, Carretera de la Fortuna s/n, 28044 Madrid (☎ 915-082 950, 💻 www.rfae.org), whose website has numerous links to aerial associations in Spain. A useful publication about aerial and other so-called 'active' sports is *Guía de Turismo Activo de España* (El País Aguilar), which includes listings of activities and companies around Spain. The Aventure Tourism website is also a useful source of information (💻 www.turismo aventura.com).

**Every year several people are killed and numerous injured in Spain as a consequence of taking part in a dangerous sport without adequate training or safety measures. Before taking up any dangerous sport, you're advised to make sure that you have adequate health, accident and life insurance and that your affairs are in order. You should also check the credentials of the company whose services you use.**

# CYCLING

Spain is one of the foremost cycling countries in Europe, where cycling is a serious sport and a relaxing pastime. Bicycles (*bicicletas*) are inexpensive in Spain, where you can buy a men's 21-speed mountain bicycle (*bicicleta de montaña*) for as little as €250 from a supermarket. Bicycles should be fitted with an anti-theft device such as a steel cable or chain with a lock. If your bicycle is stolen, report it to the local police. Bicycles can be rented in major cities and most resorts by the hour or day (e.g. €5 to €10). Not surprisingly in a country with so many hills, mountain biking is a popular sport and bikes can be rented in many mountain resorts and can even be taken on specially-adapted chair lifts to the tops of mountains.

Cycling in Madrid and other cities can be dangerous and isn't recommended (if you cycle in cities, you should wear a smog mask, a crash helmet and a crucifix). In addition to the hazards of traffic and pollution in towns and cities, cyclists must contend with the often debilitating heat, interminable hills and poor roads in many areas. However, cycling is usually pleasant in coastal areas and the flatlands outside high summer. Cyclists must use cycle lanes where provided (although there are few in Spain) and mustn't cycle in bus lanes or on footpaths. Spanish motorists usually give cyclists a wide berth when overtaking (but don't count on it), although tourists aren't always so generous, particularly those towing caravans.

It isn't necessary to wear expensive sports clothing when cycling, although a bike helmet is advisable for all riders. Head injuries are the main cause of death in bicycle accidents, most of which don't involve accidents with automobiles, but are a result of colliding with fixed objects or falls. Always buy a quality helmet that has been approved and subjected to rigorous testing. Reflective clothing is also advisable. Take **particular** care on busy roads and don't allow children onto public roads until they're competent riders.

Cycling is a popular competitive sport in Spain where over 5,000 annual cycling races and events are staged at all levels throughout the country. These include many professional races such as the tour of Spain (*Vuelta de España* – 🖳 www.lavuelta.com – in English, French and Spanish), the third most important world cycle race after the tours of France and Italy, is in its 60th year and is held over three weeks in September/October. Other national races include the tour of Andalusia and the tour of the Basque Lands. Spain has a number of top cycling teams, including Euskaltel-Euskadi and Illes Balears.

Madrid (as well as most other large towns and cities) has an annual bicycle *fiesta* in May when the roads are closed to vehicles and taken over by some 300,000 to 400,000 cyclists of all ages. There are road and track cycling clubs throughout Spain, although aspiring champions should bear in mind that they must be extremely fit to join organised trips over mountain routes. For information about clubs and competitions contact the Spanish Cycling Federation (Federación Española de Ciclismo), C/de Ferraz, 16-5º, 28008 Madrid (☎ 915-400 841, 🖳 www.rfec.com). Many companies organise cycling holidays in Spain, including TurEspaña (see page 392), Spain's national tourist board. Useful books describing many beautiful cycle routes in Spain are *España en Bici* by Paco Tortosa and María del Mar Fornés (RBA), *Cycle Touring in Spain* by Harry Dowdell (Cicerone Press) and *The Trailrider Guide: Spain: Single Track Mountain Biking* by Nathan James and Linsey Stroud (Revolution Publishing).

# FISHING

Spain is a paradise for fishermen and with 2,119km (1,317mi) of mainland coastline, over 75,000km (46,000mi) of rivers and thousands of lakes and reservoirs; it can keep even the keenest of anglers busy for a few weeks. There's excellent fishing (*pesca*) in inland waterways, including rivers, lakes and reservoirs, where a permit (*permiso de pesca*) is required. Permits are issued by the local provincial office of the Ministry of the Environment (Ministerio de Medio Ambiente, ☎ 915-976 000, 🖳 www.mma.es).

The fishing season varies depending on the particular species of fish, e.g. the trout season starts in March and the salmon season commences on the first Sunday in March. The salmon season closes on the second Sunday in July and the trout season at the end of August or September. On most rivers there are restrictions on the number of licences issued each day and on the size of fish (and often the number) that may be caught, and the bait and technique that can be employed. The most common freshwater fish include various species of trout, barbel, pike, carp, bogue, black bass, mullet, sturgeon, bream, tench and perch. Salmon are found in streams and rivers in the Cantabrian range and in Galicia, and trout are common in the upper reaches of rivers throughout Spain. Information about local fishing areas and fishing permits is available from local town halls and tourist offices. Tourist offices may also provide a fishing map (*Mapa de Pesca Fluvial*) showing where to fish and what you may catch, plus details of seasons and licences.

Sea fishing is also popular and you can fish without a licence from anywhere along Spain's coastline or rent a boat and go out to sea. Many Spaniards fish from beaches in winter. Common saltwater fish include grouper, sea-bream, mackerel, cod, tuna, mullet, bonito, swordfish and various species of shark, although sea fishing is declining in popularity, as Spanish waters are largely fished out (particularly the Mediterranean). Boat rental, perhaps with a local fisherman as a guide, and deep-sea fishing trips can be arranged throughout Spain. Sea fishing is prohibited from one hour after sunset until one hour before dawn and deep-sea fishermen need a licence from the provincial Comandancias de Marina. There are numerous regional and local fishing clubs throughout Spain.

# FOOTBALL

Football (*fútbol*), or soccer, is Spain's national sport and easily the country's most important participant and spectator sport. Spanish football fans are among the most dedicated and fervent in Europe and are matched in their fanaticism only by the Italians. Every town in Spain has a football pitch and team, and indoor football (*fútbol sala*) is also played in sports centres throughout the country. Spanish children learn to play football almost as soon as they can walk, with the most promising players being snapped up by the major clubs and coached from an early age in football schools.

Not surprisingly, Spain has many sports newspapers devoted almost exclusively to football, where every aspect of the players' public and private lives are analysed and debated. Countless TV minutes are dedicated to analysing every other move or even word uttered by a football player or manager. All news bulletins include an item on football and the 'sports section' in most news is merely a euphemism for football. Only when Spain achieves a real sporting prowess in a sport other than football (such as winning the Davies Cup in tennis) does football take a back seat!

The Spanish league is one of the most competitive in Europe and Spanish teams have enjoyed considerable success in European competitions, although the glory days of Real Madrid and Barcelona in the '50s and '60s are long gone and the successes of Spanish clubs have been overshadowed in recent years by the Italians. Spain has never been able to repeat its clubs' successes at international level and the

Spanish national team is a constant source of disappointment – Spain only won one game in the European Cup and in late 2005 was struggling to qualify for Germany 2006. The progress of the national team hasn't been helped by the influx of foreign stars in recent years (some 150 play in the first division alone), which makes it difficult for promising young Spanish players to get a game.

The Spanish league is divided into three main divisions, two of which are sub-divided into regional competitions. Division 1 (with 22 teams) and division 2a are national leagues. Division 2b is divided into four regional leagues (I central, II north, III east and IV south) and division 3 consists of local groups regionalised for financial reasons. Spanish clubs also compete in the Spanish Cup (*Copa del Rey*) and the European Cup (UEFA). The Spanish football season runs from September to June, with a break from Christmas eve until the end of January. Matches are usually played on Sundays (occasionally Saturdays), starting at 5pm, and evening matches (many televised) are also held most weeks starting as late as 9.30pm. Generally, you must queue to buy tickets on match days, although tickets for major games are sold in advance at ticket agencies in El Corte Inglés shops around the country. Tickets for the top matches start at around €10 (standing) and go up to €100 or more for seats. Hooliganism and violence are rare at Spanish football grounds and families can safely take their children to matches, although incidents of violence are on the increase, particularly at 'high-risk' matches, e.g. between Real Madrid and Barcelona.

There's a huge gulf between the top Spanish clubs and the rest regarding every aspect of the game, not least their stadiums. Real Madrid and Barcelona (Barça) in particular stand head and shoulders above the rest. Real Madrid play at the imposing 130,000-seat Santiago Bernabeu stadium, while Barcelona's home is the equally impressive 120,000-seat Nou Camp stadium. Outside the top handful of clubs, attendances at most first division matches are low. A number of division one matches are shown live on TV each week, invariably involving either (or both) Real Madrid or Barcelona, and are screened in bars throughout Spain. Gambling on football is also popular and is organised through a tote system called the *Quiniela*. Spanish football is dominated by arch rivals Real Madrid with its 'Galactic Team' of Beckham, Figo, Ronaldo and Zidane, and Barcelona (league winners in 2005), with few other teams getting a look in. Other top teams include Valencia (winners of the Spanish League and UEFA Champions in 2004), Deportivo La Coruña and Real Sociedad.

In the early '90s, Spanish football went through one of the worst periods in its history. However, like British premiership and Italian clubs, the finances of many clubs have been rescued by the vast revenue from televised football matches, although many clubs are still deep in debt. Top clubs demand instant success and tend to swap their coaches almost as often as their players change their shirts. Real Madrid has had around ten coaches in the last decade, which looks like secure employment when compared with Atlético Madrid's almost 30 coaches in the same period! Barcelona has also had its fair share of managers in the last few decades.

Spanish football is renowned for its gifted players and fluent attacking style, although there are a surprising number of sterile one-sided games, lacking in excitement and passion, when teams appear paralysed by the fear of losing. Spanish football is equally noted for its cynical 'gamesmanship' (i.e. cheating) which includes every underhand trick in the book, e.g. obstruction, body-checking, shirt-pulling, elbowing, diving, 'accidental' tripping and collisions, and faked injuries, all of which

Spanish players have perfected. Players often do their utmost to get opposing players booked or sent off.

The cheats are aided and abetted by Spanish referees, who can be wildly inconsistent while handing out red and yellow cards with abandon or losing control of matches altogether, and allowing players to get away with anything short of murder. However, their job isn't helped by players diving to the ground whenever an opposing player comes within tackling distance, although referees are guilty of falling for the most outrageous play-acting, which often leads to penalties and players being sent off. The hapless referees are crucified by TV replays, which gleefully highlight their every mistake.

# GOLF

Golf is one of the fastest growing sports in Spain (over 200,000 golfers are registered with the national federation) and is becoming increasingly popular with the Spanish, although it's still regarded by many as an elite game for rich businessmen, foreign tourists (foreigners comprise around 75 per cent of players on the Costa del Sol) and the elderly in many parts of Spain. Spain has over 250 courses with many more planned. Most courses are concentrated in the main tourist areas and islands, and include Europe's biggest concentration of golf courses along the western Costa del Sol from Malaga to Cadiz, dubbed the 'Costa del Golf'. With the exception of a few months in the summer when it's too hot, southern Spain has the perfect climate for golf, particularly during the winter. There's even a floodlit golf course for insomniacs on the Costa del Sol (the *Dama de Noche*) open 24-hours a day (a minimum of ten golfers are needed to book the course at night).

Spanish golf courses are invariably excellent and beautifully maintained. Most courses are located in picturesque settings (sea, mountain and forest), many designed by famous designers such as Robert Trent Jones, Jack Nicolas and Severiano Ballesteros and linked with real estate development. Properties on or near golf clubs (often including 'free' life membership) are popular with foreigners seeking a permanent or second home in Spain, and are among the cheapest golf properties in Europe. Some golf clubs offer golf shares for around €10,000 or €20,000, usually providing members with a number of free rounds or even free golf for life. Many golf clubs are combined with country or sports clubs and offer a wide range of sports and social facilities, including swimming pools, tennis, squash, gymnasium, snooker/pool, and a bar and restaurant.

Spain has courses to suit all standards, although there are few inexpensive public courses and it's an expensive sport. Golf used to be relatively inexpensive, but has become much dearer in recent years, although fees remain lower than in many other European countries. Most courses are owned by syndicates and have annual membership fees of from around €1,500 for a single person (couples €2,000 to €3,000) and seasonal and daily fees for non-members. Most clubs don't have a waiting list for new members or strict handicap requirements for non-members, although they usually insist on golfers wearing suitable attire.

Green fees vary depending on the club and the season, and on the Costa del Sol are usually from around €75 in winter and from €50 in summer for 18 holes. In the north of Spain, fees may be cheaper in winter than in the summer or remain the same all year round. Fees at an exclusive club such as Valderrama (Cadiz) are as high as €275 a round and you may be restricted to teeing off only at certain times, e.g. between noon and 2pm. Green fees are often reduced early in the morning, e.g. for rounds starting within one hour of opening or anytime before noon, and late in the afternoon, e.g. between 3 and 5pm. Many clubs offer reductions to couples, senior citizens and groups and have weekly rates. Note, however, that many clubs restrict non-members to off-peak times and it's often difficult for non-members to get a game at weekends and during school holidays. Playing with a member usually entitles guests to a reduction on green fees. **Third party accident insurance is obligatory and costs around €2 a day.**

You can rent golf clubs (from around €15), golf trolleys/carts (from around €5 a round or €15 for an electric trolley) and electric golf buggies (€25 to €35 a round) at all clubs. The golf cart has virtually made the caddie extinct and some courses are built in difficult terrain where it's almost mandatory to use a buggy. Some clubs include the price of a buggy in the green fees. Most clubs have a pro shop with a club professional, driving ranges, practice putting and pitching greens, and offer individual and group instruction and a full programme of competitions. Clubs and a growing number of golf schools hold regular courses for all standards from beginner to expert. Clubs are usually members of the Royal Spanish Golf Federation (Real Federación Española de Golf), C/Provisional Arroyo del Fresno Dos, 5, 28035 Madrid (☎ 915-552 682, 💻 www.golfspainfederacion.com), who produce a detailed map of Spanish golf courses listing their vital statistics and an annual competition calendar (*Calendario Oficial de Competiciones*).

Spain hosts more regular PGA European Tour events than any other country, mostly at the beginning and end of the season when the weather in northern Europe is unreliable. Valderrama hosts the Volvo Masters Tournament in autumn, the last and richest event in Europe. Spain is the second strongest European golfing country after the UK, although it has had to beat off a strong challenge from Sweden. In the last few decades, it has produced many top male professional golfers, including Severiano Ballesteros, José María Olazábel, Miguel Angel Jiménez, Manuel Piñero, José María Cañizares, Miguel Angel Martín, Ignacio Garrido, Diego Borrego, José Rivero and their latest superstar Sergio García, plus a number of top women golfers.

Golf holidays are popular in Spain and a major source of revenue for clubs, most of which welcome visitors and often offer special rates. Some hotels cater almost exclusively for golfers and offer golf holiday packages inclusive of green fees (or reduced green fees). A guide to Spanish golf courses (*Guía de Golf-España*) is available from tourist offices and many regions and provinces publish golf guides (*Golf Guía Práctica*) with maps. A number of free and subscription golf magazines are published in Spain, most with articles printed in Spanish and English, including *Andalucía Golf, Costa del Sol Golf News* and *Sun Golf*. There are numerous websites dedicated to golf in Spain, including Golf in Spain (in English, German and Spanish) which specialises in golf holidays and where you can reserve golf rounds online (💻 www.golfin spain.com). A useful guide for golfers on the Costa del Sol is the *Costa del Sol Coursefinder* with details for all the courses in the area and how to get to them. The guide can be ordered from Costa del Sol Golf News (☎ Spain 952-586 889, ✉ frank@ costadelsolgolfnews.com).

# HIKING

Spain has some of the finest hiking (*excursiones*) areas in Europe and few countries can offer its combination of good weather and spectacular, unspoilt countryside. Spain is unrivalled in Europe for its diversity of landscape, profusion of flora and fauna, and its variety of native animals and birds, many unique. Serious hikers can enjoy mountain walking in some of the most spectacular scenery in Europe. Spring and autumn are the best seasons for hiking in most of Spain, when the weather generally isn't too hot or too cold, although winter is the best time in the south of Spain. **Note, however, that some paths can be extremely dangerous in winter and are only safe in summer.**

Hiking isn't a popular sport among the Spanish, although Spain is a favourite destination for foreign hikers. It has a wealth of hiking areas, including the Basque Country, Cantabria and Asturias in the north (an area often described as 'Switzerland by the sea' containing the *Picos de Europa*), the Basque mountains and the Cantabrian Cordillera – all areas of outstanding beauty. The Pyrenees and the Ebro region are Spain's most popular and accessible hiking regions, assisted by the abundance of winter sports resorts and ski-lifts that whisk you to the mountain tops. The north of Spain has many outstanding hiking routes, the most famous of which is the old 'pilgrim's way' from Le Puy in France to Santiago de Compostela in Galicia, designated a *Grande Randonnée* (GR65) by the French. It offers some of the most beautiful scenery in Spain and takes two or more months to complete the whole route, although most hikers complete a small section at a time. A new hiking route (GR7) has been planned and signposted running from Tarifa (Cadiz) through natural areas in Andalucía, Murcia and Valencia on its way to Greece some 2,100km (1,300mi) away.

In central Spain, outstanding hiking areas include the Gredos and Guadarrama Sierras, the Alcarria region, the Sierra of southern Salamanca, the Las Hurdes of northern Extremadura, El Bierzo of western León and the Sierra Morena in the south. Andalusia also has an abundance of spectacular hiking areas, including the Alpujarras and the Sierra Nevada in Granada, the Sierra de Grazalema running from Cadiz to Malaga, and the Serranía de Ronda. Spain has nine national parks (four in the Canary Islands), including the Coto de Doñana near Cadiz, Europe's largest nature reserve, and numerous other areas designated as natural parks. For information contact the Ministry of the Environment (Ministerio de Medio Ambiente, ☎ 915-976 000, 💻 www.mma.es).

There are tens of thousands of kilometres of official footpaths throughout Spain, most of which are marked with parallel red and white stripes painted on rocks and trees, and accompanied by arrows when the direction changes. The sign of two crossed lines indicates that you should **not** go in that direction. Where paths cross they're shown by different colours, e.g. green and yellow instead of red and white. The best hiking maps are published by the Instituto Geográfico Nacional (IGN) and the Servicio Geográfico del Ejército (SGE) in scales of 1:200,000, 1:100,000, 1:50,000 and occasionally 1:25,000. The SGE series are generally considered to be more accurate and up to date than those published by the IGN, although neither is up to the standards of the best American and British maps. Editorial Alpina produces 1:40,000 and 1:25,000 map booklets for the most popular mountain and foothill areas of Spain and the Mapa Topográfico Nacional de España produce a series of 1:50,000 scale maps covering the whole of Spain and showing most footpaths and tracks. Hiking booklets containing suggested walks are published by some regional tourist organisations and maps showing city walks are available in many cities.

In mountain areas, there are over 200 refuge huts (*refugios*) for climbers and hikers, equipped with bunks and a basic kitchen, where overnight accommodation costs as little as €1.50. Some are staffed in spring and summer and provide food, although most are unstaffed and you must therefore carry your own food, sleeping bags, cooking utensils and other essentials. **Many huts are kept locked and enquiries should be made in advance about where to obtain the key.** For information contact the Spanish Mountain Sports Federation (Federación Española de Deportes de Montaña y Escalada/FEDME), C/Floridablanca, 84, 08015 Barcelona (☎ 934-264 267, 💻 www.fedme.es).

# Dangers

Hiking in Spain is no more hazardous than in other countries, although you should be aware of the dangers. Wherever you walk, you must be on the alert for savage dogs. Carry a stick or walking cane to defend yourself (pointing it at a dog is usually enough to prevent it attacking you). Don't venture too far off official paths during the hunting season, when you risk being shot by a trigger-happy hunter. Other 'natural' hazards include encounters with wild animals such as bulls, bears, wild horses, wolves, wildcats, snakes, scorpions, tarantulas and a variety of insects, e.g. mosquitoes, horseflies, ants, wasps and fleas. Your chances of meeting a wild animal or being attacked or bitten are remote, although you should take standard precautions such as checking your clothing and shoes before dressing when camping, wearing protective clothing and using insect repellent. You should also take precautions against the heat and sunstroke and **be careful not to start fires**, the lighting of which is strictly forbidden in most areas of Spain. In September 2005, a campfire started by two foreigners in Sierra Nevada destroyed over 2,200 hectares of unique woodland. If you don't speak Spanish, you should carry a phrase book when hiking in remote areas, as few people speak English (or other foreign languages). Taking a mobile phone with you is also a good idea.

Take care when walking on roads in country areas, as many have loose gravel and stones, on which it's easy to lose your footing. On narrow, winding country roads you should walk on the side of the road which affords the best view of the road ahead, as many roads have blind corners and some drivers keep close to the edge. This is the one exception when it pays to ignore the 'walk facing the traffic rule', but take care to listen for traffic approaching from behind.

A number of books about hiking in Spain are published in English, including *Trekking in Spain* by Marc Dubin (Lonely Planet), *Walking Through Spain* by Robin Neillands (Queen Anne Press) and *Lonely Planet: Walking in Spain* by Miles Roddis (Lonely Planet). There are also many books dedicated to walking in particular regions. TurEspaña (see page 392) publish a booklet, *Rutas de Montaña y Senderismo*, featuring around 50 mountain walks throughout Spain. Hiking tours and holidays are organised for hikers of all ages and fitness levels throughout Spain, and there are expatriate groups of ramblers in resort areas throughout the country. For more information contact the Spanish Mountain Sports Federation (Federación Española de Deportes de Montaña y Escalada/FEDME), C/Floridablanca, 84, 08015 Barcelona (☎ 934-264 267, 🖳 www.fedme.es). See also **Camping & Caravanning** on page 364.

# HUNTING

Hunting (*caza*) is extremely popular in Spain, which has some 35 million hectares of hunting land, including national parks, national hunting reserves, national preserves, and numerous private game reserves. The best hunting areas are the Atlantic coast, the Pyrenees and parts of Andalusia, where big game includes mountain goat (*cabra hispánica*), various species of deer, ibex, roebuck, chamois, stag, wild boar, wolf and big-horned mountain sheep. Certain animals, such as bears and lynx, are in danger of extinction and are officially protected (although people still shoot them!).

The hunting season for all game is strictly defined and there are large fines for anyone caught hunting out of season. The hunting season for small game runs from mid-October to early February and includes grouse, quail, ring dove, turtle dove, red-legged partridge, pheasant, duck, geese, bustard, water fowl, pigeon, hare and rabbit. Like the French and Italians, the Spanish kill thousands of songbirds each year, which are considered a delicacy by many people and are unprotected. There's no tradition of conservation in Spain and most hunters are inclined to shoot anything that moves. Although they won't deliberately shoot, it's advisable to steer clear of the countryside during the hunting season.

There are several kinds of hunting land, ranging from free zones where only a general licence (*permiso de caza*) is necessary, to municipal-owned local reserves, private reserves and national reserves, where a special licence is required. To hunt in a national reserve you need a hunting permit, issued by the provincial or regional office of the Ministry of the Environment (Ministerio de Medio Ambiente, ☎ 915-976 000, 🖳 www.mma.es). Special permission is also required to hunt in a private reserve (*coto privado de caza/coto vedado de caza*). The best way to hunt in Spain is to join a local club. When hunting is prohibited, it's usually denoted by a square sign divided diagonally into black and white halves.

Hunters need a medical certificate obtainable from special clinics (*Centros de Reconocimento Médico para Conductores y Armas todas las Categorías*), a firearms permit (*permiso de armas*) and third party insurance. Guns must be broken and bagged when transported on public land and they may not be used within 500m (1,600ft) of a house or in any urban zone (often ignored). Non-resident hunters may import their own firearms, although they must obtain an import certificate from their local Spanish consulate abroad (take your current firearms certificate to the consulate with a photocopy and your passport). On arrival in Spain, the import certificate and gun must be taken to the local police station, who will issue a Spanish gun permit.

There are a number of magazines devoted to hunting in Spain such as *Trofeo* and *Caza Mayor*, and regional tourist offices publish hunting leaflets and maps. Hunting trips and package holidays for hunters are organised on private estates throughout Spain (the most popular regions are Castille-La Mancha, Andalusia, Extremadura and Castille & Leon). For further information about hunting contact the Spanish Hunting Federation (*Federación Española de Caza*), C/Francos Rodríguez, 70-2°, 28039 Madrid (☎ 913-117 075, ☐ www.fedecaza.com).

# MOUNTAINEERING & ROCK-CLIMBING

Those who find hiking a bit tame may like to try mountaineering, rock-climbing or caving (subterranean mountaineering), all of which are popular in Spain. Sport climbing, where climbs are previously 'equipped' with bolts, is predominant in Spain and is the safest form. Spain is a great country for amateur rock-climbers and mountaineers, and provides a wealth of challenges and some of the best areas in Europe outside the Alps. Around 10,000 caves have been discovered in Spain, many with prehistoric rock paintings and stalactites. **Some caves are long and dangerous and should be explored only with an experienced guide.**

If you're an inexperienced climber, it's advisable to join a club and 'learn the ropes' before heading for the mountains. There are over 750 climbing clubs in Spain, many maintaining their own mountain huts and refuges. Information can be obtained from the Spanish Mountain Sports Federation (Federación Española de Deportes de Montaña y Escalada/FEDME), C/Floridablanca, 84, 08015 Barcelona (☎ 934-264 267, ☐ www.fedme.es). The FEDME also produce 1:50,000 scale maps for mountain areas (see also **Hiking** on page 403 for information regarding maps and refuges). A number of climbing books are published for the most popular regions of Spain. Comprehensive information about all aspects of mountaineering is included on the website ☐ www.spainmountains.com.

It's important to hire a qualified and experienced guide when climbing in an unfamiliar area, who are available through climbing clubs and schools throughout Spain (if you find a guide other than through a recognised club or school, ensure that they're qualified). It's important to note that Spain **doesn't** have the sophisticated mountain rescue services provided in Alpine countries and if you get into trouble you may need to rely on your own resources and those of your companions. Many climbers lose their lives each year, usually through their inexperience and recklessness. **Needless to say, it's extremely foolish, not to mention highly dangerous, to venture into the mountains without proper preparation, excellent physical condition, adequate training, the appropriate equipment AND an experienced guide.**

# RACKET SPORTS

Racket sports are popular in Spain, particularly tennis. Tennis' popularity has grown tremendously in the last few decades and there are now thousands of courts at tennis and country clubs, hotels, urbanisations, and municipal and private sports centres. Courts (many floodlit) have a variety of surfaces, including tennis-quick (fast cement court), clay (*arcilla*), cement (*hormigón*), artificial grass and plexipave. There are also indoor courts in the north of Spain, although these are rare in the south and the islands, where the weather permits outdoor tennis to be played all year round. Many tennis clubs offer a variety of other sports facilities, including swimming pools and a gymnasium or fitness centre.

Most private clubs and hotels allow guests to use their courts, with fees ranging from a around €5 an hour at a hotel to €35 for daily use of tennis courts and other facilities at a private tennis club, perhaps with a lesson and a 'free' meal included. Courts at private clubs cost from around €4 an hour during the day (€6 floodlit) to around €10 an hour (€15 floodlit) for members and up to double for non-members. Most clubs open from early morning until as late as 11pm or midnight. Many urbanisations have private tennis courts which can be used free of charge by residents (they're maintained through community fees), although floodlighting must usually be paid for via a coin meter. Courts are usually available on a first come, first served basis, although there may be a booking system in the summer season when demand is high.

Annual membership of a private club usually costs from €350 to €700 a year in a resort area, although fees can be astronomical at exclusive clubs in major cities. Weekly, monthly and six-monthly membership may also be available. Most clubs have special rates for families, children (e.g. under 18) and possibly senior citizens. Many clubs provide saunas, whirlpools, solariums and swimming pools, and most have a bar and restaurant. All clubs organise regular tournaments and provide professional coaching (individual and group lessons), and many clubs and hotels offer resident tennis schools throughout the year. Individual lessons cost from around €25 an hour. Information regarding competitions and tennis clubs can be obtained from the Royal Spanish Tennis Federation (Real Federación Española de Tenis), Avda Diagonal, 618 –2°B, 08021 Barcelona (☎ 932-005 355, 🖳 www.rfet.es).

Tennis was long regarded as an elite sport in Spain and although it remains so in some private clubs, it's now a sport of the people and one of Spain's most popular participant sports. In the last few years, Spain has become one of the world's strongest tennis countries – Spain is top of the Davis Cup rankings and was the 2004 champion. Its many top male tennis players include Albert Costa, Carlos Moya, Alex Corretja, Juan Carlos Ferrero, Feliciano López and Rafael Nadal, winner of the French Open in 2004. Among the best female players are Conchita Martínez, Virginia Ruano and Magüi Serna. Spain's top female player, Arantxa Sánchez Vicario, retired in 2002. The majority of top players come from Catalonia, the powerhouse of Spanish tennis.

Squash is gaining popularity in Spain with an increasing number of courts in many areas. There are now squash clubs in most large towns and many tennis clubs and sports centres have a number of squash courts. However, the standard is relatively low due to the lack of experienced coaches and top class competition, although it's continually improving. Rackets and balls can be rented from most squash clubs for the American version of squash, called racket ball, which is played in Spain on a squash court. Badminton isn't widely played and facilities are rare, although some sports centres have badminton courts and there are badminton clubs in some areas.

# SKIING

Skiing (*esquí*) is a popular sport in Spain, where it's growing faster than in any other European country. Spain is the second most mountainous country in Europe after Switzerland and has over 30 ski resorts in 14 provinces, where the season extends from December to April or May. The most popular form of skiing is naturally downhill (*esquí de descenso*), although cross-country (*esquí nórdico*) skiers are also catered for in many resorts. With Andorra, Spain offers the cheapest skiing holidays in Western Europe and is becoming increasingly popular with beginners and intermediate skiers wishing to avoid the high cost of skiing in the Alps. However, most of Spain's resorts aren't sophisticated or developed and most don't offer sufficient challenges to satisfy the demands of advanced skiers, particularly regarding off-piste skiing.

The majority of Spain's resorts are located in the Pyrenees in the provinces of Gerona (Nuria and La Molina), Huesca (Astún, El Cadanchú, Cerler, Formigal and Panticosa), and Lérida with Baqueira-Beret (Spain's most fashionable resort, popular with the Spanish royal family, and Europe's most extensive ski resort outside the Alps), and Boí-Taüll, Masella, La Molina and Supert-Espot. Other skiing regions include the Cordillera Cantábrica region (with the resorts of Alto Campoo, San Isidro, Valdezcaray and Valgrande Pajares), the Guadarrama and Gredos mountains north of Madrid (includes La Pinilla, Navacerrada, Puerto de Navacerrada, Valcotos and Valdesquí), Galicia (Cabeza de la Manzaneda), the Sierra de Gúdar (Teruel) and the Sierra Nevada (Granada).

Although encompassing a relatively small area, the Sierra Nevada (also called 'Sol y Nieve') near Granada is Spain's most famous resort. The Sierra Nevada is Europe's most southerly winter sports resort and a common boast is that you can ski there in the morning and swim in the Mediterranean in the afternoon. The resort is centred around the village of Paradollano at 2,100m (6,890ft), with undercover parking for 2,800 vehicles. It has 19 lifts with a capacity of over 32,000 passengers an hour, around 70km (44mi) of pistes and 30 runs, and skiing up to a height of 3,400m (11,155ft). A ski-lift pass (*forfait*) costs €35 per day in high season (public holidays, Christmas and New Year and weekends) and €27 per day in low season. There are also package deals for up to seven consecutive days and a 33 per cent discount for children under 10. Snow is generally guaranteed, as the resort has an extensive network (over 250) of snow-making machines covering many pistes. For reservations and snow and weather conditions contact ☎ 958-249 100 or visit 🖳 www.cetursa.es (information is given in English and Spanish). The Sierra Nevada website (🖳 www. sierranevadaski.com) also provides comprehensive information.

Although cheaper in Spain than many other countries, downhill skiing is an expensive sport, particularly for families. The cost of equipping a family of four is around €1,000 for equipment and clothing. If you're a beginner it's better to rent ski equipment (skis, poles, boots) or buy second-hand equipment until you're addicted, which, if it doesn't frighten you to death, can happen on your first day on the pistes. Most sports shops in Spain have pre-season and end of season sales of ski equipment.

Most resorts have a range of ski lifts, including cable cars, gondolas, chair-lifts and drag-lifts. Pistes in Spain are rated as green (very easy – *muy fácil*), blue (easy – *fácil*), red (difficult – *difícil*) or black (very difficult – *muy difícil*). Adult ski passes cost between €25 and €40 a day or €100 to €150 for five days, depending on the number of lifts provided, with passes for children costing around one-third less. Ski rental costs around €20 a day or €70 for six days and boots around half this (the smaller the resort, generally the lower the cost of ski and boot rental). Most resorts have ski schools and the larger resorts such as Sierra Nevada have Spanish and international ski schools.

Most resorts offer a variety of accommodation, including hotels, self-catering apartments and chalets. Accommodation is more expensive during holiday periods (Christmas, New Year and Easter), when ski-lift queues are interminable and pistes are often overcrowded. These periods (and school holidays in February) are best avoided, particularly as the chance of collisions is greatly enhanced when pistes are overcrowded. Outside these periods and particularly on weekdays, resorts are generally free of crowds and queues.

Mono-skiing and snow-boarding are particularly popular (and generally unrestricted) in Spain and are taught in most resorts. Other activities may include paragliding, parasailing, hang-gliding, ice-skating, snow-shoe walking, sleigh rides, climbing, snow scooters and snowmobiles. Heli-skiing, where helicopters drop skiers off at the top of inaccessible mountains, is possible in Spain. There's also night skiing on floodlit runs in some resorts.

Many winter resorts also provide a variety of mostly indoor activities, including tennis, squash, curling, heated indoor swimming pools, gymnasiums, saunas and solariums. You can find excellent food in the Pyrenees which is influenced by Basque and French cuisine, and skiers are amply provided with mountain restaurants in most resorts. There's also an excellent choice of restaurants and bars resorts, which have the most lively and cheapest (with Andorra) nightlife of any country in Europe. Spaniards aren't such fanatical skiers as other Europeans and many tend to rave all night and ski only in the afternoons, rather than ski from dawn to dusk.

For further information about skiing and other winter sports in Spain contact the Asociación Turística de Estaciones de Esquí y Montaña (ATUDEM), C/Padre Damián, 43 –1ª, Oficina 11, 28036 Madrid (☎ 913-591 557, ▭ www.atudem.org) or the Federación Española de Deportes de Invierno, Avda Madroños, 36, 28043 Madrid (☎ 913-769 930, ▭ www.rfedi.es). The latest weather and snow conditions are broadcast on Spanish television (usually on Thursday or Friday evenings) and radio, published in daily newspapers, and are available direct from resorts (which provide recorded telephone information). TurEspaña (see page 392) publish a number of brochures for winter sports fans, including *Winter Sports in Spain*, *El Turismo de Nieve en España* (in Spanish) and a skiing map (*Mapa de Estaciones de Esquí*).

# SWIMMING

Not surprisingly, swimming (*natación*) is a favourite sport and pastime in Spain, with its glorious weather, 2,000km (1,240mi) of beaches (*playas*), and a profusion of swimming pools (*piscinas*). The beach season in Spain lasts from around Easter to October, although many people sunbathe on beaches all year round in the south of Spain, and the Canaries offer year round beach weather. Most people find the Mediterranean too cold for swimming outside June to September and the Atlantic is generally warm enough only in July and August (in northern and southern Spain). Spanish beaches, almost all of which are public, vary considerably in size, surface and amenities. Surfaces include white, grey, black (in the Canaries) and even red (fine and coarse) sand, shingles, pebbles and stones. Beaches are generally kept clean all year round, particularly in popular resorts, although in some areas they're covered in rubbish and large stones and look more like waste areas than public beaches.

It's difficult to find a totally unspoilt beach, as pollution and high-rise buildings blight most Spanish beaches, although there are a few in remote areas of the mainland and the islands. The best beaches are to be found on the Atlantic coast, on the smaller islands in the Balearics (e.g. Formentera and Menorca) and in the Canaries (e.g. Fuerteventura), where it's even possible to find a deserted beach outside the main tourist season.

Most beaches are extremely crowded in summer and during school holidays, when bodies are packed in like sardines. Beaches away from the main resorts are less crowded and if you have a boat you can visit small coves that are inaccessible from the land. Most beaches have municipal guards, first-aid stations, toilets, showers, bars and restaurants, and some have special paths for those in wheelchairs. Deck chairs, beach-beds and umbrellas can be rented on most beaches, and a wide range of facilities are usually available in summer, including volleyball, pedalos and boats for rent, plus most watersports. **Dogs and camping are forbidden on most beaches.**

Many resorts have made a huge effort to clean up their beaches in recent years and the number of resorts awarded the coveted EU 'blue flag' (*bandera azul*) has risen in all areas. Around 480 blue flags were awarded to Spanish beaches in 2005 (Catalonia and the Comunidad Valenciana have the most), which is around a fifth of the total for the whole of Europe. A list of blue flag beaches and marinas can be found on ▦ www.blueflag.org. **However, some beaches are still dangerously polluted by untreated sewage and industrial waste, and bathing in some areas (particularly close to industrial towns and cities) isn't advisable.** The pollution count (which cannot always be believed) must be displayed at the local town hall: blue = good quality water, green = average, yellow = likely to be temporarily polluted, and red = badly polluted.

Topless and nude bathing is widespread and there are a number of official nudist beaches (*playas naturale/playas de nudistas*) in Spain such as the Costa Natura village situated near Estepona (Malaga) on the Costa del Sol and Almanat near Almayate (Vélez-Malaga), while on the Balearic island of Formentera it's almost standard practice. Topless bathing is permitted on all Spanish beaches, some of which have a section for nude sunbathing. Note, however, that it's possible to get arrested for nude sunbathing on some beaches. Topless bathing is less acceptable at swimming pools, although there are naturist pools in some cities and resorts.

Swimming can be dangerous at times, particularly on the Atlantic coast where some beaches have lethal currents, but even the Mediterranean can be dangerous and several swimmers drown every year. Swimmers should observe all beach warning signs and flags. During the summer months most beaches are supervised by lifeguards who operate a flag system to indicate when swimming is safe; a green flag means that it's safe (calm sea), yellow indicates possible hazardous conditions (take care) and red (danger) means bathing is prohibited. The Red Cross (*Cruz Roja/Puesto de Socorro*) operate first-aid posts on most beaches during the summer season. There are stinging jellyfish in parts of the Mediterranean and they swim near the beaches – 2005 was a particularly prolific year when warm currents swept thousands near Andalusian beaches. A comprehensive description and a rating out of 100 of all Spanish mainland and island beaches can be found on ▦ www.esplaya.com.

Most Spanish towns have a municipal swimming pool (*piscina municipal*), including heated indoor pools (*piscina cubierta*) and outdoor pools (*piscinas al aire libre*). The entrance fee to a pool varies considerably (e.g. €2 to €5 for adults) depending on whether it's an outdoor or indoor pool and its facilities and location. Many pools offer reduced-price, multiple-ticket options. Opening hours may vary day-to-day and most municipal pools don't open during the evenings. Heated indoor pools are open all year round and most outdoor pools are open only during the summer, e.g. from June to September. Public pools in cities are usually overcrowded, particularly at weekends and during school holidays, while pools in hotels and private clubs are less crowded, although more expensive. For further information contact the Spanish Swimming Federation (Federación Española de Natación), C/Juan Esplandiú, 1, 28007 Madrid (☎ 915-572 006, 🖳 www.rfen.es).

There are strict safety regulations at all public and community swimming pools. Regulations usually depend on the depth of a pool, its size (surface area in square metres) and the number of properties it serves, and are established and enforced by local municipalities. They usually include such matters as water quality and treatment, and the provision of showers, non-slip pathways, life belts, first-aid kits and lifeguards. It's usually compulsory to wear a swimming hat in a public or community pool. Usually a lifeguard must be on duty whenever a public or community pool is open (very large pools may require two lifeguards). Note, however, that many hotels and communities have pools without lifeguards. **It's important to ensure that young children don't have access to swimming pools, and private pools should be fenced to prevent accidents (also take extra care around rivers and lakes).**

Most swimming pools and clubs provide swimming lessons and run life-saving courses. Spain also has many water parks (*parque acuático*) and watersports centres where facilities include indoor and outdoor pools, water slides, flumes, wave machines, river rapids, whirlpools and waterfalls, sun-beds, saunas, solariums, Jacuzzis, hot baths and a children's area. Most water parks are open only during the summer season, e.g. from June to September.

**It's important to protect yourself against the sun to prevent sunburn and heatstroke, which includes using a high protection sun cream (factor 15 minimum, factor 25 in summer), a sun block on sensitive areas (e.g. lips, moles and nipples), and drink plenty of water.** On some beaches a body spray service is provided where you can be sprayed head to toe with sun tan lotion. Even if you think you're used to Spain's fierce sun, you should limit your exposure and avoid it altogether during the hottest part of the day in summer (noon till 5pm), wear protective clothing (including a hat) and use a sun block.

# WATERSPORTS

Spain is a Mecca for watersports enthusiasts, which is hardly surprising considering its immense coastline (7,880km/4,896mi), many islands, numerous lakes and reservoirs, and thousands of kilometres of rivers and canals. Popular watersports include sailing, windsurfing, waterskiing, jet-skiing, rowing, canoeing, kayaking, surfing, rafting and sub-aquatic sports. In addition to the Atlantic and

Mediterranean, many reservoirs and lakes are also popular venues for sailing, waterskiing and windsurfing. **Coastal resorts often have designated areas for windsurfing, waterskiing and jet-skiing, and it's forbidden to operate outside these areas.** Wet suits are recommended for windsurfing, waterskiing and sub-aquatic sports, even during the summer. Rowing and canoeing is possible on many lakes and rivers, where canoes and kayaks can usually be rented. Spain's premier canoeing event is the 22km (14mi) Descenso del Sella down the Sella river in Asturias (from Arriondas to Ribadasella), which takes place on the first Saturday in August. Surfing is popular along the Atlantic coast of the Basque Country and Cantabria: however, Lanzarote in the Canaries is the Hawaii of the Atlantic to surfers and Fuerteventura is also good. Spain also has Europe's foremost windsurfing and kitesurfing area at Tarifa. There are clubs for most watersports in all major resorts and towns throughout Spain and instruction is usually available.

Scuba-diving is a popular sport in Spain, where there are many diving clubs offering instruction and equipment and boat rental. **Scuba-diving can be dangerous and safety is of paramount importance. For this reason, many experts don't recommend learning to dive while on holiday. Holiday divers should, in any case, dive only with a reputable club, and, due to the dangers of decompression, stop diving 24 hours before taking the flight home.** A diving permit (costing around €10) is required to dive in Spanish waters and is obtainable from clubs and schools. Among the best areas for scuba divers are the seas around the Balearic and Canary islands. For information contact the Spanish Subaquatic Federation (Federación Española de Actividades Subacuáticas), C/Santaló, 15 –3°, 08021 Barcelona (☎ 932-009 200, 💻 www.fedas.es).

Spain has some of the world's best windsurfing areas, including Fuerteventura in the Canaries, El Mádano in south Tenerife, and Tarifa at the southernmost tip of Spain on the Strait of Gibraltar. Tarifa is a kitesurfers' paradise and Europe's windiest place, where winter winds from the south-west or north-east can reach up to 120kph (75mph) and the average wind speed is 34kph (21mph). There are numerous websites for windsurfers, which usually include weather reports and news of competitions (e.g. 💻 www.surferos.net and 💻 www.windtarifa.com – this site includes seven-day wind predictions). The monthly magazine, *Surf A Vela*, is a must for all windsurfing fans in Spain.

A new sport to hit Spain in recent years is canyoning, a combination of abseiling and white-water rafting consisting of descending gushing rivers, waterfalls and canyons with the aid of ropes. It can be dangerous and only 'lunatics' need apply. The best white-water area in Spain is Ribadesella in Asturias.

**Be sure to observe all warning signs on lakes and rivers.** Take particular care when canoeing, as some rivers have 'white water' patches that can be dangerous for the inexperienced. It's sensible to wear a life-jacket when canoeing, irrespective of whether you're a strong swimmer. All watersports equipment can be rented, although you're usually required to leave a large deposit and should take out insurance against damage or loss.

Spain has a wealth of marinas and harbours, many with over 1,000 berths (including Benalmádena and Puerto Banús on the Costa del Sol), which are scattered liberally along Spain's coasts. Puerto Banús near Marbella is Spain's answer to St Tropez where the rich go to sea and be seen, full of vast ostentatious yachts, flash cars and beautiful people. There are also numerous sailing clubs (*club náutico*) based at marinas and sports harbours, all of which offer tuition and courses. Crewed and uncrewed yachts can be rented in resorts, although you need a skipper's certificate or a helmsman's overseas certificate to rent an uncrewed yacht.

Despite the large number of marinas, berths can be difficult to find in summer in some areas, although temporary berths can usually be found on public jetties and harbours. Moorings can be expensive, particularly in the most fashionable resorts such as Marbella. The cost of keeping a yacht on the Atlantic coast is cheaper than on the Mediterranean or in the islands, although even here it needn't be too expensive providing you steer clear of the most fashionable berths (e.g. from as little as €15 a day for an 8 x 3 metre berth in low season to €50 a day for a 20 x 5 metre berth in high season). Races take place in many classes (such as dinghies) all year round, while yacht racing is generally restricted to between April and October, during which there are big regattas in the Balearics (where the most prestigious event is the Copa del Rey which takes place off Palma de Mallorca in August) and the Bay of Cadiz. Boating holidays are popular in Spain, where boats of all shapes and sizes can be rented in harbours and coastal resorts. For information about marinas and competitions contact the Spanish Sailing Federation (Federación Española de Vela), C/Luís de Salazar, 9, 28002 Madrid (☎ 915-195 008, 🖥 www.rfev.es).

Spain is a good place to buy a yacht, as prices are very competitive. However, a 'wandering yacht' cannot escape value added tax (VAT), as it must be levied on all yachts purchased in EU countries by EU citizens at the time of sale. Note that VAT is paid in the country of registration or destination and therefore you should compare Spain's 16 per cent VAT (*IVA*) with the country of purchase. EU residents aren't permitted to register their vessels abroad simply to avoid paying VAT, and any vessel registered outside the EU must be located there and is liable for import duties if berthed in an EU port. **All vessels kept permanently in Spain must be registered there.** Buyers from non-EU countries remain exempt from VAT, providing they export their yachts to non-EU waters. However, a foreign-registered boat can be kept in Spain and used there for six months a year by a non-resident, but must be sealed (*precintado*) when it isn't being used. Boats can be operated on Spanish tourist flag registration to avoid paying Spanish taxes.

In 2003, Valencia was chosen as the next venue for the world's oldest yachting competition, the America's Cup, which is to be held in 2007. The summer breezes in the Mediterranean around the city are deemed to be perfect for the race. Huge investment in infrastructure is underway and the city's marina and port are being extensively modified. Further information is available from the official website (🖥 www.copaamericavalencia.com).

# OTHER SPORTS & ACTIVITIES

The following is a selection of other popular sports and activities in Spain.

## Athletics

Most Spanish towns have local athletics (*atlético*) clubs which organise local competitions and sports days, including fun runs, half-marathons and marathons.

Jogging is more popular in Spain than in many other countries and there are reportedly twice as many joggers in Spain as in the UK. In recent years, Spain has become a force in middle and long-distance running.

# Basketball

Basketball (*baloncesto*) is extremely popular in Spain (second only to football throughout the country) and there are amateur clubs in all large towns and cities. Barcelona and Real Madrid are among Europe's top professional clubs and play in the European Clubs Championship group A, with matches being regularly televised.

# Billiards & Snooker

Many hotels, bars and sports clubs have billiard or snooker tables and there are billiard and snooker clubs in the larger towns where billiards, snooker and American pool can be played. Many pubs and snooker clubs in resort areas organise leagues and competitions (with cash prizes) for men and ladies.

# Bungee Jumping

If your idea of fun is jumping off a high bridge or platform with an elastic rope attached to your body to prevent you merging with the landscape, then bungee jumping may be just what you're looking for. Although late starters, the Spanish have taken to bungee jumping with a vengeance. Most venues employ purpose-built platforms and cranes (rather than natural locations), which are sometimes erected on beaches in summer.

# Gymnasiums & Health Clubs

Spain has a wealth of gymnasiums (*gimnasios*) and health clubs in cities and resort areas. Most clubs have tonnes of expensive bone-jarring, muscle-wrenching apparatus, plus saunas, Jacuzzis, steam baths and beauty treatments. Many gyms are part of a larger sports complex where facilities may include a swimming pool, tennis, paddle tennis, martial arts and squash, plus a bar, restaurant and children's playground or crèche. Dance, training and exercise classes are also offered by many sports centres and clubs.

Most clubs offer weekly, monthly or annual membership or you can just pay for individual classes on a pay-as-you-go basis. Fees vary considerably and start at around €40 a month for a single person in a resort area. There are usually reduced fees for couples, and children (e.g. under 16) accompanied by a parent may be admitted free. Individual classes are usually around €6 a session. Most clubs permit visitors, who usually pay a daily membership fee of between €5 and €10 (although it can be as high as €20 at exclusive clubs). Many clubs offer a one-day free trial or a free introductory class. Clubs are usually open from around 8am to between 10pm and midnight, seven days a week, although some close on Sundays. Some clubs are small and extremely crowded, particularly during lunch hours and early evening, and it's advisable to check the numbers at the times you wish to attend before becoming a member.

# Handball

Handball is a popular sport in Spain, as it is throughout continental Europe, and it has some of the top teams in Europe. It's played indoors on a pitch similar to a five-a-side soccer pitch, where players pass the ball around by hand and attempt to throw it into a small goal.

# Horse Riding

Horse riding is widespread in Spain, which has a long history of horse breeding and horsemanship. The Spanish or Andalusian thoroughbred is among the most famous breeds in the world and the art of horsemanship is demonstrated in many equestrian schools (such as the Real Escuela Andaluza del Arte Ecuestre in Jerez). Spain has numerous ranches, riding centres and schools (*picaderos*) where you can hire a horse by the hour or day. Instruction is provided and cross country and mountain treks on ancient shepherd's paths are organised, including day trips and tours lasting a number of weeks. TurEspaña (see page 392) provides information about riding holidays in Spain, and regional and municipal tourist offices provide details of local schools and riding centres. For more information contact the Spanish Riding Federation (Federación Hípica Española), C/Menorca, 3-4°, 28009 Madrid (☎ 914-364 200, 🖳 www.rfhe.com).

# Lawn Bowls

There are now clubs in all popular resort areas where winter and summer championships are held, including league and cup competitions. Clubs offer short-term membership to non-residents. Indoor bowls isn't played in Spain, as lawn bowls can be played throughout the year in most areas. The Spanish play their own version of bowls (*bolas*) which bears little resemblance to *boules* or *pétanque* played in France (and none at all to lawn bowls).

# Motor-racing & Motor-cycling

The Spanish are great motor racing fans and Spain stages many international races, including the Spanish formula one grand prix held at various circuits, including the *Circuito de Jarama* race track north of Madrid, the *Montmeló Circuit de Catalunya* in Barcelona or Jerez de la Frontera. Fernando Alonso is Spain's first top formula one driver with Renault and won the world title in 2005. Spain has also produced some leading rally drivers, including former world rally champion Carlos Sainz. Four-wheel driving is a popular sport in the mountains throughout Spain. Motor-cycling also has a large following in Spain, which has a long tradition of producing world motor-cycling champions (Dani Pedrosa was the 2004 world champion in 250cc) and is one of Europe's top motor-cycling nations.

# Pelota

*Pelota* (or *jai alai*) was invented by the Basques, who comprise many of the best players in north America and whose national sport it is. Every town of any size in the Basque Country (on both sides of the border with France) and many in the neighbouring provinces of Navarra and La Rioja has a three-sided court (*frontón*), on which *pelota* is played (it's also played in other parts of Spain). It's played by two or five players who throw a ball against the end wall usually with a woven basket (*chistera*) strapped to an arm, although a leather glove or even bare hands are also used (there are over 20 versions played in some 25 countries). The *chistera* combines the functions of glove and catapult, in which the ball is caught and hurled back against the wall at speeds of up to 200kmh (124mph). *Pelota* is the fastest ball game in the world and players sometimes wear crash helmets to protect themselves from being struck on the head by the ball. However, the real purpose of *pelota* is a vehicle for gambling and huge sums are wagered on top games. For information contact the Federación Española de Pelota, C/Los Madrazos, 11-5°, 28014 Madrid (☎ 915-214 299, 🖳 www.fepelota.com).

# Miscellaneous

Many foreign sports and pastimes have a group of expatriate (and also Spanish) fans in Spain, including American football, baseball, *boccia*, *boules*, ten-pin bowling, cricket, croquet, polo and rugby. Cricket is popular in many parts of Spain, where it's mainly played by zealous British expatriates with a few eccentric Spaniards to make up the numbers. There are a number of cricket clubs in Spain competing in leagues and knock-out competitions between March and November. Polo is also a popular sport and is played throughout the year at a number of clubs (including the Santa María club in Sotogrande). For information about local sports facilities and clubs, enquire at tourist offices, town halls, and embassies and consulates (see **Appendix A**).

# 17.

# SHOPPING

Spain isn't one of Europe's great shopping countries, for quality or bargains, although the choice and quality of goods on offer has improved considerably since Spain joined the European Union (EU). Prices of many consumer goods such as TV and stereo systems, computers, cameras, electrical apparatus and household appliances have fallen dramatically in recent years and are now similar to most other EU countries. Furthermore, if you're fortunate enough to get paid in a currency that has increased in value against the euro in recently, you will be pleasantly surprised how far your money will stretch.

Small family-run shops (*tiendas*) still constitute the bulk of Spanish retailers, although the shopping scene has been transformed in the last decade with the opening of numerous shopping centres (many beautifully designed) and hypermarkets. Following the trend in most European countries there has been a drift away from town centres by retailers to out-of-town shopping centres (malls) and hypermarket complexes, which has left some 'high streets' run down and abandoned. The biggest drawback to shopping in cities and towns is parking, which can be a nightmare, although many Spanish cities have improved parking facilities and pedestrianised central streets in an attempt to lure shoppers back to city centres.

With the exception of markets, where haggling over the price is part of the enjoyment (except when buying food), retail prices are fixed in Spain and shown as *Precio de Venta al Público (PVP)*. It's important to shop around and compare prices, as they can vary considerably, not only between small shops and hypermarkets, but also among supermarkets and hypermarkets in the same town. Note, however, that price differences often reflect different quality, so make sure you're comparing similar products. The best time to have a shopping spree is during the winter and summer sales (*rebajas*) in January-February and July-August respectively, when bargains (*gangas*) can be found everywhere and prices are often slashed by 50 per cent or more (the best bargains are usually clothes). If you're looking for bargains, you may also wish to try the cut-price shops which sell everything from as little as €1; most items couldn't even have been manufactured for the sale price (much of it's bankrupt stock).

Among the best buys in Spain are the diverse handicrafts which include antiques, cultured pearls, shawls, pottery, ceramics, damascene, embroidery, fans, glassware, hats, ironwork, jewellery, knives, lace, suede and leather, paintings, porcelain (e.g. Lladró from Valencia), rugs, trinkets and carved woodwork.

Shopping 'etiquette' in Spain may differ considerably from what you're used to, particularly in market places and small shops. The Spanish (and many tourists) don't believe in queuing and people often push and shove their way to the front. Don't expect shop assistants to serve customers in order; you must usually speak up when it's your turn to be served or take a numbered ticket from a dispenser. You also shouldn't expect service with a smile, except perhaps when you're being served by the owner. Shop assistants may sometimes be surly and unhelpful, and some staff give the impression they couldn't care less about your custom, although customer service has improved greatly in recent years. On the other hand, in small shops where you're a regular customer, you will be warmly received and many shopkeepers will even allow you to pay another day if you don't have enough money with you.

In major cities and tourist areas, you **must** be wary of pickpockets and bag-snatchers, particularly in markets and other crowded places. **Never** tempt fate with an exposed wallet or purse or by flashing your money around. The Spanish generally pay cash when shopping, although credit and debit cards are widely accepted. However, personal cheques (even local ones) aren't usually accepted.

For those who aren't used to buying articles with metric measures and in continental sizes, a list of comparative weights and measures are included in **Appendix D**. For information about pharmacies (chemists) see **Drugs & Medicines** on page 273.

# SHOPPING HOURS

Shopping hours in Spain vary considerably depending on the region, city or town and the type of shop. There are no statutory closing days or hours for retail outlets, except in Catalonia where shops must close by 9pm. Large shops must open on a minimum of eight Sundays and public holidays (*festivos*) a year, but the actual number depends on the region. Most regions have opted to open on eight *festivos* only except for Murcia where shops open on 12 Sundays and public holidays a year and Madrid with a record 20 *festivos* annually. Shops located in zones of 'great tourist influence' (beach resorts and historic towns) can apply to open all year round, not just during the summer months. As in other European countries, small shopkeepers (who close for *siestas* and at weekends) are having increasing difficulty competing with hypermarkets and department stores.

A big surprise for many foreigners is the long afternoon *siesta*, when most small shops close from 1.30 or 2pm until around 5pm. Apart from department stores and many large supermarkets, there's no such thing as afternoon shopping in Spain. The *siesta* makes good sense in the summer when it's often too hot to do anything in the afternoon, but it isn't so practical in winter when evening shopping must be done in the dark. However, foreigners are often divided over Spain's shopping hours, some seeing them as an inconvenience, others a bonus. Many people actually find they prefer to shop in the evening when they get used to it.

Most small shops open from between 8.30 and 9.30am until between 1 and 2pm and from around 5pm until between 7.30 and 9pm, Mondays to Fridays, and from 9.30am until 2pm on Saturdays. Note, however, that in some areas most shops are closed on Monday mornings. Department stores, hypermarkets and many supermarkets are open continually from around 9.30 or 10am, until between 8 and 10pm from Mondays to Saturdays. Department stores and hypermarkets may also open on Sundays (e.g. 10am to 3pm or noon to 8pm) and public holidays (e.g. 10am to 10pm). During the summer, shops in resort areas (particularly food shops and tobacconists) often remain open until 10 or 11pm (except in Catalonia). Shops in resort areas may also remain open longer on Saturdays and open on Sunday mornings in the summer. The OpenCor chain (part of El Corte Inglés giant) with branches all over the country opens 24-hours a day every day of the year and in major cities such as Madrid and Barcelona and some resort towns there are 24-hour, American-style, drugstores comprising a supermarket, cafeteria, tobacconist and restaurant.

In general, shops close for one whole day and one half day each week, usually on Saturday afternoon and Sunday (some shops also close on Mondays or Monday mornings). In Madrid and other cities, some shops close for the whole of August, when most people are on holiday.

# FOOD

The hallmark of Spanish cooking is the use of fresh local produce and not surprisingly, shopping for food (and eating) is a labour of love in Spain, where the range and quality of fresh food is unsurpassed. Many Spanish housewives shop daily, not because it's necessary, but out of enjoyment and the opportunity to socialise. The Spanish housewife has traditionally preferred to shop in small specialist food shops and markets, rather than in large soulless supermarkets and hypermarkets, although this is changing. Some 70 per cent of food in Spain is now purchased in self-serve supermarkets and hypermarkets and the days of the family-run shop are numbered. Those that remain survive by offering a friendly and personal service (advice, tastings, etc.), stocking local fare and providing better quality than supermarkets.

If you wish to save money on your weekly food bill, it isn't only what you buy, but where you shop that's important. In general, it's best to shop at markets and small stores where the Spanish shop. It takes more time, but is better value than shopping at supermarkets and the quality is also usually better. It helps if you speak some Spanish, although it's easy to point and say *un kilo* or *medio kilo* (half a kilo). In some areas, foreign food shops operate clubs allowing members to buy food at wholesale prices.

The Spanish haven't developed a taste for foreign foods and are parochial in their food tastes. Consequently, Spain doesn't import a lot of foreign foods, although there are specialist imported food shops in major cities and resorts with many foreign residents. Most supermarkets offer a selection of foreign foods, but don't expect to find shelves packed with imported meat, cheese or wine. **Note that if you insist on buying expensive imported foods, your food bill will skyrocket.**

## Meat

Pork (*carne de cerdo*) is the most widely consumed meat in Spain and, with chicken, the cheapest. Veal (*carne de ternera*) is also fairly common, although expensive. Beef (*carne de vaca*) and lamb (*carne de cordero*) are expensive, but usually tasty and free of BSE (although there have been isolated outbreaks). Suckling pig (*cochinillo*) and baby lamb (*cordero*) are favourite dishes in central Spain, where they're roasted in a wood or clay oven. Game is plentiful outside summer and fresh rabbit is available throughout the year. Kebab meat for barbecues is sold cubed and marinated.

Many villages and all towns have a butcher's shop (*carnicería*) selling all kinds of meat, although generally speaking, pork is the preserve of the *charcutería* (see below). Chicken (*pollo*) and eggs (*huevos*) are sold in specialist shops called *pollerías*; eggs are also sold in a *huevería* (egg shop). A *casquería* sells offal such as a bull's testicles (*cojones* – considered a delicacy in Spain) and also the meat of bulls killed during bullfights (*toro/carne de lidia*), which isn't sold in an ordinary butcher's shop (but is available in some supermarkets).

Meat is cut differently in Spain than in many other countries and is seldom pre-cut and packaged in a butcher's shop (as it is in supermarkets). Meat is usually purchased 'on the bone' or minced. Cold meat is sold by weight or by the slice (*rodaja*). Like most foods in Spain, the range of meat varies with the region, and butchers are happy to give advice on its preparation and cooking.

## Pork

Pork can be purchased from a specialist pork butcher (*charcutería*), who also sells cold meats (*fiambres*) and cheese (*queso*). Spanish raw ham is renowned and among the best in the world, although the best types are expensive. The finest Spanish ham is named after the town where it's produced, e.g. *jamón Serrano* and *jamón de Jabugo*. It's similar to Parma ham and is widely used in Spanish recipes. Cured processed ham (*jamón de York*) is also good and much cheaper than raw ham. You can buy smoked ham or bacon (*beicon*) in Spain, although it's usually of the streaky variety. Spain is also famous for its sausages, such as *chorizo* (spicy paprika) and *morcilla* (blood, sometimes with nuts). The large *chorizo* sausage is similar to salami and is intended for slicing and eating raw; a red string indicates hot and a white string mild.

# Fish

The Spanish are great fish eaters and generally eat fish around three times a week. It's usually bought from a fishmonger (*pescadería*), although shellfish is also sold at seafood restaurants (*marisquería*), which sell cooked and uncooked seafood, as well as *tapas* (see page 374). Fish is surprisingly expensive in Spain due to poor local catches and restrictive EU quotas, which mean that it must be caught in remote fishing grounds. Shellfish is reasonably priced. Fish is invariably excellent throughout Spain, even in Madrid, where fresh fish is delivered daily from the coasts.

The most common fish include bass, dorado, hake, grouper, monkfish, mullet, sea bream, salmon, sardines and trout, although they vary depending on the region. Note that the same fish may have different names in different parts of Spain or the same name may be used for several different kinds of fish. The best areas for price and variety are Galicia and the Basque Country, where most of Spain's fish is landed. Fish is cut (*cortado*), cleaned (*limpiado*), gutted (*destripado*) and scaled (*descamado*) on request. Fish are usually sorted by size and sold in fillets (*filetes*) or slices (*rodajas*) for larger fish such as swordfish and tuna. In inland towns and villages, fish is commonly sold frozen. Canned fish is also popular, particularly tuna, of which there are numerous varieties.

# Bread & Cakes

Bread (*pan*) is sold in a bakery (*panadería*) in Spain and is usually baked on the premises, even by supermarkets. A wide variety is available, although there are two main types; country bread (*pan chapata*), which is heavy and round and lasts several days, and *pan de barra*, which is a long, thin, crusty loaf similar to a French *baguette* that stays fresh for only a few hours. Among the many other types of bread available are wholemeal (*pan cateto* or *integral*), round peasant bread (*hogaza*), round bread (*gallegos*) and German bread (*pan alemán*), which is an extremely tasty dark wholegrain bread often sold in supermarkets. There are also many regional styles of loaves, usually referred to simply as *pan*.

Sliced bread (*pan de molde*) isn't sold in a bakery, although most slice bread free on request. Bread is sold by weight and prices are similar throughout Spain. Many supermarkets have a bread counter where bread is often baked on the premises. Bakers also sell French-style croissants, cakes and tarts. A *bollería* sells bread and rolls (*bollos*). Traditionally, bread and pastries weren't sold in the same shop in Spain, although bakeries nowadays sell a wide range of cakes and biscuits. If you want pastries, you must usually go to a pastry or cake shop (*pastelería* or *confitería*), which sells sweet breakfast rolls, cakes, gateaux, fruit tarts, pastries, biscuits and sweets. The best cakes and pastries are found in Catalonia and Majorca, although in general, Spanish cakes aren't up to the standards of northern European countries. The larger pastry shops often incorporate a bar or tea room (*salón de té*).

A unique Spanish treat is fried doughnuts or long fluted shapes of lightly fried dough or fritters called *churros*, usually sold at a *churrería* and costing around €0.60 a serving. They're traditionally eaten with a cup of thick, sweet, hot chocolate in which it's 'obligatory' to dip your *churros*. They're an essential part of Spanish life, particularly on Sunday mornings in winter and in the small hours of the morning after a night on the town!

## Fruit & Vegetables

Fruit and vegetables are best purchased from a market or a fruit and vegetable shop (*frutería*), rather than from supermarkets, where produce is often under-ripe or past its best. The variety and value of locally-grown fruit and vegetables in Spain is second to none, and most are available throughout the year (vegetarians can live cheaply in Spain). However, don't be influenced by the low prices and buy more than you can eat within a few days, as fruit and vegetables go off quickly in hot weather (unless stored in a refrigerator). It's easy to buy too much, particularly when prices are low, e.g. oranges at €1 a kilo, strawberries €1.50 a kilo, apples €1.50 a kilo, tomatoes €0.50 a kilo and iceberg lettuces for €0.60 each. Note that in small shops, you shouldn't handle the produce unless invited to do so, although you can usually serve yourself.

## Olive Oil

Olive oil (*aceite de oliva*) is part of the staple diet of Spaniards and merits a special mention. Spaniards consume around ten litres of olive oil per head each year (compared with around a third of a litre in many northern European countries) and have one of Europe's lowest number of deaths from heart disease (along with France, Italy and Portugal – all large consumers of olive oil). The finest quality is classified as *virgen* and is made by a single cold pressing. There are two grades of *virgen* oil, *extra* and *fino*, both green in colour. *Extra* has the least acidity and is the most expensive. Among the best olive oils are *Sierra de Segura* from Jaén and *Borjas Blancas* from Lérida, although most people have their own particular favourites. The finest oil is classified as pure olive oil (*aceite puro de oliva*). Refined (*refinado*) oil is blended with *virgen* oil and is light yellow in colour. *Puro* is a mixture of *virgen* and refined oil.

There are four controlled areas of production (*denominación de origen*) in Spain, although fine olive oil is also produced in other areas, and some 60 varieties. Olive oil can be purchased direct from producers, when you will usually be treated to a tasting as if you were buying wine. Olive oil has varying acidity (*acidez*), e.g. 0.3°, 0.4° or 0.5°, which are tasteless in salads and odourless in cooking (generally the lower the acidity, the better the olive oil). If you want more flavour, choose an acidity of 1°. Apart from its use in cooking and as a salad dressing, olive oil is also used in rolls instead of butter, which goes off quickly in hot weather, and eaten on bread sprinkled with salt.

# Cheese

There are some 300 varieties of cheese (*queso*) in Spain, although most are produced in tiny quantities and many are unknown outside Spain or the area of production. Despite the fact that cheese has been produced in Spain for over 3,500 years, the Spanish have the lowest consumption of cheese in Europe and over the years many varieties have simply vanished. Spanish cheese is mainly hard and Cheddar-like and most are an acquired taste. The hard salty *manchego* and similar cheeses are the most common (often served as a *tapa*) and can be old and ripened (*añejo*), cured (*curado*), milder and younger (*semi curado*) or very young (*tierno*). Other common cheeses are *El Cigarral*, similar to mild English Cheddar, *Cabrales*, a delicious blue sheep's cheese from Asturias, and *Idiazábel* from Navarra. Although cow's cheese (*queso de vaca*) is the most common, Spain is renowned for its sheep (*queso de oveja*) and goats' (*queso de cabra*) cheeses, which are widely available. Many cheeses are often a mixture of cow and sheep's milk. Soft fresh cheeses are also made in many areas, although they aren't often seen in shops. A wide range of foreign cheeses is available in supermarkets, including Brie, Camembert, Cheddar, Danish Blue and Edam, plus numerous processed cheeses. Dairy products are generally more expensive in Spain than in other European countries.

# Organic Food

Spain produces a vast amount of organic food, including fruit and vegetables, dairy products and meat, and an ever-growing number of farmers are switching their methods to organic farming. However, most of the organic food produced in Spain is for export (mostly to the UK and Germany) and only a small percentage of what's produced actually reaches the home market. As a consequence, organic food isn't only expensive, sometimes three times its non-organic price, but also difficult to obtain. In large cities, there are some specialist shops and large supermarket chains such as Alcampo and Hipercor stock a limited number of products. Organic eggs and chicken are relatively easy to buy and most supermarkets stock them. If you don't live near an organic food outlet, try local markets, particularly in small villages or buy direct from small farms after ensuring their produce really is organic.

## Miscellaneous Food Shops

A general store (*alimentación* or *ultramarino*) sells dairy foods, hams and other cured meats, wine, canned and packaged goods, and sometimes fresh produce and meat. In towns, many general stores have become small self-service supermarkets. A *bombonería* is a sweet shop or candy store selling a delicious assortment of hand-made chocolates, truffles and candies, all guaranteed to wreck your diet and your teeth. A *heladería* is an ice cream parlour, usually selling homemade ice cream and often combined with a café or bar. They're popular and ubiquitous in resort areas. A *herbario* is a herb and spice shop, a *lechería* a dairy shop and a *mantequería* a delicatessen selling dairy foods, wines and liqueurs (often combined with a bar). Remote areas are served by mobile shops (*venta ambulante*), which travel around the countryside selling fresh bread, meat, fish, fruit and vegetables, in addition to preserved foods.

# ALCOHOL

Drinking is an integral part of everyday life in Spain, where most people have a daily tipple. Low taxes mean that Spain has the cheapest alcohol in the EU – even cheaper than buying it duty-free. Whatever your poison, you will find something to suit your taste among the many excellent wines, beers, spirits and liqueurs produced in Spain or the numerous imported beverages. Spain is, however, most famous for its wine, particularly its sherry.

## Sherry

Sherry (*jerez*) is world famous and Spain's most celebrated export, which has been produced for hundreds of years (dominated by the English since the 16th century). Sherry takes it name from Jerez de la Frontera in Andalusia where it's produced and where three-quarters of the population is employed in its production in some way or another. It's produced mainly from the Palomino grape, which is also the only vine that the chalky soil in the south-west region of Spain will support. Sherry is matured in oak barrels and produced from a variety of vintages, using the unique *solera* method of production of progressively blending young and old wines.

There are various types of sherry to suit most tastes and occasions. Dry (*fino* or *seco*) and the medium dry (*amontillado*) are usually drunk chilled as an aperitif, while the sweet *oloroso* and *dulce* (brown, cream or amoroso) are drunk at room temperature as after dinner drinks. There's also a dry (*seco*) variety of *oloroso*. The very dry *manzanilla* has a slightly salty after taste, attributed to the salty soil of the coastal area in Sanlúcar de Barrameda where it's produced. Sherry lovers can tour the wineries (*bodegas*) in Jerez for a few euros and enjoy tastings.

# Wine

Spain has a 2,000-year history of wine production and has more acres (around 20 million) of vineyards than any country in the world, although it rates third after France and Italy in wine production. An extraordinary diversity of wines is produced in Spain, due to the country's different climatic and soil conditions, matched by few other nations. While most aren't as famous as the wines of France and some other countries, the best Spanish wines compare favourably with many classic foreign wines. Although Spain still produces oceans of mediocre 'plonk' and Spanish wine has a generally poor international reputation, it also makes some of the best value-for-money wines in Europe, including many great wines. The quality of Spanish wine has improved enormously in the last few decades, during which modern methods of production and the introduction of new grape varieties (such as chardonnay and cabernet sauvignon) have transformed wine production. However, some cheaper red wines are unreliable and it isn't unusual to find bad (e.g. corked) bottles.

## Classification

Spain has some 70 wine-producing regions, 65 of which are officially designated areas with a *Denominación de Origen (DO)* classification, indicated by a small map on the back label (labels also contain official seals, such as Rioja's 'stamp'). Regulations relating to *DO* regions include the type of grapes that can be used, yield per hectare, minimum alcohol strength, permissible amount of natural sugar, maturity process and period, bottling and labelling. Wine from another region cannot be mixed with a *DO* wine. There's also a further quality classification, *Denominación de Origen Calificada (DOC)*, which has so far been awarded only to Rioja. The designation *vino de mesa* applies to blended wine or wine made from grapes grown in unclassified vineyards, while *vino de la tierra* is local wine from a defined area that doesn't qualify for a *DO*. Note, however, that there are many excellent Spanish wine producers who choose not to belong to a *Denominación de Origen* or who produce wines that contain grape varieties which aren't permitted under *DO* regulations.

## Production Areas

Nearly every region produces wine, from sweet dessert whites to dry reds, modest table wines to fine vintages. Spanish wine regions fall into three main areas: the north, where the best wines are produced, containing the regions of Rioja, Penedés, Tarragona, Ribera del Duero and Galicia; the central zone, including La Mancha, Valdepeñas, and the coastal region of the Levante, containing half of Spain's total vineyards and producing some 35 per cent of its wine (mostly table wines) and the dry southern zone which produces (almost exclusively) apéritif and dessert wines, including sherry.

## Rioja

The most famous Spanish red (*tinto*) wine is Rioja, a strong wine high in tannin, often with a distinctive 'oaky' flavour (from the oak barrels). Some 40 per cent of Rioja is aged in barrels, the rest being drunk within one or two years of bottling. Few Spanish wines can match Rioja for price and quality and many connoisseurs believe that vintage Riojan wines can hold their own with the best France has to offer and account for nearly 40 per cent of Spanish wine sales. You usually cannot go wrong with Rioja and even the cheapest young wines are highly palatable. Good white (*blanco*) wines are also produced in Rioja, which is subdivided into three geographical areas (or sub-regions) of production: Alavesa, Alta and Baja.

Like the best French wine-producing regions, Rioja declares an annual vintage, classified as follows: poor (*mediana*), normal, good (*buena*), very good (*muy buena*) and excellent (*excelente*).

Riojas are generally released at their optimum drinking time and don't need to be kept for years before they can be enjoyed, although aged wines will continue to improve for 7 to 20 years. Riojan red wines are divided into four categories depending on the amount of aging they've undergone. The best Riojan wines are labelled *reservas* or *gran reservas* and they can reach high prices for exceptional years. *Gran reservas* (which account for just 3 per cent of total production) spend a minimum of two years maturing in oak barrels and four more in the *bodega* before being sold. A *reserva* spends at least a year in the barrel and three in the *bodega* and a *crianza*, at least a year in the barrel and another in the bottle. A *sin crianza* or *conjunto de varias cosechas* (CVC) wine isn't aged (it spends no time in oak and is fermented in stainless steel vats) and is made from a combination of vintages.

There's a huge number and variety of Riojan red and white wines, most of which are excellent quality and value for money – part of the enjoyment is experimenting and finding those that best suit your palate and pocket!

For those wanting more information, there's a Rioja Wine website (⌨ www. riojawine.com), available in Spanish, English, French and German.

## Sparkling Wines

Spanish sparkling wine made by the *méthode champenoise* or *método tradicional* is called *cava* and is often as good as French champagne and at around €5 a bottle it's much cheaper. *Cava* was actually marketed as champagne (*champán* or *méthode champenoise*) for many years, although this was prohibited after complaints from the French. It isn't, however, an inferior Spanish 'champagne', but a quality sparkling wine in its own right (it's also made with different grapes from champagne). It's usually less than a few years old and vintage *cava* is rare. Among the best-known producers are Castellblanch, Codorníu and Freixenet (Carta Nevada and Cordón Negro are top brands). *Cava* is classified by its sweetness, which includes very dry (*brut de brut, brut nature, brut reserva, vintage*), dry (*brut*), fairly dry (*seco*), semi-dry (*semiseco*), semi-sweet (*semidulce*) and sweet (*dulce*). *Rosado* or *Rose* denotes a pink wine. All *cava* wines come under the same *DO*, irrespective of where they're produced. Spain also produces lesser sparkling wines (*vinos gasificados*), which are carbonated white and rosé wines (not highly rated).

## Other Wines

Other regions worthy of special mention include Penedés, where two-thirds of Catalonia's wine is produced. Penedés is renowned for its white wines, although it also produces good reds and much of Spain's premier sparkling wine (see above). The most famous producer in Penedés is Torres, who produce celebrated red (including Sangre de Torre and Gran Coronas) and white wines (e.g. Gran Viña Sol). The main difference between the wine produced in Rioja and Penedés is that vintage Riojan wines are aged in oak and Penedés wines in the bottle. However, Spain's most exclusive and expensive wines are produced by Vega Sicilia in the Ribera del Duero wine district. They cannot be purchased in shops and are allocated by the producer. Priorato is also known for its excellent red wines. Navarra is famous for producing the best rosé wines in Spain (and is also becoming known for its reds), while Albariños of the Rías Baixas district in Galicia produces what many consider to be the best white wines in Spain. Rueda and Somontano are also noted for their white wines. Tarragona makes excellent dessert wines (*vinos generosos*) and the world's strongest red wine (up to 18 per cent proof).

## Buying Wine

Most people buy their wine from supermarkets and hypermarkets, although the quality and range of wines on offer isn't usually outstanding. An off-licence (*bodega*) usually has a larger selection of wines and other drinks than a supermarket, and the prices are usually comparable. Shops often have special offers, particularly around Christmas and New Year, when prices are reduced across the board. However, you should avoid buying expensive vintage wines from a supermarket, as they're often badly stored. Nowhere are the Spanish more parochial and nationalistic than when it comes to wine, and supermarkets stock few imported wines.

The Spanish are unpretentious when it comes to wine and don't generally take it seriously. They drink mostly young table wines (*vino corriente*) at home, which are free of tannin. At the lower end of the quality range, wine is cheaper in Spain than in many other countries, although quality wines can be as expensive as in France. At the bottom end of the market, wine is sold in cartons (*briks*) at around €1 a litre, some of which taste worse than vinegar. Inexpensive red (*tinto*), white (*blanco*) and rosé (*rosado*) wines costing around €1.50 a litre are better and include names such as *Don Simón* and *Elegido*. Slightly up market table wines (*vinos de mesa*) from Soldepeñas, Valdepeñas and Valencia (e.g. Castillo de Liria) cost from €1.50 to €2.50 a bottle. The cheapest Riojan red wines start at around €2.50, while a reasonable *crianza* starts at around €3.50. If you like dry white wine, you cannot go wrong with most from Rioja or Rueda from around €3 a bottle.

Buying wine in bulk direct from producers is possible in Spain, although it isn't common. If you live near a winery (*bodega*) you can buy wine in bulk in small glass carboys. You pay an initial deposit for the carboy and thereafter you exchange your empties for full ones (or you can bring your own container and have it filled). In many wine-producing regions, villages have a *bodega* producing strong, inexpensive wine for local consumption. It's possible to visit most Spanish *bodegas* (usually by appointment) and wine festivals are held throughout the year, particularly at harvest time. **Note that you shouldn't leave wine in a car for long periods during hot weather, as it will ruin it.**

## Books

There are numerous books about wine, a few of which are dedicated to Spanish wine, such as *The New Spain: A Complete Guide to Contemporary Spanish Wine* by J. Radford, *Spanish Wines* by Jan Read (both from Mitchell Beazley Wine Guides). There are also many Spanish guide books such as *El Gran Libro del Vino* by Mauricio Wiesenthal (Salvat) and *Guía Peñin de los Vinos de España* (Pierre Ediciones). For those who don't know when they've had enough, there's *Floyd on Hangovers* (Michael Joseph) and if you feel guilty about drinking too much wine, *Your Good Health!: The Medicinal Benefits of Wine Drinking* by Dr. E. Maury (Souvenir Press) may make you feel better.

# Spirits

Spirits are extremely cheap in Spain and the cheapest in western Europe. There are generally cheaper Spanish equivalents (*nacional*) for most imported spirits, some of which are excellent. If you want the 'real thing', don't be fooled by Spanish brands in look-alike bottles with similar brand names. Spain even produces its own gin and whisky. Spanish gin, particularly Larios (around €8 a litre), is usually excellent, although it's around the same price as Gordons, the international market leader. Spanish whisky is terrible and to be avoided. Imported gin and Scotch whisky (unknown blended brands) are available in supermarkets from around €6 for a 70cl bottle. Johnny Walker scotch costs around €9 a bottle, Smirnoff vodka around €7.50 and Bacardi rum around €12.

If you're making cocktails you may as well buy Spanish gin, vodka and white rum. Many famous French spirits are made in Spain under licence, including Benedictine, Cointreau, Marie Brizard and Pernod. They're made exactly as in France, but from Spanish wine. Spanish spirits include *Cuaranta y Tres* (similar to Southern Comfort), *Ponche* (made from brandy and herbs) and *Pacharán*, which is made from bilberries. There's even a spirit made from artichokes called *Cynar* (which tastes dreadful).

Spanish brandy (labelled *brandy* for legal reasons, but often referred to as *coñac*) has a vanilla flavour and is very good. Popular brands include *Magno, Torres Solera Selecta, Soberano* and *Bobadillo 103*. It's often drunk in coffee (for breakfast!) and in cocktails. A litre bottle of Spanish brandy costs around €5.50. *Aguardiente* (aquavits) is a strong spirit distilled from grape leftovers, skins and pips, and is one of the strongest drinks in the world (80 per cent proof). It may put hairs on your chest, but will remove your skin if you spill it and should always be drunk sitting down. *Anís*, an aniseed-flavoured drink, is also popular in Spain.

# Beer & Cider

Spanish beer is brewed in light (*dorada*), similar to the ubiquitous export lager, and dark (*negra*) varieties and is usually good. It may come as a surprise to many foreigners to find that most Spaniards prefer beer to wine. Beer is usually sold in 300ml bottles (*botellines*), but also comes in large one-litre bottles. It's strong stuff and usually contains between 4.5 and 5.5 per cent alcohol by volume. Many imported beers are available in supermarkets, although it isn't usually worth paying the extra. Among the best-known Spanish beers are *San Miguel, Cruz Campo, Aguila, Estrella* and *Mahou Cinco Estrellas*. Local regional beers are often even better than the national ones. The finest Spanish cider (*sidra*) is made in Asturias (it's also made in Galicia and León) and is best served from a barrel, although it's also bottled and sold throughout Spain. It's dry and a little cloudy and is stronger than beer. Supermarkets frequently have special offers on beer and some brands can be bought in one-litre bottles, which is cheaper than buying small bottles. Most bottles are non-returnable and are taken to bottle banks or simply thrown away.

## Health

Considering the low cost of alcohol in Spain, it may come as a surprise to find that the Spanish don't have a huge problem with alcoholism or drunkenness, which is more than can be said for many tourists and foreign residents. Expatriates who like the odd drink should carefully control their alcohol intake, as alcoholism is a big problem among foreign residents (there are many expatriate Alcoholics Anonymous groups in Spain – see page 278).

## CLOTHES

Spanish fashion has made huge strides in the last few decades and has a growing reputation on the international scene, particularly cities such as Madrid and Barcelona (which naturally hold rival fashion weeks known as '*Cibeles*' and the '*Pasarela Gaudí*', respectively). Spanish fashion reflects the Spanish character and is audacious, colourful and stylish, with vibrant colours and styles influenced by the 'gypsy' folklore of the south and the sober elegance of the north.

There's a relaxed dress code in Spain, although the Spanish are invariably well-dressed and scornful of slovenly foreigners (particularly those who dress scantily in public places away from the beaches). Spanish fashion caters mostly for the expensive and cheap ends of the market, with little in between, although in recent years, national chains offering moderately priced clothes such as the multinational giant, Zara, Mango, Pull & Bear and Massimo Dutti have appeared. If you live on the Costa del Sol, you can stock up on British clothes at shops such as Dorothy Perkins, Evans, Top Shop and Wallis in La Cañada shopping centre (Marbella). Spain isn't generally a good place to buy quality clothes at reasonable prices, although the annual sales in January and July throw up plenty of bargains. Ready-made children's clothes are excellent, but are also expensive. Spain lacks the bargain-basement clothes shops common in the US and the UK, where you can buy last season's fashions at knock-down prices, and there are also few 'vintage' (second-hand) or charity clothes shops. Markets are the best place for inexpensive clothes, but look out for counterfeit brands.

Spanish leather goods are excellent quality (but are no longer cheap) and include leather and suede coats, jackets, handbags, belts, boots and shoes (a shoe shop is a *zapatería*). Loewe is one of the best-known and most expensive brand names. Spanish shoes are good value, although they're generally made only in one width (medium). Spanish clothing and shoe manufacturers don't cater for the large sizes and fittings widely available in other European countries and North America.

El Corte Inglés department stores sell most international fashion and designer labels and international fashion shops such as Bally, Benetton, Chanel, Charles Jourdan and Maxmara have outlets throughout Spain. Other shops of note are Cortefiel (branches in some 25 cities) selling middle of the road fashion at reasonable prices; Don Algodón for fun fashion clothes for children and teenagers; Zara for inexpensive fashion clothes for men, women and children and Tokio, which has a good selection of accessories such as hats, gloves, socks and swimwear.

# FURNITURE & FURNISHINGS

Many foreigners who decide to live permanently in Spain find that it's better to sell their furniture (*muebles*), rather than bring it to Spain. In any case, foreign furniture often isn't suitable for Spain's climate and homes (antique furniture in particular often doesn't stand the heat well). Many holiday homes sold by foreigners are sold furnished, particularly apartments, although furniture may be of poor quality and not to your taste. However, buying a furnished property can represent a real bargain. If you're buying a property as an investment for letting, most developers or agents will arrange to furnish it for you.

The kind of furniture you buy depends on a number of factors, including the style and size of your home, whether it's a permanent or holiday home, your budget, the local climate, and not least, your personal taste. If you intend to furnish a holiday home with antiques or expensive modern furniture, bear in mind that you need adequate security and insurance (see pages 105 and 300).

If you're buying a large quantity of furniture, don't be reluctant to ask for a discount, as many shops will give you one. The best time to buy furniture and furnishings is during the sales (particularly in winter), when prices of many items are slashed (some shops have half price sales in winter). Many shops offer furniture packages costing from around €3,000 for a two-bedroom apartment and it's possible for residents to pay for furniture (and large household appliances) over 12 months interest-free or over five years (with interest).

A wide range of modern and traditional furniture is available in Spain at reasonable prices. Modern furniture is popular and is often sold in huge shops in commercial centres. Reasonably priced furniture can also be purchased from large hypermarkets and more exclusive furniture from department stores such as El Corte Inglés. Pine and cane furniture is inexpensive and widely available. If you're looking for classic modern furniture, you may wish to try Roche Bobois, which has over 150 shops in 22 countries.

If you're looking for antique furniture at affordable prices, you may find a few bargains at antique and flea markets in rural areas. However, you must drive a hard bargain, as the asking prices are often ridiculous. There's a large market for second-hand furniture in Spain and many sellers and dealers advertise in the expatriate press (there are also specialist newspapers for second-hand goods). There are do-it-yourself hypermarkets such as Akí and Leroy Merlin in most areas, selling everything for the home, including do-it-yourself (DIY), furniture, bathrooms, kitchens, decorating and lighting, in addition to tool rental and wood cutting. IKEA also has shops in Asturias, Badalona, the Basque Lands, Gran Canaria, Madrid, Mallorca, Seville and Tenerife (💻 www.ikea.es).

# HOUSEHOLD GOODS

Household goods in Spain are generally of high quality and although the choice isn't as wide as in some other European countries, it has improved considerably. Electrical apparatus has traditionally been more expensive in Spain than in many other European countries, although the gap has narrowed and prices are now comparable (particularly in hypermarkets and supermarkets). Spanish-made appliances, electrical apparatus and consumer goods are usually of good quality, although they're sometimes of eccentric design and not always as reliable as imported brands, which are widely available.

Bear in mind when importing household goods that aren't sold in Spain, that it will be difficult or impossible to get them repaired or serviced there (however, should you need to get something repaired, there are strict rules to protect consumers). If you bring appliances with you, don't forget to include a supply of spares and consumables such as bulbs for a refrigerator or sewing machine, and spare bags for a vacuum cleaner. Note that the standard size of kitchen appliances and cupboard units in Spain **isn't** the same as in other countries and it may be difficult to fit an imported dishwasher or washing machine into a Spanish kitchen. Check the size **and** the latest Spanish safety regulations before shipping these items to Spain or buying them abroad, as they may need expensive modifications. Spanish washing machines take in cold water and heat it in the machine, which makes machines that take in hot water (such as those sold in the US) obsolete.

If you already own small household appliances, it's worthwhile bringing them to Spain, as usually all that's required is a change of plug. However, if you're coming from a country with a 110/115V electricity supply such as the US, you need a lot of expensive transformers (see page 111) and it's usually better to buy new appliances in Spain. Small appliances such as vacuum cleaners, grills, toasters and irons aren't expensive and are of good quality. Don't bring a television or video recorder without checking its compatibility first, as televisions made for other countries often don't work in Spain without modification (see page 162). If your need is just temporary, many electrical and other household items (such as beds, cots/high chairs, electric fans, refrigerators, heaters and air conditioners) can be rented by the day, week or month. Tools and DIY equipment can also be rented in most towns. There are DIY hypermarkets such as Akí and Leroy Merlin in most areas, although DIY equipment and supplies can be more expensive than in other EU countries (many items are imported).

Spanish textiles are often of inferior quality or more expensive than in other European countries. Foreign pillow sizes (e.g. American and British) aren't the same as in Spain, although various sizes can be purchased in shops such as El Corte Inglés. If you need measuring equipment and cannot cope with decimal measures, you must bring your own measuring scales, jugs, cups and thermometers (see also **Appendix D**).

# NEWSPAPERS, MAGAZINES & BOOKS

Newspapers and magazines are sold at tobacconists, newsagents, street newsstands, railway station kiosks, and in supermarkets and hypermarkets. The Spanish aren't great newspaper readers and circulation is much lower than in most other European countries (only the Greeks, Portuguese and Albanians read fewer newspapers). Reading a newspaper in Spain is largely a middle-class habit and there's no popular tabloid or gutter press (*prensa amarilla*), as is common in many other European countries. Only ten newspapers (four of which are sports papers) sell over 100,000 copies daily nationwide and only one in five Spaniards buys a newspaper. However, each copy tends to be read by more people than in other countries, so the sales figures don't accurately reflect the total readership.

Spain's most popular and best-selling daily newspaper is *El País* (the country), founded in 1976 and published in Madrid. It's the only serious Spanish newspaper for political analysis and the best for international news. It's a liberal newspaper (although aligned with the socialist party) with a national circulation of around 2.1 million from Mondays to Saturdays and 2.53 million on Sundays (the Sunday edition includes various supplements and a colour magazine, *EPS*, itself an institution in Spain), including various regional editions. *El País* is available online by free access (usually limited to the daily edition) or subscription where subscribers have access to the newspaper's archives in their entirety (🖳 www.elpais.es). *El Mundo* (centre-right and keen on uncovering scandals involving the Socialist party) is Spain's second-largest selling newspaper with a daily circulation of around 1.4 million. *El Mundo* is available online free (🖳 www.elmundo.es). *ABC*, Spain's oldest newspaper that also publishes some regional editions (e.g. Andalusia), is also published in Madrid and is Spain's third-largest selling newspaper with a daily circulation of around 840,000. It's conservative, traditional and right wing, and changed its format substantially in 2003 in order to attract younger readers (🖳 www.abc.es, free access). *La Razón* (right, run by the ex-editor of *ABC*) is the other national newspaper, although with daily readership of around 330,000, it isn't in the same league as the other nationals.

Leading newspapers in Barcelona include *El Periódico* (the largest selling), *La Vanguardia*, and *Diari de Barcelona*, all three written in Catalan, although *La Vanguardia* is also published in Castillian. In the Basque Country, there are the Basque newspapers of *Deia* and *Eja*, which are mostly written in Basque (*Euskera*). The regional press is often right-wing and supportive of regional autonomy. Most weekly newspapers in Spain are also published on Sundays with a colour supplement. In addition to general daily newspapers, a number of highly popular sports newspapers are published such as *Marca* and *AS*, dedicated entirely to sports coverage (mostly football) and whose daily readership is far greater than that of the national newspapers. Most newspapers publish free supplements with their daily editions covering topics such as entertainment (listing local art shows, exhibitions, theatre, cinema, concerts and other leisure activities), IT, travel, art and literature, and house and home.

Over the last year, numerous free daily newspapers (e.g. *20 Minutos*, *Metro* and *Qué*) have appeared in Spain. Most are regionally or locally-based and consist of around ten pages with a round-up of local, national and international news (but no analysis or comment) plus the weather and TV programmes. The newspapers are distributed in main towns and cities and are also available on public transport.

Numerous magazines (*revistas*) are also published in Spain and are generally more popular than newspapers. Spain publishes countless glossy gossip magazines, referred to as the 'press of the heart' (*prensa del corazón*). Magazines such as *Pronto* (the best seller with a weekly circulation of around 3.54 million), *Hola*, *Diez Minutos*, *Semana* and *Lecturas* are among the ten most popular magazines in Spain, selling over 2.5m copies a week. Although they cover the private lives of the rich and famous and often epitomise bad taste, they're rarely controversial or scurrilous.

Many foreign newspapers are available in the main cities and resorts by the afternoon or the following morning. A number of British newspapers, including the *Daily Express*, *Daily Mail*, *Daily Mirror*, *The Guardian*, *The Times*, *Star* and *Sun* are printed in Spain and available on the morning of publication (including Sunday editions). Many other English-language daily newspapers are widely available on the day of publication, including *USA Today*, *International Herald Tribune* (edited in Paris), *Wall Street Journal Europe* and the *European Financial Times*. Many English and foreign newspapers produce weekly editions, including the British *International Express*, *Guardian Weekly* and *Weekly Telegraph*, all of which are available on Spanish newsstands. **Foreign newspapers cost around three times the price than in their country of origin.**

Many English-language newspapers are published in Spain, including the *Costa Blanca News*, *Costa del Sol News*, *Sur in English*, *Ibiza Sun*, *Majorcan Daily Bulletin* and *Tenerife News*. Spain also has a number of English-language monthly magazines available from newsagents throughout Spain (see **Appendix B**). Note that many Spanish and foreign newspapers and magazines can be purchased on subscription from the publishers, often at large savings over local retail prices.

Free local English-language newspapers and magazines are published in most areas and contain a wealth of information about local events, restaurants, bars, entertainment, services and shops. These include *The Broadsheet* and *Barcelona Metropolitan* (monthly) and *Euro Weekly* (regional versions, weekly). Other free newspapers and magazines are published in Dutch, Finnish, French, German and Swedish.

There are English-language book shops (*librerías*) in Spain's major cities and resort towns. There are also many second-hand book shops in resort towns that buy, sell and exchange second-hand books. Most have books in various languages, including English, Danish, Dutch, French, German and Swedish. In small towns, there are usually a few small shops selling a limited selection of books, rather than one well-stocked large book shop. Many Spanish book shops such as FNAC and the book department in the Corte Inglés also keep a small selection of English-language books.

In major cities, there are biannual book fairs and regular second-hand book markets for collectors. Generally, the price of imported books is lower in Spain than in many other European countries, although Americans will be shocked at the prices. Many expatriate organisations and clubs run their own libraries or book exchanges and some Spanish public libraries keep a small selection of English-language books.

# MARKETS

Markets (*mercados*) are a common sight in towns and villages throughout Spain, and are an essential part of Spanish life, largely unaffected by competition from supermarkets and hypermarkets. They're colourful, entertaining and fun, and an experience not to be missed, even if you don't plan to buy anything. Markets thrive throughout Spain and are the centre of life in towns and villages. Some towns have markets on only one or two days a week (always the same days), while others have daily fruit and vegetable markets from Mondays to Saturdays. In rural and coastal areas, market days are varied in local towns so that they don't clash (a list of local markets may be available from the local tourist office). There are also Sunday markets in some towns.

There are generally three kinds of markets in Spain: indoor markets, permanent street markets and travelling open-air street markets (*venta ambulante*) that move from neighbourhood to neighbourhood on different days of the week or month. There are some 8,000 travelling markets in Spain (most are in Andalusia and Extremadura), each with from 50 to 200 stands. The most popular wares are textiles and fruit and vegetables, plus shoes, perfume and toilet articles, and general household goods. Prices are often around 20 per cent lower than in shops, although much depends on your bargaining skills. There's often a large central market (*mercado central*) in cities, and many towns and neighbourhoods of large cities have indoor or covered markets. Municipal markets (*mercados municipales*) controlled by the local council are found in most towns and many large villages. Markets usually operate from 9am until 2pm, although in cities and some towns they occasionally re-open on Fridays after the *siesta*, e.g. from 5 or 5.30pm until 7.30 or 8pm.

A variety of goods are commonly sold in markets, including food, flowers, plants, clothes (markets are best for inexpensive clothes), shoes, ironmongery, crockery, hardware, cookware, linen, ceramics, compact discs (CD), arts and crafts, household wares, carpets, jewellery, watches and leather goods. Specialist markets in Madrid and other cities sell antiques, books, clothes, stamps, postcards, medals, coins, flowers, birds and pets. **You should beware of bargain-priced branded goods in markets such as watches, perfume and clothes, as they're usually fakes.**

Food markets remain highly popular, despite the proliferation of supermarkets and hypermarkets in recent years. Food is invariably beautifully presented and encompasses fruit and vegetables (including many exotic varieties), fish and shellfish, meat, dairy products, bread and cakes, and pickled vegetables, herbs and olives, and is usually sold in different sections. Food is cheaper and fresher in markets than in supermarkets, particularly if you buy what's in season and grown locally. You should arrive early in the morning for the best choice, although bargains can often be found late in the day when stallholders are packing up.

All produce is clearly marked with its price per piece or per kilo. There's no haggling over food prices, although at the end of the day an offer may be accepted. When shopping for food in markets, vendors may object to customers handling the fruit and vegetables, although you needn't be shy about asking to taste a piece of cheese or fruit. It's advisable to take a bag when buying fruit and vegetables, as carrier bags aren't always provided. When buying fruit and vegetables in markets check that the quality of produce you're given is the same as that displayed, which isn't always the case. Queues are a good sign. Local people also sell homegrown produce on the fringes of markets.

Antique and flea markets (*rastros*) are common throughout Spain, although you shouldn't expect to find many (if any) bargains in the major cities, where anything worth buying is snapped up by dealers. However, in small towns you can turn up some real bargains. Note that you shouldn't assume that because something is sold in a market it's a bargain, particularly when buying antiques (*antigüedades*), which aren't always authentic. In many cases, local shops are cheaper, particularly those selling to local residents rather than tourists. Always haggle over the price of expensive items. To find out when local markets are held, enquire at your local tourist office or town hall.

# SUPERMARKETS & HYPERMARKETS

There are supermarkets (*supermercados*) and hypermarkets (*hipermercados*) in or just outside most towns in Spain. The big advantage of supermarkets is the convenience of doing all your shopping in one place, free parking, all day opening, and you don't really need to speak a word of Spanish – a big advantage for many foreigners. Hypermarkets and large supermarkets are generally open all day from between 9 and 10am until between 9 and 10pm from Mondays to Saturdays and don't close for lunch or a *siesta*. Some also open on Sundays, although this may be only in the summer months in resorts and before Christmas. Smaller supermarkets generally open at around 9am and close earlier than hypermarkets, e.g. 7 or 8pm, or perhaps later on Fridays. Some supermarkets close for lunch, e.g. 1.30 or 2pm until 4 or 5pm, although not usually on Saturdays. Supermarkets and hypermarkets are often located in shopping centres with a variety of small shops, key cutting, shoe repair, newsagents, banks or ATMs, cafés and restaurants (often including a self-serve restaurant), toilets, public telephones, a huge free car park, and possibly a petrol station and car wash.

In addition to food and drink, most supermarkets sell household products, tableware, clothes, toiletries and hardware. The name *hipermercado* is used fairly loosely in Spain and many *hipers* are in fact small supermarkets selling a few non-food items and nothing like, for example, the vast French hypermarkets.

A 'real' hypermarket is similar to a department store (although usually on one floor) and sells everything you would expect to find in a supermarket plus books, CDs, TVs, music systems, computers, cameras, furniture, textiles, household goods, gardening equipment and furniture, domestic electrical apparatus, DIY, motoring accessories, white goods (e.g. refrigerators, freezers, washing machines), sports equipment, jewellery, bicycles, tools, kitchenware, clothes and shoes, toys, magazines and newspapers. French-owned hypermarkets such as Alcampo and Carrefour dominate the Spanish market, the main competition coming from Hipercor, owned by El Corte Inglés and Eroski. National supermarket chains include Dani, Día, Lidl, Mercadona, Plus and SuperSol, plus many smaller regional chains. Dani (Spain's cheapest supermarket in 2005) and Mercadona are among the best value for money supermarkets. There are also wholesale or cash and carry outlets in Spain such as Makro, where you need a membership card (note that some wholesale outlets don't accept credit cards).

The cost of food in Spain is slightly lower than the average for western Europe. A couple with two children can expect to spend around €120 a week on food. Note that prices often vary (even in different branches of the same supermarket) depending on the level of local competition. All supermarkets and hypermarkets have food counters for meat, fish, bread and cheese. The Spanish generally don't like to buy pre-packaged meat, fish, cheese, fruit or vegetables, but prefer to buy them to order. Some supermarkets use a number system (whereby you take a number from a roll) at certain counters (e.g. processed meat and cheese) to ensure customers are served in the correct order.

Fruit and vegetables in supermarkets are often a disappointment, with poor quality second-class produce. It's often said that the Spanish export all their best produce, which isn't difficult to believe judging by the quality in some supermarkets. Fruit and vegetables are usually weighed by an assistant and **aren't** weighed at checkouts. It's best to avoid packaged fruit and vegetables, which often contain bad produce. **Fresh produce in supermarkets is often well past its sell-by date, particularly during very hot weather when it's difficult to keep food fresh.** Always check the 'sell-by' date (*fecha de caducidad*) or date of minimum duration (*fecha de duración mínima*), particularly when buying slow-selling foods such as pre-packaged foreign cheeses and meats, as it's common to find food is out of date (and mouldy). Sometimes a 'preferably consume before date' (*consumir preferentemente antes de 'date'*), production date (*fecha de fabricación*) or packaged date (*fecha de envasado*) is shown, which mean little without a shelf-life date.

There's a huge choice of tinned vegetables and meats in Spanish supermarkets, but relatively few frozen vegetables. While there's generally an excellent selection of fresh foods, there's a poor choice of frozen and convenience (fast) foods, and microwave meals are rare. Frozen and convenience foods are also expensive and the quality leaves something to be desired. In some areas, the frozen food companies Bofrost and Agrigel operate a home delivery service of a selection of frozen foods, a convenient service, but quite expensive. Many supermarkets and specialist shops such as the British company Iceland (trading as Icelandia in Spain) cater for the tastes of foreigners, particularly in resort areas where there are many foreign residents. If you live on the Costa del Sol, you can visit Gibraltar and stock up on British foods from supermarkets such as Safeway, although the strength of the pound means it's expensive if you pay in euros.

Fresh milk is available in most supermarkets, although it may be close to or past its sell-by date (a sure sign is a bulging carton) and goes off quickly in summer. Most Spaniards and the majority of foreigners buy UHT long-life milk, which initially usually tastes awful (particularly in tea), but most people get used to it. It usually comes in skimmed (*desnatada*), semi-skimmed (*semi-desnatada*) and whole (*entera*) versions and is sold in one litre and half-litre cartons.

Although some smaller supermarkets still price items individually, most use bar code scanning. Bar codes make it difficult to check your bill (unless you have an exceptional memory), although most till receipts list all items with their name and price. Mistakes are common (usually in the retailer's favour) and you should at least verify the price of special offers. You can pay with a debit card (issued by all Spanish banks – see page 319) or credit card in most supermarkets and hypermarkets (although most require identification in the form of a passport or identity card).

Some supermarkets have their own purchase cards (*tarjetas de compra*) offering customer discounts and supermarkets may also offer free scratch cards (and other gimmicks) where you can win small prizes.

In some supermarkets, you're required to leave your shopping bags at a special counter (*consigna*) before entering, in return for which you're given a numbered disc. Most Spanish supermarkets provide free plastic bags (*bolsas*), although it's wise not to fill them with too many heavy items, such as bottles of wine! Checkout staff don't bag your purchases and take them out to your car for you, although some supermarkets have a home delivery service (sometimes you can also order by phone), which may be free when your purchases exceed a certain sum, e.g. €30 or €50. Note that it's essential to have a €0.50 or €1 coin to obtain a trolley.

All supermarket and hypermarket chains publish regular brochures and leaflets (which may be distributed to local post boxes) featuring special offers.

## Warning

In recent years, many people shopping at hypermarkets have been victims of thieves who operate in the area, particularly in the car parks. Popular tricks are stealing handbags from trolleys or distracting you when you're packing your shopping in your car while an accomplice steals your handbag or wallet. Keep an eye on your handbag and money **at all times** and **always** lock your car when you're returning the trolley. Women on their own or with children should be particularly vigilant, as they're the most likely victims.

## DEPARTMENT & CHAIN STORES

There are few department stores (*grandes almacenes*) in Spain and only one national chain, El Corte Inglés with around 80 shops. El Corte Inglés is a Spanish institution and one of Spain's top profit-making companies with branches in all cities and many large towns. It's Europe's second-largest department store chain in terms of gross sales, despite the fact that it has far fewer shops than its rivals. However, what it lacks in numbers it makes up for in size and operates huge shops with thousands of square metres of floor space.

El Corte Inglés stocks the best and most famous Spanish and international products. Shops pander to the needs of free-spending foreign shoppers and provide multilingual information desks, interpreters, tax-refunds, travel services and money changing (outside banking hours). Shops are open throughout the day from 10am until 9 or 10pm and some are also open on Sundays and public holidays (e.g. from noon to 8pm). In addition to the usual departments found in department stores, El Corte Inglés stores also have excellent (but expensive) food markets. The store accepts telephone (☎ 902-224 411) and online (🖳 www.elcorteingles.es) orders and provides free delivery for orders above a certain value, e.g. €100, or for a fee (e.g. €6) below this amount. All major credit cards are accepted and El Corte Inglés issues its own credit card, although interest rates are high on monthly accounts (some items can be purchased interest free over three months).

A number of foreign chain stores have outlets in Spain, including Benetton, Body Shop, Dorothy Perkins, H&M, Top Shop and Wallis. In addition, Britons living on the Costa del Sol can satisfy their yearning for their home high street by taking a day trip to Gibraltar, where there are branches of BHS, ELC, Mothercare and Safeway.

Some cities actively promote shopping in city centres, especially during Christmas, where discount parking or free transport is offered if you spend a certain amount (e.g. €25) in participating shops. Barcelona city centre runs a 'Bus Shopping Line' service during the Christmas period with unlimited free transport on special coaches for a day providing you spend €50 or more at certain shops.

# TOBACCONISTS'

Tobacconists' (*estancos*) are conspicuous by their yellow and dark red paintwork, and a sign depicting a yellow letter 'T' (for Tabacalera, the state-owned tobacco company) on a maroon background. Tabacalera SA is a monopoly that supplies and owns the official tobacconists' (established in 1637), which in turn supply everyone else. Cigarettes can also be purchased from machines in bars and cafes, street kiosks (*quioscos*) and from supermarkets, although these are all a bit more expensive than buying from a tobacconist.

Spanish cigarettes are usually made of strong black tobacco (*tabaco negro*) with a high nicotine content, although cigarettes made with 'blond' or Virginia tobacco (*tabaco rubio*) are also available. Note that imported brands are up to three times the price of local brands, which is why there's a lively smuggling trade (most of it through Gibraltar) costing Spain millions of euros in lost duty annually. A few foreign brands are produced in Spain under licence and are cheaper than imports. The best-selling Spanish brands are Ducados and Fortuna. Good inexpensive Spanish cigars are made in the Canary islands and imported Cuban cigars are also good value for money.

Tobacconists' are a unique institution in Spain. Not only are they the sole authorised vendors of cigarettes and other tobacco products, but they're also mini-stationers and the source of official government forms (e.g. for tax, contracts and official medical certificates) and 'state paper' (*papel del estado*), used to pay official fees for permits and licences. Note, however, that few, if any, tobacconists stock the whole range of forms or *papel del estado* and you may have to obtain them from an official government office. A tobacconist's also sells postage stamps at face value, postcards, single envelopes and writing paper, gifts and souvenirs, cigarette lighters, photographic film, and other odds and ends.

# SHOPPING ABROAD

Shopping abroad includes day trips to Andorra, France, Gibraltar, Portugal and Morocco, as well as shopping excursions further afield. A day trip abroad makes an interesting day out for the family and can save you money, depending on what and where you buy. **Don't forget your passports or identity cards, car papers, children, dog's vaccination papers and foreign currency.** Most shops in bordering towns gladly accept euros, even if they aren't within the eurozone, but usually give you a lower exchange rate than a bank. Whatever you're looking for, compare prices and quality before buying. Bear in mind that if you buy goods that are faulty or need repair, you may need to return them to the place of purchase. There are no cross-border shopping restrictions within the EU, provided all goods are for personal consumption or use and not for resale. However, there are 'indicative levels' for items such as spirits, wine, beer and tobacco products, above which goods may be classified as commercial quantities.

## Andorra

Andorra is Europe's biggest duty-free shop and considerable savings can be made on almost everything, including alcohol, tobacco products, cheese and other foodstuffs, clocks and watches, cameras, film, electrical goods, perfume, luxury goods and petrol.

## Gibraltar

Considerable savings can be made on cigarettes, petrol, foodstuffs, luxury goods (e.g. perfumes) and various consumer goods in Gibraltar. Spanish residents and visitors are permitted to import goods up to the value of €175 (€90 for under 15s), exclusive of duty-free items (see below). Note that there are often long delays for vehicles at the border crossing into Spain, as Spanish customs officers allegedly check them for drugs and tobacco. It's often advisable to park on the Spanish side of the border and take a bus or taxi (or walk) into Gibraltar town. **Make sure that you lock and secure your car against theft, as cars are sometimes stolen or broken into while their owners are shopping in Gibraltar!** Shopping hours are usually from 9am until 7pm Mondays to Fridays and 9am to 1pm on Saturdays (most shops are closed on Sundays).

## Warning

Never attempt to import any illegal goods into Spain and don't agree to bring a parcel into Spain or deliver a parcel to another country without knowing exactly what its contents are. A popular confidence trick is to ask someone to post a parcel abroad (usually to a *poste restante* address) or to leave a parcel at a particular place such as a railway station or restaurant abroad. **Beware! Parcels such as these usually contain drugs!** Many foreign truck drivers are languishing in Spanish jails having been the unwitting victims of drug traffickers (who conceal drugs in shipments of goods).

## DUTY-FREE ALLOWANCES

If you travel to or from Spain to or from another EU country, you're entitled to import goods of an unlimited value, as long as they're for personal use plus cigarettes and alcohol as listed below. Note the list is issued as a guideline only and if you import more than the amounts shown below, you must be able to show that the goods are for your personal use. If you cannot, they may be confiscated by customs officials. Note, also that guidelines are subject to change and you should check with an official source before you import large amounts:

- 800 cigarettes.
- 400 cigarillos.
- 20 cigars.
- 1kg tobacco.
- 90 litres wine (of which no more than 60 should be sparkling).
- 10 litres spirits.
- 20 litres fortified wine.
- 110 litres beer.

For each journey to a non-EU country travellers aged 17 or over (unless otherwise stated) are entitled to import the following goods purchased duty-free:

- One litre of spirits (over 22 degrees proof) **or** two litres of fortified wine, sparkling wine or other liqueurs (under 22 degrees proof).
- Two litres of still table wine.
- 200 cigarettes **or** 100 cigarillos **or** 50 cigars **or** 250g of tobacco.
- 60cc/ml of perfume.
- 250cc/ml of toilet water.
- Other goods, including gifts and souvenirs to the value of €175 (€90 for under 15s).

Duty-free allowances apply on outward and return journeys, even if both are made on the same day, and the combined total (i.e. double the above limits) can be imported into your 'home' country. It's rarely worthwhile buying duty-free alcohol when travelling to Spain, as it's usually cheaper in Spanish supermarkets and off-licences.

Special rules apply when shopping in duty-free areas such as Andorra and Gibraltar. In Andorra, the duty-free limits for those aged over 17 are:

- 1.5 litres of alcohol over 22 degrees proof **or** three litres of alcohol under 22 degrees proof **or** five litres of still table wine.
- 300 cigarettes **or** 150 cigarillos **or** 75 cigars **or** 400g of tobacco.
- 75g of perfume and 375ml of toilet water.
- Up to €175 worth of other 'agricultural' goods, although there are limits for some products such as milk (six litres), butter (1kg), cheese (4kg), sugar (5kg), coffee (1kg) and tea (200g).
- Up to €525 worth of manufactured goods (€270 for under 15s).

Duty-free allowances for Gibraltar include the following:

- 200 cigarettes **or** 50 cigars **or** 250g of tobacco.
- One bottle of spirits.
- 200 litres of petrol.
- Any other purchases to the value of €175 (€90 for under 15s).

If you're resident outside the EU, you can reclaim value added tax (VAT/*IVA*) on single purchases costing over €100. An export sales invoice is provided by retailers listing all purchases, which must be confirmed by a customs officer when leaving Spain (so keep purchases in your hand luggage). Your refund will be posted to you later or paid to a credit card account (at major airports it can also be reclaimed at a special Europe Tax-Free Shopping refund window). With certain purchases, particularly large items, it's better (or necessary) to have them sent directly abroad, when VAT won't be added. Large department stores such as El Corte Inglés have a special office where non-EU shoppers can arrange for the shipment of goods.

# INTERNET SHOPPING

Shopping via the internet is the fastest-growing form of retailing and although it's still in its infancy, sales are forecast to spiral. Shopping on the internet is very secure (secure servers, with addresses beginning https:// rather than http:// are almost impossible to crack) and in most cases, safer than shopping by phone or mail-order. There are literally thousands of shopping sites on the internet, including 🖥 www. ukshoppingpages.com and information sites, 🖥 www.shopguide.co.uk and 🖥 www. virgin.net/shopping (which has a good directory of British shopping sites).

With internet shopping, the world is literally your oyster and savings can be made on a wide range of goods, including CDs, clothes, sports equipment, electronic gadgets, jewellery, books (🖥 www.amazon.co.uk or for Spanish books 🖥 www. fnac.es), wine and computer software, and services such as insurance, pensions and mortgages. Huge savings can also be made on holidays and travel. Small high-price, high-items (e.g. cameras, watches and portable and hand-held computers) can usually be purchased cheaper somewhere in Europe or (particularly) in the US (for cameras try 🖥 www.normancamera.com), with delivery by courier within as little as three days. Several large Spanish retailers are now online, including Alcampo, Carrefour and El Corte Inglés, which like the shop, is divided into two shops, the main shop (*centro comercial*) and the supermarket (*supermercado*). Online supermarkets have most of the usual food and household products and there are facilities to record your 'usual order' to save time on future orders. Note that orders are usually only delivered within certain cities and in some cases, e.g. El Corte Inglés, you need a store card to make purchases online.

## Buying Overseas

When buying goods overseas ensure that you're dealing with a bona fide company and that the goods will work in Spain (if applicable). If possible, pay by credit card when buying by mail order or over the internet, as this offers added protection with the credit card issuer being jointly liable with the supplier. Note, however, that many card companies claim that the law doesn't cover overseas purchases, although many issuers consider claims up to the value of the goods purchased (and they could also be liable in law for consequential loss). When you buy expensive goods abroad, always have them insured for their full value.

## VAT & Duty

When buying overseas, take into account shipping costs, duty (e.g. a reduced rate of 3.5 per cent for small packages valued below around €350 and 13 per cent for clothing) and VAT (16 per cent). There's no duty or tax on goods purchased within the EU or on goods from most other countries worth up to around €30. Don't buy alcohol or cigarettes abroad, as the duty is usually too high to make it pay. When VAT or duty is payable on a parcel, the payment is usually collected by the post office or courier company on delivery.

# RECEIPTS

When shopping in Spain, insist on a receipt (*recibo* or *factura*) and keep it until you've left the shop or have reached home. This isn't just in case you need to return or exchange goods, which may be impossible without the receipt, but also to verify that you've paid. Generally speaking, a complaint won't be entertained without a receipt (so make sure that you receive one).

Under Spanish law, all products sold must be suitable for the use for which they're intended. If they aren't, then you're entitled to exchange them or obtain a full refund. It's illegal for traders to use 'small print' to try to avoid liability. You have the same legal rights whether goods are purchased at the recommended retail price or at a discount during a sale. It's advisable to keep the receipts and records of all major purchases made while you're resident in Spain, particularly if your stay is only for a limited period. This may save you time and money when you finally leave Spain and are required to declare your belongings in your new country of residence.

# CONSUMER PROTECTION

Spain has become more aware of consumer rights in recent years and there are strict consumer protection laws (particularly regarding the vital tourist industry). If you have a complaint (*reclamación*) about a product or service, you should make it, in the first instance, to the supplier or manufacturer, if possible in person. Failing that, make a complaint in writing and keep a copy of all correspondence. Note that there are special procedures for complaints against many companies, including utility companies, the post office, public transport companies, banks, insurance companies, hotels, restaurants, bars and the public health service. Your local town hall can advise you how to make a complaint.

All businesses are required by law to keep a complaints book or complaints forms (*libros/hojas de reclamaciones*), which must be produced on demand. These vary depending on the region and may be printed in Spanish and English. The form has three pages, one or two of which you receive. A request for a complaints form (or book) often results in a speedy and satisfactory outcome to a dispute, as all complaints must be forwarded to the authorities within 48 hours and businesses can be penalised if they're in the wrong.

If you fail to obtain satisfaction regarding a complaint against a local business, you should contact the Ministry of Health and Consumer Affairs (Ministerio de Sanidad y Consumo) through their local office (Oficina Municipal de Información al Consumidor/OMIC). OMIC offices are established in liaison with town halls in most towns; if there isn't a local OMIC office contact your town hall. A serious complaint may be referred to the OMIC regional office (Oficina Regional del Información al Consumidor) in the regional capital town and a business can be fined up to €15,000 if a complaint is upheld.

OMICS are supported in many areas by local housewives associations (Asociaciones de Amas de Casa), which have watchdog and educational roles. The main consumer organisation in Spain is the Organización de Consumidores y Usuarios (OCU), C/Albarracín, 21, 28037 Madrid (☎ 902-300 187, 🖳 www.ocu.org), which can provide the services of a lawyer and also has provincial offices. The OCU also runs a programme to inform tourists of their rights and help them deal with problems.

The Basque hypermarket chain, Eroski, sponsors a very useful consumer website (🖳 www.consumer.es), where you can consult consumer rights, news and advice. The website includes a free weekly e-bulletin service informing you of latest consumer news and developments. You can also subscribe to the monthly magazine.

# 18.

# ODDS & ENDS

This chapter contains miscellaneous information. Most of the topics covered are of general interest to anyone living or working in Spain, although not all are of vital importance. However, buried among the trivia are some fascinating snippets of information.

# BUSINESS HOURS

Business hours for offices in Spain are generally from 9 or 9.30am until 1.30pm and from 4.30 or 5pm until around 8pm. In summer, many businesses work from 8am through to 3pm (the end of the working day) without a break. However, in recent years many companies, particularly those operating globally, have switched to 'international' working hours, e.g. from 9am until 5pm, with a break for lunch from 1 to 2pm. It's often difficult to determine business hours in Spain and most people therefore try to do business involving telephone calls or visits in the mornings, rather than the afternoons. Note that government establishments are meticulous in keeping to their official working hours. When dealing with small businesses or the self-employed, making telephone or personal calls during *siesta* hours should be avoided.

# CITIZENSHIP

Your eligibility for Spanish citizenship depends upon your parentage, your current nationality and how long you've lived in Spain. You automatically acquire Spanish nationality if one of your parents is Spanish, you were born in Spain and one of your parents was also born there, or you were born in Spain of foreign parents who have no nationality (or you aren't entitled to claim their nationality).

Most foreigners must have held a residence permit (*residencia* – see page 78) for ten years before they can apply for Spanish nationality. The main exceptions are those who have been granted political refuge or asylum, who can apply after five years, and nationals of Latin American countries, Andorra, the Philippines, Equatorial Guinea, Portugal and Jews of Spanish origin, all of whom qualify after just two years. A one-year residence period is sufficient for someone born in Spain or born outside Spain with a Spanish mother or father, or anyone married to a Spanish citizen (even if the marriage has been dissolved). In all cases, the period of residence in Spain must have been immediately before the application. Marriage to a Spanish citizen doesn't entitle you to a work permit, although an application for one is usually granted and expedited. Foreign children aged under 18 who are adopted by Spanish parents automatically become Spanish citizens, although an adopted child aged 18 or older at the time of adoption must decide whether to choose Spanish nationality in the two years following adoption.

An application for Spanish citizenship must be made to the Minister of Justice, who can refuse it on grounds of public order or national interest. To apply for Spanish nationality you require your birth certificate, marriage certificate (if applicable), and your parents' birth and marriage certificates, all of which must be officially translated into Spanish. You also require a certificate of good conduct from the police, a statement from two Spanish citizens supporting your application, and you must show that you're a good citizen and integrated into Spanish society. Most people find it necessary to employ a lawyer to handle the paperwork involved.

Spanish law doesn't recognise dual nationality for adults and therefore a child who's entitled to choose between Spanish and another nationality must make a choice at the age of 18. A foreigner must usually renounce his former nationality (exceptions include Portuguese and Latin Americans), swear allegiance to the King of Spain, and swear to abide by the Spanish constitution and laws. Some countries (e.g. the UK) don't recognise a renunciation of nationality, irrespective of whether its citizens have taken another nationality. It's advisable to take legal advice before renouncing your nationality and becoming a Spanish citizen.

# CLIMATE

Hardly surprisingly, the overwhelming attraction of Spain for most foreigners is its excellent climate. Spain is the sunniest country in Europe and the climate (on the Costa Blanca) has been described by the World Health Organisation as among the healthiest in the world. Spain's Mediterranean coastline, from the Costa Blanca to the Costa del Sol, enjoys an average of over 300 days sunshine each year. When northern Europe is being deluged or is frozen, you can almost guarantee that the south of Spain will be bathed in sunshine. In general, May and October are considered the best months for touring, as they're generally dry and not too hot in most regions. However, there's a price to pay for all those warm days. Extremes are common with southern parts of Spain suffering drought and reservoir levels at an all-time low when at the same time, there may be widespread flooding affecting large areas in northern Spain. As they say in Spain, 'it never rains to everyone's taste' (*nunca llueve a gusto de todos*)!

Continental Spain experiences three climatic zones: Atlantic, Continental and Mediterranean, in addition to which some areas, particularly the Balearic and Canary Islands, have their own distinct micro-climates. In coastal areas, there can be huge variations in the weather simply by travelling a few kilometres inland and up into the mountains. On some islands such as Majorca, rainfall varies from 300 to 400mm (12 to 16in) in the south to over 1,200mm (47in) in the north, and some areas experience strong winds in winter while others are sheltered.

The Atlantic or green zone (*costa verde*) embraces the north-west region of the country, including Galicia (which has a mild and humid climate), the Cantabrian coast of Asturias, Cantabria, the Basque Country and the Pyrenees (dividing Spain and France). The region from Galicia's border with Asturias along the coast to the Pyrenees is the wettest area of Spain, although even here there are some 1,800 hours of sunshine a year (much more than in northern Europe). Summer coastal temperatures average around 25°C (77°F) and spring and autumn are mild. However, the region experiences high rainfall of from 900 to 2,000mm (35 to 79in) a year, particularly in winter on the coast, and inland it's cold with frequent snowfalls (Teruel and Soria provinces generally have the worst winter climate). Contrary to the popular saying, the rain in Spain certainly doesn't fall mainly on the plain – the plains are very dry and most rain falls along the northern and western coasts. Heavy snowfalls are common above 1,200m (3,937ft) in winter and although snow is rare outside the mountainous areas, most areas in the north of Spain and the Balearics occasionally experience snowfalls.

The Continental zone encompasses the central part of Spain, called the tableland (*meseta*), and the Ebro river valley. It embraces the provinces of Castile-La Mancha, Castile León and Extremadura, plus part of Aragon and Navarre, and is baking hot in summer and freezing cold in winter. Madrid is in the centre of the *meseta* and has the lowest winter temperatures in Spain, ranging from a low of 1°C (34°F) to a high of 9°C (48°F) in January. Annual rainfall in Madrid is 300 to 600mm (12 to 16in). The further you travel south from Madrid in winter the warmer it becomes (except in mountainous regions), with, for example, Seville experiencing temperate winters. Seville also experiences the hottest summers in Spain, where the temperature averages around 34°C (93°F) in July and August and often exceeds 40°C (104°F). The temperature in Ecija, between Cordoba and Seville, has exceeded 47°C (117°F) and it's appropriately known as the frying pan of Andalusia (*la sartén de Andalucía*).

The Mediterranean zone embraces the coastal regions of Spain from the French to the Portuguese borders and is split into three regions. Catalonia (including the Costa Brava) has relatively mild winters, but is also quite humid, with 500 to 800mm (20 to 31in) of rain and between 2,450 and 2,650 hours of sunshine a year. Summers are pleasant without very high temperatures. The central eastern part of the Mediterranean coast, from around Alicante to Tarragona (known as the Levante) and including the Costa Blanca (plus Valencia and Murcia), is warmer in winter than Catalonia and has lower rainfall (300 to 425mm/12 to 17in). The annual hours of sunshine are between 2,700 to 3,000 and temperatures in summer can be over 30°C (86°F). The southern coast of Andalusia (including the Costa del Sol) has slightly higher temperatures than the eastern coast (in winter and summer) and between 2,900 and 3,000 annual hours of sunshine. Annual rainfall is just 230 to 470mm (9 to 19in). In winter, the daytime temperature on the Costa Blanca and Costa del Sol often reaches a pleasant 15 to 20°C (59 to 68°F), when the Spanish habitually dress in overcoats and the foreigners in shorts or bathing costumes.

Andalusia includes the most arid part of Spain in the province of Almeria and also the area with the highest rainfall in the whole of Spain in Grazalema in the province of Cadiz. Most rain in Andalusia falls in the winter months, with some areas having as little as 200mm (8in) a year, which may all fall in one or two days, causing flash floods. The Mediterranean coast is also subject to cold winds from the north and north-east which bring snow to the Pyrenees and the *meseta* in winter. The Costa del Sol can be extremely windy in winter (it was originally called the 'windy coast' or *Costa de Viento* until the tourist ministry's marketing men got to work) and parts of the Atlantic coast of Cadiz, Costa de la Luz, experience a particularly strong wind called the *levante*, which can blow for days at a time (great for windsurfers). The mountain ranges of the hinterland help protect the coastal regions from climatic extremes and funnel warm air from the *meseta* to the coast in summer.

The Balearic Islands have a Mediterranean climate with mild winters and hot summers, tempered by cool sea breezes (the most pleasant summer climate in Spain).

Annual sunshine is similar to the Levante, while annual rainfall is higher at between 450 and 650mm (18 to 26in).

The Canary Islands boast the best year-round climate with warm winters and temperate summers, and temperatures of between 20 to 27°C (68 to 81°F) throughout the year. Hours of sunshine are similar to the Costa del Sol. Rainfall is low and varies from less than 100mm (4in) a year on Fuerteventura and Lanzarote to 750mm (30in) in the inland areas of Gran Canaria and Tenerife. The inland region of Tenerife experiences around 3,400 annual hours of sunshine – the highest in Spain.

Approximate average daily maximum/minimum temperatures for some major cities are shown below in Centigrade and Fahrenheit (in brackets):

| Location | Spring | Summer | Autumn | Winter |
|---|---|---|---|---|
| Barcelona | 18/11 (64/52) | 28/21 (82/70) | 21/15 (70/59) | 13/6 (55/43) |
| Cadiz | 20/13 (68/55) | 27/20 (81/68) | 23/17 (73/63) | 15/9 (59/48) |
| Granada | 20/7 (68/45) | 34/17 (93/63) | 23/10 (73/50) | 12/2 (54/36) |
| Madrid | 18/7 (64/45) | 31/17 (88/63) | 19/10 (66/50) | 9/2 (48/36) |
| Malaga | 21/13 (70/55) | 29/21 (84/70) | 23/16 (73/61) | 17/8 (63/46) |
| Palma | 19/10 (66/50) | 29/20 (84/68) | 18/10 (64/50) | 14/6 (57/43) |
| Santander | 15/10 (59/50) | 22/16 (72/61) | 18/12 (64/54) | 12/7 (53/45) |
| Seville | 24/11 (75/52) | 36/20 (97/68) | 26/14 (79/57) | 15/6 (59/43) |
| Tenerife | 24/17 (75/62) | 28/20 (83/68) | 28/21 (82/69) | 20/14 (68/58) |
| Valencia | 20/10 (68/50) | 29/20 (84/68) | 23/13 (73/55) | 15/6 (59/43) |

# NATURAL PHENOMENA

Spain experiences many violent, cold/hot, dry winds, including the *terral* in southern Spain, the *tramontana* in Catalonia, Minorca (Balearics) and the Pyrenees, and the *solano* in Cadiz. Although they're rare, southern Spain is prone to earthquakes; however, the strongest usually measure only a maximum of around 5.0 on the Richter scale and they rarely cause any damage or injuries. In summer, forest fires are a danger throughout the country and along with droughts, pose a serious long-term threat to the landscape, which resembles a desert in many areas (some 15 per cent of the country's surface has a serious erosion problem). Flash floods can be very dangerous, particularly in mountainous areas (over 80 people died in 1996 when flash floods struck a campsite in Biescas in northern Spain). Flash flooding is also common in seemingly dry stream or river beds, which when it rains hard, quickly turn into treacherous fast flowing water. **Never attempt to cross a stream or river when it's raining hard even in a 4x4 vehicle**. In October 2005, three foreigners were drowned while crossing a swollen river in their car in Catalonia.

Frequent weather forecasts (*pronósticos* or *el tiempo*) are given on television, radio and in daily newspapers. A quick way to make a **rough** conversion from Centigrade to Fahrenheit is to multiply by two and add 30 (see also **Appendix D**).

# CRIME

Spain's crime rate is among the lowest in Europe, although it has increased dramatically in the last decade and petty crime continues to increase. The Spanish generally have a lot of respect for law and order, although 'petty' laws (such as illegal parking and making too much noise) are usually ignored. In villages away from the tourist areas, crime is almost unknown and windows and doors are usually left unlocked. As in other countries, major cities have the highest crime rates and Alicante, Barcelona, Madrid, Malaga, Seville and Valencia are among the worst. Many cities are notorious for 'petty' crime such as handbag snatching, pickpockets and thefts of and from vehicles. Stealing from cars, particularly those with foreign registrations, is endemic throughout Spain, although car theft was down by nearly 14 per cent in 2004. You should **never** leave anything on display in your car, including your stereo system, which should be removed when parking in cities and towns (in some areas it will be gone within 15 minutes). Even storing valuables in your boot (trunk) isn't advisable, as thieves may force them open and steal the contents. In cities, it's advisable to park in 'guarded' car parks, although they take no responsibility for a car's contents.

The most common crime in Spain is theft, which embraces a multitude of forms. One of the most common is the ride-by bag snatcher on a motorbike or moped. Known as the 'pull' (*tirón*), it involves grabbing a hand or shoulder bag (or a camera) and riding off with it, sometimes with the owner still attached (occasionally causing serious injuries). It's advisable to carry bags on the inside of the pavement and to wear shoulder bags diagonally across your chest, although it's better not to carry a bag at all (the strap can be cut) and wear a wrist pouch or money belt. You should also be wary of bag-snatchers in airport and other car parks, and never wear valuable jewellery and watches in high-risk areas. Motorcycle thieves also smash car windows at traffic lights to steal articles left on seats, so stow bags on the floor or behind seats.

Tourists and travellers are the targets of some of Spain's most enterprising criminals, including highwaymen, who pose as accident or breakdown victims and rob motorists who stop to help them. Don't leave cash or valuables unattended when swimming or leave your bags, cameras or jackets lying around on chairs in café or bars (**always** keep an eye on your belongings in public places). Beware of gangs of child thieves in cities such as Madrid and Barcelona, pickpockets and over-friendly strangers. Always remain vigilant in tourist haunts, queues and anywhere there are large crowds, and **never** tempt fate with an exposed wallet or purse or by flashing your money around. One of the most effective methods of protecting your passport, money, travellers cheques and credit cards is with an old-fashioned money belt. There has been a spate of muggings in some cities in recent years.

Foreigners are often victims of housebreaking and burglary, particularly holiday homeowners, which is rife in resort areas, especially in the province of Alicante where housebreaking crimes have risen dramatically over the last few years. Always ensure that your home is secure (see page 105) and that your belongings are well insured (see page 300), and never leave valuables lying around. It's advisable to install a safe if you store valuables or cash in your home. Even having a guard dog may not help, as professional thieves may try to kill it and cut telephone lines to prevent owners from calling the police. In some areas, it isn't unusual for owners to return from abroad to find their homes ransacked. Many developments and urbanisations are patrolled by security guards, although they usually have little influence on crime rates and may instil a false sense of security. It's advisable to arrange for someone to frequently check your property when it's left unoccupied. Petty theft by gypsies, who wander into homes when the doors are left open, is common in some parts of Spain.

Violent crime is still relatively rare, although armed robbery has increased considerably in the last decade or so. However, despite the fact that there's an estimated three million guns in Spain, they're rarely used by crooks. Muggings at gun or knife-point are also rare in most towns, although they're becoming more common in some areas and sexually-related crime has increased greatly in Madrid. There are no particular dangers for women travelling alone in Spain, although hitchhiking isn't recommended. Sexual harassment is no longer a big problem, although women (particularly blondes) may be the subjects of unwanted attention in some areas. It's advisable for lone women to use taxis rather than public transport late at night.

The most common source of violent crime in Spain comes from Euskadi ta Azkatasuna (ETA), meaning 'Basque homeland and liberty', the Basque terrorist organisation, which has been waging a struggle for independence since 1959. ETA has lost much of its support in recent years due to indiscriminate bombings, kidnappings and murder, and isn't supported by the vast majority of Basques. The ETA political party, Herri Batasuna (HB), receives around 15 per cent of the vote, although HB was declared illegal in 2003. ETA's campaign of violence has claimed over 1,000 lives in the last 30 years and it continues to murder members of the police and security forces (and random other victims). It isn't, however, a threat to most foreigners in Spain and its activities are largely confined to Madrid and the north of Spain.

The Costa del Sol has earned an unsavoury reputation as a refuge for criminals and fugitives from justice, hence its nickname the 'Costa del Crime', although in recent years the Costa Blanca and Costa Brava have also attracted the wrong sort of tourists. Spain previously had no extradition treaty with most other European countries, although this changed with Spain's entry into the European Union (EU). A new threat in recent years has come from foreign organised crime syndicates, who take advantage of open frontiers and use Spain as a safe haven from the law in their home countries. Much organised crime (particularly money laundering and drug trafficking) on the Costa del Sol is centred on Marbella and mostly involves foreigners, including the Russian Mafia (the police have identified around 20 different criminal organisations or 'gangs' on the Costa del Sol in recent years).

One of the biggest dangers to most foreigners in Spain isn't from the Spanish, but from their own countrymen and other foreigners. It's common for expatriate 'businessmen' to run up huge debts, through dishonesty or incompetence, and cut and run owing their clients and suppliers thousands of euros. In resort areas, confidence tricksters, swindlers, cheats and fraudsters lie in wait around every corner and newcomers must constantly be on their guard (particularly when buying a business). Fraud of every conceivable kind is a fine art in Spain. Always be wary of someone who offers to do you a favour or show you the ropes or anyone claiming to know how to 'beat the system'. **If anything sounds too good to be true, you can bet it almost certainly is.** It's a sad fact of life, but you should generally be **more** wary of doing business with your fellow countrymen in Spain than with the Spanish.

Although the increase in crime in Spain isn't encouraging, the crime rate remains relatively low, particularly violent crime. This means that you can usually safely walk almost anywhere at any time of day or night, and there's absolutely no need for anxiety or paranoia about crime. However, you should be 'street-wise' and take certain elementary precautions. These include avoiding high-risk areas, particularly those frequented by drug addicts, prostitutes and pickpockets. When you're in an unfamiliar city, ask a tourist office, policeman, taxi driver or local person whether there are any unsafe neighbourhoods – and avoid them! You can safely travel on public transport in Spanish cities at night. As with most things in life, prevention is better than cure. This is particularly true when it comes to crime prevention in Spain, where only a small percentage of crimes are solved and the legal process is agonisingly slow. It's also important to have adequate insurance for your possessions. Report all crimes to the police, but don't expect them to take any interest in your case.

See also **Car Crime** on page 258, **Household Insurance** on page 300, **Home Security** on page 105, **Legal System** on page 460 and **Police** on page 469.

# Domestic Violence

Domestic violence is an ever increasing problem in Spain, where hardly a day seems to go by without a woman being murdered or injured by her partner or husband. In many cases, the woman has reported the man to the police on several occasions, but little has been done to protect her or the man has violated a court order. Urgent measures, including mobile phones connected to a police 'hotline' for high-risk victims, faster court cases and increased police vigilance are being introduced. Further information about what to do if you're a victim of domestic violence or feel threatened by your partner is available from the Woman's Institute (Instituto de la Mujer, ☎ 900-191 010). Calls are free and lines are open 24-hours a day.

# Drug Dependency

Drugs are often behind the motivation for most crime in Spain's major cities. Drug addiction is a huge and growing problem throughout Spain, and drug addicts (and prostitutes) are a common sight in many towns and cities. Spain is the major gateway for cocaine and hashish into Europe and drugs are easy to obtain, particularly in the cities. It's an offence to possess soft drugs such as hashish, although the law tends to turn a blind eye to its use and it's openly smoked in many bars and clubs. However, the possession and use of hard drugs such as heroin and cocaine is strictly prohibited. Spain is particularly harsh in its treatment of foreign drug dealers (of whom there are many), who can be held on remand for years without trial (much of the organised crime in Spain such as drugs and prostitution is run by foreigners). **Foreigners travelling to and from Spain in private or commercial vehicles must** take particular care when exporting goods or freight from Spain, as cargoes are frequently found to contain hidden drugs.

# Prisons

Spain rates third in the number of prisoners per 100,000 inhabitants in Europe after Hungary and the UK, and the prison population has more than doubled over the last fifteen years (Spanish prisons house some 30 per cent more prisoners than they were designed for). There are conflicting reports about the treatment of prisoners, with some claiming it to be inhumane and others exemplary. While conditions in Spanish prisons vary considerably, most are no worse than those in other European countries and many foreigners actually prefer to do their time in Spain. Spain houses over 13,400 foreigners in its jails (nearly a quarter of its prisoners), half of whom are from the EU and a large percentage are serving sentences for drug offences.

# GEOGRAPHY

Spain or the Kingdom of Spain (*reino de España* or *Estado Español*) is the second-largest country in Western Europe after France, and is often referred to as 'the old bull hide' (*la piel de toro*), because a map of the country resembles a stretched out bull hide. It covers an area of 492,463km² (190,154mi²) of the Iberian Peninsula or 504,749km² (194,898mi²) including the Balearics and the Canary Islands. The mainland is 805km (500mi) from north to south and 885km (550mi) from east to west. Spain's mainland coastline totals 2,119km (1,317mi).

The Balearic Islands off the eastern coast comprise the islands of Majorca, Ibiza, Menorca and Formentera and cover an area of 5,014km² (1,936mi²), while the Canary Islands, situated 97km (60mi) off the west coast of Africa, cover an area of 7,272km² (2,808mi²). Spain also has two North African enclaves, Ceuta and Melilla, which have been held by Spain since the 15th century and are, not surprisingly, claimed by Morocco. In July 2002 in a major military exercise, Morocco occupied the tiny island of Perejil inhabited by a few goats and flew the Moroccan flag in an act of provocation. The incident sparked off a major diplomatic incident between the two countries and Spain 'reclaimed' the island a few days later. Diplomatic relations were not resumed until early 2003. The small islands of Peñón de Vélez, Alhicemas and Xhafarinas off the Moroccan coast also 'belong' to Spain.

The Pyrenees in the north form a natural barrier between Spain and France and Andorra, while to the west is Portugal. To the north-west is the Bay of Biscay and the province of Galicia, with an Atlantic coast. In the east and south is the Mediterranean. The southern tip of Spain is just 16km (10mi) from Africa across the Straight of Gibraltar.

Spain consists of a vast plain (the *meseta*) surrounded by mountains and is the highest country in Europe after Switzerland, with an average altitude of 650m (2,132ft) above sea level. The vast plateau of the *meseta* extends over an area of over 200,000km² (77,000mi²) at an altitude of between 600 and 1,000m (2,000 and 3,300ft). Mountains hug the coast on three sides with the Cantabrian chain in the north (including the Picos de Europa), the Penibetic chain in the south (including the Sierra Nevada with the highest peaks in Spain) and a string of lower mountains throughout the regions of Catalonia and Valencia in the east. The highest peak on the peninsula is the *Pico de Mulhacen* in the Sierra Nevada range (3,482m/11,423ft), which is topped by Mount Teide (3,718m/12,198ft) on the Canary island of Tenerife.

Spain's main river is the Ebro, from which the Iberian peninsula gets its name, and the only Spanish river flowing into the Mediterranean. Others include the Douro, Guadalquivir, Guadiana, Tagus and Tajo, all of which flow into the Atlantic. Half of Spain's soil is unproductive or barren and some parts of the south-east are almost desert (many Spaghetti westerns are made inland from Almeria). At the other extreme, the *huerta* of Valencia and the Guadalquivir valley are extremely fertile and the northern coast of Cantabria, Asturias and Galicia are green and lush with forests and pasturelands.

# GOVERNMENT

Following the death of General Franco in 1975, the Spanish constitution of 31st October 1978, arguably the most liberal in western Europe, heralded a radical transformation from a dictatorship to a democratic government. The most important task of the constitution was to devolve power to the regions, which were given their own governments, regional assemblies and supreme legal authorities. The central government retains exclusive responsibility for foreign affairs, external trade, defence, justice, law (criminal, commercial and labour), merchant shipping and civil aviation. Spain has been a member of the United Nations (UN) since 1955, the North Atlantic Treaty Organisation (NATO) since 1982 and the European Union (EU) since 1986, and is also a permanent observer member of the Organisation of American States (OAS).

## Parliament

The national parliament (*las Cortes Generales*) has two chambers, the lower of which is the Congress of Deputies (*Congreso de los Diputados*) and the upper the Senate (*senado*). The Congress consists of 350 members representing Spain's 50 provinces and the North African enclaves of Ceuta and Melilla. Each province is an electoral constituency, with the number of deputies depending on its population. Members of Congress are elected by a system of proportional representation for four years. The Senate has 259 members, directly elected by a first-past-the-post system. Each province provides four members plus additional members in the Balearic and Canary islands, where extra members represent the various islands, making a total of 208 members. The 17 autonomous regions also elect one senator each and an additional member for each one million inhabitants, totalling a further 51 members. The Senate has the power to amend or veto legislation initiated by Congress.

Under Spanish law, the official result of a general election is made public five days after the vote, in order to allow sufficient time for recounts and disputed results. After the members have been sworn in, the King of Spain meets with the party leaders and asks one of them to form a government, which must then be ratified by parliament. The leader of the party of government becomes the president (*presidente*) of Spain and has his official residence in the Moncloa Palace in Madrid.

The Constitutional Court (*el tribunal constitucional*) is responsible for ensuring that laws passed by parliament comply with the constitution and international agreements to which Spain is party.

The Judiciary is independent of the government, with the highest legal body being the General Council of Judicial Power (*Consejo general del Poder Judicial*), which has 20 independent members and is headed by the president of the supreme court (*tribunal supremo*).

## Present Government

A general election was held on 14th March 2004, three days after the bombing attack by Al Qaeda in Madrid, which left 191 people dead and over 1,500 injured, many seriously. The Socialists (Partido Socialista Obrero Español/PSOE, who governed Spain from 1982 to 1996), led by José Luís Rodríguez Zapatero, won with 164 seats against the Partido Popular's (PP) 148. Political analysts generally agree that the Madrid bombings, which the PP blamed on ETA, were the final straw for a majority of Spaniards, who were already disenchanted by the PP's handling of several affairs – among them the *Prestige* oil disaster in Galicia, where miles of pristine coast was irreparably damaged along with the livelihood of thousands.

Other parliamentary parties include the following: Convergencia i Unió/CiU (10 seats) and Esquerra Republicana/ERC (8 seats), both Catalán regional parties, the latter left-wing and with republican aspirations and the former right-wing and conservative; Partido Nacionalista Vasco/PNV, the Basque nationalist party (7 seats); the United Left (Izquierda Unida/IU with 5 seats) with its worst results in history; Coalición Canaria/CC (3 seats), the Canary Islands nationalist party and several other very small nationalist parties from Galicia, Catalonia and Aragón.

The PSOE have opted to rule as a minority government, but plan to reach consensus in parliament with as many parties as possible when necessary. Their willingness to listen and enthusiasm for dialogue rather than confrontation is currently a welcome breath of fresh air on the Spanish political scene. The fact that the cabinet is made up of an equal number of men and women, and that the vice-president is a woman are also seen as welcome moves.

## Autonomous Regions

Spain has 17 autonomous regions (*comunidades autónomas*), shown on the map in **Appendix E**, each with its own president, government (*gobierno* or *junta*), administration and supreme court (plus its own flag and capital city). The regions are funded by the central government and the regions of the Basque Country, Catalonia, Galicia and Andalusia are responsible for matters such as economic development, education, health, environment, police, public works, tourism, culture, local language and social security. The other regions have less autonomy and fewer responsibilities. The people of the Basque Country, Catalonia and Galicia have also been recognised as separate ethnic groups and have the right to use their own languages in education and administration. With the increasing influence of the Basque and Catalan regional parties in national politics, the whole question of regional power and autonomy has taken on a new significance. All regions are currently revising their Autonomy Statutes and the Catalan draft is proving a particular headache for regional and national politicians, mainly because the draft proposes calling Catalonia a 'nation' and aspires to collect all taxes instead of the regional percentage only. Both these proposals are rejected by many Spaniards outside Catalonia.

# Provinces

Each province has its own administration (*diputación*) that is responsible for a range of services, including health (hospitals, nursing homes), public works (including roads), sports facilities (such as public swimming pools) and social clubs (e.g. for youths and the elderly). The civil governors (*gobernadores civiles*), who were head of the provincial governments, have been replaced by sub-delegates (*subdelegados del gobierno*), who co-ordinate the work of the different government offices in the provinces.

# Municipalities

A municipality is run by a council consisting of a number of councillors (*concejales*), each of whom is responsible for a different area of local services. The council is headed by the mayor (*alcalde*), and has its offices in the local town hall (*ayuntamiento*). The official population of a municipality includes everyone who's registered in the list of inhabitants (*padrón municipal*). Entry in the *padrón municipal* is a requirement for inclusion on the electoral roll (*censo electoral*) and the right to vote in local elections every four years. Although it isn't mandatory for foreigners to register in their community, it's important to register, as the funds that municipalities receive from central and regional governments are based on the official number of inhabitants. Theoretically the more government funds a municipality receives, the lower the local taxes.

The responsibilities of municipalities include rubbish collection, street cleaning, street lighting, drinking water, sewage disposal/treatment, road access and maintenance, public health controls, cemeteries, schools, urban planning, traffic control, consumer protection and policing. Municipalities with over 5,000 inhabitants must also provide public parks, a public library and markets, and those with over 20,000 must also provide civil protection, social services, fire prevention, public sports facilities and a municipal slaughterhouse.

Many town halls have a chronic liquidity problem, due to a combination of inefficiency (many Spanish communities are among the worst run in the EU), over-manning and a failure to collect taxes. It's ironic that while municipalities are quick to fine residents for late payments, they are themselves the worst payers of bills in Spain and have run up debts of many millions of euros. Some are so bad at paying their bills that they have great difficulty in finding companies willing to supply or work for them, and municipal workers often have to strike to get paid (some towns cannot even afford to insure their police cars). The financial situation of many councils is critical, many of which are paying thousands of euros a day in interest charges on their debts, and has been described as a financial time-bomb. As a result of town halls debts, property taxes have risen sharply in recent years and are expected to go even higher.

# Corruption

One of the most topical issues in Spain during the last few years has been corruption among public officials, including illegal financing of political parties, tax avoidance, fraud, bribery, institutionalised sleaze, nepotism, misappropriation of public funds, illegal patronage, influence-peddling and kickbacks. Spain has been described (in the Spanish press) as the most corrupt society among the original 15 members of the EU and corruption permeates political and public life at every level.

# Foreign Voting Rights

The voting rights of non-EU residents depend on whether a bilateral agreement exists between Spain and their home countries. Foreigners must be registered on the electoral roll to vote in local elections. Foreign nationals of EU countries resident in Spain have been able to vote and stand as councillors in local elections since 1999. Candidates must be able to express themselves in a dignified manner in Spanish and have a good knowledge of their municipality and the local government laws in Spain. The non-political organisation *Ciudadanos Europeos* has long promoted voting rights for European Union citizens resident in Spain and other European countries and fielded candidates in local elections in 1999.

With the new voting rights for foreigners, it's expected that they will be taken more seriously by their town halls in future (at least in municipalities where there's a sizeable resident foreign population). Many town halls already have employees who speak English and other foreign languages, and in municipalities where there are a large number of foreign residents there are often special foreigners' departments (*departamentos de extranjeros*). However, foreigners usually pay a disproportionate amount of taxes for what they receive in return, particularly non-resident homeowners, and their investment in Spain is out of all proportion to the number of votes they receive. Local councils in resort areas often ignore the needs of certain communities and urbanisations, particularly those mainly populated by non-resident foreigners, and spend (waste) the vast bulk of their revenue beautifying their main town centre.

EU Residents of Spain are allowed to vote in European elections for Members of the European Parliament (MEPs), but cannot vote in Spanish general elections.

# Gibraltar

The ownership of Gibraltar (a British colony) has long been a thorn in the side of Spain's rulers and on occasion it flares up. Although relations have improved, they remain strained and in recent years Spain has increased its diplomatic efforts (and obstruction) in its efforts to regain sovereignty over Gibraltar. Both the British and Spanish governments make concerted efforts to resolve the problem of Gibraltar sovereignty, although proposals are generally met with opposition from the Gibraltarians, who are unwilling to give up their status.

Spain also has concerns over the high level of crime associated with Gibraltar, including tobacco smuggling, drug-running and money-laundering. The smuggling of cigarettes and hashish is carried out openly in Gibraltar under the eyes of the local police, although there have been crackdowns in recent years.

# LEGAL SYSTEM

If you're seeking legal advice, ask around among local residents and obtain recommendations. This way you will usually find out not only who to employ, but more importantly who to avoid (wrong legal advice is often more expensive in the long term than having none at all). Always obtain an estimate (*presupuesto*) of costs in advance, if possible in writing, and shop around and compare fees from a number of lawyers, as they can vary considerably. The estimate should detail exactly what the lawyer will do for his fees. If you consult a number of legal 'experts' about the same matter, you're highly unlikely to receive exactly the same advice.

The Spanish legal system is excruciatingly slow (i.e. largely at a standstill) and there's a backlog of hundreds of thousands of cases throughout Spain, which means that it takes years for many cases to come to court. Even local courts can take five years to hear a case, although delays are usually up to two years for minor offences and up to four years for serious offences. **This means that you should do everything possible to avoid going to court by taking every conceivable precaution when doing business in Spain, i.e. obtaining expert legal advice in advance**. If things do go wrong it can take years to achieve satisfaction and in the case of fraud the chances are that those responsible will have gone bust or disappeared. Note that even when you have a foolproof case there's no guarantee of winning and it may be better to write off a loss as experience. Local courts, judges and lawyers frequently abuse the system to their own ends and almost anyone with enough money or expertise can use the law to their own advantage. In recent years, public confidence in Spain's legal system has been rocked by a succession of scandals.

## Lawyers

If you're buying property in Spain, investing in or starting a business, applying for a work permit or making a will, you should employ the services of an experienced Spanish lawyer (*abogado*). You may be able to obtain a list of lawyers from your local embassy or consulate (see **Appendix A**). Suggested lawyers' fees are set by provincial professional bodies (*Ilustre Colegio de Abogados*), although individual lawyers often set much higher fees. However, fees are usually lower than those charged by lawyers in northern European countries, with a simple consultation of less than half an hour costing from €30. When preparing contracts involving a sum of money, e.g. property or land purchase, fees are calculated as a percentage of the sum involved. 'No win, no fee' lawsuits are illegal in Spain.

Always try to engage a lawyer who speaks your mother tongue. In some areas, lawyers who speak English and other foreign languages are common and they're used to dealing with foreigners and their particular problems. In cases where a lawyer is obligatory and your income is below double the Spanish minimum wage (see page 39), you can apply for free legal assistance (*abogado de oficio*). The college of lawyers appoints a lawyer to assist you, although they won't take as much interest in your case as a private lawyer would. In cases involving sums over €900 the services of a barrister (*procurador*) is required. If you don't receive satisfactory service you can complain to the local professional college. Common complaints include long delays, poor communication, high fees and overcharging (particularly with regard to property transactions involving foreigners).

## Gestores

A *gestor* is an official agent licensed by the Spanish government as a middleman between you and the bureaucracy. This speaks volumes for the stifling and tortuous Spanish bureaucracy, which is so complicated and cumbersome that it's necessary for citizens to employ a special official simply to do business with the government! It isn't **compulsory** to employ a *gestor*, but without one you must usually speak fluent Spanish (or have an interpreter), possess boundless patience and stamina, and have unlimited time to deal with the mountains of red tape and obstacles that will confront you. However, if you have the time and can speak reasonable Spanish, you will find it extremely 'educational' to do your own paperwork.

A *gestor's* services aren't generally expensive and most people find it worthwhile employing one. They usually work in a *gestoría*, where a number of experts may be employed dealing with different matters, including employment and residence permits; establishing and registering a business; obtaining a driving licence, tourist plates or registering a car; social security and property contracts. A *gestor* can help you in your dealings with any government body or state-owned company. **The quality of service provided by *gestores* varies considerably and they cannot always be relied upon to do a professional job (some have been known to take money and do absolutely nothing).**

## Notaries

A notary (*notario*) is a public official authorised by the government, who's most commonly engaged in property transactions. He doesn't deal with criminal cases or offer advice concerning criminal law. *Notarios* have a monopoly in the areas of transferring real property, testamentary (e.g. of wills) and matrimonial acts, which by law must be in the form of an authentic document, verified and stamped by a *notario*. In Spain, property conveyancing is strictly governed by Spanish law and can be performed **only** by a *notario*. In respect to private law, a *notario* is responsible for administering and preparing documents relating to property sales and purchases, inheritance, wills, establishing limited companies, and buying and selling businesses. He also certifies the validity and safety of contracts and deeds. If you need irrefutable proof of delivery of a letter or other documents, they should be sent via a *notario*, as nobody can deny receiving a document delivered through his offices.

## Property Administrators

A property administrator (*administrador de fincas*) is a licensed professional who's qualified to handle all matters connected with owning and managing property in Spain, particularly property in an urbanisation where there's a community of owners. His duties include calling meetings, taking minutes, advising residents, collecting fees, paying taxes and paying bills.

## Courts

Like French law, Spanish law derives from the *Code Napoléon*. The lowest court is the justice of the peace (*juez de la paz*), dealing with simple matters such as property complaints between neighbours. Neither party need have legal counsel and simple cases are usually resolved at this level. Civil cases are decided by a *juzgado/tribunal de primera instancia*, where most cases start. The next highest court is a district court presided over by a district judge (*juez de distrito*), where you need a lawyer. It handles more serious matters, e.g. unpaid debts for goods and services or failure to meet the conditions of a contract. Criminal cases are held before a local *tribunal de primera instancia e instrucción*, followed in order of importance by an *audiencia provincial*, *audiencia territorial*, *audiencia nacional*, *tribunal superior de justicia* and the Supreme Court (*tribunal supremo*) in Madrid. Trial by jury for criminal trials was reintroduced in 1996 after 57 years' absence. A jury consists of nine people, seven of whom must agree to establish a guilty verdict. You have the right of appeal in all cases.

## Arrest

If you're arrested you have the right to make a statement in the presence of your lawyer or one nominated by the police if you don't have one, and the right to an interpreter. You also have the right to advise a member of your family or another person of your arrest or in the case of a foreigner to contact your consul. You can be held for up to 72 hours without charge, after which you must be charged and brought before a court or freed. You cannot be held longer without a judicial order. **However, if you're remanded in custody, you can be held for years while a case is being 'investigated'.**

## Complaints

If you have a complaint against someone, for example your neighbour for making too much noise or your local authority for not collecting your rubbish, and your appeals fall on deaf ears, you can make an official complaint (*denuncia*) to the police. There are ombudsmen in most regions who handle certain complaints and queries, many with staff who speak English and other foreign languages. If you have a complaint concerning the way EU laws are interpreted or are being broken in Spain, you should complain to your European member of parliament. You can also bring a lawsuit against the Spanish state. However, you should expect to wait a long (long) time for your case to be heard.

## Reforms

At the end of 1999, the Spanish parliament approved a new version of the Law of Civil Judgement designed principally to speed up the courts and the legal process in Spain. Legal experts and lawyers' representatives were generally opposed to the reforms because, although the reforms looked excellent on paper, they would come to nothing unless the government injected vast sums of money into the legal system. For example, for more employees and computers to modernise it and to allow the reforms to take place – it's no good having a law that gives a debtor 20 days to appeal if you haven't got the staff at the court to inform the debtor and carry out other essential duties. Needless to say, the reforms became law in 2001 without the extra investment!

Included is a 'small claims' (maximum €30,000) system designed to assist the self-employed and small businesses to collect their debts. The creditor completes a form claiming his payment, which must be accompanied by some form of proof of the debt and lodges it with the court. The services of a solicitor or barrister aren't required. The debtor then has around 20 days to pay or explain why he won't be paying. If the 20 days pass without the debtor doing either, then the judge immediately proceeds to an embargo of the debtor's goods and/or property. While many other aspects of the new law have yet to come to fruition because of lack of investment, the 'small claims' procedure has been very successful and claims are generally resolved quickly.

**Never** assume that the law in Spain is the same as in any other country, as this often **isn't** the case and some Spanish laws are bizarre. Note that it's illegal for anyone to be without some form of personal identification in Spain and you should carry your residence permit (see page 78) or passport at all times (you can be asked to produce it by a policeman). Certain legal advice and services may also be provided by your embassy or consulate in Spain, including, for example, an official witness of signatures (Commissioner for Oaths). A useful book for Spanish residents and property owners is *You and the Law in Spain* by David Searl (Santana). See also **Consumer Protection** on page 444, **Crime** on page 452 and **Police** on page 469.

# MARRIAGE & DIVORCE

Despite the falling number of marriages and church attendances in Spain, a church wedding with all the trimmings remains the dream of most Spanish girls. Marriage bureaux are common in cities, with applicants (of all ages) paying a fee of from

€150 to €300 to meet an unlimited number of prospective partners with no time limit. Surprisingly, nearly 70 per cent of Spaniards below the age of 30 live with their parents.

To be married in a Roman Catholic church in Spain at least one partner must be Roman Catholic; a divorcee isn't permitted to marry in a Spanish church if the previous marriage was solemnised in church. A certificate of baptism is required plus a declaration from your former parish priest that you're a Roman Catholic and are free to marry. You receive a certificate from the priest, which must be presented within one week to the local civil registry in order to obtain an official marriage certificate. Couples also receive a 'family book' (*libro de familia*) when they marry, which is the official registration of a couple and their children. It's necessary for children to present this when they apply for their own identity card, social security card and when they marry or divorce (or when someone dies).

In order for two non-Catholic foreigners to marry in Spain, one must have lived (and have been domiciled) in Spain for at least two years. Marriages are held at Spanish civil registry offices and are presided over by a judge (church weddings for non-Catholics in Spain aren't legally recognised). If you're divorced or widowed, you must produce an official divorce or death certificate. A divorced person requires a legal declaration (*certificado de ley*) drawn up by a lawyer and legalised by a Spanish consul in the country of origin. Some foreigners find it easier to get married abroad, e.g. Britons and Americans can get married in Gibraltar, where couples are married in a registry office in front of two witnesses. Many foreigners can also be married at their country's embassy in Spain.

# Homosexual Marriages

As from July 2005, homosexual couples have the right to marry (Spain is only the third country in the world to allow this) and therefore enjoy the same rights as heterosexual married couples. In the first few months after the law was passed, some 600 homosexual couples had got married in registry offices. In September 2005, the main opposition party, the Partido Popular, presented an appeal against the law before the Constitutional Court on the grounds that the Spanish Constitution only permits marriage between a man and woman. Legal experts are divided on whether the appeal will prosper or not.

# Common-law Partners

Unmarried couples (including homosexuals) can register their union at a special registry in many towns and receive a formal certificate allowing them to claim social security and benefit from life insurance policies. **However, common-law partners generally have no property rights in Spain and are treated as unrelated individuals if they don't have official documentation.** The regions of Andalusia, Aragón, Balearics, Basque Lands, Catalonia, Madrid and Navarra recognise common-law partners if they're officially registered for tax and inheritance purposes and there have been several highly-publicised court cases where common-law partners' rights have been recognised.

# Divorce

New divorce legislation, designed to make divorce by mutual consent quicker and easier, was approved in 2005. Under the legislation (known as *divorcio directo*), a couple wishing to divorce must have been married for a minimum of three months (less if there's domestic violence), neither party needs to present any grounds for divorce and there's no minimum period of separation required beforehand. If the couple have children, they can agree to have equal custody of the children. The paperwork is relatively straightforward and the services of a lawyer shouldn't be required. A divorce in court is only necessary if the parties cannot agree on the terms of the divorce or the divorce isn't by mutual consent.

Foreigners who were married abroad can be divorced in Spain and only one of the partners need be a resident.

# MILITARY MATTERS

In 2001, military service was abolished. The government is in the process of forming a professional army of some 150,000 soldiers, which came into being in 2002, although there's a major shortage of soldiers and the Ministry of Defence is running high profile recruiting campaigns.

Spain is a signatory to the treaty banning nuclear weapons and has been a member of NATO (*OTAN* in Spanish) since 1982, although there has been widespread opposition, particularly to American bases in Spain. Defence spending in Spain is around 2 per cent of gross domestic product (GDP) and less than 20 per cent of what the UK, France and Germany spend. Spanish troops in Iraq were brought back to Spain in June 2004 fulfilling one the Socialist's main election promises to huge public acclaim and some international criticism, notably from the Bush administration. Spain has troops on UN peacekeeping missions in several countries, including Afghanistan, Haiti and Kosovo.

# PETS

If you plan to take a pet (*animal de compañia* or *mascota*) to Spain, it's important to check the latest regulations. Make sure that you have the correct papers, not only for Spain, but for all the countries you will pass through to reach Spain. Particular consideration must be given before exporting a pet from a country with strict quarantine regulations, such as the UK.

# Spanish Regulations

A maximum of two pets may accompany travellers to Spain. A rabies vaccination is usually compulsory, although this **doesn't** apply to accompanied pets (including dogs and cats) coming directly from the UK or for animals under three months old. However, if a rabies vaccination is given, it must be administered not less than one month or more than 12 months before export. A rabies vaccination is necessary if pets are transported by road from the UK to Spain via France. Pets over three months old from countries other than the UK must have been vaccinated against rabies not less than one month and not more than one year before being imported. If a pet has no rabies certificate it can be quarantined for 20 days.

Two official certificates are also required: one signed and stamped by a vet declaring that the animal has been vaccinated against rabies and the second which is a signed declaration by the owner of the pet stating that the animal has been under his supervision for three months before its importation into Spain. Both certificates are in Spanish and English and are valid for **only** 15 days after they've been signed. The certificates can be obtained from Spanish consulates abroad and can also be downloaded from Spanish consulate websites. Some animals require a special import permit from the Spanish Ministry of Agriculture and pets from some countries are subject to customs duty.

# British Regulations

The Pet Travel Scheme (PETS – now under the auspices of the EU pet passport scheme) replaces quarantine for qualifying cats and dogs. Under the scheme, pets must be micro-chipped (they have a microchip inserted in their neck), be vaccinated against rabies, undergo a blood test and be issued with a 'health certificate' (passport). **Note that the PETS certificate sometimes isn't issued until six months AFTER the above have been carried out!** In the UK, EU pet passports are issued by Local Veterinary Inspectors (LVI) only. In other EU countries, passports are issued by all registered vets.

The scheme is restricted to animals imported from rabies-free countries and countries where rabies is under control – 22 European countries plus Bahrain, Canada and the US. However, the current quarantine law will remain in place for pets coming from Eastern Europe, Africa (including the Spanish enclaves of Ceuta and Melilla), Asia and South America. To qualify, pets must travel by sea via any major British ferry port, by train via the Channel Tunnel or via Bristol, Gatwick, Heathrow or Manchester airports. Only certain carriers are licensed to carry animals and these are listed on the Department for Environment, Food and Rural Affairs (DEFRA) website (🖳 www.defra.gov.uk/animalh/quarantine). For additional information about the PETS scheme, contact DEFRA (☎ UK 0870-241 1710, ✉ pets. helpline@defra.gsi.gov.uk).

The regulations cost pet owners around £200/€300 (for a microchip, rabies vaccination and blood test), plus £60/€90 a year for annual booster vaccinations and around £20/€30 for a border check. Shop around and compare fees from a number of veterinary surgeons.

British pet owners must complete an Application for a Ministry Export Certificate for dogs, cats and rabies susceptible animals (form EXA1), available from DEFRA at the above address. DEFRA contact the vet you've named on the form and he performs a health inspection. You then receive an export health certificate, which must be issued no more than 30 days before your entry into Spain with your pet.

# General Information

If you're transporting a pet to Spain by boat, you should notify the ferry company. Some companies insist that pets are left in vehicles (if applicable), while others allow pets to be kept in cabins. **If your pet is of nervous disposition or unused to travelling, it's best to tranquillise it on a long sea crossing.** A pet can also be shipped to Spain by air. Animals are permitted to travel to most airports in Spain.

If you intend to live permanently in Spain, most veterinary surgeons (*veterinarios*) recommend that you have a dog vaccinated against rabies before arrival. Dogs should also be vaccinated against leptospirosis, parvovirus, hepatitis, distemper and kennel cough, and cats immunised against feline enteritis and typhus. **Note that there are a number of diseases and dangers for pets in Spain that aren't found in most other European countries.** These include the fatal leishmaniasis (also called Mediterranean or sandfly disease), processionary caterpillars, leeches, heartworm, ticks (a tick collar can help prevent these), feline leukaemia virus and feline enteritis. Obtain advice about these from a veterinary surgeon on arrival in Spain. Take extra care when walking your dog, as some have died after eating poisoned food in rural areas. Poisoned bait (e.g. meat laced with strychnine) is laid in some areas by hunters and poachers to control natural predators such as foxes, wolves and lynx (poisons are also laid in some urbanisations to keep down the feral cat population).

Veterinary surgeons are well trained in Spain, where it's a popular profession, and emergency veterinary care is also available in animal clinics (*clínica veterinaria*), many of which provide a 24-hour emergency service. Veterinary surgeons and animal clinics advertise in English-language publications in Spain. Health insurance for pets is available from a number of insurance companies. The premium is around €75 a year for a dog and €40 for a cat, which covers owners against veterinary fees (e.g. up to €1,500 a year), travel abroad, complementary medicine, third party liability (e.g. €50,000), accidental death and theft.

There are kennels and catteries (*residencias para animales de compañía*) throughout Spain, many of which advertise in Spanish English-language publications in resort areas (make sure they're registered and bona fide establishments). Book well in advance if you plan to leave your pet at a kennel or cattery, particularly for school holiday periods. Fees are around €4 a day for a cat and from €6 a day for a dog, depending on its size (there may be a small discount for more than one pet). **Pets must be vaccinated.**

There may be discrimination against pets when renting accommodation, particularly when it's furnished, and the statutes of community properties can legally prohibit pets. Many hotels accept pets such as cats and dogs, although they aren't usually permitted in restaurants, cafés or food shops (except for guide dogs). Information about hotels accepting dogs and other animals can be found on numerous websites, including 🖥 www.onlydog.com and 🖥 www.perros.com.

# Dogs

All dog owners are required to register their dogs and have them tattooed with their registration number in an ear or have a microchip inserted in their neck. Registration costs around €15 to €30 and there are fines for owners who don't have their dogs registered. Irrespective of whether your dog is micro-chipped, it's advisable to have it fitted with a collar and tag with your name and telephone number on it and the magic word 'reward' (*recompensa*). All municipalities have rules (*ordenanzas*) regarding the keeping of dogs, which require a health card if they're older than three months. In public areas, a dog must be kept on a lead (and muzzled if dangerous) and wear a health disc on its collar. Dogs are prohibited from entering places where food is manufactured, stored or sold; from sports and cultural events and are banned from beaches.

In response to several killings and maiming by dogs in Spain, the government introduced extensive legislation for dangerous dogs with strict regulations regarding ownership of such dogs. Under the legislation there are eight breeds defined as 'dangerous': Akita, American Staffordshire Terrier, Dogo Argentino, Fila Brasileiro, Japanese Tosa, Pit Bull, Rottweiler and Staffordshire Bull Terrier. 'Dangerous' breeds also include dogs that have all or most of the following characteristics: a strong and powerful appearance; a strong character; short hair; shoulder height between 50 and 70 cm **and** a weight of over 20kg (44lb); square and robust head with large jaws; wide and short neck; broad and deep chest; robust fore legs and muscular hind legs. If you aren't sure whether your dog has most of these characteristics, you should consult your vet. If your dog is 'dangerous' you need a special licence. In order to obtain the licence (available from local councils). the owner must be over 18, have no criminal record, undergo psychological and physical tests and have compulsory third party insurance for €120,000. A 'dangerous' dog must be muzzled and on a lead no longer than two metres in public areas. In private areas, if the dog isn't securely enclosed, it must be muzzled.

It's common in Spain for owners to let their dogs roam free (in Spain dogs go for walks on their own), although owners of unsupervised dogs are held responsible for any damage they cause. Dogs that chase cyclists and mopeds are a nuisance in some towns and Spain has a growing problem with bands of wild dogs attacking sheep and other domestic animals. One of the most unpleasant consequences of dog ownership in Spain is the vast amount of excrement deposited on Spanish streets, which is an increasing health hazard, particularly for young children. You must **always** watch where you walk and keep an eye on children. It's illegal not to clean up after your dog in a public area, although few people do so. **Note that the chemicals used in swimming pools are a health hazard for dogs and if you allow your dog to swim in your pool, you should hose it down afterwards.**

Legislation against cruelty to animals was introduced for the first time in 2003. The Spanish aren't sentimental about animals and aren't a nation of animal lovers, which is confirmed by the many owners who simply abandon their pets when they go on holiday. Many Spaniards (and foreigners) own dogs simply to guard their homes and many bark continually, particularly at night. They're often tied up for 24 hours a day, although fed and watered regularly, and may be left on their own for days or weeks at a time. However, the Spanish aren't a nation of animal abusers and most Spaniards love and care for their pets as much as owners in any other western European country. There are animal protection organisations and animal shelters run by foreigners in many resort areas.

Most criticism is reserved for Spain's treatment of its working animals (among the worst in the EU) and the ritual abuse of animals in what have been described as 'barbaric medieval practices'. Among the targets of animal rights' campaigners are bullfighting, where horses are often killed in addition to the bulls; the use of live ponies on roundabouts (the 'living carousel'), which are often forced to work for hours on end without a rest or food or water and stone-pulling competitions by horses and donkeys in the Basque Country, where many die in the attempt to haul huge stones weighing hundreds of kilos.

# POLICE

Spain has a high ratio of police officers to inhabitants and three police forces, often with confusing and overlapping roles, although the government plans to amalgamate the three forces to improve co-ordination and make better use of skills and resources. The main forces are the local municipal police (*policía municipal/local* or *guardia urbana*), the national police (*policía nacional*) and the civil guard (*guardia civil*), all of whom are armed. Some autonomous regions have their own police forces, including the Basque Country (where they wear red *boinas* or berets) and Catalonia (the *Mosses d'Esquadra*). Spain also has an elite special operations group (*Grupo Especial de Operaciones*/GEO) responsible for combating terrorism and dealing with other extreme situations, in addition to guarding Spanish ambassadors and embassies abroad. Other 'police' forces include the port police (*policía de puerto*) in sea ports, whose jurisdiction is limited to the property of the local *junta del puerto*, and armed guards (*vigilantes jurados*) employed by banks and security companies.

## Municipal Police

The municipal police are attached to local town halls in towns with a population of over 5,000. They wear blue uniforms with white-chequered bands on their hats and sleeves, and usually patrol in white or blue cars. Municipal police deal with minor crime such as traffic control, protection of property, civil disturbances and the enforcement of municipal laws. In large cities, municipal police often have multilingual offices and some towns have mounted police. They're the most sympathetic Spanish police force. In resort areas, the local police often speak English and during the summer spend most of their time dealing with drunken (mostly British) tourists. On-the-spot fines are imposed for a range of offences. However, in some towns, local police are heavy-handed and can be a law unto themselves and aren't averse to using illegal methods.

## National Police

The national police 'replaced' the despised 'armed' police (*policía armada*). The *policía armada* were much hated and feared, but the national police are now 'quite popular'. They're stationed in towns with a population of over 20,000 and deal with serious crime such as theft, rape and muggings, and are also used to control demonstrations and crowds. Other duties include guarding embassies, railway stations, post offices and army barracks in most towns and cities, when they're armed with submachine guns. The national police are housed in a police station (*comisaría de policía*), many of which have a foreigners (*extranjeros*) department dealing with matters such as residence permits (see page 78). There are also plain clothes policemen (*cuerpo superior de policía*) in urban areas.

# Civil Guard

The civil guard patrol Spain's highways and rural areas, often on motorcycles (which operate in pairs), and deal with road accidents. They also act as immigration officers and frontier guards and use helicopters to combat crime. In villages, there are usually barracks (*cuartel*) instead of a police station. The civil guard is a military force and was traditionally headed by a general, although this is no longer the case. They wear avocado green uniforms and olive-green caps, which have replaced the black, patent-leather, tricorn hats now worn only on ceremonial occasions. They're one of the world's most efficient police forces and have a reputation for honesty and courtesy.

Spanish police are generally extremely helpful and go out of their way to be of assistance. However, corrupt policemen dealing in drugs, prostitution and other organised crime aren't uncommon, and a disturbing number of policemen have run amok with their guns. There have been reports of stolen goods disappearing into thin air after having been 'recovered' by the police (they're supposed to be displayed at police departments, e.g. for 18 months, after which they're sold at auction if not claimed). Spanish police are sometimes colour prejudiced, particularly with regard to Africans.

If you need to contact the police in an emergency, you can dial ☎ 091 for the national police or, in some towns, ☎ 062 for the civil guard. You must usually dial a local number for the municipal police, although dialling ☎ 092 may get you connected to the local police station or get your message relayed. The telephone numbers of local police stations are listed at the front of telephone directories. If you lose anything or are the victim of a theft, you must report it in person to the local police and make a complaint (*denuncia*). This must usually be done within 24 hours if you intend to make a claim on an insurance policy. The report form, of which you receive a copy with an official stamp for your insurance company, may be printed in English and Spanish. **If you don't speak Spanish, you should have a fluent Spanish speaker with you**, although in some tourist areas you can make a complaint in a number of foreign languages. Note that you can now make a complaint by telephone (☎ 902-102 112) or by the internet (🖳 www.policia.es). Once you've made the complaint, you're given a number that you can take to the nearest police station after 10am the following day and within 72 hours. When you arrive you present the number to the official and you're given a signed and stamped copy of the complaint. Telephone and internet complaints are given priority and it saves you having to queue for hours at the police station waiting for your turn. **However, you cannot** make a complaint by telephone or internet if you're reporting a violent crime or you can identify a criminal by name.

See also **Traffic Police** on page 252, **Car Crime** on page 258, **Crime** on page 452 and **Legal System** on page 460.

# POPULATION

The population of Spain is around 43.2 million and has steadily increased over the last 20 years, mainly due to the influx of foreign residents from Africa, Central and South America and retirees (from the UK, Germany, Belgium, the Netherlands and Scandinavia). Spain has one of the lowest birth rates in the world, although births increased by 8 per cent in 2001 (mainly immigrant children). However, during the latter half of the 20th century the population of half of Spain's provinces decreased, as people abandoned the countryside for the cities. Now just nine provinces are home to half the population, and Madrid and Barcelona alone account for over 25 per cent of Spain's population. Some 75 per cent of the population is concentrated on the perimeters of Spain (including the Balearic and Canary Islands) and Madrid.

Spain has an average population density of around 80 inhabitants per $km^2$ (200 per square mile), one of the lowest in Europe and just one sixth of the Netherlands' and one-third of the UK's. However, it varies enormously from region to region. For example, the regions of the Basque Country and Madrid comprise just over 3 per cent of the land area and are home to some 18 per cent of the population, while the regions of Extremadura, Castile-La Mancha, Castile León, Aragon and Navarre make up half of Spain's land area and have a smaller population than the Basque Country and Madrid. Some 75 per cent of Spaniards live in towns with over 10,000 inhabitants. In resort areas, the population figures don't include the often large number of foreigners who live in Spain all year round, but don't register as residents.

The largest conurbations are Madrid, Barcelona, Bilbao and Valencia and the largest cities Madrid (3.1 million), Barcelona (1.58 million), Valencia (785,700), Seville (705,000) and Zaragossa (639,000). The most densely populated areas are the provinces of Madrid and Barcelona, both of which have around 600 inhabitants per $km^2$ (some 1,600 per $mi^2$). Barcelona is the fourth most densely populated city in the world. The most sparsely populated areas are the provinces of Soria, Teruel and Guadalajara with 10 to 12 inhabitants per $km^2$ (26 to 31 per $mi^2$).

# RELIGION

Spain is a Christian country where some 81 per cent of the population claims to belong to the Catholic Church and less than 1 per cent Protestant. The majority of the world's religious and philosophical movements have religious centres or meeting places in the major cities and resort areas, including English (e.g. Anglican) and American churches. The right to freedom of religion is guaranteed under the Spanish constitution, although some extreme sects are prohibited.

There have traditionally been close relations between the state and the church, although Catholicism is no longer the state religion and the Catholic Church has lost much of its previous influence under Franco. In fact, Spain is fast turning its back on its Catholic past and increasingly passing laws contrary to the church's teaching (such as divorce and abortion). Like a number of other countries, Spain is finding it difficult to attract new recruits to the priesthood and has had to resort to importing priests from Latin America (while convents have imported teenage nuns from India). The shortage is reaching crisis proportions, with some 3,000 priests retiring each year and just 250 new ordinations. However, although many Spaniards are ambivalent about religion and church attendances are falling, around 20 per cent of the population attends mass regularly and many Spanish families still spend more than €2,000 on a child's first Holy Communion.

Spain has a wealth of historic churches and cathedrals, many in desperate need of restoration, including the cathedral of Santiago de Compostela, one of the most important holy places in Christendom (it once rivalled Rome) and a place of pilgrimage since the ninth century. **It's necessary to dress appropriately to enter places of worship and if you're wearing shorts (short trousers, not underwear!), a vest or have bare feet, you won't be admitted.** Women may also be refused entry if they're wearing short skirts or 'scanty' tops. Like churches, shrines and sanctuaries are holy places and should be treated with respect.

Foreign church services are listed in English-language publications such as *SUR in English* on the Costa del Sol, and include all major and many minor religions. Notices of Catholic services are posted outside churches and at strategic points in towns (mass is held in foreign languages in some churches).

# SOCIAL CUSTOMS

All countries have their own particular social customs and Spain is no exception. As a foreigner you will probably be excused if you accidentally insult your host, but you may not be invited again.

When you're formally introduced to a Spaniard you should say 'good day' (*buenos días señor/señora/señorita*) or 'good evening' (*buenas tardes*) and shake hands (a single pump is enough). Spanish men shake hands on meeting and again on departing, whether it's a casual meeting in the street or a formal occasion. If you're in doubt as to whether a woman is married or single, wedding rings are worn on the fourth finger of the right hand (not the left), although mature women should be addressed as *señora*. 'Good afternoon' (*buenas tardes*) is used instead of 'good day' (*buenos días*) after lunch, which can **start** as late as 3pm until 9 or 10pm. 'Good night' (*buenas noches*) is usually used when going to bed or leaving a house late at night. 'Goodbye' is *adiós* or less formally you can say see you later (*hasta luego*).

'Hi' or 'hello' (*¡hola!*) is used among close friends and young people, often accompanied by 'how are you?' (*¿qué tal?*) or 'what's new?' (*¿qué hay?*). In more formal language, 'how are you?' is *¿cómo está usted?*, to which the reply is usually 'fine, thank you, and you?' (*muy bien, gracias, ¿y usted?*). A common reply when being formally introduced is 'delighted' (*encantado/a*). Elderly friends are often addressed as 'male' (*don*) and 'female' (*doña*), followed by their Christian name (considerable courtesy and respect is shown to women and the elderly in Spain). When someone thanks you (*gracias*), it's polite to reply 'it was nothing/you're welcome' (*de nada*). **When talking to a stranger it's polite to use the formal form of address (*usted*) and not the familiar form (*tú*) or someone's Christian name until you're invited to do so.** However, nowadays the *tú* form is much more widely used and *usted* is reserved mainly for business and when addressing older people.

Male and female acquaintances kiss each other, usually on both cheeks. If a lady expects you to kiss her she will offer her cheek. The 'kiss' is deposited high up on the cheek, never on the mouth (except between lovers), and isn't usually really a kiss, but a delicate brushing of the cheeks. Close family and male friends embrace.

You should introduce yourself before asking to speak to someone on the telephone. Although the traditional *siesta* is facing a battle for survival, it isn't advisable to telephone between the *siesta* hours (e.g. 2 to 5pm) when many people have a nap. If you call between these times, it's polite to apologise for disturbing the household.

Family surnames are often confusing to foreigners, as the Spanish often have two surnames (possibly linked by 'and', e.g. *y* or *i* in Catalan), the first being their father's and the second their mother's. When a woman marries she may drop her mother's name and add her husband's, although this isn't usual. Spanish children are usually named after a saint and a person's saint's day (*santo*) is as important a celebration as their birthday (*cumpleaños*), both of which are occasions on which it's traditional to entertain your family and friends.

If you have an appointment with a Spaniard don't expect him to arrive on time, although being more than 15 minutes late is considered bad manners. If you're going to be more than 15 minutes late for an appointment you should telephone and apologise.

The Spanish say 'good appetite' (*que aproveche/buen apetito*) before starting a meal. If you're offered a glass of wine, wait until your host has made a toast (*¡salud!*) before taking a drink. If you aren't offered a (another) drink it's time to go home.

Spanish men and women are almost invariably well groomed and style and fashion are important, although they often dress casually. It's advisable to dress conservatively when doing business or visiting government offices on official business. There are few occasions when formal clothes are necessary and there are very few dress rules in Spain (except in respect to places of worship). Spaniards consider that bathing costumes, skimpy tops and flip-flops or sandals with no socks are strictly for the beach or swimming pool, and not for example, the streets, restaurants or shops.

# THE SPANISH ROYAL FAMILY

The Spanish monarchy was restored to the throne in 1975 after 44 years, following the deposition of King Alfonso XIII in 1931 and 39 years of dictatorship under General Franco, who named the current King as his 'heir'.

The King (*el Rey*) of Spain is Juan Carlos I, who's married to Queen (*la Reina*) Sofía of the Greek royal family. They have one son, Prince Felipe, Prince of Asturias and heir to the throne, and two daughters, the Princesses Elena and Cristina. Princess

Elena was married to Jaime de Marichalar amid much pomp and ceremony in Seville cathedral in 1995, Spain's first royal wedding for 89 years (King Juan Carlos and Queen Sofía were married in Athens in 1962). Princess Cristina was married in 1998 to Iñaki Undangarín in Barcelona. In May 2004, Prince Felipe finally got married to Letizia Ortiz, a journalist and newsreader on La Primera's 9pm news. Her commoner origins, plus the fact that she was divorced caused certain disquiet among the more conservative sections of Spanish society, but Letizia, now Princess of Asturias, has been warmly welcomed by the Spanish royal family and is popular with the majority of Spaniards who believe that the Prince should marry whoever he wishes. Their first child and Felipe's heir was born in November 2005.

The royal family live in the *Palacio de la Zarzuela,* a few miles to the north-west of Madrid and also have use of the *Palacio de Marivent* in Palma de Mallorca. The King pays taxes and the Spanish royal family is one of the least expensive to maintain in Europe. The King is the supreme commander of the armed forces and has a considerable personal influence on politics, although his powers are strictly limited by the constitution. His duties include the promulgation of laws and decrees, the calling of elections and referendums, and the appointment of ministers.

In addition to the royal family, the Spanish aristocracy comprises numerous hereditary and non-hereditary title holders, many of whom received their titles from the King. The leading nobility in Spain number some 400 and have the title of *grandee* (*los grandes de España*) in addition to their other titles. There are also some 2,500 nobles (including marquises, counts, viscounts, barons and lords) who don't merit the title of *grandee*, and a large number of 'knights' (*hidalgos*), although the title is no longer used. A title confers no economic or legal privileges on the holder, although they have considerable social cachet in the right circles.

# TIME DIFFERENCE

Most of Spain is on Central European Time (CET), which is Greenwich Mean Time (GMT) plus one hour. The exception is the Canaries, which from October to March are on Western European Time or GMT and from April to September on CET. The Spanish mainland changes to summer time in spring (the end of March), when they put their clocks forward one hour. In autumn (at the end of September), clocks are put back one hour for winter time. Time changes are announced in local newspapers and on radio and television.

Times in Spain, for example in timetables, are usually written using the 24-hour clock, when 10am is written as 10h and 10pm as 22h. Midday (*mediodía*) is 1200 and midnight (*medianoche*) is 2400; 7.30am is written as 07.30. Note, however, that *mediodía* can also refer to lunchtime, which can be anytime between 2 and 4pm. The 24-hour clock is never referred to in speech, when 7am is *las siete de la mañana* and 7pm is *siete de la tarde*. The international time difference in winter (October to March) between Madrid at noon (1200) and some major international cities is shown below:

| MADRID | LONDON | JO'BURG | SYDNEY | AUCKLAND | NEW YORK |
|--------|--------|---------|--------|----------|----------|
| 12 noon | 11am | 1pm | 10pm | 12 midnight | 6am |

# TIPPING

Tipping isn't a common practice among the Spanish. Hotel, restaurant and café bills usually include a 15 per cent service charge (plus 7 per cent VAT/*IVA* or 16 per cent for 5-fork restaurants), usually shown on the bill as *servicio incluido*. When it isn't indicated, most people assume that service is included. However, even when service isn't included the Spanish rarely leave tips (*propinas*), although they may leave a few small coins. The only exception to this rule is in expensive or fashionable establishments where 'tips' may be given to secure a table (or guarantee a table in future). Many foreigners follow international practice and tip as they would in other countries.

The 'no tipping' practice usually extends to other businesses and services, including taxi drivers, porters, hotel staff, car park attendants, cloakroom staff, shoeshine boys, ushers (cinemas, theatres and bullrings) and toilet attendants, although you can give a small tip if you wish. Even at Christmas the Spanish rarely give tips, although Spanish employers usually give their employees a hamper or a few bottles of wine. If you're unsure whether you should tip someone, ask your Spanish neighbours, friends or colleagues for advice (who will probably all tell you something different!). Large tips are considered ostentatious and in bad taste in Spain.

# TOILETS

Although it has had a poor reputation in the past for its public toilets (*aseos públicos*), Spanish toilets are now among the cleanest in Europe and most are spotlessly clean (although toilet paper is sometimes a luxury). However, you will still find the occasional dirty toilet, possibly without a seat, and there are some Turkish-style squat toilets in use in rural areas. The Spanish have a number of words for the toilet, including *servicios* (the most commonly used), *baño* (literally bathroom), *aseos*, W.C., *retretes* and *sanitarios*. To ask where the toilet is you say *¿Dónde están los servicios por favor?* or simply *¿Hay servicios por favor?*. The usual signs are ladies (*damas*) and gentlemen (*caballeros*), although you may also see women (*señoras*) and men (*señores*). Doors may also be marked simply with an 'S' (*señoras*) or 'C' (*caballeros*) or with signs depicting the silhouette of a woman or man.

Public toilets are few and far between in Spain, although there are toilets in bars, cafés, restaurants, hotels, department stores, supermarkets, shopping centres, railway stations, museums and places of interest, on beaches and near markets. Bars, hotels, cinemas and department stores must, by law, offer their facilities free of charge to anyone (although it's customary to buy a drink when using the toilet in a bar or café). There are modern coin-operated public toilets with soap, hot water, towels and air-conditioning in some cities and resort areas.

Many cafés and restaurants have their toilets located at the rear of the building with access from outside (not from the restaurant) and some public toilets have an automatic, timed light switch, where you're plunged into darkness after around one minute. Toilets at petrol stations are usually locked and you must ask the attendant for the key. The latest craze in night clubs in Barcelona are designer communal toilets for men and women, which may even have see-through glass doors on the cubicles! **Toilet paper (*papel higiénico*), which is usually very thin in Spain, isn't provided in many toilets and it's advisable to carry some with you when travelling.** One of the reasons is that many Spanish toilets are unable to handle paper, which should be deposited in the basket provided.

# 19.

# THE SPANISH

Who are the Spanish? What are they like? Let's take a candid and totally prejudiced look at the Spanish people, tongue firmly in cheek, and hope they forgive my flippancy or that they don't read this bit (which is why it's hidden away at the back of the book).

A typical Spaniard is courteous, proud, enthusiastic, undisciplined, tardy, temperamental, independent, gregarious, noisy, honest, noble, individualistic, boisterous, jealous, possessive, colourful, passionate, spontaneous, sympathetic, fun-loving, creative, sociable, demonstrative, irritating, generous, cheerful, polite, unreliable, honourable, optimistic, impetuous, flamboyant, idiosyncratic, quick-tempered, arrogant, elegant, irresponsible, an *aficionado*, hedonistic, contradictory, an anarchist, informal, self-opinionated, corrupt, indolent, frustrating, vulgar, voluble, helpful, friendly, sensitive, a traditionalist, insolent, humorous, fiery, warm-hearted, chauvinistic, bureaucratic, dignified, kind, loyal, extroverted, tolerant, macho, frugal, self-possessed, unabashed, quarrelsome, partisan, a procrastinator, scandal-loving, articulate, a *bon viveur*, inefficient, conservative, nocturnal, hospitable, spirited, urbanised, lazy, confident, sophisticated, political, handsome, chaotic and a football fanatic.

You may have noticed that the above list contains 'a few' contradictions (as does life in Spain), which is hardly surprising as there's no such thing as a typical Spaniard. Apart from the differences in character between the inhabitants of different regions, such as Andalusia, the Basque Country, Catalonia, Galicia and Madrid, the population also includes a potpourri of foreigners from all corners of the globe. Even in appearance, fewer and fewer Spaniards match the popular image of short, swarthy and dark, and the indigenous population includes blondes, brunettes and redheads.

Although not nearly as marked or rigidly defined as the British or French class systems, Spain has a complex class structure. The top drawer of Spain's aristocrats are the 400 or so grandees, who are followed at a respectable distance by myriad minor nobles, all of whom tend to keep to themselves and remain aloof from the hoi polloi. Next in pecking order are the middle class professionals, the lower middle class white-collar workers, the blue-collar working class and the peasant underclass. These are followed by assorted foreigners, a few of whom have been elevated to the status of 'honorary' Spaniards (usually after around 100 years' residence). At the bottom of the heap, below even the despised drunken tourists, are the gypsies (*gitanos*), Spain's true aristocrats. Gypsies are treated as lepers by many Spaniards (except when they're celebrated flamenco artists or bullfighters) and are even less desirable as neighbours than the *Moros* (Moroccans).

Spaniards are often disparaging about their compatriots from other regions. Nobody understands the Basques and their tongue-twister of a language, the Galicians are derided as being more Portuguese than Spanish, and the Andalusians are scorned as backward peasants. However, the most widespread antagonism is between the cities of Madrid and Barcelona, whose inhabitants argue about everything, including the economy sport, history, politics, culture and language. Catalans claim that *Madrileños* are half African, to which they reply that it's better than being half French. However, although they're proud of their regional identity, most Spanish aren't nationalists or patriotic and have little loyalty to Spain as a whole.

Most Spaniards live in harmony with the foreign population, although many foreigners (colloquially dubbed *guiris*, from the word *ghirigay* meaning gibberish) live separate lives in tourist 'ghettos', a million miles away from the 'real' Spain. The Spanish don't consider the concrete jungles of the Costa del Sol, Costa Blanca, Majorca and parts of the Canaries to be part of Spain, but a plastic paradise created for and by foreigners so that pasty-faced tourists can fry in the sun and get drunk on cheap booze. However, although the Spanish aren't generally xenophobic, they're becoming more racist and many would happily eject the gypsies, Arabs and North Africans from their country. They don't care much for the Portuguese either, who are the butt of their jokes (when they aren't about the Andalusians). It's an honour for a foreigner to be invited to a Spaniard's home, although it's one rarely granted. Nevertheless, Spaniards do occasionally marry foreigners, much to the distress of their parents.

Usually when Spaniards and foreigners come into contact (conflict), it concerns official business and results in a profusion of confrontations and misunderstandings (few foreigners can fathom the Spanish psyche) and does little to cement relations. Spain has among the most stifling (and over-staffed) bureaucracy in Western Europe (even worse than the French!) and any encounter with officialdom is a test of endurance and patience. Official offices (if you can find the right one) often open only for a few hours on certain days of the week; the person dealing with your case is always absent; you never have the right papers (or your papers and files have disappeared altogether); the rules and regulations have changed (again) and queues are interminable (take along a copy of *Don Quixote* to help pass the time). It's all part of a conspiracy to ensure that foreigners cannot find out what's going on (and will hopefully therefore pay more taxes, fines, fees, etc.).

Official inefficiency has been developed to a fine art in Spain, where even paying a bill or using the postal service (a world-class example of ineptitude) is an ordeal. The Spanish are generally totally disorganised and the only predictable thing about them is their unpredictability. They seldom plan anything (if they do, the plans will be changed or abandoned at the last moment), as one of the unwritten 'rules' of Spanish life is its spontaneity. Spain has been described as part advanced high-tech nation and part banana republic, where nothing and nobody works.

Almost as infuriating as the bumbling bureaucracy is the infamous *mañana* syndrome, where everything is possible (*no problema*) 'tomorrow' – which can mean later, much later, some time, the day after tomorrow, next week, next week, next month, next year or never – but **never, ever tomorrow** (the Spaniard's motto is 'never do today what you can put off until *mañana*'). When a workman says he will come at 11 o'clock, don't forget to ask which day, month and year he has in mind. Workmen (especially plumbers) don't usually keep appointments and, if they do deign to make an appearance, they're invariably late (and won't have the right tools or spares anyway). The Spanish are good at starting things but not so good at finishing them (hence the numerous abandoned building sites in Spain).

The Spanish are dismissive of time constraints and have no sense of urgency, treating appointments, dates, opening hours, timetables and deadlines with disdain (it's said that the only thing that begins on time in Spain is a bullfight). If you really need something done by a certain date, **never** tell a Spaniard your real deadline. It's significant, however, that the Spanish have a much lower incidence of stress-related disease than north Europeans, which is somewhat surprising in the noisiest country in Europe and the second loudest in the world (after Japan). Over half the inhabitants of Spanish cities endure noise levels well in excess of the World Health Organisation's 'healthy' limit of 65 decibels. Most noise is caused by traffic, lustily supported by pneumatic drills, jack hammers, chain-saws, mopeds (usually without silencers), car horns, alarms, sirens, radios, televisions, *fiestas*, fireworks, car and home music systems, discos, bars, restaurants, incessantly barking dogs, loud neighbours, screaming children and people singing in the streets. In Spain, a normal conversation is two people shouting at each other from a few feet apart (not surprisingly, Spaniards are terrible listeners). Spanish cities are the earthly equivalent of Dante's hell, where inhabitants are subjected to endless noise. Maybe creating a din is the Spanish way of releasing tension? Spaniards don't care to waste time sleeping (except in the afternoons) when they can party and cannot see why anyone else should want to.

Spanish men are world champion hedonists and are mainly interested in five things: sex, football, food, alcohol and gambling (not necessarily in that order). The main preoccupation of the Spanish is having a good time and they have a zest for life matched by few other peoples. They take childish pleasure in making the most of everything and grasp every opportunity to make merry. The Spanish are inveterate celebrants and, when not attending a *fiesta*, family celebration or impromptu party, are to be found in bars and restaurants indulging in another of their favourite pastimes: eating and drinking.

Spaniards have a passion for food, which consists largely of *paella* and *tapas* and is always swimming in garlic and olive oil. Like the French, they eat all the objectionable bits of animals that 'civilised' people throw away (e.g. pigs' ears and bulls' testicles) and will eat any creatures of the deep, the more revolting-looking the better (e.g. octopus and squid). They're particularly fond of baby food (baby suckling pig, baby lamb, baby octopus), which is preferable to 'grown-up' food as it's easier to fit into the ubiquitous frying pan (when not eaten raw, like their ham, all food is fried in Spain). Contrary to popular opinion, the Spanish are a nation of animal lovers: they will eat anything that moves. They do, however, have an unsavoury habit (at least most foreigners think so) of 'playing' with their food and can often be seen chasing their steak around a ring before dinner (*¡Olé!*).

When not eating (or playing guitars or flamenco dancing), the Spanish are allegedly having sex – Spanish men have a reputation as great lovers, although their virility isn't confirmed by the birth rate, which is one of the lowest in the world. In any case, most of their conquests are drunken tourists (only too keen to jump into the sack with anything in trousers), so their reputation doesn't bear close scrutiny. (A recent survey found that the average Spaniard makes love badly and infrequently: just 71 times a year compared with the world average of 109 – how do they know these things?) Their macho image has taken a further pounding in recent years as women have stormed most male bastions and today are as likely to be found in the university, office, factory, professions or the government, as in the home or the church.

Most Spaniards are anarchists and care little for rules and regulations, generally doing what they want when they want, particularly regarding motoring (especially parking), smoking in public places, the dumping of rubbish and paying taxes. Paradoxically they've taken to democracy like ducks to water and are passionate Europeans, firmly believing in a united Europe and the euro (so would you if you'd had to put up with the peseta!). However, like most sensible people they care little for their politicians, whose standing has plummeted to new lows in the last decade following a spate of corruption scandals.

The Spanish are sensitive to criticism, particularly regarding their history and traditions. Whatever you do, don't ask an old man 'what he did in the Civil War' or mention Franco, the Falklands or Gibraltar. Spaniards are intolerant of other people's views; criticism of Spain is reserved for the Spanish (who do it constantly) and isn't something to be indulged in by ignorant foreigners.

Since throwing off the shackles of dictatorship in 1975, Spain has resolutely turned its back on the past and embraced the future with gusto. In the last quarter of a century, the country has undergone a transformation influencing every facet of life. However, although most changes have been for the better, many people believe that the soul of traditional Spain has been lost in the headlong rush towards economic development. The modern Spaniard is more materialistic than his forebears and has taken to the art of making a fast buck as quickly as any North American immigrant ever did. Progress has, however, been purchased at a high cost and has led to a sharp increase in crime, drug addiction, alcoholism, poverty, begging, and the devastation of unspoilt areas by developers hell-bent on smothering the country in concrete and golf courses. Despite being hard hit by the recession in the '90s, the country has made a strong recovery in recent years and has one of the most promising outlooks of any EU country.

Despite the country's problems, the Spanish enjoy one of the best lifestyles (and quality of life) of any European country and, indeed, any country in the world; in Spain work fits around social and family life, not vice versa. The foundation of Spanish society is the family and community, and the Spanish are noted for their close family ties, their love of children and care for the elderly (who are rarely abandoned in nursing homes). Spain has infinitely more to offer than its wonderful climate and rugged beauty and is celebrated for its arts and crafts, architecture, fashion, night-life, music, dance, gastronomy, design, sports facilities, culture, education, health care and technical excellence in many fields.

For sheer vitality and passion for life the Spanish have few equals, and whatever Spain can be accused of it's **never** dull or boring. Few other countries offer such a wealth of intoxicating experiences for the mind, body and spirit (and not all out of a bottle!). But the real glory of Spain lies in the outsize heart and soul of its people, who are among the most convivial, generous and hospitable in the world. If you're willing to learn Spanish (or at least make an effort) and embrace Spain's traditions and way of life, you will invariably be warmly received by the natives, most of whom will go out of their way to welcome and help you. Spain is highly addictive and, while expats may occasionally complain, the vast majority wouldn't dream of leaving and infinitely prefer life in Spain to their home countries. **Put simply, Spain is a great place to live (provided you don't have to do business there).**

*¡Vivan los españoles! ¡Viva España!*

# 20.

# MOVING HOUSE OR
# LEAVING SPAIN

W hen moving house or leaving Spain, there are many things to be considered and a 'million' people to inform. The checklists contained in this chapter will make the task easier and may even help prevent an ulcer or nervous breakdown – providing of course you don't leave everything to the last minute.

# MOVING HOUSE

When moving house **within** Spain the following items should be considered:

● If you're renting accommodation, you must usually give your landlord one or two months notice (refer to your contract) and have your deposit refunded. Your notice letter should be sent by registered post (*certificado*).

● Inform the following, as applicable:

 – Your employer;

 – Your present town hall and the town hall in your new municipality;

 – Your local social security and income tax offices;

 – If you have a Spanish driving licence or a Spanish registered car and are remaining in the same province, you should return your licence and car registration document (*permiso de circulación*) and have the address changed (see page 227). If you're moving to a new province you should inform both your current and new provinces;

 – Your electricity, gas, telephone and water companies;

 – Your insurance companies (e.g. health, car, house contents and private liability); hire purchase companies; lawyer; accountant and local businesses where you have accounts. Take out any new insurance, if applicable;

 – Your banks and other financial institutions such as stockbrokers and credit card companies. Make arrangements for the transfer of funds and the cancellation or alteration of standing orders and/or direct debits (any regular payments);

 – Your family doctor, dentist and other health practitioners. Health records should be transferred to your new practitioners;

 – Your children's schools. If applicable, arrange for schooling in your new community (see **Chapter 9**). Try to give a term's notice and obtain copies of any relevant school reports and records from current schools;

 – All regular correspondents, subscriptions, social and sports clubs, professional and trade journals, and friends and relatives. Arrange to have your post redirected;

 – Your local consulate or embassy if you're registered with them (see page 91).

● Return any library books or anything borrowed.

● Arrange removal of your furniture and belongings, or rent a van if you're doing your own removal.

● **Ask yourself (again): 'Is it really worth all this trouble?'.**

# LEAVING SPAIN

Before leaving Spain for an indefinite period the following items should be considered **in addition** to those listed above under **Moving House:**

- **Check that your own and your family's passports are valid.**

- Give notice to your employer, if applicable.

- Check whether any special entry requirements are necessary for your country of destination by contacting the local embassy or consulate in Spain, e.g. visas, permits or inoculations. An exit permit or visa isn't required to leave Spain.

- You may qualify for a rebate on your income tax (see page 330) and social security payments (see page 288).

- If you have contributed to a supplementary pension scheme, a percentage of your contributions may be repaid (see page 295), although the pension company will require proof that you're leaving Spain permanently.

- Arrange to sell anything you aren't taking with you (car, furniture, etc.). Find out the procedure for shipping your belongings to your country of destination (see page 107) and arrange shipment. Check with the local embassy or consulate in Spain of the country to which you're moving (for a list of see **Appendix A**). Special forms may need to be completed before arrival. If you've been living in Spain for less than two years, you're required to re-export all personal effects imported duty-free from outside the European Union (EU), including furniture and vehicles (if you sell them you may be required to pay duty).

- If you have a Spanish registered car that you intend to take with you, you can drive on your Spanish plates for a maximum of three months before changing them.

- Pets may require special inoculations or may have to go into quarantine for a period (see page 465), depending on your destination.

- Arrange health, travel and other insurance (see **Chapter 12**).

- Depending on your destination, you may wish to arrange health and dental check-ups before leaving Spain. Obtain a copy of your health and dental records.

- Terminate any loans, lease or hire purchase contracts, and pay all outstanding bills (allow plenty of time as some companies are slow to respond).

- Check whether you're entitled to a rebate on your road tax, car and other insurance. Obtain a letter from your Spanish motor insurance company stating your no-claims bonus.

- Make arrangements to sell or let your house or apartment in Spain.

- Check whether you need an international driving licence or a translation of your Spanish or foreign driving licence for your country of destination.

- Give friends and business associates in Spain an address and telephone number where you can be contacted abroad.

*¡Buen Viaje!*

# APPENDICES

## Appendix A: USEFUL ADDRESSES

### Embassies & Consulates

Embassies are located in the capital Madrid; many countries also have consulates in other cities (British provincial consulates are listed on page 334). Embassies and consulates are listed in the yellow pages under *Embajadas*. Some countries have more than one office in Madrid and, before writing or calling in person, you should telephone to confirm that you have the correct office.

**Algeria:** C/General Oraá, 12, 28006 Madrid (☎ 915-629 705).

**Angola:** C/Serrano, 64, 28001 Madrid (☎ 914-356 166).

**Argentina:** C/Pedro de Valdivia, 21, 28006 Madrid (☎ 915-710 500, 🖳 www.portalargentino.net).

**Australia:** Pza Descubridor Diego Ordás, 3, 28003 Madrid (☎ 913-536 600, 🖳 www.spain.embassy.gov.au).

**Austria:** Paseo de la Castellana, 91, 28046 Madrid (☎ 915-565 315, 🖳 www.bmaa.gv.at/madrid).

**Belgium:** Paseo de la Castellana, 18, 28046 Madrid (☎ 915-776 300, 🖳 www.diplobel.org/spain).

**Bolivia:** C/Velázquez, 26, 28001 Madrid (☎ 915-780 835, 🖳 www.mcei-bolivia.com).

**Brazil:** C/de Fernando el Santo, 6, 28010 Madrid (☎ 917-004 650, 🖳 www.brasil.es).

**Bulgaria:** C/Travesia de Santa Maria Magdalena, 15, 28016 Madrid (☎ 913-455 761).

**Cameroon:** C/Rosario Pino, 3, 28020 Madrid (☎ 915-711 160).

**Canada:** C/Núñez de Balboa, 35, 28001 Madrid (☎ 914-233 250, 🖳 www.canada-es.org).

**Chile:** C/Lagasca, 88, 28001 Madrid (☎ 914-319 160).

**China:** C/Arturo Soria, 113, 28043 Madrid (☎ 915-194 242, 🖳 www.embajadachina.es).

**Colombia:** C/General Martínez Campos, 48, 28010 Madrid (☎ 917-004 770).

**Costa Rica:** Paseo de la Castellana, 164, 28046 Madrid (☎ 913-459 622).

**Croatia:** C/Claudio Coello, 78, 28001 Madrid (☎ 915-776 881).

**Cyprus:** Paseo de la Castellana, 45, 28046 Madrid (☎ 915-783 114).

**Czech Republic:** Avda. Pío XII, 22-24, 28016 Madrid (☎ 913-531 880, 🖳 www.mfa.cz/madrid).

**Cuba:** Paseo de la Habana, 194, 28036 Madrid (☎ 913-592 500, 🖳 www.ecubamad.com).

**Denmark:** C/Claudio Coello, 91, 28006 Madrid (☎ 914-318 445, 🖳 www.embajadadinamarca.es).

**Ecuador:** C/Velázquez, 114, 28006 Madrid (☎ 915-627 215/216).

**Egypt:** C/Velázquez, 69, 28006 Madrid (☎ 915-776 308).

**El Salvador:** C/General Oraá, 9, 28006 Madrid (☎ 915-628 002, 🖳 www.embasalva.com).

**Estonia:** C/Claudio Coello, 91, 28006 Madrid (☎ 914-261 671, 🖳 www.estemb.es).

**Finland:** Paseo de la Castellana, 15, 28046 Madrid (☎ 913-196 172, 🖳 www.finlandia.es).

**France:** C/Salustiano Olózaga, 9, 28001 Madrid (☎ 914-238 900, 🖳 www.ambafrance-es.org).

**Gabon:** C/Francisco Alcántara, 3, 28002 Madrid (☎ 914-138 211).

**Germany:** C/Fortuny, 8, 28010 Madrid (☎ 915-579 000, 🖳 www.embajada-alemania.es).

**Greece:** Avda. Doctor Arce, 24, 28002 Madrid (☎ 915-644 653).

**Guatemala:** C/Rafael Salgado, 3, 28036 Madrid (☎ 913-440 347).

**Haiti:** C/Marqués del Duero, 3, 28001 Madrid (☎ 915-752 624).

**Honduras:** Paseo de la Castellana, 164, 28046 Madrid (☎ 915-790 251, 🖳 www.embahonduras.es).

**Hungary:** C/Fortuny, 6, 28010 Madrid (☎ 914-137 011, 🖳 www.embajada-hungria.org).

**India:** Avda. Pío XII, 30-32, 28016 Madrid (☎ 902-901 010, 🖳 www.embajadaindia.com).

**Indonesia:** C/Agastia, 65, 28043 Madrid (☎ 914-130 294, 🖳 www.embajadaindonesia.es).

**Iran:** C/Jerez, 5, 28016 Madrid (☎ 913-450 112, 🖳 www.embajadairan.es/madrid).

**Iraq:** C/Ronda de Sobradiel, 67, 28043 Madrid (☎ 917-591 282).

**Ireland:** Paseo de la Castellana, 46, 28046 Madrid (☎ 914-364 093).

**Israel:** C/Velázquez, 150, 28002 Madrid (☎ 917-829 500, 🖳 www.embajada-israel.es).

**Italy:** C/Lagasca, 98, 28006 Madrid (☎ 914-233 300).

**Ivory Coast:** C/Serrano, 154, 28006 Madrid (☎ 915-626 916).

**Japan:** C/Serrano, 109, 28006 Madrid (☎ 915-907 600, 🖳 www. embjapon.es).

**Jordan:** Paseo General Martinez Campos, 41, 28010 Madrid (☎ 913-191 100).

**Korea:** C/González Amigó, 15, 28033 Madrid (☎ 913-532 000).

**Kuwait:** Paseo de la Castellana, 141, 28046 Madrid (☎ 915-792 467).

**Latvia:** C/Alfonso XII, 52, 28014 Madrid (☎ 913-691 362).

**Lebanon:** Paseo de la Castellana, 178, 28046 Madrid (☎ 913-451 368).

**Libya:** C/Pisuerga, 12, 28002 Madrid (☎ 915-635 753).

**Lithuania:** C/ Pisuerga, 5, 28002 Madrid (☎ 917-022 116, 🖳 www. emblituania.es).

**Luxembourg:** C/Claudio Coello, 78, 28001 Madrid (☎ 914-359 164, 🖳 www.mae.lu/espagne).

**Malaysia:** Paseo de la Castellana, 91, 28046 Madrid (☎ 915-550 684).

**Malta:** Paseo de la Castellana, 45, 28046 Madrid (☎ 913-913 061).

**Mauritania:** C/Velázquez, 90, 28006 Madrid (☎ 915-757 007).

**Mexico:** Carrera de San Jerónimo, 46, 28014 Madrid (☎ 913-692 814, 🖳 www.embamex.es).

**Monaco:** C/Villanueva, 12, 28001 Madrid (☎ 915-782 048).

**Morocco:** C/Serrano, 179, 28002 Madrid (☎ 915-631 090, 🖳 www. maec.gov.ma/madrid).

**The Netherlands:** Avda. del Comandante Franco, 32, 28016 Madrid (☎ 913-537 500, 🖳 www.embajadapaisesbajos.es).

**New Zealand:** Plza. de la Lealtad, 2, 28014 Madrid (☎ 915-230 226, 🖳 www.nzembassy.com/spain).

**Nicaragua:** Paseo de la Castellana, 127, 28046 Madrid (☎ 915-555 510).

**Nigeria:** C/Segre, 23, 28002 Madrid (☎ 915-630 911).

**Norway:** Paseo de la Castellana, 31, 28046 Madrid (☎ 913-103 116, 🖳 www.noruega.es).

**Pakistan:** Avda. Pío XII, 11, 28016 Madrid (☎ 913-458 986, 🖳 www. embajada-pakistan.org).

**Panama:** C/Claudio Coello, 86, 28006 Madrid (☎ 915-765 001).

**Paraguay:** Paseo Eduardo Dato, 21, 28010 Madrid (☎ 913-082 746).

**Peru:** C/Príncipe de Vergara, 36, 28001 Madrid (☎ 914-314 242).

**Philippines:** C/Eresma, 2, 28002 Madrid (☎ 917-823 830).

**Poland:** C/Guisando, 23 bis, 28035 Madrid (☎ 913-736 605, 🖳 www.polonia.es).

**Portugal:** C/Pinar, 1, 28006 Madrid (☎ 917-824 960).

**Romania:** Avda. Alfonso XIII, 157, 28016 Madrid (☎ 913-504 436, 🖳 www.embajadarumana.com).

**Russia:** C/Velázquez, 155, 28002 Madrid (☎ 915-622 264).

**Saudi Arabia:** C/Doctor Alvarez Sierra, 3, 28033 Madrid (☎ 913-834 300, 🖳 www.arabiasaudi.org).

**Slovakia:** C/Pinar, 20, 28006 Madrid (☎ 915-903 861).

**Slovenia:** C/Hermanos Bécquer, 7, 28006 Madrid (☎ 914-116 893).

**South Africa:** C/Claudio Coello, 91, 28006 Madrid (☎ 914-363 780, 🖳 www.sudafrica.com).

**Sweden:** C/Caracas, 25, 28010 Madrid (☎ 917-022 000, 🖳 www.swedenabroad.com/madrid).

**Switzerland:** C/Núñez de Balboa, 35, 28001 Madrid (☎ 914-363 960, 🖳 www.eda.admin.ch/madrid).

**Syria:** Pza. Platerías Martínez, 1, 28014 Madrid (☎ 914-203 946).

**Thailand:** C/Joaquín Costa, 29, 28002 Madrid (☎ 915-632 903).

**Tunisia:** Avda Alfonso XIII, 64, 28016 Madrid (☎ 914-473 508).

**Turkey:** C/Rafael Calvo, 18, 28010 Madrid (☎ 913-198 064, 🖳 www.tcmadridbe.org).

**United Arab Emirates:** C/Capitán Haya, 40, 28020 Madrid (☎ 915-701 001).

**United Kingdom:** C/Fernando el Santo, 16, 28010 Madrid (☎ 917-008 200, 🖳 www.ukinspain.com).

**United States of America:** C/Serrano, 75, 28006 Madrid (☎ 915-872 200, 🖳 www.embusa.es).

**Uruguay:** Paseo Pintor Rosales, 32, 28008 Madrid (☎ 917-580 475).

**Venezuela:** C/Capitán Haya, 1, 28020 Madrid (☎ 915-981 200).

**Vietnam:** C/ Arturo Soria, 201, 28043 Madrid (☎ 915-102 867, 🖳 www.embavietnam-madrid.org).

# British Provincial Consulates in Spain

**Alicante:** British Consulate, Plaza Calvo Sotelo, 1/2, 03001 Alicante (☎ 965-216 190, ✉ enquiries.alicante@fco.gov.uk).

**Barcelona:** British Consulate-General, Edif. Torre de Barcelona, Avda. Diagonal, 477-13, 08036 Barcelona (☎ 933-666 200, ✉ barcelonaconsulate@ ukinspain.com).

**Bilbao:** British Consulate-General, Alamada de Urquijo, 2-8, 48008 Bilbao (☎ 944-157 600, ✉ bilbaoconsulate@ ukinspain.com).

**Ibiza:** British Vice-Consulate, Avenida de Isidoro Macabich, 45, 07800 Ibiza (☎ 971-301 818, ✉ britishconsulate@fco.gov.uk).

**Las Palmas de Gran Canarias:** British Consulate, Edif. Cataluña, Luis Morote, 6-3, 35007 Las Palmas (☎ 928-262 508, ✉ LAPAL-Consular@ fco.gov.uk).

**Madrid:** British Consulate-General, Paseo de Recoletos, 7/9, 28004 Madrid (☎ 915-249 700, ✉ madridconsulate@ ukinspain.com).

**Malaga:** British Consulate, Edif. Eurocom, C/Mauricio Moro Pareto, 2-2º, 29006 Malaga (☎ 952-352 300, ✉ malaga@fco.gov.uk).

**Menorca:** Honorary British Vice-Consulate, Sa Casa Nova, Cami de Biniatap, 30, Es Castell, 07720 Menorca (☎ 971-363 373).

**Palma de Mallorca:** British Consulate, Plaza Mayor, 3D, 07002 Palma de Mallorca (☎ 971-712 445, ✉ consulate@palma. mail.fco.gov.uk).

**Santa Cruz de Tenerife:** British Consulate, Plaza Weyler, 8-1, 38003 Santa Cruz de Tenerife (☎ 922-286 863, ✉ tenerife. enquiries@fco.gov.uk).

# Major Property Exhibitions

Property exhibitions are common in the UK and Ireland, and are popular with prospective property buyers who can get a good idea of what's available in a particular area and make contact with estate agents and developers. Below is a list of the main exhibition organisers in the UK and Ireland. Note that you may be charged a small admission fee.

**Homes Overseas** (☎ 020-7002 8300, 🖥 www.blendoncommunications. co.uk). Homes Overseas are the largest organisers of international property exhibitions and stage a number of exhibitions each year at a range of venues in both the UK and Ireland.

**International Property Show** (☎ 01252-720652, 🖥 www. international-propertyshow.com). The International Property Show is held several times a year in London and Manchester.

**Spain on Show** (☎ 0500-780 878, 🖥 www.spainon show.com). Spain on Show organises several annual property exhibitions at venues around the UK, including Northern Ireland.

**Town & Country** (☎ 0845-230 6000, 🖥 www.spanish property.uk.com). This large estate agency organises small Spanish property exhibitions at venues around the UK and Ireland twice monthly.

**World Class Homes** (☎ 0800-731 4713, 🖥 www.worldclass homes.co.uk). Exhibitions organised by World Class Homes are held in small venues around the UK and feature UK property developers only.

**World of Property** (☎ 01323-726040, 🖥 www.outbound publishing.com). The *World of Property* magazine publishers (see **Appendix B**) organise three large property exhibitions a year, two in the south of the UK and one in the north.

## APPENDIX B: FURTHER READING

# English-language Newspapers & Magazines

Unless otherwise stated, addresses and telephone numbers are in Spain.

**Absolute Madrid,** Palacio de Miraflores, Carrera de San Jerónimo 15, 2, 28014 Madrid (☎ 914-547 268, 💻 www.absolutemagazine.com). Free monthly magazine.

**Absolute Marbella,** Office 21, Edif Tembo, Avda Rotary International, 29660 Puerto Banús, Malaga (☎ 902-301 130, 💻 www.absolute magazine.com). Free monthly magazine.

**Barcelona Metropolitan,** (☎ 934-514 486, 💻 www.barcelona-metropolitan.com). Free monthly magazine.

**The Broadsheet,** (☎ 915-237 480, 💻 www.thebroadsheet.com). Free monthly magazine.

**Costa Blanca News,** C/ Alicante 9, Polígono Industrial La Cala, Finestrat, Alicante (☎ 965-855 286, 💻 www.costablanca-news.com). Weekly newspaper published on Fridays.

**Costa del Sol News,** CC Las Moriscas Local 10, Avda Juan Luis Peralta, 29629 Benalmádena Pueblo, Malaga (☎ 952-448 730, 💻 www.costadelsolnews.es). Weekly newspaper published on Fridays.

**Euro Weekly** (☎ 952-561 245, 💻 http://euroweeklynews.com). Weekly free newspaper.

**Essential Marbella,** (☎ 952-766 344, 💻 www.essential magazine.com). Free monthly magazine.

**Everything Spain,** PO Box 326, Sittingbourne, Kent ME9 8FA, UK (☎ 0870-403 0335, 💻 www.everything spainmag.co.uk). Monthly lifestyle and property magazine.

**Homes Overseas,** Blendon Communications, 1st Floor, 1 East Poultry Avenue, London EC1A 9PT, UK (☎ 020-7002 8310, 💻 www.homesoverseas.co.uk). Monthly property magazine.

**The Ibiza Sun,** (💻 www.ibiza-spotlight.com). Free weekly newspaper.

**Island Connections,** (☎ 922 750 609, 💻 www.newscanarias.net). Fortnightly newspaper published in the Canary Islands.

**Living Spain,** Albany Publishing, Tunns Cottage, Olney, Bucks MK46 4AE, UK (☎ 01234-710 992, 💻 www.livingspain.co.uk). Bi-monthly lifestyle and property magazine.

**The Mallorca Daily Bulletin** (☎ 971-788 400, 💻 www.majorcadailybulletin.es). Daily newspaper for the Balearics.

**Property News**, Jarales de Alhamar, Calahonda, 29647 Mijas-Costa, Malaga (☎ 952-931 603, 🖳 www.property-spain.com). Free monthly newspaper.

**Property World**, Ctra de Cádiz Km 202, Urb la Buganvilla, Mijas Costa, Malaga (☎ 952-587 575, 🖳 www.propertyworldmagazine.com). Free monthly magazine.

**Spanish Homes Magazine**, (☎ UK 020-8318 1532, 🖳 www.spanishhome-smagazine.com). Monthly property magazine.

**Sur in English**, Diario Sur, Avda. Doctor Marañón, 48, 29009 Malaga (☎ 952-649 741, 🖳 www.surinenglish.com). Free weekly newspaper.

**Tenerife News**, (☎ 902-346 001, 🖳 www.tennews.com). Free fortnightly newspaper.

**Valencia Life**, (🖳 www.valencialife.net). Quarterly magazine.

**Villas & . . .**, SKR Española, SL, CC Diana 3-31, 29680 Estepona, Malaga (🖳 www. villas.com). Monthly property magazine with articles in English, French, German and Spanish.

**World of Property,** 1 Commercial Road, Eastbourne, East Sussex BN21 3XQ, UK (☎ 01323-726040, 🖳 www.outbound publishing.com). Quarterly property magazine.

# Books

The books listed below are just a selection of the hundreds written about Spain. For example, in addition to the general tourist guides listed, there are numerous guides covering individual cities and regions of Spain. The publication title is followed by the author's name and the publisher's name (in brackets). Note that some titles may be out of print, but may still be obtainable from book shops or libraries. Books prefixed with an asterisk are recommended by the author.

## Living & Working in Spain

**\*\*The Best Places to Buy a Home in Spain**, Joanna Styles (Survival Books)

**\*\*Costa Blanca Lifeline**, Joanna Styles (Survival Books)

**\*\*Costa del Sol Lifeline**, Joanna Styles (Survival Books)

**\*\*Making a Living in Spain**, Anne Hall (Survival Books)

**Choose Spain**, John Howells & Bettie Magee (Gateway)

**Introducing Spain**, B.A. McCullagh & S. Wood (Harrap)

**Life in a Spanish Town**, M. Newton (Harrap)

**\*\*Living and Working in Spain**, David Hampshire (Survival Books)

**\*Madrid Inside Out**, Arthur Howard & Victoria Montero (Frank)

**Simple Etiquette in Spain**, Victoria Miranda McGuiness (Simple Books)

**Spain: Business & Finance** (Euromoney Books)

**Traditional Houses of Rural Spain**, Bill Laws (Collins & Browns)

**You and the Law in Spain**, David Searl (Santana)

## General Tourist Guides

**AA Essential Explorer Spain** (AA)

**Andalucía Handbook**, Rowland Mead (Footprint)

**\*Andalucía: The Rough Guide** (Rough Guides)

**\*Baedeker's Spain** (Baedeker)

**Berlitz Blueprint: Spain** (Berlitz)

**Berlitz Discover Spain**, Ken Bernstein & Paul Murphy (Berlitz)

**\*Blue Guide to Spain: The Mainland**, Ian Robertson (Ernest Benn)

**\*Cadogan Guides: Spain**, Dana Facaros & Michael Pauls (Cadogan)

**Collins Independent Travellers Guide Spain**, Harry Debelius (Collins)

**Daytrips Spain & Portugal**, Norman Renouf (Hastings House Pub)

**Excursions in Eastern Spain**, Nick Inman & Clara Villanueva (Santana)

**Excursions in Southern Spain**, David Baird (Santana)

**\*Eyewitness Travel Guide: Spain**, Deni Bown (Dorling Kindersly)

**Fielding's Paradors in Spain & Portugal**, A. Hobbs (Fielding Worldwide)

**\*Fodor Spain** (Fodor)

**\*Fodor's Exploring Spain** (Fodor's Travel Publications)

**\*Frommer's Spain's Best-Loved Driving Tours**, Mona King (IDG Books)

**Guide to the Best of Spain** (Turespaña)

**\*Inside Andalusia**, David Baird (Santana)

**The Insider's Guide to Spain**, John de St. Jorre (Moorland)

**\*Insight Guides: Spain** (APA Publications)

**Lazy Days Out in Andalucía**, Jeremy Wayne (Cadogan)

**\*Let's Go Spain & Portugal** (Macmillan)

**\*Lonely Planet Spain** (Lonely Planet)

**\*Madrid**, Michael Jacobs (George Philip)

Madrid: A Traveller's Companion, Hugh Thomas (Constable)

*Michelin Spain Green Guide (Michelin)

*Michelin Red Guide: España, Portugal (Michelin)

Off the Beaten Track: Spain, Barbara Mandell & Roger Penn (Moorland)

*Paupers' Barcelona, Miles Turner (Pan)

Rick Steves' Spain & Portugal, Rick Steves (John Muir Publications)

*Rough Guide to Andalucía, Mark Ellingham & John Fisher (Rough Guides)

The Shell Guide to Spain, David Mitchell (Simon & Schuster)

Spain: A Phaidon Cultural Guide (Phaidon)

Spain at its Best, Robert Kane (Passport)

Spain: Everything Under the Sun, Tom Burns (Harrap Columbus)

Spain on Backroads, Duncan Petersen (Hunter Publishing)

*Spain: The Rough Guide, Mark Ellingham & John Fisher (Rough Guides)

Special Places to Stay in Spain, Alistair Sawday (ASP)

Time Off in Spain and Portugal, Teresa Tinsley (Horizon)

*Time Out Madrid Guide (Penguin)

Travellers in Spain: An Illustrated Anthology, David Mitchell (Cassell)

Welcome to Spain, R.A.N Dixon (Collins)

*Which? Guide to Spain (Consumers' Association and Hodder & Stoughton)

## Travel Literature

*As I Walked Out One Midsummer Morning, Laurie Lee (Penguin)

*Between Hopes and Memories: A Spanish Journey, Michael Jacobs (Picador)

*The Bible in Spain, George Borrow (Century Travellers Series)

*Cider with Rosie, Laurie Lee (Penguin)

Gatherings in Spain, Richard Ford (Dent Everyman)

*Handbook for Travellers in Spain, Richard Ford (Centaur Press)

Iberia, James A. Michener (Fawcett)

*Jogging Round Majorca, Gordon West (Black Swan)

In Search of Andalucía, Christopher Wawn & David Wood (Pentland Press)

*In Spain, Ted Walker (Corgi)

*A Rose for Winter, Laurie Lee (Penguin)

*Spanish Journeys: A Portrait of Spain, Adam Hopkins (Penguin)

*South from Granada, Gerald Brenan (Penguin)

*A Stranger in Spain, H.V. Morton (Methuen)

Two Middle-aged Ladies in Andalusia, Penelope Chetwode (Murray)

*A Winter in Majorca, George Sands

## Food & Wine

*AA Essential Food and Drink Spain (AA)

*The Best of Spanish Cooking, Janet Mendel (Santana)

The Complete Spanish Cookbook, Jacki Passmore (Little Brown)

*Cooking in Spain, Janet Mendel (Santana)

Delicioso: The Regional Cooking of Spain, Penelope Casas (Alfred A. Knopf)

A Flavour of Andalucía, Pepita Aris (Chartwell)

*Floyd on Spain, Keith Floyd (Penguin)

The Food and Wine of Spain, Penelope Casas (Alfred A. Knopf)

404 Spanish Wines, Frank Snell (Santana)

Great Dishes of Spain, Robert Carrier (Boxtree)

*The 'La Ina' Book of Tapas, Elisabeth Luard (Schuster)

Mediterranean Seafood, Alan Davidson (Penguin)

**Rioja and its Wines, Ron Scarborough (Survival Books)

Shopping for Food and Wine in Spain (Santana)

*Spanish Cooking, Pepita Aris (Apple Press)

*The Spanish Kitchen, Pepita Aris (Wardlock)

The Spanish Table, Marimar Torres (Ebury Press)

*Spanish Wines, Jan Read (Mitchell Beazley)

The Spanishwoman's Kitchen, Pepita Aris (Cassell)

The Tapas Book, Adrian Linssen & Sara Cleary (Apple Press)

Tapas, Silvano Franco (Lorenz)

*The Wine and Food of Spain, Jan Read & Maite Manjón (Wedenfeld & Nicolson)

The Wine Roads of Spain, M&K Millon (Santana)

## Miscellaneous

**The Art of Flamenco**, DE Pohren (Musical News Services Ltd)

*****Blood Sport: A History of Spanish Bullfighting**, Timothy Mitchell (University of Pennsylvania Press)

**Cities of Spain**, David Gilmour (Pimlico)

**Dali: A Biography**, Meredith Etheringon-Smith (Sinclair-Stevenson)

*****A Day in the Life of Spain** (Collins)

*****Death in the Afternoon**, Ernest Hemingway (Grafton)

**Gardening in Spain**, Marcelle Pitt (Santana)

**The Gardens of Spain**, Consuela M. Correcher (Abrams)

*****In Search of the Firedance**, James Woodall (Sinclair-Stevenson)

**The King**, Jose Luis de Vilallonga (Weidenfeld)

*****Nord Riley's Spain**, Nord Riley (Santana)

*****On Foot Through Europe: A Trail Guide to Spain and Portugal**, Craig Evans (Quill)

*****Or I'll Dress You in Mourning**, Larry Collins & Dominique Lapierre (Simon & Schuster)

**La Pasionaria**, Robert Low (Hutchinson)

**Shooting Caterpillars in Spain**, Alex Browning (Survival Books)

**Spain: A Literary Companion**, Jimmy Burns (John Murray)

**Spain's Wildlife**, Eric Robins (Santana)

**Trekking in Spain**, Marc S. Dubin (Lonely Planet)

*****Walking Through Spain**, Robin Neillands Queen Anne Press)

*****Wild Spain**, Frederic Grunfeld & Teresa Farino (Ebury)

*****Xenophobe's Guide to the Spanish** (Ravette)

## APPENDIX C: USEFUL WEBSITES

The following list contains some of the many websites dedicated to Spain as well as websites containing information about a number of countries. Websites about particular aspects of life and work in Spain are mentioned in the relevant chapters.

## Spanish Websites

**About Spain** (🖥 www.aboutspain.net). Information about specific regions.

**All About Spain** (🖥 www.red2000.com). General tourist information.

**Andalucia** (🖥 www.andalucia.com). Comprehensive information about the region of Andalusia in English.

**Barcelona** (🖥 www.xbarcelona.com). Information including job opportunities and useful tips for foreigners living in Barcelona.

**Escape to Spain** (🖥 www.escapetospain.co.uk). General information and a property guide to the Costa Blanca, Costa Brava and Costa del Sol.

**Expatica** (🖥 www.expatica.com). An excellent compendium of general information about living and working in Spain.

**Ideal Spain** (🖥 www.idealspain.com). Information about many aspects of living in Spain.

**JobtoasterSpain** (🖥 www.jobtoasterspain.com). Comprehensive employment portal offering vacancies in several locations in Spain, including the Costa del Sol, Barcelona, Granada, Cadiz.

**Madrid Man** (🖥 www.madridman.com). A wealth of useful and continually updated information about living and working in Madrid including an 'ask the expert' facility.

**Spain Expat** (🖥 www.spainexpat.com). Information about living in Spain, including an 'ask the legal expert' facility. The site has particularly good links.

**Spain For Visitors** (🖥 http://spainforvisitors.com). Good general information about visiting Spain.

**Spanish Forum** (🖥 www.spanishforum.org). A wealth of useful and continually updated information about all aspects of living and working in Spain, including a free monthly e-newsletter.

**Spanish Property Insight** (🖥 www.spanishpropertyinsight.com). One of the best websites on property with the emphasis on up-to-date, useful and impartial information. The site includes a forum and a free monthly e-newsletter.

**Survival Books** (🖳 www.survivalbooks.net). Survival Books are the publishers of this book and *Buying a Home in Spain, The Best Places to Buy a Home in Spain* and *The Wines of Spain*. The website includes useful tips for anyone planning to buy a home, live, work, retire or do business in Spain.

**TurEspaña – Spanish National Tourist Office** (🖳 www.tour spain.co.uk or 🖳 www.spain.info).

**Travelling in Spain** (🖳 http://travellinginspain.com). Information about Spanish cities with particular emphasis on Madrid.

**TuSpain** (🖳 www.tuspain.com). General information with the emphasis on buying property and residential matters.

**Typically Spanish** (🖳 www.typicallyspanish.com). Information about a wide range of topics.

**UK in Spain** (🖳 www.ukinspain.com). The British embassy's official site includes a wealth of useful information about aspects of living and working in Spain. Go to the section 'Advice to tourists and residents in Spain'.

## General Websites

**Americans Abroad** (🖳 www.aca.ch). This website offers advice, information and services to Americans abroad.

**Australians Abroad** (🖳 www.australiansabroad.com). Information for Australians concerning relocating plus a forum to exchange information and advice.

**British Expatriates** (🖳 www.britishexpat.com). This website keep British expatriates in touch with events and information about the UK.

**ExpatBoards** (🖳 www.expatboards.com). The mega site for expatriates, with popular discussion boards and special areas for Britons, Americans, expatriate taxes, and other important issues.

**Escape Artist** (🖳 www.escapeartist.com). An excellent website and probably the most comprehensive, packed with resources, links and directories covering most expatriate destinations. You can also subscribe to the free monthly online expatriate magazine, Escape from America.

**Expat Exchange** (🖳 www.expatexchange.com). Reportedly the largest online community for English-speaking expatriates, provides a series of articles on relocation and also a question and answer facility through its expatriate network.

**Expat World** (⌨ www.expatworld.net). 'The newsletter of international living.' Contains a wealth of information for American and British expatriates, including a subscription newsletter.

**Expatriate Experts** (⌨ www.expatexpert.com). A website run by expatriate expert Robin Pascoe, providing invaluable advice and support.

**Family Life Abroad** (⌨ www.familylifeabroad.com). A wealth of information and articles on coping with family life abroad.

**Foreign Wives Club** (⌨ www.foreignwivesclub.com). An online community for women in bicultural marriages.

**Francopats** (⌨ www.francopats.com). Online expatriate community.

**Real Post Reports** (⌨ www.realpostreports.com). Provides relocation services, recommended reading lists and plenty of interesting 'real-life' stories containing anecdotes and impressions written by expatriates in just about every city in the world.

**Southern Cross Group** (⌨ www.southern-cross-group.org). A website for Australians and New Zealanders providing information and the exchange of tips.

**Third Culture Kids** (⌨ www.tckworld.com). A website designed for expatriate children living abroad.

**Travel Documents** (⌨ www.traveldocs.com). Useful information about travel, specific countries and documents needed to travel.

**Travel for Kids** (⌨ www.travelforkids.com). Advice on travelling with children around the world.

**Women of the World** (⌨ www.wow-net.org). A website designed for female expats anywhere in the world.

**World Travel Guide** (⌨ www.wtgonline.com). A general website for world travellers and expatriates.

**Worldwise Directory** (⌨ www.suzylamplugh.org). This website run by the Suzy Lamplugh charity for personal safety, providing a useful directory of countries with practical information and special emphasis on safety, particularly for women.

## APPENDIX D: WEIGHTS & MEASURES

Spain uses the metric system of measurement. Those who are more familiar with the imperial system of measurement will find the tables on the following pages useful. Some comparisons shown are only approximate, but are close enough for most everyday uses. In addition to the variety of measurement systems used, clothes sizes often vary considerably with the manufacturer (as we all know only too well). Try all clothes on before buying and don't be afraid to return something if, when you try it on at home, you decide it doesn't fit (most shops will exchange goods or give a refund).

### Women's Clothes

| | | | | | | | | | | |
|---|---|---|---|---|---|---|---|---|---|---|
| Continental | 34 | 36 | 38 | 40 | 42 | 44 | 46 | 48 | 50 | 52 |
| UK | 8 | 10 | 12 | 14 | 16 | 18 | 20 | 22 | 24 | 26 |
| US | 6 | 8 | 10 | 12 | 14 | 16 | 18 | 20 | 22 | 24 |

### Pullovers

| | Women's | | | | | | Men's | | | | | |
|---|---|---|---|---|---|---|---|---|---|---|---|---|
| Continental | 40 | 42 | 44 | 46 | 48 | 50 | 44 | 46 | 48 | 50 | 52 | 54 |
| UK | 34 | 36 | 38 | 40 | 42 | 44 | 34 | 36 | 38 | 40 | 42 | 44 |
| US | 34 | 36 | 38 | 40 | 42 | 44 | sm | med | | lar | xl | |

### Men's Shirts

| | | | | | | | | | | |
|---|---|---|---|---|---|---|---|---|---|---|
| Continental | 36 | 37 | 38 | 39 | 40 | 41 | 42 | 43 | 44 | 46 |
| UK/US | 14 | 14 | 15 | 15 | 16 | 16 | 17 | 17 | 18 | - |

### Men's Underwear

| | | | | | | |
|---|---|---|---|---|---|---|
| Continental | 5 | 6 | 7 | 8 | 9 | 10 |
| UK | 34 | 36 | 38 | 40 | 42 | 44 |
| US | sm | med | | lar | | xl |

**Note:** sm = small, med = medium, lar = large, xl = extra large

### Children's Clothes

| | | | | | | |
|---|---|---|---|---|---|---|
| Continental | 92 | 104 | 116 | 128 | 140 | 152 |
| UK | 16/18 | 20/22 | 24/26 | 28/30 | 32/34 | 36/38 |
| US | 2 | 4 | 6 | 8 | 10 | 12 |

## Children's Shoes

| Continental | 18 19 20 21 22 23 24 25 26 27 28 29 30 31 32 |
|---|---|
| UK/US | 2  3  4  4  5  6  7  7  8  9  10 11 11 12 13 |
| Continental | 33 34 35 36 37 38 |
| UK/US | 1  2  2  3  4  5 |

## Shoes (Women's and Men's)

| Continental | 35 | 36 | 37 | 37 | 38 | 39 | 40 | 41 | 42 | 42 | 43 | 44 |
|---|---|---|---|---|---|---|---|---|---|---|---|---|
| UK | 2 | 3 | 3 | 4 | 4 | 5 | 6 | 7 | 7 | 8 | 9 | 9 |
| US | 4 | 5 | 5 | 6 | 6 | 7 | 8 | 9 | 9 | 10 | 10 | 11 |

## Weight

| Avoirdupois | Metric | Metric | Avoirdupois |
|---|---|---|---|
| 1oz | 28.35g | 1g | 0.035oz |
| 1lb* | 454g | 100g | 3.5oz |
| 1cwt | 50.8kg | 250g | 9oz |
| 1 ton | 1,016kg | 500g | 18oz |
| 2,205lb | 1 tonne | 1kg | 2.2lb |

## Length

| British/US | Metric | Metric | British/US |
|---|---|---|---|
| 1in | 2.54cm | 1cm | 0.39in |
| 1ft | 30.48cm | 1m | 3ft 3.25in |
| 1yd | 91.44cm | 1km | 0.62mi |
| 1mi | 1.6km | 8km | 5mi |

## Capacity

| Imperial | Metric | Metric | Imperial |
|---|---|---|---|
| 1 UK pint | 0.57 litre | 1 litre | 1.75 UK pints |
| 1 US pint | 0.47 litre | 1 litre | 2.13 US pints |
| 1 UK gallon | 4.54 litres | 1 litre | 0.22 UK gallon |
| 1 US gallon | 3.78 litres | 1 litre | 0.26 US gallon |

**Note:** An American 'cup' = around 250ml or 0.25 litre.

## Area

| British/US | Metric | Metric | British/US |
|---|---|---|---|
| 1 sq. in | 0.45 sq. cm | 1 sq. cm | 0.15 sq. in |
| 1 sq. ft | 0.09 sq. m | 1 sq. m | 10.76 sq. ft |
| 1 sq. yd | 0.84 sq. m | 1 sq. m | 1.2 sq. yds |
| 1 acre | 0.4 hectares | 1 hectare | 2.47 acres |
| 1 sq. mile | 2.56 sq. km | 1 sq. km | 0.39 sq. mile |

## Temperature

| °Celsius | °Fahrenheit | |
|---|---|---|
| 0 | 32 | (freezing point of water) |
| 5 | 41 | |
| 10 | 50 | |
| 15 | 59 | |
| 20 | 68 | |
| 25 | 77 | |
| 30 | 86 | |
| 35 | 95 | |
| 40 | 104 | |
| 50 | 122 | |

**Notes:** The boiling point of water is 100°C / 212°F.

Normal body temperature (if you're alive and well) is 37°C / 98.4°F.

## Temperature Conversion

Celsius to Fahrenheit: multiply by 9, divide by 5 and add 32. (For a quick and approximate conversion, double the Celsius temperature and add 30.)

Fahrenheit to Celsius: subtract 32, multiply by 5 and divide by 9. (For a quick and approximate conversion, subtract 30 from the Fahrenheit temperature and divide by 2.)

## Oven Temperatures

| Gas | Electric | |
|-----|-----|-----|
| | °F | °C |
| - | 225–250 | 110–120 |
| 1 | 275 | 140 |
| 2 | 300 | 150 |
| 3 | 325 | 160 |
| 4 | 350 | 180 |
| 5 | 375 | 190 |
| 6 | 400 | 200 |
| 7 | 425 | 220 |
| 8 | 450 | 230 |
| 9 | 475 | 240 |

## Air Pressure

| PSI | Bar |
|-----|-----|
| 10 | 0.5 |
| 20 | 1.4 |
| 30 | 2 |
| 40 | 2.8 |

## Appendix E: MAP

The map opposite shows the 17 autonomous regions and 50 provinces of Spain (listed below). The maps on the following pages show airports with scheduled services from the UK and Ireland (see **Appendix F**), high speed train (AVE) routes, and motorways and other major roads.

**Galicia**
1. A Coruña
2. Lugo
3. Pontevedra
4. Ourense

**Asturias**
5. Asturias

**Castilla y León**
6. León
7. Palencia
8. Burgos
9. Zamora
10. Valladolid
11. Soria
12. Salamanca
13. Avila
14. Segovia

**Cantabria**
15. Cantabria

**La Rioja**
16. La Rioja

**País Vasco**
17. Vizcaya
18. Guipúzcoa
19. Alava

**Navarra**
20. Navarra

**Aragón**
21. Huesca
22. Zaragossa
23. Teruel

**Cataluña**
24. Lleida
25. Girona

26. Barcelona
27. Tarragona

**Extremadura**
28. Cáceres
29. Badajoz

**Castilla La Mancha**
30. Guadalajara
31. Toledo
32. Cuenca
33. Ciudad Real
34. Albacete

**Madrid**
35. Madrid

**Comunidad Valenciana**
36. Castellón
37. Valencia
38. Alicante

**Andalucía**
39. Huelva
40. Seville
41. Córdoba
42. Jaén
43. Cádiz
44. Málaga
45. Granada
46. Almeria

**Murcia**
47. Murcia

**Baleares**
48. Baleares

**Canarias**
49. Santa Cruz de Tenerife
50. Las Palmas de Gran Canaria

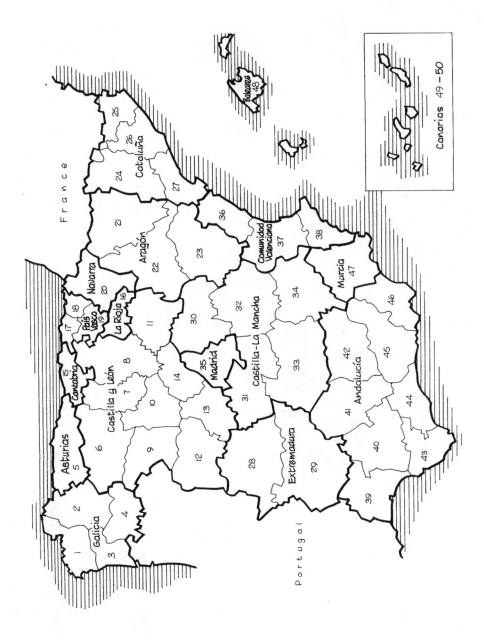

# INDEX

# C

# G

# H

# I

# S

# T

# LIVING AND WORKING SERIES

**Living and Working** books are essential reading for anyone planning to spend time abroad, including holiday-home owners, retirees, visitors, business people, migrants, students and even extra-terrestrials! They're packed with important and useful information designed to help you **avoid costly mistakes and save both time and money.** Topics covered include how to:

- Find a job with a good salary & conditions
- Obtain a residence permit
- Avoid and overcome problems
- Find your dream home
- Get the best education for your family
- Make the best use of public transport
- Endure local motoring habits
- Obtain the best health treatment
- Stretch your money further
- Make the most of your leisure time
- Enjoy the local sporting life
- Find the best shopping bargains
- Insure yourself against most eventualities
- Use post office and telephone services
- Do numerous other things not listed above

**Living and Working** books are the most comprehensive and up-to-date source of practical information available about everyday life abroad. They aren't, however, boring text books, but interesting and entertaining guides written in a highly readable style.

**Discover what it's really like to live and work abroad!**

Order your copies today by phone, fax, post or email from: Survival Books, PO Box 3780, YEOVIL, BA21 5WX, United Kingdom (☎/🖅 +44 (0)1935-700060, ✉ sales@survivalbooks.net, 🖥 www.survivalbooks.net).

# BUYING A HOME SERIES

*Buying a Home* books, including *Buying, Selling & Letting Property*, are essential reading for anyone planning to purchase property abroad. They're packed with vital information to guide you through the property purchase jungle and help you **avoid the sort of disasters that can turn your dream home into a nightmare!** Topics covered include:

- Avoiding problems
- Choosing the region
- Finding the right home and location
- Estate agents
- Finance, mortgages and taxes
- Home security
- Utilities, heating and air-conditioning
- Moving house and settling in
- Renting and letting
- Permits and visas
- Travelling and communications
- Health and insurance
- Renting a car and driving
- Retirement and starting a business
- And much, much more!

*Buying a Home* books are the most comprehensive and up-to-date source of information available about buying property abroad. Whether you want a detached house, townhouse or apartment, a holiday or a permanent home, these books will help make your dreams come true.

**Save yourself time, trouble and money!**

Order your copies today by phone, fax, post or email from: Survival Books, PO Box 3780, YEOVIL, BA21 5WX, United Kingdom (☎/🖷 +44 (0)1935-700060, ✉ sales@survivalbooks.net, 🖳 www.survivalbooks.net).

# OTHER SURVIVAL BOOKS

**The Alien's Guides:** *The Alien's Guides to Britain and France* will help you to appreciate the peculiarities (in both senses) of the British and French.

**The Best Places to Buy a Home in France/Spain:** The most comprehensive homebuying guides to France and Spain, containing detailed profiles of the most popular regions for home-buying.

**Buying, Selling and Letting Property:** The most comprehensive and up-to-date source of information on buying, selling and letting property in the UK.

**Earning Money From Your Home:** Essential guides to earning income from property in France and Spain, including short- and long-term letting.

**Foreigners in France/Spain: Triumphs & Disasters:** Real-life experiences of people who have emigrated to France and Spain, recounted in their own words.

**Lifelines:** Essential guides to life in specific regions of France and Spain. See order form for a list of current titles in the series.

**Making a Living:** Essential guides to self-employment and starting a business in France and Spain.

**Renovating & Maintaining Your French Home:** The ultimate guide to renovating and maintaining your dream home in France.

**Retiring Abroad:** The most comprehensive and up-to-date source of practical information available about retiring to a foreign country.

**Shooting Caterpillars in Spain:** The hilarious experiences of an expatriate who sent to Spain in search of . . . she wasn't quite sure what.

**Surprised by France:** Even after living there for ten years, Donald Carroll finds plenty of surprises in the Hexagon.

### Broaden your horizons with Survival Books!

Order your copies today by phone, fax, post or email from: Survival Books, PO Box 3780, YEOVIL, BA21 5WX, United Kingdom (☎/📠 +44 (0)1935-700060, ✉ sales@survivalbooks.net, 💻 www.survivalbooks.net).

| Qty. | Title | Price (incl. p&p) | | | Total |
|---|---|---|---|---|---|
| | | UK | Europe | World | |
| | The Alien's Guide to Britain | £6.95 | £8.95 | £12.45 | |
| | The Alien's Guide to France | £6.95 | £8.95 | £12.45 | |
| | The Best Places to Buy a Home in France | £13.95 | £15.95 | £19.45 | |
| | The Best Places to Buy a Home in Spain | £13.95 | £15.95 | £19.45 | |
| | Buying a Home Abroad | £13.95 | £15.95 | £19.45 | |
| | Buying a Home in Australia & NZ | £13.95 | £15.95 | £19.45 | |
| | Buying a Home in Cyprus | £13.95 | £15.95 | £19.45 | |
| | Buying a Home in Florida | £13.95 | £15.95 | £19.45 | |
| | Buying a Home in France | £13.95 | £15.95 | £19.45 | |
| | Buying a Home in Greece | £13.95 | £15.95 | £19.45 | |
| | Buying a Home in Ireland | £11.95 | £13.95 | £17.45 | |
| | Buying a Home in Italy | £13.95 | £15.95 | £19.45 | |
| | Buying a Home in Portugal | £13.95 | £15.95 | £19.45 | |
| | Buying a Home in South Africa | £13.95 | £15.95 | £19.45 | |
| | Buying a Home in Spain | £13.95 | £15.95 | £19.45 | |
| | Buying, Letting & Selling Property | £11.95 | £13.95 | £17.45 | |
| | Earning Money From Your French Home | £11.95 | £13.95 | £17.45 | |
| | Earning Money From Your Spanish Home | £11.95 | £13.95 | £17.45 | |
| | Foreigners in France: Triumphs & Disasters | £11.95 | £13.95 | £17.45 | |
| | Foreigners in Spain: Triumphs & Disasters | £11.95 | £13.95 | £17.45 | |
| | Costa Blanca Lifeline | £11.95 | £13.95 | £17.45 | |
| | Costa del Sol Lifeline | £11.95 | £13.95 | £17.45 | |
| | Dordogne/Lot Lifeline | £11.95 | £13.95 | £17.45 | |
| | Normandy Lifeline | £11.95 | £13.95 | £17.45 | |
| | Poitou-Charentes Lifeline | £11.95 | £13.95 | £17.45 | |
| | Provence-Côte d'Azur Lifeline | £11.95 | £13.95 | £17.45 | |
| | Living & Working Abroad | £14.95 | £16.95 | £20.45 | |
| | Living & Working in America | £14.95 | £16.95 | £20.45 | |
| | Living & Working in Australia | £16.95 | £18.95 | £22.45 | |
| | Living & Working in Britain | £14.95 | £16.95 | £20.45 | |
| | Living & Working in Canada | £16.95 | £18.95 | £22.45 | |
| | Living & Working in the European Union | £16.95 | £18.95 | £22.45 | |
| | Living & Working in the Far East | £16.95 | £18.95 | £22.45 | |
| **Total carried forward (see over)** | | | | | |

# ORDER FORM

| Qty. | Title | Price (incl. p&p) | | | Total |
|---|---|---|---|---|---|
| | | | Total brought forward | | |
| | | UK | Europe | World | |
| | Living & Working in France | £14.95 | £16.95 | £20.45 | |
| | Living & Working in Germany | £16.95 | £18.95 | £22.45 | |
| | L&W in the Gulf States & Saudi Arabia | £16.95 | £18.95 | £22.45 | |
| | L&W in Holland, Belgium & Luxembourg | £14.95 | £16.95 | £20.45 | |
| | Living & Working in Ireland | £14.95 | £16.95 | £20.45 | |
| | Living & Working in Italy | £16.95 | £18.95 | £22.45 | |
| | Living & Working in London | £13.95 | £15.95 | £19.45 | |
| | Living & Working in New Zealand | £16.95 | £18.95 | £22.45 | |
| | Living & Working in Spain | £14.95 | £16.95 | £20.45 | |
| | Living & Working in Switzerland | £16.95 | £18.95 | £22.45 | |
| | Making a Living in France | £13.95 | £15.95 | £19.45 | |
| | Making a Living in Spain | £13.95 | £15.95 | £19.45 | |
| | Renovating & Maintaining Your French Home | £16.95 | £18.95 | £22.45 | |
| | Retiring Abroad | £14.95 | £16.95 | £20.45 | |
| | Shooting Caterpillars in Spain | £9.95 | £11.95 | £15.45 | |
| | Surprised by France | £11.95 | £13.95 | £17.45 | |
| | | | | **Grand Total** | |

Order your copies today by phone, fax, post or email from: Survival Books, PO Box 3780, YEOVIL, BA21 5WX, United Kingdom (☎/🖨 +44 (0)1935-700060, ✉ sales@ survivalbooks.net, 🖥 www.survivalbooks.net). If you aren't entirely satisfied, simply return them to us within 14 days for a full and unconditional refund.

I enclose a cheque for the grand total/Please charge my Amex/Delta/Maestro (Switch)/MasterCard/Visa card as follows. (delete as applicable)

Card No. _ _ _ _   _ _ _ _   _ _ _ _   _ _ _ _   Security Code* _ _ _

Expiry date _____ Issue number (Maestro/Switch only) _____

Signature _____ Tel. No. _____

NAME _____

ADDRESS _____

_____

* The security code is the last three digits on the signature strip.